SEMIOTICS 1988

Edited by

Terry Prewitt
University of West Florida

John Deely
Loras College
Universidade Federal de Minas Gerais, Brasil

Karen Haworth
University of West Florida

UNIVERSITY
PRESS OF
AMERICA

Lanham • New York • London

Proceedings of the Thirteenth Annual Meeting
of the Semiotic Society of America
27–30 October 1988
Cincinnati, Ohio
Hosted by the University of Cincinnati
Organized by Gila Safran–Naveh

Copyright© 1989 by

The Semiotic Society of America

All rights reserved

Printed in the United States of America

The title of the Annual Proceedings Volumes
is the property of the Semiotic Society of America

This book is co-published by arrangement with the
Semiotic Society of America

This book is also a volume
in the University Press of America series
SOURCES IN SEMIOTICS (SIS)
under the general editorship of
John Deely and Brooke Williams

ISBN: 0–8191–7478–5 (alk. paper)
LCN: 84–640162

All University Press of America books are produced on acid-free paper.
The paper used in this publication meets the minimum requirements of American
National Standard for Information Sciences—Permanence of Paper for Printed Library
Materials, ANSI Z39.48–1984. ∞

CONTENTS

Editors' Preface   xi

I. SEMIOTIC MODELING

1. Myrdene Anderson
Knowledge Dynamics:
Evolution and Development in Semiotic Environments   3

2. Stanley N. Salthe & Myrdene Anderson
Modeling Self-Organization   14

II. PSYCHOLOGICAL PERSPECTIVES ON SEMIOTIC MODELS

3. Donald J. Cunningham
Abduction and Affordance: J. J. Gibson and Theories of Semiosis   27

4. James C. Lundy
She Understood Him: "All Too Well"   34

5. Donna E. West
Form and Use Differences in the Acquisition of
Speech Participant Signifiers: Evidence from Blind Children   38

III. SEMIOTIC INTERPRETATION OF MUSICAL MODELS

6. William DeFotis
The "Music" in Barthes' *A Lover's Discourse*   53

7. William P. Dougherty
Reading Beethoven's Readings: Toward a Semiotics of Song   57

8. Gayle A. Henrotte
Hjelmslev's Glossematics and Music: The Sign May Be an Illusion   66

IV. COMPUTER SCIENCE MODELS

9. Walter J. Savitch
Semen, Demonic Possession, and the Common Cold   77

10. Robert T. Swank
Metaphor, Myth, and Computer Language   83

V. SESSIONS OF THE CHARLES S. PEIRCE SOCIETY

11. André De Tienne
Peirce's Early Semiotic Analysis of Representation   93

12. Nathan Houser
Peirce's Pre-Phenomenological Categories   103

13. Sandra B. Rosenthal
The Ultimate Logical Interpretant and the Dynamical Object   109

14. David Savan
Peirce and the Trivium   116

15. Thomas L. Short
Why We Prefer Peirce to Saussure   124

VI. EXPANSIONS OF PEIRCEAN SEMIOTICS

16. John Deely
Semiosis: The Subject Matter of Semiotic Inquiry   133

17. Jeffrey R. DiLeo
A Semiotic Classification of Proper Names   143

18. Terrance King
The Relation between Peirce's Realism and His Idea of the Sign   150

19. James J. Liszka
Peirce, Saussure, and the Concept of Transvaluation   156

VII. SEMIOTIC DIRECTIONS IN PHILOSOPHY

20. Vincent Colapietro
Recovering the Agent after Decentering the Subject   165

21. David Lidov
Locke's Formula and the Scope of Semiotics   173

22. Ralph A. Powell
Epistemology's Minimal Cause as Basis of Science   180

23. Thomas A. Sebeok
The Notion 'Semiotic Self' Revisited   189

24. Scott Simpkins
The Fear of the Arbitrary Sign   196

VIII. SEMIOTICS AND RELIGION

25. Robert S. Corrington
Faith and the Signs of Expectation — 203

26. Judith Porges Hollander
Playing Cards with the Witch: Tarot Reading and Psychotherapy — 210

27. Felicia E. Kruse
The Interior Castle as Mystical Sign — 215

IX. SEMIOTICS OF DECEPTION

28. Tullio Maranhão
Longing for Presence in the Semiotic of Deception — 225

29. Floyd Merrell
The Sign of Deceit — 232

30. Terry J. Prewitt
The Exposed Exotic Dancer:
A Semiotic of Deception in Porno-Active Ritual — 241

31. Machiko Takayama
April Fool and Halloween: A Semiotic Analysis of the Lie — 248

32. Inge Crosman Wimmers
Figures of Deception in *A La Recherche Du Temps Perdu* — 254

X. LITERARY SEMIOTICS: CRITICAL THEORY

33. Jackson G. Barry
Defining a Narrative Signifier — 263

34. Vittoria Borsò
The Literature of Silence: A Concern of Semiotics? — 268

35. David K. Danow
Dialogue and Monologue — 277

36. Erika Freiberger
Poetics of Illusion: Gogol's Fantastic Stories — 283

37. Michèlle M. Magill
Intertextual and Intratextual Analysis:
The Holy Grail in Julien Gracq's Work — 291

38. Steven C. Scheer
The Illusion of Reading: Deconstructive *versus* Semiotic Theories — 298

39. Anthony J. Tamburri
Aldo Palazzeschi's *'riflessi'*:
Retrospective Reading and Reverse Intertextuality ... 303

40. Eva Tsuquiashi-Daddesio
Saint-Loup and the White Rabbit: Intertextual Fiction and Reality ... 311

XI. LITERARY SEMIOTICS: DISCOURSE ANALYSIS

41. Thomas C. Daddesio
The Role of the Paratext in *The Name of the Rose* ... 319

42. R. Lane Kauffmann
Rotpeter's Revenge: Kafka's "Report to an Academy"
as Critique of Anthropecentrism ... 324

43. Mary Libertin
Deely's Semiotic as *Doctrina* and Joyce's "Process of Mind" in *Ulysses* ... 331

44. Norma Procopiow
The Semiotics of Narrative: Narrative, Prisoners, and Social Meaning ... 336

XII. ELIAS CANETTI: TRADITION AND TRANSFORMATION

45. David Darby
A Fiction of Detection: The Police Enquiry in Elias Canetti's *Auto-da-Fé* ... 343

46. Kristie A. Foell
Absence as Presence: Sigmund Freud in the Works of Elias Canetti ... 350

47. Steven J. Rosen
Canettian and Freudian Approaches to Swift ... 356

XIII. SEMIOTICS OF POETIC DISCOURSE

48. Beverly Seaton
The Pragmatical Dimension of Reserve in John Keble's *The Christian Year* ... 367

49. Scott Simpkins
Negative Capabilities: Shifting Signs in Keat's "Ode to a Nightingale" ... 374

50. Sid Sondergard
"Pain is perfet misery": Reading the Miltonic Discourse of Violence ... 380

XIV. SEMIOTICS AND GENDER AWARENESS

51. Thomas F. Broden
Gallic Semiotic Subjects and Feminism: Greimas, Duras, *et Al.*   391

52. Martha M. Houle
The Play of Illusion in a Map of Love: *La Carte de Tendre* (1654)   397

53. Linda Kintz
Permeable Boundaries, Femininity, and Violence   404

54. Katherine S. Stephenson
Luce Irigary: Theoretical and Empirical Approaches
to the Representation of Subjectivity and Sexual Difference
in Language Use   412

XV. CAMILLO AND THE ILLUSION OF COLLECTIVE MEMORY

55. Curt Dilger
Theater and Architecture: A Parallel Experience   421

56. Homa Fardjadi
Camillo's Theatre and the Automaton   429

57. Donald Kunze
The Cone of Vision:
Delirious History and Optical Mnemonics in Vico and Camillo   436

58. David Leatherbarrow
Architecture and the Illusion of Perfect Memory   447

XVI. SEMIOTICS OF FILM, TELEVISION, THEATER

59. Ian C. Henderson
Max Headroom: Televisual Invention and Edison Carter   455

60. Richard J. Leskosky
The Illusion of Reality and the Reality of Illusion in Animated Film   460

61. Milan Palec
Scenography: The Semiotics of Violence   466

62. Mary Ann Frese Witt
Murder as Sign and Cycle in *Les Negres*   471

XVII. SEMIOTICS OF ART

63. Lev Manovich
Perceptual Semiotics:
Functions of Repetitions in an Image   479

64. Deborah L. Smith-Shank
Art History *versus* Art Mythology: The Semiotic Tension 487

XVIII. SEMIOTICS AND POSTMODERN CULTURE

65. Jay Knaack
Garbage Pail Kids: Recognition and Adaptation   495

66. Richard L. Lanigan
Popular Political Signs: Jesse Jackson's Presidential Candidacy
as Depicted in Editorial Cartoons   501

67. Thomas E. Lewis
Semiotics in the Streets: Hyperrealism and the State   507

68. William Pencak
Stamping Out History: National Identity on Postage Stamps 516

XIX. SEMIOTIC ACCOUNTS OF LINGUISTIC CONCEPTS

69. Alexander F. Caskey
'Language as Work and Trade' as Metaphor   523

70. Joseph DeChicchis
The Semiotics of Mayan Imperatives   528

71. Michiko Hamada
Speaking as Signs of Embodiment:
Japanese Terms for Self-Reference and Address   536

72. Alicia Sakaguchi
International Planned Languages:
An Essay on their Definition and Limitation   544

XX. "PROXEMIOTICS"

73. Rui-hong Guo
Jokes, Transgression, and Laughter   553

74. Richard A. R. Watson
The "Classical" Proxemiotics of the Encounter   559

XXI. SEMIOTIC HISTORIOGRAPHY

75. Stephan Bleier
Horkheimer, Adorno, Foucault: The Term "Subject" in the Enlightenment   573

76. Julio Pinto
The Question of the Subject in Semiosis: Peirce and Lacan   578

77. Anthony F. Russell
The Semiotic of Maurice Blondel's Logic of Action   583

INDEX   589

Supporting Subscribers   598

EDITORS' PREFACE

This volume marks a new production level for the annual SSA Proceedings. A detailed historical commentary on the development of the SSA proceedings volumes can be found in the Editor's prefaces of *Semiotics 1982*, *Semiotics 1984*, and *Semiotics 1985*. In this *Semiotics 1988* volume, we add to the historical notes an account of two extremely positive changes in the ongoing project, both of which have occurred since 1984. First, all of the volumes from *Semiotics 1984* through the present have been completed on a schedule coinciding with the annual SSA meeting. The process of manuscript completion has worked well to assure the timely appearance of our combined scholarly work. With an annual production process in place, moreover, editorial attention has shifted more strongly toward enhancing the appearance of the volumes. This has been aided by the "Style Sheet for Proceedings Papers" (Deely 1984: 715-739; 1986) which provides the opportunity for the membership to directly contribute to the "proceedings cycle" through careful and consistent manuscript preparation. The use of a common submission format has saved editorial time on the the whole. Perhaps more important, the common bibliographic organization and sectioning of volumes reflects a unity of purpose for the society's diverse academic efforts. More importantly, the attention in recent years to accurately represent each meeting helps build a continuing sense of "American Semiotics".

The "look" of the proceedings enhances the ability of the volume to communicate our common interests to those who consider themselves outside the semiotic canopy. *Semiotics 1987* and *Semiotics 1988* bring the volumes to a new and attractive tier of appearance, consistent with the longer trend of enhancement. The text is produced in more handsome fonts which achieve a near-typeset appearance. The technology supporting these changes has streamlined the annual production effort and size of volumes. Our goal of *representing* the meeting means the inclusion of more papers (there was a fifty percent increase in submissions this year). The stylistic changes introduced over the past two years are in part designed to hold page increases to a minimum while incorporating more papers. All of these changes are essential if we are to make the scholarly impact we all would like to see across the many disciplines we represent.

We gratefully acknowledge the efforts of the following individuals who worked diligently to assure the efficient production of this proceedings volume: Amy Brown, Scott Ceier, Cecily Fruchey, Stephanie Jones, Hermine Kraßnitzer, Franz Rulitz. We also extend our thanks for support from Douglas Friedrich, Provost of the University of West Florida, John Fulton, Dean of Arts and Sciences, and Gary Howard, Dean of Freshmen, all of whom provided support for student assistants who worked on the volume. Finally, we thank Karen Brotherton and the staff of the UWF Computer Services, as well as Gregory Lanier and Ronald Miller, for technical assistance they provided on several manuscripts.

SSA PROCEEDINGS STYLE MANUAL REFERENCES

DEELY, John.
- 1984. "Style Sheet for the Proceedings Papers of the Semiotic Society of America", in *Semiotics 1984*, ed. J. N. Deely (Lanham, MD: University Press of America, 1985), 715-739. See gloss on 1986 below.
- 1985. "The Project of the Proceedings", Editor's Preface to *Semiotics 1984*, ed. John Deely (Lanham, MD: University Press of America, 1985), ix-xii.
- 1986. "Semiotic Society of America Style Sheet", *The American Journal of Semiotics* 4.3/4, 193-215.
- 1986a. "A Style Sheet for Semiotics", Editor's Foreward to *Semiotics 1985*, ed. John Deely (Lanham, MD: University Press of America, 1985), iii-vi. This style sheet incorporates a device called "Historical Layering" which requires for the first time in principle that all works used in the preparation of research be referenced by a date taken from within the lifetime of the author of the work. It is a critical device equally useful in the sciences and the humanities, and, when applied, establishes an invariant reference base for primary sources with a clear account of their relation to later editions used.

DEELY, John and Jonathan EVANS.
- 1987. "Editors' Preface" to *Semiotics 1982*, ed. John Deely and Jonathan Evans (Lanham, MD: University Press of America, 1987), explaining the origins of the SSA Style Manual (1984, 1986 above).

I

SEMIOTIC MODELING

KNOWLEDGE DYNAMICS:
EVOLUTION AND DEVELOPMENT IN SEMIOTIC ENVIRONMENTS

Myrdene Anderson
Purdue University

Prolegomenon

Knowledge in dynamical systems--whether living ones or their extensions in machines--arises from little-understood processes in phylogenetic, ontogenic, and historical time, the last both cultural and experiential in nature. Even though the particular processes and products of knowledge may remain empirical questions, we do now have a working understanding of the behavior of dynamical systems in general, from which cogent hypotheses about knowledge can be drawn to focus future discourse and investigation.

Open Temporal Systems

Crucial to any discussion of the semiotic behavior of knowledge, is the role of very different temporal trajectories, from deep-time biology, to meso-time culture, to various scales of surface-time experience of the more elemental units of knowledge-generation, knowledge-negotiation, knowledge-conservation, and knowledge-dissipation. In considering cultural phenomena--such as the interplay of information, knowledge, meaning and machines--the human organism has often been taken as the natural or convenient unit of analysis, and also as an autonomous actor wielding intentionality and unilateral decision-making skills. Both these scales of complexity bear closer scrutiny for the operation of knowledge at levels above, below, and outside the individual, and for the more realistic script available to human actors. Of course, critical discourse in any field first centers on unpacking the conventional units of time, of space, of matter/energy, of information--and of all the above, as well. We assume this reassessment bears fruit when done in a reflexive and nonmechanical fashion.

In this regard, we should guard against modeling knowledge, or any other putative hierarchical structure, as successively embedded *or* successfully expanding Chinese boxes. This visual habit clouds the empirical question of how the hierarchization process behaves, either through upward/outward dynamics and/or downward/inward dynamics, and/or otherwise. It also hampers representing interaction between levels, perhaps noncontiguous ones, taken as incommensurable and essentially hermetic in the model, regardless of the degree of "interactional complexity" (following Wimsatt 1980a, 1980b) acknowledged. In addition, it sidesteps crucial issues concerning any concomitant heterarchy and the identification of appropriate or at least interesting units of analysis.

Knowledge as Means and Ends

The polysemous character of "knowledge" renders a number of other distinctions, however provisional, important for pragmatic reasons. First, we should resist the temptation to assume that knowledge will always or necessarily reduce to, or project into, natural human verbal language formulations; there exist other digital and numerous analogue "languages" in the human repertoire which do not lend themselves to "linguistic" treatment--take skills, as an example, one particularly relevant to human-artifact interaction (see Harper 1987).

Second, in conjunction with this, a mechanical distinction of left- and right-brain functions may bootstrap as a heuristic, but can boomerang as tautology. "Localizing" performance of spatial, non-linear skills in the right hemisphere, for instance, begs several important questions: for starters--what relationship obtains between the cerebral hemispheres and their patently connecting corpus callosum, and whence these over-determined and dichotomous coordinates of "space" and "time"?

Third, knowledge connotes a product and storage parameter; it may go without saying a compensating consideration needs to be given the processes involved--the flows, episodic and level, which feed into, out of, and through knowledge stores--some probably best described as cascading, curso-genetic, execution-driven phenomena often contributing to throughput.

Fourth, as the keystone for our argument about the nature and culture and semiotics of knowledge, we provide a foundation for considering knowledge environments as constituting ecological and ethological dynamical self-organizing systems, shaped by two processes ordinarily called evolution and development. While these terms have most currency in biology, we assume that biological evolution and biological development constitute but special cases of the phenomena of metaevolution and metadevelopment in nonequilibrium dynamical systems generally, although we retain the shorter, more common words as generic terms. We then attend to the explication of and discrimination between evolutionary and developmental processes, which concepts we find exceedingly utile. Only with this background can one proceed to study knowledge in tractable semiotic and ecosystemic terms.

An ecosystem condenses in co-evolutionary space-time when guilds of synergistic interactants (cooperative, competitive, or otherwise) form enduring relations through essergetic exchange of matter/energy and information. Most natural ecosystems do not exhibit strictly evolutionary behavior, however, but rather exhibit a developmental character (Ulanowicz 1986). This emphatically applies to the ecological phenomenon of succession. Knowledge systems, and historical process, too, exhibit stages--sometimes in apparent recurrence as cycles--in developmental fashion, while simultaneously participating in an evolutionarily open trajectory. These formal notions need to be related to each other before their nontrivial application to substantive phenomena; the exercise is not mere classification. As with the assignment of structure and functions in a system, that for evolution and development reflects the context and angle of the observer; structure at one level and from one perspective may represent function through another, and evolution accessed at one level and from one perspective may bear the imprint of development from another, and vice versa.

Both evolution and development concern irreversible change, whether gradual, continuous transitions of degree, or punctuated, discrete transformations of kind; both are found in open, self-organizing, far from-equilibrium, dissipative structures; both are also non-deterministic and teleonomic, but to different extents. Development, conventionally viewed as a symptom of evolution, generates individual tokens of a type in a manner somewhat deterministic, quite temporally-sequenced, and marginally teleologic, or at least equifinal, as compared with evolution. However, one must be cautious in employing the individual organism as the exclusive metaphor for a unit of analysis appropriate to development, as observed by Leo W. Buss (1987). The significance of developmental dynamics for the semiotic ecology of knowledge rests on the feature of stages in ontogeny shaped largely by a concatenation of initial and boundary conditions, contrasting with the open trajectory of phylogeny for evolution, discussed by Stanley N. Salthe (1988). Salthe describes evolution as the accumulation of historical information leading to uniqueness of type, and development as stereotypical emergence of individuality of token, often through stages from immature (associated with maximization of gross energy flow, à la Lotka and the Odums), to mature, to postmature or senescent (accompanied by minimization of entropy production, à la Prigogine).

Any thorough exploration of the relevance of metaevolution and metadevelopment to the semiotic dynamics of knowledge perforce includes exegeses on the embedded concepts of selection (natural and artificial) and epigenesis; vertical hierarchy and lateral heterarchy; metastability; exogenous perturbation and endogenous fluctuation; habitat, niche and Umwelt; competition and cooperation; generalization and specialization; density and scale; order, disorder, and chaos; prediction and control; and entropy and negentropy. These concepts receive general treatment by Prigogine and Stengers (1979), Barbieri (1985), Brooks and Wiley (1986), Campbell (1982), Casti and Karlqvist (1986), Conrad (1983), Gatlin (1972), Hutchinson (1978), Nauta (1972), Odum (1969, 1981), Oyama (1985), Sober (1984), Ulanowicz (1986), and Wicken (1987), among others, of course.

The fifth aspect of the semiotic behavior of knowledge systems treated here concerns their ethology, if you will, as much as their ecology. How knowledge systems and their vehicles differentially replicate and survive, and how these processes intercalate with epigenesis, synergistically and otherwise, gives us some insight into the interpenetration and independence of embodied versus machine knowledge. As cultural evolution and development continue in concert--while humans and their implements (which variously substantiate, facilitate, dramatize, and sometimes even negate the human situation in an Umwelt, à la von Uexküll) become increasingly confused and even interchangeable--the moment ripens for a measured appraisal of the ontological status of the human condition, of knowledge, and of "our" tools and toys--ideas paramount among them, but also machines and artifacts in general. Material culture is no less equivocal for being, some assume, manifest in "reality." Clearly, two concepts demand out attention in dealing with both the material and immaterial, and with both biology and culture: neoteny and death, as recognized by Montagu (1981) and Gould (1977).

The types generated and culled in evolution lead to still other types; the tokens generated and maintained in development realize themselves. It is crucial to acknowledge the near-viral behavior of cultural tools and toys, and also of that phenomenon called "artificial life" (Langton 1988), although "synthetic life" might be a more auspicious cover term (Anderson 1987).

At this juncture, the temptation for cautious and/or playful speculation about the future overpowers scholars such as Margulis and Sagan (1986a, 1986b), Simons (1985), and Wesley (1974). What, really, is our coevolutionary and coadaptational relationship with knowledge-conserving and knowledge-dissipating machines? And if we comprehend this, can all parties agreeably parse "power" and "responsibility" (Anderson 1987, 1988)?

Knowledge and Life as Information and Energy

Although knowledge readily conflates with stored information in ordinary language, scholars have tried to distinguish these, from each other, and from the notion of meaning (e.g., Campbell 1982; Nauta 1972), in that meaning emerges situationally in a nondeterministic fashion which cannot reduce to elemental units or processes. In a similar vein, life implicates information, and thereby necessitates a parallel consideration of meaning. We return to semiotic issues of meaning and interpretation later in this essay. At this juncture we set out some thoughts on the relationships and life, and of information and energy, in all their permutations and combinations.

Life most concerns the discipline of biology; in fact, the description of biology as the study of living things may appear incontestable. Yet biology does not presume to define "life"; rather, it assumes it. The definition of "living, organic, growing, developing, replicating things" remains a semiotic issue rather than a biological one (Anderson 1989). Another problem, alluded to above, has to do with the "thing" in "living things", which too readily suggests "organism", and lays bare the cultural emphasis on material instantiations in space, at the expense of dealing with the pregnance of temporal process. In any event, too-literal interpretation of biology as the study of living things would reduce biology to the study of development, to the exclusion of evolution. In fact, the majority of biologists carry out their iterations of biological method without reference to either evolution or development; for some, these remain the ground, as life itself, for the figures of their investigation, while others do not even connect their practice to theory.

Evolution and Development:
Biology and Culture of Artifactual Informatics

For this purpose we assume that evolution and development refer to generic processes in dynamical systems, without foreclosing the possibility that there could emerge still other fundamental self-organizing processes coordinate with evolution and development.

While linked and feeding into and out of each other, evolution and development are distinguishable with reference to units participating in reproduction, selection, and epigenesis. As a consequence, the evolutionary process generating the phylogeny of kinds of things is open-ended, nondeterministic, and teleonomic; following Salthe (1988), evolution labels the irreversible accumulation of historical information, leading to unique and non-predictable types. The manifestation of evolutionary process generating ontogeny--that is, the developmental process generating individual tokens of things--is somewhat deterministic, temporally-sequenced, and marginally teleologic, or at least equifinal. Both evolution and development concern irreversible change, whether continuous transitions of degree (sometimes appearing gradual) or punctuated, discrete transformations of kind (sometimes appearing sudden); issues associated with scale and the status of observation can render these distinctions problematic. Gradual and punctuated evolution correspond roughly with growth and differentiation in development. Development, for instance, subsumes a continuous process of growth and decay as well as a tandem discontinuous process through stages comprising maturation and senescence. But, to repeat, both genres of processes are open, self-organizing, far-from-equilibrium, dissipative structures; both are also basically non-deterministic and teleonomic; but to different extents.

Since semiotics already tackles biology and culture (see, for instance, Koch 1986; Hoffmeyer and Emmeche 1989), with little extra courage it might as well go all the way to deal with the emergent in culture. Electronic knowledge environments, as tools and toys and other symptoms of culture, arise as a result of the application of other knowledge and information, in the organism and in the society. Such knowledge systems not only derive from other knowledge, but they obligate still other knowledge and information in their maintenance. If, in addition, the users desire confidence in either prediction or control, then sizeable energy investments must accompany those of information. This is because of the negentropic behavior of information which obeys its own dynamic within the sometimes limiting but often enabling constraints of semiosis.

Pattern, order, and organization in spatial, temporal, and substantial systems are symptoms of and also sources for information. For instance, information in both "environment" and genome integrate to shape epigenesis and phenome at various organismic levels in development, while within evolution, information bestows phenomena with form leaving tracks for the ambitious to reconstruct phylogenies.

Information, Knowledge, Meaning

Considerable confusion surrounds these notions. Even though they not infrequently have been conflated and confounded, we suggest they be distinguished with care. In the canons of information science, information operationally reduces to energy, through the equivalence of information with the reciprocal of entropy. This engineering sense of information renders it utterly redundant and uninteresting. Rather, energy systems bear information, but the latter will not reduce to the former.

In real and open systems, neither energy nor information, neither entropy nor negentropy, collapse neatly onto each other. In such environments, one must settle for provisional interpretation of meaning, rather than either prediction or control, although information, knowledge and meaning are all embedded in the infinitely regressive matrix of particular and generic human culture.

At the reductionist-inductivist end of a spectrum--or rather a maze--of approaches to information, knowledge, and meaning, lies the assumption that information exists a priori, only later to be organized into knowledge structures and endowed with meaning through normative habits and values. The holistic-synthetic view inverts this implicational hierarchy; when combined with an appreciation of the human culture-bearer's biological heritage (Anderson et al 1984, von Uexküll 1940), it appears that meaning emerges from the negotiation of experience constrained by individual ontogeny and species phylogeny, if not coevolutionary phylogenies.

The environment of human knowledge, machine-aided or otherwise, is simultaneously experiential, cultural, and biological. It cannot be divorced from deep past time or future fantasies. It cannot be analyzed as discrete atoms or enlarged through projection and/or arithmetic manipulation. It defies both simplistic reduction and mechanical accumulation.

Replication, Selection, Epigenesis

In the biological realm, species maintain themselves through recruitment of replicated units such as organisms. Organisms, shaped by their genotype, negotiate a phenotype by means of interacting with and incorporating aspects of the extra-genomic and extra-somatic environment.

The developing, replicating units and their aggregations are sites of various orders of variation, from mutation and meiotic recombination to gene flow (through population migration) and genetic drift (within population isolates). On this inhomogeneous ground operates the figure of selection, a compound of differential reproduction and differential survival, such that the range of genomic and phenomic instantiations of a species are never constant through time. Richard Dawkins (1976) introduces another level pertaining to culture, namely the memomic. The meme as a unit of replication would have a memome collocation and various meta-phenomic realizations when integrated in actual environments (Henson 1987).

Epigenesis describes the emergence of morphological structure in developing systems, and has been most unambiguously applied to the ontogeny of individual biological organisms (Buss 1987, Gould 1977). At other orders of magnitude and in other genres of developing systems, morphogenesis comprises analogous stages of immaturity or juvenility (high throughput, resilience to perturbation, growth, increase in qualitative complexity), maturity (homeostatic plateau, increase in quantitative complication, replication), and post-maturity or senescence (increase of rigidity leading to eventual loss of recovery from insult) (Salthe 1988).

Looking at organismic pathways per unit of biomass, the juvenile executes and consumes high rates of both information and energy, in stark contrast with the senescent's low rates of information and energy throughput. At the intermediate maturity of a system, a multi-modal, bifurcating environment generates the storage and flow of both information and energy leading to authority structures, reproduction, so-called power, knowledge, wisdom, and the issues surrounding altruism. Nicholas Maxwell (1984) distinguishes knowledge from wisdom, the former as an information store and the latter knowledge compounded by a humanistic ethic.

Morphogenesis in general and epigenesis in particular are frequently ignored, under-appreciated, or misunderstood in the operation of dynamical systems. These entail cascades in trajectories as well as oscillations around equilibrium attractor sinks. Morphogenesis precedes, enters into, and ensues in other manifestations from replication and selection.

Machine knowledge potentially slices through these orders of magnitude, from genome to phenome to memome to metaphenome. Here again, our layer-cake of imagery of nested structures and neatly contingent functions may interfere with an appreciation of the enabling and limiting constraints pertaining to culture in general, and human-artifact knowledge environments in particular.

Storage, Retrieval, Interpretation

In any system, information and energy mutually entail, although never in the redundant clasp portrayed by closed-systems cybernetics. Other parameters and variables apply as well, most dramatically those of continuous flow and those of discrete storage, and their other permutations.

Knowledge has often been assumed to be a static store of information, subject in the worst case to entropy, or decay of access and retrieval pathways. The semiotically more realistic worst case might be summed up as negentropy. Given the promiscuous hybridization of information, and the few constraints shaping its interpretation, and the incessant redigestion accompanying analogues to memory, stored information can never be passively suspended between loss and retrieval.

Retrieval, moreover, need not be accompanied by intentional pursuit, and intention need not be exclusively satisfied by the targeted information. Interpretation in every case imposes historico-psycho-socio-culturo-linguistic grids of over-determination in conjunction and under-determination in disjunction.

Knowledge enters discourse tagged as store rather than flow, product rather than process, spatial rather then temporal, information rather than energy--yet all permutations of these modalities apply. On reflection, one extreme limit for knowledge--a hermetic store of information--hardly qualifies as other than a stereotype. At another extremity--execution-driven, curso-genetic application of information--knowledge constantly reconfigures itself in self-obsolescence.

Prediction, Intentionality, Control

One of the more poignant lessons from biosystems ecology concerns illusions of rationality in human affairs. "Rationality" manifests itself through knowledge management: the selection, accumulation, application, and culling of information. These processes assume discrete and uncontaminable units of information, which behave in recoverable and projectable analytic pathways, and which respond to the imposition of artificial selection. Human intentionally, presumably situated in culture, would determine the targeted desirable features to select-in (the prototypic conditions of artificial selection) and/or the undesirable features to select-out (more typical of the "survival of the least unfit" of natural selection). Intentionally condenses in decision matrices, each node with a finite-state outcome, usually bimodal.

Virtually nothing in the empirical world resembles this closed-analytical-system scenario. Human intentionality premeditates, prescribes, invests in, anticipates, some future; these are costly operations in terms of drain on present time and other resources, such as information, energy, and space. Charmed by the myth of rationality, humans imagine time-binding through prediction and control. Much of positivistic science is phrased in terms of prediction, with control tacked on by the applied sciences such as engineering and education.

In point of fact, perfect prediction maps onto perfect control, but neither state resembles any ecological, ethological, or sociocultural reality or possibility. More often, prediction remains a game for simulation-jocks and gamblers, dealing predominately in informatics, while control consumes parents, police, and polity, often heavily invested in energetics.

All such systems, nonetheless, are powerfully shaped by their temporal trajectories--any emerging present contains the past. And all dynamical systems which persist in both developmental and evolutionary modes, do so through some synergistic concatenation of replication, selection-in, selection-out, epigenesis, and morphogenesis.

Succession Dynamics as Development

Any relatively predictable trajectory, any oscillation around an equilibrium state, any cycling around an attractor sink, any equifinalistic outcome, will be best described as developmental. Ecological succession of co-adapted (usually through co-evolution) guilds of species follows the life-span descriptive metaphors of juvenile (or expanding, colonizing, frontier, pioneer, immature), to mature (often attributed to the misnomer, "climax"), to senescent (the ultimate in "climax", seldom attained given real-world vagaries).

Ecological development potentially feeds into evolutionary trajectories in a number of ways. Individuals, communities, species, and guilds, all function as units of replication, selection, and morphogenesis, although seldom in synchronization; indeed, actual synchronization endangers the system. For example, if and when the units of replication and selection collapse onto each other, and at the same time eclipse morphogenesis, development precludes evolution and vice versa.

The Ecological Theater and the Evolutionary Play

In Hutchinson's metaphorical ecological theater and evolutionary play (1965), the dialectic lies in the intersection of energetic-space with informational-time . . . reduced crudely to other dimensions, we could describe it as a story of food and sex (Anderson 1988; Margulis and Sagan 1986a, 1986b). Another way of handling the theater and play, one particularly suited to the case of knowledge, is the linguistic convention of paradigm-stores and syntagm-realizations, connected by a recursive cursogenetic program.

It is necessary to specify the ethological actors, as well. In speaking of humans, the ethological actors are the products of both evolution and development, in interpenetrating orders involving both biology and culture, and choice, chance, and necessity. Particularly in social species--and after all, most are--the ethological script is shaped by ad hoc expedience, autotelic dissipation, and perceived desiderata. Given the potential links between knowledge and action, and action and norms, one expects, and receives, prescriptions and proscriptions about ethical responsibility attached to the loci of stored and exercised knowledge (e.g., Fardon 1985). One of these has come to be known by its acronym, R & D, for research and development. Sure enough, R & D maintains its vigorous appearance of early development by swiftly switching projects as they become mature (and hence imminently senescent) or complicated. In such a scenario, the ecological theater in its developmental mode corresponds to tragedy, insofar as the constraints argue for certain outcomes and preclude others, while the evolutionary play corresponds to comedy, insofar as the script remains nonprescriptive, open, and by definition nothing but surprises.

REFERENCES

ANDERSON, Myrdene.
   1987. "The Conduct of Artificial Life." Manuscript in conjunction with the Symposium, Artificial Life, Los Alamos National Laboratory, September 1987.
   1988. "Food and Sex", *Semiotica* 72.3-4, 361-374.
   1989. "Biology and Semiotics" in *Semiotics and the Individual Sciences* Bochum Publications in Evolutionary Cultural Semiotics 10, ed. Walter A. Koch (Bochum: Studienverlag Dr. Norbert Brockmeyer, forthcoming).

ANDERSON, Myrdene, John DEELY, Martin KRAMPEN, Joseph RANSDELL, Thomas A. SEBEOK, and Thure von UEXKÜLL.
   1984. "A Semiotic Perspective on the Sciences: Steps Toward a New Paradigm", *Semiotica* 51.1-2, 7-47.

BARBIERI, Marcello.
   1985. *The Semantic Theory of Evolution* (Chur, London, Paris, and New York: Harwood Academic Publishers).

BROOKS, Daniel R., and E. O. Wiley.
   1986. *Evolution as Entropy: Toward a Unified Theory of Biology* (Chicago and London: The University of Chicago Press).

BUSS, Leo W.
   1987. *The Evolution of Individuality* (Princeton, New Jersey: Princeton University Press).

CAMPBELL, Jeremy
   1982. *Grammatical Man: Information, Entropy, Language, and Life* (New York: Simon and Schuster).

CASTI, John L., and Anders KARLQVIST, editors.
   1986. *Complexity, Language, and Life: Mathematical Approaches* (Berlin: Springer-Verlag).

CONRAD, Michael.
   1983. *Adaptability: the Significance of Variability from Molecule to Ecosystem* (New York and London: Plenum Press).

DAWKINS, Richard.
   1975. *The Selfish Gene* (Oxford: Oxford University Press).

FARDON, Richard.
   1985. *Power and Knowledge: Anthropological and Sociological Approaches*, proceedings of a conference (December, 1982) at the University of St. Andrews (Edinburgh: Scottish Academic Press).

GATLIN, Lila L.
   1972. *Information Theory and the Living System* (New York: Columbia University Press).

GOULD, Stephen Jay.
   1977. *Ontogeny and Phylogeny* (Cambridge and London: Harvard University Press).

HARPER, Douglas.
   1987. *Working Knowledge: Skill and Community in a Small Shop* (Chicago: The University of Chicago Press).

HENSON, Keith.
   1987. "Memetics: the Science of Information Viruses", *Whole Earth Review* (winter) 57, 50-55.

HOFFMEYER, Jesper, and Claus EMMECHE.
    1989. "Code-duality and the Semiotics of Nature", in *On Semiotic Modeling*, ed. Myrdene Anderson and Floyd Merrell, *Semiotica* (special issue, forthcoming).
HUTCHINSON, G. Evelyn.
    1965. *The Ecological Theater and the Evolutionary Play* (New Haven: Yale University Press).
    1978. *An Introduction to Population Ecology* (New Haven: Yale University Press).
KOCH, Walter A.
    1986. *Evolutionare Kultursemiotik: Skissen zur Grundlegung und Institutionalisierung von integrierten Kultur-Studien* (Bochumer Beitrage zur Semiotik, 10); English version: *Evolutionary Cultural Semiotics: Essays on the Foundation and Institutionalization of Integrated Cultural Studies* (= Bochum Publications in Evolutionary Cultural Semiotics, 6) (Bochum: Studienverlag Dr. Norbert Brockmeyer, 1986).
LANGTON, Chris.
    1988. "Toward Artificial Life", *Whole Earth Review* (Spring) 58, 74-79.
LOTKA, A. J.
    1925. *Elements of Physical Biology* (Baltimore: Williams and Wilkins).
MARGULIS, Lynn, and Dorian SAGAN.
    1986a. *Microcosmos: Four Billion Years of Evolution from our Microbial Ancestors* (New York: Summit Books).
    1986b. *Origins of Sex: Three Billion Years of Genetic Recombination* (New Haven: Yale University Press).
MAXWELL, Nicholas.
    1980. "Science, Reason, Knowledge, and Wisdom: a Critique of Specialism", *Inquiry* 23, 19-81.
MONTAGU, Ashley.
    1981. *Growing Young* (New York: McGraw-Hill Book Company).
NAUTA, Doede, Jr.
    1972. *The Meaning of Information* (The Hague and Paris: Mouton Publishers).
ODUM, E. P.
    1953. *Fundamentals of Ecology* (Philadelphia: W. B. Saunders, third edition, 1971).
ODUM, Howard T.
    1969. *Environment, Power, and Society* (New York: John Wiley).
    1981. *Energy: Basis for Man and Nature* (New York: McGraw-Hill Book Company).
OYAMA, Susan.
    1985. *The Ontogeny of Information: Developmental Systems and Evolution* (Cambridge: Cambridge University Press).
PRIGOGINE, Ilya, and Isabelle STENGERS.
    1979. *La nouvelle alliance: metamorphose de la science* (Paris: NRF, Gallimard, Biblioteque des sciences humaines). Page citations are to the English trans. *Order Out of Chaos* (New York: Bantam Press, 1984).
SALTHE, Stanley N.
    1985. *Evolving Hierarchical Systems: Their Structure and Representation* (New York: Columbia University Press).
    1988. "Self-organizing of/in Heirarchically-structured Systems" Manuscript (August 1988).

SIMONS, Geoff L.
   1985. *Biology of Computer Life: Survival, Emotion, and Free Will* (Cambridge: Birkhauser, Boston).

SOBER, Elliot.
   1984. *The Nature of Selection: Evolutionary Theory in Philosophical Focus* (Cambridge, Massachusetts: The MIT Press).

UEXKÜLL, Jakob von.
   1940. "Bedeutungslehre", *Bios* 10 (Leipzig: Johann Ambrosius Barth), trans. as "The Theory of Meaning" by Barry Stone and Herbert Weiner, in *Semiotica* 42.1, 25-82. Page references are to the English translation.

ULANOWICZ, R. E.
   1986. *Growth and Development* (Berlin: Springer-Verlag).

WESLEY, James Paul.
   1974. *Ecophysics: The Application of Physics to Ecology* (Springfield, Illinois: Charles C. Thomas, Publisher).

WICKEN, Jeffrey S.
   1987. *Evolution, Thermodynamics, and Information: Extending the Darwinian Program* (Oxford: Oxford University Press).

WIMSATT, W.C.
   1980a. "Reductionistic Research Strategies and their Biases in the Units of Selection Controversy", in *Scientific Discovery: Case Studies*, Boston Studies in the Philosophy of Science 60, ed. T. Nickles (Dordrecht: Reidel).
   1980b. "Robustness, Reliability and Multiple Determinism in Science: the Nature and Variety of a Powerful Family of Problem-Solving Heuristics", in *Knowing and Validating in the Social Sciences: a Tribute to Donald T. Campbell*, ed. M. Brewer and B. Collins (San Francisco: Jossey-Bass).

MODELING SELF-ORGANIZATION

Stanley N. Salthe
Brooklyn College of the City University of New York

Myrdene Anderson
Purdue University

Abstract

Foremost among the tasks facing a semiotically-informed modeling of natural open systems is the recognition and representation of self-organization. This forces attention on process, time, and energetics to complement the conventional semiotic bias toward structure, space, and informatics. While self-organization might be captured in numerous operational idioms, we suggest that the fundamentally distinctive formal structures of (a) *development* (intrinsic predictability) and (b) *evolution* (unexpected change through change in contextual meaning) constitute the warp and woof of virtually all observations on systems undergoing change, and that, since these represent complementary orientations toward phenomena generally, interaction of these styles of change within systems can lead to generic models of enormous utility in many fields.

The Dynamics of Change

We take change to be fundamental to most discourses today. Constancy, stability, and predictability seem increasingly to have been the desiderata of dominant social classes, in a dominant society, in its prime. The relevance of this state of affairs to our predilections for modeling will become abundantly clear as we go on.

Change has been dealt with in two general ways in western discourses. On the one hand, we have Newtonian systems that change only when impinged upon by perturbations from outside the system (e.g., Darwinism, behaviorism, and so on). On the other hand, we have approaches deriving from Hegel and being elaborated now under the rubric of 'self-organization'. The former are well-known and semiotically relatively simple. We will explore the latter.

It is crucial to emphasize at the outset that we discuss semiotically-interesting systems in a general way and at their utmost abstract. But this does not mean that they are either exotic or trivial; rather, they are commonplace. Indeed, they are the only systems we know, either as ordinary mortals or as semioticians. Their ubiquity does not render them pushovers for our compulsive modeling, however. Any modeling necessarily hangs suspended between the Scylla of reduction and the Charybdis of projection, and negotiates upstream through the rapids of undecidability, uncertainty, and incompleteness. Any model insults the phenomenon modeled, in that the model will at best represent a single translation of that phenomenon, which simultaneously exists in many modalities (Rosen 1985). Any model likewise reflects the conscious, unconscious, and nonconscious motivations of the modeler, the centripetal self-indulgent pull of the playful scientist's modeling 'in' means-oriented exploration, the centrifugal push of consumer-oriented descriptive models 'of' and generative models 'for' (Anderson 1988).

Constancy and change are endemic in our discourse about the universe, but constancy is itself viewed as being maintained through conservation principles entailing modification at other levels in a system (Conrad 1983). Therefore we take *change* as the more fundamental, ubiquitous, unmarked. Change can be apprehended as process or through its product-consequences, as degree or kind, as digital or analogue, as continuous, gradual or transition *or* as discrete, punctuated or tranformational. In any case, change is too often transparent to the observer, and when not utterly transparent, may be intransigently opaque to satisfactory description, let alone explanation. In other cases, apparent change seduces the observer, who thereupon becomes blind to the properties simultaneously conserved. The challenge of any intellectual enterprise must be to construct the fundamental principles of change embedded in the habits of conservation and dissipation in self-organizing systems.

Self-Organization

Systems interesting to semioticians fall under this rubric of self-organized and self-organizing systems, regardless of whether we view them as natural or cultural, as physical or metaphysical, as thing-like structures or process-like functions, as containers or connectors, as informatics or energetics, as arbitrary or imperative, as accidental or deliberate, as overdetermined or underdetermined, as enduring or ephemeral, or as trivial or profound. In short, change in organisms, ecosystems, and social systems can be viewed as dynamically self-organizing. This means (1) that the system is internally driven to change, (2) that the system becomes more complex and organized with time, (3) that it does so in active contact with a fluctuating and occasionally perturbing environment, from which it accumulates traces that lead to its individuation, and (4) that the results of this process contribute to an intensification of agency in the system. Agency is that property of systems by which their unique individuality is reflected in the results of their interactions.

Changing systems are driven in ways describable abstractly most conveniently using thermodynamic discourse. A dissipative system is open at some level to flows of matter/energy (*mattergy*) and information (altogether essential energy or *essergy*, to some). The system shreds this free external essergy, incorporates by throughput some of the essergetic structure into the organization of the system, and discards less-ordered by-products or wastes back into the external environment. The energy is dissipated in form, behavior, and heat, while the information stored in the matter is dissipated into new configurations and heat. In all of this, entropy is produced within the system, some exported as heat and relatively disordered waste products, while some is retained by complication that increases the number of states the system can access. When this number of states gets large, individuality can be expressed more fully. Natural examples of such systems are driven into being by systems larger than themselves, then grow, elaborate to varying degrees, and eventually senesce, perhaps becoming absorbed by other burgeoning systems. Most of them are eventually recycled. Thus, self-organizing systems emerge, persist, transform themselves and other systems, and dissolve entirely or into other systems in a *temporal* trajectory, far from equilibrium. Hence, these are irreversible, nonlinear, and motivated (habitual or teleonomic) phenomena, but at the same time, because of individuation by way of evolution, they are also nondeterminate, relatively unpredictable, irreducible, and just plain complex.

Their complexity comes in several complexions and derives from several factors. One has to do with the scale and level of entry into the system by the observer. In the final analysis we are concerned with *human* interpretation, as it is enabled and limited by all the constraints inherent in phylogeny, ontogeny, culture history, language, and individual experience--and further by unmotivated accident. All our prosthetic sensory extensions and all our synthetic cognitive intensions notwithstanding, our construction of any subject/object of inquiry reflects our human perspective. We access and project into significance only certain 'real' and 'imagined' properties of our universe, and which of these are more or less important, adequate, or viable--for us or to the system itself--is seldom convincingly apparent.

Of course, another factor in complexity *is* complexity. Zooming in on a system from the outside, we risk oversimplifying the system by some finite deductive law-like principles, assuming we 'crack' the system at all. From this perspective--if we perceive an organized system in the first place--we are apt to see the regularities at the expense of the stochastic aberrations, which as noise may be reincorporated into the system in its hierarchizing trajectory anyway; we certainly don't appreciate the incessant drama of fluctuations which wash out at other levels. We view an instantiation of an individual *token* of phenomena, and find some possibly predictive *developmental* regularities by comparing its behavior with that of other tokens of the same type.

On the other hand, elbowing out into a system from the inside, we risk overcomplicating the system. From the inside our perspective privileges an intimate awareness of the unique trajectory *type*, subject to inscrutable and/or random behavior of internal and external forces, and conclude that the system can, at best, only be described post hoc as an *evolutionary* one--there being no others with which to compare it.

Development and Evolution

Change has conventionally been constructed in two quite different ways, labeled *development* and *evolution*. As a minimal way of distinguishing them, we note that development is a *predictable irreversible change*, while evolution is the *irreversible accumulation of historical information*--that which mediates individuation.

We will return in more graphic detail to this criterial distinction between development and evolution. For the moment, we offer some of their key signatures, before further discussing self-organization per se. Development and evolution are both irreversible temporal trajectories, with which we'd be more familiar were our terminology consistently employed. *Development* consists of the emergence in increasing specification of a somewhat predictable set of stages during the individuation of a token, from (physiological and ecological) configurations labeled immature to mature to senescent. Thus, development is formally closed by termination from senescence, while evolution is formally completely open. Organisms in their ontogeny *develop*, but so do societies and temper tantrums, and so does the universe insofar as we find its inception and ensuing history conforming to thermodynamic developmental patterns. Even though we infuse ordinary discourse with developmental metaphors, as a generic process, development has been under-recognized by almost all fields in this century, including biology, in part because of the exploration of the evolutionary paradigm (Salthe 1985, 1986, 1988a, 1988b, 1988c, 1988d, 1988e, 1989).

Evolution consists of utterly unpredictable emergence through the accumulation of some subset of historical information in a unique token of a classificatory type. Species *evolve* in their phylogenies when viewed and interpreted after the fact, and so do culture and personalities, as does the cosmos insofar as we emphasize its singular path of surprising entropy-driven self-organizing events.

Even though development and evolution constitute two different discourses on change in self-organizing systems, they are virtually two sides of that coin insofar as these processes intercalate and implicate each other. Not only does one precipitate the other, but their relation to the observer's scale and purpose suggest which interpretation is natural or primary. It bears repeating that biological development and biological evolution are but special cases of these formal modalities of change in dynamical systems.

Given that one can form a class or, better, a *type* of changing systems, development and evolution are related as follows: the commonalities of change shown among tokens of the type, because they allow prediction, are read as developmental changes. The unique aspects of the trajectories of the heterogenous tokens are taken to be evolutionary. So, any definable type--temper tantrums, societies, earthly planets--does both. The earth is an interesting case insofar as we have only one exemplar of it. Here we see the power of the thermodynamic connection. It can be seen that the earth has followed most of the predicted transformations of dissipative structures, and so can be taken as a token of that type, showing its characteristic developmental features. So, similarities over systems of very different scale and material embodiment can be taken as signs of membership in a single type.

Whether we take development or evolution to be the most fundamental depends on our orientation. If we are structuralists, and believe that structures are immanent in the world, development seems prior. In our society, so enamored of prediction and control, this seems an appropriate attitude. Evolution on this view is the result of failure to conform to the rules, partly caused by generalized friction. Evolution here is an embroidery on preordered developmental regularities. On the other hand, if we see process as primary, we see development as reflecting mere statistical parameters, always more stable and predictable than the actual unique instances on which they are based. These instances are theoretically capricious and constrained only by contingent boundary conditions and/or historically-bound internal stored information which itself comes in part from past boundary conditions. These constraints are then the source of the observed regularities. They are not structures because they are entirely contingent. On this view, development is emergent from collections of instances of evolutionary trajectories. In any case, it is development that is of interest to us here because it has a kind of structure or form. Evolution is a mere willy-nilly accumulation in which anything can happen given propitious conditions.

Modeling Development

Development is invariably labeled by a series of stages. Analysis of many examples allows us to postulate that these labels mark a series of ontological steps toward whatever we take to be the most developed condition of the system under observation. For organisms, it would be the human adult or mind; in Figure 1, it is taken to be the self-organized machine ('machine' being here defined as the most specified kind of individual there can be); for eschatological purposes, it has been taken to be the Godhead, for political purposes, the state. The developmental trajectory is in this way structured so as to be capable of carrying meaning. Formally, these ontological steps make a nested system of classes (called levels) of increasing specification transitively related, so that, in the well-known Linnaean hierarchy, a human being is also a mammal and also, just as fully, a thermodynamically open system.

To some extent, one can view the developmental aspect of change in self-organizing systems as traversing a specification hierarchy of nested types as also illustrated in Figure 1 (Salthe 1988d), with actual emergence the outcome of a dialectic between intrinsic habit and extrinsic constraint with stochastic factors operating within each as well as on their compounding. Development, consequently, is the traversing of a specification hierarchy from the least to the most highly specified condition. We suggest that systems of lower specification carry, rather than strictly determine, the more specified stages. The medium of carriage is largely energy flow. Each achieved stage in the early part of the trajectory has a greater intensity of energy flow through it, so that the system can achieve a greater range of distinct stages within each narrower specialization. The potential number of these states has increased insofar as the system has also grown and become more complicated in form, giving it a greater range of actual configurations. Even by default, the more elaborate system is, the more room there is for inappropriate states--this is an entropic aspect of senescence. So, more highly specified stages are in this sense generally more entropic. Each achieved stage supplies enabling constraints allowing the system to broach yet more intense being.

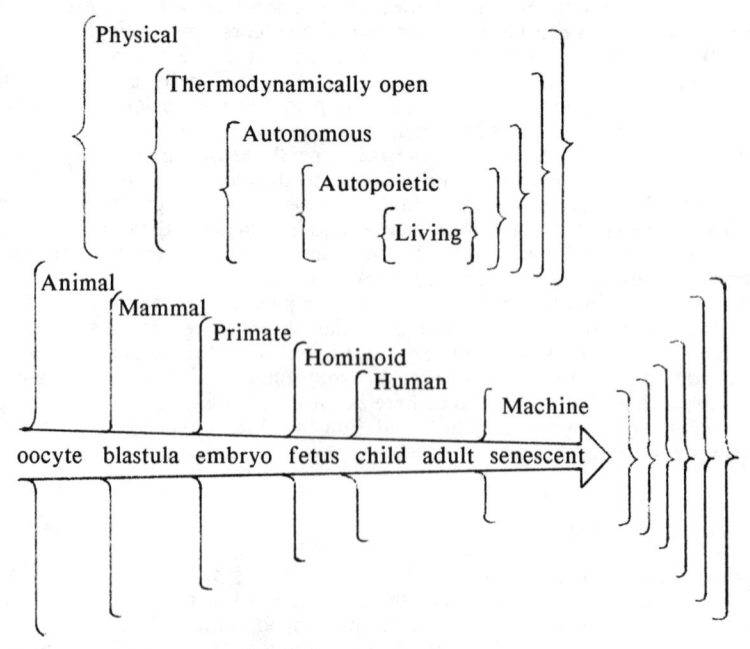

Figure 1. A Homocentric Specification Hierarchy.

Figure 2 makes the further point that selection among possibilities for further development is formally representable by a dichotomous key. An autopoietic system can become, say, living--or instead elaborate into some other kind of abiotic, autopoietic system. On this chart we follow up only those possibilities leading to humans, our favorite species. Twisting the above specification hierarchy into its perverse recursiveness, we have a cornucopia or yin-yang taxonomy of systems.

> Dynamic material (versus Cognitive)
> > Thermodynamically open (versus Isolated)
> > > Autonomous (versus Dependent)
> > > > Autopoietic (versus Without internal information constraints)
> > > > > Living (versus Abiotic autopoietic)
> > > > > > Symbolic cultural (versus Nonsymbolic)
> > > > > > > Cognitive (versus Material)

Specification hierarchy (to southeast)--　　carrying medium
largely *enabling* constraints--semiotic　　largely *energy*

Implication hierarchy (to northwest)--　　infecting vector
largely *limiting* (regulating)　　largely *information*
constraints--semiosic

Figure 2. Relating Specification and Implication.

If we can scan back over the hierarchy from the most highly-specified stage, we could interpret it as an implication hierarchy. Being alive implies that the system is also autonomous, and also that it is a material system. The higher levels, once they have been reached, can be seen to integrate, interpret, infect, or to harness or domesticate the lower ones. Each achieved stage sets constraints upon, and regulates, the less specified aspects of its being. James Lovelock's (1979, 1988) Gaia hypothesis concerning the planet earth as a living organism is predicated on just this contagious property. Each achieved state is *less* entropic than the preceding one in the sense that it has become restricted to fewer possible *kinds of* states. (Notice, however, that a higher level system made up of these developing entities would become potentially *more* entropic as more different kinds and tokens emerge from the accompanying individuation.) What we have is an accumulation of stored informational constraints. This developmental trajectory concept was an important part of C.S. Pierce's cosmology of the continued elaboration of 'habits' at the expense of vague and creative potentialities.

Note that empirically there is a definite optimal state of maturity in these developing systems, which state inevitably collapses into senscence. Thermodynamically immature systems burgeon as the intensity of their energy flow increases. They are maximizing their gross energy throughput--the Lotka/Odum 'maximum power principle'. And this continues for a while even after the intensity of energy flow has begun to decline because the system is still growing and still storing information at significant rates. In this way, complication continues to increase even while the energy intensity of the system drops. Complication is the antithesis of flexibility, and flexibility is necessary for surviving perturbations. Hence, with the increasing number of internal constraints on behavior, the system becomes so rigid in its own ventures (this component of its entropy decreases), that it cannot homeostat successfully against perturbations. Because of this, its actual behavior becomes even more entropic by way of entropy flow from the environment, until it surpasses boundaries consistent with the continuation of its type, and is then recycled.

The complication referred to in the last section is actually embodied in evolved, historically-gleaned form. It carries the individuation of the system. As the development of the surface of the earth (a kind of primary succession of ecosystems) has gone on, organic evolution has produced more and more kinds of organisms on the earth--more and more kinds of ontogenetic developments. As the ontogenetic development of an organism takes place, more and more cell types come into being, more and more particular neuronal configurations emerge, more and more traces of historical accidents of all kinds accumulate, so that each becomes more different from any of the others of its type. As a hurricane develops, it is subject to more and more contingent perturbations which deflect its track and strength from the average for its kind. The developmental attitude has informed us that changes will take place at certain rates and in certain patterns. The *actual* changes that take place at any level are *not* predictable. Thus, we know in advance that a blastula will be succeeded by a gastrula in development of certain kinds of organisms. But in the history of living systems this transition was presumably discovered as a response to some historical perturbation in the past. Since then, it has become part of the internally-held stored information of the system, and is now subject to but minor fluctuations--a habit was formed.

Modeling Evolution

As we can see from this discussion, modeling self-organization boils down to modeling development. It is the only change that we construct as knowable. Only it reflects our semiosis. Evolutionary change is meaningless in the sense that it is change we cannot anticipate because--as Robert Rosen (1985) has pointed out--all models are of necessity incomplete. That there are mammals on earth instead of *wrnps* or *uieees* or *R2D2s* has no systemic meaning for us; it is the result of historical accident and *could not* have been modeled by anyone. This means that our own presence here could not have been anticipated by *any* model, nor the reasons why this individual and not another is struck down in an epidemic. Perhaps we could identify predisposing attributes, yet these are only enablements. It still requires an exact arrangement of contingencies to explain causally. It is effectively a random event, in the sense of Gregory Chaitin (1975). It could only be modeled by a string of *ifs*--if this, if that ... until we have constructed the whole event rather than a model of it. This has been called a 'continuous series explanation' (Dray 1964). If, in addition, we are startled by the event, it would be a *'how-possibly!'* explanation.

Whereas development has a genuine shape, evolution has no intrinsic shape, and phylogeny can only be tenuously interpreted and approximated post hoc through its temporal traces in a particular system--using as clues a critical inspection of extant ontogeny alongside any fortuitously-found and temporally-situated fossil forms.

Less confidently, we could proffer an evolutionary curve for the higher-specified trajectories which reverses that of development. The developmental throughput trajectory largely deals in energy flow, with a peak early in the immature stage. As sheer speculation, we could explore some generic evolutionary throughput trajectory as being largely in information flow, and that flow peaking in a late (senescent? preterminal?) 'stage'.

We have several reservations about this model. It does render evolution as an embroidery on development. Moreover, its most convincing instantiations--for some, anyway--will take contemporary human socioculture as a reference point--as did

Teilhard de Chardin (1959) in a decidedly developmental and homocentric prognosis of evolution. Thoughtful critics and mindless media concur that these are times of increasingly rapid cultural change, that we live in an information age. These litanies pass uninspected and merge with postmodern cosmological dogma. Any overdetermined, too-easily-rationalized paradigm must be suspect, at least to the extent that one is then obliged to foreground its provisionality. Do we actually have a qualitative or quantitative metric to impose on this grid of perceived gradual and/or punctuated cultural change? This challenge will lie fallow until our next collaboration.

Modeling Self-Organized Systems

Hence, the developmental model of the system *is the system* in the sense of systems science. We suggest that its semiotic structure is basically the interpenetration of the specification and implication hierarchies. Acts of specification (the making of distinctions and choices), carried by energy transformations, could be taken as supplying Aristotelian material and efficient causes. The structural of the model itself is the formal cause. Most interestingly, we also have final causes in the model --the string of implications back to the beginning, the string of informational constraints. Since the series is knowable, it is effectively being constructed as a higher-level entity--a trajectory--which could be said to exist completely and simultaneously at a higher-level cogent moment, as represented in Figure 3. That higher-level existence justifies the presence of final cause in respect to events measured by lower-level cogent moments. Insofar as these moments come and go without any change in the upper-level situation, that which was present at the beginning of a lower-level event is still present at its end.

Note again, history, evolution, and individuation are in this model only as general potentialities, probabilities, possibilities, as 'if...then' statements. The perturbations producing them come either from outside the system or from within it. The latter might be thought part of the system and hence accessible to modeling-- but not so. Many of them are amplifications of lower-level events formally not in the system description, others are simply fluctuations of the system itself at its own scale. Both of these (and any creativity!) seem to be modelable only as probability distributions.

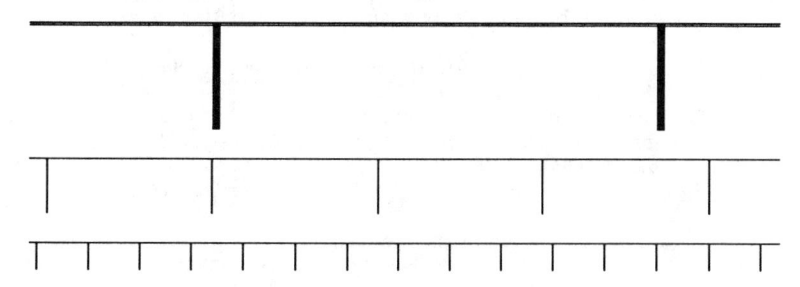

Figure 3. Incommensurable Levels and Scales of Cogent Moments.

Finally, we can see from this why games, like baseball, can be of such absorbing interest. The developmental aspects are forefronted, stereotyped, and well-knowable. The possibility of outside perturbations, unlike in the real world, are carefully circumscribed to give a thrilling edge, but they are not allowed to destroy the game.

Modeling as a Self-Organizing Exercise

We suggest that modeling can be an end in itself (models 'in' the abductive, suspenseful inspiration from something), as well as means to ends (models 'of' something or generative models 'for' something) (Anderson 1988). Modeling in any of these modalities will exhibit the same patterns of self-organization discussed here.

Any temporal activity will have its developmental spurts and starts and its conclusions or abandonment. Those abductive leaps which synergize each insight correspond to the immature peaks in throughput. The fine-tuning and final touches increase the specificity of the individual token product. The model can then either die or go to heaven, where it finds itself incessantly replicated and reincarnated and reinterpreted, with each of these facsimile homologues and analogues (Gould 1988) having its own ontogenetic trajectory.

The same modeling activity, seen through its phylogenetic trajectory of increasing uniqueness of type as it reflects the differential accumulation of information, will be an instance of evolution. G. Evelyn Hutchinson, in an oft-cited essay (1965), refers to the ecological theater and the evolutionary play. The ecological theater focuses on the spatial and atemporal dynamics of horizontal 'ecology' and its paradigm store of similarity and potentially, and the evolutionary play focuses on the temporal and aspatial links of 'genealogy' and its syntagm flow of contiguity and realization (Anderson 1989; Lounsbury 1959; Salthe 1985).

Keeping to the dramaturgical metaphor, we suggest that evolution, with its nondeterminate and unpredictable emergence, corresponds to an open-ended comedy. (As an aside, this bears comparison with Walter A. Koch's notions of tension and suspense [Koch 1985a, 1985b].) Development, with its equifinal outcomes, its entropy-driven scenarios, corresponds to a closed and constrained tragedy. Underdetermined evolution epitomizes surprise, overdetermined development, suspense.

REFERENCES

ANDERSON, Myrdene.
- 1985. "Synthetic Potential Within, Beyond, and Through Semiotics," *Semiotics 1984*, edited by John Deely (Lanham: University Press of America), 363-372.
- 1986a. "From Predator to Pet: Social Relationships of the Saami Reindeer-herding Dog," *Central Issues in Anthropology* 6:3-11.
- 1986b. "Expansion, Contraction, Containment, Contamination, and Other Frontier Phenonmena" (Manuscript, January 1986).
- 1988. "Thinking Through Tinkering; Tinkering Through Thought," *Semiotics 1987*, edited by John Deely (Lanham: University Press of America), 31-41.
- 1989. Paradigms of Evolution and Paradigms of Culture," *Culture and Evolution*, edited by Walter A. Koch (Bochum, West Germany: Brockmeyer).

CHAITIN, Gregory J.
- 1975. Randomness and scientific proof. *Scientific American* 232.1:47-52.

CONRAD, Michael.
- 1983. *Adaptability: The Significance of Variability from Molecule to Ecosystem* (New York and London: Plenum Press).

DRAY, William.
- 1964. *Philosophy of History* (Englewood Cliffs, New Jersey: Prentice-Hall, Inc.).

GOULD, Stephen Jay.
  1988. "The Heart of Terminology," *Natural History* 97.2:24-31.
HUTCHINSON, G. Evelyn.
  1965. *The Ecological Theater and the Evolutionary Play* (New Haven: Yale University Press).
KOCH, Walter A.
  1985a. "Tension and Suspense: On the Biogenesis and the Semiogenesis of the Detective Novel, Soccer, and Art," in *Linguistic Dynamics: Discourses, Procedures and Evolution*, edited by Thomas T. Ballmer (Berlin and New York: Walter de Gruyter), 279-321.
  1985b. "The Biology of the Theatre: On the Semiogenisis of Drama and Related Cultural Events," in *On the History and Theory of Drama and Theatre/Zur Geschichte und Theorie des Dramas und Theaters*--On occasion of the international symposium at Bochum, April 1984, edited by Herta Schmid and Heinrich Steinkueheler (npp:np), circa 35 pp.
LOUNSBURY, Floyd G.
  1959. "Similarity and Contiguity Relations in Language and Culture," in *Report of the 10th Annual Round Table; Georgetown University Monograph Series on Language and Linguistics* 12, edited by Richard S. Harrell (Washington, DC: Georgetown University), 123-128.
LOVELOCK, James E.
  1979. *Gaia: A New Look at Life on Earth* (Oxford: Oxford University Press).
  1988. *The Ages of Gaia: A Biography of Our Living Earth* (New York: W.W. Norton).
ROSEN, Robert.
  1985. *Anticipatory Systems: Philosophical, Mathematical, and Methodological Foundations* (New York: Pergamon Press).
SALTHE, Stanley N.
  1985. *Evolving Hierarchical Systems: Their Structure and Representation* (New York: Columbia University Press).
  1986. "The Logic of Self-organization in a Hierarchical System" (Manuscript; modified October 1988).
  1988a. "Development and Evolution: Attitudes Toward Change" (Manuscript, March 1988).
  1988b. "Styles of Change in Self-organizing Systems" (Manuscript, May 1988).
  1988c. "The Relationship Between Natural Selection and Self-organization" (Manuscript, July 1988).
  1988d. "Self-organization of/in Hierarchically Structured Systems" (Manuscript, August 1988).
  1988e. "The Logic of Self-organization in a Hierarchical System" (Manuscript, October 1988; modification of 1986).
  1989. "Kali Theory," *On Semiotic Modeling*, edited by Myrdene Anderson and Floyd Merrell, *Semiotica* (forthcoming).
TEILHARD DE CHARDIN, Pierre.
  1959. *The Phenomenon of Man*, translated by Bernard Wall (New York, Harper and Row).

II

PSYCHOLOGICAL PERSPECTIVES ON SEMIOTIC MODELS

ABDUCTION AND AFFORDANCE
J.J. GIBSON AND THEORIES OF SEMIOSIS

Donald J. Cunningham
Indiana University

In previous papers at the Semiotic Society of America and elsewhere (Cunningham 1987, 1988, in press) I have explored the implications of semiotic models of cognition like Deely's (1982, 1986) Umwelt model and Eco's (1976) model Q. Today I want to respond to a criticism of these models which has been frequently raised, appropriately in my view. These critics have argued that semiotic models eventually lead to solipsism; that is, these models seem to imply (if not avow) that organisms can know nothing that they themselves have not created or experienced.[1] While semiotic models often propose that semiosis arises from an interaction between the physical world and the cognizing organism via signs, little is said about the nature of the elements which are interacting and how the outcome is influenced (or not) by those elements. Robert de Beaugrande (1987), in a paper presented last year at this meeting, raised many important issues relevant to this discussion and proposed a non-classical model of semiosis. Drawing upon insights from quantum science, he proposes that we consider multiple realities and shows how semiosis can operate in both ordinary experience (the seemingly deterministic world in which we all appear to find ourselves) and in the non-deterministic world of quantum mechanics. In this paper, I am going to try to portray the semiosis of ordinary experience of terrestrial animals, primarily humans, by considering the nature of the physical world from the perspective of J. J. Gibson's (1979) ecological approach to visual perception. I start with the assumption that although we can not know the physical world directly, it surely exists and as such has features which constrain the sign processes. As I dash across the street, I *will* endeavor to avoid the onrushing traffic in the belief that the cars are real and not the product of my own unique semiosis. Given the relatively consistent nature of sign structures which humans within a particular context develop, what does this suggest about the nature of the physical world?

Deely's model is fundamentally a sensation based model. The physical world is presented to us as bundles of features which we some how synthesize into a perceptual object - a process which sounds a lot like traditional encoding models of perception where impoverished stimulus information arrives at a receptor (e.g., the retina) and is somehow operated on by information processing mechanisms until the information is reorganized into a form consistent with our existing knowledge. But if these features can be combined and recombined in an infinite number of ways, what is the reason for the preeminence of some arrangements over others? Could it be that perception is a function of structures in the physical world, not simply decomposed features and/or constructions of the perceiving organism?

This is essentially the question raised by J. J. Gibson (1979) in his ecological approach to visual perception.[2] Gibson begins with a notion all too rare in academic psychology, that his theory of perception must account for *ordinary* perception, that of organisms moving about in their environment, seeing the ordinary things of daily life. Why, he asks, would it be the case that if perception was simply a construction from sensed features (and impoverished ones at that) that our perceptions seem to agree so well with the environment through which a multitude of observers move?

Gibson rejects the sensation based theories of perception which regard the perceiver as a passive receiver of impoverished stimulus energy on the basis of which the perceiver transforms a retinal image into a percept. These theories have been developed largely within the context of experimental tasks where the subject's head is immobilized or where he is asked to fixate on a point so that he will not scan the pattern which is exposed. Presentations are usually of very short duration to likewise minimize scanning. Gibson characterizes these tasks as *snapshot* or *aperture* vision since they resemble the vision one might experience looking though the shutter of a camera. Gibson's ecological optics abandons the sensation-perception distinction and proposes instead an ecological model of an active perceiver confronting an information rich stimulus environment by moving about, by turning his head, by scanning --the very action that aperture vision tasks seek to prevent.

Gibson's notion of environment is actually very compatible with the idea of the Umwelt. For Gibson, an environment is that which organisms perceive, not the physical world which a physicist might describe. The term refers to the "surroundings" of an organism on a scale appropriate for terrestrial animals (i.e. in terms of terrains, objects, and events which are appropriate for organisms on this planet - sizes between inches and kilometers, times between seconds and years, etc.). For Gibson, the words *organism* and *environment* are an inseparable pair.... each implies the other. One can not talk of an environment in general but only of an environment with respect to a particular animal.

The terrestrial environment, unlike the physical environment, consists of a medium, substances and surfaces that separate the medium from substances. The medium for humans is the gaseous atmosphere, the "air" which permits unimpeded locomotion from place to place, seeing, smelling, hearing and touching of substances. In our world, the medium has absolute axes of reference such as the vertical axis defined by gravity and the horizontal axis defined by the ground. Substances are the "things" of the world, the objects or "furniture" which occupy the terrestrial surface. Unlike the medium, substances do not permit locomotion or transmit light. Substances are heterogeneous whereas the medium is relatively homogeneous. Surfaces separate the medium from substances. It is at the level of surface where all of the action in visual perception takes place. We do not perceive the medium or substances but only surfaces where the medium and substances meet. A surface is said to have a layout (form), texture, the property of being lighted or shaded and the property of a certain fraction of the illumination falling on it.

To make a very long story much too short, visual perception arises when structured information from surfaces is perceived. The ambient optical array (this structured information available in light) is described by Gibson as visual solid angles with a common apex at the point of observation. They are angles of intercept which change as the observer moves or the surface(s) under observation move. But other aspects of the array do not change (e.g. the layout and reflectance). The perceptual system monitors those things that change and those things that persist and from this information, perception is developed. Perception is thus a process which develops from the interaction of an active perceiver in an informationally rich environment which is constantly in flux. In other words, for Gibson, the information for perception is in the light, not in the prior knowledge, cognitive processes or needs of the perceiving organism. The organism detects those aspects of the world which persist and those which change and registers them or "resonates" to them. The process of "tuning" is raised to account for perceptual learning and development; that is, for example, we become more adept at reading radar screens or whether a person is friendly by gaining experience in extracting the relevant invariants from the information flux.

By now some of you may be wondering if I have lost my mind by presenting such an undoubtedly realist model to semioticians who believe fervently that all the universe is "perfused with signs" or perhaps composed exclusively of signs. Gibson's notion that we directly pickup perceptual information from the environment seems wildly incompatible with the idealism implied by Peirce's statement. Even within academic psychology, Gibson's position is held as out of the mainstream, championed only by a small group of former students. But while Gibson's metatheory is certainly a realist position (for example, Gibson denies any meaningful role to memory, knowledge or inference in the perceptual process), the theory itself was undoubtedly moving much closer to an interactive position at the time of Gibson's death. The realist stance was taken to distance his position as clearly as possible from the dominant information processing view of perception where impoverished sensations are augmented by such processes as memory and inference into percepts. Gibson's criticism of those views has never been successfully countered, in my opinion. For example, if visual perception is based solely on the impoverished information arriving at the retina, then we must postulate some entity (the homunculus?) which must look at the retinal image and elaborate it. But this entity must then also have an eye (retina) and mind which we must then account for. Furthermore, if perception is a process of elaboration, then the perceiver must already have knowledge of what is being perceived and the physical world is thereby rendered irrelevant. These are telling criticisms but Gibson clearly went too far in the opposite direction by denying any role for the perceiving organism. Yet a sympathetic reading of his work reveals a genuinely interactive or, in my view, semiotic stance which avoids the necessity of adopting either a realist or idealist stance.

Of primary importance for our purposes here is Gibson's theory of affordances. As noted above, Gibson considers the environment to be the surfaces that separate substances from the medium in which animals live. But environments also *afford* things (such as shelter, locomotion, etc.). There is information in light for perception but also for the perception of what surfaces afford. To perceive something is to perceive what it affords, its value or meaning. To quote Gibson "The affordances of the environment are what it offers the animal, what it provides or furnishes, either for good or ill" (1979: 127). But affordances do not exist independent of an animal; the term refers to both the environment and animal. "An affordance is neither an objective property nor a subjective property; or it is both if you like... (it) points both ways, to the environment and the observer" (1979: 129). The terrestrial surface, for example may be horizontal, flat, extended and rigid, thus affording support to certain terrestrial animals. But this affordance is relative to particular terrestrial animals, not an abstract property of the physical world.

The process of perceiving affordances is called "information pick-up", unfortunately the least developed aspect of Gibson's theory. Affordances are invariants available in the ambient optic array and perception of affordances results from monitoring those aspects of the ambient optic array which persist and those which change. Note that this conception places the affordance in the light, not in the needs or motives of the observer. The potential affordance of a paper clip as a replacement for fishhook is available whether or not it is perceived by a particular organism to which the affordance is relevant.

In my current thinking, the concept of affordance is very relevant to semiotic models of cognition. In Deely's model, for example, abduction is a mode of inference whereby organisms attempt to make sense of the world by creating sign structures. In essence this process has been likened by Shank (1987) to "reading" the environment. But is our reading free to take any possible form? Can the Umwelt we create be entirely independent of those aspects of the environment relevant to us as a species or as an individual? A fruitful area of research for semioticians will be to investigate the possibilities of affordance-like constancies in our worlds. I fully appreciate the fact that I am making a hugh leap from a model of visual perception to one of cognition, especially a model of cognition with the scope of semiotics. I personally believe the leap is justified and moves us away from the criticism of solipsism.[3]

If you can read beyond the realist rhetoric, Gibson's book is filled with thought provoking ideas and insights and I recommend it to you. Let's consider a few of these.

Terrestrial versus Physical Environment

Much of Gibson's theory depends on a distinction between the environment at an ecological level versus the environment that a physicist might describe. He is interested in describing environments in terms of those aspects of it that have an impact on animals. As mentioned above, environments at this level of description imply an animal that is surrounded; indeed, the animal could not exist without this environment. You can not, therefore, describe a terrestrial environment in absolute terms, but only with reference to a particular animal (e. g., you could describe a rock, a field, a plain, etc; your choice of level of description would depend upon the particular animal being considered). So the "facts" of the physicist may or may not have relevance in describing the terrestrial environment of a particular animal. To take an extreme example, the fact that the world is round has no impact on the perception of most animals; for all intents, the world may safely be regarded as flat since that information is available in the ambient light. Likewise, if a substance goes out of existence (e.g., water evaporates) in the ecological environment, it no longer has an impact on the organism (or has a different one) while at the level of physics, of course, matter is conserved. A description of the environment at this ecological level is sorely needed and Gibson's work is a useful start.

Space and Time

In a related vein, Gibson questions the relevance of the concepts of space and time for perception. The physicist assumes the existence of space which the objects of the world inhabit. According to Gibson, however, terrestrial animals perceive space only because there are objects in the world: that is, we are not born with some *a priori* notion of space which we then apply to the objects of the world; rather, the experience of seeing some objects go out of sight or occlude others leads us to the perception of space. It is thus the structured information in the ambient optic array which serves as the basis for us noticing that the terrestrial environment is cluttered, not some innate sense.

Likewise, the flow of abstract time has no reality for terrestrial animals. We perceive not time but events and only those events relevant to us at some level. Humans can not ordinarily perceive a glacier advancing but can certainly perceive a snowball heading for our head.

In light of these observations, Gibson has attempted to describe the substances and events of the world in terms of their layout and in terms of what they afford, rather than in terms of concepts like time and space. For instance, an enclosure, a layout of surfaces that surrounds the medium to some degree (e.g., a cave or a hut) can afford shelter, a hiding place, etc. Likewise an event such as a change of layout due to rotations of an object (a rolling ball) can afford bowling, moving ammunition to the cannon, injury from an imminent collision (as in the famous scene from *Raiders of the Lost Ark*), etc. In perceiving these objects and events, the animal is monitoring those aspects of the optic array which persist and those which change. He is extracting invariants.

Ambient Light

Gibson bases his notions of visual perception on information available in ambient light rather than radiant light. Light from a single source is a relatively rare occurrence in the terrestrial world. The light we experience is many times reflected and it is the reflected light which has structure, contains information about reflecting surfaces. Much of the traditional literature on perception is based upon radiant light or minimal amounts of ambient light, and is thereby largely irrelevant to ordinary perception. Likewise, organisms explore the ambient light by moving about, turning their heads and it is this active role that allows the perceiver to extract invariants. This is not possible with radiant light.

Places

The concept of place is an interesting one. A place is a location in the environment. While a physicist might describe a place as a point in space with respect to some coordinate system, that is not how an animal perceives a place. This room, for instance can be described as to what floor it is on, in which hotel, in which city, and in terms of what it affords. Many places have no definite boundaries, such as places where food is to be found, places of danger, etc. In these cases, a place seems to be more a region than a defined area. Despite the ambiguity of the concept of places, it seems to be central for a theory of perception (and semiosis). The terrestrial environment or the habitat of an animal might be said to consist primarily or exclusively of places. What is it that persists about a place, and what changes? What invariants can be extracted? Gibson presents an elaborate and farfetched example of a "hiding place" which I will not repeat here but I think the concept is an interesting one within the context of this theory an deserves serious attention.

The Role of the Perceiver

An important aspect of Gibson's theory is the perceiver's awareness of self in the process of perceiving the environment. Egoperception accompanies exteroception and is inseparable from it: "Perception has two poles, the subjective and the objective, and information is available to specify both. One perceives the environment and coperceives oneself" (1979: 126). The animals body occludes part of the optic array but as the animal moves, previously hidden parts of the array come into view and others disappear. It seems to me that the deliberate control of movement which is postulated here is essential in the process of extracting invariants. Perceptual learning and development would be difficult, if not impossible, if we were limited to displays which were not subject to our own manipulation.

I could go on but perhaps this is enough to convince you that Gibson, despite his realist rhetoric, has some useful ideas which might be incorporated into semiotic models of cognition. The perception of affordances seems to me to be a natural extension of abduction. Both of these processes assume, in my view, that we will eventually be led to ever more adequate conceptions of the terrestrial world. Like Peirce, I believe that our inquiry will eventually lead us closer to the dynamic object, to an understanding of the world as it *is*, unmediated by signs. But since this quest is of the nature of *all* cognition, why should our theoretical and/or empirical inquiry be any different?

NOTES

[1] Not everyone regards solipsism as a problem. Thomas A. Sebeok has recently remarked, "I am a solipsist and proud of it." (Sebeok, Lamb and Regan 1987: 12)

[2] It should be stressed here that Gibson's work is limited largely to visual perception and can only be analogously applied to other forms of perception and to other cognitive processes.

[3] Gibson himself has recognized that some version of solipsism is inevitable: "Just as there are no material objects in an (optic) array but only invariants to specify objects, so are there no material events in the (optic) array but only the information to specify events" (Gibson 1979: 102).

REFERENCES

BEAUGRANDE, Robert de.
    1987. "Semiotics and Control Systems: Toward a Non-Classical Model of Communication". Paper presented at the annual meeting of the Semiotic Society of America, Pensacola, Florida, October, 1987.
CUNNINGHAM, Donald.
    1987. "Outline of an Educational Semiotic", *American Journal of Semiotics* 5, 201-216.
    1988. "Abduction and Affordance: A Semiotic View of Cognition". Paper presented at the annual meeting of the American Educational Research Association, New Orleans, April, 1988.
    In press. "Semiotic Aspects of Pedagogy", in *Handbook of Semiotics*, ed. Roland Posner (Berlin: Walter De Gruyter).
DEELY, John.
    1982. *Introducing Semiotic* (Bloomington: Indiana University Press).

1986. "The Coalescence of Semiotic Consciousness", in *Frontiers in Semiotics*, ed. John Deely, Brooke Williams and Felicia Kruse (Bloomington: Indiana University Press).

ECO, Umberto.
    1976. *A Theory of Semiotics* (Bloomington: Indiana University Press).

GIBSON, J.
    1979. *The Ecological Approach to Visual Perception* (Boston: Houghton Mifflin).

SEBEOK, T., LAMB, S. and REGAN, J.
    1987. *Semiotics in Education: A Dialogue* (Clairmont, CA: College Press).

SHANK, Gary.
    1987. "Abductive Strategies in Educational Research", *American Journal of Semiotics* 5, 275-290.

SHE UNDERSTOOD HIM: "ALL TOO WELL"

James C. Lundy
Southern Illinois University at Carbondale

"The President's Speech" is a chapter in Oliver Sacks' *The Man Who Mistook His Wife for a Hat*. Sacks is a neurologist who feels himself ". . . a naturalist and physician both. . . equally drawn to the scientific and the romantic, and continually sees both in the human condition" (1987: vii). It is this reason humans fall "radically into sickness".

The essay, "The President's Speech", is a case study of a patient on an aphasia ward, who watches a televised speech by the president of the United States. The aphasics on the ward, who though intelligent, are rendered incapable of understanding written or spoken language by organic neural damage. They are, however, able to understand most of what is said to them. That is, they understand "speech" but not "language". Natural speech consists of an utterance, which involves more than mere word-recognition. Therefore, according to Merleau-Ponty, "The aphasic still knows how to put words together" (1973: 5). He further states, "Since the possession of language depends upon the integration of phonemes, inversely, aphasia must result in the destruction of the phonemic system" (1973: 25). That is aphasics negate language. So, Sacks argues, ". . . expressiveness. . . is perfectly preserved in aphasia, though understanding of words be destroyed" (1987: 81).

"Either he is brain-damaged, or he has something to conceal" (Sacks 1987: 84) claims Emily D., a patient from the aphasia ward, speaking of the President's speech. While Emily D. is on the aphasia ward, she actually does not have aphasia but, instead, a form of "tonal" agnosia. For Emily D., the expressive qualities of voice are gone, however, words (and grammatical constructions) are perfectly understood. That is, Emily D. understands "language", but not "speech". Therefore, the aphasics and Emily D. perform precisely the opposite functions in obtaining meanings. The aphasics preserve, even enhance, the cognitive meaning of "expressive" speech.

To Kristeva any utterance serves a dual purpose which she refers to as the "symbolic" and the "semiotic". The "symbolic" names the referential function of the utterance (Holenstein 1976: 156); it is the interpretive way in which the speaker is situated as a relation to reality. The "semiotic" names the unconscious of the utterance, such as rhythm and gesture, Lacan argues ". . . what the psychoanalytic experience discovers in the unconscious is the whole structure of language" (1977: 147). However, in this discovery Kristeva realizes that language is not accepted "into" the unconscious. Because, the unconscious is the ". . . unspoken precondition of linguistic systematization" (1984: 78). The unconscious shows, ". . . that thetic signification. . . constitutes the subject without being reduced to his process precisely because it is the threshold of language" (1984: 45).

In poetic language the semiotic is emphasized. Kristeva refuses to accept the notion that all utterances are equal. No utterance is without the duality of both the symbolic and the semiotic; meaning is generated through their relationship. There is a dialectical interplay between the symbolic and semiotic. The thetic is a "break" in the signifying process (1984: 43). It posits a "gap" between the signifier and the signified. Emily D. is "already" in this thetic phase. This duality in establishing ". . . the positing of the thetic. . . is a permanent struggle to show the facilitation of drives within the linguistic order itself" (1984: 81).

Kristeva is against fixed categorical distinctions. She is concerned with codebreaking. Her stress is on the symbolic and semiotic "released" through the breaking of codes. For Merleau-Ponty, aphasia is a ". . . loss of speech, related to a disorder of the speech organs. . . the aphasiacs is not someone who no longer speaks, but rather someone who speaks less or in another fashion" (1973: 69). This leads Merleau-Ponty to "the idea of a two-functioned language". There would be: 1) a concrete language, whose role would be to respond to actual situations; 2) a categorical language, which considers the word in itself as a purely abstract entity and which responds to fictitious situations or to "problems". "Aphasia would lead language back to its first function," (1973: 70) says Merleau-Ponty. That is, the patient with aphasia would lose the "possibility" of the second function, a categorical language.

For Kristeva, the subject is not a unitary entity, but a "split subject". The "split subject" is both the subject of enunciation and the subject of utterance. The symbolic and the semiotic depends on what Kristeva calls the *chora*, which is "different from that of symbolic law but nevertheless effectuates discontinuities by temporarily articulating them and then starting over, again and again" (1984: 26). That is, to "negate" something is to "create" something new. The chora is the "point" where you can see structure emerging; it is the "blank space" about to happen.

". . . but the sick and their sickness drives me to thoughts which, perhaps, I might otherwise not have" (Sacks 1987: vii). Sacks further states, "constantly my patients drive me to question, and constantly my questions drive me to patients--thus. . . there is a continual movement from one to the other" (1987: vii). So, Sacks is concerned with restoring the human subject to a "who" as well as a "what". Kristeva says the human subject needs a semiotic as well as a symbolic. Sacks also sees the necessity of "a gulf" between the psychical and the physical: Kristeva's chora. The scientific and the romantic come together.

For Kristeva, there is a revolution in poetic language when the semiotic overruns the symbolic. That is, poetic language occurs when "speech (*parole*) overcomes "language" (*langage*). "Normal" human beings are taught to look for the semiotic only in such "poetic language", e.g., Joyce, Lautréamont, Mallarmé (because it is the "not-yet-intelligible"). "Normals" are not looking for the semiotic in "The President's Speech". Kristeva's subject in process/on trial is the subject in whom the semiotic continually negates the symbolic. The subject continually arrives at a new position (*langue*). When the semiotic overruns the symbolic, speech negates language by becoming "the spoken". The more sensuous, desiring part (the semiotic) negates the abstract, law-governed part (the symbolic).

While desire (the semiotic, Emily D.) is founded on drives, Kristeva sees drives as "dividing the subject" unconsciously from desire. Without this "division", there is a "lack" that ". . . brings about the unitary *being* of the subject" (1984: 131). This subject, conscious of desire, who ". . . lives at the expense of his drives. . .", is the subject in search of language (the symbolic, aphasics, "normals"). The Freudian theory of drives is viewed by Kristeva ". . . as a transition from the psychical to the somantic. . . drives. . . both connect and differentiate. . ." (1984: 167).

Emily D. is not deceived by the President, because her symbolic perception is "enhanced". She can negate the symbolic and look, instead, at the semiotic. However, the aphasics are deceived by the President, because their semiotic is "enhanced". They are looking at the symbolic. In other words, poetic language is an "unleashing" of the unconscious drives (the instinctual, the semiotic) (Bové 1984: 218). Drives articulate the semiotic chora which is ". . . a nonexpressive totality formed by the drives and their stases in a motility that is as full of movement as it is regulated" (Kristeva 1984: 25). Drives are ". . . always ambiguous, simultaneously assimilating and destructive. . .". This dualism ". . . makes the semiotized body a place of permanent scission" (1984: 27).

So, for Emily D. the semiotic is her "unconscious" drive. She can resist language, her "conscious" drive, by incorporating it, and be "aware" of the semiotic. For aphasics, on the other hand, the semiotic is their "conscious" drive. They resist speech, and "unleash" their "unconscious" drive of language. "According to Jakobson, in aphasiacs, there subsists a system of phonemes, a unity, a degenerated whole that nevertheless remains systematic as a result of this continual reequilibration" (Merleau-Ponty 1973: 25). Merleau-Ponty adds, "in aphasia it is not the innate instrument that is lost, but the possibility of using it in certain cases" (1973: 25). "Normals" have the possibility of both, but typically, look to the symbolic. To resist the use of language (the symbolic) is to project the unconscious (the semiotic) into an antisocial role. That is, Emily D. is trying to "free herself from authority" (Bové 1984: 224).

Kristeva's subject in process/on trial is the subject who "breaks free" of culture's codes (the symbolic, language) and whose signifying practice (semiotic, speech) becomes " poetic language". When the semiotic negates the symbolic, "poetic language" occurs. Because the aphasics "understand" and have an "enhanced" semiotic, they seek the symbolic; they strive "toward" authority. However, Emily D. because she "understands" and has an "enhanced" symbolic, she seeks the semiotic. She is trying to "free herself from authority".

Even as Jakobson applies his theory of the two axes of the paradigmatic and the syntagmatic to aphasia it, necessarily, implies a "loss". He ". . . distinguishes two main types of aphasia, depending on whether the paradigmatic axis of selection or the syntagmatic axis of combination is impaired" (Holenstein 1976: 143). If the "problem" is in the former axis, he calls it a "similarity disorder"; if it is in the latter axes, he calls it a "contiguity disorder" (Jakobson 1971: 292). In either case, while the functions of paradigmatic and syntagmatic axes are reversible, language is still lost.

Sacks sees a paradox with "The President's Speech". So-called "normal" human beings, so says Sacks, were, indeed, fooled. The question is: why? The answer, for Sacks, is the President's cunningly deceptive word-use (symbolic) combined with deceptive tone (semiotic). Only the brain-damaged, the aphasics and Emily D., remained undeceived. In other words, the President's rhetoric "reifies" the "normals" and "repressed" the aphasics, but "frees" Emily D. She recognizes her unconscious drive; she is not deceived. Because the President is "closed to change" he negates the semiotic (Bové 1984: 225).

The key word is "combined". "Normals" always combine the symbolic and semiotic; although they do not reflect on it or feel it. However, the aphasics "understand" the semiotic and therefore "enhance" the symbolic; they move toward authority. Emily D., on the other hand, "understands" the symbolic and, therefore, "enhances" the semiotic; she is trying to free herself from authority. The aphasics negate the semiotic. Emily D. negates the symbolic. The symbolic must be "negated" to give way to the desire of the semiotic. However, this "negation" is Kristeva's "new negativity". "Negativity constitutes the logical impetus beneath the theses of negation and that of the negation of negation, but it is identical to neither since it is, instead, the logical functioning of the movement that provides the theses" (1984: 109). Negativity operates ". . . on the border between 'consciousness' and 'unconsciousness'" (1984: 121). So, while "normals" negate, the "brain-damaged" actually combine. This is why Emily D. claims, from the beginning, that the President is either brain-damaged (combines) or, that he has something to conceal (negates). She would "understand" him in either case, because she is "continually arriving at a new position". The President is "normal". Contrary to Sacks, the President made a digital (either/or) choice in the language/words he selects. He cannot let his language "combine" with his sensuous meaning or speech (he has something to conceal). It is precisely because of the image of the speaker in "The President's Speech", unwillingness to allow for a "combination" or "reversal" of the semiotic and the symbolic, that he "fooled" the "normals," as well as the aphasics, but not Emily D.

REFERENCES

BOVÉ, Carol.
    1984. "The politics of desire in Julia Kristeva," *Boundary 2* XII.2 (Winter), 217-228.
HOLENSTEIN, Elmar.
    1976. *Roman Jacobson's Approach to Language: Phenomenological Structuralism*, trans. Catherine Schlebert and Tarcisus Schlebert (Bloomington: Indiana University Press).
JAKOBSON, Roman.
    1971. "A linguistic classification of aphasic impariments", in *Selected Writings Vol. II* (The Hague: Mouton), 289-306.
KRISTEVA, Julia.
    1984. *Revolution in Poetic Language*, trans. Margaret Waller (New York: Columbia University press).
LACAN, Jacques.
    1977. *Écrits: A Selection*, trans. Alan Sheridan (New York: W.W. Norton).
MERLEAU-PONTY, Maurice.
    1973. *Consciousness and Acquisition of Language*, trans. Hugh J. Silverman (Evanston: Northwestern Univeristy Press).
SACKS, Oliver.
    1987. "Preface" and "The President's Speech", in *The Man Who Mistook His Wife for a Hat: And Other Clinical Tales* (New York: Harper & Row) vii-x and 80-84.

FORM AND USE DIFFERENCES IN THE ACQUISITION OF SPEECH PARTICIPANT SIGNIFIERS: EVIDENCE FROM BLIND CHILDREN

Donna E. West
State University of New York at Cortland

Much investigative effort has been expended on the question of possible differences in onset of "I" for blind children, for which conflicting findings exist (Fraiberg, 1977, Urwin, 1977, 1978, Rowland, 1980, Mulford, 1981, 1983). Little attention, if any, has been given to a more qualitative approach, i.e., unconventional predeictic form and use, and incidence of grammatical case, once deictic use prevails over nondeictic use. To settle for a quantitative analysis only, obscures the course of acquisition, and the issue of use, and reduces the acquisition process to nothing more than instantiations of adult form. Such an approach undermines the semiotic assumption that all entities are signs, and that all signs have meaning, by failing to consider the legitimacy of non-adult predeictic forms, as well as the onset and use of the full range of case forms in novel contexts. A semiotic analysis provides insight into which representational aspect of the target sign is contributing to an increased or decreased use of the predeictic or deictic form (index, icon, or symbol). Hence, apart from a semiotic analysis the function of index in deictic use, particularly its place in the acquisition process could not be understood. Furthermore, if index is primarily a visual phenomenon, blind children are likely to experience a greater reliance on symbolic features.

Fraiberg (1977) has been the only investigator to have considered deictic versus nondeictic use, albeit merely in terms of first person, and primarily focusing on subject form to the exclusion of possessive and objective forms ("my", "mine" and "me"). Her analysis revealed that although the blind children's onset of production of the subject "I" was within range for sighted children, their creative use of "I" (in contexts other than stock phrases) was not found until they had reached a mean age of 4:10--mean age for sighted children, 3:0 (Fraiberg, 1977, Loveland, 1980). Fraiberg attributes the difference to a state of prolonged egocentrism brought about by a delay in self representation in play, without consideration to the possibility that other conventional/unconventional forms may have been used for self representation, and without having recorded the course of acquisition of other person pronouns.

Additional evidence from Urwin (1977) and Mulford (1981, 1983) has suggested that no difference in acquisition of person deictics exists by calculating frequencies alone, and by focusing nearly exclusively on subject forms. Moreover, Mulford could make few claims regarding the acquisition process itself since her data were taken from blind children who had exceeded five years of age. The present investigation (West 1986) considers both the issue of course of acquisition (predeictic forms and use) as well as the character of deictic use (comparisons in frequencies of grammatical case forms). The advantage to this analysis is that it attempts to describe a complete account of pre- and postdeictic acquisition in which children are active deductive thinkers within a universe of signs whose representational features can be used to their advantage, as opposed to the more prescriptive approach. From this perspective, the following hypotheses have been developed:

1) Differences do not exist in onset of deictic use of first person forms between blind and sighted children;

2) Blind children's use of first person deictics is not noticeably different from sighted children's;

3) Blind children experience a delay in onset of the deictic use of second person forms;

4) Blind children use second person deictics differently than do sighted children.

Data were gathered from two blind children (Bonny, Libbie) and a sighted child (Eric) whose ages at the study's onset are: 2:4, 2:10 and 2:5, respectively (see Table for age at each visit). A natural speech sample was taped bimonthly for the course of one year. The sessions took place at the children's homes and a familiar adult was present on every occasion. Frequencies were calculated from either first person or second person productions and not from the entire speech corpora. Two cognitive tasks to measure degree of comprehension of speech participant roles were likewise tape recorded.

The children were requested to orient an object with an intrinsic top (hexagonally shaped canister) in the case of Task 1. In the case of Task 2, the object to be oriented had an intrinsic front (familiar doll/teddy). Three trials for each deictic were given in which the investigator made the request as follows: "Make the canister so I/you can get some candy." or in the case of Task 2, "Make the doll/teddy so I/you can kiss it." (for validity see Loveland, 1980). The present design is a modification of Loveland's design in that she requested that the subjects "Make the teddy so I/you can see it." which is hardly effective in the case of blind children and/or blind investigators. The coding scheme categorizes response patterns as: egocentric (code 1)--in all three trials for the deictic, the orientation point was the child him/herself; initial decentration (code 2a)--object is oriented such that either speech participant can have access to its intrinsic side; partial deictic contrast (code 2b)--orientation is successful in one of the three trials; full deictic contrast (code 3)--successful orientation in at least two of the trials for each deictic.

Age of Participants at Each Visit

VISIT NO.	Bonny	Libbie	Eric
1	2:4	2:10	2:5
2	2:6	3:0	2:7
3	2:8	3:2	2:9
4	2:10	3:4	3:1
5	3:1	3:7	3:3
6	3:4	3:10	3:6

Hypothesis 1 is supported since onset differences were not found. Deictic use prevailed over nondeictic use at similar ages for all children, between 3:0 and 3:4 (see Table 1.1). It appears that age, rather than blindness, was the primary determining factor in the acquisition process.

Table 1.1

Relative Frequencies of Deictic Use Across Visits
First Person

VISIT NO.	Bonny	Libbie	Eric
1	.05	.22	.34
2	.10	.89	.20
3	.10	.93	.32
4	.12	.92	.37
5	.15	.94	.80
6	.89	1.00	.93
MEAN	.24	.87	.59

The largest differences in trends and frequencies occurred between the blind children, precluding that blindness had a substantial effect on acquisition of first person deictics. Findings from the cognitive task performance are in accord with onset similarities, since the children demonstrated full perspective-taking awareness by age 3:1 (see Table 1.2). All of the children arrived at the highest level prior to the point at which deictic use prevailed over nondeictic use, except for Bonny's performance on Task 1. Secondary factors such as degree and quality of experience, may have influenced the onset of deictic use, since the blind children's experiences were so diverse. Hence, the claim of Hypothesis 1--that no differences exist in rate of acquisition of first person deictics, is supported since any differences among children are ascribed to the interacting effect of age and experience.

Table 1.2

Cognitive Task Performance

VISIT NO.	Bonny Task 1	Task 2	Libbie Task 1	Task 2	Eric Task 1	Task 2
1	1	1	1	2.b	1	1
2	1	1	1	3	1	1
3	2.a	2.b	3	3	2.b	2.b
4	2.a	3	3	3	3	3
5	2.a	3	3	3	3	3
6	2.a	3	3	3	3	3

Nonetheless, differences in the course of acquisition were revealed, indicating that use differences exist between the two groups. This finding provides disconfirming evidence to the claim of Hypothesis 2--that use differences in first person do not exist. The forms which the blind children used as first person signifiers did not match those of the sighted child. Proper names and third person pronouns, which were used to refer to self, were produced by the blind children exclusively, and they produced a higher incidence of verb plus noun without a subject morpheme, e.g.,

"Want cookie." relative to the sighted child (see Table 2.1). Eric's developmental forms were of a different character: Productions of proper name and third person pronouns did not occur, while production of the form schwa plus optional verb plus noun was frequent, e.g., "/ ə / want cookie." It is likely that Eric employed his own proper name to refer to self prior to data collection since it has been documented that sighted children use this predeictic form rather extensively (Loveland, 1980). It is exceedingly unlikely, however, that Eric ever produced a third person pronoun to signify self since this form has never been documented for sighted children to my knowledge. Documentation for blind children does exist (Andersen, 1982). She reports that all of her blind subjects frequently produced "she"/"he" for self reference during the acquisition process.

Table 2.1

Total Absolute and Mean Relative Frequencies for Predeictic Forms
First Person

	Bonny n	Bonny f	Libbie n	Libbie f	Eric n	Eric f
Prop.	29	.17	18	.31	0	.00
3 P. Pro.	27	.16	8	.14	0	.00
Recip.	15	.09	1	.02	2	.03
schwa+(V)+N	10	.03	10	.85	45	.36
V + N	83	.48	13	.22	12	.19
Syn.	2	.01	7	.12	4	.06

It is curious that the blind children used the third person forms to refer to self since doing so appeared to deemphasize their role as speaker in the speech event (conversational exchange) and perhaps in the narrated event as well (event spoken about). Since the third person pronoun conventionally refers to someone outside of the speech event, the blind children's use obscures speaker participation, which may in turn, limit the degree to which others engage them as speech partners. Although the use of these third person forms does not preclude entirely participation in the narrated event, their use suggests that someone other than the speaker is the referent. Consequently, the speaker's role in the narrated event is likewise obscured. The blind children's function in both events is unclear, because "she"/proper name is interpreted to refer to non-speech participants who play a role in the narrated event only, such that they could never be speakers.

The primary factor contributing to such third person uses in course of acquisition could be the incidence with which others use such third person forms in reference to the blind children which gives rise to a decreased likelihood of participation in conversational exchanges. Consequently, the act of deemphasizing the role of the self in the speech event and in the narrated event on the part of the blind children may not have been deliberate at all; rather it may have been a function of their particular experiences as blind children. Failure to perceive extralinguistic indexical cues (eye-gaze directed toward the addressee) which initiate verbal interaction, is likely to have had linguistic consequences. Lack of such access may have contributed to less frequent participation in speech exchanges, and to the increased frequency with which others spoke about them. Limited practice as a speech partner might, in turn, limit the degree to which one initiates such exchanges, thus affecting the frequency with which the speech event is maintained and refined. Parents of the blind subjects may have spoken for them more frequently than parents of the sighted subject, and other adults may have less frequently addressed the blind children because of the lack of facility to engage them by means of novel attention-getting strategies. As a consequence, the degree to which the blind children experienced reference to them as non-speech partners could account for the incidence of third person self referents.

The sighted child's performance is in accord with this line of reasoning, since his speech input included exposure to similar patterns. His older brother is blind, and Eric was exposed to speech patterns similar to those of the blind children, even though he was not the addressee. Despite this, his speech record shows no incidence of self reference by the same means, indicating that lack of experience in speech events, rather than imitation of adult form is the primary determinant.

A semiotic analysis reveals that the indexical function is, for the most part, not operating when proper names are used: It appears not to be critical that index be present extralinguistically as an accompanying gestural cue. In the case of full-fledged nominals, successful reference can occur by use of the symbolic function alone because of its more explicit general meaning, especially for proper names. Thus, their substitution was likely to have been deliberate on the part of the blind children. Perhaps they were still unaware that their voice functions as index when the pronoun "I" is used, in that its symbolic meaning is more vague than that of proper names. Avoidance of indexical means to successfully refer could be a consequence of the inherent visual realization of most indexes--signs' indexes may be restricted nearly exclusively to access in the visual modality, especially for a prelinguistic child.

Like the previous pre-deictic third person forms, the blind subjects' higher relative frequency of verb plus noun without a subject morpheme could have been a result of lack of experience in speech participant roles. The absence of a morpheme to clarify the person participant may be symptomatic of their relative inexperience as speakers. Since the person referents of the schwa forms (/ ə / plus (verb) plus noun) always signified self reference, their meaning was never unclear; but person referents of the form verb-plus-noun, because they did not consistently refer to the self, were often unclear. Instances of v-plus-n were used as imperatives by the blind children. The greater production of this predeictic form on the part of the blind subjects may likewise be resultant from their paucity of experience as speech participants. Hence, use of these predeictic third person forms appeared to be a function of: 1) blindness, in that conversational cues were not accessible, and 2) quality of experience--the degree to which others drew them into the conversation, and the means which they used to do so.

An early form for which no differences were observed between the groups was the use of "you" for "I" (pronoun reciprocation). The frequencies were extremely low for all subjects relative to the other developmental forms (see Table 2.1). These data suggest that direct imitation is not a primary means of acquisition. The subjects seldom referred to themselves as "you" despite the fact that "you" was frequently used in reference to them. The children's equally low incidence of syncretic utterances likewise supports the claim that direct imitation is, for the most part, not operating (see Table 2.1). Cutsforth (1932) and Maxfield (1936) have found a high proportion of echolalic and perceverative utterances on the part of their blind subjects, which is not in accord with the present findings. Such stereotypic patterns were found to be rather extensive in the speech records of a subject from whom data were gathered for the present study, but which were not analyzed because of a diagnosis of a concomitant learning disability. Perhaps Cutsforth's and Maxfield's sample consisted of children with other handicapping conditions, or children whose experience was limited as a result of residential school affiliation.

Even though the blind children's course of acquisition of first person diverged somewhat from the sighted child's course, their onset of deictic use is rather similar when age and performance levels are matched. The subjects arrive at virtually the same developmental level at approximately the same age. Hence, Hypothesis 1 is supported while support is not found for Hypothesis 2. Differences in course of acquisition are in actuality use differences, because the predeictic third person forms which were employed by the blind children were made to signify something other than the conventional.

Comparisons of the production of grammatical case forms of first person likewise casts some doubt on the claim of Hypothesis 2--that differences in use of the deictic first person pronouns between groups does not exist, by the fact that blind subjects produced certain of the case forms more often relative to other first person case forms. Their mean proportions of the determiner "my" were higher than Eric's (see Table 2.2).

Table 2.2

Total Absolute and Mean Relative Frequencies of Grammatical
Forms of Deictic Referents--First Person

	Bonny n	f	Libbie n	f	Eric n	f
Sub. ("I")	44	.83	252	.68	67	.74
D.O. ("Me")	1	.02	35	.09	6	.07
I.O. ("Me")	0	.00	8	.02	1	.01
Det. ("My")	7	.13	69	.19	10	.11
Poss. P. ("Mine")	1	.02	5	.01	6	.07

Sub.: Subject; D.O.: Direct Object; I.O.: Indirect Object; Det.: Determiner; Poss. P.: Possessive Pronoun

By contrast, the pronoun "mine" was the more frequent form for Eric. This finding is not surprising in light of blind children's need to make explicit the referent for the addressee. The nominal which accompanies "my" functions to disambiguate the intended referent for addressees of blind children, whereas eye-gaze is sufficient for addressees of sighted children. The blind children appeared to depend strongly on linguistic symbolic means for purposes of successful reference. Such means, although helpful, do not substitute entirely for the inability to employ visual indexing, since no indication of spatial location is given. Spatial indexing can further disambiguate the referent if other similar potential referents happen to be present.

While "this" and "that" refer to an object on which the speaker is focusing,"my" plus nominal and "mine" possess the additional feature of belonging, perhaps not merely to current objects of ownership, but to potential ones as well. Loveland (1980) found a rather high incidence of these possessives in the speech of two-year olds which may have been a function of their strong inclination to identify what belongs to them, which is also in accord with Piaget's claim that egocentrism prevails at this age. Unlike the incidence of the possessive determiner, the fact that the determiners "this" and "that" were not more frequently used by the blind subjects relative to the pronoun counterparts, further supports the contention that ownership identification prevails at this point in the developmental course (West, 1988).

If this line of reasoning is valid, the possessive determiners may have served a second major purpose for the blind subjects, that of expressing their desire for an object which is not within reach. They may have functioned as imperatives to request that the adult make accessible to them the desired object. The sighted child appeared to have had less of a need to make such requests because objects are more accessible to seeing children. Given this logic, blind children experience a greater propensity to use the determiner to access far objects (objects beyond their "personal space") than to access near ones (those within their "personal space"). This motivation may partially account for their higher mean proportions of the determiner as opposed to the pronoun, since presumably the field of reference which lies beyond the blind children's personal space (near space) is greater than that of seeing children, if reach determines near space. Because the sighted subject had the benefit of the visual field, which affords simultaneous and sustained access to the potential field of referents, and because visual indexing strategies (eye-gaze, pointing) were effectual, his reliance on linguistic symbolic means, namely, the accompanying nominal was not critical. This difference in type of cues for successful reference (index versus symbol) appears to be responsible for the deictic use differences between the groups.

Differences were not found in production of any of the remaining case forms. Age appears to determine use regarding the subject form. All three children exhibited a marked increase in frequency at about the same age, between 3:0 and 3:3 (see Table 2.2). The greater difference in frequency occurred between the blind children which also suggests that age and not blindness was responsible--the age differential was greater between the blind children. Age, however, may only have had an indirect affect.

Cognitive developmental factors such as decentration may have had a more direct influence. Piaget and Inhelder (1969: 93-96) claim that at about three years of age children begin to decenter. They become aware of self as a member of a universe of other selves. This awareness is a precursor to a deictic use of "I" since awareness of agent with respect to conversational roles (speaker versus addressee versus person spoken about) rests upon the more basic notion of self as distinct from others. In addition, it rests upon the awareness that all person perspectives are potentially valid, such that they can assume identical, as well as distinct functions in any one event. A sense of self as speaker is founded upon an additional differentiation between participant roles in the speech event, and a strong sense of self as agent in the narrated event. The subject's use of "I" in creative contexts by 3:3 presumes the mastery of several skills: decentration, speech role differentiation, speech/narrated event differentiation, and participant function in the narrated event.

The incidence of the direct and indirect object forms "me" was so low as to preclude comparisons across subjects (see Table 2.2). Their low incidence is consistent with findings which suggest that such grammatical case forms are later productions by children in general relative to other case forms (Bates, 1979).

The findings for first person onset support the respective hypothesis since all of the children experienced a striking increase of deictic use over nondeictic use by 3:4, which is within normal range. The claim of Hypothesis 2--that use differences do not exist, however, is tenuous, because different predeictic forms were produced by the blind children which have never been documented for seeing children, and because some difference was revealed in deictic use, namely, degree of production of the grammatical case of possessive determiner versus possessive pronoun. Although the blind and sighted subjects' performance was similar regarding production of grammatical subject and direct and indirect object forms, the differences were sufficiently striking to question the Hypothesis.

No confirmation for the claim of Hypothesis 3--that a difference in onset of deictic second person exists between groups, can be found. The frequencies of the blind subjects deictic productions were quite disparate, whereas Libbie's and Eric's frequencies were nearly identical (see Table 3.1). Their mastery of the deictic second person was nearly complete, since deictic productions far exceeded nondeictic productions prior to data collection, except for Bonny whose deictic use never prevailed over nondeictic use, even at 3:4 after which no further data were taken. In addition, Bonny is the only subject who acquired first person deictics prior to those of second person (see Table 1.1 and Table 3.1). Cognitive task performance may shed some light on Bonny's divergence. Her performance on Task 1 was strikingly different from her performance on Task 2, which suggests some developmental disadvantage for her with respect to the other children (see Table 1.2). Second person onset patterns cannot be attributed to age since trends were not observed for any of the children.

Table 3.1

Relative Frequencies of Deictic Use Across Visits
Second Person

VISIT NO.	Bonny	Libbie	Eric
1	.00	.92	1.00
2	.00	1.00	1.00
3	.25	1.00	1.00
4	.37	1.00	1.00
5	.00	1.00	1.00
6	.25	1.00	1.00
MEAN	.16	.996	1.00

Perhaps Bonny's less diverse experiences overall contributed to the delay in second person onset, and to the slight developmental disadvantage in perspective-taking. Since Bonny had never attended preschool, and had little interaction with peers, the opportunity to engage in turn-taking exchanges was less likely than for Libbie, who had extensive opportunities in the preschool setting and in the home setting, as well. Limited experience in turn-taking exchanges may result in delayed understanding of reciprocal speech participant roles, especially in the case of blind children, because visual access to others' behavioral contribution to events is frequently unavailable. Their further participation in turn-taking behaviors could contribute to greater use of linguistic index, if one assumes that index is operative in reciprocal exchanges. Hence, differences in early experience are likely to have had a major effect on the degree to which the children referred to their addressee's participation in events.

Findings from predeictic use disconfirm the respective hypothesis (Hypothesis 4) since experience and not blindness appears to account for any existing differences. The lack of congruence between the blind children, in addition to the fact that few predeictic forms were produced, make comparisons across children difficult. Bonny, the youngest, had the only documented use of third person forms to refer to addressee--proper name use and the person pronoun "she" (see Table 4.1). It was observed that proper name use was extensive in speech input to Bonny, which was much less so in input to the other children.

Table 4.1

Total Absolute and Mean Relative Frequencies for Predeictic Forms
Second Person

	Bonny		Libbie		Eric	
	n	f	n	f	n	f
Prop.	31	.84	1	1.00	0	.00
3 P. Pro	2	.05	0	.00	0	.00
Recip.	4	.11	0	.00	0	.00

Use of this proper name form deemphasizes the role of the addressee in the speech event and in the narrated event as well, since the form suggests that the referent is a part only of the narrated event. Identification of the addressee as a participant is obscured by a form typically used in reference to non-speech partners only. For example, the fact that Bonny's mother was the addressee in the question "Mommie cookin?" was not clear in the linguistic context. The extralinguistic context confirmed that the mother was the addressee because no other possible addressees were present, and because she deliberately faced her mother. Bonny's paucity of experience in linguistic turn-taking exchanges, together with the frequency with which proper names were substituted for "you" in speech input to Bonny, could well have contributed to frequent productions of such unconventional forms.

The findings regarding case only weakly support Hypothesis 4. Although differences were apparent in degree of use of the possessives, the frequencies of all forms were low, precluding comparisons. While all the children produced the subject form most often, which was also the case for first person, the blind children produced the possessive determiner somewhat more frequently than did Eric. Eric's frequency of possessive pronoun exceeded that of the blind children (see Table 4.2). This pattern is similar to that of first person forms, and indicates the need for linguistic symbolic disambiguation on the part of the blind children. The findings for second person possessives indicate that the latter reasoning is more valid to account for such use differences. The second person referents are not likely to be employed as imperatives, unlike first person possessives. "Your X" is seldom used to access an object beyond the speaker's personal space; it makes explicit both the object of ownership and the individual owner who is someone other than the speaker. Therefore, the high frequency of second person possessive determiners are attributed to a need to disambiguate rather than to a means of accessing objects.

Table 4.2

Total Absolute and Mean Relative Frequencies of
Grammatical Forms of Deictic Referents--Second Person

	Bonny		Libbie		Eric	
	n	f	n	f	n	f
Sub. ("You")	5	.71	83	.56	26	.79
D.O.("You")	0	.00	20	.14	3	.09
I.O. ("You")	0	.00	12	.08	0	.00
Det. ("Your")	2	.29	28	.19	2	.06
Poss. P. ("Yours")	0	.00	4	.03	2	.06

Sub.: Subject; D.O.: Direct Object; I.O.: Indirect Object;
Det.: Determiner; Poss. P.: Possessive Pronoun

The frequencies for the remainder of the case forms, namely, the direct and indirect objects are rather low, make comparisons across children less than meaningful (see Table 4.2). Libbie produced the highest frequency of object forms which can be attributed to her more advanced age and more mature referencing system. The low frequencies of the object forms for second person cannot be attributed to the overall complexity of second person, but to the complexity of object forms in general. The findings for first person support this since object forms were likewise seldom produced (see Table 2.2). "Me" and "you" most often identify a speech participant as taking a less active role in the narrated event because the participants assume a benefactor or receiver role. Perhaps such roles are less salient to younger children in comparison to agentive or initiator roles, as Bates (1979) suggests.

The fact that "you" is isomorphic across case provides a still stronger explanation for the low frequencies of second person as opposed to first person productions (see Table 1.1 and Table 3.1). Presumably, if a single form has more than one function, the distinct functions are obscured. Becoming aware of the functions seems to demand more mature cognitive skills when each function is not represented by a distinct signifier. The findings indicate that this may have been operating, since the oldest subject, Libbie, revealed the highest frequencies.

From the findings regarding use of predeictic productions and postdeictic case forms Hypothesis 4 is weakly supported at best. No difference is found in the types of predeictic forms produced, as was the case for first person. In addition, only small differences are revealed in case use. Nevertheless, vocative use (use of addressee's proper name to accompany "you") provides substantial evidence to support the Hypothesis. Vocatives are used by the blind children during the course of the visits, while the sighted child's productions occurred at the last visit only (see Table 4.3). Thus, it appears that the blind subjects discovered their effectiveness at earlier ages, perhaps as a consequence of the ineffectiveness of visual indexing for addressee disambiguation. Vocatives function as partial substitutes for visual index in that they provide explicit semantic information to single out the intended addressee from a host of potential addressees, in addition to providing a rather effective means of securing the addressee's attention. It appears that the blind subjects substitute linguistic symbolic signifiers for the sighted child's visual index (eye-gaze, pointing) which is likewise operating for object disambiguation, i.e., frequent use of possessive determiners. An increased need to use vocatives, in addition to an early awareness of their effectiveness to successfully refer, may have given rise to a greater likelihood of participation in the speech event for these blind children. Vocative use could contribute to their success as speakers to secure and maintain the listener's attention, and as addressees, because as a consequence, others are likely to become aware of alternative attention-getting strategies particular to blind children. This more symbolic substitute (vocatives) could well have provided the experience necessary to master deictic use, since person deictic use depends on a differentiation in the speech event between speaker/listener roles, and the further application of speech role participants to their function in the narrated event. Limited practice in the speech event, as initially seems to be the case for blind children, may preclude an early awareness of such differentiations.

Table 4.3

Absolute and Relative Frequencies of Vocatives

	Bonny		Libbie		Eric	
VISIT NO.	n	f	n	f	n	f
1	4	.06	8	.04	0	.00
2	6	.09	22	.08	0	.00
3	11	.08	36	.16	1	.02
4	2	.03	9	.05	0	.00
5	4	.04	9	.03	0	.00
6	3	.03	49	.15	6	.04
TOTAL(n) & MEAN(f)	30	.05	133	.10	7	.01

The blind children appear not to experience a delay in onset of first or second person deictic use, perhaps because they use alternative strategies to successfully address others, as well as to have others address them. Their appropriate use of possessive determiners and vocatives seems to have been a major determinant in similarities in deictic use onset--to demonstrate a distinct but effective means of differentiating the referent object/person from other potential referents. A semiotic analysis suggests that blind children's development of these alternative means is somewhat more complex than seeing children's use of visual index, simply as a result of the more symbolic character of linguistic signifiers which must alone be sufficient to disambiguate. Accompanying indexes provide an additional signifier in an additional modality to secure simultaneous identification, and verification, which is not possible in the case of linguistic symbolic means when used in isolation. If this logic is correct, it indicates the greater function of linguistic signifiers for blind than for sighted children, and in turn, their dependence on symbolic signifiers to the exclusion of indexical ones.

REFERENCES

ANDERSEN, E.
    1982. Personal communication, the University of Southern California in March.
BATES, E.
    1979. *The Emergence of Symbols: Cognition and Communication in Infancy* (New York: Academic Press).
CUTSFORTH, T.D.
    1932. "The Unreality of Words to the Blind", *The Teachers Forum* 4, 86-89.
FRAIBERG, Selma.
    1977. *Insights from the Blind: Comparative Studies of Blind and Sighted Infants* (New York: Basic Books, Inc.).
LOVELAND, Katherine.
    1980. *Development of the Objective Self-Concept: Some Implications of Perceptual Development for Language Acquisition* (Ithaca: Cornell University, unpublished doctoral dissertation).
MAXFIELD, K.E.
    1936. *The Spoken Language of the Blind Preschool Child: A Study of Method* (New York: Columbia University, unpublished doctoral dissertation).

MULFORD, Randa.
- 1981. *Talking Without Seeing: Some Problems of Semantic Development in Blind Children* (Stanford: Stanford University, unpublished doctoral dissertation).
- 1983. "Referential Development in Blind Children", in *Language Acquisition in the Blind Child, Normal and Deficient*, ed. Anne E. Mills (London: Croom Helm), 89-107.

PIAGET, Jean and Barbel INHELDER.
- 1969. *The Psychology of the Child* (New York: Basic Books, Inc.).

ROWLAND, C.N.
- 1980. *Communicative Strategies of Visually Impaired Infants and their Mothers* (Oklahoma City: University of Oklahoma, unpublished doctoral dissertation).

URWIN, C.
- 1977. "I'm coming to get you: Ready, steady, go!" in *The Child's Representation of the World*, ed. G. Butterworth (New York: Plenum), 139-156.
- 1978. "The development of communication between blind infants and their parents", in *Action, Gesture, and Symbol: The Emergence of Language*, ed. A. Lock (New York: Academic Press), 78-108.

WEST, Donna.
- 1986. *The Acquisition of Person and Space Deictics: A Comparison Between Blind and Sighted Children* (Ithaca: Cornell University, unpublished doctoral dissertation).
- 1988. "The Critical Function of Tactile Index in Blind Children's Use of Deictics", in *Semiotics 1987*, ed. John Deely (Lanham, Maryland: University Press of America), 128-141.

III

SEMIOTIC INTERPRETATION OF MUSICAL MODELS

THE "MUSIC" IN BARTHES' *A LOVER'S DISCOURSE*

William DeFotis
College of William and Mary

This book's explicit purpose--the affirmation of a discourse irrelevant to officialdom, to all the "languages" of authority--compels me not only to speak of it in the first person but also to adopt a tone bordering on the confessional: I desire to account for my continuing attraction to it. At the same time, I am not interested in simply relating "personal reflections", as if they were somehow distinguishable from analytical insights. I am more interested in seeing how my desire to re-read and re-think *A Lover's Discourse* enters me into a process which is perhaps analogous to its content, since in fact this book's triumph--its most spectacular analytical virtuosity--is that its structure mirrors the discourse, being discussed--that the book is, does, what it's talking about. This I think accounts for this text's resistance to any "detached" reading; that is, in order to make any sense of it at all, you have to enter into the structure of a lover's discourse with no hope of finding and extracting principles or conclusions from it. Thus *A Lover's Discourse* does not create an officialdom of intimacy; I think the last thing Barthes would have wanted is to be looked at as an authority on the language of love. What this book does create is a context--a "site"--in which and with which it is possible to conceive of and describe a non-authoritarian language.

And here enters the first paradox: all the while Barthes is affirming and celebrating this discourse of solitude, of illogic--of all the modes foreign to the claims of intelligent political discourse--he makes it implicitly clear that the lover's discourse is constantly preoccupied with matters of control and power. For instance (Barthes 1978: 37-38):

> There is a scenography of waiting: I organize it, manipulate it, cut out a portion of time in which I shall mime the loss of the loved object and provoke all the effects of a minor mourning. This is then acted out as a play ... Waiting is an enchantment: I have received *orders not to move*.

Or (Barthes 1978: 51):

> The amorous *glue* is indissoluble; one must either submit or cut loose: accommodation is impossible (love is neither dialectical nor reformist).

The assertion that love is not reformist easily follows from the idea that the lover's "outbursts of language . . . occur at the whim of trivial, of aleatory circumstances" (Barthes 1978: 3)--that is, not in direct response to clearly understood events, and thus not aimed at "reforming" anything. But the notion that the discourses of love are not dialectical--that they do not adhere to rules of argumentation, of order, or to the transforming power of reason, in short, that they create no narrative--this notion is trickier. Barthes repeats this assertion that love is not dialectical in various contexts in the book, and elevates it to a sort of principle of organization--or perhaps non-organization--with the book's layout. But there is an enriching contradiction in the placement and tone of his anecdotal examples involving "X", the Other. In these examples there is an inescapable flirtation with narrative, with the story of lovers "I" and "X". For example (Barthes 1978: 41):

> X, who left for his vacation without me, has shown no signs of life since his departure: accident? post-office strike? indifference? distancing maneuver? exercise of a passing impulse of autonomy ("His youth deafens him, he fails to hear")? or simple innocence? I grow increasingly anxious, pass through each act of the waiting-scenario. But when X reappears in one way or another, for he cannot fail to do so (a thought which should immediately dispel any anxiety), what will I say to him? Should I hide my distress --which will be over by then ("*How are you?*") Release it aggressively ("*That wasn't at all nice, at least you could have . . .*") or passionately ("*Do you know how much worry you caused me?*")? Or let this distress of mine be delicately, discreetly understood, so that it will be discovered without having to strike down the other. ("*I was rather concerned . . .*")? A secondary anxiety seizes me, which is that I must determine the degree of publicity I shall give to my initial anxiety.

Each of the lover's imagined responses at the return of X Barthes would call a *figure*: "the body's gesture caught in action and not contemplated in repose" (1978: 4). Although the prospect of each of these figures may suggest to us (or to the lover) various narratives, the performance of any one of them in the actual presence of X will not come off as part of any logical succession of events but will explode, vibrate in and of itself "like a sound severed from any tune" (1978: 6). And its "reverberations" for the lover overwhelm any sense of it as an event in a narrative. Barthes (1978: 93) writes:

> . . . if I keep a journal, we may doubt that this journal relates, strictly speaking, to *events*. The events of amorous life are so trivial that they gain access to writing only by an immense effort: one grows discouraged writing what, *by being written*, exposes its own platitude: "I ran into X, who was with Y" "Today X didn't call me" "X was in a bad mood", etc.: who would see a story in that? The infinitesimal event exists only in its huge reverberation: *Journal of my Reverberations* (of my wounds, my joys, my interpretations, my rationalizations, my impulses): who would understand anything in that? Only the Other could write my love story, my novel.

And in this book, the Other never speaks, never tells the love story; the discourse under study here is the lover's, not the beloved's--the desirer's, not that of its object.

Thus the subject of this book is a mode of expression whose source of energy is desire and whose means greatly expand the range of gesture typical of more prosaic modes of expression. It is in this sense that *A Lover's Discourse* can be read as a fantastical anatomy of music. It is not accidental that the imagery is often musical: "vibration", "reverberation", and most important, the related notions: rhythm, repetition, timing. This imagery is useful in that it deemphasizes the "content" of the lover's utterance and concentrates on the expressive power of its movement and of the accidental moment which sets it off. The accidental moment may be internal; it may be absurd. It may confuse present and past, present and absent. Barthes' (1978: 15-16) discussion of absence can be read as the exegesis of a musical paradigm: the serenade to an empty window.

> Endlessly I sustain the discourse of the beloved's absence: actually a preposterous situation; the other is absent as referent, present as allocutory. This singular distortion generates a kind of insupportable present; I am wedged between two tenses, that of the reference and that of the allocution: you have gone (which I lament), you are here (since I am addressing you). Whereupon I know what the present, that difficult tense, is: a pure portion of anxiety.
>
> Absence persists--I must endure it. Hence I will *manipulate* it: transform the distortion of time into oscillation, produce rhythm, make an entrance onto the stage of language . . . .

At its extreme, the lover's "oscillation" may be entirely internal (Barthes 1978: 200) :

> What echoes in me is what I learn with my body: something sharp and tenuous suddenly wakens this body, which, meanwhile, had languished in the rational knowledge of a general situation: the word, the image, the thought function like a whiplash. My inward body begins vibrating as though shaken by trumpets answering each other, drowning each other out: the incitation leaves its trace, the trace widens and everything is (more or less rapidly) ravaged. In the lover's Image-repertoire, nothing distinguishes the most trivial provocation from an authentically consequent phenomenon; time is jerked forward (catastrophic predictions flood to my mind) and back (I remember certain "precedents" with terror): starting from a negligible trifle, a whole discourse of memory and death rises up and sweeps me away: this is the kingdom of memory, weapon of reverberation--of what Nietzsche called *ressentiment*.

Barthes also uses the metaphor of reverberation externally--acoustically, as it were --meaning *resonance*. Its absence is silence (Barthes 1978: 167):

> (Like a bad concert hall, affective space contains dead spots where the sound fails to circulate. The perfect interlocutor, the friend, is he not the one who constructs around you the greatest possible resonance? Cannot friendship be defined as a space with tonal sonority?).

With the metaphor of sonority, Barthes makes a palpable connection between amorous "space" and musical "space".

What I'd like to suggest is that within a temporal expressive mode such as music, there exist innumerable actions, rhythmically inflected movements, which are analogous to what Barthes calls "figures" in the lover's "thesaurus". These movements --whether they be the recognizable rhythmic inflection of a commonly known dance type, or a completely idiosyncratic action--are, like the lover's "figures", understandable as *signs* to the extent that they are a *performance*--that is, to the extent that their meaning is a matter of timing. The timing, the performance, illuminates what might otherwise be an empty gesture--or more accurately: an empty signifier. This gives music's and the lover's signs a sort of delicious precariousness, unlike the kinds of signs whose source of energy is not desire but rather something more simply reactive, prosaic, unambiguous--such as those of an auctioneer or a traffic cop. Music's or lover's signs are not aimed to give a true or false image of anything; they instead nod both to their immediate history and possible fulfillment. Thus these signs function neither as reality nor as illusion but as gestures. Music exists in that expanse of human gesticulation from the most public to the most private--that is, all the way from ritual to tears--with rhythmic possibilities far richer than those of language. If one "textually" described this range of gestural possibilities in music, one might use the two terms Barthes (1977: 181) himself transposed from Julia Kristeva in his essay "The Grain of the Voice": *pheno-song* ("everything in the performance which is in the service of communication, representation, expression") and *geno-song* ("a signifying play" focused on "the voluptuousness of its sounds-signifiers", its "diction"). *Pheno-song* is oratorical; its venue is the breath. *Geno-song* is visceral; one is more conscious in its performance of the movements of hands and tongue.

The language Barthes chooses when invoking musical qualities ignores music's oratorical power--it's capacity for grand public gesture--except in the case of an illustration he makes (1978: 175) of the figure "obscene" ("Love's Obscenity"):

> "Evening at the Opera: a very bad tenor comes on stage; in order to express his love to the woman he loves, who is beside him, he stands facing the public. I am this tenor: like a huge animal, obscene and stupid, brightly lighted as in a show window, I declaim an elaborately encoded aria, without looking at the one I love, to whom I am supposed to be addressing myself." [Barthes' quotation marks]

This exception proves the rule that the focus here is on the *geno-song*, with its kinship to choreography, where a body's movements are aimed to incite a kinesthetic response, a sympathetic inner movement. And like music as embodied in *geno-song*, the structures of amorous language are akin to dancing or mime rather than oratory. In that moment of affinity to body movement may lie the intersection of possible musical and verbal meanings--in the figures, the gestures of a lover's discourse.

REFERENCES

BARTHES, Roland.
    1978. *A Lover's Discourse--Fragments* (Richard Howard, trans. New York: Hill and Wang).
    1977. "The Grain of the Voice", *Image-Music-Text* (Stephen Heath. trans. New York: Hill and Wang).

READING BEETHOVEN'S READINGS: TOWARD A SEMIOTICS OF SONG

William P. Dougherty
Plymouth State College

The art song is an interdisciplinary object whose signification arises from the intricate synthesis and antithesis of poem and music--each of which in themselves are constituents of separate and noncomplementary modes of discourse. As a consequence, the genre suggests that its analytic sphere embrace an epistemological and methodological outlook that incorporates mono-disciplinary perspectives while it simultaneously transcends them. That is, the analysis of the art song requires an analyst not only to examine the salient characteristics of the poem and of the music but to use that examination to inform an exploration of the larger semiotic complex generated by the combination of the two art forms. Attention to this larger and more elusive complex engages musical and poetic analysis such that each contributes as fertile resources to the quest to explicate the significance of the *lied*.

Figure I indicates the location of a semiotics of song in relation to the abstract processive elements of a song and to the disciplines which might inform it. The purpose of this compounded version of Jakobson's communication model (Jakobson 1960) is not to suggest that the functions of the various constituents of this process are necessarily equivalent or that the model floats intact across different stylistic periods or different types of song. Indeed, the ways in which the elements of this model interact and intersect are largely a product of a song's function or of a particular view of the nature of musico-poetic relationships. My concern today, though, is with the art song of the common-practice era and more specifically with a semiotic approach to two of Beethoven's *lieder*; to that end, Figure I illustrates diagrammatically a special node between the poetic mode of discourse and the musical mode of discourse. The juncture where the composer-as-addressee becomes composer-as-addresser has been labeled the "composer-as-reader", and insofar as listeners are readers of a composer's specially transformed reading process, I should like to define and refine this crucial concept with respect to both its realization in a musical setting and its function in the signification process. (Although the loose sketch of relationships presented in Figure I has an attractive symmetry about its design, it should become apparent in the following discussion that my remarks ultimately fall under the aegis of a musical semiotics; that is, I am trying to cultivate an important plot within that field.)

Figure 1. Location of a Semiotics of Song.

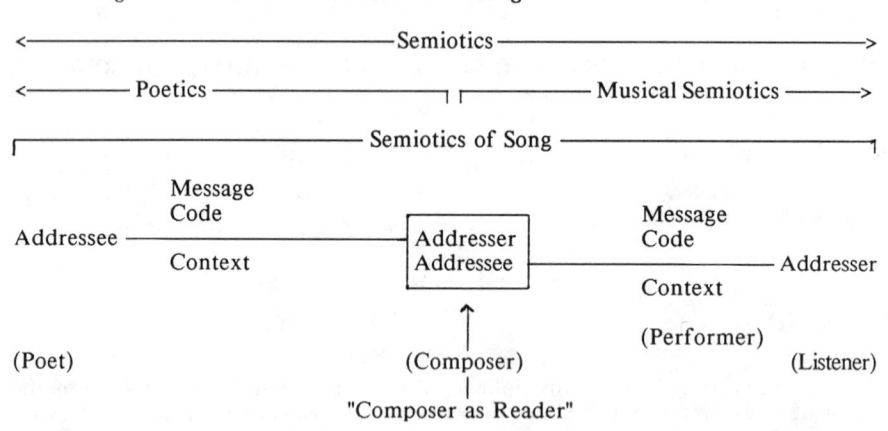

```
<─────────────────── Semiotics ───────────────────>
<────── Poetics ──────┐  ┌────── Musical Semiotics ──────>
┌─────────────── Semiotics of Song ───────────────┐

              Message                  Message
              Code        ┌─────────┐  Code
Addressee ────────────────┤Addresser├──────────────── Addresser
              Context     │Addressee│  Context
                          └─────────┘
                               ↑      (Performer)
 (Poet)                    (Composer)              (Listener)
                               │
                       "Composer as Reader"
```

In many discussions of the art song, the analytic spotlight is invariably used to illuminate the ability of music to support, underlie, or otherwise enhance the meaning of the text where the degree of correspondence between music and text is highlighted with apparently intentional examples of "word painting"--a troublesome label since it metaphorically adds yet another ingredient--painting--to an already thick artistic stew. Typically, we are shown trembling tremolos, sighing appoggiaturas, doleful modal borrowings, or the musical depiction of phenomena mentioned in the text. In addition, many analytic discussions detail the ways in which music--particularly the accompaniment--creates a "mood" or an "atmosphere" that is loosely correlated to one seemingly implied in the text. Although explicit criteria defining these "moods" are frequently absent, their identification is generally considered appropriate and uncontentious, at least in terms of their descriptive power.

Undoubtedly, both of these compositional techniques can be traced to 16th-century notions espousing the view that music was subservient to the requirements of the text. Nevertheless, an analytic emphasis on them implicitly relegates the composer-as-reader to the position of a gifted but obsequious translator of words into music; a transcriber, if you will, whose measure of success is largely proportional to his or her ability to depict musically images contained in the text while he or she simultaneously maintains the structural integrity of the poetry. Indeed, this was Goethe's concept of the quintessential song composer, and it is an opinion that is perpetuated in and guides many present-day examinations of the composer's relationship to the *lied*. For instance, Anneliese Landau (1980: 5, 11) feels that "the greatest challenge for the composer is to listen to the innate music of [the] poem and write it down to create the lied. . . . The lied strives to bring out the innate music of the poem; its music is an exaggerated 'reading aloud' of the poem."

The problem with this analytic tactic is not that correlations between text and music are non-existent; indeed, their pervasiveness is ample evidence of their importance. Rather, the problem is that an analytic framework that exclusively focuses on surface analogies and correspondences avoids investigating the play of significations that is generated by musical and poetic relationships as they motivate and confront one another. That is, if the art song places poem and music in an uneasy and uneven symbiosis whose surface and background convergences, compromises, and confrontations constitute a discursive space, then the song can be treated as a multi-leveled and multi-planar discourse where the web of significations is spun as much by musical and poetic confrontations as by convergences. Indeed, the convergences, compromises, and discontinuities that occur between semiotic systems suggest more background coding correlations whose province lies beyond the purely musical and poetic systems, and once its nature is clarified, this potentially infinite space perfused with compounded sign-functions may well shed light on the structures allowing us to find musico-literary relationships in the first place. In any case, though, a starting point for the examination of this nested set of relationships in the art song is the concept of the composer-as-reader.

To explicate and define the composer's interpretive response to a poem insofar as it is manifested in a musical setting, we posit a special reading process that allows for the transmutation of text into musical setting. Steven Scher (1986: 156) observes that this directed interpretive ability enables a composer to perceive in his or her reading certain structural, semantic, and emotive features and properties which possess a signifying potential extending beyond the text's inherent literariness. Once recognized and internalized, these features and properties suggest certain compositional strategies, and consequently the musical setting emerges from a specially charged reading process. We may say, then, that for the composer-as-reader the text is an autonomous semiotic entity whose rules of combination, syntax, and content admit of expressive possibilities amenable to treatment in another mode of discourse with entirely different rules of combination, syntax, and content.

The notion of a composer-as-reader implies a dynamic process wherein the composer appropriates a text and shapes the musical material--both on the surface and at structural levels--to animate some particular conception of the text. Music and poetry enter into a symbiotic relationship, however unstable, wherein the product of their merger is largely determined by the composer's idiosyncratic reading process. As such, the setting is a reading, and the poem, stripped of its potential for other possible readings, is both assimilated in and transmuted by the setting. Moreover, in the setting, the composer-as-reader presents one--not the only--reading of the text. The setting is thus simultaneously one of selection, in that a composer appropriates a possible reading from among many, and one of circumscription, in that a composer will strive to delineate musically his or her specific reading at the expense of other possible readings. Consequently, the setting is both a synthesis and an antithesis of poetry and music; the richness and ambiguity resonating across the poem's multiple readings, qualities that often attract composers to texts in the first place, are unable to free themselves from the composer's specific reading. Lawrence Kramer (1984: 127) observes that a setting "does not *use* a reading; it *is* a reading, both in the critical as well as the performative sense of the term".

Two other observations are pertinent to this general framework. First, composers are not, and historically have not been restricted to the poet's intentions, either conceptually or formally. Susanne Langer (1953) avers that a composer "annihilates" the poem when setting it to music, and Edward T. Cone (1974) convincingly argues that a poet's persona is *not* one of the three personas participating in the dramatic unfolding of a song. Thus, the old debates about the merits of through-composed settings of strophic poems or about "unauthorized" textual repetitions are largely misdirected; the composer manipulates the phonetic, syllabic, metric, and structural elements of the poem to achieve an expressive end. Second, a musical setting, like a poem, is temporal. Stanley Fish (1972) contends that patterns of signification evolve through time during the text's presentation; consequently, the reader may posit various hypotheses that are altered, dropped, or reshaped during the course of the reading. This description of an abductive-like reading strategy perhaps becomes audible in a song as it threads its way through the multivalent tapestry of the text, in the process implying, confirming, or denying varying and vying significatory possibilities.

This broadly sketched framework can be illustrated tangibly--if briefly--by an examination of Beethoven's two setting of "An die Hoffnung". That a composer should set the same text more than once is a curious phenomenon, and critics who have noted this fact often argue that multiple settings of the same text represent a composer's struggle to attain the ultimate musical interpretation of the text. It should be clear from earlier comments that I would argue the opposite: the composer, rather than searching for some "ideal" setting, instead treats the text as an expressive structure that supports several musical readings--readings with valuable and revealing intertextual relationships.

Beethoven's settings of "An die Hoffnung" appropriate a text extracted from a longer poem titled *Urania*, written in 1801 by Christian August Tiedge (Figure 2). Beethoven's first setting of the poem was published in 1805 as Op. 32, and his second version was published in 1816 as Op. 94.

The poem is an apostrophe to hope, invoking a personified vision of hope to comfort a solitary and desolate sufferer. The contrast between the redemptive power of hope and the deserted sufferer is strikingly, if unevenly, captured by the imagery of the poem, and this opposition between hope and sufferer is also maintained musically in Beethoven's settings. But beyond the more surface correlations, the settings also strive for larger interpretive goals. Beethoven contends with this text, and insofar as he exploits nodal points of disjunction in the closure of text and music, he lifts the settings to a different expressive plane than that entertained in the poem. Indeed, Beethoven confronts, wrestles with, and ultimately re-defines the poem's assumption that hope's redemptive powers are easily and freely earned by one at the nadir of despondency.

In Tiedge's poem, the most potent images of hope's restorative strength occur in the final lines of the first and third stanzas, and it is precisely at these points in his settings that Beethoven openly oppugns the poetic imagery, particularly in defying the closure of these lines. In the strophic setting of Op. 32 (Example 1), the closure implied by the final lines of the first and third stanzas is musically denied when the dominant harmony of measures 20 and 21 regresses to a vii^0_6/V in measure 22 while the melodic descent of these same measures--a line implying tonic arrival both on the surface and at structural levels--is diverted. Musical closure does not coincide with poetic closure, then, until measure 31--a ten-measure interruption that necessitates the repetition of the final lines of the stanzas. By denying and then affirming these lines, Beethoven has seemingly provided ironic commentary on the exclamation point following stanzas 1 and 3: that is, in measure 22 the exclamation point is perhaps more of a question mark, if you will, indicating a tentative poetic proposition that is not musically asserted until measure 31.

The comparable lines in the *da capo* aria setting of Op. 94 are even more strikingly undermined, and the musico-poetic confrontation generated by the conflict wends its way across the surface, structural, formal, and expressive features of the setting in a more circuitous manner (Example 2). In this setting, the image of an angel counting tears at the end of the first stanza is again accompanied by an interrupted cadence that avoids harmonic and melodic closure. Indeed, the apparent deceptive cadence of measure 38 (i.e., V_7 to IV_6) slides to a vii^{06}_5/V, the same chord found at this juncture in Op. 32. But in the Op. 94 setting, the diminished-seventh chord is enharmonically resolved to the subtonic for a *forte* repetition of the apostrophe to hope. The effect of this discontinuity is that the final line of the stanza is repeated three times before harmonic and melodic closure is reached in measure 45. Moreover, the disjunction between musical and poetic closure has been established compositionally, and the role of tonic G to signal musical closure or nonclosure through arrival or avoidance is exploited throughout the remainder of the song.

The second stanza receives a chromatic setting that rapidly tonicizes several keys. In the final line (Example 3), though, G minor is strongly implied in measure 57; this implication, however, is thwarted when the octave D's of measure 58--contextually heard as dominant--turn out to be tonic, and the setting moves into D minor for the beginning of the third stanza. During this stanza, a cadence in G is implied again in measure 62. Once more, though, the arrival of tonic is avoided, and the setting slides into B major for the poem's final lines.

It is left to the final lines to move from B Major to G Major, and Beethoven bridges the somewhat distant tonal areas by tonicizing C Major--the Neapolitan of B and the subdominant of G. Instead of a "textbook" modulation from C Major to G Major, though, the song abruptly shifts from an F-major chord to the dominant-seventh chord of G Major on the last word of the poem (m. 69). The abrupt harmonic movement, the setting of *Sonne* on a dominant-seventh chord, and the melisma, *decrescendo*, and *fermata* conspire to undercut and disrupt the strongest and most luminescent poetic treatment of hope's power.[1] Indeed, Beethoven has musically denied the closure of the entire poem, and after a brief transition to regain the setting's energy, Beethoven's compositional solution to counterbalance the chromaticism and dissolution of textual and musical closure is to repeat the entire first stanza.

Figure 2. An die Hoffnung, By Christoph August Tiedge from *Urania*.

Die du so gern in heil'gen Nächten feierst,	You who so gladly on holy nights celebrate,
Und sanft und weich den Gram verschleierst,	and softly and gently veil the sorrow
Der eine zarte Seele quält,	which tortures a tender soul,
O Hoffnung! laß, durch dich emporgehoben,	O Hope, let, by you raised up,
Den Dulder ahnen, daß dort oben	the sufferer suspect that on high
Ein Engel seine Tränen zählt!	an angel counts his tears!
Wenn, längst verhallt, geliebte Stimmen schweigen;	When, long hushed, loving voices are silent;
Wenn unter ausgestorbnen Zweigen Verödet die Erinnrung sitzt:	when, under dead branches, memory, desolate, sits:
Dann nahe dich, wo dein Verlassner trauert,	then approach where your deserted one mourns,
Und, von der Mitternacht umschauert,	and, enveloped by midnight,
Sich auf versunkne Urnen stützt.	supports himself on subsided urns.
Und blickt er auf, das Schicksal anzuklagen,	And if he raises his eyes to accuse fate,
Wenn scheidend über seinen Tagen Die letzten Strahlen untergehn:	when, departing upon his days, the last rays set:
Dann laß ihn, um den Rand des Erdentraumes	then let him, around the border of this earthly dream
Das Leuchten eines Wolkensaumes Von einer nahen Sonne sehn!	see the hem of a cloud illuminated by the nearby sun.

In both of these settings, on different levels and with different musical means, the immediacy of poetic closure has been subverted by the music. Music and text create a compound sign whose respective expressive planes are at times oppositional, and at these points of discontinuity, it is as if the music shows the text to be a lie; that is--given the theme of this conference--the illusion of the poem becomes apparent through the reality of the music.

Relationships between poem and music in the art song are complex and diffuse: they operate as a multi-leveled discourse whose significance is determined by surface, structural, and systematic parallels, compromises, and discontinuities. Our task as readers of a composer's reading is to attempt to track often elusive relationships through a labyrinth of significatory possibilities.

NOTES

[1] Incidentally, the juxtapositioning of F-major and D-major chords in measures 68 and 69 is similar to the progression on the word *Hoffnung* after the interrupted cadence at the end of the first stanza (see m. 38).

REFERENCES

CONE, Edward T.
   1974. *The Composer's Voice* (Berkeley: University of California Press).
FISH, Stanley E.
   1972. *Self-Consuming Artifacts: The Experience of Seventeenth-Century Literature* (Berkeley: University of California Press).
JAKOBSON, Roman.
   1960. "Closing Statement: Linguistics and Poetics." In *Style in Language*, ed. Thomas A. Sebeok (Cambridge, MA: M.I.T. Press), 350-377.
KRAMER, Lawrence.
   1984. *Music and Poetry: The Nineteenth Century and After* (Berkeley: University of California Press).
LANDAU, Anneliese.
   1980. *The Lied: The Unfolding of Its Style* (Washington, D.C.: University Press of America).
LANGER, Susanne K.
   1953. *Feeling and Form* (New York: Charles Scribner's Sons).
SCHER, Steven.
   1984. "Comparing Poetry and Music: Beethoven's Goethe Lieder". In *Sensus Communis: Contemporary Trends in Comparative Literature*, ed. János Riesz, Peter Boerner, & Bernhard Scholz (Tübingen: Gunther Narr), 155-165.

EXAMPLE 1. Beethoven, *An die Hoffnung*, Op. 32 (mm. 17-33).

EXAMPLE 2. Beethoven, *An die Hoffnung*, Op. 94 (mm. 36-47).

EXAMPLE 3. Beethoven, *An die Hoffnung*, Op. 94 (mm. 56-73).

HJELMSLEV'S GLOSSEMATICS AND MUSIC:
THE SIGN MAY BE AN ILLUSION

Gayle A. Henrotte
Cleveland State University

Louis Hjelmslev (1899-1965) was a linguist and semiotician, and the founder of the glossematic theory of signs. Hjelmslev defines form, substance, expression, and content as the basis of glossematics (Hjelmslev 1961: 47-60). These definitions and his discussion, however, cannot yet be applied easily to the analysis of specific works of music, because they are theoretical concepts and not analytical methodologies. They address the problem of the concept of sign and as such apply to the development of semiotic theory. Up to now, the function of semiotics in music has been to ferret out the different kinds of perspectives which apply to all aspects of the perception of music (Henrotte 1987). Semiotics has allowed us to distinguish between the music and the verbal report of it, that is, to recognize the perspectives of composer, performer, listener, analyst, and theorist, and to indicate the relationship of each of these agents to music. But semiotics has no comprehensive methodology for dealing with the analysis of the production and/or perceptions of each of these agents. The most fruitful analyses of music are still by musicologist who happen to be semioticians, not by theoretical semioticians who are, first of all, linguists and philosophers.

Hjelmslev's glossematics is a theory of sign based on algebra but articulated through linguistic data; its object is to describe principles of pure form. It seems to me, that if we look at music from the perspective of pure form, we arrive at such principles behind musical structures as repetition and variation. These concepts are so pervasive, however, in *all* structures that to claim them as particular to music is naive. The more abstract theory becomes, the more and more general its statements appear. This generality is a problem for interdisciplinary work, and as such, the price one has to pay for attempting to apply a theory such as Hjelmslev's to a non-linguistic discipline. Where music theory and linguistic theory meet is the level of meta-theory, the level at which semiotic theory begins to work. At this level, objects of analysis are so far removed from the theory, that by the time principles of sign relationships are articulated, the level of theoretical description tends to make that abstraction sound naive. The identification of concepts such as repetition and variation then sound equally naive to linguist and musician.

I have encountered the problem of explaining music theory at the semiotic level to linguists recently in my dissertation (Henrotte 1988), which is a study of music analyses based wholly or in part on linguistic principles. My explanations are satisfying neither to the linguist nor to the musicologist, because I have had to speak in generalizations in order to bridge the wide gap between linguistics and music. The premises of the two fields are diametrically opposed. Music is art, whereas language, as viewed by the linguist, is a mental and/or social phenomenon, not an aesthetic one. Analyses of musical and linguistic data proceed from different perspectives. In the examination of an artwork, aesthetic value is a major factor. Such a factor, however, is not an element of linguistic analysis. If the musicologist considers pure form at the deepest level of his analysis, it will be to articulate deep, underlying formal principles for the formation of artistic wholes. In the examination of pure form, the linguist *may* consider social relevancy, ethnic background, or psychological formatting in his analysis, but he will *never* consider the questions of aesthetic balance which are basic to any music analysis.

The object/datum which the music analyst considers is music as the conscious creation of a composer intended for performance in real time. The linguist, on the other hand, considers utterances in general as indications of an innate quality of speech which all humans possess. What attracts musicologists to linguistics is, I think, the focus of such thinkers as Hjelmslev (1961), Chomsky (1957), and Montague (1974) on the form behind utterances. This is what attracted Leonard Bernstein (1976) in Chomsky's (1957) view of language and what has fostered over thirty years of music analysis based on linguistics. The thinker in music who comes closest to Hjelmslev's view of algebraic semiotics is Benjamin Boretz ("Meta-variations," 1970) dismisses sound as an inherent element in music and claims that it is merely incidental to music ("Nelson Goodman," 1972) since music exists, for him, in the aesthetic interplay of pure form.

The application of the theory of glossematics to the development of a methodology for analyzing music is beset with difficulties. Let us examine some of the precepts of Hjelmslev's thinking. As Trabant (1987: 90, 1.1) has said: Hjelmslev "is nothing less than the originator of... a general science of signs... based on immanent and structural linguistics." Hjelmslev developed what he himself called *glossematics*, i.e. the science of pure form. "As a science of *general* sign structures, glossematics is a science of theoretical possibilities and not of manifest realities. Hjelmslev's view of glossematics as a type of algebra should be viewed this way, for like algebra, glossematics is a discipline of possible constructs that do not have to be made manifest in particular substances" (Trabant 1987: 96, 2.2.4). The application of such a cognitive model would, then, seem to offer insurmountable problems to the music analyst, but not to the theorist.

Hjelmslev's approach to glossematics begins with the identification of the sign (Hjelmslev 1961: 102). For him, this is merely ascertaining whether whatever is identified as the sign is interpretable or not. Then he proceeds to an exhaustive description of the concept of sign based on structural planes which he identifies as the planes of expression and content (Sebeok 1986: 247), both of which have sub-elements of substance and form. It is the analysis of these two kinds of form, which, Hjelmslev claims, are the object of glossematics. Form is, for Hjelmslev, a constant, manifested pattern while substance is the variable manifestation of form (Hjelmslev 1961: 106). For Hjelmslev, the sign is an interdependence of content-form and expression-form, both of which can be analyzed exhaustively the same way (Hjelmslev 1961: 96-101). Unlike Saussure, Hjelmslev's analysis of the sign begins with text; his "starting point is the text and the system behind it" (Sebeok, 1986: 247). Once he has the text as the object of analysis, he differentiates between the planes of content and expression. Each of these planes has two levels: form and substance. Hjelmslev proposes explicit rules for the analysis (description) of each level. Such descriptions are self-contained, exhaustive, and simple. For Hjelmslev, it is in the interaction of the form levels that the sign appears. The sign is a function--an interdependence of content-form and substance-form. For Hjelmslev, both content-form and expression-form can be analyzed the same way into their respective smallest units. The sign is more than the text, though, for it is a formal relation existing on any level of the analytical continuum (Eco 1986: 944-945). Hjelmslev then applies this analysis to various levels (Hjelmslev 1961: 125). For him, no totality can be isolated; an individual instance reflects a general system foreseen schemata (Hjelmslev 1961: 126). The content-form of the sign is made up of its specific divisions in relation to referent function, while the expression form is the way zones of expressive meaning are divided (Sebeok, 1986: 248). For Hjelmslev, form is a patterned, structural constant which is pure and non-substantial; it does not have to be articulated; its most important aspect is its virtuality. Substance, on the other hand, is variable and articulating.

Hjelmslev has developed his theory of glossematics from the examination of texts. The theory generates a methodology for defining meaning as abstract, pure, and non-substantial. The identification of form as a basis for uncovering meaning depends on the type of sign system being analyzed. For Hjelmslev, the rules for forming extended structures are to be found in language; these rules are (Hjelmslev 1961: 4) independent of any specific purpose value, be it logical, aesthetic, or ethical, and they can therefore apply as well to data other than language. Hjelmslev's analysis of text is an exhaustive process. For instance (Hjelmslev 1961: 115), the categories of expression upon which he bases a textual analysis include stylistic forms, styles, stylistic values, media, tones, and idioms. These can be combined to produce hybrid texts such as belletristic, slang, lecture style, pulpit style, and chancery style (Hjelmslev 1961: 116). Is this an hierarchic analysis or only the exhaustive analysis of one level?

Does this summary of basic premises in Hjelmslev's view of semiotics allow us to extract a methodology for the meaningful analysis of specific music works? I say no, because the distance between Hjelmslev's concept of pure form and the manifestation of the specific artwork is too great. In attempting to ascertain whether Hjelmslev's concepts can be applied effectively to the analysis of a specific piece, it would seem best to analyze the piece and then to uncover those elements which can be described as pure form. These elements should differ from universals in music, because, if they are truly semiotic structures, they will be found in all forms.

I have not attempted an exhaustive analysis of the "Victimae paschali laudes" (*Liber Usualis* 1934: 780; Parrish and Ohl: 10) but have rather concentrated on its motivic structure in the (1) interplay of recurring melodicals, intervals and mode tones; in the (2) relationship of text to phrase beginnings and endings; and in the (3) melodic curves at the beginnings and ends of phrases (see Examples 1 and 2). What I have not considered is the historical and musical form of the sequence as well as the place of this particular chant within the entire Gregorian repertoire. (Such matters would be included in an examination of substance in the type of analysis envisioned by Hjelmslev.) The examination of the concatenation of the smallest units of the piece reveals the interaction of superimposed levels of structure which do not coincide but overlap. The analysis (see Example 2) indicates the kinds of motivic and modal (tonal) manipulation at work in this short effective piece.

The piece is a single-line Easter chant set to a partially rhymed Latin hymn (sequence). The tone of the text is joyful but subdued, and this mood is reflected in a melodic setting which tends to reach the highest pitch when Christ is mentioned in the text and to descend at the ends of the phrases. The basic motion of the chant is step-wise. Leaps are generally no larger than a perfect fourth, with fifths occurring between phrases. Within the phrases certain melodic patterns predominate: the neighboring tone, patterns with [third plus second], and patterns with [second plus third]. The most prominent tone in the melody is "d", the final, or resting tone, followed in importance by "a", the dominant. These are the tones which serve as beginnings and endings of most phrases and are the focal points for the motives which make use of the neighboring-tone and filled-in fourths. When the same melody is used for different texts, the words do not always begin and end on the same tones in the two settings. However, the composer was not unaware of the text as is seen at the beginning of verse 8 which corresponds musically to verses 2 and 3. An extra "a" in verse 8 accommodates an extra syllable while maintaining the basic outline of the melody. The setting of the rhymed poem is syllabic, that is, there occurs one tone for each syllable of text. Only rarely does the composer engage in slight melismas (more than one tone per syllable). These occur effectively in verses 5 and 7 at the rhymes "ventis/gentis" and "mea/laeam".

What the identification of the smallest units of this piece indicates is an intricately woven structure which operates at various levels simultaneously: (1) the harmonic level, by stressing the final and tonic; (2) the melodic level by stressing (a) the interval of the fourth, (b) descending patterns at the ends of lines, and (c) varying patterns of seconds and thirds. A perusal of each element in the analysis (see Example 2) reveals how these elements are used linearly throughout the piece. Underlying structural patterns emerge which do not coincide with the flow of music in real time, but are part of its deeper level of organization: (1) the neighboring tone patterns ascend and descend in a rainbow-like curve on each of the tones between the final and the dominant; (2) the succession of fourths within the piece follow, first, an ascending pattern, then a descending pattern as the line ascends to the highest point; a second ascent is made followed by a descending one with ascending open fourths before the next climax; (3) the melodic patterns made up of seconds and thirds use ascending and descending patterns; after the climax the patterns descend to the lowest tone; (4) the beginnings and endings of phrases stress the final and dominant with fleeting reference to the mediant, and then only half way through the piece after the "tonic" has been well established; (5) the phrase endings tend to descend, a feature typical of Gregorian chant, and therefore to be expected even in a joyous sequence; (6) the beginnings of phrases exhibit more variety than the endings; (7) upward motion is balanced by descent: and (8) the interval of the fourth, a prominent interval in the piece as a whole, is as well the basic interval for phrase beginnings. The piece is highly structured, not in the antecedent-consequent logic structure of the Classical masterpieces with which we are perhaps most familiar, but in an hierarchical texture operating at various levels--from what is actually heard, to deeper level principles of repetition and variation. These levels operate simultaneously in the piece, and although not all of them are heard, still all are important for the coherence of the work.

What Hjelmslev can bring to the process of music analysis is the identification not only of surface events but of underlying structures as well. Here, in the "Victimae paschali laudes", the underlying forms are articulated by harmonic structure, basic intervals, and recurring melodic manipulations of those intervals. Such elements were part and parcel of the composer's craft in the era in which this hymn (sequence) was composed. By recognizing these elements, we become aware of medieval style as it was experienced by contemporary composers. We consciously analyze patterns which were used unconsciously by medieval composers. If music is the sign of its times, then, by the recognition of immanent patterns in the style, we are becoming conscious of the music at its sign level--at the interaction of the non-substantial, pure expression- and content-forms. The music we experience is the concrete evidence of the now consciously conceived underlying structures.

Hjelmslev identified not only expression and content, but also the *form* of expression and content as the elements of the sign in the theory of glossematics. In music, expression and content are not isomorphic as they are in language, but are inherent in each other; each is the message of the other. Hjelmslev asks us to look at the sign on its own terms without substance evidence (from the world). He finds structure in the interacting levels of the sign. I submit that if we consider a musical work as a whole to be a sign (for this is the only kind of musical evidence we have), the overlapping and interweaving of each level of analysis will uncover the depth of the concept of the musical sign which, hidden in the interplay of harmony, rhythm, and text renders a surface form which proves that the sign is not an illusion.

REFERENCES

BERNSTEIN, Leonard.
    1976. *The Unanswered Question* (Cambridge, MA: Harvard Univ. Press).
BORETZ, Benjamin.
    1970. "Meta-Variations: Studies in the Foundations of Musical Thought (1)" *Perspectives of New Music* 8.1, 1-74.
    1972. "Nelson Goodman's *Language of Art* from a Musical Point of View" in *Perspectives on Contemporary Music Theory*, ed. Benjamin Boretz and Edward T. Cone (New York: W.W. Norton).
CHOMSKY, Noam.
    1957. *Syntactic Structures* (= Janua Linguarum, Series Minor, 4) (The Hague: Mouton).
ECO, Umberto.
    1986. "Sign Function", in *Encyclopedic Dictionary of Semiotics*, ed. Thomas A. Sebeok (Berlin: Mouton de Gruyter), 943-946.
HENROTTE, Gayle A.
    1987. "Music as Sign". Unpublished paper presented at the annual meeting of the Semiotic Circle of California at the University of California at San Diego, 1987.
    1988. "Language, Linguistics, and Music: A Source Study". Unpublished dissertation, University of California at Berkeley.
HJELMSLEV, Louis.
    1961. *Prolegomena to a Theory of Language*, the second revised trans. by Francis J. Whitfield of *Omkring sprogteoriens grundlœggelse* (Copenhagen: Ejnar Munksgaard, 1943), incorporating "several minor corrections and changes that have suggested themselves in the course of discussions between the author and the translator" (Madison, Wisconsin: University of Wisconsin Press).
Liber Usualis.
    1934. Edition No. 801 (Tournai), 780.
MONTAGUE, Richard.
    1974. *Formal Philosophy. Selected Papers of Richard Montague*, ed. Richmond H. Thomason (New Haven: Yale Univ. Press).
PARRISH, Carl and John F. OHL.
    1951. "Victimae Paschali" in *Masterpieces of Music before 1750* (New York: W.W. Norton), 8-10.
SEBEOK, Thomas A. (General Editor).
    1986. *Encyclopedic Dictionary of Semiotics* (Berlin: Mouton de Gruyter).

TRABANT, Jürgen.
1987. "Louis Hjelmslev: Glossematics as General Semiotics" in *Classics of Semiotics*, ed. M. Krampen, K. Oehler, R. Posner, T. Sebeok, and T. von Uexküll (New York: Plenum, 98-108).

EXAMPLE 1. Gregorian Chant (Sequence) "Victimae paschali laudes"

72   SEMIOTICS 1988

EXAMPLE 2a. Analysis.

Beginnings and ends of phrase-sections

Directions of phrase endings

Beginnings of phrases

INTERPRETATION OF MUSICAL MODELS / Henrotte

EXAMPLE 2b. Analysis.

Neighboring tones

The perfect fourth

Tonal focus

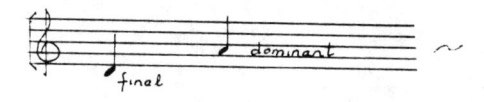

Melodical

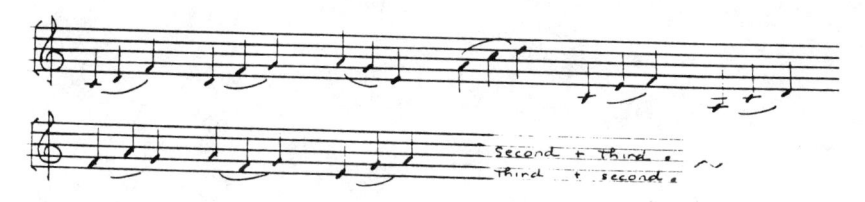

IV

COMPUTER SCIENCE MODELS

SEMEN, DEMONIC POSSESSION, AND THE COMMON COLD

Walter J. Savitch
University of California, San Diego

The metaphor of the computer program permeates everyday speech and appears in virtually all metaphoric forms. A few examples will illustrate the variety of forms that this metaphor can take:

(1) Do you think I'm a computer?

(2) That plan has a few bugs in it.

(3) This match was programmed to start yesterday.

The first is a straightforward overt, conscious metaphor that might be said in response to a demand for detailed figures on your expenses for the last year. The second is a frozen metaphor. This usage of the word "bug" comes to us from the notion of a "bug" in a computer program. However, the word has entered the lexicon and now stands on its own. Many people who use sentence (2) are unaware of the fact that this has anything to do with computers. Sentence (3) uses the term "programmed" in a sense that is older than the notion of a computer program. *The Oxford English Dictionary* cites this exact phrase as appearing in print in 1896, and cites other related usage as early as 1661. Yet, many people would read (3) as a metaphor to a computer program. The computer program metaphor recurs in many forms and contexts. In this paper I wish to focus on just one of those contexts, namely the use of this metaphor in what might, loosely speaking, be called scientific theories. I will survey a few conspicuous examples of the computer program metaphor in this context. In particular, all of the items listed in the title will be seen to be instances of the computer program metaphor. I will contend that the computer program metaphor may exemplify a new phenomenon involving metaphor, or at least a phenomenon that has previously received little attention.

The Mind as Computer Program

One of the most famous examples of this metaphor is the theory which says the mind is a computer program and the body is a computer which executes this program. The extreme position, which holds that this is literally true, is known as the *Strong A.I. Thesis*. Researchers in Artificial Intelligence hold a variety of positions ranging all the way from a weak metaphoric reading all the way to embracing the Strong A.I. Thesis without qualification.

The Strong A.I. Thesis has a compelling emotional appeal to those who miss the notion of a soul, but who feel compelled to adhere to a code of strict rational, scientific materialism. The Strong A.I. Thesis offers an escape from this emotional bind. Viewing the mind as a computer program fits well with modern scientific materialism. Yet, it offers all the emotional appeal of an immortal soul. The mind as a computer program is an abstract entity. Like all abstract entities it transcends physical reality. The abstract notion of a program (even a particular program) is as immortal as the number five. But, the mind as a computer program offers more immediate and more down-to-earth satisfaction than that. It offers immortality in the most immediate and physical sense. If the computer wears out, one can down-load the program and install it in a new computer, and one can continue to do this ad infinitum. When the body/computer wears out, the mind/program can be transferred to another computer, perhaps made of silicon, perhaps made of meat. It matters little what form the body/computer has. Technology will eventually produce the form one wants. If you want meat, just wait in silicon for a few millennia. The technology for even a silicon afterlife is not available today and may never be available, but the promise is there. The Strong A.I. Thesis implies that, in principle, immortality is "scientifically" achievable. Although its proponents might not approve of this phrasing, it would not be incorrect to paraphrase the Strong A.I. Thesis as stating that "Your immortal soul is a computer program."

In this paper I am not concerned with the truth or falsity of the Strong A.I. Thesis. I am only interested in language and meaning. However, one argument commonly given against the thesis will be instructive to look at. It has been argued that the Strong A.I. Thesis is simply one more example of a simple, general phenomenon: the metaphor of the dominant technology applied to ourselves as the center of our universe. In Freud's time the brain was compared to a steam engine. When the technology changed, this argument continues, the steam engine metaphor was replaced by the computer metaphor. The implication in this line of argument is that the computer program metaphor is a transient phenomenon and so has no claim to intrinsic truth or long term significance. As already stated, the truth or falsity of the Strong A.I. thesis is not at issue here. However, I will contend that the mind/computer program metaphor is more than a brief transient phenomenon. That it is more than simply the metaphor of the dominant technology.

The Metaphor Defined

In this paper we will eventually see that the origins of the computer program metaphor are less obvious then one might at first think. Indeed I am not able to explain its origin. The surface form of the metaphor, on the other hand, is easy to characterize. The metaphor consists of an analogy to the two items computer program and computer. For example, the analogy of the mind to a computer program and the body to a computer. For the purpose of this analogy, the relevant properties of the metaphorical computer program are that it is nonphysical, information laden, and can be viewed as instructions or commands. The relevant properties of the computer are that it is physical, that the metaphorical program can enter it, and that it is controlled by the metaphorical program.

These properties certainly obtain in the case of the mind as a computer program metaphor. In this metaphor the mind is viewed as something nonphysical. This does not mean that it need be mystical or even mysterious. It may be a very dull program, much like a simple accounting program, straightforwardly written to take care of a multitude of possibilities, large but otherwise uninspiring. However, it is not physical just as a simple accounting program is not physical. In this metaphor the mind is an abstract entity. Moreover, it is viewed as being information laden. All the information that a human being has is viewed as residing in the mind. Thus far, the fit is perfect. However, most user of this metaphor would not immediately think of the mind as a set of instructions or commands. This is apparent mismatch is a common occurrence with the computer program metaphor. Often, as in the case of the mind, the metaphorical program does not seem to consist of commands or instructions until we consider how it interacts with the metaphorical computer. The disembodied mind does not appear to be instructions, but when it is placed in the body it is the source of commands. It tells the body what to do. The body also fits the analogy. It is physical. It contains the metaphorical program (the mind) and it is controlled by the metaphorical program.

Virus as Program and Program as Virus

From the point of view of modern medical science a virus, such as a common cold virus, is nothing but a piece of genetic material encased in a simple delivery package. The virus enters its host and controls it. The genetic material is the virus. What matters is the instructions contained in the genetic material. It is physical only in so far as a book or computer program is physical. There is some physical medium which manifest it, but it is pure instructions. Indeed, scientists often speak of genetic material as programs. The metaphor is overt and conscious. Our description of viruses applies equally well to sperm. To modern biology, life is but the carrying out of (and perhaps the modification of) programs. The programming language is the genetic code. The computer program theme is at the heart of modern biology.

In virtually all cases, the computer program metaphor folds in on itself. The metaphor is almost always bidirectional. One metaphor says that the mind is a program, but we also speak of a computer (meaning both the computer and the program) as an "electronic brain". The virus metaphor has also reversed itself in recent years. We now have a class of computer programs know as "computer viruses". These are programs which surreptitiously enter a computer and gain control of it. A computer virus takes over control supplanting the computer's rightful programs. Like a true virus, a computer virus reproduces and spreads to other computers. A recent *N.Y. Times* article talks about a computer virus that rapidly spread across the nation shutting down many major computer installations (including much of the installation in my own department).

The Universe as Computer

Staring from our perspective as human beings, we have seen the computer program metaphor within our concept of self and have seen some examples of the metaphor in our concepts of microscopic phenomena. We now turn away from ourselves again, but in the other size direction. One of the oldest computer metaphors is the metaphor of the universe as a computer. We can see its roots in the notion of the universe as the "plan of God", but recent scientific thought brings the metaphor into sharper focus. Scientist who are at least on the fringe of respectability advance the view that the universe is a computer following a computer program. In the view of some this computation even has a goal. In their view the program is computing an answer. The idea goes back at least as far as *Genesis*. God made good and evil, started that program running on the computer of the temporal world of man, and is still waiting for the outcome of the computation.

If you want to know the outcome of an experiment, you may compute the answer based on theory or you may run the experiment, which in the cases at hand means running a program. In some cases, the fastest way to arrive at the answer is to run the experiment (program). In fact, it is not difficult to show that there are such programs. There are programs whose final result cannot be determined except by running them (or by doing something that takes at least that long). Is the universe an attempt to answer one such question? (if it is answering any question at all). One possibility is that the question of say good and evil, is relatively easy to formulate and understand (at least for God), but is one of those questions for which it is logically impossible to answer in less time than it takes to run the obvious program, namely letting the universe happen. Even God might be bound by such laws of logic and so have a reason for running the program.

The idea of the universe as computer is perhaps best known from science fiction writing. In *The Hitchhiker's Guide to the Galaxy* the planet earth is a computer designed to run one particular program in order to answer one particular question, although certainly a very large question. The question is the answer to "Life the Universe and Everything", a question perhaps not unrelated to God's question in *Genesis*.

A related notion is the *Gaia Theory*. It can be found in both science fiction writing and the work of the what might be termed the fringe of the scientific community. The Gaia Theory holds that the planet is a single organism. If this is combined with the Strong A.I. Thesis and the Plan-of-God Thesis, we get a complete circle of metaphors. The planet is an organism. The organism is a computer. God's computer program is run on the computer of the planet.

Demons and Other Old Metaphors

Let us return to the argument which says that the computer program metaphor is "just" the metaphor of the dominant technology. There is one fatal flaw in that line of reasoning: The computer program metaphor predates the invention of the computer program! We have already seen that something like the computer program metaphor is involved in the ancient view that the universe is the plan of God. That may not be exactly the computer program metaphor, but it is certainly close and other examples are more conspicuous.

The duality of mind and body is a view that predates the computer program. Moreover, it fits the metaphor. The body is physical. The mind can enter and leave the body. The mind gives instructions to the body. Some might have to substitute the word "soul" for "mind" before they recognize the analogy, but that is of no consequence to the issue of whether or not the metaphor has been use. The metaphor is old, clear, and well know. The Strong A.I. Thesis may or may not have any claim to truth, but, it has been a prominent thought pattern for a very long time. As a metaphor, the Strong A.I. Thesis predates A.I. Indeed, it predates computer programs in general.

Perhaps the clearest thought pattern which fits the computer program metaphor is the notion of demonic possession, and this too is a notion that predates the computer era. The demon is viewed as a spirit. It may be manifest in some physical form, but that physical form is incidental, a mere carrying case. The demon is typically clever and often close to omniscient. In any event, the demon is certainly information laden. The person possessed is viewed as physical (at least by comparison). The demon can enter and leave the body. In fact it can enter different bodies much like a program run on different computers. The demon can enter and leave the body along with its effects, just as a program can enter and leave a computer.

This metaphor goes in both directions. A rather ill-defined class of programs are know as demons. The term is so widely used in the Unix operating system that a rather benign, even friendly, demon has come to be the symbol of that operating system. (The term in this context may originally have been used in a slightly different sense of demon as indicated by the spelling, "daemon", normally used in this context. However, in usage this distinction is typically not kept in mind.) This typical folding in or reversing of metaphor is, as I have noted, typical of the computer program metaphor, but in this case the details are rich enough to touch most of the cases we have discussed.

A human being has its native program before and after being possessed by a demon. That is the metaphor of the Strong A.I. Thesis. Since the normal program is disrupted by the demon, demons are a different kind of program. Specifically, it appears that demons were the first computer viruses, a view that leads to the following chain of metaphors: The demon is a computer virus. A virus is a computer program. Certain classes of ("real") programs are know as demons.

Other Theories of Metaphor

In order to put this work into perspective, I will briefly relate it to two representative works on theories of metaphor, one on metaphor in everyday speech and one on literary uses of metaphor. Specifically, I will consider Lakoff and Johnson's famous book on metaphors in everyday speech (Lakoff and Johnson 1980) and Umberto Eco's analysis of metaphor in *Finnegans Wake* (Eco 1979).

If, as I have claimed, the computer program metaphor did indeed exist before the computer, then this particular metaphor does not fit easily into Lakoff and Johnson's theories of metaphor. In their book *Metaphors We Live By* they tacitly assume that metaphors are created as analogies to known things. My view of the computer program metaphor does not stand in opposition to their views, but it does say that their view is not complete.

Eco's analysis of metaphor in *Finnegans Wake* is really orthogonal to the view I have presented here, but is, in at least one sense, congenial to my claim that the computer program metaphor predates the computer. In Eco's view a metaphor arise as the result of a metonymic chain, often an obscure and personal chain of associations. In Eco's view, the analogy which short-circuits the chain and which we recognize as the metaphor is often added later. It is not inconsistent with Eco's view that a metaphor might arise for reasons unrelated to the analogy perceived in later readings.

Conclusions

I have explored the computer program metaphor and some of its more interesting aspects. I have more questions than answers. However, I would like to highlight one aspects of the metaphor that deserve further study: How can the computer program metaphor predate the computer? It is as though the computer program metaphor was a thought pattern waiting for its primary exemplar. To use a meta-metaphor it was a ghost metaphor which came to life.

REFERENCES

A complete set of references would be many times as long as the text of this article, and would not be of much help. The concepts are widespread and pervade our culture. The reader can easily fill in one of the many appropriate reference for each of the classical points of view. Below I have listed only a few of the more recent sources which I have used. Unfortunately, I do not know of a good reference for the Gaia Theory. My sources of information on the Gaia Theory have been special PBS television and radio programs. The Reference by Asimov is a good example of its use in the science fiction genre. [*Editors' note*: the basic published exposition of the Gaia hypothesis is J. E. Lovelock, *Gaia: A New Look at Life on Earth* (Oxford: Oxford University Press, 1979).]

ADAMS, D.
    1979. *The Hitchhiker's Guide to the Galaxy* (New York: Pocket Books).
ASIMOV, I.
    1986. *Foundation and Earth* (New York: Ballantine Books).
ECO, U.
    1979. *The Role of the Reader: Explorations in the Semiotics of Text* (Bloomington: Indiana Univ. Press).
LAKOFF, G. and M. JOHNSON.
    1980. *Metaphors We Live By* (Chicago: The Univ. of Chicago Press).
The Oxford English Dictionary.
    1971. (Oxford: Oxford Univ. Press).
The New York Times.
    1988, Nov. 4 (Vol. 138, No. 47,679, page 1), "'Virus' in Military Computers Disrupts Systems Nationwide".
UNIX Programmer's Reference Manual-4.3 Berkeley Software Distribution.
    1986. (Berkeley, Calif: Computer Science Division, Dept. EECS).

METAPHOR, MYTH, AND COMPUTER LANGUAGE[1]

Robert T. Swank
The Johns Hopkins University

I. Introduction

Computers and language, necessarily paired, are uneasy partners. Many computer activities are unobserveable and, therefore, difficult to comprehend, making the use of metaphor important as a guide to the mysterious, as well as for simple naming and descriptive purposes. We will examine the evolution of a computer language mythology, showing how a metaphor that represents a false reality grows into a myth that obstructs the use of verbal and computer language and leads to the destruction of computer information. The consequences of computer programmers acting as metaphor police and the programmer/user relationship as a type of author/reader relationship are also discussed. Because computer systems are living language arenas, strategies for the constructive use of metaphor are also explored.

II. Metaphor in Computer Language

A. Computing as an Arena for Metaphor

Metaphor is well-suited to computer language because the essential functions of the computer are hidden from sight. The functional unit of the computer is the bit, a binary on/off state, usually existing on a magnetic medium. The computer user deals with the larger units--characters, records and files--which loosely correspond to the printed character, line on a page, and some group of pages. While there are correspondences, the reality of the computer cannot be completely understood through metaphors. Moreover, the human brain, another poorly understood device, is often used as a grand metaphor for the computer, making the operation of a computer even more fearsome and mysterious for the novice. This vacuum of human reason and understanding in the world of the ultimate rational machine creates an atmosphere where metaphor has strong possibilities for use, in direct proportion to the level of technological alienation in the computer user.

B. Descriptive Metaphor

The use of metaphor and other symbolic forms allows people to grasp new concepts, particularly abstract concepts, by using something they already understand as a reference point, filter or conduit. The need for metaphor is strong in computer language, because many computer functions are neither concrete nor observable. Often, one must simply trust that computer data exist, based upon clues or information reported by the computer, rather than through any sense information. For example, in the VM (Virtual Machine) operating system, there are two kinds of disk storage, temporary and permanent. To explain the *functional* differences, the *disk is a garage* metaphor might be used:

> Storing data on a permanent disk is like parking one's car in a garage, while temporary disk is similar to street parking. The garage is superior to street parking because it is safer, but there is a limited amount of space. One may use street parking outside one's house when one has visitors or if one buys another car. While it is possible to expand the size of one's garage, it is hardly a practical short-term solution. As with street parking, to get temporary disk one must compete with other drivers for a limited amount of space. Also, one would not want to leave one's car parked on the street for long periods, as it may get towed for street cleaning or ticketed as an abandoned vehicle.

This shows the difference between two unknown computer devices in terms of their functions, explaining *what* in terms of *how*. As computer users become more experienced, they rely less on the metaphors and more on their own experiences.

Similarly, computer functions can be described in terms of other computer functions, using the same metaphorical constructions as in the previous example. For example, someone experienced with the DOS operating system on a PC would understand that temporary disk in VM is like RAM (random access memory) on a PC. While there are vast differences between the signifier and the signified, the *temporary disk is a RAM* metaphor alerts one to certain functional similarities. In these cases, metaphor is not meant to be an end, but a conduit for meaning, a ladder that one kicks away after climbing up it.

C. Naming Metaphors

In the current discussion, "naming" metaphors are those metaphors that become elements of the computer language. For example, the *disk is a garage* descriptive metaphor, is a much weaker use of metaphor than if the program that allocated disk was named "GARAGE". The descriptive metaphor is optional, while the naming metaphor must be accepted by anyone using the GARAGE program. A name metaphor has more authority than a descriptive metaphor and stands by itself, independent of the namer. Poor descriptive metaphors may be forgotten, while naming metaphors are indelibly fixed to the computer program and are more likely to spawn additional naming and descriptive metaphors.

In the past, computer languages consisted of rather dull names for computer objects and functions. However, some new systems, such as the Apple MacIntosh, use icons to represent computer functions. For example, rather than explaining that erasing a file is like putting a piece of paper in a trash can, the MacIntosh represents the computer functions with pictures, or icons, of those objects and the user manipulates the icons on the computer screen, putting the computer file into the computer trashcan, eliminating the mental images that one might draw in one's mind, and probably restricting creativity.

Traditionally, the closer one gets to the computer's inner logic, the less metaphor is used, probably due to the lack of correspondence between objects in the natural world and the logical workings of a computer. Assembly languages, "low level" languages, deal with bits, bytes and registers, and are highly codified, rarely using metaphors outside of the standard code. A higher level language, such as Fortran, encourages more metaphor and, for example, will speak of opening a file and writing to a printer. The highest level, where the user is most removed from the computer's logic and structure, is the MacIntosh, where the user manipulates icons.

III. The Protect Metaphor

The computer users studied here are graduate students and researchers who use a mainframe computer to analyze data, principally using "canned" software packages, such as SPSS or SAS, rather than programming languages such as Fortran, Cobol, or Assembler. Most have medical or social science backgrounds, with few having experience in computer programming concepts.

The computer is an IBM mainframe, running the CMS operating system, a subset of VM, in which the user communicates with the computer through commands whose syntax is similar to natural language English. Users can create synonyms for existing functions and name programs with simple words, with few constraints. Files have simple three part names, for example:

MY DATA A

MY NEWDATA A

PHONE BOOK B

with the first two parts being constrained to eight alphanumeric characters each and the third part signifying the location of the file (disk A, B, etc.)

When the School's computing center was set up in 1981, CMS was chosen, in part, because it is easy to learn. Users work interactively and it appears that each person has their own computer or virtual machine (VM). Like all mainframe systems, there are systems programmers who install software, write programs, and maintain hardware. For our purposes, systems programmers and programmers are synonymous. Systems programmers have special privileges to alter or access information on the computer, as well as the ability to bring the system "up" or "down". The term "user" signifies a computer user, or end-user, who may have virtually no computer skills or may have skills equal to or exceeding those of the systems programmers. Users have no special privileges and are, technologically, at the mercy of the systems programmers.

In CMS a user's data are stored on fixed-size disk storage areas. If a user's disk fills up, there is no easy way to increase the size. One remedy is to request a larger disk, called temporary disk, that is borrowed from a pool of disk shared by all users. This temporary disk is a work area that is used during one session. Any work that the user wants to save can be transferred to magnetic tape or the user's permanent disk before the temporary disk is released. While permanent disk remains intact after the session is ended, temporary disk is wiped clean and returns to the pool. Additionally, the data on the temporary disk is erased if the user accidentally ends the session (logs off) or if the computer crashes.

Creation of a temporary disk is not a simple process, so a systems programmer wrote a program that made its creation easier by combining several steps. For example, the following commands are needed to create a temporary disk of size 50:

    CP DEFINE T3380 AS 505 50

    FORMAT 505 A

    ACCESS 191 B

One minor problem appeared. After the temporary disk was created, one could accidentally write over or erase files on the permanent disk. Rather than modify the original program, the programmer erased it and wrote a program called PROTECT that created a temporary disk and PROTECTed or locked the user's permanent disk. Instead of entering the three commands above, the user simply typed "PROTECT 50".

The first generation of users knew that PROTECT had two functions--to create a new temporary disk and lock the permanent one--with the latter function protecting the user from himself or herself.

Because the creation of temporary disk is not standard from system to system, it is important that users understand the basic concepts behind the shortcut. There was steady turnover in the student population from year to year; the original users moved on, taking with them the knowledge of the primary purpose of PROTECT. For new users, the name of the program implied its secondary purpose. The poor matching of name and function created a tension that pushed metaphor into myth, as users sought to resolve the tension by extending the metaphor.

The name "PROTECT" was not useful in conveying the concept of permanent and temporary disks, because the primary function was not represented in the name metaphor. PROTECT signifies an action, but the object of protection is missing. Therefore, it was necessary to add another layer of descriptive metaphor, such as the *disk is a garage* metaphor. Users distorted the PROTECT metaphor and spoke of temporary disk as PROTECT disk and PROTECT space. "Protect space" sounds like a very nice place: safe, comfortable, eternal, with no hint of technological alienation. "Temporary disk", however, sounds short-term and insecure, as it ought to. The PROTECT myth evolved from those attributes signified by the phrase "protect space", rather than "temporary disk".

The power of the myth can be seen in the transformation of physical dimensions. The magnetic surface of a disk is two dimensional, while "protect space" implies the addition of a third dimension. Users, grasping for meaning, made the disk more real by giving it three-dimensional form. However, the use of the term "space" was unfortunate. A "protect box", "protect balloon", or even "protect tent" would have been better. The term "space" is three-dimensional, but has no form, substance, or bounds--it is not self-contained--it is infinite and envelops all in its universe.

People spoke of protect space as if it was an aura surrounding the user, rather than a place where data was stored. Unlike floppy diskettes, the mainframe disks cannot be observed or touched by the user. The user's temporary disk is hidden among hundreds of other virtual disks within a large blue metal box. In reality, one's data are *on* a flat disk, while people spoke of being *in* protect space. Not only was their data now three-dimensional, but *they were in this space*. Therefore, any threat to protect space implied an attack on the occupants of that space. This identification made changes to the PROTECT program difficult and helped the myth to grow. Three-dimensional users seemed to like three-dimensional metaphors for two-dimensional collections of one-dimensional bits.

New users familiar with the temporary disk concept, expected to find a short-cut program, but were greeted with the mythology of PROTECT. The level of devotion to the PROTECT myth varied, with the highest levels among students who worked late at night or on weekends, when the mystery of computing is highest due to the lack of technical support staff. Users passed on knowledge of the intricacies of PROTECT in the computer room. The users can hardly be ridiculed for developing the mythology, since they were extending the metaphor that was given to them by a systems programmer. The word "protect" had to be used by them, even though all but one systems programmer had abandoned it in favor of more technical language.

Users needed help to resolve the tension between mythic meaning and personal experience. The PROTECT metaphor was extended with verbal descriptive metaphors such as "protect space". One systems programmer extended the myth with several programs, using PROTECT-type name metaphors such as REPROTect and UNPROTect. A peripheral function, the creation of a temporary disk, something that one might never use, was now the center of mythic computing.

Some people became so attached to the PROTECT myth that they used the unstable temporary disk *instead of* the secure permanent disk for their normal work. Therefore, if the system crashed, people lost not just a few hours of work, but days or weeks worth.

The PROTECT metaphor was so pervasive that the letter "P" became a prefix and synonym for PROTECT, for example, PSave, PEdit, and PFile, while "P" is the obvious abbreviation for permanent disk and "T" that of temporary disk. The data on the insecure temporary disks were called PROTECT(ed) files, not those files on their permanent disk that were actually protected. Users referred to their temporary disk as their "P" disk. This was confusing because the operating system automatically named disks with the letters A through Z. The real "A" disk was referred to as the mythical "P" disk, but the real "P" disk was also called the "P" disk.

Users were developing a code that was internally contradictory and untranslateable. Metaphor was originally used to bridge the gap between the user and technology, relieving alienation. Because the PROTECT myth created more distance and tension between human and machine, a different sort of alienation was created. The users were choosing the *kind of meaning and non-meaning* that they preferred. The alienating void of technical jargon not-knowing was eschewed in favor of the more comforting mythical not-knowing. Over time, protect *space* became a reality for users: metaphor was no longer a conduit for meaning, but a barrier that isolated users from the systems programmers and the true computer concepts. Protect space, boundless in conception, was a prison of language.

The lead systems programmer believed that all shortcuts, such as PROTECT, were the mark of an inferior computer user. However, as systems programmer, he had access to unlimited amounts of permanent disk and, therefore, rarely needed temporary disk. Because there was no sensibly named short-cut program, the user was forced to choose between the cumbersome technical language of the systems programmer and the language of the myth. The programmer's indifference to this language problem caused the user to choose the false but more accessible language of PROTECT.

To resolve tension in the PROTECT universe and create a human symbol for their technological problems, some users imagined the systems programmers as digital Satans, causing or at least being indifferent to their problems. When the computer crashed, users often complained to the systems programmer, suspecting foul play, even though he had warned them against using a temporary disk as a long-term storage area.

In 1986, about four years into the Age of Protect, a new systems programmer decided to eliminate PROTECT, because it caused many problems for users and, consequently, programmers. A more sensibly named and technically superior program, called TDISK, was written but was largely ignored. Users stayed with PROTECT, yet still complained about its consequences. They simply never believed that something named "protect" could harm them. The written text had immense authority, more authority than the authors of the text, the programmers. The systems programmers misjudged the power of PROTECT and failed in their attempt to use reason against it. PROTECT was briefly removed and replaced with TDISK, but this action caused panic among a few of the students and protests from some of the faculty.

Guessing that the metaphor of the computer as a mechanical brain was more mysterious and powerful than any other myth, a new strategy was devised. Instead of trying to topple the PROTECT myth as outsiders, the systems programmers worked against it from within the larger mythic structure. They programmed the computer to berate the PROTECT myth. The computer allowed PROTECT to be invoked, but the PROTECT program now confessed its inferiority and suggested using the superior TDISK program. Eventually, when PROTECT, UNProtect, and REProtect were invoked they simply referred the user to the TDISK program.

Some time after the death of PROTECT, it was discovered that a small and quiet cult of users had copied the PROTECT programs to their private disks and continued to use them. Ironically, the systems programmer who wrote some of the PROTECT programs left the computing center at the time of the demise of PROTECT, taking copies of PROTECT to his new computing center, and is rumored to still lead the PROTECTors.

IV. Conclusion

The intention of the computing center was not to sterilize language, by removing symbolic forms, but simply to eliminate one particular metaphor that had, like a mutant virus, grown out of control. Creative use of metaphor may help the computer user to understand or remember a program. For example, a program that searches through files for some word or phrase is called FERRET. A program that erases old programs is called SCIMITAR. The use of metaphor in the computer industry has become rampant is recent years and its overuse may make people immune to it. One of the most infuriating language problems occurred when IBM released the new version of a program called "TAPE DUMP". It was called VMFPLC2, but there was no VMFPLC1, and it is almost never used, due to the name.

In places where there is a lack of concrete information, metaphor will "stick" easily, making it essential that the naming corresponds to the real function. The correspondence can be judged, by the effects and side-effects of the name, by the extension of the metaphor, by how it spawns other metaphors and how it aligns with competing metaphor systems.

Given that the computer environment is fertile ground for the development of metaphor, those who control the language of the computer need to accept some responsibility for the meaning that the language creates and the consequences of faulty metaphor. Computer programmers who create components of computer languages that are shared by others, especially those less technically skilled, must understand the enormous impact that the language they create has on others. Programmers need not police the language of others, but should set good examples and provide well-thought out names for computer functions. While much effort here has been spent on showing the mythologizing of the computer by users, the same process occurs for programmers. Users embrace metaphor and create myths to resolve the alienation that comes from a lack of control of their environment, while programmers create myths to celebrate their control over technology. The systems programmers are the more destructive mythologizers, because they have the knowledge that the users need, but often hide it behind technical jargon and technological elitism.

From computer guru to neophyte, the power of metaphor and myth is strong. While people get caught up in the illusions of technology, the purpose of computers is simply that of a tool. Creativity that is centered *around* the tool, such as the mythologizing of PROTECT, is wasted energy. It is essential for programmers to realize that the computer is the *medium* through which they communicate to users. If programmers understand that the language they use transmits meaning to other people, much like the relationship between an author and a reader, they may find their work better received and the alienation that technology creates will be lessened.

NOTES

[1] We wish to thank the students of the School of Hygiene and Public Health for their participation in the ongoing and unintended experiments in computer language. Special thanks also go to Catherine Jackson for her insightful comments and criticism.

V

SESSIONS OF THE CHARLES S. PEIRCE SOCIETY

PEIRCE'S EARLY SEMIOTIC ANALYSIS OF REPRESENTATION[1]

André De Tienne
Catholic University of Louvain and the Peirce Edition Project

1. Introduction

That Peirce wrote his celebrated essay "On a New List of Categories" in 1867 is a well known fact. Many a scholar has insisted on 1867 as being the "most decisive year" (Fisch 1984: xxi) and turning point in Peirce's philosophical career. Indeed, the five papers he presented at the American Academy of Arts and Sciences (1867: 12-86) justify such a claim beyond discussion. However, little is it reflected that Peirce's 1867 presentation of the "New List" stemmed from a several-year-long research in logic and metaphysics, and that Peirce's categorial quest had already reached completion by the end of 1866. As a matter of fact, Peirce gave his first public presentation of the "New List" not in 1867, but in 1866 in his eighth and ninth Lowell Lectures (1866a: 471-488).[2] Several scholars (Lohkamp 1970: 202-203; Buzzelli 1974: 205-206; Esposito 1976: 346) have justly remarked that the germs of many important later doctrines (like the critical common-sensism, for instance) could be found easily in the earlier writings, preceding 1867. It is my purpose to show that this is also true of Peirce's semiotic theory, a theory already quite elaborate in its early stage. What follows is a tentative account of the development of the theory of representation between 1859 and 1865.

2. Brief Reminder: Kant and Peirce

In order to fulfill this objective, I must first recall briefly some of the basic epistemological ideas Peirce entertained following his critical reading of Kant. In the first place, Peirce sought to revise the noumenon-phenomenon distinction by rejecting Kant's notion of a noumenon as an uncognizable transcendental object. Though it is true we cannot have an immediate representation of the things that are out of us, and we cannot think them, yet we are able to think *of* them, or to have a mediate representation of them, and it is absurd to say that things may exist without being of-thinkable in this way. All unthought must therefore be thought-of, otherwise we could not even suspect its existence. Everything is thus representable.

In the second place, unsatisfied with Kant's logically flawed table of categories, Peirce strove to find a set of categories so fundamental that they were a necessary part of every cognition. Inspired by his reading of Schiller's Aesthetic

Letters, Peirce was soon convinced of the operative importance of formal triadism. The first triad he fashioned was that of I, IT, and THOU, where *I* stood for the internal element, *IT* for the external element, and *THOU* for the intermediate element that allows the other two to congregate and make up experience. At about the same time, Peirce came to distinguish three "stages of thought" in Kant's table of categories, those of Null or Simple, Positive, and Perfect, where the Positive stage represents the actual outcome of the blending of the two extremes. It is interesting to examine how the latter triad was applied by Peirce in his earliest manuscripts, in order to account for the possibility of representation.

3. The "Three Stages of Thought" Analysis

One of Peirce's earliest manuscripts is titled "Analysis of Creation". By "creation" Peirce understands the "realization of abstractions ... in thought and in feeling" (1861a: 9), that is to say, the bringing forth of a "modification" of consciousness. Considering an actual modification of consciousness as a Positive stage of thought, our philosopher (1861b: 37) wants to determine the nature of the combination of Null and Perfect that is embodied in such a modification:

> The less a modification of consciousness is such, the more it approaches that nonentity which we have called *things-or-thing* which it becomes in ceasing to modify the consciousness at all, but the more it is a modification of consciousness the more it approaches being a pure *abstraction* which is a modification of consciousness without even personality or number.

In other words, a modification of consciousness or representation arises from the union of the manifold of sense (things-or-thing) on the one hand, and of a pure formal abstraction on the other. This gives us the following Null-Positive-Perfect triad:

⎧Things-or-thing		⎧Thing		⎧Substance
⎨Modification of consciousness	or	⎨Feeling	or	⎨Predicate
⎩Abstraction		⎩Pure Form		⎩Predicable
(1861b: 37)		(1861c: 13)		(1861c: 13)

In another essay, titled "The Modus of the IT" (1861: 47), Peirce adds:

> The relations of the triad being apprehended, it will be clear that which is in the sensible world can only enter the mental world by having in it a *revelation* which is in the abstract world.

As soon as 1861, then, Peirce entertains the idea that a representation is the result of a triadic interplay in which two "absolutes" (the substantial manifold of sense and the pure abstract form) are conflated to produce an actual sensible representation of something. Peirce's primary intention is to show how a quality becomes attributed to an object given to the senses. His earliest theory is that something can be thought of only if it is revealed through an abstraction, whose embodiment carries it into the mental world of representations. Which is the same as saying that something can exist only through qualities. Even though Peirce will change the structure of his triad somewhat in the ensuing years, he will never question this basic epistemological principle.

4. Representation and Truth

Let us now make another step. In his "Treatise on Metaphysics" (1862:65-84), Peirce, among other things, defines the three different kinds of truth or agreement between a representation and its object in terms of verisimilitude, veracity, and verity. *Verisimilitude* indicates an agreement based on a resemblance or sameness between representation and object, and Peirce calls the representation involved in such a relation a likeness or *copy*. *Veracity* refers to an agreement based not on a resemblance, but just on a constant connection, the result of an arbitrary convention, between the representation and its object. The representation involved in such a relation is called a *sign*. Finally, when the agreement is based on a relation similar to that which prevails between a substance and its accidents, or between a subject and its predicates, the correspondence between the representation and its object is total and is called *verity*. The representation itself is called a *type* or *symbol*. The correspondence or truth is said to be total because, as already suggested, "the unity of substance implies perfect correspondence of qualities" (1862: 80). I shall come back later to this threefold division of truth and representation, which is crucial to a proper understanding of Peirce's early semiotic analysis of representation.

5. From Noumenon to Representation

Copy, sign, and symbol are the three forms of representation in general, and as such they share the same general structure. In order to delineate Peirce's early analysis of representation, the best thing to do is to examine his 1865 writings, in which the two terms representation and symbol acquire a specific sense--even though Peirce is not always consistent in his use of them. The reason of his occasional inconsistency can be understood by giving a look at his classification of the sciences which can be found either in (1865: 174-175) or in (1865c: 304).

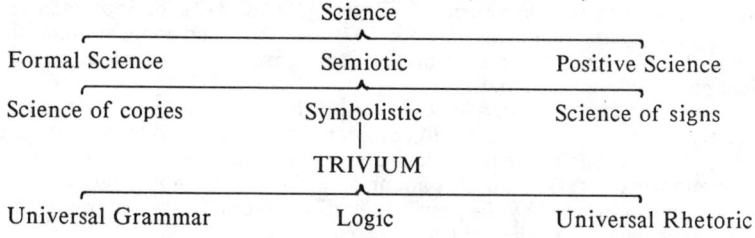

```
                          Science
         ┌─────────────────┴─────────────────┐
   Formal Science        Semiotic        Positive Science
   ┌─────┴─────┐                         ┌─────┴─────┐
Science of copies      Symbolistic       Science of signs
                           │
                        TRIVIUM
              ┌────────────┼────────────┐
      Universal Grammar   Logic    Universal Rhetoric
```

The first division is based on the fundamental trichotomic distinction I, Thou, and It, reformulated in the triad Form, Representation. and Thing or Matter. Semiotic is the name Peirce gives to the general science of representations, and Symbolistic is the name for the more specific science of symbols, which is itself composed of three subordinate sciences, one of which is Logic, the science of the reference of the symbol to its object. As Peirce happens from time to time to use the word "logic" to designate also either Semiotic or Symbolistic, it is not always evident to determine on which of those levels he is speaking when resorting to the word "symbol". Besides, as he proceeds through his triadic analysis of representation, Peirce generates tens and tens of triads whose internal elements are constantly renamed or changed of position, so that it is hard to apprehend clearly the rationale of the many successive changes. What I am going to do is to offer a tentative reconstruction, or more accurately, a tentative reordering of the different conceptual triads Peirce brings forward.

As has already been said several times, Peirce holds that everything is representable, and that a noumenon, if it exists, must be knowable. In the essay "An Unpsychological View of Logic" (1865d: 313), he reformulates the phenomenon-noumenon distinction accordingly:

> [The noumenon] is the regularities of the form which induce the objectification of the phenomenon ... . The notion of the noumenon is nothing more than the expectation of a recurrence of those regularities--a hypothesis that everything seen is matched by something not seen. It results from this similarity between phenomenon and noumenon that the latter is analyzable into the same elements as the former.

Peirce derives the triadic elements of the noumenon from those of the phenomenon. I shall however reverse the order of presentation, starting with the most basic triad, that of the noumenon.

Triad no. 1[3]
- Pure or Substantial Form
- Noumenal or Substantial Matter
- Accidents or Concept or Logos

(1865d: 307-308, 313)

The claim that a noumenon is composed of those three fundamental elements, one of which (accidents) is a representative element, sets the path for all subsequent analyses. In one way or another, this triadic pattern will have to be repeated faithfully, since every representation is a reflection of its object, and ultimately a reflection of its origin, the intelligible noumenon. This noumenon includes in itself what Peirce calls "Accidents", or Concept: the representative element "prescinded from all substance whether form or matter" (1865d: 313), or separated from "the material and mental element" (1865d: 307). So the noumenon contains in itself, through the Concept, the possibility of its cognizability, which is Peirce's basic critical common-sensist belief.

As they are presented in triad no. 1, the three elements are each viewed separately. It is however possible to consider them in their dynamic relation to one another; this will enable us to explain better the regularities of cognition. If every phenomenon is the reflection of a noumenon, the actual knowledge of a phenomenon must be conditioned by the possibilities of cognition contained in the noumenon. This necessity generates the next triad of elements:

Triad no. 2
- Qualities
- Thing(s)
- Representation in general, or Object

(1865d: 307, 314)

These three aspects are related to one another very closely and make up the possibilities of cognition; as such, as Peirce also says, they constitute the substrata of phenomena. The *qualities* are all the attributes predicated of the thing and constitute the "mental" or "internal" representation of the "thing". The *thing* is the "noumenon" so far as it induces the mental representation; it is matter combined with quality. And the *object* is an "external representation" resulting from the combination of the accidents with the material and mental elements.

As the three fundamental elements of a noumenon have been defined both analytically and synthetically, I come now to the next triad in the chain of derivation, that of the *phenomenon*. By phenomenon, Peirce understands any "actual cognition" (1865d: 307) considered objectively in its distinctive elements (in contradistinction to a *representation*, which is a cognition considered subjectively in the internal dialectic of its elements). Every phenomenon has, not very surprisingly, three aspects:

Triad no. 3
{ Qualities
  Reality
  Image
(1865d: 307)

Qualities are those characters that permit us to differentiate one phenomenon from another and constitute the *form* of the phenomenon. *Reality* refers to the phenomenon when it is objectified or thought-of, "reproduced in the imagination" Peirce says (1865d: 313); as such it allows the phenomenon to enter our consciousness as an IT, or a propositional subject: as something containing *matter*. *Image* is that aspect in which the phenomenon is regarded as a representation of something not present: the noumenon. This word, image, is well chosen because it conveys the definition of a phenomenon as an actual and accurate reflection of the noumenon. As in triad no. 1, these three phenomenal elements are viewed separately from each other. Peirce gives a different but equivalent formulation of them in the tenth Harvard Lecture (1865a: 274):

Triad no. 4
{ Form: the relation between a representation and thing prescinded from both representation and thing.
  Matter: that for which a representation might stand,
   or   prescinded from all that could constitute a relation
  Thing: with any representation.
  Image: a representation prescinded from thing and form.

Triad no. 4 is the same as triad no. 3, though its elements recall those of triad no. 1, noumenality put aside. Now, as in triad no. 2, Peirce needs to form a triad in which those three elements are not viewed separately but in their dynamic relation to one another, so as to account for the structure of an actual cognition taken subjectively, that is to say, of a representation proper.

6. Peirce's 1865 Conception of Representation

In the unfinished essay "Logic of the Sciences" (1865f: 323-326), Peirce presents a radicalized notion of representation:

> In the present work instead of being restricted to something within the mind, [the term *representation*] will be extended to things which do not even address the mind. ...
> We must ... admit that a thing in its attributes is a representation of the same thing in itself.
> We can ... apply induction to *all that is*, in the widest sense; and so find the character of the *summum genus*. Whatever is immediately

> present to us, will be instances of *what is*. These instances ... are representations ... [because they are] *taken* as instances. Hence, we presume that *whatever is* is a representation... The *Summum Genus*, or What is, is representation, then.

To assert that everything is a representation is of course to deny that something could not be a representation. As Peirce will say in 1868, "*cognizability* (in its widest sense) and *being* are not merely metaphysically the same, but are synonymous terms" (1868: 208). Berkeley in his days had coined the phrase *esse est percipi*; Peirce, making a step further, could have written *esse est repraesentari*.

Let us come now to the triadic structure of a representation. Peirce's technical definition (1865f: 330) is as follows:

> Representation is the character of standing to a subject for an object upon some ground.

From there we get triad no. 5:

Triad No. 5 { Ground
              Object
              Subject

Peirce gives another equivalent formulation of triad no. 5 in his tenth Harvard Lecture, namely triad no. 6 (1865a: 274):

Triad no. 6 { Logos
              Object
              Equivalent Representation

The *ground* or *logos* is a form or quality embodied in the object, or in the subject, or in both, and is the occasion of their being brought together in a representation. The *object* is the thing represented or stood for; it is endowed with a form and corresponds with an actual representation. The *subject* or *equivalent representation* is an image which translates another representation as a representation. It is "that which is determined by the representation to agree with it in its reference to the object on [some] ground" (1865f: 335). Peirce makes clear that the subject is not a human mind, though it can be a human representation; it is to be understood logically, not psychologically.

7. Connotation, Denotation, Information

So much for the triadic structure of representation. As we have seen earlier, Peirce distinguished the three kinds of representation (copy, sign, and symbol) for the first time in 1862. In his 1865 writings, he reworks this division extensively, mostly on the basis of an important logical investigation in the subject-predicate relation. In the last but one Harvard Lecture, Peirce (1865a: 275) remarks that

> so far as the object of a representation contains the *thing*, so far the representation *stands for* something, and so far it *denotes*. And so far as its object embodies a form, so far the representation has a meaning and so far it *connotes*.

Thus, the *denotation* of a representation is its direct reference to its object, and its connotation is its indirect reference to its ground through the denotation of the object. Peirce calls *extension* of a representation the sum of all its objects of denotation, and he calls *comprehension* of a representation the sum of all its objects of connotation or qualities. He then observes the presence of a balance between extension and comprehension: the more the extension of a term is increased, the more its comprehension decreases; the more objects the term applies to, the less common characters it connotes. Conversely, the more the comprehension increases, the more the extension decreases; the more qualities are added, the less objects will be found that share them. This logical principle can be translated into the following formula:

COMPREHENSION x EXTENSION = CONSTANT (1865a: 276).

However, the case may happen that when the comprehension is increased, the extension does not decrease and remains the same, or *vice versa*; this happens only when the increase is due to the addition of an equivalent representation. An addition to the comprehension that does not disturb the extension, Peirce calls it *information*. Thus the formula becomes:

COMPREHENSION x EXTENSION = INFORMATION (1865a: 276).

Peirce defines information as "the amount of comprehension a *symbol* has over and above what limits its extension" (1865b: 287); "the information of a term is the measure of its superfluous comprehension" (1866: 467).[4] This definition refers to the word "symbol" (of which a term is a species), and it is not by chance. As a matter of fact, Peirce's 1865 distinction between copy, sign, and symbol (1865a: 272), rests heavily on the denotation-connotation analysis.

> Every symbol *denotes* by *connoting*. A representation which *denotes* without connoting is a mere *sign*. If it *connotes* without thereby *denoting* it, it is a mere copy.

A *copy* is a representation which refers to its object by resembling it; as such it does not denote the object, but just connotes it: it just shows how the object looks. Referring to triad no. 5, Peirce defines a copy as "a representation whose subject and object depend immediately upon the ground and not upon any character of either. ... It is this sort of representation ... which a picture is" (1865f: 328). Saying that a *copy* is a representation whose ground is contained both in the object and the subject amounts exactly to saying that a copy is a representation which connotes without denoting, since the representation is determined by the ground to refer to the ground itself.

A *sign* is a representation which accords with its object without any real correspondence; as such it does not connote the object but just denotes it: its applicability to a thing "depends only upon a convention which establishe[s] precisely what it should denote" (1865d: 308). In the terms of triad no. 5, a sign is "a representation whose object is determined by its subject; that is to say whose Ground is a character of the Subject. ... If two men agree to have a certain sign denote certain things, that sign is a representation of this kind" (1865f: 328). A proper name, for instance, is a sign in that sense.

8. Information and Symbol

Since neither a copy nor a sign have at once comprehension and extension, they provide no information. *Symbol* is the only species of representation that gives information, and the remainder of this paper will be spent presenting Peirce's definition and analysis of the symbol (1865a: 273):

> A symbol *denotes* by virtue of *connoting* and not *vice versa*, hence the object of connotation determines the object of denotation and not *vice versa*, in the sense in which the subject of a proposition is the term determined and the predicate is the determining term.

Peirce's theory is that a symbol cannot denote an object unless it connotes its qualities. This of course is in concordance with his basic belief that "a thing in its attributes is a representation of the same thing in itself" (1865f: 324). If we recall that Peirce defines the information of a term as the amount of its superfluous comprehension, we should understand Peirce's next contention easily, that every symbol has information. Indeed, as he argues in the last Harvard Lecture, a symbol must connote *reality* in order to denote at all. Now, as everything is cognizable and has attributes, it must also have reality, and reality is a part of that superfluous comprehension which has no effect on the extension of the symbol--therefore every symbol has information.

In the terms of triad no. 5, Peirce defines a symbol as "a representation whose subject depends upon its object" (1865f: 328), which means that the ground of the representation is a character of the object. In the terms of triad no. 6, the symbol is defined as "[that which] stands for its *object*, ... translates its *equivalent representation*, [and] ... realizes its logos" (1865a: 274). The symbol "realizes its logos": this means that the symbol relates to the form or ground embodied in the object by bringing it to the light and showing it as being truly attributed to the object; only by connoting the ground in this way can the symbol "stand for the thing", or denote it as the legitimate owner of the different characters making up its ground. This double work of connotation and denotation is possible only through the translation of an equivalent representation, because it is precisely the equivalent representation which symbolizes the object both immediately--by denoting it--and mediately--by connoting its character. The result of this symbolic process will be the creation of *information*.

"As every symbol is determined in three ways," Peirce says, "symbols, as such, are subject to three laws. ... The first law is Logic, the second Universal Rhetoric, the third Universal Grammar" (1865a: 274). Universal Grammar is the science of the reference of symbols to qualities, Universal Rhetoric is the science of the reference of symbols to equivalent representations, and Logic is the science of the relations of symbols to their objects--and only to their objects. "Yet," Peirce adds in MS 726 (1865e: 28), "as the objects have three elements, matter, form, and accidents, logic comes to deal with the reference to these". This last assertion brings us back to triad no. 1, so that the loop is looped, and I feel entitled to stop my account of Peirce's early semiotic analysis of representation here.

NOTES

[1] This article has been made possible through a grant from the Belgian National Fund for Scientific Research, where I am an Aspirant. It is a slightly revised version of the paper I read in Cincinnati. I wish to thank the editorial staff of the Peirce Edition Project, Indiana University at Indianapolis, for their unfailing and most generous assistance.

[2] The eighth Lowell Lecture is no longer extant, but evidence in Lowell Lecture IX suggests clearly that Peirce presented his categories already in Lecture VIII.

[3] Triads no. 1 to 6 are all presented in the I-It-Thou order for the sake of consistency, even though Peirce did not necessarily present them in that order.

[4] There seems to be some kind of tension involved in Peirce's analysis. On the one hand, he insists on the symbol as "denoting by virtue of connoting" and not *vice versa*, which means that the function of connotation is to determine the denotation--as a result of which the information is the measure of superfluous comprehension. On the other hand, Peirce also says that "when the comprehension is increased there is an increase of either extension or comprehension without any diminution of the other of these quantities" (1866: 465), which means that the information should also be the measure of superfluous *extension*. However this conclusion, though implied, is never explicitly drawn by the author.

REFERENCES

BUZZELLI, Donald E.
    1974. *The "New List of Categories": A Study of the Early Philosophy of Charles Sanders Peirce* (New York: Fordham University, Ph.D. dissertation, U.M.I. GAX74-19639).

ESPOSITO, Joseph L.
    1976. "Peirce's Early Speculations on the Categories", in *Proceedings of the C. S. Peirce Bicentennial International Congress* (held in Amsterdam in June 1976), ed. Kenneth L. Ketner et al. (Lubbock, Texas: Texas Tech Press, Graduate Studies 23, 1981), 343-346.

FISCH, Max H.
    1984. "The Decisive Year and its Early Consequences", Introduction to *Writings of Charles S. Peirce: A Chronological Edition*, ed. Peirce Edition Project (Bloomington: Indiana University Press), vol. 2, xxi-xxxvi.

LOHKAMP, Richard J.
    1970. *The Meaning and Significance of Charles S. Peirce's "On a New List of Categories"* (South Bend: University of Notre Dame, Ph.D. dissertation, U.M.I. GAX71-19081).

PEIRCE, Charles S.
1861-1868. The historical layering in this entry is based on the "Chronological List" provided in the editorial apparatus of the *Writings of Charles S. Peirce: A Chronological Edition*, vol. 1 1857-1866, vol. 2 1867-1871, ed. Peirce Edition Project (Bloomington: Indiana University Press, 1982, 1984). Standard abbreviated reference to this edition is by capital W, followed by the volume number, colon, and page number. MS + number refers to the manuscripts as arranged in *Annotated Catalogue of the Papers of Charles S. Peirce*, ed. Richard S. Robin (University of Massachusetts Press, 1967), with pagination referring to the Institute for Studies in Pragmaticism numeration.
1861. "The Modus of the It", in W 1:47-49.
1861a. "Analysis of Creation", in MS 1105:2-11.
1861b. "§1 Of Forms", in MS 922:36-38.
1861c. "A Classification", in MS 919:13-15.
1862. "A Treatise on Metaphysics", in W 1:65-84.
1865. "Harvard Lecture I", in W 1:162-175.
1865a. "Harvard Lecture X", in W 1:272-286.
1865b. "Harvard Lecture XI", in W 1:286-302.
1865c. "Teleological Logic", in W 1:303-304.
1865d. "An Unpsychological View of Logic to which are appended some applications of the theory to Psychology and other subjects", in W 1:305-321.
1865e. "Chapter II. Connotation, Denotation, Information", in MS 726: 28-36.
1865f. "Logic of the Sciences", in W 1:322-336.
1866. "Lowell Lecture VII", in W 1:454-471.
1866a. "Lowell Lecture IX", in W 1:471-488.
1867. "The American Academy Series", in W 2:11-86.
1868. "Questions Concerning Certain Faculties Claimed for Man", in *Journal of Speculative Philosophy* 2, 103-114 reprinted in W 2:193-211.

PEIRCE'S PRE-PHENOMENOLOGICAL CATEGORIES

Nathan Houser
Indiana University

In Peirce's eleventh Lowell Lecture of 1866, he told the story of a young boy who could only articulate three words. The cause of this curious deficiency is not important, although it should be said that the child was, otherwise, quite capable. The complete lexicon of the child consisted of these words: "name", "story", and "matter". Peirce (1866: 501) continues the story of the boy as follows:

> He says *name* when he wishes to know the name of a person or thing; *story* when he wishes to hear a narration or description; and *matter*--a highly abstract and philosophical term--when he wishes to be acquainted with the cause of anything. *Name, story,* and *matter,* therefore, make the foundation of this child's philosophy. What a wonderful thing that his individuality should have been shown so strongly, at that age, in selecting those three words out of all the equally common ones which he heard about him. Already he has made his list of categories, which is the principal part of any philosophy.

Peirce went on to point out the profundity of this curious classification, and how, by including "name" in his list, the child had improved on Aristotle. I mention this story for three reasons. First, to remind you that from the beginning of his philosophical life Peirce was much interested in the subject of categories. In fact, if you look at Volume 1 of the new chronological edition of Peirce's writings, you will see that the preponderance of his earliest writings deal with categories. Second, I wanted to point out that Peirce's approach to philosophy was architectonic. He held that philosophy should be built up from a foundational categorical structure. Third, I thought it worth noting that in starting with a search for categories Peirce was following some of the greatest thinkers. In the story, only Aristotle is mentioned. But Kant, especially, and Hegel as well, were also architectonic philosophers whose works inspired Peirce.

It is not news to anyone here that Peirce was interested in categories or that he made important contributions in that regard. The triad, sign, object, and interpretant, will be mentioned again and again during these meetings in Cincinnati, and it will probably be mentioned more than once that Peirce's semiotic categories bear some relation to his more general categories: firstness, secondness, and thirdness.

But only a few of us will ever have attempted to discover the nature of the relations between Peirce's categories in different fields of thought, and still fewer are likely to have exercised ourselves over the problem of the priority ordering of Peirce's various classifications. More than likely, if we are semioticians, we have tended to regard Peirce's semiotic classifications as fundamental.

Those of us (probably the ones concentrated in this room) who *have* struggled with Peirce's thought along these lines, and who have tried to fathom the sometimes juryrigged structure that brings it together into a unified system, know very well how foundational his categories are. They are the key to the organization of his whole philosophy. In mathematics we find one, two, three; or first, second, and third. In the logic of relatives we find monads, dyads, and triads. In phenomenology we find feeling, action, thought; or primisense, altersense, medisense; or what sounds suggestively mathematical (some might say deceptively so): firstness, secondness, and thirdness. In normative logic we find sign, object, interpretant; icon, index, symbol; term, proposition, argument; abduction, induction, deduction; and many other familiar triads. In metaphysics we find possibility, actuality, destiny; chance, law, habit; and mind, matter, evolution.

These are only a few of the seemingly countless triads that pervade Peirce's work. In the absence of a principle of organization to bring order and significance to this great collection of triads, one is in danger of contracting vertigo, and may even come to suspect Peirce of hucksterism or gimmickry. Peirce knew of these risks. "There is a class of minds", he said, "to whom any proposal of a three-fold philosophical distinction acts like a red rag before a mad bull" (Peirce 1913: 31-32). But as we know, Peirce had good reasons for his affinity for triads; moreover, few Peirce scholars doubt that he organized his thought according to at least relatively clear structural principles. Assuming this to be true, it is incumbent on those of us who hope to penetrate to the depths of Peirce's thought to pay serious heed to his architectonic motivation, and to seek to uncover the skeletal structure on which his philosophy hangs. I hope, with this paper, to make a small contribution to the great ongoing task of exposing the structure of Peirce's thought.

It has long been recognized that Peirce's thought evolved over the course of his working life, and that when it is viewed as timeless one is bound to find some terminological conflicts and even some theoretical incongruity. Yet it is usually agreed, by even the most historically-minded Peirce scholars, that Peirce's *fundamental* categories, those which *somehow* support the rest, are his phenomenological categories: firstness, secondness, and thirdness. There is good reason for this, for firstness, secondness, and thirdness, as formal categories of experience, are, as we shall see, the most fundamental *philosophical* categories. But what of his mathematical categories, one, two, three; or his relational categories, monad, dyad, triad? Are they not more fundamental, more abstract, than the phenomenological categories? I believe that they are, but the status of these pre-phenomenological categories remains obscure.

My chief reason for holding that Peirce regarded his mathematical and mathematical-logical categories as more fundamental than, and therefore as basic to, his phenomenological categories, is the relative placement of mathematics and phenomenology in his classification of the sciences. Inspired by Comte and other 19th Century philosophers (Kent 1987: 23-30), Peirce undertook early on in his career to work up a table of the sciences arranged in their order of dependency on each other. A science is dependent on another if it must appeal to it for its principles. The most fundamental science, according to Peirce's "perennial classification" (Kent 1987: 121 ff.), the only science independent of all others, is mathematics. The independence of mathematics does not preclude what we might call "a significant working relationship" between mathematics and subsequent (dependent) sciences. Mathematics may, perhaps must, appeal to subsequent sciences for problems and data. But mathematics does not appeal to any other science for its fundamental principles or structure. On the other hand, every other science, being subsequent to mathematics, must appeal either directly or indirectly to mathematics for its principles. The next science after mathematics is philosophy, which is subdivided in order of dependency into phenomenology, the three normative sciences of esthetics, ethics, and logic, and metaphysics. Phenomenology is closest to mathematics, but is dependent on it.

If one takes seriously Peirce's architectonic approach to philosophy--his view that the method of philosophy should be to first formulate or discover some fundamental ideas, or a fundamental structure, and from this basic foundation to build a philosophic system--and, also, his classification of the sciences in which mathematics is shown to be the fundamental science, one seems compelled to accept the mathematical categories as the most basic, the most fundamental, set. It is my thesis that Peirce's mathematical categories are pre-phenomenological in this sense, and that their appearance in all subsequent sciences, including phenomenology, is in a less abstract, more fleshed-out, form.

This line of reasoning seemed unproblematic at first, but of late I have encountered some difficulties. As fate would have it, I have come up against a triad of problems. First, there are a number of passages, not all of them early ones, in which Peirce appears to regard the phenomenological categories as primary. Second, his placement of logic in the classification of sciences is ambiguous: sometimes Peirce seems to include logic within mathematics and at other times he clearly includes it within the normative sciences. Third, as Murray Murphey has pointed out, Peirce's architectonic ambitions may be incompatible with his classification of the sciences. In one way or another, each of these difficulties raises doubts about my thesis.

The first difficulty is, perhaps, the easiest to dispel. Usually, when Peirce asserts the priority of the phenomenological categories he is discussing the foundations of philosophy. Philosophy, as we already noticed, is composed of three main branches of which phenomenology is first. Philosophy, as a positive science, deals with the world of experience. Mathematics, on the other hand, is a hypothetical science. It is not unlikely that when Peirce asserts, or implies, that phenomenology provides the fundamental categories, he has the positive sciences in mind. He means to say that phenomenology is first *in philosophy*, and that the fundamental *philosophical* categories are firstness, secondness, and thirdness. What is left unsaid is that there are pre-philosophical categories that are more abstract, more fundamental, than their phenomenological counterparts.

This does not wholly dispose of the first difficulty, however, for there are passages where Peirce appears to at least equate the abstractness and formality of the phenomenological categories with that of the mathematical categories. There is even a passage where Peirce says that "the connection of [his] categories with the numbers 1, 2, 3, although it affords a convenient designation of them, is a very trivial circumstance" (Peirce 1898: 339). I mentioned already that because Peirce's thought grew and developed during his more than fifty years of mature thought it is not surprising to find an occasional inconsistency or incongruity. It would be convenient to dismiss Peirce's troublesome remarks, especially his early ones, accordingly. Or I could point out cases of what appear to be aberrations in Peirce's thought where it seems likely that he merely gives the wrong impression because of an unusual perspective or emphasis. But I don't pretend that I could solve all of the problems so easily. However, as I cannot hope to dispel all doubts in the short time I have, I will pass on to the second difficulty.

The second difficulty concerns the placement of logic in the classification of the sciences. Strictly speaking, logic is the third normative science, which in turn is the second branch of philosophy. This poses a problem because Peirce often identifies the logical categories as the fundamental ones. One reply is to point out that Peirce came to regard the logic of relatives, and formal logic in general, as a branch of mathematics, and to reserve for philosophical logic the normative fields: speculative grammar, critical logic, and speculative rhetoric. Thus when Peirce refers to logic he may mean either the mathematical subject or the philosophical one, and often great care is needed to determine which is meant (Houser 1988). It is my recollection that when Peirce refers to logical categories as fundamental he has the mathematical branch in mind. But this difficulty leads to the third one, which I shall now take up.

The third difficulty for my thesis results from the traditional conception of architectonic as the foundation of philosophy upon a logical, not mathematical, structure. Murphey (Murphey 1961) has clearly articulated this problem. He points out that Kant showed that "it is the fact that cognition must have a certain logical form which enables us to argue that whatever is necessarily true of anything which can be known in such a cognition is true of all we can know" (Murphey 1961: 368). Thus, it is from a logic of cognition that the architectonic philosopher must set out. Peirce's architectonic program was thwarted, according to Murphey, by his classification of the sciences. By locating logic with the normative branches of philosophy, Peirce precluded the Kantian approach to architectonic; he could not found philosophy on his logic. Peirce tried to overcome this difficulty by introducing his science of phenomenology at the head of philosophy, a science whose principal purpose was to abstract from experience a fundamental set of categories. But, according to Murphey, phenomenology could yield many different sets of categories, and which one we should choose as the foundation of our philosophy is far from evident. According to Peirce, phenomenology yields those categories which coincide with the fundamental mathematical-logical relations: monad, dyad, and triad. But why should we opt for this set of categories unless we realize that relative predicates are necessary for cognition? And how can we know that without appealing to a logic of cognition? Phenomenology shows us that it is *possible* to abstract a set of categories that corresponds to the mathematical ones, but it does not provide a rationale for embracing those categories. Murphey concludes that "it is impossible to regard Peirce's phenomenological treatment of the categories as anything more than a quite unsuccessful sleight of hand" (Murphey 1961: 368). According to Murphey, the justification for the phenomenological categories would have to come from normative logic, in particular from speculative grammar, which might be regarded as a logic of cognition; but Peirce's architectonic precludes such an appeal to normative logic. Thus Peirce's classification of the sciences is incompatible with his architectonic program. If Murphey is right, then the ground for my thesis vanishes.

But is Murphey right? The crux of his argument is that architectonic philosophy must be based on a logic of cognition. But why must this be so? It is not surprising, of course, that Kant held this view. There was no logic of relations to suggest to him the foundational potential of the fundamental categories of relation. But Peirce was a close intimate of the basic relations, and had a deep belief in their universal applicability. Murphey cannot understand how mathematical categories can compel the allegiance of a systematic philosopher, but he forgets, I believe, that even mathematical relations reserve places for relates and correlates--things in the world, if you like. It is just that the mathematician isn't interested in what things, if any, are related. I do not feel the impact of Murphey's claim that the formal (mathematical) logic of relations fails to provide a structure which phenomenologists can expect to find central to experience. Charles Hartshorne, in his attempt to blunt Murphey's argument, agrees (Hartshorne 1964: 457). But he muddies the water a little by trying to close the gulf between mathematics and phenomenology. "Between formal logic and phenomenology", he says, ". . . mutual harmony might well be a suitable relationship, rather than one-way dependence. For both topics seem comparable in universality". He thus feels confident in saying that "all thought must in some sense have form as well as matter, and the universal forms incarnate in the matter of experience can only be or correspond to the universal forms utilized in thought" (Hartshorne 1964: 457). He thereby disposes of Murphey's threat, but at some cost to Peirce's classification of the sciences. As I have indicated above, I do not think we have to pay this price, for I believe the mathematical treatment of relations can be expected to guide phenomenology without conflating mathematics and phenomenology. I, therefore, hold that Peirce's architectonic as well as his classification of the sciences can survive Murphey's challenge.

I realize, of course, that I have not entirely disposed of the difficulties I raised for my thesis that there are pre-phenomenological categories which must be regarded as the structural basis for Peirce's entire system of thought. And I have not discussed priority levels within mathematics to ascertain the dependency order of the various pre-phenomenological triads: 1, 2, 3; first, second, third; monad, dyad, triad; and no doubt others. Nor have I taken up the ramifications of my thesis. This is a short paper, and one must not expect too much.

What I hope to have shown is that my thesis is at least plausible, and how one might set out to establish it. I have given a preliminary account of the relation between Peirce's classification of the sciences and his architectonic, and have indicated how integral these doctrines are to any case for the importance of any particular set of categories. I hope to have given a glimpse of the underlying unity, or unifiability, of Peirce's thought, and to have made a modest contribution to the revelation of its forbidding structure.

I will conclude with a remark about the programmatic upshot of what I have said. If Peirce's system of thought is judged to be architectonic, as it usually is, and as Peirce himself believed, then either the standard Kantian conception must be replaced by an architectonic based on mathematical categories *or* Peirce's mature classification of the sciences must be rejected. The rejection of Peirce's classification of the sciences is a high price to pay for a traditional architectonic. But if that price isn't paid, we must make a convincing case for the claim that mathematical categories can have a priori applicability to experience. Even more, we must explain why the fundamental relations of mathematics may be taken a priori as the structuring principle of experience.

REFERENCES

HARTSHORNE, Charles.
    1964. "Charles Peirce's 'One Contribution to Philosophy' and his Most Serious Mistake", in Moore and Robin 1964: 455-474.
HOUSER, Nathan.
    1988. "The Significance of Logic as Semiotic", in *Semiotics 1987*, ed. John Deely (Lanham, MD: University Press of America, 1988), 404-413.
KENT, Beverley.
    1987. *Charles S. Peirce: Logic and the Classification of the Sciences* (Kingston and Montreal: McGill-Queen's University Press).

MOORE, Edward C. and Richard S. ROBIN, eds.
    1964. *Studies in the Philosophy of Charles Sanders Peirce*, Second Series (Amherst: University of Massachusetts Press).

MURPHEY, Murray.
    1961. *The Development of Peirce's Philosophy* (Cambridge: Harvard University Press).

PEIRCE, Charles S.
    The writings of Peirce referred to in this entry are from various sources: 1. The Charles S. Peirce Papers, Manuscript collection in the Houghton Library, Harvard University (photocopies at the Peirce Edition Project in Indianapolis). Reference to the Peirce manuscripts is either by the Robin (1967, q.v.) *Catalogue* numbers or the Peirce Edition Project numbers. 2. *Writings of Charles S. Peirce: A Chronological Edition*, ed. Max H. Fisch et al (Bloomington: Indiana University Press, 1982, 1984). Three volumes published to date. 3. *Collected Papers of Charles Sanders Peirce*, ed. Charles Hartshorne, Paul Weiss, and Arthur Burks (Cambridge: Harvard University Press, 1931-1958), in eight volumes. 4. *The New Elements of Mathematics*, ed. Carolyn Eisele (The Hague: Mouton, 1976), in 4 volumes.

    1866. "Lowell Lecture XI", published in *Writings* 1.491-504, with title supplied by editors. Peirce Edition Project MS 132.
    1898. "Detached Ideas continued and the Dispute between Nominalists and Realists", Robin MS 439. Published in *New Elements* 4.331-46.
    1913. "A Study of How to Reason Safely and Efficiently", Robin MS 681 (unpublished).

ROBIN, Richard S., ed.
    1967. *Annotated Catalogue of the Papers of Charles S. Peirce* (Amherst, Massachusetts: University of Massachusetts Press).

THE ULTIMATE LOGICAL INTERPRETANT AND THE DYNAMICAL OBJECT

Sandra B. Rosenthal
Loyola University, New Orleans

The following examination of the relation between the ultimate logical interpretant and the dynamical object will proceed by way of Peirce's understanding of the internal structure of the meanings through which we grasp a world of perceived objects. Peirce claims that the problem of the meaning of intellectual concepts can only be solved by the study of the interpretants, or proper significant effects of signs (1907: 5.475), and he suggests that the nature of meaning is based upon and understood in terms of the nature of signs (1902: 8.119; c.1904: 8.191). As T. L. Short points out (1986: 110), Peirce did not presuppose an unanalyzed notion of meaning, but rather explicates meaning in terms of his semiotic. For Peirce, human conduct is itself a cognitive semiotic process. His pragmatic theory of meaning would seem to be part and parcel of his semiotics.

A focus on the significance of the semiotic character of the internal structure of meaning can best begin with Peirce's unique appropriation of pragmatic schemata, and the best access to this is through his discussion of mathematics. In making his well known distinction between theorematic reasoning or reasoning as diagrammatic, and trivial corollarial reasoning, Peirce claims that diagrammatic or schematic reasoning involves the introduction of an element of novelty in the deductive process, "through the formation in the imagination of some sort of diagram, that is, iconic representation . . . as skeletonized as possible" (1911: 2.778). Though the aspect of iconic representation is usually stressed in discussions of Peirce's understanding of diagrammatic reasoning, two key qualifications made by Peirce should be here observed. First, such a diagram involves both visual and muscular "imagery" by which it is seen that "the conclusion is compelled to be true by the conditions of the construction of the diagram" (1911: 2.778). Secondly, though he speaks of the formation of the diagrammatic representation "in the imagination", he clarifies this by stressing that ultimately schematic structure is not understood as a generalization of imagined instances but as a product of a predictive rule" (1903: 4.478). Thus the diagrammatic reasoning of mathematics involves, ultimately, a predictive rule generative of the action-image matrix of a schematic structure. This schematic imagery allows for the introduction of novelty into mathematical reasoning which corollarial reasoning does not allow (1902b: 4.233), for the novelty of theorematic reasoning is attained by the construction of schematic imagery in which new relationships come to be recognized. However, such novelty is the novelty of a creative construction for the discovery of what is already contained in or allowed by the starting point, for various schemata are constructed according to alternative possibilities virtually contained in the thesis (1902b: 4.233).

In mathematics, then, schemata bring to light relationships implicitly operative in rule guided activity through the interrelationship of predictive or generative rule, activity, and imagery. A series of schemata generated represent alternative possibilities of a predictive rule. And Peirce, after carefully developing the position that theorematic reasoning, as opposed to corollarial reasoning, depends upon experimentation with individual schemata, concludes that "in the last analysis, the same thing is true of the corollarial reasoning too . . . Only in this case, the very words serve as schemata" (1902: 4.233). Accordingly, the difference becomes not whether or not schemata are employed, but rather whether or not the schemata are exemplified in words or are "specially constructed", the latter belonging to theorematic or mathematical reasoning proper. And, to say that words are employed as schemata, for Peirce, would seem to indicate that meaning, beneath the level of language, employs schemata, for "meaning enters into language by determining it" (c.1900: 1105). Thus he states that the pragmatist will "hold that everything in the substance of his beliefs can be represented by the schemata of his imagination" (1902a: 288). The function of schemata embodied in common sense perceptual awareness is expressed in Peirce's explanation (1906: 293) that

> The Diagram remains in the field of perception or "imagination", and so the Iconic Diagram and its initial Symbolic interpretant taken together constitute what we shall not too much wrench Kant's term in calling a schema, which is on the one side an object capable of being observed, while on the other side it is a general.

In light of the above analysis of schemata, the ensuing discussion will briefly sketch their function within the internal structure of the concept. Peirce's pragmatic stress on meaning in terms of habits of response is, of course, well known, but the language in which it is usually expressed tends to hide from view the full nature of its relational structure. Meanings for Peirce are to be understood as relational structures emerging from behavioral patterns, relational structures in which sensuous recognition and conceptual interpretation represent two ends of a continuum rather than an absolute difference in kind. His view that sensuous recognition involves interpretive aspects can be found in his view that there are no first impressions of sense (1905: 5.416; 1893: 7.465). And, all cognition for Peirce involves the perceptual in the sense that it logically involves an iconic presentation of the cognized object. One implication of diagrammatic reasoning is, in Peirce's words, that "Icons have to be used in all thinking" (c.1900b: xxi). Peirce's view that conceptualization requires imagery is open to some confusion. Though Peirce says he will "go so far as to say that we have no images even in actual perception" (1905a: 5.503), what he is rejecting is the definition of image as an absolutely singular representation, a representation absolutely determinate in all respects (1868: 5.298-299). He objects to Kant's understanding of the schema because Kant separates it from the concept, failing to recognize that a schema for the application of a concept to the data of experience is as general as the concept (1905a: 5.531). In the schematic aspect of conceptual meaning there is to be found the inseparable mingling of the sensuous and the relational as the vehicle by which we think about and recognize objects in the world.

This mingling can best be understood in terms of the relation between habit as the ultimate logical interpretant and schematic structure as the logical interpretant. Peirce holds that every logical interpretant includes within itself both the emotional

and energetic interpretants. A physical object concept contains the structure of action related characters. As Peirce observes, "How otherwise can a habit be described than by a description of the kind of action to which it gives rise, with the specification of the conditions and the motive" or intended result? (l907: 5.491). The relation between possible conditions, acts, and results is present in the very structure of the logical interpretant or schematization of the habit. Further, schemata are constituted by the generality of "kinds", and as such represent principles or possibilities in terms of which sensory content can emerge within experience, as opposed to the manifold of particulars organized by them. What serves as the particular stimulus or "condition" within the structure of the logical interpretant is what Peirce calls the ponecipuum (1903a: 7.648), which is itself an epistemically functional universal. And, if the act is dependent upon the stimulus, condition, or sensory content, then different sensory conditions will give rise to different acts and results. The ultimate logical interpretant as the living habit binds together into a systematic unity the various possibilities, thus making the unified diversity of logical interpretants possible. The concrete meaning, as the disposition or habit, is the source of the generation of explicit schemata, each of which makes precise for conscious awareness some aspect of the concrete meaning, some selection from the inexhaustible range of possibilities. Conceptual meaning thus includes the total set of possible appearances and possible transformations via appropriate responses to other appearances as controlled by habit as a rule of generation and organization. This dispositional rule fills in a resultant schematic appearance with the results of other possible acts, given other possible
conditions, thereby endowing the result of an act with "intentional objectivity". Thus, what is apprehended is not an appearance only, but a perspective of an object. Habit thus does more than unify three pre-existent elements. Only as habit performs its function of unifying sensory conditions and reactions does schematic structure emerge at all. As Peirce notes, the schema, or logical interpretant or "general idea" is "the mark of the habit" (1898: 7.498). By general idea here is of course not meant a Lockean type of generality but rather the generality of a schematic aspect.

Peirce, in appropriating Kantian schemata within the internal structure of meaning, thus takes from Kant the fundamental insight that concepts are empirically meaningful only if they contain schematic possibilities for their application to sensible experience. Further, the imagery which makes possible the application of a concept cannot be abstracted out from sense experience but rather must be provided before meaningful perceptual content can emerge within experience. However, Peirce's pragmatic appropriation of these insights radically alters Kant's understanding of the schema. Such a schema is no longer a product of productive imagination as distinct from the understanding as the faculty of judgment. Rather, both understanding and imagination are unified and transformed into the creative functioning of habit as providing a semiotic unity between knower and known. The significance of this transformation is well expressed in the claim that Peirce forces the function of judgment out of its dominant position, replacing it by the sign function (Oehler 1987: 59).

A disposition or concrete meaning cannot be inspected as such, but it is inspectable in any aspect. Explicit aspects can be continually generated for inspection, though the rule of generation will never be exhausted by the schemata and, hence, never in principle completely inspected. A disposition is concrete, and any attempt to make it clear and explicit requires an abstraction from this concreteness. For this reason, a meaning is never fully determinate but always further determinable. Further, the concreteness of living habit provides the conceptual counterpart of the "that which has" characteristics, and the "that which has" can never be exhausted by the qualitative lawfulness which it incorporates. And, as representing a "that which has", or a possible existent individual, there is a further indeterminateness. An object as a concrete individual includes not just those characteristics necessary for its being a particular type of object, but also necessarily includes the indefinite specificity of having or not having other characteristics. The ultimate logical interpretant incorporates an objectivity as that to which essential characteristics must apply and to which an indefinite number of non-essential characteristics may or may not apply, and it will cancel out as "unreal" those characteristics which do not fit consistently within the range constituted by the perceptual unity. Thus, the specificity of meaning which lies in the ultimate logical interpretant as the rule of generation includes within itself a basic indeterminateness both in relation to the total meaning and in relation to the specificity of the concrete, existing object denoted.

For Peirce, meaning is indeterminate in that there is in principle always more to specify. And, its application to the world is indeterminate further, in that the very meaning intends that to which the attribution of a limitless number of non-essential characteristics is always possible. For Peirce, "no concepts, not even those of mathematics, are absolutely precise" (1906b: 6.496). Further, no individual, in its concrete individuality, can be precisely grasped. For example, "When I see a thing, I do not see that it is not sweet, nor do I see that it is sweet; and therefore, what I see is capable of logical division into the sweet and the not sweet" (1870: 3.93). Further, such an individual "thing" is not, ontologically, what Peirce means by an absolute individual, which "cannot exist, properly speaking" (1870: 3.93). An absolute individual would be a bare reaction event, an abstraction from the concreteness of existence as a continuous process, as a continuity of events. Thus, the individual thing of perceptual experience, in its concreteness, is not an "absolute individual" (1903b: 478).

Here it must be stressed that the difference between the concreteness of an existing object and a set of qualities is not the difference between extension and intension. Rather, the intensional meaning contains the meaningfulness of the concreteness of objectivity or "existence" as that which can never be reduced to a set of qualitative aspects or structural relations, for quality is Firstness, and structural relation is Thirdness, while the "that which has" qualities and relations incorporates Secondness, or the concreteness of existence, and this concreteness is built into the very meaning intended. Thus, meaning identifies an individual existence as an instance of a kind, not as a uniquely concrete individual, but it also provides the meaningful recognition that concrete individuality provides an "always more". We can denote objects rather than collections of qualities because our meanings embody the basis of the concreteness of objectivity, of concrete existence, of the "that which incorporates" certain lawful modes of behavior and certain qualitative possibilities. The ultimate logical interpretant, as living habit, provides the meaning of the dynamical bond. The meaning of the concreteness of reacting Secondness embodying qualitative lawful continuities is included in the concreteness of habit as rule, and is represented in the perspectival aspect of schematic structure.

It has been held that Peirce's argument that no sign can profess to completely express or represent all the properties of the object of the sign does not mainly follow from a phenomenological analysis of the sign relation, but from certain metaphysical assumptions (Almeder 1980: 32). According to the above analysis, however, this incompleteness is a phenomenological dimension of the awareness of habit as a readiness to respond to more than can ever be specified, which manifests itself in the ability of the ultimate logical interpretant to generate an indefinite number of schematic forms or logical interpretants representing aspects of an object, each logical interpretant being at once a sign calling forth further logical interpretants.

In making the distinction between the logical interpretant and the ultimate logical interpretant, Peirce holds that logical interpetants are themselves signs which must have logical interpretants, while the ultimate logical interpretant, though it may be a sign in some other way, is not a sign in the same way in which the logical interpretant is a sign (1907: 5.476; 5.491). This can be seen in two senses. First, any logical interpretant is a sign which is interpreted by other logical interpretants within the sign system of the concept. The ultimate logical interpretant, however, as the "self analyzing" habit (1907: 5.491), as that concreteness of living habit which generates but can never be exhausted by any number of logical interpretants, is not a sign for any intra-systematic logical interpretant but rather every such logical interpretant is in a sense a sign of it. As was indicated above, the logical interpretant is the mark of the habit or ultimate logical interpretant. Second, a sign stands for its object not in all respects but in some respect, while the ultimate logical interpretant, as that which generates the possibility of the grasp of objects in some respect, incorporates the object in its indefinite entirety. Logical interpretants can represent forms or features of objects because the ultimate logical interpretant allows for the grasp of an object as a concrete individual. Interpretants can refer to objects only because we can intend objects as referents.

This focus on objects, however, leads directly to Peirce's recognition of the need "to distinguish the Immediate Object, which is the Object as the Sign itself represents it, and whose Being is thus dependent upon the Representation of it in the Sign, from the Dynamical Object, which is the Reality which by some means contrives to determine the Sign to its Representation" (1906a: 4.536). Peirce notes that collateral observation is needed for the dynamical object, and by collateral observation he means previous acquaintance with what the sign denotes (1903c: 8.179-181).

According to Peirce the indexical relation of referring cannot occur unless the mind is already acquainted with thing denoted. Collateral experience of the object is possible because our meanings by their very nature refer to the concreteness of objects having the indeterminateness of an indefinite number of features or aspects. And, past experience of the acquaintance with the dynamical object can lead to the incorporation of more features into the network of logical interpretants potentially available for actualization by the ultimate logical interpretant. For Peirce, the very possibility of "collateral experience requires that a habit has been established in him by which that word calls up a variety of attributes" (1903: 8.178).

The process of incorporating past experience into the
structure of the ultimate logical interpretant corresponds neither to definition nor stipulation but rather corresponds most closely to the creative process which Peirce calls abduction, though what are here fixed by such creative activities or abductive processes are not empirical hypotheses asserting the applicability of meanings but rather the very structure of the meanings themselves. As Peirce states, "An abduction is Originary in respect to being the only kind of argument which starts a new idea" (1902: 2.96). Habit, as creatively structuring, always brings a "more than" to the organization of past experiences, though it is these past experiences which in fact "nourished" the habit in which they are now contained (1907: 5.491). This is not a vicious circle, but a cumulative process in which the very structure of the ultimate logical interpretant in its relation to logical interpretants allows for the experience of the dynamical object, while the acquaintance with particular aspects of the dynamical object allows for the fuller development of the sign system incorporated within the ultimate logical interpretant. The development of the sign system is an ever evolving process, but at any moment it has an internal systematic structure unified by the organizing creativity of habit. The systematic structure concerns the sign nature of any meaning qua meaning. The genesis and maintenance of the system concerns its

relevance to, and workability within, the ongoing context of experience. In this way habit creates the immediate object under the constraints of the dynamic object which is its ultimate referent.

It may at first seem surprising that Peirce views abduction in terms of the icon rather than the index (1902: 2.96). Indexical relations, however, are dependent upon the abductive formation of meanings, on the internal structure of the concept, not the reverse. Until incorporated into a network of logical interpretants under the rule generated activity of the ultimate logical interpretant, there is no isolatable dynamical object. The dynamical object apart from the structure of meaning is the whole of nature in its indeterminate richness, for apart from our meaning structures, nature as ontologically "there" is for Peirce a continuum which "swims in indeterminacy" (1897: 1.171-172), while the dynamical object as the referent of a sign is that which can be singled out from a surrounding environment (1909: 8.314). There is a two way direction operative in which the dynamic object in its metaphysical dimension puts constraints on the ultimate logical interpretant, while the ultimate logical interpretant determines what will count as restraints imposed by the dynamical object in its semiotic relation. The dynamical object is the goal of interpretation, but this goal is possible only through the generation of an interpretant series whose structure is dependent upon the ultimate logical interpretant, and which will endure only if it serves to objectify the indeterminate richness of reality in workable ways. This entire dynamic can perhaps be summed up in Peirce's succinct but cryptic claim that "There is no *thing* which is in itself in the sense of not being relative to the mind, though things which are relative to the mind doubtless are, apart from that relation" (1868: 5.311).

REFERENCES

ALMEDER, Robert.
    1980. *The Philosophy of Charles Sanders Peirce* (New Jersey: Rowman and Littlefield).
OEHLER, Klaus.
    1987. "Is a Transcendental Foundation of Semiotics Possible? A Peircean Consideration", *Transactions of the Charles S. Peirce Society*, 23.1 45-63.
PEIRCE, Charles Sanders.
    1868. "Some Consequences of Four Incapacities", *The Journal of Speculative Philosophy*, 2, 140-157. Reprinted in *Collected Papers of Charles Sanders Peirce*, in 8 volumes, 1-6 ed. Charles Hartshorne and Paul Weiss, 7-8 ed. Arthur Burks (Cambridge, Massachusetts: Harvard University Press, 1931-1958). Page reference in the present essay is to the CP reprint, 5.264-5.314.
    1870. Memories of the American Academy, 9, printed in CP 3.93.
    1893. Chapter VI for *Grand Logic*, printed in CP 7.465.
    1897. Untitled manuscript intended as part of a lecture, printed in CP 1.171-1.172.
    1898. Unpublished papers on habit, printed in CP 7.498.
    c. 1900. Several starts of manuscripts, printed in Harvard Microfilm Edition, section 1105.
    c. 1900b. *New Elements of Mathematics*, 4, ed. Carolyn Eisele (The Hague: Mouton Press, 1976).
    1902. Partial synopsis of a proposed work in logic, printed in CP 2.96.

1902a. Materials for Monist article, printed in Harvard Microfilm Edition, Section 288.
1902b. Manuscripts of Minute Logic, printed in CP 4.233.
c. 1902. Partial drafts of a review, printed in CP 8.119.
1903. "Logical Tracts, no.2", printed in CP.
1903a. "Telepathy", an unpublished manuscript which appears in CP 7.648.
1903b. Syllabus of a course lecture. Printed in Harvard Microfilm Edition, section 478.
1903c. Unfinished letter, printed in CP 8.178-8.181.
c. 1904. Draft of a review. Printed in CP 8.191.
1905. What Pragmatism Is", *The Monist* 15, 161-181. Page reference in this essay is to the CP reprint 5.416.
1905a. Unpublished manuscript on Critical Common-Sensism. Printed in CP 5.502-5.537.
1906. Unpublished manuscript. Printed in Harvard Microfilm Edition, Section 293.
1906a. "Prolegomena to an Apology to Pragmaticism", *The Monist* 16, 492-546. Page reference in the present essay is to the CP reprint, 4.536.
1906b. "Answers to Questions Concerning My Belief in God", unpublished manuscript printed in CP 6.496.
1907. Unpublished paper which appears in CP 5.464-496 under "A Survey of Pragmaticism", a title supplied by the editors.
1909. Letter to William James. Printed in CP 8.314.
1911. (Dictionary of Philosophy and Psychology), 2, ed. J. M. Baldwin (New York: Macmillan). Page reference in this essay is to CP reprint.

SHORT, T. L.
1986. "What They Said in Amsterdam: Peirce's Semiotic Today", *Semiotica*, 60.1/2, 103-128.

PEIRCE AND THE TRIVIUM[1]

David Savan
University of Toronto

Peirce's semeiotic is a way of thinking which asks for growth and new departures. Both Gerard Deledalle and Thomas Sebeok, in different ways, have shown how Peirce's pioneering work may be extended. I would like to honor them and further their kind of work by exploring the relation between semeiotic and methodeutic, the theory of the method for studying and testing methods. It was here, Peirce believed, that semeiotic would show its value. In this short paper I wish to make a beginning on this project by considering Peirce's unique achievement in showing the structural unity underlying the hitherto separate and independent sign theories in the traditional trivium--grammar, logic, and rhetoric. I will focus on Peirce's work from 1865 through 1868. His later work on methodeutic grew out of his early theory of semeiotic rhetoric.

In 1865, when his semeiotic first took on a definite and clear shape, Peirce recognized that his new analysis of symbols showed how the classical trivium could be deepened, extended, and unified. In the opening sentence of his Harvard lectures of that year, he said, "I ask your attention to one of the studies of the ancient Trivium . . ." (Peirce 1865: 162). He then proceeded to outline his new theory of representation and concluded that this "gives a trivium consisting of Universal Grammar, Logic, and Universal Rhetoric . . ." (Peirce 1865: 175).

Let me begin by turning back to the ancient trivium. What, within the trivium, was the role of sign theory? For the ancient Greeks, a *sema* is a physical object or mark, which, when it is noticed by the properly prepared interpreter, leads to the recognition of something beyond the sign's appearance. Often, a *sema* also signals some specific kind of action. For example, Hesiod tells the farmer that the cry of the cranes is a *sema* that the autumn remains have arrived and that ploughing should begin. The word *semeion* is more general. A *semeion* may be a set of words or actions or things which are evidence of something further. From a *semeion* something further may be inferred.

Aristotle, in closing the *Prior Analytics* (c.350-344BC: 70a), made a *logical* analysis of signs; he defined a sign as a proposition serving as the explicit premiss in an enthymematic argument. The object of the sign, the signatum, is the proposition which is the conclusion of the enthymeme. The argument is refutable, not apodictic. We can not infer reliably to the signatum. That a woman is of a sallow complexion is taken to be a sign that she is pregnant. However, Aristotle says, this sign sometimes and perhaps often fails. Aristotle is thinking of natural signs. Why then does he say that it is the *proposition* that is the sign? Presumably, because he recognized that nothing in nature, simply taken as a state of affairs, is in itself a sign. Something is a sign only if it is so related to something further that an inference from the one to the other is justified, even if the inference is not a necessary inference. Thus suppose it is tacitly assumed that pregnant women are sallow. That this woman is sallow is then a sign that she is pregnant, even though the syllogism is formally invalid; the premisses do lend some support, however weak, to the conclusion.

The logical theory of natural signs was carried further by Chrysippus and the Stoic logicians. For the Stoics too a sign is a proposition. It is the "proposition which forms the antecedent in a sound conditional, being revelatory of the consequent" (Sextus Empiricus c.200fl: Adv.Math. VIII.245). Proof is a species of sign, since the premisses of a proof can be expressed as the antecedent of a conditional proposition, of which the conclusion of the proof is the consequent. The Stoics added to the Aristotelian analysis not only the insights of their propositional logic, but also the epistemic condition that a sign must be more evident than its object.

John Locke, who was sometimes quoted on this matter by Peirce, followed Aristotle and the Stoics when he wrote that one of the three major divisions of all science is *semeiotic*, "which is aptly enough termed also *logic*" (1690, Bk.IV, Ch. 21).

Next, how are signs related to words, in classical grammar? In the *De Interpretatione* Aristotle outlined very succinctly his semeiotic theory of words. Words are *symbols* because the word sounds (or writing) are *signs* (*semeia*) of mental experience, and the mental experience is, in turn, a likeness (*homoioma*) of that to which the word refers. Although the languages of mankind differ, the mental experiences of which the various speech sounds are signs are the same for all human beings. In this way, through the concept of the *symbol* Aristotle reconciled the two theories of naming discussed in Plato's *Cratylus* (c.385BC). The symbol is a synthesis of the arbitrary and conventional connection between a sound and a mental image, on the one hand, and a relation of conaturality or resemblance between mental image and external thing on the other.

According to Sextus Empiricus (c.200fl: Adv.Math. VIII.11-12) the Stoics held a somewhat different theory of names. Two physical things are involved, the sound (or writing, e.g. "Dion") and the external physical thing named (e.g. the man, Dion). The sound is the signifier (*semainon*), and what is signified (*semainomenon*) is an immaterial third entity, the *lekton*. The *lekton*, i.e., what is communicated, is shared by all who speak a common language and not understood by those who do not understand the language, even though they may hear the sound "Dion" and also see the man.

Locke, who was quoted with approval on this matter in Peirce's first Harvard lecture, follows in the footsteps on both Aristotle and the Stoics. "Words . . . can properly and immediately signify nothing but the *ideas* that are in the mind of the speaker . . . (Further, men) suppose their words to be marks of the ideas in the minds also of other men with whom they communicate . . . (in addition) they often suppose their words to stand also for the reality of things" (1690, Bk.III, Ch. 2, para. 4, 5; quoted in Peirce 1865: 170-171).

The third member of the classical trivium, rhetoric, is defined by Aristotle (c.335-334BC: 1355b26) as "the faculty of discovering the possible means of persuasion in reference to any subject whatever". Persuasion depends on three things: (1) proof, (2) the ability of the persuader to move the feelings of the listeners (or readers) in an appropriate way, and (3) the style of presentation. The three are conveniently summarized as *docere*, *movere*, and *delectare*. Aristotle introduced his theory of signs only in the first of these, proof. The enthymeme is a rhetorical syllogism, and persuasion by the use of examples is rhetorical induction (c.335-334BC: 1356b). Since rhetorical speech and writing is usually concerned with matters that are contingent and subject to differing judgments, the premises of rhetorical syllogisms and rhetorical inductions will usually be signs, and the support they give to their conclusions will be less than conclusive. It is ironic that Aristotle's theory of natural signs was not applied by him to natural science but to rhetorical persuasion.

Apart from the application of sign theory to rhetorical argumentation, it seems to have had no bearing upon the other two divisions of rhetoric--emotion and style. Aristotle was followed in this by later rhetoricians--Cicero, the author of *Ad Herrenium* (Anonymous c. 85BC), Quintilian, and Augustine, for example.

Two things should be noticed in summing up the classical trivium. One is the fact that there seems to be no conception that verbal symbols and natural signs may share some generic common character. Second, and associated with the quite separate treatment of verbal symbols and natural signs, no theory, no philosophical analysis, is offered to justify bringing together grammar, logic, and rhetoric into the systematic association of the trivium. Among other advances it makes, Peirce's semeiotic remedies these two deficiencies.

Peirce's semeiotic stands directly and consciously within the tradition linking semeiotic with logic, a tradition running from Aristotle and the Stoics through Locke, "All symbolization is inference (and) . . . inference is symbolization. They are the same notions", Peirce wrote in 1865 (1865a: 280). Echoing the Stoic thesis that proof is a species of sign, he went on to say that "Logic comes under the genus symbol" (1865d: 329). It is Peirce's new conception of a symbol that brings grammar, logic, and rhetoric together under a general theory of symbols. "The third and last kind of representations are *symbols* or general representations . . . To this class belong all *words* and all *conceptions*. Most combinations of words are also symbols. A proposition, an argument, even a whole book may be, and should be, a single symbol (1866: 468). Echoing these words more than thirty years later, Peirce (c. 1900: 239) wrote that "a whole literature is a sign". Thus the study of symbols is foundational for the study of words, inferences, and literature--grammar, logic, and rhetoric.

Peirce was acutely aware of the originality and power of his new conception of a symbol. His opening Harvard lecture of 1865 bubbles with excitement. What is the source of the extraordinary power of the symbol? A symbol is a representation, a sign. Like all signs, a symbol has three essential relations. First, it must embody some form, character, or quality in virtue of which it is a sign. Second, it must refer to or denote some real thing. What Peirce intends here is put most clearly and succinctly in a letter written in 1900 to Georg Cantor. "No man can communicate any information to another without referring to some *experiences* known to be shared by him and the person whom he addresses" (Peirce 1900: 770; cf. 1865a: 282). Third, a sign or representation must be interpretable or translatable or representable by some further sign. It must address itself to a possible further symbol. It must *imply* something further.

Nevertheless, a copy--in later writings, Peirce calls it an *icon*--is a representation but not a symbol. It resembles its object through sharing a quality with that object. An arbitrary mark, conventionally agreed upon--later called an *index*--is also a representation but not a symbol. It lacks generality, and identifies only the specific object with which it is actually connected. A symbol, on the other hand, is a sign simply because it is interpreted by some further symbol to be a sign. The symbol need not resemble its object iconically, nor need it have any actual indexical connection with its object. A word, for example conveys a concept which has nothing to do with the shape of the writing or the sound of the utterance. Nor need it have anything to do with the specific things with which the word was connected in the past. The word has acquired a nature of its own simply through being interpreted by further signs. "The symbol has acquired a nature, which may be described thus, that when it is brought before the mind certain principles of its use--whether reflected on or not--by association immediately regulate the action of the mind; and these may be regarded as laws of the symbol itself which it cannot *as a symbol* transgress" (1865: 173).

"I here announce the great and fundamental secret of the logic of science" (1866: 465). The secret so enthusiastically announced is that every symbol implies some further equivalent symbol which is its interpretant, and thus every symbol itself is implied by (or is the interpretant of) some prior symbol. "The process of getting an equivalent for a term is . . . the process of nutrition of terms by which they get all their life and vigor and by which they put forth an energy almost creative--since it has the effect of reducing the chaos of ignorance to the cosmos of science. Each of these equivalents is the explication of what there is wrapped up in the primary--they are the surrogates, the interpreters of the original term. They are new bodies animated by the same soul. I call them the *interpretants* . . ." (1866: 464-465). An icon and an index, being signs, must *be able* to be interpreted by interpretants. A symbol, however, must *in fact* be interpreted by interpretants. For a symbol, to be is not only to be symbolizable. Its being is to be symbolized. The principles or rules through which a symbol grows, animating interpretant after interpretant, are the principles of the three fundamental forms of inference--hypothesis (later to be called abduction), induction, and deduction. That is precisely what Peirce meant when he wrote that symbolization and inference are the same (1865a: 280).

Given this new conception of representation, and specifically of the concept of the symbol, Peirce was able to show the unity of the trivium and the systematic relations within the triad. Representational space is three dimensional, and the analysis of any symbol must, finally, include all three dimensions. The trivium is therefore the study of the three dimensions of symbols and the way that, together, they constitute a single symbolic space. Every symbol must have, first, some form or character in virtue of what it is significant. Second, every symbol must at least purport to refer to some object which exists independently of the symbol. Third, every symbol must be translated into some further symbol which interprets it--its interpretant.

Consider now what this implies for a semeiotic trivium--a grammar of symbols, a logic of symbols, and a rhetoric of symbols. The grammar of a language sets out the principles of the construction of meaningful expressions in that language. Peirce began to explore, as early as 1865, semeiotic grammar--what he tentatively called Universal, General, Formal, or Speculative Grammar. Its principles would govern the construction of meaningful symbols and combinations of symbols. In his lectures of 1865 and 1866 he envisaged three divisions within semeiotic grammar. One, it will classify the types or forms of symbols. The later classification of qualisigns, sinsigns, legisigns, icon, index, symbol, etc., would fall within this first division. Two, it will distinguish the systematic variations a symbol exhibits in various contexts. Peirce compared this to "the distinctions between such words as *creative, creation, create*" (1865c: 309). Three, semeiotic grammar will lay down the principles for the meaningful combinations of symbols, and thus distinguish complex expressions which make sense from those which are nonsense (1865: 174). In sum, semeiotic grammar is the study of the elements and the generation of significant symbols.

Logic, Peirce wrote, "is the science of the conditions which enable symbols in general to refer to objects" (1865: 175). This is not the place to criticize or evaluate this conception of logic as the theory of formal truth conditions. What is important here is to recognize that Peirce deliberately framed his definition so that it would include the formal conditions on the discovery and testing of truths through induction and hypothesis (later called *abduction*). Every symbol must at least purport to refer to the real world existing independently of that symbol. Otherwise it represents nothing and is not a symbol at all. "A symbol may be a mere fiction; we may know it to be a fiction; it may be intended to be a fiction and the form of the word may hint that intention, as in the case of abstract terms such as *whiteness, nonentity*, and the like. But the symbol itself always pretends to be a true symbol and hence implies a reference to real things . . ." (1865b: 287; cf. 1865a: 276). Peirce distinguished the nonsense resulting from a violation of logical rules from the nonsense resulting from a violation of grammatical rules. Grammatical nonsense is *meaningless*. Logical nonsense is *absurd*. Examples of logically absurd nonsense that Peirce offers are "I know that my opinion is false, but still I hold it", and "This very proposition is false" (1865: 174-175).

Semeiotic rhetoric could be said to be Peirce's most radical and most fruitful departure from the classical trivium. Some thirty years later Peirce will refer to it as "the highest and most living" member of the trivium (c.1895: 333). In his first Harvard lecture of 1865 Peirce already understood semeiotic rhetoric (named by him Universal, General, Formal, or Speculative Rhetoric) to be "the science of the formal conditions of intelligibility of symbols" (1865: 175), or the relation of a symbol "to any language as being translatable, which I call . . . its power of appealing to the mind" (1865: 174). From the very beginning, Peirce held the view that the human being is a symbol, and that a mind is a consistent set of interpretants into which a symbol may be translated (1866b: 490-504). It is for this reason that a symbol's rhetorical power of appealing to a mind is equivalent to that symbol's translatability into a variety of interpretants.

I have already remarked that from Aristotle to Richard Whately[2] classical rhetoric had been divided into persuasion by argument, by emotion, and by style--*docere, movere*, et *delectare*. Peirce's new conception of semeiotic rhetoric proposed a similar division into the force with which a symbol addresses itself to thought, to feeling, and to attention (1866b: 491, 499). First, consider the force of a symbol as it addresses its interpretant mind through argument. The premisses of an argument are a symbol of which the conclusion is the interpretant. This interpretant "is no part of the argument but is the assent to it" (1866a: 478). This distinction between premisses and interpretant-conclusion is a rhetorical distinction, Peirce wrote, and hence it is a distinction between two kinds of *belief*. In assenting to the conclusion of an argument we assent to "that which is believed in on account of a belief in the (premisses)" (1865c: 320). So while semeiotic logic deals with propositions, semeiotic rhetoric is concerned with beliefs. Peirce suggests further that while logic is concerned with conclusions which follow apodictically, rhetoric concerns itself with beliefs which follow with various degrees of assent from prior beliefs which may exert various degrees of force. "Experience shows that of the most rigid and careful inductions and hypotheses only an infinitesimal proportion are never found to be in any respect false" (1866: 470). Clearly, Peirce followed traditional classical rhetoric in asserting that rhetorical argumentation yields only fallible beliefs.

The second division of semeiotic rhetoric is feeling, under which is included sensation as well as emotion. In addition to the emotions, Peirce's examples of feeling are the sense of beauty, pleasure, and color, (1866a: 472). "An emotion is always a simple predicate substituted by an operation of the mind for a highly complicated predicate" (1868: 229). An emotion is "a sort of mental name. To assign a name to a thing is to make a hypothesis. It is plainly a predicate which is not in the *data*" (1866a: 472). Like any hypothesis, an emotion groups together certain situations as similar to one another. A variety of situations are similar, for example, in being outrageous, or in being threatening, etc. "When I communicate my thought and my sentiments to a friend with whom I am in full sympathy, so that my feelings pass into him and I am conscious of what he feels, do I not live in his brain as well as in my own--most literally? . . . Man is conscious of his interpretant, his own thought, in another mind--I do not say immediately conscious--is happy in it, feels himself in some degree to be there" (1866b: 498-499). Indeed, the three Christian sentiments of love, hope, and faith, are required as the ultimate validating interpretants of all valid semeiosis (1869: 270-272; cf. 1878: 652-655). I have discussed Peirce's semeiotic theory of emotion in detail elsewhere (Savan 1981). Here I wish only to point to the fact that his theory of emotion is a subdivision of his semeiotic rhetoric. It is an account of one of the three different modes in which a symbol addresses its interpretant.

The third division of classical rhetoric is the study of style. What counterpart, if any, could Peirce find for style in semeiotic rhetoric? It is this aspect of semeiotic rhetoric which appears to have given him the most trouble. On this problem his views changed most markedly over time. There is a short passage in the concluding Lowell lecture of 1866 (1866b: 497) in which it is suggested that the ultimate interpretant of all symbols is metaphorical, if by *metaphor* is meant "broad comparison on the ground of characters of a formal and highly abstract kind". However, in these papers of the 1860's Peirce settled, for this subdivision of semeiotic rhetoric, on the power of attention and the resultant habit (1866b: 491-496). The connection between attention and habit is that attention is a denotative relation in which a symbol picks out a specific part or aspect of some existent external to that symbol. While this is a particular and singular act, its interpretant is general. It may affect memory, so that we re-identify the same phenomenon on different occasions (1868: 232). As well, it may be interpreted by the nervous system, so that a given pattern of activity is elicited by similar phenomena (Ibid.). This constitutes a habit of action, so that habits are inductions based on instances of attention (1866b: 491), as emotions are hypotheses which simplify complex predicates.

In what way are attention and habit correspondent, in semeiotic rhetoric, to style in classical rhetoric? Peirce does not tell us, and I can only suggest a plausible answer. One of the chief functions of literary or oratorical style is to catch the attention of the reader or hearer, to hold that attention, and to enhance it. One of the chief functions of semeiotic rhetoric is to fix our attention upon a particular symbol and its object, thus leading to the *fixation of the belief* and habit which are the interpretants of the symbol. Peirce's pragmaticism, his conception of the fixation belief, and his interest in a method for the development of methods of inquiry, all are outgrowths of his early theory of semeiotic rhetoric.

NOTES

[1] *Editor's Note*: An earlier version of this paper under the same title appears in *Cruzeiro Semiotico* No. 8 (January 1988, Associação Portuguesa de Semiotica), 50-56. The citations, including diverse references to C. S. Peirce's writings and other philosophical references, have been historically layered and listed individually in this version.

[2] Richard Whately, Archbishop of Dublin, was the author of a widely consulted *Rhetoric* and *Logic*. Both were familiar to Peirce.

REFERENCES

ANONYMOUS.
c. 85BC. *Rhetorica ad C. Herrenium De Ratione Dicendi*, ed. Harry Caplan (Loeb Classical Library, Cambridge: Harvard University Press, 1954). This work was long attributed incorrectly to Cicero.

ARISTOTLE.
c. 350-344BC. *Prior Analytics*, originally probably undifferentiated from *Posterior Analytics*, but textually segregated in very early manuscripts, appears in *Prior and Posterior Analytics*, ed. and trans. by John Warrington (New York: Dutton, 1964) and numerous other editions.

c. 335-334BC. *Rhetorica*, trans. W. Rhys Roberts, in Vol. XI of *The Works of Aristotle*, ed. W. D. Ross (attributed to c.335-334BC, Oxford: Clarendon Press, 1924).

c. 330BC. *De Interpretatione*, trans. Boethii, in *Aristoteles Latinus*, Vol. II, parts 1-2, ed. L Minio-Paluello (Bruges and Paris: Desclée de Brouwer, 1965). English trans. by E. M. Edghill, *On Interpretation*, in *The Basic Works of Aristotle*, ed. Richard McKeon (New York: Random House, 1941).

PEIRCE, Charles S.
References to the *Writings of Charles S. Peirce: A Chronological Edition*, Vol. I, ed. M. H. Fisch, et al. (Bloomington, Indiana: Indiana University Press, 1982), and Vol. II, ed. E. C. Moore, et al. (Bloomington, Indiana: Indiana University Press, 1984) are listed below as W followed by pages. Citations in *Collected Papers of Charles Sanders Peirce*, 8 volumes, 1-6 ed. P. Weiss and C. Hartshorne, 7-8 ed. A.W. Burks (Cambridge, Mass.: Harvard University Press, 1931-1958) are listed below as CP, volume number, and paragraph number. Listings in *New Elements of Mathematics*, ed. C. Eisele (The Hague: Mouton, 1976) are abbreviated NEM, volume number, and page number.

1865. "Harvard Lecture I", W 1.162-175.
1865a. "Harvard Lecture X", W 1.272-286.
1865b. "Harvard Lecture XI", W 1.286-302.
1865c. "An Unpsychological View of Logic to which are appended some applications of the theory to Psychology and other subjects", W 1.305-321.
1865d. "Logic of the Sciences", W 1.322-336.
1866. "Lowell Lecture VII", W 1.454-471.
1866a. "Lowell Lecture IX", W 1.471-488.
1866b. "Lowell Lecture XI", W 1.490-504.
1868. "Some Consequences of Four Incapacities", *Journal of Speculative Philosophy* 2, 140-157, reprinted in W 2.211-242.
1869. "Grounds of Validity of the Laws of Logic: Further Consequences of Four Incapacities", *Journal of Speculative Philosophy* 2, 193-208, reprinted in W 2.242-272.
1878. "Three Logical Sentiments", CP 2.652-655, part of "The Doctrine of Chances", *Popular Science Monthly* 12, 604-615, reprinted in CP 2.645-668 as corrected in 1893 for inclusion as part of *Grand Logic*.
c. 1895. "The Nature of Assertion", originally part of "That Categorical and Hypothetical Propositions are one in essence, with some connected matters", CP 2.333.
c. 1900. "Kaina Stoicheia", NEM 4, 235-263.
1900. "Letter to Georg Cantor", NEM 3/2, 767-771.

PLATO.
  c. 385BC. *Cratylus*, in *The Collected Dialogues of Plato Including the Letters*, ed. Edith Hamilton and Huntington Cairns, trans. by Benjamin Jowett (Bollingen Series LXXI; New York: Pantheon Books, 1961), 421-474.

SAVAN, David.
  1981. "Peirce's Semeiotic Theory of Emotion", *Proceedings of the C.S. Peirce Bicentennial International Congress*, ed. K.L. Ketner, J.M. Ransdell, et al. (Lubbock, Texas: Texas Tech Press, 1981), 319-33.

SEXTUS EMPIRICUS.
  c. 200fl. "Adv. Math VIII" ("Against the Logicians"), in *Sextus Empiricus*, Loeb Classical Library Edition of his Greek text with facing English trans. by R. G. Bury (London: Heinemann, 1917-1955), in 4 volumes.

WHY WE PREFER PEIRCE TO SAUSSURE

T.L. Short
Kenyon College

The issue posed by contrasting Peirce and Saussure is well-understood and has been discussed by, among others, Benveniste, Eco, and Sebeok. In the words of Emile Benveniste (1985: 228), the question is, "What is the place of language among the systems of signs?"

Eco (1976) has detailed the history, of more than two millenia, of the recognition of a distinction between natural signs, such as medical symptoms, and conventional meaning. He has also emphasized a point to which I will return at the end of my remarks, that there is a troubling class of cases, such as animal cries, that do not fit easily into either category.

In general, then, the problem is one of defining the object of our study. Is it language, primarily, and other systems of conventional meaning that are either like or derivative from language? That is Saussure's view. Or does it also include natural signs and likenesses, so that language is only one type among other types of sign and is not paradigmatic of the whole class? That is Peirce's view.

I

Saussure himself, at the outset of his seminal treatise, suggest that the difficulty we confront is peculiar to our study: "Other sciences", he says, "work with objects that are given in advance and that can then be considered from different viewpoints; but not linguistics". This is totally false. Benveniste (1985: 231) replicates the error when he writes, "We could not conceive of a science uncertain of its object". On the contrary, it is characteristic of science to be uncertain of its object.

Take Galileo, for example. He continued the Aristotelian and Medieval study of motion, but reconceived motion's nature, taking what we now call "inertia" to be its essence, so that it was not the continuance of motion but changes in motion that require to be explained. In this way he eliminated a problem the Aristotelians were unable to solve, namely, the problem of explaining projectile motion. My point is that in a scientific advance the very object of study is reconceived. But that's not all. For with such reconception the boundaries of the study also change. From the pre-Galilean point of view, celestial motion and terrestrial motion were radically different kinds of motion and necessarily the objects of different sciences, employing different methods, but from Galileo's point of view, each was inertial motion subject to change by the influence of imposed forces. Hence, after Galileo we had one physics of earth and the heavens alike.

There is, then, nothing special about linguistics or semiotics having to define its own object and fix its own boundaries: that is just what serious intellectual work, scientific or not, always involves. But how is this defining of object, this fixing of boundaries to be accomplished? There was nothing in the received meanings of such words as "motion" or in the known phenomena that made Galileo's choice inevitable. Similarly, Saussure's approach and Peirce's are equally conjectural. Each is a stab in the dark, albeit in different directions.

That does not mean that the delimitation of our field of study is arbitrary or merely a matter of taste. It means only that we cannot determine which is the right choice until after--perhaps long after--the choice itself has been made. Different ways of conceptualization have to be tried, and the one that eventually proves to yield the best results is the one we will decide is right. Decisions in inquiry are justified by what comes after them, and not--or not entirely--by what comes before them. The centrality of conjecture to intellectual work makes the future-directedness of that work essential to any claim it may have to objectivity. Time is of its essence.

Saussure and Benveniste did not make a simple blunder when they suggested that a science requires its boundaries to be fixed in advance. Rather, they were assuming the older definition of "science", namely, as a completed *system* of knowledge. It was Saussure's contemporary, Charles Peirce, who first recognized that the definition has limited interesting applicability and does not fit that which had come to be called "science".[1] Peirce argued that science is best conceived of as a *process*, one without fixed results, fixed methods, or fixed definitions. Definitions are temporary guideposts. Consistently with this view, Peirce regarded his own archetectonic of the departments of inquiry as a provisional guide to future work-- a guide based on the uncertain ground of past experience.

Thus, summing up one lesson of history to date, Peirce defined "science" as the life of a community bound together by its interest in truth, hence, by its resolve to form and to test conjectures. What counts as a test is itself a matter of on-going discovery: we are always coming across more rigorous, more revealing ways of discriminating between competing ideas.

The question for us, then, is whether we have as yet any reason to suppose that Saussure's approach to language and related phenomena is more fruitful than Peirce's or vice versa. It is not too early to form a preliminary assessment of their prospects. Where we shall place our own bets--that is, that to which we decide to devote our limited resources--depends on such provisional judgments. But it is fortunate that we do not all make the same judgment.

II

Saussure defines "semiology" as the study of "the life of signs within society". This excludes natural signs, but includes much that would not ordinarily be thought of as having a meaning: for example, Saussure mentions customs. The common denominator is the purely conventional coupling of a material signifier with a concept signified, such as a word and the idea it expresses or such as the physical act of grasping someone's hand, pumping it up and down, and the meaning which that act has for those for whom it is a custom. So defined, semiology includes linguistics as one part among others. But Saussure also makes linguistics a model for the other parts. For, he says, "Signs that are wholly arbitrary realize better than the others the ideal of the semiological process". Yet, in so saying, Saussure admits that some signs are not wholly arbitrary.

Peirce, however, defines "semeiotic" as the study of all sign phenomena, where by "sign" he means something having both an object that it signifies and an interpretant in which it is interpreted as signifying that object. The interpretant can remain an unactualized potentiality, grounded in some relation the sign has to its object. Thus, the causal relation of *most* smoke-like vapor to fire makes *any* such vapor a (*fallible*) sign of fire, since knowledge of that relation would justify a probable inference from the observed vapor to fire as its supposed cause. Similarly, resemblance and convention ground interpretation. Hence, linguistic and other conventional signs belong, on Peirce's view, to a much wider class of phenomena than are comprised in Saussure's semiology; and, of this wider class, language is far from paradigmatic.

That, then, is one difference between Peirce and Saussure: Saussure achieves theoretical unity by limiting his study to conventional, hence, to man-made signs, while Peirce spreads the net wider.

Another difference is that Saussure (i.1906-1911: 65-70) defines "sign" as the union of material signifier and the concept it signifies, whereas Peirce (i.1867-1897: passim), following the lead of ordinary language, identifies the sign with the signifier. That something is a sign only in virtue of its relation to the object signified does not mean that the latter is *part* of the former, any more than a mother is a complex of woman and child. No, a mother is just one person and her child is somebody else. Peirce's logic of relations tells us that something can be what it is because of its relation to *another*. To insist that x can be essential to y only be being part of y, is to deny the logic of relations: it is to return to the scholastic metaphysics of substance and attribute.

Furthermore, Peirce admits more kinds of signs than does Saussure. Since Saussure makes the abstract structures of language, and not their concrete uses in speech, to be the subject of his study, his "material signifier" is actually a general type of articulated sound or written mark. This is an example of what Peirce meant by 'legisign' (see Short 1982). But in addition to legisigns, Peirce also admits qualisigns and sinsigns, that is, qualities and singular entities that are signs. There are many types of sinsign on Peirce's view. Among others, some are significant because of the legisigns they replicate. Now Saussure is famous for having emphasized that language has a diachronic as well as a synchronic dimension. The diachronic is that in which language evolves over time. But since that evolution takes place through concrete uses of language, it seems to me that Peirce's scheme is better able to accommodate diachronic studies than is Saussure's, since it, unlike Saussure's, contains within a single theoretical perspective both language and speech, both legisigns and their replications.

Finally, on Peirce's view, the thing signified is not normally a concept. The very idea that every sign--even every linguistic sign--must be associated with a mental entity is a part of the Cartesian inheritance that Peirce was particularly anxious to reject. On Peirce's view, concepts are themselves signs, requiring interpretation. The interpretant may be conceptual--that is, it may be a sign of a verbal type--but it could also be a feeling or an action. Admittedly, the interpretants of legisigns are abstractions, much as Saussure intended by his idea of content. The trouble is that we cannot find an illuminating account of "the content plane" unless we step outside the confines of Saussurean semiology. Saussure places a heavy explanatory burden on a term he leaves painfully vague. Peirce, by contrast, tells us that the interpretant of a legisign is a rule that determines how its replicas are to be interpreted, and since his semeiotic embraces those replicas and the acts by which they are interpreted, he can give us a complete explication of the meaning of legisigns--an explication internal to his doctrine of signs. The failure of Saussurean semiology to provide such an explication results in a further problem, that it is unable to explain the relation of language to the real world.

These last three differences are very important, and tell, I believe, decisively in Peirce's favor. But I do not have time to develop that theme here. Here, I shall restrict my attention to the first difference, that Saussure's semiology is limited to conventional signs while Peirce's semeiotic is a much broader study. I shall argue that on this ground alone we should prefer Peirce to Saussure.

III

So far, it may seem that Peirce's semeiotic and Saussure's semiology are, although different, complementary. Why shouldn't we approach the same phenomena sometimes with a narrower and sometimes with a broader perspective? Well, I am not denying that one can learn from Saussure. Yet each thinker claimed not simply a point of view but *that unique* point of view which reveals the objective order or natural classification of the phenomena under consideration. Saussure (i.1906-1911: 9) said that

> Language ... is a self-contained whole and a principle of classification. As soon as we give language first place among the facts of speech, we introduce a natural order into a mass that *lends itself to no other classification* (My emphasis).

Similarly, Peirce wrote that

> If the question were simply what we *do* mean by a sign, it might soon be resolved. But that is not the point. We are in the situation of a zoologist who wants to know what ought to be the meaning of 'fish' in order to make fishes one of the great classes of vertebrates.

Each, in other words, meant to cut nature at nature's joints, and since they were cutting the same beast but not in the same places, at least one of the two missed the joints. The issue is whether language, in order to be understood, has to placed in a wider perspective, as just one type of sign-activity among many others, including those that do not depend upon conventions. Saussure thinks not.

Eco and others have tried to meld Peirce's theory with Saussure's by arguing that all signs, including natural signs and likenesses, are mediated by a conventional code. This is the most extreme form of conventionalism, since it makes every object of cognition conventional; as such, it is at odds with the rest of Peirce's philosophy. It denies the possibility of a naturalistic account of the development of language, society, and mind, and it denies the possibility of objective knowledge. Furthermore, it contradicts Peirce's clearly stated view that significance is sometimes grounded in non-conventional relations, e.g., causal relations.

Of course, one can try to argue that Peirce was mistaken in this regard. One can claim that a natural sign signifies what it does only because the causal relation or likeness in which that significance is grounded has been represented in a general theory, hence, in a verbal structure. That, however, is a bad argument. Admittedly, the words employed are significant by convention; but it does not follow that what they signify is conventional. And it is the causal relation or likeness and not the theory that justifies or grounds the interpretation. If the theory alone justified the interpretation, then a false theory would be just as good as a true one. Since the truth of the theory matters, it must be the relation it represents, and not the theory itself, that grounds the significance of the natural sign. Besides, this attempt to argue that natural indices are conventional overlooks the fact that lower animals interpret natural signs without benefit of verbal theories. The panther tracks his prey by following its spoor.

I take it, then, that Peirce's theory does not reduce to Saussure's. To see why it is preferable to Saussure's, I should like to turn again to Benveniste, who sees the difference between Peirce and Saussure as I do but who rejects Peirce's view as being too broad and argues, consistently with Saussure, that all the signs embraced by semiology must be interpreted in language. "Language occupies a special position in the universe of sign systems", he says, because "The signs of society can be interpreted integrally by those of language, but the reverse is not so" (1985: 236). By interpreting a system of signs Benveniste means stating its code in another system. But his view that language is the ultimate interpreter seems to me a paradox from which Saussurean semiology cannot escape. The paradox is this: if only the most sophisticated of sign systems can interpret all the others, then how shall that system be understood? Comprehension, I submit, cannot begin at the most rarified level, and yet that is what Saussurean semiology implies.

Peirce's theory provides a radically different and more coherent perspective. Diachronically and synchronically, it relates the structures of human language to more primitive signs--signs which occur and are interpreted independently of any system of conventional meanings. Thus it provides for a naturalistic account of the development of language and for an account of linguistic meaning in terms of the uses of language in speech and the relation of speech acts to simpler forms of semeiosis (see Short 1981). These two accounts are connected, since the uses of language in specific speech acts requires the cooperation of the *same* non-linguistic signs that preceded language and prepared the way for language. For example, pointing picks out the objects to which concrete nouns may be applied. If such gestures and other non-linguistic signs had no meaning apart from their interpretation in language, then language itself would be a meaningless game that could never have developed.

There is, of course, a kind of meaning, and, hence, a kind of interpretation that emerges first at the linguistic level. Peirce is certainly opposed to any form of reductionism. But if the claim of Eco, Benveniste, and company is only that nothing has *such* meaning until interpreted in language, then their claim is a mere tautology. Meanwhile, Saussurean semiology ignores the fact that this linguistic meaning, though it is not reducible to more primitive forms of semeiosis, is nevertheless dependent on them, while they are *not*, in turn, dependent on it.

IV

It is no surprise that the differences between Peirce and Saussure derive from Peirce's triadism as opposed to Saussure's dyadism. The triadic, end-directed process of interpretation accounts for significance without Peirce's having to posit any inexplicably mentalistic "conceptual content"--either as object or as interpretant. Hence, he can recognize interpretants, processes of interpretation, and signs that are not functions of the human mind, human language, or social convention.

It is instructive in this connection to consider the class of signs to which Eco (Eco et al. 1983) has drawn our attention: signs, like the barking of a dog, that are related to their objects neither by the causal connection of natural indices nor by the conventions of human society. Although Benveniste claims that all that has survived of Peirce's semeiotic is the icon/index/symbol trichotomy, it is in fact Peirce's qualisign/sinsign/legisign trichotomy that enables us to put barking dogs in their proper place. For a legisign is an abstract type that has come into existence in order to be replicated, because replications of it can serve some purpose, and a legisign can come into existence either through biological evolution, as in the case of the cries of animals, or through social convention, as in the case of human languages. Peirce's category of the legisign therefore bridges the chasm between nature and artifice.

Let us dwell for a moment on dogs' barking. Eco has shown that its classification is an ancient problem; Peirce, so far as I know, did not realize this. Hence, it is quite unexpectedly that the basic principles of his semeiotic yield its solution. It is precisely such unanticipated successes that reassure us about the truth of a theory.

I do not mean to suggest that Peirce's semeiotic solves all problems. A science in the modern sense of that term is marked by fruitful questions, not final answers. But there is a difference between a problem that appears capable of solution and one that, seeming unsolvable, stands as evidence against the assumptions in terms of which it is framed. I suggest that the evidence to date indicates that Peirce's theory is more fruitful--not of reams of publications, but of solid advances in understanding--than is Saussure's.

NOTES

[1] My representation of Peirce's ideas is drawn mainly from Chapters 2 and 3, Volume II of *The Collected Papers of Charles Sanders Peirce* (Peirce i.1867-1897) and the collected letters of C.S. Peirce to Lady Welby (see Hardwick 1977), material dated after 1900.

REFERENCES

BENVENISTE, Emile.
    1985. "The Semiology of Language", in *Semiotics, An Introductory Anthology*, ed. R. Innis (Bloomington, IN: Indiana University Press).
ECO, Umberto.
    1976. *Semiotics and the Philosophy of Language* (Bloomington, IN: Indiana University Press).
ECO, Umberto, et al.
    1983. "'Latratus Canis' or: the Dog's Barking", originally presented to the Convention on Animals in the Middle Ages held at Spoleto by the Centro Italiano di Studi sull'Alto Medioevo, revised English version in *Versus* 38/39, 1-38; second revised version under the title "Latratus Canis" in *Tijdschrift voor Filosofie* 47.1 (March, 1985), 3-14. The version used here, synthesizing all the earlier papers and incorporating historically layered references, appears in *Frontiers in Semiotics*, ed. John Deely, Brooke Williams, Felicia Kruse (Bloomington, IN: Indiana University Press, 1986), 63-73.
HARDWICK, Charles, ed.
    1977. *Semiotic and Significs: The correspondence between Charles S. Peirce and Victoria Lady Welby* (Bloomington, IN: Indiana University Press).

PEIRCE, C.S.
 i. 1867-1897. Chapters 2 and 3, *The Collected Papers of Charles Sanders Peirce*, Volume II, ed. Charles Hartshorne and Paul Weiss (Cambridge, MA: Harvard University Press, 1932); Chapter 2, originally in *Proceedings of the American Academy of Arts and Sciences* 7 (April 9, 1867) includes additions and corrections of 1897; Sections 1 and 2 of Chapter 3 apear in *John Hopkins 'Studies in Logic'*, ed. C.S. Peirce (1883), rewritten in 1893 for *Grand Logic*; Section 3 of Chapter 3 was written in 1893.

SAUSSURE, Ferdinand de.
 i. 1906-1911. Lectures delivered at the University of Geneva and published from auditors' notes by Charles Bally and Albert Sechehaye with the collaboration of Albert Riedlinger under the title *Cours de Linguistique Générale* in 1916; critical edition prepared by Tullio de Mauro (Paris: Payot, 1972). English trans. with an introduction and notes by Wade Baskin, *Course in General Linguistics: Ferdinand de Saussure* (New York: McGraw-Hill).

SEBEOK, Thomas.
 1971. "'Semiotics' and Its Congeners", in *Frontiers in Semiotics*, ed. John Deely, Brooke Williams, and Felicia Kruse (Bloomington, IN: Indiana University Press, 1986), 255-263.

SHORT, T.L.
 1981. "Semeiosis and Intentionality", *Transactions of the Charles S. Peirce Society*, 17.3, 197-223.
 1982. "Life Among the Legisigns", *Transactions of the Charles S. Peirce Society*, 18.4, 285-310.

VI

EXPANSIONS OF PEIRCEAN SEMIOTICS

SEMIOSIS:
THE SUBJECT MATTER OF SEMIOTIC INQUIRY

John Deely
Universidade Federal de Minas Gerais, Brasil
Loras College, USA

If we ask what it is that semiotic studies investigate, the answer is, in a word, action. The action of signs. This peculiar type of action, corresponding to the distinctive type of knowledge the name semiotics properly characterizes, has long been recognized in philosophy in connection with investigations of the various types of causality. For example, some of the most difficult and extended passages in Poinsot's early attempt (1632a) to systematize the foundations of semiotic inquiry arise from the need to make this heretofore peripheral topic of natural enquiry central to the establishment of semiotic: see, for example, Questions 2-5 in Book I of his *Treatise on Signs*. And more recently, in this same context of inquiry, Ralph Powell (1986, 1988) has managed to indicate how central this neglected and previously obscure type of causality is to the whole problematic of epistemology, once its semiotic character has been recognized.

Not until about 1906, however, was the peculiar action of signs singled out as a distinct field of possible inquiry in its own right and given a proper name. The investigator singling out this field in its own right, rather than through its adjacency with other lines of immediate investigation, was Charles Sanders Peirce, and the name he assigned to it was *semiosis*. At this point the doctrine of signs turned a fundamental corner in its development: Peirce saw that the full development of semiotic as a distinct body of knowledge required a dynamic view of signification as a process. It could not be merely a question of the being proper to signs ontologically considered. There is also the further question of the becoming this peculiar type of being enables and sustains itself by. It is not just that there are, let us say, symbols. There is also the fact that symbols grow.

Semiosis as a type of activity is distinctive in that it always involves three elements, but it is even more distinctive in that one of these three elements need not be an actual existent thing. In all other types of action, the actors are correlative, and hence the action between them, however many there be, is essentially dyadic and dynamical: for it to occur, both terms must exist. A car cannot hit a tree unless the tree is there to be hit, but sign can signify an upcoming bridge which is no longer there. Galileo's eyes and telescope engaged in a dynamic interaction with light from the stars. But over and above this dynamic interaction he essayed opinions concerning the celestial spheres which turned out not to exist. And yet the nonbeing of these spheres contributed to Galileo's imprisonment and propositions concerning them cited as the ground for the serious sanctions taken against Galileo by the authorities.

Peirce calls the action as such between existent things "brute force" or "dynamical interaction". It may be physical, or it may be psychological. In either case, it takes place between two subjects of physical existence, and is, in a terminology we shall be obliged to both clarify and insist upon along our way, always and irreducibly a *subjective interaction*. Subjective interactions, whether psychical or physical, are always involved in the action of signs, but they surround the semiosis as its context and condition, while always falling short of the action of signs proper. In other words, while the action of signs always involves dynamical interactions, dynamical interactions need not always involve the action of signs.

The distinctiveness of semiosis is unavoidable when we consider the case of two things existing affected in the course of their existence by what does not exist, but if we understand what is distinctive about it, that distinctiveness remains unmistakable even when the three terms involved in a semeiosy happen also to be all three existent. Peirce gives the example of the rise of the mercury in a thermometer, which is brought about "in a purely brute and dyadic way" by the increase of ambient temperature, but which, on being perceived by someone familiar with thermometers, produces also the idea of increasing warmth in the environment. This idea as a mental event belongs entirely to the order of subjective and physical existence, no more and no less than does the rising mercury and the relative presence or absence of warmth in the atmosphere. It is, as Peirce puts it, the "immediate object" of the thermometer taken as a certain type of sign, namely, one indexical of an environmental condition.

The object of the thermometer as a sign is the relative warmth of the surroundings. The object of the idea of the thermometer as a sign is no different. However, the thermometer prior to being read is involved only in dynamical interactions. On being read a third factor enters in, the factor of interpretation. The thermometer on being seen may not be recognized as a thermometer: in that case, besides being a subject of physical interactions, that is to say, a thing, it becomes also a cognized or known thing, an element of experience or object. But if it is both seen and recognized as a thermometer, it is not only a thing become object but also an object become sign. As a thing it merely exists, a node of sustenance for a network of physical relations and actions. As an object it also exists for someone as an element of experience, differentiating a perceptual field in definite ways related to its being as a thing among other elements of the environment. But as a sign it not only stands for itself within experience and in the environment, but for something else as well, something besides itself. It not only exists (thing), it not only stands to someone (object), it also stands to someone for something else (sign). And this "something else" may or may not be real in the physical sense: what it indicates may be misleading, if, for example, the thermometer is defective.

In this case, its immediate object, the idea it produces as sign, becomes in its turn a node of sustenance for a network of relations presumed to be physical but which in fact, because of the defective nature of the thermometer being observed, is merely objective. Here we encounter a primary phenomenon semiotic analysis is obliged to take into account: divisions of things as things and divisions of objects as objects are not the same and vary independently, the former being determined directly by physical action alone, the latter being mediated indirectly by semeiosy, the action of signs.[1]

The immediate point to be noted is this: Divisions of objects as objects and divisions of things as things may happen to coincide, as when the thermometer seen and recognized is also functioning properly; or they may happen to diverge, as when the thermometer seen and recognized is, unbeknownst to its interpreter, deceptive by defect. But even when they coincide, the two orders remain irreducible in what is proper to them.

The idea of surrounding temperature produced by the thermometer as sign represents to the interpreter of the thermometer something that it itself is not, namely, the presumed condition of the environment indexically represented by the thermometer. As a mental representation, that is to say, a psychological reality, it belongs to the order of subjective existence and is the immediate object of the thermometer as sign. But, within that order, it also functions to found a relation to something other than itself, namely, a condition of the environment surrounding the thermometer, which condition is both objective (known) and physical (something existent besides being known), presuming the thermometer accurate, or merely objective but deviant from the physical situation rather than coincident with it, presuming the thermometer defective. As founding this relation, in every case objective, in some cases coincidentally physical as well, the idea itself produced by the thermometer has in turn produced "the proper significate outcome" of the thermometer as sign. This Peirce calls the *interpretant*, a unique and important notion, the key to understanding the action of signs as a process, a form of becoming, as well as a kind of being, and over and above the unique essential structure which makes signification possible in the first place.

Peirce suggests (c.1906: CP 5.4730 that "it is very easy to see what the interpretant of a sign is: it is all that is explicit in the sign itself apart from its context and circumstances of utterance". In the case at hand: the sign is the thermometer; the context and circumstances of its utterance are the ambient temperature producing a certain level of the mercury correlated--accurately or inaccurately, as we have seen--with a scale, the whole of which apparatus is seen and recognized as a temperature measuring device; and what is explicit in the sign itself apart from this context and these circumstances is representation of something other than the thermometer, namely, the ambient temperature, as being presumably at what the thermometer indicates it to be, although this may be wrong due to defect in the mechanism. In other words, all that is explicit in the sign itself apart from its context and circumstances of utterance is "its proper significate outcome", the objective element of the situation, irreducible to the dynamical interactions involved, and establishing channels and expectations along which some of the interactions will be diverted in ongoing exchanges.

In our example, the idea of the thermometer enabling the thermometer to function as a sign was in the first instance a mental representation. However, and this is a very important point, the interpretant of a sign "need not be a mental mode of being", nor, as we have seen, is it as mental mode of being that the idea produced by the thermometer functioned as interpretant. Whether a given interpretant be an idea or not, what is essential to it as interpretant is that it be the ground upon which the sign is seen to be related to something else as signified, which signified in turn becomes a sign relative to other elements in the experience of the interpreter, setting in motion the chain of interpretants on which semiosis as a process feeds. In other words, what is essential to the interpretant is that it mediate the difference between objective and physical being, a difference which knows no fixed line; and this is the reason why, at the same time, the triadic production of the interpretant is essential to a sign, and the interpretant need not be a mental mode of being, although, considered as founding a determinate relation of signification for some animal, it will be.

We see now with greater clarity the difference between the action of signs and the action of things: the former is purely objective, always at once involving and exceeding the latter, while the latter is purely subjective, or, what comes to the same thing, physical or psychic, and restricted to the order of what exists here and now.[2]

Wherever the future influences a present course of events, therefore, we are confronted by semiosis. Never confined to what has been or is, semiosis transpires at the boundary between what is and what might be or might have been. Linguistic signs may well be "the ideological phenomenon par excellence", as Vološinov said 1929: 13); but action of signs, as providing the general subject matter of semiotic inquiry, extends well beyond what we call "language", even though it is only through language that this range can be brought to light for us as inquirers. Why this is so we shall eventually see.

To appreciate at once the privileged and at the same time restricted role of linguistic signs in semiosis, however, it is necessary to get these peculiar signs into a larger perspective revealing something of the other processes, no less semiosic, on which the possibility and actuality of linguistic semioses depend. For this purpose, it is useful to outline in broad terms a number of levels within semiosis. These levels, of course, can be further distinguished indefinitely for purposes of specialized research and investigation. Here it will be enough to bring out in a synoptic way the prospective scope of semiotic inquiry, an effort which will have the additional merit perhaps of neutralizing the vestigial inclinations to positivism and modern idealism that often in practice corrupt the semiotic standpoint by assimilating it to what is irretrievably presemiotic in the previous era and most recent epoch of philosophy.

The highest level of semiosis so far as our experience goes is also the one closest to us: *anthroposemiosis*. Anthroposemiosis from one point of view includes all the sign processes that human beings are directly involved in, and from another point of view names those sign processes which are species-specifically human. From the latter point of view, anthroposemiosis includes first of all language, and secondly those sign systems which come after language and which further structure perception and modify the environment even for species of animals other than human, although the understanding of these postlinguistic changes in what is proper to them is possible only in and through language.

For this reason, language has come to be called in Eastern European circles of semiotic development the "primary modeling system", and the rest of human culture and civilization a series of "secondary modeling systems". However, as Sebeok in particular has taken pains to point out (1987), this way of describing the situation is not entirely satisfactory, because it is grounded, as is apparent, in a derivative understanding of anthroposemiosis. More fundamentally and inclusively, anthroposemiosis comprises, as we have said, all the sign processes that human beings are directly involved in. From this point of view, language itself is already a secondary modeling system, not the primary one, even though, relative to the distinctively human cultural traditions and developments of civilization, language is the proximate enabling medium and sustaining network of semiosis. Proximate to language, however, is the larger semiotic web of human experience which intricately interweaves linguistic semiosis with perceptual semioses shared in common with other biological species, and delicately depends upon endosemiotic networks within the body whereby the human organism itself is sustained by a complex network of symbioses without which the human individual would perish, and which network proves in its own right to be a thoroughly semiosic one.

In addition, the very interaction between human being and physical environment, whereby, for example, a person noting the sky anticipates stormy weather and prepares accordingly, gives rise to further strands of the semiotic web linking the human being not only with conspecifics and not only with other animals, but also with the general realm of physical surroundings in the largest sense. From this point of view, anthroposemiosis forms a seamless whole with all of nature, and the appropriate metaphor is not that of language as a primary modeling system, but the ancient one of man as the microcosm. Anthroposemiosis is the most complex form of semiosis not because it harbors unique modes of semiosis, beginning with language. It is the most complex form because, besides harboring uniquely high and complex developments, it harbors at the same time all the other semiosic developments as well, and depends upon them in achieving whatever is unique and specific to itself, beginning with language.

The semiosic processes of perception and sensation which are common to other animals besides the human defines the level and zone of what Sebeok and Wells first characterized as *zoösemiosis* (Sebeok 1963: 74). To their original coinage I add the umlaut, to prevent the misunderstanding which I have actually encountered, whereby this rich realm has been unwittingly reduced in hearers' minds to the study of sign systems among captive animals.

Like anthroposemiosis, zoösemiosis can be regarded from two standpoints. From one point of view, zoösemiosis is concerned with the overlap of semiotic processes shared between human animals and other animal forms. However, this point of view provides only part of the story, for each animal species, and not only the human one, develops also species-specific semiotic modalities, and these are also the province of zoösemiotic investigations. The splendid work of von Frisch (1962, 1967) unraveling the species-specific semiosis of bees, or of Kessel (1955) in uncovering the species-specific symbolic component in mating activities of balloon flies, provide landmark examples of zoösemiotic analysis beyond the study of semiotic systems shared between human and other animals (although humans do indeed mate, and benefit too from the dance of bees). From this point of view, we see an entire regrouping of naturalist studies which have their own distinguished traditions under a new label more appropriate to and specificative of what naturalists have been trying to accomplish all along. Like anthroposemiosis, zoösemiosis comprises a series of microcosms and species-specific objective worlds as well, each one of which is entangled in natural processes of physical interaction (secondness) as well as in semiosic processes of objective interaction within and across species, the whole of which forms an interlocking network of irreducibly semiotic relations, many of which are physical as well as objective.

Most recently, a third macroscopic realm and level of semiosis within nature has been surveyed and established by the distinguished work of Martin Krampen and his coworkers under the rubric of *phytosemiosis*, the semiotic networks of plants. Here again a twofold standpoint is possible. There is undoubtedly semiosic interaction between plants and various species of animals, as the many insect victims of plants such as the notorious "venus fly-trap" mutely testify. It is surely remarkable, for example, that many plants grow in a form which is sexually deceiving to species of insect on which the propagation or nutrition of the plant depends. The plant world is replete with these astonishing examples of the extrinsic formal causality at the heart of sign activity. But there is also the question of semiosis within the plant world itself, as the recent discovery that trees are able to inform one another of zones of infection, for example, raises.

Here we reach a boundary line, which we may nonetheless cross by the means of abduction, that is to say, the formulation of some hypothesis suggesting new ideas for the further extension of the boundaries of semiotic activity to include the realm of so-called inorganic nature, both chemical and physical, ideas which need to be developed, tested, and further refined or even rejected by whole teams of workers.

Besides the three main levels of semiosis which have been briefly described above and which are firmly established regions of sign activity, there is reason to think that sign activity has also been at work in an anticipatory way even at inorganic levels before the advent of life in nature, as is suggested by the formula established by Poinsot (1632a: 126/3-4): "it suffices to be a sign virtually in order to signify in act". This formula derives from carefully considering the fact that all that pertains to secondness and dyadic interaction in semiosis belongs to signs strictly through what in them provides the foundations or fundaments whence result or might result relations of representation of another in which signifying consists formally as thirdness.[3] Sign activity in the inorganic realm would, according to this formula, occur less visibly and in the background, then, but virtually and as a matter of fact throughout the material realm.

On this hypothesis, there is not only the macroscopic realm of *biosemiosis* whose three main levels have been outlined and named, already with plenty of indication of microscopic subcurrents equally semiosic, as in the case of endosemiosis stated by Sebeok. There is also the more inclusive macroscopic realm of evolution in general, let us call it *physiosemiosis*, an activity virtual by comparison with biosemiosis but no less replete with the objective causality whereby the physical interaction of existing things is channeled toward a future different from what obtains at the time of the affected interaction. This a process whereby first stars and then planetary systems develop out of a more primitive atomic and molecular "dust", but which in turn give rise to conditions under which further complexifications of atomic structure become possible and then, inevitably, some of them actual as well (such as an oxidizing atmosphere, to choose a local example), continuing the process, as I have shown elsewhere (1969: shown, that is, as definitively as anything can be shown in the absence of directly observed data), inevitably along an overall trajectory pointing to the establishment of biosemiosic phenomena.

On this hypothesis, semiosis, as providing the subject matter of semiotic investigation, establishes nothing less than a new framework and foundation for the whole of human knowledge, not only for the so-called human and social sciences, as we have already seen from the partial tradition of semiology after Saussure, but for the so-called "hard" or natural sciences as well, precisely as they too arise from within and depend in their development upon experience and the processes of anthroposemiosis generally, as the wholistic tradition of semiotics after Peirce has begun to outline.

In many basic respects this is a contemporary development, but it draws its nourishment from long ago and has its own distinguished lineage of pioneers and precursors. In particular, we see here a contemporary development fulfilling the prophecy of Winance (1983: 515): "It is in the tradition of Peirce, Locke, and Poinsot that Logic becomes Semiotic, able to assimilate the whole of epistemology"--which we may take as a synecdoche for the human sciences--"natural philosophy as well"--where 'natural philosophy' is also taken synecdochically for the natural sciences including, as Aquinas noted (c.1269: Book I, lectio 1, n. 2), "even metaphysics". Representing our answer to the question of what semiotics investigates integrally, that is, including in a single scheme both what is firmly established and what we abductively extrapolated therefrom, we may outline the overall subject matter of semiotic investigations thus:

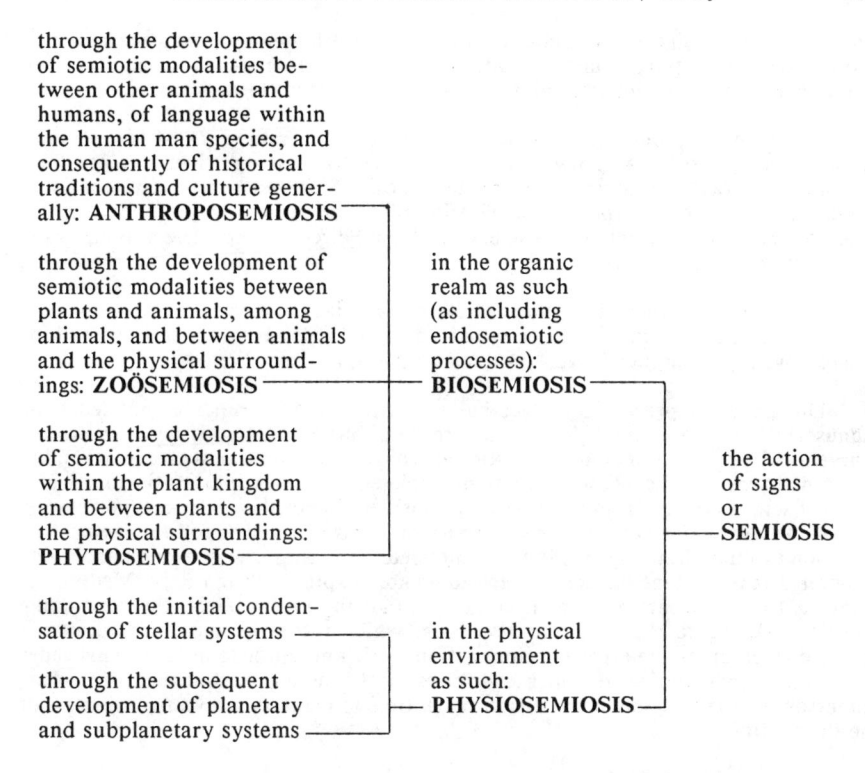

through the development of semiotic modalities between other animals and humans, of language within the human man species, and consequently of historical traditions and culture generally: **ANTHROPOSEMIOSIS**			
through the development of semiotic modalities between plants and animals, among animals, and between animals and the physical surroundings: **ZOÖSEMIOSIS**	in the organic realm as such (as including endosemiotic processes): **BIOSEMIOSIS**		
through the development of semiotic modalities within the plant kingdom and between plants and the physical surroundings: **PHYTOSEMIOSIS**		the action of signs or **SEMIOSIS**	
through the initial condensation of stellar systems	in the physical environment as such: **PHYSIOSEMIOSIS**		
through the subsequent development of planetary and subplanetary systems			

Regardless of our hypothetical extension of semiosis beyond the boundaries of the biological community--whether, that is, we wish to stick with the firmly established levels or wish also to consider the possibilities of a physiosemiosis in nature antecedent to and subtensive of the later and more restricted phenomena of biosemiosis--it is clear at this point that semiotics is the name for a distinctive series of investigations, distinctive for the same reason that any investigation is distinctive, namely, by reason of what it studies, in the present case, semiosis. But how is such an activity as semiosis possible in the first place?[4]

NOTES

[1] The contrast between objective being and the subjective order of physical existence was noted early in the development of an explicitly semiotic consciousness, for example, in the work of Cajetan (1507). But its centrality to the doctrine of signs only gradually came into view. Like the geological fault presaging major changes in the lay of the land, the inherent difference between objective and physical existence at the heart of being made it inevitable that dynamical interactions, overall, would give rise to directional changes, and with them to transformations of crude atomic

structures to the point where semiotic animals would wander where once cosmic dust and random interactions obtained. But this takes us too far from the simplicity of our example and the fundamental point it makes for the doctrine of signs.

[2] Peirce's way of putting this is obscure, outside the framework of his technical semiotic: thirdness, he says, always presupposes the brute interactions of secondness which also always presupposes the dream world which secondness differentiates, firstness. For present purposes, clarification of this technical way of phrasing the situation may safely be left to the exegetes of the Peircean texts. The aim here is to reach a more general audience.

[3] In current parlance, it is the vehicle of the sign, rather than the sign itself formally, that, for example, can be washed away in a flood, fall over on something passing by, or, at another leave, "produce a sense impression", etc.

[4] This paper as presented in October was drawn from a since completed book manuscript entitled *Basics of Semiotics*, to be published later this year by Indiana University Press. The concluding question was omitted from the oral presentation, but is retained here to indicate the essential incompleteness of the consideration of diverse levels of semiosis apart from the balancing consideration of the uniform type of being proper to signs which subtends the diversity of levels and makes for a common type of action throughout the levels. In the completed book, thus, the question concluding Chapter 3 (the present paper) is the lead-in to Chapter 4 ("Signs, the Medium of Semiosis") which treats of what is common to all the levels. Thus, the concluding question relating to the larger context from which the present paper is drawn is retained to preclude the erroneous impression, which might be taken from this paper in isolation, that semiosis comprises a series of "Chinese boxes". I thank Myrdene Anderson for alerting me to the difficulty in time to make this *caveat* for readers of the Proceedings.

REFERENCES

AQUINAS, Thomas.
   c.1269. *In decem libros ethicorum Aristotelis ad Nicomachum expositio*, ed. R. Spiazzi (3rd ed.; Turin: Marietti, 1964).

CAJETAN, Thomas de Vio.
   1507. *Commetaria in summan theologicam. Prima pars* (Rome), reprinted in Sancti Thomae Aquinatis Doctoris Angelici Opera Omnia, vols. 4 and 5 (Rome: Leonine, 1888-1889).

DEELY, John.
   1969. "Animal Intelligence and Concept-Formation", *The Thomist* XXXV.1 (January and April), Part I 75-149, Part II 251-342.
   1982. *Introducing Semiotic. Its History and Doctrine* (Bloomington: Indiana University Press).
   1982a. "On the Notion of Phytosemiotics", in *Semiotics 1982*, ed. John Deely and Jonathan Evans (Lanham, MD: University Press of America, 1987), 541-544; reprinted with minor changes in Deely et al. 1986: 96-103.
   1988. "The Semiotic of John Poinsot: Yesterday and Tomorrow", major discussion of reviews of and theoretical issues in the 1631-1632 work of Poinsot 1632a (entry below), *Semiotica* 69.1/2 (April), 31-127.

1989? *Basics of Semiotics* (Bloomington, IN: Indiana University Press).
FRISCH, Karl von.
    1962. "Dialects in the Language of Bees:, *Scientific American* 207, 79-87.
    1967. *The Dance Language and Orientation of Bees* (Cambridge, MA: Harvard University Press).
KESSEL, Edward L., ed.
    1955. *A Century of Progress in the Natural Sciences, 1853-1953* (San Francisco: California Academy of Sciences).
KRAMPEN, Martin.
    1981. "Phytosemiotics", *Semiotica* 36.3/4, 187-209, substantially reprinted in Deely et al. 1986: 83-95.
PEIRCE, Charles Sanders.
    c. 1906. Excerpt from "Pragmatism (Editor [3])", published under the title "A Survey of Pragmaticism" in *CP* 5.464-496.
POINSOT, John.
    1631. *Artis Logicae Prima Pars* (Alcalá, Spain). The opening pages 1-11a14 of this work and the "Quaestio Disputanda I. De Termino. Art. 6. Utrum Voces Significant per prius Conceptus an Res" pages 104b31-108a33, relevant to the discussion of signs in the *Secunda Pars* of 1632 (entry following), have been incorporated in the 1632a entry (second entry following, q.v., pp. 4-30 and 342-351 "Appendix A. On the Signification of Language", respectively), for the independent edition of that discussion published by the University of California Press. The Reiser edition of Poinsot's work (Vol. I; Turin: Marietti, 1930: pp. 1-247, arranged by columns--a, b--and line numbers within each column) was used as source for the Latin text.
    1632. *Artis Logicae Secunda Pars* (Alcalá, Spain). The Reiser edition of this work (also arranged as described in preceding 1631 entry; Vol. I; Turin: Marietti, 1930: pp. 249-839) was used as source for the Latin text.
    1632a. *Tractatus de Signis*, subtitled *The Semiotic of John Poinsot*, extracted from the *Artis Logicae Prima et Secunda Pars* of 1631-1632 (above two entries) and arranged in bilingual format by John Deely in consultation with Ralph A. Powell (First Edition; Berkeley: University of California Press, 1985), as explained in Deely 1985, q.v. Pages in this volume are set up in matching columns of English and Latin, with intercolumnar numbers every fifth line. (Thus, references to the volume are by page number, followed by a slash and the appropriate line number of the specific section of text noted--e.g., 287/3-26.)
POWELL, Ralph A.
    1986. "From Semiotic of Scientific Mechanism to Semiotic of Teleology in Nature", in *Semiotics 1986*, ed. John Deely and Jonathan Evans (Lanham, Maryland: University Press of America, 1987).
    1988. "Degenerate Secondness in Peirce's Belief in God", in *ACPA Proceedings* LXII.
SEBEOK, Thomas Albert.
    1963. "Review of Communication among Social Bees; Porpoises and Sonar; Man and Dolphin", in *Language* 39.3, 448-466, partially reprinted in Deely et al. 1986: 74-75, to which excerpt page reference is made in this volume.
    1987. "Language: How Primary a Modeling System?", in *Semiotics 1987*, ed. John Deely (Lanham, Maryland: University Press of America, 1988), 15-27.

VOLOŠINOV, V. N.
   1929. *Marksism i filosofiia iazyka. Osnovnye problemy sotsiologicheskogo metoda v nauke o iazyke*, translated by Ladislav Matejka and I. R. Titunik as *Marxism and the Philosophy of Language* (New York: Seminar Press, 1973), to which translation page references are keyed.

WINANCE, Elenthère.
   1983. Review article in *Revue Thomiste* 83.3, 514-516.

A SEMIOTIC CLASSIFICATION OF PROPER NAMES

Jeffrey R. DiLeo
Indiana University, Bloomington

I. Introduction

    The study of proper names has a rich history. Philosophies of language, from Plato's *Cratylus* through Wittgenstein's *Philosophical Investigations*, have discussed and debated the nature of proper names. Although semiotic concerns have been raised by many philosophies of language throughout history, in no other philosophy of language do they have a more central and crucial role than in the work of Charles Sanders Peirce.
    While pursuing the study of signs, Peirce sought to interweave and relate semiotic concerns to all aspects of his philosophy of language. Peirce was a systematic thinker, and believed that it was not in his "power to study anything,--mathematics, ethics, metaphysics, gravitation, thermodynamics, optics, chemistry, comparative anatomy, astronomy, psychology, phonetics, economic, the history of science, whist, men and women, wine, metrology, except as a study of semiotic . . ." (Peirce 1908: 85-86). Although in many instances, philosophical issues pertaining to language amount to semiotic questions, Peirce's conception of philosophy is broader than his theory of signs. One need only to recall his classification of the sciences to verify this.[1] Nonetheless, Peirce's approach to problems in the philosophy of language might be described as "semiotico-philosophico".
    This paper will examine the significance and meaning of Peirce's classification of proper names within his ten classes of signs.[2] The development of arguments as to why Peirce's semiotic classification of proper names is unambiguous and exclusive within the ten classes of signs will serve a dual purpose. Not only will it provide an overview of the way in which his semiotic accommodates a classic topic in the philosophy of language, but it will also reveal how Peirce deals with a major problem in semiotics, specifically that of the unambiguous classification of semiotic phenomena. In evaluating Peirce's semiotic classification of proper names, the interdependent character of philosophical and semiotic concerns utilized in maintaining its exclusiveness and lack of ambiguity should become evident, although it cannot be developed in this essay. Let us begin by refreshing our memory, albeit superficially, as to how the ten classes of signs are determined, and what exactly they are, before examining Peirce's explicit classification of proper names amongst them.

II. Peirce's Ten Classes of Signs: A Glance

A "sign" is defined by Peirce as "anything which is so determined by something else, called its Object, and so determines an effect upon a person, which effect I call its Interpretant, that the latter is thereby mediately determined by the former" (Peirce 1908: 80-81). As such, a sign is the subject of a triadic relation, involving the *sign* in itself, an *object* or what the sign stands for, and an *interpretant* or the equivalent sign which the first sign creates in the mind of the person apprehending it. Thus, based on the triadic nature of the sign, he distinguished three *divisions* of signs: (1) the sign in itself, (2) the sign as related to its object, and (3) the sign as interpreted to represent an object.

In turn, because all phenomena whatsoever possess three aspects of being, each of these three divisions of signs must be specifiable under the categories of Firstness, Secondness, and Thirdness. As a result, each of the three divisions become trichotomies. The subdivisions of the divisions are as follows: the first division (trichotomy) is subdivided into the *qualisign*, a quality which is a sign; the *sinsign*, an actual existent thing or event which is a sign; and the *legisign*, a law which is a sign. The second division is subdivided into the *icon*, a sign which refers to the object that it denotes merely by virtue of characters of its own, and which it possesses just the same, whether the object exists or not; the *index*, a sign which refers to the object that it denotes by virtue of being really affected by that object; and the *symbol*, a sign which refers to the object that it denotes by virtue of a law. Finally, the third division is subdivided into the *rheme*, a sign of qualitative possibility for its interpretant; *dicisign*, a sign of actual existence for its interpretant; and *argument*, a sign of law for its interpretant (Peirce c.1903: 138-146).

Consequently, the application of Peirce's principle (c.1903: 2.235-237), which claims that a First is determined only by a First; a Second is determined only by a Second or a First; and a Third is determined by a Third, a Second or a First, to the three trichotomies yields Peirce's ten classes of signs: (1) (rhematic iconic) qualisign; (2) (rhematic) iconic sinsign; (3) rhematic indexical sinsign; (4) dicent (indexical) sinsign; (5) (rhematic) iconic legisign; (6) rhematic indexical legisign; (7) dicent indexical legisign; (8) rhematic symbolic (legisign); (9) dicent symbolic (legisign); and (10) argument (symbolic legisign) (Peirce c.1903: 2.254-264).[3]

III. A Semiotic Classification of Proper Names

Peirce defined a "proper name" as "a name of anything considered as a single thing; and this thing which the Proper Name denominates must have been one with which the Interpreter was already acquainted by direct or indirect experience" (Peirce 1908a: 32). Within his ten principle classes of signs, Peirce (1904: 35) explicitly classifies proper names as *rhematic indexical legisigns*. The classification of proper names as rhematic indexical legisigns is significant not only for giving both direct and indirect insight into his philosophy of language, and theories of names, naming and proper names, but also because it places proper names in a unique relationship among other semiotic phenomena. Although it would be ideal to embark on an extended discussion as to how and why a proper name is a rhematic indexical legisign, such a discussion would take this paper well beyond its limits. Nevertheless, it is important to have a general understanding as to what the classification of proper names as rhematic indexical legisigns means before any consideration of alternative classifications.

In a letter to Lady Welby, Peirce (1904: 32) claims that a proper name, considered as a legisign, "has a definite identity, though usually admitting a great variety of appearances". He (Peirce 1904: 33) goes on to tell Lady Welby that, as an index, a proper name is a sign determined by its object by virtue of being in a real relation to it. Finally, Peirce (1904: 34) explains to Lady Welby that as a rheme, a proper name is "any sign that is not true nor false, like almost any single word," and also that a proper name is "defined as a sign which is represented in its signified interpretant as *if it were* a character or mark".

Given these cursory remarks on the rhematic, indexical and legisign aspects of proper names that Peirce wrote to Lady Welby on October 12, 1904, some of the general characteristics of proper names may be summarized as follows: a) proper names do not have truth values, viz., proper names are rhematic; b) proper names have a definite identity, although they are usually admitted through an appearance, viz., proper names are legisigns; c) proper names have a real relationship with their dynamic object, viz., proper names are indexical. From these three general characteristics of proper names, and characteristics derivative from them, it is possible to develop a complete theory of proper names.[4]

At this point, we know some important points concerning proper names. Among them are Peirce's classification of proper names within his ten classes of signs, and a general understanding as to what it means to make this classification. With this we can now ask a major question of his semiotic classification of proper names as rhematic indexical legisigns: Are there any other viable classifications of proper names among the remaining nine classes? That is to say, could Peirce classify proper names as one or more of the remaining nine classifications? If so, would his position remain consistent?

IV. A Consideration of Alternative Classifications

In pursuing the possibility of alternative semiotic classifications of proper names, it must be assumed that each of the three subdivisions of each of the three divisions (trichotomies) of signs is not exclusive, but rather comprise an inclusive disjunction.[5] This implies that if it is assumed that something is to be classified as a legisign, then it is not inconsistent to also classify it as a qualisign and/or a sinsign. If we were to assume that the subdivisions within the divisions are exclusive, rather than inclusive, it would be superfluous to ask whether or not something which Peirce tells us is a legisign, is also a qualisign and/or a sinsign. If the subdivisions within the divisions were exclusive, then there should not be the problem of the ambiguous classification of semiotic phenomena: If something is classified as a legisign, then there is no possibility that it is also a sinsign and/or a qualisign.

In order to conduct a complete survey of the possible alternative semiotic classifications of proper names systematically, we shall examine each of the three divisions of signs, attempting to show that proper names are exclusively classifiable within each division of signs. Let us begin by examining the first division of signs, which represents the sign in itself, and ask if it is possible that a proper name could be a qualisign and/or a sinsign as well as a legisign.

If a proper name were a qualisign, then like a legisign it would not be an individual thing. It would differ in that it would be "the mere quality of an appearance" and would not be "exactly the same throughout a second" (Peirce 1904: 33). Unlike a legisign, which "has a definite identity, though usually admitting a great variety of appearances," a qualisign "has *great similarity*, & cannot differ without being called quite another qualisign" (Peirce 1904: 33).

As a qualisign, a proper name would not have its law-like character or definite identity, and would signify through its abstractable quality--through the Firstness of quality. This would mean, for example, that if I said the word "Plato" to identify the person to whom I wish to speak, there would be some quality of the spoken word "Plato" essential to it as a sign of the person to whom I wish to speak. But of what quality is the spoken word "Plato" a sign? What quality, abstractable from the individual occurrence of the sound of my saying "Plato" would signify the person to whom I wish to speak? It seems certain that any quality abstractable from the sound of my saying "Plato" is completely irrelevant to it as a proper name. Clearly, a proper name is not a qualisign, thus eliminating the possibility of classifying proper names as rhematic iconic qualisigns.

A proper name considered as a sinsign, would be an individual, actual, existent thing or event which is a sign. As such, a proper name such as "Plato," could be found five times on a single page, and Peirce would contend that they would count as five words. However, in another sense of the word "word," there is but one word "Plato" in the English language; "and it is impossible that this word should lie visibly on a page or be heard in any voice, for the reason that it is not a Single thing or a Single event" (Peirce 1906: 4.537). Peirce would claim that the one word in the English language, "Plato," "does not exist; it only determines things that do exist" (Peirce 1906: 4.537). Such a word--a proper name--is termed a "Type" or legisign by Peirce (c.1903: 2.246), whereas "a Single event which happens once and whose identity is limited to that one happening or a Single object or thing which is in some single place at any one instant of time, such event or thing being significant only as occurring just when and where it does, such as this or that word on a single line of a single page of a single copy of a book . . ." is called a "Token," or a sinsign (Peirce 1906: 4.537).

Peirce contends that in order that a proper name, or a legisign (type) may be used, it has to be embodied in a sinsign (token) which shall be a sign of the proper name (legisign), and thereby the object the proper name (legisign) signifies. A sinsign (token) of a legisign (type) is an "Instance" of the legisign (Peirce 1906: 4.537) Thus, a proper name, which is clearly a legisign, has a very definite relation to a sinsign. A proper name is general for Peirce, hence it can only function through an instance or "Replica" of itself, but this instance or replica of itself, in turn, involves qualisigns. Accordingly, a proper name or legisign, may have many different sorts of sinsigns. Thus, even though the use of proper names, or legisigns, involves sinsigns and qualisigns, a proper name is not itself a sinsign or a qualisign. With this, three more alternative classifications may be eliminated: rhematic iconic sinsigns, rhematic indexical sinsigns, and dicent indexical sinsigns. Let us now turn our attention to the second division of signs--icon, index and symbol--which concern the relation of a sign to its object (Peirce 1904: 33).

Given that a proper name is a legisign, we must first consider whether or not a proper name can be an "iconic" legisign. Peirce defines an iconic relation as one of likeness or resemblance between the sign and the object, wherein the sign has some quality or character that it shares with its object regardless of whether or not its object actually exists. An iconic legisign is for Peirce (c.1903: 2.258) "any general law or type, in so far as it requires each instance of it to embody a definite quality which renders it fit to call up in the mind the idea of a like object". Furthermore, the mode of being of an iconic legisign is that of governing single replicas or tokens, i.e., iconic legisigns exist only through tokens or replicas which the legisign governs. Examples of iconic legisigns are a diagram or an architectural blueprint, apart from its factual individuality or the word "word". Thus, as an iconic legisign, a proper name will share some resemblance of form or structure with its object, but is this at all possible?

The proper name "Plato" could not be said to have an iconic relation with its object because it is simply absurd to claim that "Plato," per se resembles in form or structure some quality characteristic of its object. Even when a proper name is indicative of or denotes a particular quality of its object, for example, the proper names "Slim" or "Shorty", it is not an iconic legisign because there is nothing in the structure or form of the proper name "Shorty" that resembles its object. It is by convention, not iconicity, that "Shorty" evokes an image of "shortness", which in turn resembles its object. As such, "Shorty" is better understood as a common name, rather than a proper name, given the conventionality of its relation to its object.

One way "Shorty" might be considered to have an iconic resemblance with its object would be if it were written with letters lower in height relative to the other letters in the passage. Better yet, a short man could be sketched or caricatured on a sheet of paper to resemble, in some way, an object. In turn, this sketch or caricature might be considered the proper name of the object which it resembles. Even though both of these examples might be considered iconic legisigns, they are not proper names without a real existential relationship with their objects. Proper names are always indexical. Hence, rhematic iconic legisign is not a viable semiotic classification for proper names. Even though a proper name might share an iconic relationship with its object, it must also have an indexical relationship with the self-same object. Next, we must consider whether or not a proper name has a symbolic relation to its object.

A symbol is a sign which is determined by its object "only in the sense that it will be so interpreted" and "depends either upon a convention, a habit, or a natural disposition of its interpretant..." (Peirce 1904: 33). Peirce (c.1902: 329) writes that a

> proper name, when one meets with it for the first time, is existentially connected with some percept or other equivalent individual knowledge of the individual it names. It is then, and then only, a genuine Index. The next time one meets with it, one regards it as an Icon of that Index. The habitual acquaintance with it having been acquired, it becomes a Symbol whose Interpretant represents it as an Icon of an Index of the Individual named.

Thus, according to Peirce, a proper name is only a genuine index if one has not met with it before. The point of positing that proper names are genuine indices only on the first meeting with them is that after this the proper name serves to order and retrieve information concerning some existing or fictitious object. The next time one meets with the proper name, it is no longer a genuine index, but is to be regarded as an icon of that index, or what Peirce calls a subindex or hyposeme. It is interesting to note that habitual acquaintance with a proper name eventually renders a symbolic relationship to its object. This leads to the question as to whether or not this symbol is a proper name.

We must remember that a proper name has an inherent indexical connection with its object, whereas a symbol does not. This implies that a symbol can be considered in relation to any object depending on the relation of the symbol to its interpretant, whereas a proper name has some real (existential) relation with its object. This existential relation that a proper name has with its object exists as a matter of brute fact, known only through experience and not uniquely identifiable only through a general description.

Peirce (1906: 4.544) claims that

> [a]ll general, or definable words, whether in the sense of Types or of Tokens, are certainly Symbols. That is to say, they denote the objects that they do by virtue only of there being a habit that associates their signification with them. As to Proper Names, there might be a difference of opinion, especially if the Tokens are meant. But they should probably

be regarded as Indices, since the actual connection (as we listen to talk), of Instances of the same typical words with the same Objects, alone causes them to be interpreted as denoting those Objects.

When a proper name takes on a symbolic relation to its interpretant, it becomes, in effect, a common name (or common noun). In renouncing its real existential relation to its object, and shifting to a symbolic relation to its interpretant, a proper name does not function as a 'genuine' proper name, but more like a common noun. Whereas "[e]very language must have proper names . . . " (Peirce c.1902: 2.328), Peirce (1904:33) claims that common nouns are not a necessary part of speech.

For Peirce, proper names must always be regarded as indices, even though they loosely might be thought of as symbols. Thus, because a proper name does not have a symbolic relation to its object, it cannot be classified as either a rhematic symbolic legisign, dicent symbolic legisign or an argumentative symbolic legisign. With eight possible classifications of the proper name having been eliminated, there is only one more classification to consider: dicent indexical legisign, which brings us to a consideration of Peirce's third division of signs.

The third division of signs is concerned with logical arguments and has to do with the way in which the sign is represented by its interpretant. This division of signs corresponds to "the old division Term, Proposition, and Argument" (Peirce 1904: 33). Peirce (1904:33) explicitly states that a rheme, or a "Term is simply a class-name or proper-name". A rheme is a not a proposition, nor does it express a proposition--it is a "blank form of proposition" (Peirce 1906: 4.560). Peirce states that "[t]he readiest characteristic test showing whether a sign is a Dicisign or not is that a Dicisign is either true or false . . ." (Peirce c.1902: 2.310). From this "characteristic test," one can easily determine that a proper name is not a dicisign, for Peirce (1904: 34) has already told us that a proper name is a "sign that is not true nor false". Thus, proper names fail Peirce's characteristic test for dicisigns, or propositions: a proper name is not a dicisign. With the elimination of dicisign, the last possible alternative semiotic classification of proper names, that is, dicent indexical legisign, has been disqualified as a possible classification.

V. Concluding Comments

The classification of semiotic phenomena into unique categories is an aim of any complex, semiotic, classificatory system such as Peirce's. This aim, in turn, leads to the well-documented and fiercely debated question as to which category various semiotic phenomena should occupy. Any theory of sign classification should exhibit a precise method and criteria whereby varying semiotic phenomena can be assigned a unique status in the classificatory scheme. One is less likely to criticize a system that is capable of consistently classifying semiotic phenomena uniquely, than one that does not. It also seems plausible that the more semiotic phenomena that the classification system is capable of uniquely classifying, the less controversy the system is liable to attract.

This paper considered the classification of one specific type of semiotic phenomena: proper names. Although the proper name is probably not the most problematic semiotic phenomenon to classify, its classification exhibits the fact that the criteria whereby semiotic phenomena are classified can be determined by and reflect more than semiotic concerns. Peirce is able to maintain a unique classification for proper names by allowing his criteria for the semiotic classification of proper names to reflect both the semiotic and the philosophical nature of proper names.[6]

NOTES

[1] Peirce (1903: 1.180-202) classified Theoretical Science into the Sciences of Discovery and the Sciences of Review. Under the former, he lists Mathematics, Philosophy and Idioscopy, further dividing Philosophy into Phenomenology, Normative Science and Metaphysics. The suborders of Normative Science are Esthetics, Ethics and Semiotic (or Logic). The families of Semiotic are Speculative Grammar, Critic, and Methodeutic.

[2] Given the length restrictions of this paper, it will be possible to consider only Peirce's classification of proper names within his ten classes of signs, while postponing the lengthy task of pursuing his classification of proper names within the sixty-six and/or 59,049 classes of signs.

[3] According to Peirce, designations among the ten classes in parentheses are superfluous (Peirce c.1903: 150).

[4] This claim is defended by and based on work that I have done elsewhere on this subject.

[5] The assumption of exclusiveness might, at times, seem contrary to Peirce's intention. For example, in his October 12, 1904 letter to Lady Welby, Peirce (1904: 34) claims that ". . . a sign is either of the nature of an appearance, when I call it a *qualisign*; or secondly, it is an individual object or event, when I call it a *sinsign* . . . or thirdly, it is of the nature of a general type, when I call it a *legisign*." It is debatable whether or not this statement should be read as an exclusive or an inclusive disjunction. For the sake of argument, I will assume that it is inclusive.

[6] I wish to acknowledge the generous assistance given to me by Nathan Houser and Dinda L. Gorlee.

REFERENCES

PEIRCE, Charles S.
  c. 1902. "Syllabus", which appears in the *Collected Papers of Charles Sanders Peirce*, in 8 volumes, 1-6 ed. Charles Hartshorne and Paul Weiss, 7-8 ed. Arthur Burks (Cambridge, Massachusetts: Harvard University Press, 1931-58). Referred to as CP followed by the volume and paragraph numbers. This piece is CP 2.309-331.
  c. 1903. "Nomenclature and Divisions of Triadic Relations, as far as they are determined", which appears in the CP 2.233-2.272.
  1903. *A Syllabus of Certain Topics of Logic*, 5-9, which appears in CP 1.180-202.
  1904. Letter to Lady Welby dated 12 October 1904, which appears in *Semiotic and Significs: The Correspondence between Charles S. Peirce and Victoria Lady Welby*, ed. Charles Hardwick, (Bloomington: Indiana University Press, 1977): 22-36.
  1906. "Prolegomena to an Apology for Pragmaticism", *The Monist* 16 (October), 492-546, reprinted in the CP 4.530-572. Page reference in the present essay is to the CP reprint.
  1908. Letter to Lady Welby dated 23 December 1908, which appears in Hartwick (1977), 73-86.
  1908a. "Chapter I. Common Ground (Logic)", MS 612.

THE RELATION BETWEEN PEIRCE'S REALISM AND HIS IDEA OF THE SIGN

Terrance King
Wayne State University

Consider the sense of symmetry evoked by binary oppositions like *right/left, good/bad, nature/culture*. By "sense of symmetry" I mean the correlative equivalence binary oppositions like these generate, a sense of mutual dependency in which each of the terms simultaneously excludes yet invokes its companion. As William Blake puts it, "opposition is true friendship" (c. 1793: 42) because the difference that separates two binary terms depends upon an underlying sameness. In the 50s Jakobson, who applied formal Saussurean principles to oppositional equivalence (1956: 55-82), argued that is was a result of one of two basic language operations of the brain. Jakobson's work succeeded in raising an old question about the connection between language and the world in a new and interesting way: does the equivalence of binary oppositions indicate a capacity to structure the world through language or does it show the mind's ability to discover relations already in the world? Or put another way, are binary oppositions rhetorical instruments involving power or are they cognitive tools involving truth? The complexity of the problem is indicated by the fact that in order to ask this very question, we have to already assume that there are at least a few binary oppositions that are rhetoric-exempt, namely, *rhetoric/ knowledge, power/truth*, and *language/world*. With this kind of circulatory is it any wonder why Jakobson identified the principle of oppositional equivalence with a rhetorical trope, namely, metaphor? In my discussion of Peirce a little further into this paper, I will argue that the upshot of Jakobson's work is the suggestion that rhetoric is integral to language function and that it is therefore impossible to distinguish, in any firm and unrevisable sense, rhetoric and knowledge, power and truth, language and world.

Since the 50s the rhetorical status of binary oppositions has emerged as a significant area of concern across a number of disciplines engaged in the study of language. In the research of those working in Jakobson's own tradition--people like Henning Anderson (1974), Michael Shapiro (1976), and James Liszka (1985)--a case has been made for a rhetorical dimension of binary opposition that Jakobson himself did not consider. For in this more recent work, we find evidence for the view that at every level of language, from phoneme to myth, the so-called symmetry of binary opposition is in fact an illusion necessary to the rhetoric of this form: it is argued that instead of just a simple correlativity along, say, a horizontal plane, there is a culturally imposed hierarchy down a vertical axis. Rhetorically speaking (in the actual language use of Western cultures, say) one does not have a purely symmetrical geometry of right versus left, good versus bad, nature versus culture, but an asymmetrical hierarchy where one term presents itself as superior to its companion, a case of right *over* left, good *over* bad, nature *over* culture. And in founding deconstruction, Derrida--even though his response is to Husserl rather than Jakobson--makes the same point from a philosophical angle, declaring that in Western philosophical discourse binary oppositions are hierarchizing gestures of language that protect vested ideological and metaphysical interests.[1]

I

This problematic of the rhetoric of binary opposition seems far removed from Peirce, who at the other end of this century was committed to using language in the relatively unworried manner of the previous age, namely, that of nineteenth-century system building, which in his case was modestly aimed at explaining quite literally everything. There is pervasive in Peirce's thinking a scientistic point of view that does not see language itself as problematic but treats it rather as something that should ideally work as only a transparent instrument of the scientific mind. As the title of his well-known essay, "How to Make Our Ideas Clear" (1878), plainly indicates, language is to be treated, not as a complication involving thinking, but simply a tool *of* thinking. Even if Peirce were engaged in the issues of today, he would not likely take sides with deconstruction, since his philosophy aims to build a positive and totalistic model of the world. Moreover, the thrust of his architectonic theory is explicitly anti-nominalist: there is, he believed firmly, a real world beyond the language categories we use to represent this world. And yet Peirce's realism is, to say the least, quite unlike most theories one would call realist. The reason of course is that what is real for him is the sign, and if a semiotic realism is to be consistent, it cannot in any way afford to have only an uncomplicated--i.e., instrumental--view of language. And as it turns out, there is nearly as much evidence for this other, more complicated view of language in Peirce as there is for his instrumental perspective. For even during the middle years when "How to Make Our Ideas Clear" was written, the relation between thinking and language does not appear in his prose as only a simple agent-versus-tool connection but one in which cognition and language seem to fuse as a single identity. In his later years, this identity tends to be more explicitly portrayed: "It is wrong to say that a good language is *important* to good thought, merely; for it is the essence of it. . . . Every symbol is a living thing, in a very strict sense that is no mere figure of speech" (1903: 2.220, 222).

But the most interesting turn of Peirce's realism is that his critique of nominalism turns out to be an attack against a dualistic perspective, and one that (even though his language is not explicit in this respect) emerges in effect as a brilliant analysis of the rhetoric of binary opposition. In other words, Peirce's realism does not, in the manner of a positivistic realism, utilize and uphold binaristic categories; it rather assumes a philosophical position that serves to expose binaristic categories for what they are at least in part, namely, rhetorical gestures--language as a force rather than language as a transparent medium. Peirce most of all opposes the atomistic point of view he believes binaristic categories induce, the opinion that the most elemental issues involve questions about self-contained essences like "mind" as opposed to "matter", "word" as opposed to "referent", "law" as opposed to "process". He argues rather that the more fundamental the issue, the greater the need for a holistic perspective in which, in a most basic respect, there is everywhere operative a principle of continuity, in which nothing is so discrete and distinct from something else that it can symmetrically implicate it as an absolute opposite. Thus to describe this monistic, holistically conceived universe, Peirce builds into his model a kind of inherent instability: he has asymmetrically derived triadic categories replace symmetrically conceived binary categories and thereby, even in spite of his own idealist modifications, portrays an evolutionary world without center or circumference, origin or destiny.

In Peirce's model, it is a question, not on one hand, of a centralized self-identity (namely, the mind) interpreting on the other hand its symmetrical opposite (the world) but of one sign interpreting another sign to create a third sign, which itself, may, down the road, serve as the interpretant of another sign to create still another, and so on indefinitely. Let us take the case of someone reading a book containing numerous photographs. Peirce would agree with common sense that the brain events of a reader would interpret the verbal and iconic events of say a particular page, but he would insist in addition that information is also generated from the opposite direction, that in fact the verbal and iconic signs of the page interpret the brain events of the reader: both sets of signs participate together in a process-as-a-whole that generates new signs in the form of, for example, fresh ideas and spur-of-the-moment annotations. We can speak here of a domain of semiotic interaction, but it is misleading to divide this domain into two wholly separate realms--of, say, interior mental signs on one hand and exterior physical signs on the other, or again, of cultural signs (the verbal symbols) as opposed to natural signs (the iconic images of the photographs). It is better here to speak of only a *conversation* of signs and to note that within this conversation there is no executive center, no "mind" governing the process. This is not to say, of course, that Peirce would regard an activity like reading a book as purposeless, but rather that he would frame his notion of purpose within the holistic terms of the whole process. And since he refuses to limit his notion of semiotic process by applying a binary notion of a definable beginning and end--the view of an infinite "semiosis"--his idea of purpose becomes in practical terms identifiable with only the local coherence of a given domain of interaction at a particular point in time. Any domain of sign-interaction like the activity of an individual and a book mutually interpreting one another may be viewed as a "whole" in only a limited and relative sense, for any given whole may itself, on a different order, function as a sign within another domain made coherent by a subsuming order of purpose. And so on and so on. Hence in Peirce's idea of the sign there is a recursive principle in which the same triadic pattern of development repeats itself indefinitely and generates in the process a newness in which variety and scale quite literally have no knowable limit.

II

It might be argued at this point that my use of the word *purpose* to suggest a principle of coherence amounts to talk about law but that in spite of Peirce's attempt to overcome the symmetrical lock-up of all binary opposition, there is still the inevitable dualism between process and law, between for example the activity of reading a book and all the principles (psychological, linguistic, environmental) that regulate the activity of reading a book. But Peirce might ask in return why it is necessary to conceive of law as some static fiat extrinsic and opposite to process. Why not view law, he might ask, as merely an aspect of the self-same process, only taken now in its "tendency . . . to behave in a similar way under similar circumstances in the future" (c. 1906: 5.487). In Peirce, in other words, all law is law-in-time, what he calls "habit", a disposition toward coherence and regularity arising to constitute a particular domain, developing within this domain, and across time, perhaps transmuting into new forms.

In Peirce, then, we find a radical attempt to eliminate the sense of separateness and self-containment generated by binary terms: any domain of semiotic interaction is one with the habits disposing this domain toward coherence, and similarly, the individual signs composing the domain are one with the domain as a whole. In fact the generality of the individual signs lies at the core of Peirce's notion of realism. Of course from an atomistic point of view his unitary realism may seem quite ridiculous. For under an atomism, after all, a law is one kind of distinct existent, an individual sign another, and the collective reality of the general domain in which signs interact still another. But within Peirce's holistic concept, law and process, individuality and generality, all constitute the same sign. We recall that the medieval debate between nominalism and realism arose over this problematic relation between individuality and generality: the realists maintained that both generality and individuality are part of the world, while the nominalists argued that the world reveals only individual essences and that generality belongs only to the categories of the language which we use to talk about the world but which, according to nominalism, the realists mistakenly attribute to the world itself.

For Peirce, however, the mistake lies rather with nominalism: universals--or what he calls "generals"--may indeed be identified with language, but all the rest of the world also reveals generals because this all-the-rest-of-the-world is continuous with language. They are both forms of sign process. The semiotic activity of language is paradigmatic of the evolving universe, and in either case the sign is both individual and general at the same time. Whereas for the nominalists, the real world is a substantive object atomistically composed of individual essences, for Peirce this substantiveness is a mirage created by--he can read as saying tacitly--the essentializing rhetoric of binary oppositions. For practical reasons we may need to treat the world as a fixed solid, and in this sense this process of essentialization may be altogether necessary, but such reasons do not in any way justify the idea that it is in fact such. As W.B. Gallie points out (1966: 153-156), Peirce's realism is *relational* and not "substantival": if I see an individual rose in a garden, its redness is real, not because--as medieval realists believed--the abstract property redness exists somewhere as an individual essence, but because this rose in all its properties occurs relationally within some context, a context of law. In a semiotic sense this context of law is nothing but a given domain made up of habits and signs interacting in certain ways. Permit me to stress one more time that between part and whole, law and process, sing and sign-governing-whole, there is for Peirce no absolute distinction. Information is here growth, development, change; and as such it is determined, not by any term taken by itself alone but by the whole--i.e., the particular domain of interaction--in which it occurs and the habits that make this whole cohere at a certain point in time.

Hence, if posed the question, "What is the nature of truth?" Peirce would not base an answer on a firm binary correspondence between mind and reality but only on the kind of conversational model I mentioned earlier, a conversation, let us imagine it, among various types of interlocutors, with each one sharing *both* difference and sameness with all the rest. Now in a semiotic sense, remember, these interlocutors are nothing but signs engaged in the kind of interpretive interaction I described in the case of someone reading a book. And so, since any interlocutor-sign within this conversation--and this could be a human being, of course--is identified not with its individuality alone but with the whole of which it is a part, Peirce is free to characterize truth, not with some state of self-identity an individual may feel he or she holds, but with the accord or consensus ideally achieved within the general domain--call it the "institutional whole"--which Peirce believes constitutes a person as much as individuality does. "A person", he explains, "is not absolutely an individual. . . . The man's circle of society (however widely or narrowly this phrase may be understood), is a sort of loosely compacted person, in some respects of higher rank than the person of an individual organism" (1905: 5.421).

III

Peirce's trust in institutional consensus does suggest that he is eager to contain the question of truth within a notion of utopian closure. Truth, in other words, still seems to be idealized within the closed terms of some self-contained immanence, only now we are asked to call it an institution rather than a subject. And of course it is not just any institution that is so privileged, but Peirce's own, namely, the scientific community. Two contradictory impulses are discernible in Peirce. On one hand, he readily admits to the revisability of any and all assertions, including his own. For as his evolutionary notion of fallibilism makes clear, the truth of any assertion is integral to a limiting past, with all its accumulated insight and bias, and to a limiting future with all its unpredictable possibleness. On the other hand, his founding notion of pragmatism also makes it clear that he is loathe to apply these fallibilistic constraints to science as a whole; and science, while it would readily admit to the provisionality of its work as practice, nevertheless envisions its work as a whole as a *progress*, which involves the very reduction of a future as an "unpredictable possibleness". In effect, Peirce replaces an atomistic and naive scientism--namely, positivism--with a more coherent, holistically conceived scientism.

But a scientism nevertheless. Where I part company from Peirce lies not in his scientific optimism *per se*--in which truth is envisioned as an ideal at the end of a navigable line of closer and closer approximations. It is rather in the way he suggests that this optimism is justified on a universal scale by the logic of his own semiotic model. By this logic, rather, scientific optimism can be justified, not in universal, but only local terms, the unavoidably parochial terms of scientific rationality itself, which it a habit--one of many--of making sense of the world. In Peirce, then, binary opposition comes in through the back door as it were, appearing now as the final truth holding between science and the world. And yet here at the end I don't want to sound as if I'm dismissing Peirce or, worse, pretending to provide a definitive interpretation of his achievement. I merely want to suggest that all of Peirce--his contradictions as well as his insights--seem to indicate that any inquiry into what is truly real must include the issue of binary opposition as part of its problematic.

NOTES

[1] Perhaps Derrida's most explicit enunciation of the relation between hierarchizing binary categories and Western philosophy appears in his *Limited Inc*.: "All metaphysicians have proceeded thus, from Plato to Rousseau, from Descartes to Husserl: good before evil, the positive before the negative, the pure before the impure, the simple before the complex, the essential before the accidental, the imitated before the imitation, etc. This is not just *one* metaphysical gesture among others; it is the metaphysical exigency, the most constant, profound, and potent procedure" (1977: 236).

REFERENCES

ANDERSON, Henning.
    1974. "Towards a Typology of Change: Bifurcating Changes and Binary Relations", in *Historical Linguistics* (= North Holland Linguistic Series 12a-12b), ed. Henning Anderson and Charles Jones, 2 vols. (Amsterdam: North Holland) 2, 17-60.

BLAKE, William.
    c.1793. "The Marriage of Heaven and Hell", in *The Complete Poetry and Prose of William Blake*, ed. David V. Erdman (Berkeley: University of California Press, 1982), pp. 33-45.

DERRIDA, Jacques.
    1977. *Limited Inc.*, supplement to *Glyph 2* (Baltimore: John Hopkins University Press), with Samuel Weber's English translation in *Glyph 2* (1977), 162-254.

GALLIE, W.B.
    1966. *Peirce and Pragmatism* (New York: Dover).

JAKOBSON, Roman and Morris HALL.
    1956. *Fundamentals of Languages* (The Hague: Mouton).

LISZKA, James Jakob.
    1985. "Mythic Violence: Hierarchy and Transvaluation", *Semiotica*, 54.1-2, 227-249.

PEIRCE, Charles Sanders.
    1860-1908. *The Collected Papers of Charles Sanders Peirce*, in 8 vols., 1-6 ed. Charles Harshorne and Paul Weiss, 7-8 ed. Arthur W. Burks (Cambridge: Harvard University Press, 1931-1958). Abbreviated as CP with numbers to the right indicating volume and paragraphs.
    1878. "How to Make Our Ideas Clear", in *Popular Science Monthly* 12 (Jan.), 286-302, reprinted in CP 5.388-410.
    1903. "The Ethics of Terminology", in *Syllabus of Certain Types of Logic* (Boston: Alfred Mudge and Son), pp. 10-14, reprinted in CP 2.219-226.
    1905. "What Pragmatism Is", *The Monist* 15 (April), 161-181, reprinted in *CP* 5.411-437.
    c.1906. Survey of Pragmatism, unpublished ms. reproduced in CP 5.464-496.

SHAPIRO, Michael.
    1976. *Asymmetry: An Inquiry into the Linguistic Structure of Poetry* (New York: North Holland Publishing Company).

PEIRCE, SAUSSURE, AND THE CONCEPT OF TRANSVALUATION

James Jakób Liszka
University of Alaska

I want to show that despite their many dissimilarities, there is a family resemblance between Peirce's notion of the interpretant and Saussure's concept of value. I also want to show how a semiotic operation I call *transvaluation* can be developed out of their synthesis.

According to Peirce, a sign is a sign by virtue of establishing a triadic relation between itself, its referent and what Peirce calls its interpretant (1905: 5.484). An interpretant in its singular sense is any particular sign which can be developed, inferred from some previous sign, i.e., what Peirce calls "translated" (1906: 5.509; 1898: 5.594); 1893: 4.127); 1868: 5.284). In its more general and formal sense, the interpretant is a rule of such sign translation; and in its ultimate sense, the interpretant is a habit or rule of action which establishes a mode of interpretation for some interpreting agency (1909: 110; c.1906: 5.476). The interpretant embodies the triadic aspect of the sign-relation, for it coordinates, on the one hand, the sign's ability to refer to an object, that is, its extension, with the sign's intension, that is, as constituted by its relation to other signs which form a system with it.

Already in the early development of the concept of the interpretant, Peirce emphasizes its function as the synthesizer or coordinator of sense and reference, breadth and depth. Peirce called the result of this coordination, *information* (c.1903: 3.608), which I like to hyphenate since it exploits a certain ambiguity in the term. One the one hand, it suggests that meaning accrues through structuration, i.e., giving form to non-meaningful differences. It is in-formation in that the differences which organize a system of signs become meaningful through the mediation of a referent, i.e., that act of anchoring the system in another outside of itself. At the same time, the referent, which may itself be a sign belonging to a different set of differences receives meaning through its coordination with another system. On the other hand, the effect of such coordination creates information in the normal sense of creating a set of meaningful messages for some interpreting agency. As Peirce expresses it information, as the quantity of the interpretant, is the area of breadth and depth, sense and reference (c.1867a: 2.49). That means, as articulated in propositional analysis, information simultaneously establishes the depth of a breadth term and the breadth of a depth term. Let me give an example.

The traffic light coordinates two systems of signs, the set of vehicular operations associated with stopping a car and the acceleration of the vehicle, on the one hand, and red and green lights on the other. Red and green as a part of a color system stand in certain relation of difference, defined physically, physiologically and psychologically. Physically, red is the most salient color to the human eye and green is consubstantial with red; psychologically, red is said to have an irritating effect on human perceivers, while green a soothing one. Culturally, red and green have various conventional employments as well. Stopping and making a vehicle go are contrary operations which can also be articulated as a set of differences. The interpretant of the traffic light correlates a set of differences between signs in one system with that of another. At the formal level the interpretant is the rule as found in the books of the state or province; the ultimate interpretant is the habit or rule of action that is established in drivers and exemplified by the disposition to stop at read lights and go at green ones. Prior to this correlation, the difference between red and green have a sense, so to speak, but are meaningless. They simply exemplify a system of differences without being anchored in a meaning-giving correlation. On the other hand, 'stopping' and 'going' are now not just vehicular operations, but are now reorganized by means of the interpretant of the traffic light. They acquire a higher meaning by being correlated with a symbol that is purposefully designed to control traffic at intersections. As we know, for Peirce, symbol and purpose are intimately connected (c.1904: 4.261).

Despite the many differences between Peirce and Saussure, Saussure's concept of value may not necessarily be included among them. Michael Shapiro argues, in fact, that Peirce's interpretant is comparable to Saussure's notion of value (1983: 7), which I also believe to be the case; Christian Stetter argues that Saussure's chapter on value contradicts the claim that Saussure never held a triadic view of the sign (1979: 125, 127).

The traditional criticism of Saussure in light of Peirce is that Saussure's theory relies on a dualistic or dyadic theory of signs while Peirce's is triadic (Deledalle 1976a, 1976b; cf. Boone 1979). But I think this is due more to a confusion between what Saussure calls *signification* (i.1906-1911: 117) and his concept of value. Signification, as the correlation between a specific signans and signatum can only be understood and, in fact, has its possibility, in the value of the sign--"without 'value'," Saussure writes, "signification would not exist" (i.1906-1911: 117). As Saussure says in his own words, the "ultimate law of language is that nothing can reside in a single term. Since signs are correlated to what they designate, a sign cannot designate without understanding its relation to the other signs with which it forms a system" (a.1911: 63). This is why Barthes argues that Saussure increasingly concentrated on the notion of value which eventually becomes more important than that of signification (1964: 54).

Saussure uses an economic model to explain his notion of value as it applies to language which, as Roy Harris emphasizes, has an advantage over the geometric model (value as the cut through two amorphous substances), in that it assumes a coordination between two already organized systems. In the economic model, value is the means of coordination, rather than a principle of organization (1987: 220ff). According to this economic model, values are always composed: 1) of a *dissimilar* thing that can be *exchanged* for the thing of which the value is to be determined; and 2) of *similar* things that can be *compared* with the thing of which the value is to be determined (i.1906-1911: 115). To determine what a five-franc piece, for example, is worth, one must know that it can be exchanged for a fixed quantity, such as bread, and that it can be compared with a similar value of the same system, e.g., one-franc piece (i.1906-1911: 115). By analogy, a word can be exchanged for something dissimilar, an idea; but besides, it can be compared with other words, its value relies on the comparison with similar values, with other words that stand in opposition to it (i.1906-1911: 115). I venture to say that in this respect that the ability of the word to be exchanged for something dissimilar to itself, an idea or object, is comparable to the notion of reference; while the comparison of a sign within a system of signs is equivalent to the notion of sense. Saussure emphasizes that both factors, the ability of the sign to be exchanged *and* compared, "are necessary for the existence of value" (i.1906-1911: 115). The value of the sign, then, is not simply its relation with other signs in *its* system, but its relation with signs or objects *outside* of its system as well. The value of the sign, then, involves both its referential and connotational aspect, so that a signifier refers to a signified only through the mediation of the system of signifiers, while, the system of signifiers coalesces into a meaningful difference by means of its anchorage in a reference. Consequently, to the extent that value is the coordination of relations between signata and signantia, and, among signantia, in Saussure, and the interpretant is the coordination of sense and reference of a sign, then value and the interpretant are family related notions. In the end for Saussure, "a linguistic system is a series of differences of sounds combined with a series of differences of ideas; but the pairing of a certain number of acoustical signs with as many cuts made from the mass of thought engenders a system of values; and this system serves as an effective link between the phonic and psychological elements within each sign" (i.1906-1911: 120). Thus, "language is only a system of pure values" (i.1906-1911: 111).

There is no doubt that Saussure serves as an inspiration for the classical structuralist understanding of language. As exemplified by Jakobson, a sign generally belongs to a system of signs which is organized paradigmatically and syntagmatically. Using a phonological model, a system is an organization of embedded levels in which relations are established among units within any one level and among units between different levels. A syntagm is a cut through the sign system which reveals a sign at one level as composed of signs from a lower level. A paradigm is typically a binary comparison of units or signs within a certain level of the system. For example, the English phonemes, /p/ and /b/, form a paradigm, since they are contrasted by one difference syntagmatically.

So far this is the classical structuralist explication of language in which the latter is a system of signs moving from the lowest level of distinctive features to the more complex level of the grammar and lexicon. But, as Jakobson had already recognized as early as 1932--and something which Andersen and Shapiro have argued more recently, the organization of relations among signs in a system is not a set of purely symmetrical relations, but is rather a *valuative* relation, characterized in terms or markedness on the paradigmatic level and by rank on the syntagmatic one. Indeed, according to Jerome Bruner, Jakobson argued that "the most primitive and important distinction in language was between the marked and the "unmarked" (1984: 163).

Generally speaking markedness refers to the valuative relation between the two poles of an opposition which establishes an asymmetry between them. Students of markedness have disagreed on the exact attributes of that concept, but, generally speaking, most agree on the following properties (cf. Lyons 1987; Comrie 1976, 1983; Andrews 1984; Brakel 1983; Battistela 1986):

1. *Optimality*: the marked term is derivative of the unmarked. More specifically, the marked term requires the background, so to speak, of the marked one. Whenever /ü/ occurs in a language, /i/ is also present, making /i/ unmarked.

2. *Indeterminateness*: the unmarked term has more referential scope, the marked term provides more information but less referential scope. 'Man', for example is

unmarked in comparison to 'woman', since it can mean both '*Homo sapiens*' and the male species of homo sapiens.

3. *Simplicity*: the unmarked term is usually less elaborate in either its morphosyntactic make-up or in its acoustic or articulatory nature. For example, 'I *walk* to the store' as opposed to 'I walk*ed* to the store', makes the latter marked.

4. *Unrestricted Distribution*: the unmarked term has greater freedom to combine with other linguistic elements. This is related to the phenomenon of *neutralization*. For example, in the opposition between host/hostess, in the plural, the unmarked term (host) is typically used, as in 'Your hosts are Mr. and Mrs. Hill'.

An excellent non-linguistic example of markedness is found in perception, as noted by Ann Treisman. In her work, she showed that there is a certain "search asymmetry" among perceivers when targeting a certain feature in the context of its perceptual opposite. For example, if a single curved line is placed in the background of straight lines, the curved line "pops-out," that it requires less search time, then the obverse case, where a straight line is targeted with a background of curved lines. The latter involves a "serial search," and requires more time to find. In this case, as Treismann suggests (1986), straightness is coded as the absence of curvature, or the unmarked feature, curvature generating more activity on the retina than straightness, i.e., curvature is the more complex or focussed member of the opposition. This is also true in the case of long lines (unmarked) versus short ones (marked), and vertical lines (unmarked) versus oblique ones (marked).

Rank, on the other hand, is the measure of asymmetry in a syntagm. Based mostly on the work of Andersen (1979), rank has been shown to be a useful tool for phonological typology and shows how one vowel system may differ from another.

Although the notion of rank is extremely useful for linguistic typology, it can be modified for use in the analysis of other sign systems. Generally speaking, given a syntagm, the highest ranked feature is typically the feature which will represent a certain signatum regardless of the combination of other features in the syntagm. For example, in stylized representations of happy faces, all other cues may be eliminated, but the smile must remain in order to represent that emotion. In this case the smile is of high rank with respect to the representation of happiness, just as the frown is with respect to the representation of sadness. Thus, although each feature is of high rank in regard to its respective emotional response, paradigmatically, the smile and the frown form a marked relation. In most social situations (the normal presentation of self, portraiture, greeting, etc.), the smile is considered unmarked, while the frown is marked (the well-known physiological fact which requires more complex musculature to produce a frown in a way confirms its marked character).

If the interpretant is a rule of translation which organized sense and reference of signs and value, understood in the Saussurean sense, is the coordination of differences within a system of signs and between systems of signs, and, if the notions of markedness and rank are considered as the most developed notion of value, then the marriage between these three concepts, interpretant, value and hierarchy (markedness and rank), leads to the notion of transvaluation. More specifically, I will want to argue that transvaluation, in its most comprehensive form, is a rule-like semiosis which re-evaluates the perceived, conceived or imagined markedness and rank relations of the features of a referent by means of the markedness and rank relations of the features of its sign. Transvaluation occurs as a valuative translation of the referent into a sign medium which reevaluates it generally in terms of a teleology defined by the semiotic agency. It is precisely by means of valuation of the referent that the sign-signified relation is made coherent, i.e., allows signification to accrue. The referent is given a meaningful order via transvaluation. Let me illustrate this idea with an example of a minor trope, euphemism.

Troping proves to be a good example of the application of the notion of transvaluation, especially if it is couched in the language of displacement, viewed essentially as a process of value disruption. More specifically, it has to do with the disruption of hierarchy qua rank, i.e., in the sense in which Freud originally defined it: displacement is a process in the dream-work which differentiates the dream from the dream-thought by centering the important elements of the dream-thought, i.e, those with the greatest psychical value, differently in the manifest dream (Freud 1900: 305). In effect "a complete transvaluation of all psychical values" takes place between the material of the dream-thought and the manifest dream (1900: 330).

Of course, using the terminology of Freud, Jakobson labelled metonymy as displacement. This is prime example since in metonym, a part of high (perceptual, sensual or conceptual) rank is used to represent the whole, as in "sail" for ship, or "wheels" for car. But displacement in terms of rank is evident in other tropes, especially euphemism.

We must keep in mind the social function of euphemism first. Its purpose is to represent something that may be perceptually distasteful or improprietous in a relatively proprietous way. This indeed parallels the formal displacement on the linguistic level, and there are essentially two types: (1) those that involve a decentering of rank, and (2) those that concern the inversion of rank (ironic euphemism). In the first, a (perceptually, sensuously, cognitively) lower ranked feature which is contiguously associated with or similar to the referent is used to represent the referent: e.g., "sleeping together". People who have sex often sleep together as a consequence, or use a bed for the sexual act. Thus what is immediately associated with the event, or of low sensual rank serves as its representation in the euphemism. Other examples include: 'kicked the bucket', 'dark meat' for leg, 'sewing machine' for machine gun, 'my place or yours'. In the case of the inversion of rank, a low-ranked signatum is represented by a higher ranked signans: honeybucket, honeydripper.

Vulgarisms on the other hand, in their social function, intend to devalue the listeners or some social group, and their linguistic form assimilates this function. In the vulgarism, the higher ranked (i.e., perceptually prominent) part of the signatum is used to represent the signatum by likening to or associating it with something of lower value. Examples of vulgarism by contiguity include, bodice ripper, chestcutter, skinhead, kisser, cutthroat, 'the old in an out'. Examples of vulgarism by similarity include: porking, humping, egghead, skinhead, snotrag.

To return to the earlier example of the red light, a transvaluative analysis shows that we do not have a simple correlation of formal differences between one system and another, but the correlation is made coherent through the displacement or assimilation of the *valuative* relations in each system. The difference between red and green is a valuative difference, so that given the physiological and psychological evidence, red appears marked in the context of green. On the other hand, it is much more important to stop at an intersection than not to go once one is stopped, and most of the traffic laws focus on the former rather than the latter. Consequently there is a kind of markedness assimilation in which the marked term in one system represents the marked term in the other, and the ranking of the terms is also evident, for example, in the arrangement of the traffic signal. Red is at the top, green at the bottom, or sometimes the red light is larger than the green light.

The notion of transvaluation retains the best features of Peirce's interpretant and Saussure's value, and integrates them in such a way as to remedy their limitations. By arguing that the correlation between sign and referent is a valuative relation, specifically in terms of markedness and rank, this emphasizes the connection between sign and value left wanting in Peirce (cf. 1902: 24). By arguing that such a valuative correlation is effected by means of a triadic, rule-like process, bounded by a teleology, this emphasizes the pragmatic dimension that is lacking in Saussure's semiology. Transvaluation ensures that sign, purpose and value are incorporated holistically into an analysis of semiotica.

REFERENCES

ANDERSEN, Henning.
    1979. "Phonology as Semiotic", in *A Semiotic Landscape*, ed. S. Chatman, et al. (The Hague: Mouton) 377-81.
ANDREWS, Edna.
    1984. *A Theoretical Foundation for Markedness: Asymmetry in Linguistics from a Mathematical Perspective*. Ph.D. dissertation (Ann Arbor: University Microfilms).
BARTHES, Roland.
    1964. *Éléments de Sémiologie* (Paris: Editions du Seuil). References to the English translation by A. Lavers and C. Smith, *Elements of Semiology* (New York: Hill and Wang, 1967).
BATTISTELA, Edward.
    1986. *Markedness: The Evaluative Superstructure of Language*. Unpublished manuscript.
BOON, James.
    1979. "Saussure/Peirce á propos Language, Society and Culture", *Semiotica* 6, 83-100.
BRAKEL, George.
    1983. *Phonological Markedness and Distinctive Features* (Bloomington: Indiana University Press).
BRUNER, Jerome.
    1984. *In Search of Mind* (New York: Harper and Row).
COMRIE, Bernard.
    1976. *Aspect* (New York: Cambridge University Press).
    1983. *Language Typology and Linguistic Universals* (Chicago: University of Chicago Press).
DELEDALLE, Girard.
    1976a. Peirce ou Saussure, *Semiosis* 1, 7-13.
    1976b. Saussure et Peirce, *Semiosis* 2, 18-24.
FREUD, Sigmund.
    1900. *Die Träumbedeutung*. References to the English trans., by J. Strachey, *The Interpretation of Dreams*. (New York: Avon, 1965).
HARRIS, Roy.
    1987. *Reading Saussure* (La Salle, Illinois: Open Court).
LYONS, John.
    1977. *Semantics*. 2 vols. (Cambridge: Cambridge University Press).
PEIRCE, Charles Sanders.
    1867. "Upon Logical Comprehension and Extension", *Proceedings of the American Academy of Arts and Sciences* 7, 416-32. Reprinted in *The Collected Papers of Charles Sanders Peirce*, in 8 volumes, 1-6 ed. C. Hartshorne and P. Weiss, 7-8 ed. A. Burks (Cambridge, MA: Harvard University Press, 1931-1958) 2.351-2.434.
    1868. "Questions Concerning Certain Faculties Claimed for Man", *Journal of Speculative Philosophy* 2, 103-114.
    1893. Chapter XVII. *Grand Logic*. Unpublished Book. Appears in CP 4.85-4.152.

1898. "Detached Ideas on Vitally Important Topics", Cambridge Lectures. Lecture Number 3.
c.1902. *Minute Logic.* Unpublished manuscript. Appears in CP various.
c.1903. "Nomenclature and Divisions of Dyadic Relations". Unpublished Manuscript. Appears in CP 2.571-608.
c.1904. *Kaina stocheia.* Unpublished manuscript. Appears in *The New Elements of Mathematics*, ed. C. Eisele (The Hague: Mouton, 1976) 4, 14-163.
1905. "Issues in Pragmatism", *The Monist* 15, 481-499. Reprinted in CP 5.438-462.
1906. "Prologomena to an Apology for Pragmatism", *The Monist* 16: 492-546. Reprinted in CP 4.530-572.
1909. Letter to Lady Welby, dated Feb. 24. Appears in *Semiotics and Significs: The Correspondence Between Charles Peirce and Victoria Lady Welby*, ed. C. Hardwick (Bloomington: Indiana University Press, 1977).

SAUSSURE, Ferdinand de.
i.1906-1911. Lectures delivered at the University of Geneva and published from auditors' notes by C. Bally and A. Sechehaye under the title *Cours de linguistique générale*, trans. by W. Baskin as *Course in General Linguistics* (New York: McGraw-Hill, 1966).
a.1911. Unpublished manuscript. Appears as "Notes inedites de F. de Saussure", *Cahiers Ferdinand de Saussure* 12 (1954).

SHAPIRO, Michael.
1983. *The Sense of Grammar* (Bloomington: Indiana University Press).

STETTER, Christian.
1979. "Peirce and Saussure", *Kodikas/Code* 1, 124-149.

VII

SEMIOTIC DIRECTIONS IN PHILOSOPHY

RECOVERING THE AGENT AFTER DECENTERING THE SUBJECT

Vincent Colapietro
St. Mary's College of Minnesota

With the dramatic successess of the natural sciences in the modern period, the demythologizing of the cosmos--or, to use Max Weber's expression, the disenchantment of nature (*die Entzauberung der Welt*)--was inevitable. One consequence of this was that the natural world has come more and more to be seen as a domain in charge of itself, not one ruled by an external power or transcendent agent. That the world is, at least in some measure, a cosmos and not a chaos has come to be explained in terms of the world itself and not in terms of something (traditionally, Someone) outside of the world. With the rise of modernity, then, kingly rule lost credibility as a legitimate source not only of political but also of cosmic order. Since the ultimate source of cosmic order was traditionally conceived as a fatherly as well as kingly being, the rejection of such a source may be viewed as patricide as well as regicide.

With certain developments within the human "sciences" in the post-modern period (developments closely associated with the names of Marx, Nietzsche, Freud, and Saussure), the decentering to the subject was unavoidable. One result of this is that individual human beings have come more and more to be seen as no longer masters of their own houses, rulers of their own souls, but rather as arenas of conflict, stages upon which ideologically charged signifiers seemingly of their own accord perform a play of differences (cf. Hume 1739: 253). While the demythologizing of the cosmos encouraged granting an autonomous status to the natural world, the decentering of the subject fosters accepting the heteronomous constitution of the human subject (Smith 1988, 156).

If granting autonomy to nature can be seen as patricide, refusing to grant a stable identity and genuine autonomy to any individual person might be construed as a form of homicide and, in reference to oneself, an instance of suicide (cf. Foucault 1966: 385-6). But those advocating this refusal (e.g., Foucault, Barthes, Derrida) sse their advocacy in terms of emancipation rather than annihilation and, in reference to themselves, in terms of self-liberation rather than self-destruction. For what is being challenged by these thinkers is the identity of the individual as conceived by liberal humanism (cf. Smith 1988: 137). This humanism is an ideology unaware of itself as such. More specifically, it is an ideology tied to the emergence and continuation of a specific form of economic production. This form is, of course, capitalism. So conceived, such humanism is a relatively new tradition loudly proclaiming universality while actually perpetuating the opposite (e.g., ethnocentrism and phallocentrism). It is in this light, of course, that we ought to place the self-avowed anti-humanism of some prominent structuralist and post-structuralist thinkers, perhaps most notably Claude Lévi-Strauss and Michel Foucault (cf. Giddens 1979: 38).

The decentering of the subject has been one of the central preoccupations of contemporary theorists, especially struturalist and post-structuralist thinkers (Giddens 1979: 9-48, 1987: 73-108). The radical critique of the Cartesian *cogito* is the way those working within the field of semiotics have attempted to put language or, more generally, systems of signs at the center of our discourses about ourselves, thereby pushing an ahistorical, trans-linguistic consciousness not simply to but actually beyond the periphery of such discourses--in other words, pushing such consciousness entirely out of bounds.

Given the two figures principally responsible for the contemporary founding of semiotic investigation, this should not be surprising. For what constitutes the field os semiotics today has been deeply informed by not only Saussure's *semiologie* (the "*science that studies the life of signs within society*" [i.1906-1911: 16]) but also Peirce's semeiotic ("a cooperative coenoscopic attack upon the problems of the nature, properties and varieties of Signs, in the spirit of XXth century science" [Peirce 1911: 22). Regarding the investigation of signs, there are, of course, profound differences between Saussure and Peirce (see Short 1989). However, for both of these thinkers, it was imperative to displace private, individual consciousness from the prominent position it had come to occupy in post-medieval thought. In *Cours de linguistique générale* Saussure privileged language (*langue*) over speech (*parole*) and, moreover, denied language is "a function of the speaker; [rather] it is a product passively assimilated by the individual" (i.1906-1911: 14). It is a system of signs in which the only essential thing is the arbitrary conjunction of signifier and signified (i.1906-1911: 15, 67-68). In "Some Consequences of Four Incapacities", Peirce (1868) noted that while Cartesianism "teaches that the ultimate test of certainty is to be found in the individual consciousness", he himself held that "to make single individuals absolute judges of truth is most pernicious".

Moreover, in Peirce's definition of "semiosis" (the activity of a sign), the interpretant replaces the interpreter (Fisch 1983: 59); in Saussure's definition of the sign (*signe*) the signifier (*signifié*) signifies not a person who establishes a correlation but of one of the correlates in the arbitrarily fixed relation constitutive of signfication. "The signifier . . . is fixed, not free, with respect to the linguistic community that uses it. The masses have no voice in it, and the signifier *chosen by language* could be replaced by no other" (Saussure i.1906-1911: 71; emphasis added). In both Peirce's semeiotic and Saussure's *semiologie* (especially as these have been appropriated by contemporary theorists), signs appear to be granted not only be a life but also an agency of their own, whereas those beings we ordinarily designate as agents (persons or organisms) seem to be reduced to one of the loci in which (in the case of Peirce) the evolution of interpretants or (in the case of Saussure) the play of difference takes place. To view a being exclusively as such a locus amounts to denying that the being is *a* source from which signs flow and *a* power by which they are directed. In such a view, the focus is on an impersonal and self-contained system of signs to the exclusion of personal and self-directed users of signs.

However, Peirce is far better equipped than Saussure to make room for agency within his theory of signs. Indeed, while at the highest level of generality the interpretant in effect replaces the interpreter, at lower levels Peirce's finely nuanced conception of the interpretant provides a straightforward way to conceive rational consciousness. Peirce was, in his won words, "a convinced Pragmaticist in Semeiotic" (1908: 78); and if pragmaticism means anything, it means the endeavor to render our thinking concrete by connecting it with not only how persons are disposed to respond in certain circumstances, when guided by certain motives.

It is one thing to say that semiosis in general--indeed, in the most general form conceivable--is explicable without reference to agents (i.e., utterers and interpreters of signs) (Fisch 1983: 59). It is quite another to claim that the distinctive forms of human semiosis are intelligible apart from embodied agents, flesh-and-blood actors engaged in day-to-day struggles and, on occasion, even life-and-death conflicts. Whatever any one of these forms os semiosis is, it is not simply a play of signifiers operating of their own accord. Yet this is how these forms are frequently depicted. For example, Jacques Derrida, one of the most masterful and ingenious interpreters of texts, explicitly disavows his own agency in his role as interpreter. "I would never say every interpretation is equal, but *I* do not select. The interpretations select themselves" (Smith 1988: 47). This is but a specific instance of a general tendency in Derrida's thinking to efface the "I": what we are left with is (in Derrida's own words) "a more or less anonymous multiplicity" (Smith 1988: 48). In this tendency, Derrida bears a resemblance to Nietzsche who claimed in *The Twilight of the Idols* (1889: 49):

> The 'inner world' is full of phantoms and false lights: the will is one of them. The will no longer moves anything, consequently no longer explains anything--it merely accompanies events, it can also be absent. The so-called 'motive': another error. Merely a surface phenomenon of consciousness, an accompaniment of an act, which conceals rather than exposes the *antecedentia* of the act. And as for the ego! It has become fable, a fiction, a play on words: it has totally ceased to think, to feel and to will!

For Nietzsche and Derrida, to see the self as a play on words liberates us from one of the most crippling conceptions in Western culture (*the* individual).

Semiotics is both a highly abstract and formal discipline *and* focuses and engaged critique. This point merits emphasis: that semiotics is, in the hands of certain practitioners, a highly theoretical undertaking does not preclude it from being, in the hands of other practitioners, a potentially *emancipatory* discipline in Jürgen Habermas's sense--a discipline capable of unmasking the forms of dominance as a first step toward overthrowing these forms (1968). For semiotics in either of these orientations, questions regarding agency and autonomy are crucial. More specifically, there is a need to explore the possibility of recovering the human agent after decentering the human subject.

The need for such a recovery has been underscored by (among others) Anthony Giddens in a variety of works (e.g., 1979, 1987) and Paul Smith in *Discerning the Subject*, an important recent contribution to one of the most crucial issues within semiotic theory. "The theme of the decentering of the subject is", according to Giddens, "without doubt one which must be taken seriously by anyone interested in modern philosophy or social theory. But while the basic perspective surely must be accepted, the particular mode in which it is elaborated within structuralism and post-structuralism remains defective" (1986: 89; cf. 98). This mode is defective, according to Giddens, because in the process of decentering human subjectivity it eliminates human agency. Hence, "it is essential to insist upon the need for an interpretation of the agent, rather than the subject, and of agency rather than subjectivity alone. 'Subjects' are first and foremost agents" (1986: 98). What is required is, accordingly, a social science with the conceptual resources to portray human beings as "knowledgeable, capable agents".

In *Discerning the Subject*, Smith observes: "current conceptions of the 'subject' have tended to produce a purely *theoretical* 'subject,' removed almost entirely from the political and ethical realities in which human agents actually live and . . . a different concept of the 'subject must be discerned or discovered" (1988, xxix). What is needed is "to produce a notion of subjectivity which sill satisfy both the demands of theory and the exigencies of practice . . ." (Smith 1988, xxxii). Either within this notion itself or complementary to it some conception of agency must be reinstalled. For "a person is not simply determined and dominated by the ideological pressure of any overarching discourse . . . but is also the agent of a certain *discernment*. A person is not simply the *actor* who follows ideological scripts, but is also an *agent* who reads them in order to insert him/herself into them--or not" (1988, xxxiv-xxxv).

The capacity of agents to read such scripts and to make such decisions is what Smith calls discernment. But, in his usage, this term also means something more. In fact, what he means by dis-cerning can only be grasped in reference to his attempt to play upon "two rarely used English words--'to cern' and 'to cerne'" (1988: xxx). "To cern" in general means "'to accept an inheritance or a patrimony'"; in Smith's book, "the cerning of the subject" means (in part) accepting "a western philosophical heritage in which the 'subject' is construed as the unified and coherent bearer of consciousness" (1988: xxx). In contrast, "to cerne" means, in general, "'to encircle' or 'to enclose'" and, more specifically in Smith, to limit in an excessively narrow way the definition of the human agent (1988: xxx). Thus, in Smith's double pun, to discern the subject is (1) to reject a central tenet of our intellectual heritage and (2) to refuse to enclose human agency within the excessively narrow limits of the dominant conceptions of human subjectivity. However, both of these senses of dis-cernment are ultimately subordinate to the more immediately practical capacity to insert ourselves into ideological scripts--or to refuse to do so. To insert ourselves into the dominant practices, institutions, and discourses or not, to take part in or to take arms against--that is the question. A *discerning* agent is acutely aware of the subtle as well as obvious forms in which this fundamental option appears again and again in the everyday life of any historically situated person.

As indicated above, decentering the subject means repudiating the *cogito*. In turn, this repudiation means at least two things: first, refusing to take the Cartesian *cogito* or individual consciousness as the *central* datum of philosophical reflection, as the absolutely solid bedrock upon which we can build the edifice of knowledge; second, refusing to conceive the *cogito* in the manner of Descartes, i.e., as an individual substance only contingently connected with a body (1641: 146, 148), other minds (p. 155), and the world (1637: 101). The Cartesian *cogito* does not simply designate the actual views of a historical thinker regarding the nature and importance of consciousness; it also symbolizes a dominant perspective in western thought, namely, the perspective which privileges consciousness as something given at the outset and something transparent to itself. From this perspective, consciousness is a unitary or indivisible substance; in the view of its critics, consciousness is a set of fractured and fragile processes made possible by language (Giddens 1979, p. 38). Put another way, the Cartesian *cogito* is an absolutely stable and unified being, while the decentered subject is a kaleidoscopic intersection of precarious processes.

In "Consciousness and the Unconscious", Paul Ricoeur claims: "Everything that can be said about consciousness after Freud seems to me to be contained in the following formula: Consciousness is not a given but a *task*" (1969, 108). After Descartes, the "I" is identified with consciousness, but this consciousness is unconscious of the unconscious, of the other within the "I". Moreover, the "I" of the Cartesian *Cogito* is a disembodied subject: "I shall consider myself as having no hands, no eyes, no flesh, no blood, nor any senses . . ." (1641: 148)--nor presumably any genitalia. However, after Freud, the "I" must be conceived as an *engendered* subject and, due to the processes by which the "I" becomes en-gendered (processes involving repression), the "I" must be conceived as a *split* subject (consciousness/the unconscious); since the unconscious is that dimension called into being by repression.

Before continuing, let us consider the character of so many assertions in postmodern discourse, a character especially apparent in discussion of the subject and, thus, directly relevant to our concern. The impetus for this consideration is Ricoeur's remark that, after Freud, consciousness must be viewed as a task, not as a datum. As John Dewey observed, humankind in general tends "to think in terms of extreme opposites. It is given to formulating its beliefs in terms of *Either-Ors*, between which it recognizes no intermediate possibilities" (1938: 17). This general tendency is at work in Ricoeur's specific remark, for there is no necessity to look at consciousness either as a task or a given. Stated positively, consciousness may be *both* a gift and a project, something given by the graciousness of powers other than ourselves and something won by our own efforts.

In general, many of the assertions is most-modern discourse strike the "common reader" (in Virginia Woolf's sense) as unqualified, undialectical, unempirical. In his review of *The Return of Grand Theory of the Human Sciences* (an anthology edited by Quentin Skinner dealing with, among others, Lévi-Strauss, Althusser, Foucault, and Derrida), Frederick Crews severely criticizes what he sees as a dominant feature of both structuralist and post-structuralist thought, namely, their "theoreticism". Crews defines "theoreticism" as "frank recourse to unsubstantiated theory, not just as a tool of investigation but as an anti-empirical knowledge in its own right" (1986: 37). It "is less a specific position than a mood of antinomian rebellion and self-indulgence" (1986: 39). This "mood comes down to us from the later Sixties--from a sense of the criminal inhumanity in science and technology, a revulsion against dry rationality, a cherishing of direct intuitive belief, and a willing surrender to intellectual, political, and spiritual counter-authorities" (1986: 39). This mood is unmistakably evident in Roland Barthes' *The Pleasure of the Text*, a work in which the author attempts to liberate the subject from the prison of a single identity, thereby enabling the subject to enjoy the ecstasy of a diffused selfhood or (in Derrida's terms) "an anonymous multiplicity" (cf. Eagleton 1983: 141). For such a liberated subject, the "text is (or should be) that uninhibited person who shows his behind to the Political Father" (Barthes 1973: 53; cf. Eagleton 1983: 141). Crews (1986: 42) sees this antinomian mood as "an ironic counterpart of positivism--a heaping up, not of factual nuggets, but of movement slogans that are treated as fact".

Is "the decentering of the subject" one such slogan? While this expression may be used as a slogan, it can and, indeed, must be rooted in the experience of our interactions with others. the expression refers primarily not to what Foucault, Lacan, and others say but to what we experience. No doubt, what these and other theorists say can help us discern more sharply what we experience. Even so, it is helpful to recall here that, for Peirce, semeiotic is a part of philosophy and, in turn, philosophy is a species of science in the very modest sense of a discipline required to evaluate its assertions in light of experience.

John Dewey suggests a way of defining the term "subject" that simultaneously can be linked to the disclosures of our everyday experience and the discourses of contemporary theorists. In *Experience and Nature* Dewey defines both object and subject in a two-fold way. On the one hand, the object is "that which objects, that to which frustration is due. But it is also the objective; the final and eventual consummation . . ." (1925: 239). On the other hand, the "subject is that which suffers, is subjected and which endures resistance and frustration; it is also that which attempts subjection of hostile conditions; that which takes the immediate initiative in remaking the situation as it stands".

The subject in this sense is nothing other than the human organism in its fateful involvement in a complex environment. Such an organism is both a being subjected to the pressures and impositions of others *and* a being capable of countering these pressures and opposing these impositions. Such an organism is not only a being who has suffered and bears the scars of suffering and degradation, but also a being who rebels and possesses the capacity to resist injury and exploitation.

The recovery of human agency requires nothing more--nor less--than the recollection of our embodied selves. Given such recollection, there is nothing mysterious in our being continuously subjected to the impositions of others nor in our being characteristically able to resist such impositions. If one desires to resist the seductive images of bourgeois culture, one can only do so by moving beyond an anonymous multiplicity toward some personal integration. It takes integrity to resist, let alone to rebel. While such integrity is always far more fragile and less coherent than we ordinarily suspect, it is as real and enduring as our dispositions to respond in certain circumstances, in certain ways.

In *The Captive Mind* Czeslaw Milosz describes a way of seeing he calls "the vision of the cobblestones" (1951: 39):

> A man is lying under machine-gun fire on a street in an embattled city. He looks at the pavement and sees a very amusing sight: the cobblestones are standing upright like the quills of a porcupine. The bullets hitting against their edges displace and tilt them. Such moments in the consciousness of a man *judge* all poets and philosophers. Let us suppose, too, that a certain poet [or philosopher] was the hero of the literary cafes [or establishment], and wherever he went was regarded with curiosity and awe. Yet his poems [or philosophy], in such a moment, suddenly seem diseased and highbrow. The visions of the cobblestones is unquestionably real, and poetry [or philosophy] based on an equally *naked* experience could survive triumphantly that judgment day of man's illusions.

We have only to ask the question, "How do most of the dominant theories of human subjectivity look to I's (i.e., subject) sprawling under fire on cobblestones?" to know the answer. My point is not to grant a license to dismiss, out of hand, any theorist, movement, or "method". What Peirce said of "classical German philosophy"--namely, it is "a rich mine of philosophical suggestions", though upon its argumentative side it is of little weight--may also be said of much contemporary theoretical discourse (c.1897). My point *is* that the subject is more than what even Smith, a thinker concerned with recovering agency, contends; that is, the subject is more than "the series or the conglomeration of *positions*, subject-positions, provisional and not necessarily indefeasible, into which a person is called momentarily by the discourses and the world that he/she inhabits" (Smith 1988: xxxv). The view of the subject as simply a locus in which conflict and contradiction occurs (rather than also a source from which resistance and innovation emanates) is perhaps best seen as an unwitting portrait of victimized consciousness. In addition, the Derridean view of human subjectivity as "anonymous multiplicity" is perhaps more an unconscious reflection of bourgeois culture than it is a means for resisting the manipulations and degradations of that culture. The "I" called into being by the text of this moment, an "I" without continuity or integrity, is a portrait of above all else--the consumer, the principal product of capitalist production. Thus, I resist the temptation to buy this new improved view of subjectivity; an it is I who deliberately does this.

REFERENCES

BARTHES, Roland.
    1973. *Le Plaisir du texte* (Paris: Editions du Seuil).
CREWS, Frederick.
    1986. Review of *The Return of the Grand Theory in the Human Sciences* in *The New York Review of Books* (May 29).
DES PRES, Terrence.
    1978. "Czeslaw Milosz: The Poetry of Aftermath" in *The Nation*, 227.23 (December 30), 241-3.
DESCARTES, René.
    1637. *Discourse onthe Method of Rightly Conducting the Reason and Seeking for Truth in the Sciences*, trans. Elizabeth S. Haldane and G.R.T. Gross in *The Philosophical Works of Descartes* (corrected reprint edition; New York: Dover, 1955, I: 79-130).
    1641. *Meditations on First Philosophy*, trans. Elizabeth S. Haldane and G. R. T. Gross, in *The Philosophical Works of Descartes* (corrected reprint ed.; New York: Dover, 1955), I, 131-199.
DEWEY, John.
    1925. *Experience and Nature*. All references to this work in my paper are to the 1958 Dover Publications, Inc., edition.
    1938. *Experience and Education* (New York: Kappa Delta Pi)
EAGLETON, Terry.
    1983. *Literary Theory*. (Minneapolis: University of Minnesota Press).
FISCH, Max.
    1983. "Just *How* General Is Peirce's General Theory of Signs?" All references to this essay are to *Peirce, Semeiotic, and Pragmatism* (Bloomington: Indiana University Press, 1986), edited by Kenneth Laine Ketner and Christian Kloesel.
FOUCAULT, Michel.
    1966. *Les Mots et les choses* (Paris: Editions Gallimand).
GIDDENS, Anthony.
    1979. *Central Problems in Social Theory* (Berkeley: University of California Press).
    1987. *Social Theory and Modern Sociology* (Stanford: Stanford University Press).
HABERMAS, Jürgen.
    1968. *Erkenntnis und Interesse* (Suhrkamp Verlag).
HUME, David.
    1739. *A Treatise of Human Nature*. All references are to L.A. Selby-Bigge edition (Oxford: Clarendon Press, 1973).
MILOSZ, Czeslaw.
    1951. *Zniewolony Umysl* (Instytut Literacki), trans. as *The Captive Mind* by Jane Zielonko (New York: Vintage, 1959).
NIETZCHE, Friedrich Wilhelm.
    1889. *Götzen-Dämmerung, oder: Wie man mit dem Hammer philosophirt*, trans. as *Twilight of the Idols, or How to Philosophize with the Hammer* with *Antichrist* by R. J. Hollingdale (Baltimore, MD: Penguin Books, 1968).
PEIRCE, Charles Sanders.
    1868. "Some Consequences of Four Incapacities", originally published in *Journal of Speculative Philosophy* 2, 140-157; reprinted in CP 5.264-317.
    c. 1897. Untitled ms. published in full as CP 1.3-7. The same manuscript is titled "Religion, Science, and Fallibilism) in *Annotated Catalogue of the Papers*

of *Charles S. Peirce*, ed. Richard S. Robin (University of Massachusetts Press, 1967).
- 1908. Letter to Lady (Victoria) Welby dated "1908 Dec. 23.), published in *Semiotic and Significs: The Correspondence Between Charles S. Peirce and Victoria Lady Welby* (Bloomington: Indiana University Press, 1977), ed. Charles S. Hardwick with the assistance of James Cook.
- 1911. "A Sketch of Logical Critic." Unpublished manuscript appearing as MS 675 in Robin 1967.

RICOEUR, Paul.
- 1969. "Consciousness and the Unconscious", trans. by Willis Domingo in *The Conflict of Interpretations: Essays in Hermeneutics*, ed. Don Ihde (Evanston, IL: Northwestern University Press, 1974), 99-120, originally published as *Le Conflit des interprétations: Essais d'herméneutique* (Paris: Editions du Seuil).

SAUSSURE, Ferdinand.
- i. 1906-1911. Lectures delivered at the University of Geneva and published from auditor's notes by C. Bally and A. Sechehaye under the title *Cours de linguistique générale*, trans. by W. Baskin as *Course in General Linguistics*, (New York: McGraw-Hill, 1966).

SHORT, T. L.
- 1989. "Why We Prefer Peirce to Saussure", *Semiotics 1988* (see above, 124-130).

SMITH, Paul.
- 1988. *Discerning the Subject* (Minneapolis: University of Minnesota Press).

LOCKE'S FORMULA AND THE SCOPE OF SEMIOTICS

David Lidov
York University, Toronto

In *Frontiers in Semiotics*, John Deely characterizes semiotics (as he does elsewhere) as a "higher order of understanding, of which scientific understanding forms only a substructure" (Deely, 1984: 270). I hope that what follows will pose some questions about this position. But I will defer the purely doctrinal question of what semiotics ought to be, in order to develop first what may seem a more picayune question, which is whether a semiotics to which scientific understanding is subordinate is (again quoting Professor Deely) "what Locke calls for". Locke's famous adumbration of semiotics is not a systematic doctrine, of course, and I will not attempt to impute one to him. But the *Essay* as a whole establishes certain semiotic *attitudes* which seem to me to bear in a direction quite different from that suggested either by the brief phrases of Deely's which I quoted above or the more elaborate analyses he provides in the same volume's first essay and final footnotes (ibid.: 23-5, 288).

I do think that Deely is on target in suggesting that Locke may still be a neglected figure in the history of semiotics.[1] Peirce paraphrased Locke's preface (1690: 58) in calling himself a backwoodsman and seems to echo many concerns broached throughout the *Essay*. But almost everybody else quotes just the last page. What lies between the Preface and the Coda deserves more explication. I don't want to suggest that I am more than a novice student of its meanderings. Its reasoning is not always compelling; its categories seem to well deserve their present desuetude. But its semiotic relevance is undeniable. I use the word 'attitude' deliberately and non-technically. My impression is that while the fairly unanimous criticism of Locke as unsystematic is valid, there is still a unity of attitude linking his concepts and judgments which merits the serious and respectful attention from semioticians which Peirce clearly accorded it.

The scope of semiotics remains an unsettled, fundamental issue in semiotic theory. Sebeok identifies a "major tradition" coming to us from classic sources, including Locke, directly or via Peirce and characterized by its attempt to regulate (at least) the foundations of all knowledge and consciousness--let us call this "pansemiotics"--and a "minor tradition" originating with Saussure and, because it draws its methodology from linguistics, limited to what might be encompassed in a view of culture as a translinguistic phenomenon. Locke obviously belongs with the pansemiotitions, not with the translinguists, not merely by chronology, not merely because he explicitly articulates some distinct characteristics of non-linguistic signs, but because of his broad philosophic orientation.

Nevertheless, I'm not sure this dichotomy is fair to Locke: In some ways, the *Essay* suggests a mediating position. The difference I mean to stress is not just a question of how a few phrases are turned; it is a fundamental difference of positions in the study of knowledge and consciousness. Locke doesn't propose a unified system for viewing knowledge and consciousness and never suggests we will discover one. He is content to open up lines of enquiry and advance certain fundamental principles. This is not at all the same thing as finding or founding a master discipline. The *Essay* as a whole is not fully systematic partly because it engages different ways of understanding in a dialogue with each other. Although the *Essay* is not self-reflective to the point of identifying dialogue as its own method, Locke is certainly explicit (when he discusses forbearance) about the relation of social tolerance to the growth of knowledge. Obviously, social tolerance is not logical tolerance, but in emphasizing the provisional nature of most knowledge, which he regards as based on probability, not certainty, and in contrasting *a priori* principles to true hypotheses (p. 400) Locke has laid the basis for an understanding of dialogue as a principle of the advancement of knowledge. To see how essential this tolerance is in Locke's overall *theoretical* direction, I suggest we consider closely what his attitude is about logic, itself.

Locke concludes the *Essay on Human Understanding* with his suggestion that semiotics--a new kind of logic--should be added to the classically established divisions of knowledge, the natural and the practical. Deely has explicated some of the content of this richly suggestive passage by referring us to the context for Locke's terminology in the Aristotelian tradition. Here I want to focus on its context in the *Essay* itself.

For a naive modern reader, such as myself, one puzzle about Locke's last page is why it is last. Could this suggestion have been made at the beginning of the book? What is it he feels he has not done in the previous 400 pages that the new logic would do? Saussure makes his proposal for a new science early in his course. In Locke's case one gets a first impression that his proposal is either an afterthought or an affectedly modest appraisal of his own efforts. Has he not already been unfolding the new logic? And where is the old logic in his scheme of things?

Internally, the remark has to be understood as referring, in the first instance, to Chapter XVII of Book IV, the chapter on Reason, which is devoted primarily to Locke's criticism of the syllogism, perhaps the one place in the *Essay* where we sense a somewhat acid tone (ibid.: 416-22). While he is prompt to acknowledge Aristotle's contribution, Locke has no sympathy with the promulgation of syllogistic doctrine. It is worthwhile to be clear what Locke's offensive is not. He is not primarily veiling an *ad hominem* attack on scholastics and he is not merely rehearsing some version of the familiar diatribe about counting angels on pinheads. And he is not, in any substantial way, elaborating the logical opposition of deduction and inference. What Locke does here is something like what Peirce does with the notion of abduction: he shifts the problematics of logic from the investigation of the intrinsic structure of certainty, which syllogism provides--and Locke accepts that result (ibid.)--to the problem of observing the nature of actual thinking. In other words, Locke is evaluating logic as a psychology of thinking. It appears in his examples (which, by the way, suggest that thinking is enthematatic) that Locke's new logic is to be an empirical study of the thinking process and its tools.

The old logic was concerned only with the relations of propositions to each other and with their application to the world. It did not permit any difficulties to be imposed on this domain by the careful consideration of perception and cognitive processing. The old logic was strictly doctrinal and deductive. In Locke's view it had become quite stale, for his interest is the cognitive and perceptual problems the logic did not encompass. He approaches these questions as a reporter, an observer of common experience. Perhaps in calling this method empirical, when it still lacks any method of testing and cross-checking, we overstate the case, but Locke certainly moves logic away from the old doctrinal method and towards the standpoint of an emerging empirical physics. I want to emphasize the possibly too familiar point that Locke's idea of logic and Locke's idea of *semiotika* owes quite a bit to the model of physics; it certainly does not subordinate physics. And I don't think that's a failure of system on his part so much as a unity of attitude.

The old logic really was a prerequisite to all other knowledge, both in practical pedagogy and in its epistemological status. The new logic has more scope, but also a lower status. The old logic was in status exactly what Deely and Sebeok seem to suggest semiotics should be: a doctrinal discipline regulating our most fundamental knowledge. Locke is moving logic in the opposite direction.

His proposal to bypass the old logic, which was the foundation of knowledge, or, perhaps, to take it for granted, and to institute a new one, semiotics, which would be one of three *investigative* sciences amounts to trading prestige for vitality of content. Considering the how great the prestige of the old logic was, the proposal has to come at the end of the book, with the full weight of Locke's explorations behind it, to have any credibility.

The concepts which form the apex of his whole investigation are those of 'probability' and 'assent'. His analyses of these ideas rest on a tripod. Clear representation is one leg--that's semiotics; sensation as the independent source without for our ideas is a second--that leads to physics; and integrity among men sharing the enterprise of knowledge is a third--that's ethics. This edifice tips if you make any one leg do the work of two.

* * * * *

Now I have said where I think Locke stands in the matter of epistemological hierarchy, but I haven't shown why I think it matters and why I regard his attitude as wise notwithstanding the obvious inadequacies of his analyses and arguments. To do this I must turn from Locke to criticize what I see as more radical alternatives within pansemiotics.

Let us dispose first of all with what we might call "naive pansemiotics". By this I mean the kind of theory that emerges if Locke's own line of enquiry is transformed into an *a priori* dogma--an exaggeration I do not find in his book but which does seem implicit in some programmatic claims for contemporary semiotics. This argument that semiotics is foundational for all other knowledge runs something like this: "All knowledge is mediated by signs. We do not actually know anything immediately, because all knowing is sign-making. In our effort to grasp the truth of things, signs are like gloves on our grasping fingers that stand between us and our experience. Any idea we have of our experience must be a construction that depends on the gloves as a vehicle for our impressions. The I or we that does the knowing is essentially a collection of these representations as is the universe without that we construct. Therefore, to know anything at all, we'd better start by examining those gloves, the signs". As a description of our ultimate circumstance in the universe, this perspective may be consistent, but the proposed regimen doesn't follow from the diagnosis. Indeed, if we pursue the analysis, our situation in the world is appears even more isolated than the description so far indicates. What happens when we try to feel the gloves? It always turns out that there is a second pair inside the first. We can't feel the gloves immediately. We know signs only by representing them with other signs. When you are paying attention to what I mean, you scarcely hear my words. Since, no sign is the same as its object, we do not know signs more immediately than anything else. The monstrous self-consciousness of semiotic theory and its continuous explosions of technicalities is a direct symptom of the fact that we can't get at the nature of signs any more directly than we can get at the nature of anything else.

Taken to its implicated conclusion, this perspective turns out to be a great equalizer of enquiries. It suggests that we do all of our learning and knowing without the benefit of immediate experience, whatever that would be. If we do learn everything we know mediately, knowledge of signs, however illuminating, has no special priority. It is (as Locke's arrangement suggests) one of the alternative ways of being conscious of the universe and not the peak of a hierarchy.

Now let us consider the problem from a second point-of-view, the semiotics outlined by Deely in the work mentioned and, somewhat more fully, in his *Introducing Semiotic* (1982). For Deely, semiosis is prior to any differentiation of subjective from objective worlds. His signs are relations, not gloves. To the question whether grass is green in itself or whether the impression of green is a property of a visual faculty, Deely's semiotic will answer that green is a natural and necessary *relation* between grass and a visual faculty. His is an approach which suggests Peirce's, if we can conceive of Peirce's abstracted from its prior ontology (and with indices then preceding icons). In Deely's scheme the notion of a physical reality is gradually extracted from the encompassing objective world of signs first, as congruences of experience point to physical invariants (e.g., the intraspecies success of camouflage) and second, more spectacularly, as language creates a critical sign consciousness. Unlike the "naive" perspective that we trace back to Locke, we do not know *through* signs here but in signs. Though it has some gaps,[2] it is a neat system, but I think Deely has made some excessive claims for it. Perhaps this excess concerns the doctrine's outward dressing more than its logical core.

Nevertheless, dressing or core, what is at stake is still the claim for semiotics as "a higher order of understanding". I think Deely makes a very elementary mistake here of confusing semiotics and semiosis. In the epistemology he develops, our construction of physical reality requires as a prerequisite our *critical* apperception of our own stipulated signs. To know the world, we must first or at least simultaneously develop a critical semiosis. This is not semiotics. Sign consciousness, in itself, is not semiotics. Ophelia distributing her flowers has intense sign consciousness, but she is not semiotician. The critical study of signs with respect to their significations of something entails semiosis. Only the critical study of signs with respect to their *capacity to signify* entails semiotics. It is semiosis--a very critical, sophisticated semiosis--that gains epistemological priority in Deely's system, not semiotics.

The confusion between semiosis and semiotics, which you might think would be impossible for us, really seems to be endemic and to have a lot to do with the suspicion of vagueness, aggrandizement and false advertising which hangs over our enterprise.

For example, a typical weak argument for the priority of semiotics involves the claim that particle physics has become aware of its own metaphorical status, hence semiotic, now that laws of indeterminacy take account of the observer. That is not accurate. Nuclear physicists, like any others who have an imaging or communication problem, can develop a deeper consciousness of semiotic issues, but that is a sideline for them. The discipline of physics *per se* is still confined to constructing a model of physical reality. It is true that physics now takes more elaborate account of the observing subject, but that is another matter altogether, evidence of its ever more sophisticated semiosis, perhaps. Physics takes no account of itself as an observation *theory*. Only a discipline which internally represents its own theory as an object of investigation should be said to be semiotic. Some physicists have become more aware of the metaphorical basis of physics, but physics has not.

A thorough and unified pansemiotic perspective courts the disadvantage common to unitary and absolute descriptions like pure solipsism or ethical theories of pure self-interest. The grand synthesis itself gives us no handle on "the differences that make a difference". These must then be recreated inside the system. In Deely's system, the catastrophe (in the popular mathematical sense of the word) which separates subjective, objective and physical realities occurs with language. He has a lot to say about the character of the power of language, but does not analyze its source.[3] If the features of language which account for its power were spelled out, we might see two doctrines here not one: a translinguistic castle with a pansemiotic basement. Perhaps we approach a dividing line here between the interests of semiotics considered as a part of philosophy and the interest of general semiotics as a special discipline. The former will be more sensitive to unities, the latter to differences. However, as a theorist interested in general semiotics, I find it suggestive, that by eschewing questions of epistemological priority, Locke bridges this division in proposing a framework which we could think of as a dialogue among essentially different types of knowledge.

Building on that framework, we might want to recognize a way of knowing peculiar to physics (in Locke's broad sense of the term) a mode of consciousness that attributes properties or appearances to their objects without full *consciousness* of appearances as signs. We could also posit a way of knowing peculiar to ethics, displayed in a subject's unselfconscious knowledge that a certain action is objectively right or wrong without any admission that the value is determined by a judgement. These modes for apprehending the world are as basic to our lives as knowing meanings. We should not lose sight of the differences and *oppositions* between these kinds of knowledge simply because we can view all these three types of knowledge as sign structures. They are different as semiosic strategies.

* * * * *

I will try to show that my by now rather widely scattered points of argument have some relation to each other via a brief exercise in application. The example posed for us this weekend is the topic of reality and illusion. There is no such thing as an illusion among physical phenomena or ethical values. An illusion has to be a sign. But there is no such thing either as a purely semiotic criterion for distinguishing illusion from reality. As an instance, let us consider what the reality is of the $500,000,000 that was lost on the New York Stock Exchange on Black Monday. Here is a semiotic vista of representations of representations that seems at first to recede without end. What could be a more exemplary semiotic construction than changes of values of options on futures flashing across a pixel board or through a modem? The experts I've asked so far assure me that the loss was real, but if so, was that wealth real the Friday before? According to those who claim the market was inflated, some of it must have been an illusion.

Look at this scene first as the *Umwelt* of a fully immersed participant, say an individual trader. She has a semiotic consciousness, a semiotic epistemology, for she knows she's in a somewhat arbitrary "numbers game". But the whole tension and reactivity of the system depends on her perception (or the community's or the system's perception) of "hard facts" at its horizon: belief in real (physical) labor and goods at one end of the ticker tape and belief in necessary ethical (or unethical) truths--interests and obligations--at the other.

Now consider how we will model this nexus as detached, semiotic observers. We have to paraphrase those perceived thresholds between figures and facts. Deely can express them as functions of the participants' critical understanding, but note that he can only frame, not duplicate, the acts of critical judgement; those acts are semiosic but not semiotic.

A richer model, which, let me acknowledge, may have no bearing at all on the classical problems which Deely's work reanimates, might acknowledge an inherently dialogical relation between semiotic and other modes of apprehending the world. From this position we can offer a more dynamic interpretation of the realities and illusions of such a nexus as in the stock market example: Illusion is a label that one domain foists on the constructions of another. In *practice*, semiosis and semiotics, even where they seize the same sets of data, tend to be *opposite* motions of thought. Critical judgement in the traders' world, or any other active world, demands a measure of semiotic *unconsciousness* as a condition of action. Typically, judgement is expressed as a refusal to acknowledge the arbitrary representational content of a sign ("An honest day's work", "A buck is a buck", "*Gotta* look out for No. 1").

The reality status of the whole nexus is not a vacuous problem, but may become one if we don't acknowledge the inadequacy of any one framework, even semiotics, to capture all modes of consciousness of it.

It is for this reason that a semiotic attitude like Locke's, which pursues lines of enquiry without formulating a unified dogma might be intellectually more valuable than either a pan-semiotics which plays Atlas to all of science or a trans-linguistics which risks reducing semiotics to a display of current fashions in literary criticism. What Locke's position loses in logical closure is well compensated by the gain in its dialogical situation. The principle empirical finding of semiotics would seem to be the permanence and ubiquity of the dialectic of autonomous structure and extrinsic influence. We must ask ourselves if the doctrine of signs, itself, is well served if we construct it as an autonomous structure, wherein conversation is orderly but strictly intramural.

NOTES

[1] I refer here to the "promisory note" issued in Deely 1984: 288 n. 3, concerning the to-be-explored synedoches in Locke's concluding chapter of 1690. In fact, at least partial payment on that note was made in an essay by Deely which I did not learn of in time to take account of in this text, "John Locke's Place in the History of Semiotic Inquiry", in *Semiotics 1986*, 406-418. How this essay might affect my reflections here I leave to another time.

[2] Deely's signs aggregate in webs which progress in sophistication through sensation to perception to stipulation and understanding, but it is not clear how they are fit to do so. Peirce's interpretants are always inadequate and transcendent in relation to their object, leading to re-representations which promise semiotic *progress*. Deely's relations, at their lowest level are depicted by him as merely associating with each other, *via* some unnamed and unexamined capacity for association: e.g., sensations of color get attached to forms. The process seems a mixture of whimsical physiological fragments. What if we learned that retinal receptors only fire in groups? Would shape then precede color? Or should we wonder how color gets *abstracted from* shape in the first place?

[3] Except to emphasize that language is stipulated, but domestic pets respond to stipulated signs, too.

REFERENCES

LOCKE, John.
    1690. *An Essay Concerning Human Understanding*, ed. A.D. Woozley (New York: Meridian, 1964).

DEELY, John.
    1982. *Introducing Semiotic, Its History and Doctrine* (Bloomington: Indiana University Press).
    1984. "Semiotic as Framework and Direction" in *Frontiers in Semiotics*, ed. J. Deely, B. Williams, and F. E. Kruse (Bloomington: Indiana University Press, 1986), 264-71.

DEELY, John, Brooke WILLIAMS, and Felicia E. KRUSE.
    1986. *Frontiers in Semiotics* (Bloomington, IN: Indiana University Press).

EPISTEMOLOGY'S MINIMAL CAUSE AS BASIS OF SCIENCE

Ralph A. Powell
Aquinas Institute--St. Louis

Introduction

    Peter Strawson among British philosophers and Willard Van Orman Quine among American philosophers are probably more respected by other philosophers than anyone else writing on philosophy in English. Now these two philosophers agree in two negative statements in Epistemology:

    1) We do not have rational control of our certitude of the existence of the external world (Strawson 1985: 13-19).

    2) We do not have rational control of our certitude of the existence of minds in the human bodies around us (Quine 1973 : 54;1976: 223; 1981:17).

Yet these two certitudes are obviously the basis of science. For science is about the external world as observed by some scientists and replicated by others in the same scientific discipline. But this paper holds that our certitudes of the existence of an external world and of other minds in human bodies results from rationally controllable causality. But it is a kind of causality of a very peculiar sort. However, this type of causality is such as to explain that it does not give rational certitude about the existence of things of everyday life, such as people, sheep and tables. For the type of causality here proposed as the basis of science is a minimal kind of causality. And this minimal type of causality does not permit us to discern the existence of any individual bodies such as people, sheep and tables. Hence, Strawson and Quine would be right in saying that science is not based on the known existence of the everyday world of people, sheep and tables.

    This minimal cause is prior to the well known Aristotelian four causes, the agent, the final, the formal and the material cause. For these four causes are the causes of individual bodies in their action and in their existence. The agent and final cause are causes of its action, and the formal and material causes are causes of its individual existence. Now a minimal cause that does not require knowledge of the existence of individual bodies is prior in knowledge to these four causes. Now this prior type of cause is manifest in the history of science. For it expresses what is most evident in the motion of moving bodies: namely to be either orderly motions by having determinate destinations (Newton's first law of motion: or to be losing orderliness by increase of entropy (the second law of thermodynamics). Now orderliness of motions does not require that the moving bodies be individual existent bodies. For the historic paradigm of orderly motions since Copernicus has been the solar system. But the sun and the planets are not individual existent bodies.

This paper will be divided as follows: 1) temporal relations as manifest destiny of moving bodies, 2) specification of temporal relations as minimal causality, 3) temporal relations do not distinguish what common sense calls individual bodies from heaps of rubbish, 4) scientific mechanism as specified by this minimal type of causality is the minimal scientific knowledge of reality.

1. Temporal Relations as Manifest Destiny of Moving Bodies

Opening your mouth as your hand raises your food-laden fork is a real temporal relation of the two moving bodies. It is a mind-independent relation, not a mere imaginary one, since the opening mouth and the approaching fork must be moving in mutual relation, or else the food will be deposited on your face, instead of in your mouth. Now that real temporal relation is a real effect distinct from the two moving bodies, since the relation is not itself a moving body.

This distinction of the relation from the moving bodies can be seen as follows. Using your tongue to keep food between your jaws as you chew, you instinctively avoid biting your tongue. Your moving tongue and moving jaw are in temporal relations to each other. The two moving bodies cause two temporal relations between them. Your moving jaw is temporally related to your tongue, and your tongue is temporally related to your moving jaw, so that biting of your tongue does not usually occur. Now your moving tongue is not the same as the temporal relation of your tongue to your moving jaw. For your tongue could have the same motion even if your jaw were stationary. But then there would be no temporal relation of your moving tongue to your moving jaw. Hence the temporal relation of your moving tongue to your moving jaw is not the same as your isolated moving tongue. Their mutual temporal relations are distinct from the moving bodies themselves.

Temporal relations can also be seen in inanimate bodies as real effects really distinct from the moving bodies that cause them. Speeding on an interstate highway in a chain of cars at 65 miles an hour, one must keep some distance from the car ahead and from the car behind, if one is to avoid an accident. Hence the temporal relations between the cars speeding at 65 miles an hour is a mind independent relation, whether the drivers think about it or not. Yet the temporal relations of a car from the one ahead and from the one behind is distinct from the speed of any one car, since any one car all alone could be speeding at 65 miles an hour on the interstate, but then the temporal relations to the car ahead and to the car behind would not exist. Hence these mind independent relations are real effects of any given car having speed enough to hold its place with the car ahead and with the car behind. It is the real ordering to something ahead and to something behind which cannot be reduced to the mere speed of moving at 65 miles an hour that the car would have if it were all alone on the highway. Hence the real temporal relations involved in this chain of cars are real effects distinct from the speeding cars. If the lead car suddenly stopped and the chain of cars piled up into one another, the temporal relations linking them together would become evident. Let me take another example. The Niagara river is destined to flow over the falls until winter freezes it. Only the change to bitter winter alters the destiny of the river water as it approaches the falls. The moving water at the brink of the falls is a three dimensional body. But its summer-time destiny to flow over the falls is not a three dimensional body. It is a real temporal dimension that lacks three dimensions just because it is destiny for an immediate future that does not yet exist. That immediate temporal dimension is a real temporal relation caused by the moving waters of the Niagara river.

We experience real temporal relations by contrast with imaginary temporal relations. Everyone experiences the imaginary motion of the scenery while motoring in the country. For example, the posts of a fence speed backwards at 65 miles an hour in imaginary motion. One discounts this illusory motion in order to perceive one's real motion forward at 65 miles an hour. It is the contrast of the real motion of the car with the imaginary motion of the backward flying fence posts that enables us to perceive our real motion forward.

Similarly, physicists discount the apparently incompatible measurements of their time and distance from events by adjusting their known movements relative to one another to the constancy of the speed of light. Thus the physicists as themselves moving bodies destined to move in determinate ways relative to one another, are moving bodies mutually measured by the speed of light as destined to be in constant real temporal relation to all moving bodies (Hawking 1988: 21-29; Jammer 1967: 5, 398). Now according to Newton's first law of motion, all moving bodies are destined to constant motions in a straight line unless acted upon by a new force. Hence their presently destined straight line motions are the effects of their present motions.

2. Specification of Future Temporal Relations as Minimal Causality

Minimal causality is that which produces the minimal effect. Now a moving body produces a *determinate destiny which lacks all three spatial dimensions*. Yet it is nevertheless a *real effect, namely a real temporal relation*. Now a real effect that lacks all three spatial dimensions is surely a minimal effect. Moreover all four of the Aristotelian causes, and philosophy has never found any other kinds of causes, produce greater effects. Those four causes are: the agent cause, the final cause, the formal cause, and the material cause. The agent cause causes bodily motion, so its effect is a three dimensional reality. The agent's effect is therefore greater than a temporal relation which lacks all three spatial dimensions. The final cause causes the agent cause to act, so its effect also has three dimensions, and hence it is also greater than a temporal relation. The formal and material cause are mutual causes to each other in producing a real individual body; so their effect is also a three dimensional one. And consequently their effect is also greater than a temporal relation which lacks all three spatial dimensions. Hence, in sum, all four causes known to philosophy produce effects greater than a real temporal relation. And so moving bodies as causing these real temporal relations are producing the minimal known effects.

Since the effect produced by this minimal cause lacks all three spatial dimensions, *the effect lacks an intrinsic formal cause*. For an intrinsic formal cause is just the cause whose reciprocal causality with the material cause produces a real individual body, as said above. Nevertheless temporal relations *have a determinate species*, because they constitute the determinate future destiny of a moving body. The moving body determines the species of its destiny as to keep moving in a straight line. Now the temporal relation thus specified lacks any intrinsic nature. Hence, temporal relations have only got *extrinsic formal specification*. The cause of this merely extrinsic formal effect was called by the Scholastics, *an extrinsic formal cause* (Poinsot 1632: 602b38-603a10).

3. Temporal Relations do not Distinguish What Common Sense Calls Individual Bodies from Heaps of Rubbish

From the point of view of common sense, there is a big difference between a human being and a heap of rubbish, and the difference is not only some mysterious thing called human rights. For a human being is a product of nature, and so enjoys biological unity as an individual body, while a heap of rubbish is just a chance effect lacking the unity of an individual body.

Now common sense distinguishes individual bodies by the fact that they occupy different parts of three dimensional space. But since temporal relations lack all three spatial dimensions, they do not enable us to distinguish one individual body from another. Thus for example, in an airplane traveling at 600 miles an hour, the passengers are also traveling at 600 miles an hour. But so too a heap of rubbish which stewardesses have collected after a meal is also travelling at 600 miles an hour. Now a passenger is some kind of a product of nature, and is perceived by common sense as an individual body. But the heap of rubbish is perceived by common sense as just bits of paper and garbage thrown together, and is not perceived as an individual body. However, as bodies moving through the air at 600 miles an hour, the heap of rubbish is related to the outside air just like any passenger is. Hence, the temporal relation does not discern what common sense calls an individual body from a heap of rubbish. The solar system as understood since Copernicus as a system of temporal relations is a classic example of temporal relations that do not distinguish individual bodies from chance collections of bodies. For no one believes that the earth or the moon is an individual body, although they are parts of the solar system.

4. Scientific Mechanism as Temporal Relations Specified by Extrinsic Formal Causality is Minimal Scientific Knowledge of Reality

Recall the epistemological stance of Strawson and Quine, two outstanding British-American philosophers. They say that we have no rational control over our certitudes about the existence of an external world, and about the existence of minds in other people's bodies (Strawson 1985: 13-19; Quine 1973: 272). Now the disappearance of people, sheep and tables would indeed follow from science's exclusive use of extrinsic formal causality, just as Quine says is the case for science. For temporal relations cannot discern the existence of individual bodies. And since extrinsic formal causality is the minimal possible causality of the minimal effect, namely temporal relations, science could be content with such an explanation on the grounds of Occam's razor. However, extrinsic formal causality does explain the mind independent existence of temporal relations. So mind independent reality would furnish the data of science. Hence *science would not be driven to nonrational belief in the existence of an external world*.

Still extrinsic formal causality may not be the adequate answer to the epistemological challenge of Strawson and Quine to the rational basis of science. It seems that even with personal understanding of extrinsic formal causality, one could still need nonrational belief in the existence of minds in other human bodies. For science does not refer to anyone's conscious experience. Hence, even if one person understood about knowledge of extrinsic formal causality, that person would only have *scientifically unverified conscious experience*, and other people's bodies would be understood scientifically as mechanisms totally devoid of consciousness. One's own consciousness would leave *one all alone in the universe*. That indeed was *the historic stance of the whole of classical modern philosophy* from Descartes until it lost its dominance in this century. Therefore, nonrational belief in other people's minds would still be necessary in order to have the data observed by one scientist replicated by the observations of other scientists. For replication by other scientists is required for verification in the logic of science in the twentieth century.

In reply to this second argument for nonrational control of the basis of science, the following must first be noted. The idea of the individual mind isolated and alone in the universe is not and never has been the opinion of either common sense or of science. It was a philosophic thesis which derived from Descartes and dominated classical modern philosophy until recent generations. Now, according to Descartes, a human mind was: 1) a spiritual substance completely independent from matter in general; *and* 2) independent of its human body in particular; *and* 3) needing no empirical information whatever from the material world, since all its perceptions, feelings and ideas were innate. One's own human body and all human bodies as well as any body whatever are merely mechanisms ruled exclusively by the laws of mechanics. Hence, on observing the movements of other human bodies, one could never conclude to the existence of a spiritual substance within that mechanism. Consequently, one was an isolated mind all alone in the universe.

However, the thesis of the isolated mind all alone in the universe is challenged today by several disciplines. In philosophy, many philosophers have accepted the argument of Wittgenstein that all or almost all individual experience is expressed in public language (Wittgenstein: 1936-1949, nos. 262-268). Hence, an isolated individual mind is impossible. For social psychology, the self which individuals experience shares its life with other persons (Fraser 1987: 722). According to Peirce, the mentor of so many American semioticians, an isolated personal existence is an illusion (Peirce 1893: 4.68). For Sebeok, the semiotic self lies in a biologically and socially determined, yet individually variable, zone of privacy that keeps strangers at a distance (Sebeok 1979: 45 and 267). Hence the semiotic self is embedded in social distances to others; it is not a mind isolated and alone in the universe. Therefore, philosophers following Wittgenstein, social psychologists, and semioticians like Peirce and Sebeok, show that scientists can replicate one another's data in a rational manner, because personal experience is communicable to others. Hence, the second argument for nonrational control of the basis of science is false.

I now proceed to give my argument for extrinsic formal causality as the basis of science. Whether we move our own bodies, or other bodies move around us, we are almost constantly dealing with bodies in motion. Now what we actually experience as external stimuli are past events in the physical environment. For "[m]any scores of milliseconds must pass before any change in the world can be registered by a sense organ or interpreted by a brain" (Rabbitt 1987: 670). But the destiny of motions from now into the immediate future is what we usually perceive. For, estimating where the stimulus of a moment ago destines a moving object to be now, that is what we usually perceive. For example, an instant after a fly is hit, the major league outfielder turns his back on the hitter, and races fifty feet backwards, turns his head, holds up his gloved hand and catches the baseball. As we walk down a crowded sidewalk, we weave our way through the oncoming crowd by estimating which way other persons are going to move past us. According to Rabbitt (1987: 672), *people can reduce to zero milliseconds the time lapse between reception of a stimulus and the physiological reaction time required to interact with an object, precisely because we perceive the immediate future course of motions.* Evolution has formed our perception to estimate the immediate future of moving bodies in our vicinity. In eating, we automatically estimate the time to open our mouth as the fork laden with food approaches its destination. As our tongue pushes food between our chewing jaws, we automatically remove it from the serious wounds it could suffer if our powerful chewing would pierce our tongue. All these ordinary experiences of everyday living are perceptions of the immediate future of bodies in motion.

Now perception of the immediate future of moving bodies is perception of real temporal relations. Hence, perception of real temporal relations is an ordinary experience of everyday life. Moreover, the future destiny of moving bodies constitutes the elementary experimental law of physics, namely Newton's first law of motion: namely, a body not acted on by any other force will keep moving in a straight line at the same speed. Newton's first law of motion plainly declares the immediate future of a moving body, and that is what is meant by a real temporal relation. Therefore, the basic law of experimental science concerns real temporal relations, and real temporal relations are matters of perception in everyday living. *Hence, both science and everyday common sense find a basis in mind independent realities, namely in real temporal relations.* However, real temporal relations do not manifest the existence of any existent bodies, since they merely concern a future that does not yet exist. And a future that does not yet exist is not an existent body. For future destiny of a moving body is not any one of its three spatial dimensions, but it is nevertheless a real dimension. And that real dimension is the object of Newton's first law of motion.

Hence, some peculiar deliverances of philosophy of science come to make sense in the light of real temporal relations, taken as the basic mind independent data of science. First of all, Positivism is right in holding that the data do not reveal the intrinsic nature of things. For real temporal relations do not have any intrinsic nature. Secondly, the theory-ladenness of facts makes sense, inasmuch as facts concern some type of body. But real temporal relations as basic data do not require any specific type of body, since they do not have any intrinsic nature, whereas bodies do have some type of intrinsic nature and so must be bodies of some specific kind. Now physics sometimes uses field theory, which dispenses with the existence of all individual bodies; sometimes it uses the theory of invisible bodies such as sub-atomic particles and atoms; and sometimes it uses the theory of visible bodies such as crystals (Quine 1981: 17; Powell 1985: 48). Hence, it is the use of one or the other of these theories which determines what type of body is a fact. Now all other facts presuppose some type of body of which they are facts. Therefore, all facts are theory-laden, if we hold that the basic data are real temporal relations.

Now science is concerned with real temporal relations only inasmuch as they are discovered to be the specific destiny of identifiable motions. For example, biological or electro-chemical motions are found to specify real temporal relations so as to constitute mechanical systems of temporal relations. However, science itself consists of language. And the articulated sounds of human words have destinies which are not fully determined by any biological or electro-chemical motions. Indeed, the temporal relations between the sounds of human words constitute mechanical systems of real temporal relations which radio or telephone can transform into their own proper kinds of energy. But the manifest destiny of sounds of scientific words in radio waves is still specified by conscious thought. Never mind that the radio waves do not think. The extrinsic formal causality of thought is still the specifier destining those radio waves. *It is just because science pursues mechanistic understanding, content with mere extrinsic formal causality, that it can dispense with public experience of specifying private thinking.* Just as the astronomer produces apodictic proof of the existence of a star by motions observed which cannot otherwise be explained, although that star itself cannot be observed, so the specific destinies of words manifest the extrinsic formal causality of private thought which can never itself be publicly observed.

Fortunately, this analysis is confirmed by a recent revolution in psychology. Prof. Roger Walcott Sperry reports that, in the last fifteen years, the predominate paradigm in contemporary psychology places "mind in a control role above matter in the brain". The new paradigm displaces the reductionist paradigm which placed matter in control of mind. The new paradigm grants matter a subordinate role in determining mind (Sperry 1987: 165). This paradigm shift in psychology confirms the above analysis in the following way. Sperry says that the new paradigm does not hold for interaction between mind and electrochemical processes. "Mind is conceived to move matter in the brain and to govern, rule and direct neural and chemical events without interacting with "...them (Ibid.). *Now it is precisely the function of extrinsic formal causality to displace the agent and final causes by a more elementary cause which is not committed to explaining how interaction could be understood.* Thus the solar system is explained as a mechanism specified by extrinsic formal causes without needing any explanation by agent causes, (let alone by final causes which have not been recognized by science since the 17th century). For, Einstein's general relativity precisely eliminated gravitational forces from explanation of the solar system, by substituting the curvature of space-time for gravitational forces (Hawking 1988:29-30). Now gravitational forces are agent causes, whereas the curved space-time that governs the path of the earth around the sun is *an excellent example of extrinsic formal causality.* I say that the space-time curvature which governs the path of the earth around the sun is an excellent example of extrinsic formal causality, because that path consists of specified temporal relations between the earth and the other bodies of the solar system. Hence, these specified real temporal relations are plain cases of extrinsic formal causality.

Finally, the specification of human language in the medium manifests human thought as largely free from determination by neural and electro-chemical forces, according to contemporary psychology. Now what fundamentally specifies human thought by extrinsic formal causality is the destined future motion of moving bodies. But this destined immediate future motion is *entirely by chance respecting the three spatial dimensions of matter, since it depends on the chance influence of previous forces upon the body in question.* Hence, the fundamental specification of thought consists in that which occurs entirely by chance respecting the spatial three dimensional structure of matter. *Now the three spatial dimensions constitute the intrinsic nature of matter.* Hence, what fundamentally specifies thought is not determined by the intrinsic nature of matter. Therefore, the fundamental specification of human language in the medium as largely free from neural and electrochemical forces is explained by the fundamental specification of human thought by extrinsic formal causality.

This basic specification by extrinsic formal causality constitutes that minimal causality which merits to be called the epistemological level of causality. For it is at this level of causality that we find both the mechanical causality characteristic of experimental science, and the freedom characteristic of all the works of human civilization.

We are now in position to discuss Quine's claim that the existence of people, sheep and tables is a belief of great survival value in town and jungle for man and beast alike; but that it would be senseless to speak of a motive for this archaic and unconscious posit (Quine 1973: 54; 1976: 249). To this I reply that people, sheep and tables are public signs for mind directed cerebral mechanisms genetically and culturally conditioned. Hence, people, sheep and tables are not signs inasmuch as they are individual existent bodies, but as mechanical signs apt to stimulate genetically and culturally conditioned mind directed cerebral mechanisms. Hence, Quine's position is true to the extent that, at the epistemological level, the enculturated Western certitude that people, sheep and tables are existent individual bodies is only a mind dependent belief of great survival value for town life in the West. But, nevertheless, people, sheep and tables as public signs are mind independent mechanisms consisting of specified temporal relations. The epistemological level leaves undecided the difference between the Western belief in the existence of individual human beings, sheep and tables and the Buddhist belief which denies mind independent existence to people, sheep and tables.

But the great gain of seeing the unresolved difference between Western belief and Buddhist belief is that it lays bare the fact that, at the minimal and foundational epistemological level, we experience real temporal relations specified by motions that occur by chance respecting the intrinsic nature of bodies. So these relations are not specified by the intrinsic nature of bodies. And, consequently, human thought is not originally specified by the biochemical forces which are found only in individual existent agents. Therefore, the freedom of thought is manifested by this historic difference between Western and Buddhist beliefs.

The Western and Buddhist difference of beliefs over the existence of individual bodies manifests the difference between beliefs and scientific knowledge. Just as the drivers in a chain of cars on an interstate highway perceive their real speed ahead at 65 miles an hour by counterdistinction to the believable motion of fence posts flying backwards at 65 miles an hour, so the truth of scientific mechanism of specified temporal relations is perceived as scientific knowledge of mind independent reality by contrast to these opposed historical beliefs of the West and of the Buddhists.

It is not true that unanimity of beliefs is characteristic of scientific knowledge. Rather the contrast between irreconcilable beliefs with replicated data is the usual path of scientific progress, as believable hypotheses are refuted by verifying the real mechanisms of mind independent reality. That contrast between belief known to conform to mind independent reality at a given time and under a certain respect, with a contrary opinion known not to conform to mind independent reality at the given time and under the same respect is the meaning of the Aristotelian principle of contradiction (Aquinas 1268-1270: 2212). *Now the truth of mechanism that excludes the existence of individual bodies is only true at the epistemological moment of first contact with mind independent reality by the minimal epistemological causality of extrinsic formal causes.* That verified belief in extrinsic formal causality is not a belief contrary to belief in the existence of individual bodies as caused by agent, final, formal and material causes. For, these other causes are not experienced at the epistemological moment. The distinction of these different types of causes is indispensable for understanding the epistemological redominance of mechanism in modern science.

REFERENCES

AQUINAS, Thomas.
    c.1269-1272. *In Duodecim Libros Metaphysicorum Aristotelis Expositio*, ed M. R. Cathala and Raymond M. Spiazzi (Turin: Marrietti, 1950); available in English trans. by John P. Rowan, *Commentary on the Metaphysics of Aristotle* (Chicago: Regnery, 1961), 2 vols.

FRASER, Colin.
    1987. "Social Psychology", in Gregory 1987: 721-723.

GREGORY, Richard L., Editor.
    1987. *The Oxford Companion to the Mind* (Oxford: Oxford University Press).

HAWKING, Stephen A.
    1988. *A Brief History of Time: from the Big Bang to Black Holes* (New York, Bantam Books).

JAMMER, Max.
    1967. "Motion", in *The Encyclopedia of Philosophy*, ed. Paul Edwards (New York: The Free Press), Vol. 5, 396-399.

PEIRCE, Charles Sanders.
    1893. *The Grand Logic*, Chapter 6, alternative version, in CP 4.53-74.

POINSOT, John.
    1632. *Tractatus de Signis*, edited and subtitled *The Semiotic of John Poinsot*, ed. John Deely (Berkeley: University of California Press, 1985).

POWELL, Ralph.
    1985. "The Evidential Priority of Unindividuated Realities: The Philosophy of Science of Willard Van Ormand Quine", in *Semiotics 1985*, ed. John Deely (Lanham, MD: University Press of America), 45-55.

QUINE, Willard Van Orman.
    1973. *The Roots of Reference* (La Salle, IL: Open Court).
    1976. *The Ways of Paradox* (Cambridge, MA: Harvard University Press).
    1981. *Theories and Things* (Boston: Belknap Press of Harvard University Press).

RABBITT, P.A.M.
    1987. "Reaction Times", in Gregory 1987: 671-672.

SEBEOK, Thomas A.
    1989. *The Sign & Its Masters* (Lanham, MD: University Press of America).

SPERRY, Roger Walcott.
    1987. "Consciousness and Causality", in Gregory 1987: 164-166.

STRAWSON, Peter.
    1985. *Skepticism and Naturalism: Some Varieties* (New York: Columbia University Press).

WITTGENSTEIN, Ludwig.
    1936-1949. *Philosophische Untersuchungen*, English trans. as *Philosophical Investigations* with facing German text by G.E. Anscombe, 2nd edition (Oxford: Basil Blackwell, 1958).

THE NOTION 'SEMIOTIC SELF' REVISITED

Thomas A. Sebeok
Research Center for Language and Semiotic Studies
Indiana University, Bloomington Campus

The topic I am going to talk about is called "the semiotic self", and I have to put this into a context so you will understand why I am doing this. Many years ago there was a conference held in Germany that was convened by Thure von Uexküll. Our late President Shands was there, and I was asked there to talk on the subject of the semiotic self. I then did that and wrote a paper which I published in a book called *The Sign & Its Masters*, which John Deely has recently accepted for his series in a revised edition (1989). As I was preparing this for Deely, I said to myself 'This is really a very poor chapter, and I don't like it at all'. So I said to myself 'The whole question of the semiotic self has to be rethought.' Whereupon I sat down and rethought it, and wrote a second paper which, since I have written it, I have also rethought--of course, that's what science is all about, constant thinking, and there is no end--and so what I am going to tell you about is some of the more recent ideas about this notion of semiotic self, which is perhaps a strange notion.[1]

Fortunately for you I don't have a blackboard, so I will have to verbalize these things to some extent. I'll tell you how I conceive the self.

I think that animals have a two-layer skin, as it were, of 'self-hood'. The first one is strictly biological, but with semiotic overtones. The other is strictly semiotic but accurate in biology. Let me explain what I mean by the first 'skin', as it were, the 'semiotic skin'. It is equivalent to the immune system. That is, the immune system is an enormous organ going throughout all vertebrate and animal bodies, which has a function of recognizing two things, the self and the other--*ego, alter*. The history of the immune system is very interesting. If you know anything about microbiology-- and if you don't, you should read Lynn Margulis's and Dorion Sagan's (1986) book called *The Microcosmos*--the most ancient and the first semiotic opposition in living nature is self-recognition and other-recognition. The most primitive bacteria are capable of doing this, and as evolution progressed this became more and more elaborate and finally (not *finally*, but finally as of this moment) this is all incorporated in what is called the immune system, namely, the recognition of invaders.

There is an extraordinary Danish scholar whose name is Niels Jerne[2], and in 1984 he gave a Nobel address, wherein what he said, without going into details, was that the immune system is not just a semiotic system, but it is precisely a generative grammar type semiotic system. By this he means that the immune system is made up of rules--you see, when you have invaders coming in the body, they can be infinite in number. The body cannot predict what kind of a bug it will encounter, and, in fact, the immune system can protect you against all existing bugs, and also those which don't exist, those which you can synthesize in laboratories, for example. (The exception to this of course is in cases of a malfunctioning, mis-semiosis, which our doctors call a carcinoma, AIDS, or whatever. These are semiotic events which malfunction at the junction of the immune system with the external world. But in most cases it works.)

Now of course the problem for immunologists--and you will find this in the work of Medawar[3], for example, who also won the Nobel Prize for the realization of the problem--is, how on earth can the body know in advance what it will encounter throughout life, and how it can react to things which don't even exist which it might or might not encounter.

The answer is the same as Noam Chomsky gave to the question of how do we recognize sentences which we have never heard before, and all linguists know this, that all but a few simple cliches are novel. The answer is, of course, a generative type grammar.

So the first definition of the self is that which is defined by the parameters of this interesting generative grammar which is called the immune system. However, this is a problem for the immunologists, not for semioticians. You can see that it has semiotic aspects, but it is basically a problem for molecular biology.

So then I asked myself, 'Is there anything else?' And I got the answer 'Yes'. Here we go back to the work of the great Swiss animal psychologist, Professor Heini Hediger (1980), who, already in 1936 in his unpublished dissertation, discovered that all animals have an invisible bubble, as it were, surrounding their biological entity, their body, and this is a bubble which has a rather precise definition in terms of distance from the self, which might be variable under certain contextual circumstances--it might expand, it might contract, but every animal has this. It can be artificially reduced to zero, namely, in a context of animal taming, or specifically in domestication. By this I mean, for example, that any child can go up to a cow and pat it: the cow has been domesticated. To put it semiotically, domestication means the reduction of this distance to zero and breeding for a zero distance.

I hope I am being reasonably clear about this. Wild animals of course behave differently, and human beings are among these wild animals. We all carry this bubble around us. This bubble expands and contracts depending on the context. Obviously when you make love, it diminishes; when you are engaged in hostility, it enlarges. But this is rule-governed. Each culture has very strict rules about limits beyond which you can or cannot go.

Let me give you very briefly a glimpse of how this works. I wish Paul Bouissac were here; he could explain to you very well how circus animals are trained.[4] You have a ring, and in the ring you have, let us say, a tiger, and the problem for the trainer is a very complicated one. He has on the one hand to work with the tiger or tigers, as the case may be, and, on the other hand he has a semiotic relation with the audience. Let's keep that apart, it's another problem. The trainer appears with a whip and a chair and appears, like in the old movies, to dominate--because *Homo sapiens* is superior to the other animals--to dominate these cats. That's what the audience sees.

But what really happens is that we know precisely what the tiger's personal space is, and if you have a tiger in one spot and you want the tiger to have to move back, you just intrude into the space. The whip is not to beat the animal. It is simply an indexical device: you intrude it into the space, and to the extent that you intrude it the tiger will move backwards. When you withdraw it the tiger will go back to its so-called secondary territory. So you can control animals simply by the manipulation of their personal spaces.

This is a long story. It has been particularly studied by an anthropologist called Edward Hall (1959, 1966) who invented a term for this, proxemics, which is essentially the study of the personal space of human beings, and not only of personal space but of personal time, because time-space in this respect are the same. I just refer you to the problem of American invitations to parties. If you're invited to a dinner, and your hostess says "Dinner at six", you'd better not show up at seven or you'll never be asked again. On the other hand, if you're invited to a cocktail party at six, in America it's perfectly okay to arrive at seven. So your context will define when personal time-space can be violated.[5] And every culture has this kind of set of rules, and Hall studied these among Arabs, the Japanese, West Germans, and Americans, and so on.

I'm just mentioning that this is the background of this double layer skin, the immune system on the one hand and this invisible bubble on the outside which I'd like to discuss further but for the moment can only refer you to the work of Hall.

Now, the question is, what is the closest link in the body with the self? And the answer, which dawned on me only long after I had written my original paper, is, obviously, memory.[6] Memory has two aspects. It is a physical repository of information, and it is also a social construct. The reasons for this are quite straightforward.

Each organism requires information--I use "information" in the everyday sense, not in the Shannon and Weaver (1949) sense--about certain experiences in its past to enable that individual to steer with reasonable certitude of survival in a specific Umwelt. When I end the sentence with the word "Umwelt" I conjure up a whole image of Jakob von Uexküll who, in my opinion, was one of the all-time great semioticians. His semiotic framework--and you must remember that Jakob von Uexküll was an experimental and theoretical biologist who never heard of Peirce, never heard of Saussure, never heard of semiotics--was among the most important of all time. The similarity with Peirce, by the way, derives from a quite obvious fact: he was a neo-Kantian, and Peirce, although Peirceans don't want to admit this, was of course a neo-Kantian as well. That is why von Uexküll is similar to Peirce, and to Cassirer, and that is why René Thom refers to him all the time--but this is by the way.[7]

How memory works has recently been explored in a marvelous autobiography by François Jacob (1988), with his central guiding metaphor, his *statue interior*. Let me read you a brief passage:

> I have been sculpting it [his interior statue] since my childhood. It gives my life continuity. It is the most intimate part of me, the hardest kernel of my character. I have been shaping this statue all of my life. I have been constantly retouching, polishing, refining it.

And then comes a very semiotic sentence--Jacob is one of the great semioticians of France:

> Not a gesture, not a word [nonverbal communication, probably], has but been imposed by the statue within

which is his metaphor of how the self is shaped, as it were, internally, by this very great man. And also we have people like Karl Popper (1977) who says that "the self is like a living organism. It extends through a stretch of time from birth to death".

Again here is an interesting question (and by the way I want to say that the self is not identical with consciousness, this is a terrible confusion that some people perpetuate, but it is not identical): what is the difference between consciousness and the self? One of the differences is that consciousness is interrupted by sleep, the self is never interrupted, the self is continuous from conception until death.

Jacob interestingly raises this same question. I was very struck by this. Jacob says "Why doesn't the system slip, so that after sleep has disassembled the mind, its memory and will, the mechanism is not reassembled somewhat differently to form a different person, a different me." In other words, he's asking why is Jacob who wakes up the same Jacob who fell asleep. A very interesting question we ought to have time to discuss. There is in fact a book about this called *Self-Consistency*, (Lecky 1945) and the question is how do we maintain this self-consistency.

We do it by many techniques. In the old days, of course, by oral tradition, and this is what folklore really is all about, but literate peoples do something else. They invented the diary. The diary is a way of keeping track of the self. They invented the intimate journal. This is an old literate technique. But later we have other devices, we have a photo-album. Every boring American family when you go there brings out a photo album. What are they doing when they are showing you these boring pictures? They are reaffirming the consistency of the self. And, God help us, home movies! Now there are comparable technical accoutrements. You know, I have been to a dinner recently where they played the tape of their children crying at birth.

It's obvious that these are simply techniques for maintaining the self.

But, skipping over a lot, let me ask what are the twin functions of memory in our lives? On the one hand, it is amalgamative, in the sense that I have been discussing. And also it is archival. And of course its sources in both cases are genetic on the one hand and semiotic on the other. Here again, one is inherited by Darwinian means, and one by Lamarckian means. By the way, a very exciting book by Todorov (1982) in this connection is about the discovery of America, but it is precisely a discussion of the same problem--what is meant by the semiotic self--of people like Christopher Columbus, for example, or de las Casas.

Well, four more minutes, the moderator says. I would love to have four more hours. I would have liked to tell you about how these things are done--fingerprinting, for example--and by the way about Alphonse Bertillon (1888, 1893), a great semiotician who nobody mentions in this connection; notice his titles, *service de signalement, . . . instructions signalétique*. He was perfectly aware of what he was doing. And if you want to know more about these early people who have written about this, look at the marvelous article by Carlo Ginzburg (1983) in a book that Eco and I edited called *The Sign of Three* in which he puts together various pursuers phenotypic clues from three different fields, art historians (particularly Giovanni Morelli), psychoanalysts (Freud), and of course the great Sherlock Holmes.

I also would like to point out to you that there are many physiological devices by which this can be done, most of them quite familiar. But I would like to point out just one book written by a German novelist called Patrick Süskind (1985), called *Das Parfum*, and here the semiotic self of the anti-hero, a very horrible man called Grenouille, is constructed entirely out of odors. Like a dog he lives in a realm of smell, and I quote from here (Süskind 1985: 149):

> . . . *the* odor of a human being doesn't exist--any more than *the* human countenance. [as shown by Paul Ekman] Every human being smelled different, no one knew that better than Grenouille, who recognized thousands upon thousands of individual odors and could sniff out the difference of each human being from birth on. . . . each individual's

aura hovered as a small cloud of more refined particularity. . . . the highly complex unmistakable [semiotic] code of a *personal* odor . . . .

Now I have many other examples, but I have run out of time. I may mention in conclusion that my approach to the semiotic self differs from that of Singer (1980) mainly in that my approach is much more biological. His approach is in the tradition of Alfred Schutz (1955, 1962) and Charles Morris (1948-1949), a semiotic tradition of a very theoretical and literate kind. I come from a different tradition, more strictly biological, but the two intermesh.

NOTES

[1] *Editor's note:* This paper is a transcription of the remarks made by Professor Sebeok in the session on Semiotics and Cognitive Sciences chaired by Judith Hollander. Because of the informal nature of this presentation, citations of published sources cover only those works discussed or elaborated upon in the talk. Readers seeking a fuller bibliographic treatment should consult the three publications noted by the author, namely, Sebeok 1977, 1979, 1989a.

[2] Niels K. Jerne shared in the 1984 Nobel Prize in Medicine for his work with immunology.

[3] Sir Peter Brian Medawar received the Nobel Prize for Medicine in 1960.

[4] See, for example, Bouissac's (1976) *Circus and Culture: A Semiotic Approach* and his contribution to *The Clever Hans Phenomenon* (Sebeok and Rosenthal 1981).

[5] There is a very interesting study of violent murderers, prisoners. If I had a blackboard I would show you how you can almost predict who will be a murderer by delineating the personal space of let's say the average human being from that particular social class as a circle with the person in the center, whereas a violent person would have a personal space of an oval type with the person being at the rear end. This is very much like an old movie when you have a bar-room scene where the bad guy sits up against wall and puts his chair up against the wall. Why? Because his personal space is such that he cannot bear being invaded from the rear, so he protects that, and then there is a large space in the front which means that you can't really come close to him before he draws and shoots back. It's a certain violent type.

[6] There is memory of a personal nature, and there's institutional memory. For instance, I have been at Indiana for forty-six years. I have had an enormous number of changes in administrators. In fact, the joke is that I have had twenty college deans. Now when a college dean comes in, a new one, every administrator calls up and says, "Now Tom, I hear you've been here forty-six years. Could I use your memory?" And then I have a very long lunch with some Dean and tell him what he should have known when he accepted the job. And the reason he must know this of course is that he is constructing an institutional self by analogy.

[7] Works of von Uexküll and Thom cited in other papers by the author include, for example, von Uexküll 1909, 1940; Thom 1973.

REFERENCES

BERTILLON, Alphonse.
   1888. *Service de signalements*
   1893. *Identification anthropométrique: Instructions signalétiques* (Paris: Melun).

BOUISSAC, Paul.
   1976. *Circus and Culture: A Semiotic Approach* (Bloomington, IN: Indiana University Press).

GINZBURG, Carlo.
   1983. "Clues: Morelli, Freud, and Sherlock Holmes" in *The Sign of Three*, ed. Umberto Eco and Thomas A. Sebeok, (Bloomington, IN: Indiana University Press), Chapter 4, 81-118.

HALL, Edward T.
   1959. *The Silent Language* (Garden City, NY: Doubleday).
   1966. *The Hidden Dimension* (Garden City, NY: Doubleday).

HEDIGER, Heini.
   1980. *Tiere Verstehen: Erkenntisse eines Tierpsychologen* (Munich: Kindler Verlag).

JACOB, François.
   1988. *The Statue Within* (New York: Basic Books).

LECKY, Prescott.
   1945. *Self-Consistency: A Theory of Personality* (New York: Island Press).

MARGULIS, Lynn and Dorion SAGAN.
   1986. *Microcosmos* (New York: Summit Books).

MORRIS, C. W.
   1948-1949. "Signs about Signs about Signs", *Philosophy and Phenomenological Research* 9, 124-127.
   1970. *The Pragmatic Movement in American Philosophy* (New York: George Braziller).

POPPER, Karl R. and John C. ECCLES.
   1977. *The Self and Its Brain* (Berlin: Springer-Verlag).

SCHUTZ, Alfred.
   1955. "Symbol, Reality and Society", in *Symbols and Society*, ed. Lyman Bryson, Louis Finkelstein, Hudson Hoagland, and R.M. MacIver (New York: Harper and Brothers).
   1962. *Collected Papers, Volume I: The Problem of Social Reality*, ed. I.M. Natanson (The Hague: Martinus Nijhoff).

SEBEOK, Thomas A.
   1977. "The Semiotic Self", discussion paper presented at the Werner-Reimers-Stiftung, in Germany, and subsequently included as Appendix I in Sebeok 1979: 187-207.
   1989. *The Sign & Its Masters* (= Sources in Semiotics VIII, ed. John Deely and Brooke Williams; Lanham, MD: University Press of America, 1989), reprint in corrected form with a new Author's Preface and an added Editor's Preface, of original imprint under the same title (Austin, TX: University of Texas Press, 1979).
   1989a. "The Semiotic Self Revisited", in *Sign, Self, and Society*, ed. Benjamin Lee and Greg Urban (Berlin: Mouton de Gruyter).

SEBEOK, Thomas A., and Robert ROSENTHAL
   1981. *The Clever Hans Phenomenon: Communication with Horses, Whales, Apes, and People*, ed. Thomas Sebeok and Robert Rosenthal, *Annals of the New York Academy of Sciences* (New York: New York Academy of Sciences).

SHANNON Claude E., and Warren WEAVER.
1949. *The Mathematical Theory of Communication* (Urbana: University of Illinois Press).
SINGER, Milton
1980 "Signs of the Self: An Exploration in Semiotic Anthropology", *American Anthropologist* 82.3, 485-507.
SÜSKIND, Patrick.
1985. *Das Parfum* (Zurich: Diogenes Verlag), translated as *Perfume: The Story of a Murderer* by John E. Woods (New York: Alfred A. Knopf, 1986).
TODOROV, Tzvetan.
1982. *La Conquête de l'Amérique* (Paris: Éditions de Seuil).

THE FEAR OF THE ARBITRARY SIGN

Scott Simpkins
South Dakota State University

Ferdinand de Saussure's assertion that the linguistic sign is constructed arbitrarily ("The bond between the signifier and the signified is arbitrary" [i.1906-1911: 67]) frequently elicits uneasiness from semioticians. In his study on *The Fashion System*, for instance, Roland Barthes (1967: 215) attempts to emend this "error" by Saussure as he asserts that

> ... in language the equivalence of the signifier and the signified is (relatively) unmotivated . . . , but it is not arbitrary; once this equivalence is established [he gives as an example the word "cat" equalling a cat or the concept of cat], it cannot be overlooked if we are to make full use of the system of language, and it is because of this that we can say, correcting Saussure, that the linguistic sign is not arbitrary: a general law narrowly limits the power of those who use the system: their freedom is combinative, not inventive.

As is evident from this example by Barthes, the notion of the arbitrary sign seems to imply that signification is an illusory--or even impossible--process if signs lack any sort of motivational basis, or even more frightening, if the individual sign user is granted full latitude in sign use. Saussure's contention undermines the superstructure of sign function, positing a system which has no objective mechanism--a system, in fact, that can hardly be called a system since it is regulated by that least regulatable of entities: the sign user.

Jacques Derrida's suggestion that Saussure's term is "grossly misnamed" illustrates this disdain for the implications of subjectivity that arbitrariness elicits. In his *Of Grammatology*, he asserts that "from the moment that one considers the totality of determined signs, spoken, and *a fortiori* written, as unmotivated institutions, one must exclude any relationship of natural subordination, any natural hierarchy among signifiers or orders of signifiers" (1967: 44). Apparently, in this case, arbitrariness wields a threat for every institutionalized form of communication, implying perhaps that such institutions are derived from a "natural", rather than relational, logic, as Derrida suggests. It stands as a type of value-less realm in which nothing is certain or discernable from the viewpoint of rational decoding. The sign, then, appears to effectively promote a polysemousness which denies communication to any useful extent.

But, rather than a threat to the semiotic enterprise, the arbitrary sign should be viewed as a basic principle of sign construction and production. We need to remember Charles S. Peirce's remark that a sign is "something which stands *to somebody* for something in some respect or capacity"--in other words, that the individual involved in sign usage plays a significant, perhaps *the* significant, role in communication (c.1897: 98). In this manner, Ludwig Wittgenstein's observation that "bububu" could be used to mean "If it doesn't rain I shall go for a walk", seems far less like a threat of semiotic anarchy--and more like an acknowledgement of the process of signification (1945: 18e).

Jonathan Culler has succinctly pointed out the importance of recognizing the relational nature of both signifiers and signifieds in regard to Saussure's notion of "arbitrariness". Instead of an act of naming, the use of language depends upon designations which correspond to the signifier employed and the signified it transmits through signification. On either end of this act, the sender's intention and the decoder's perception of that intention are mediated only through the use of the sign, a liaison which is weakened by the subjective evaluation on the part of each individual involved, yet strengthened at the same time by the communal interaction which both have experienced before and use to bring about each future interaction. As Culler (1976: 14-15) notes:

> since the relation between signifier and signified is arbitrary, since there is no necessary reason for one concept rather than another to be attached to a given signifier, there is therefore no defining property which the concept must retain in order to count as the signified of that signifier. The signified associated with a signifier can take any form; there is no essential core of meaning that it must retain in order to count as the proper signified for that signifier. The fact that the relation between signifier and signified is arbitrary means, then, that since there are no fixed universal concepts or fixed universal signifiers, the signified itself is arbitrary, and so is the signifier.

Thus, when Saussure asserts that "in language there are only differences", it is clear that this element of selection and identification undertaken in the signification process is, or can be, entirely determined by both the sender and receiver of a message (Saussure i.1906-1911: 120). A sender could have an extremely unusual and idiosyncratic plan in mind when employing a signifier; a receiver could likewise take a signifier and connect any possible association to it when decoding it. If this condition were considered as a likely outgrowth of Saussure's contention, it is easy to see how a linguist such as Roy Harris could conclude that if the nature of language usage is considered to be "intrinsically open-ended and indeterminate", "speech communication would be at the mercy of unpredictable innovation, and the basis for a systematic identification of linguistic signs would be lost" (Harris 1984: 234). When both the sender and receiver have, in effect, total control over sign usage, this line of argument suggests, then the notion of system no longer applies. This is the consequence of "arbitrariness" that stands as perhaps the single most dangerous threat to the semiotic project. Or, at least, so it seems.

Rather than an unfortunate choice of words, however, Saussure's selection of "arbitrary" is perfectly suited to describe the paradoxical scene of signification. Accordingly, the preoccupation that semioticians reveal through their attempts to decode--and largely emasculate--Saussure's use of the word "arbitrary" further indicates the slippery, undecidable quality which it, as an emblem of the enterprise of language, displays so graphically. In addition to suggesting an act of choice, "arbitrary" can also indicate capriciousness or randomness--as well as tyranny or despotism. All of these connotations, of course, reverberate within our discussions of the term, ostentatiously illustrating the very situation that Saussure was trying, I would argue, to describe.

In fact, Saussure contends that the most desirable concept of the sign is its necessary arbitrariness. "Signs that are wholly arbitrary", he suggests, "realize better than the others [that are not entirely arbitrary] the ideal of the semiological process." For, it is through the arbitrary designation of the sign, through a communal, social agency, that signs work most successfully. As Saussure (i.1906-1911: 68; emphasis added) notes:

> every means of expression used in society is based, in principle, on collective behavior or--what amounts to the same thing--on convention. Polite formulas, or instance, though often imbued with a certain natural expressiveness (as in the case of a Chinese who greets his emperor by bowing down to the ground nine times), are nonetheless fixed by rule; it is this rule *and not the intrinsic value of the gestures* that obliges us to use them.

But Saussure, not unlike those who have written in his wake, attempts to salvage the sign from the abyss of subjectivism that haunts our reception of the word "arbitrary", thereby revealing in his own endeavors a similar fear of the implication of arbitrariness. His insistence on the need to rein in the usages and, more importantly, potential alterations of the sign demonstrates this as he attempts to rationalize a need for sign control. "The word *arbitrary* ... calls for comment", he observes. "The term should not imply that the choice of the signifier is left entirely to the speaker (... the individual does not have the power to change a sign in any way once it has become established in the linguistic community); I mean that it is unmotivated, i.e. arbitrary in that it actually has no connection with the signified" (Saussure i.1906-1911: 68-69). It is through institutionalized signification, Saussure argues, that we are able to decode the sign in a manner which leads to probable semiotic proficiency-- and thus effective communication. Still, if the signifier is not "connected with the signified", an infinite number of potential associations which produce signification is acknowledged. And it would seem that arbitrariness--random, personal associations--would be quite possible for each individual decoder.

However, Saussure tries to rescue "arbitrariness" from its largely negative connotation by declaring that this situation is responsible for protecting, rather than endangering, language. Because it is both mutable and immutable, Saussure contends, language functions within a shielded economy while simultaneously avoiding the stagnation characteristic of closed systems.

> As [language] is a product of both the social force and time, no one can change anything in it, and on the other hand, the arbitrariness of its signs theoretically entails the freedom of establishing just any relationship between phonetic substance and ideas. The result is that each of the two elements united in the sign maintains its own life to a degree unknown elsewhere, and that language changes, or rather evolves, under the influence of all the forces which can affect either sounds or meanings. (Saussure i.1906-1911: 76).

Change, nonetheless, is inevitable and its influence remains a source of anxiety for those--including Saussure--who depend upon signs for communication. "Mutability is so inescapable that it even holds true for artificial languages", Saussure notes. "Whoever creates a language controls it only so long as it is not in circulation; from the moment when it fulfills its mission and becomes the property of everyone, *control is lost*" (p. 76, emphasis added). This poses a significant threat to language through the implication that it lacks a grounding force of rationale or certainty. As Saussure admits, language is different from those cultural institutions and practices--he cites laws and customs as examples--which have established "natural relations" with the entities associated with them because these "human institutions . . . all have of necessity adapted the means employed to the ends pursued" (p. 75). But language, to the contrary, is "limited by nothing in the choice of means, for apparently nothing would prevent the associating of any idea whatsoever with just any sequence of sounds" (p. 76). Because the sign by nature is arbitrary, "Language is radically powerless to defend itself against the forces which from one moment to the next are shifting the relationship between the signified and the signifier" (p. 75). This powerlessness creates much of the anxiety associated with "arbitrariness" by suggesting that language cannot, in fact, be controlled and employed within objective, logical perimeters: when the law of language is seen as being beyond the law, no law reigns ultimately. Language usage, then, is a lawless enterprise.

Through syntagmatic and associative relations, however, Saussure contends that the sign is maintained with the confines of a system. These two elements, he says, "are what [limit] arbitrariness" (p. 133).

It is important to ask at this point why arbitrariness should be limited. It would seem, as Saussure himself observes, that the very nature of the linguistic sign presupposes, and *remains vital* because of, its arbitrary superstructure. Yet, the explanation is clear: if the sign can be entirely arbitrary, language appears to lose its communal basis, that very element which guarantees the successful interaction of communication which language presumably serves. As a result of this dilemma, and a potential strategy for resolving it, Saussure insists that "the limiting of arbitrariness" is the "best possible basis for approaching the study of language as a system." Because the "whole system of language is based on the *irrational* principle of the arbitrariness of the sign", he says, this principle "would lead to the worst sort of complication *if applied without restriction*". He adds that since "the mind contrives to introduce a principle of order and regularity into certain parts of the mass of signs", "relative motivation" has been introduced to effect this control. Because, Saussure argues, "there is no language in which nothing is motivated", the application of degrees of motivation allows us to find that restriction, that rational control which ensures semiotic security (p. 133, emphasis added). Although Saussure had previously claimed that signs can be "radically motivated, i.e. unmotivated", his strategic use of motivation as a factor of regulation is clear. Through the systematic analysis of varying degrees of motivation, we can more accurately describe the mechanisms behind a wide range of signs; but, if the possibility of motivation is not granted, we are left with only convention, a factor which resists much of our systematizing and, therefore, undermines the basis of semiotic analyses.

Yet Saussure realizes that this creates an apparent paradox, and he is quick to draw our attention to it. "Even in the most favorable cases", he notes, "motivation is never absolute" (p. 132). In other words, the element of usage always affects the signification process to various degrees depending upon each sign situation. Thus, he suggests that we have to be aware of the potential for motivation while also realizing that arbitrariness can come into play and unhinge any assumed logical association.

This is where the desirability of arbitrariness becomes evident, since it so visibly displays the organic nature of language as an ever-changing system of relations with no ultimately fixed values. It is hardly ironic, accordingly, when Saussure concludes that "the arbitrary nature of the sign is really what protects language from any attempt to modify it" (p. 73). This need for protection is merely another way of ignoring the real activity of arbitrariness as Saussure attempts to turn our conception of it toward a positive valuation. But such protection is not necessary when the inherent effect of arbitrariness is recognized as inherent--an element that cannot be eliminated by systematization or taxonomical categorization. Signs can signify anything that the sender and receiver want them to signify. They always have--and this is something we have to learn to embrace rather than shunning it with the hope that it will resolve itself if we ignore it or deny its implications for semiotics. "Arbitrariness" does not make all systemization obsolete or even endanger it--it merely draws attention to its limitations, its weak links, and thus produces a stronger analysis as a result.

REFERENCES

BARTHES, Roland.
    1967.   *Systéme de la Mode* (Paris: Editions du Seuil); trans. as *The Fashion System* by Matthew Ward and Richard Howard (New York: Hill and Wang, 1983).

CULLER, Jonathan.
    1976.   *Ferdinand de Saussure* (New York: Penguin Books).

DERRIDA, Jacques.
    1967.   *De la Grammatologie* (Les Editions de Minuit); trans. as *Of Grammatology* by Gayatry Charavorty Spivak (Baltimore: The Johns Hopkins Press, 1976).

HARRIS, Roy.
    1987.   *Reading Saussure: A Critical Commentary on the Cours de Linguistique Générale* (LaSalle, Illinois: Open Court).

PEIRCE, Charles Sanders.
    c. 1897.   "What is a Sign? Three Divisions of Logic", in *Philosophical Writings of Peirce*, ed. Justus Buchler (New York: Dover Publications, 1955), 98-101.

SAUSSURE, Ferdinand de.
    i. 1906-1911.   Lectures delivered at the University of Geneva and published from auditors' notes by Charles Bally and Albert Sechehaye, in collaboration with Albert Riedlinger, under the title *Cours de Linguistique Générale*, trans. into English by Wade Baskin as *Course in General Linguistics* (New York: McGraw Hill, 1966).

WITTGENSTEIN, Ludwig.
    1945.   *Philosophical Investigations*, trans. G.E.M. Anscombe, 3rd ed. (New York: Macmillan, 1968).

VIII

SEMIOTICS AND RELIGION

FAITH AND THE SIGNS OF EXPECTATION

Robert S. Corrington
The Pennsylvania State University

      The reality and experience of faith has been articulated in a variety of ways, each attesting to a particular and limited conception of the human process and its relation to the divine. What is needed is a generic account that will exhibit the basic features of faith regardless of the finite and historically determined perspectives within which faith is located. In most cases, at least, faith has been sharply demarcated from belief insofar as belief is tied to the logical structure of assertive judgments of the form "S is P". The affirmation of a predicate, be it a quality or an event, of a given subject entails that such a predicate can be brought under circumscribed forms of inquiry and possible validation. The reality of faith, on the other hand, is of a radically different logical nature. As Paul Tillich has persuasively argued, faith is the state of being grasped by an ultimate concern (Tillich 1963). In the sheer bindingness of this concern, all mere beliefs about the divine nature are broken open by that which can not be the bearer of predicates or a subject within which or upon which such predicates could inhere.
      If faith is fundamentally different from belief, it follows that it can not be rendered in the same semiotic terms as those that pertain to beliefs. To believe that something is the case is to articulate and ramify signs and interpretants as they serve to illuminate and embody the object of belief. Thus, for example, to assert that the divine is complex in its nature is to struggle toward a specific series of signs that will exhibit the various forms and orders of the complexity of God. Each sign series will be related to the other relevant series that together flesh out the contour of God's complex ways of being. For the Christian, for instance, beliefs about God's incarnation in the slumbering orders of nature will be expressed in a body of signs that make the incarnation actual to a community of believers. It makes sense to say that some signs are more compelling than others or that some interpretants promise to facilitate further inquiry into the divine nature. Yet none of this semiotic material clarifies the deeper and more problematic phenomenon of faith.
      In being grasped by an ultimate concern the human process is inverted and shriven of its semiotic plenitude and compelled to go beyond the semiotic richness of its religious beliefs. Mere preliminary concerns, always concretized in communally available sign systems, cannot replace the ultimate import of the elusive 'object' of faith. The signs of the determinate religions, to use Hegel's formulation, become curiously suspended in the moment of faith and recede in the face of that which is

not a sign or a body of interpretants. Our theological beliefs are finite and determinate and thus can fit in with the rest of our interpretive life. But the movement away from belief toward faith requires that the finite give way to the infinite. This process is already foreshadowed in the unconscious. Hegel, lecturing in 1827 shows this quite clearly (1827: 423):

> Instead the genuine other of the finite is the infinite, and this is not bare negation of the finite but is affirmative, is being. . . . This affirmative process is the process of our spirit; it brings itself about unconsciously within our spirit; but philosophy is having the consciousness of it. We bring the same thing to pass when we raise ourselves up to God. Thus the infinite itself is at first something finite or negative. The second [moment] is that it is something affirmative. There is a progression through different determinations, and it is by no means an external one but is rather necessity itself. This necessity is the deed of our spirit.

The human process is compelled by its own unconscious momentum to move beyond determinate beliefs toward that infinite that cannot be circumscribed or delimited by the 'sum' of finite affirmations. Hegel brings us to the moment of transition in which semiotic plenitude is overturned by the higher power of the infinite.

But this transition to the non-finite is more than the drive of the concept toward transparency. In spite of his innovations and insights, Hegel erred in seeing faith in terms of conceptual encompassment. The deeper reality of faith lies in the unconscious potencies that speak to us from beyond our categories. Hegel's panlogism affirms that the world is a self-contained cosmos that only awaits proper categorial analysis. Faith would be but one moment within the quest for totalization. Yet Hegel, more forcefully than anyone before him, brings us to the threshold of faith but does not allow us to understand the more elusive presence of that which is not graspable by our sign systems. The true power of faith lies in its absolute refusal to become bound by any categorial analysis no matter how fecund. This negation of a bound totality has been seen more clearly by Jürgen Moltmann, a theologian who remains in dialogue with Hegel. Writing in his *Theology of Hope*, he states (Moltmann 1965: 92):

> Hence every view which sees the world as a self-contained cosmos, or history as a universal whole that contains and manifests the divine truth, is broken down and transposed into the eschatological key of 'not yet.' Our knowledge, as a knowledge of hope, has a transcendent and provisional character marked by promise and expectation, in virtue of which it recognizes the open horizon of the future of reality and thus preserves the finitude of human experience.

The "not yet" hovers over the faith experience and makes it permeable to that which is without a contour or semiotic shape. To be grasped by an ultimate concern is, on the deepest level, to be grasped by the fundamental not yet that speaks from out of the unconscious potencies of the self and nature. If Hegel ignored the not yet in his drive toward the luminous plenitude of the category, Moltmann reminds us that our thought systems are themselves shriven by the open horizon that cannot be filled in.

The human process lives between and among meaning-horizons that give it its fundamental wealth of signs. To live in the innumerable orders of nature and history is to be buffeted by the cultural and natural signs of these various meaning-horizons. A horizon of meaning can be defined as the location of actual and potential signs. No horizon is fully isolated and must interact with other horizons and their internal sign systems. More importantly, all cultural horizons derive their dynamism and hermeneutic clarification from the orders of nature. Nature is permeated by its own intrinsic sign systems and meanings and serves as the enabling condition for all cultural systems.

The basic contour of the self thus emerges from out of the felt pressures of these horizons. Belief systems attain some kind of survival value according to the practical strategies of the sign using organism. Yet, within the protean unconscious of the self, an unconscious that is universal and rooted in the vast evolutionary structures of nature, lies this deeper potency of the not yet, that is, of the open horizon that cannot be reduced to a cluster of signs (Corrington 1987).

The movement from belief to faith, as the movement from bound to open horizons, entails a painful and dramatic emptying of the self. Hope, as concretized in the promise of a new personal identity, destroys the old self. Moltmann, referring to the faith experiences of Martin Luther, makes this clear (1965: 91):

> The event of promise does not yet bring him to the haven of identity, but involves him in the tensions and differentiations of hope, of mission, and of self-emptying. If revelation encounters him as promise, then it does not identify him by disregarding what is negative, but opens him to pain, patience and the 'dreadful power of the negative', as Hegel has said.

Analogous to the loss of a closed and bound cosmos is the loss of the self and its attendant sign systems. If self identity in the pre-faith stage can be seen as sustained by innumerable signs and meanings, then the new identity emerging out of hope will make such an identity impossible. The power of the negative is actually the gift of the not yet that breaks open the semiotic self to something not filled with semiotic content. The liberating power of expectation is initially experienced as the wrath that consumes the plenitude of the self and leaves it dangling over an abyss seemingly devoid of all transforming power.

Finite subjectivity deludes itself that it has attained that radical openness that will bring it into contact with the potencies of the divine. The loss of the merely subjective, as a moment with the experience of faith, is only possible through the eschatological perspective that brings the power of the not yet out of the unconscious into the center of the finite subject. The illusory plenitude of the ego is dispersed into the negating abyss of the not yet conscious. Hegel, while over stressing the role of pure thought, fully understands this negation of finite subjectivity. He states (1827: 446-447):

> It is part of knowing the true that one should dismiss one's subjectivity, the subjective fancies of personal vanity, and concern oneself with the true purely in thought, conducting oneself solely in accordance with objective thought. This negation of one's specific subjectivity is an essential and necessary moment.

The sign using organism becomes freed from its own semiotic richness by the unconscious potency of the not yet that negates all finite self will. The signs at its disposal become permeable to the ever receding movement of the open horizon of the not yet. From the standpoint of the threatened subjectivity, this negations appears in the guise of death, of an impending loss of center and meaning that will destroy the integrity of the self. But another interpretation will appear to the self on the other side of this seeming shipwreck.

The loss of finite subjectivity and its internal sign systems prepares the way for an eschatological transformation of human nature. The signs of mere belief overcome their opacity to ultimate import by foundering in the not yet. In being overturned, these signs become transparent to possibilities of transformation in nature, history, and the human process. An ordinary sign becomes a sign of expectation when its semiotic density is negated to allow for an empty radiance open to the not yet conscious. Moltmann describes this process as it is exhibited in the self (1965: 91-92):

> Thus the promised identity of man leads into the differentiation of self-emptying. He gains himself by abandoning himself. He finds life by taking of death upon him. He attains to freedom by accepting the form of a servant. That is how the truth that points forward to the resurrection of the dead comes to him.

Behind the mythological understanding of the resurrection is the deeper existential truth of the power of the not yet that enters into the region provided by the shipwreck of the finite self. Put in different terms, the semiotic self, that is, the self of "personal vanities", is reborn through the transformation of its internal sign systems. The new self is gathered into the movement of expectation and thus lets go of its previous identity.

All of the orders of creation are quickened by the power of expectation that gently undermines the tyranny of the powers of origin. Put in evolutionary terms, expectation provides the open spaces within which novelty and creativity can emerge for sign using organisms. Without the presence of the not yet, evolution would consist in the blind reiteration of the structures of origin. The potency of the not yet, retained forever in the unconscious of nature, goads evolutionary ramification toward a richer unfolding of its various forms of consciousness. While this unfolding is not governed by an intrinsic or final goal, it retains a fundamental restlessness that points eternally toward the not yet.

When signs of belief become signs of expectation they leave the realm of death and negation and allow the positive contour of the divine to emerge. Faith, as the human clearing within which this transition occurs, is remolded on the other side of negativity. In this renewal, the finite self is brought into proximity with the divinity that speaks from out of the not yet. In what remains we will exhibit the correlation of faith and the divine. While the experience of the not yet lies beyond all signs, the experience of the divine can be rendered into semiotic terms. Put in different language, God stands between the abyss of the not yet and the orders of creation (including history and the human process). As such God lives between the poles of the ontological difference and participates in post-semiotic and semiotic reality. Only in distinguishing between God and the not yet are we able to show how faith lives in an ambiguous relation to semiotic structures. Thus far we have emphasized the negative dimensions of faith. It is necessary to emphasize the positive.

In passing through the shipwreck of the finite subject, faith becomes permeable to transcendence. This is first experienced in those complexes of nature that reveal the potencies of God. Some orders of creation reveal a power of Being that is not evident in other orders. For example, the divine is manifest in certain musical structures but is curiously absent in many others. Where this power of Being appears, the music points to an ultimate import that cannot be reduced to the formal, material, or expressive qualities of the work itself. Faith is quickened and given an objective correlate in its encounters with these fragmentary and ofttimes elusive traces of God. The power of great works of art comes from the promise of transcendence, that is, of the eschatological transformation of human nature. Faith, in this first positive dimension, is not a belief about the traits of these works but is the response to the power of Being embodied in them.

Phenomenologically, the first dimension of faith is manifest in those experiences tinged or permeated with a sense of power and mystery. Finite subjectivity is opened to an elusive actuality than is incomparable to ordinary experience. Rudolf Otto has probed into the nature of this first dimension and has exhibited its structure in terms of the tension between the daunting and the fascinating (1963: 31):

> These two qualities, the daunting and the fascinating, now combine in a strange harmony of contrasts, and the resultant dual character of the numinous consciousness, . . . is at once the strangest and most noteworthy phenomenon in the whole history of religion. The daemonic-divine object may appear to the mind an object of horror and dread, but at the same time it is no less something that allures with a potent charm, and the creature, who trembles before it, utterly cowed and cast down, has always at the same time the impulse to turn to it, nay even to make it somehow his own.

In the orders of nature, this fascination with that which breaks into the ordinary causal realm gives the impression of the miraculous. These traces of God are not, however, violations of the causal order, but marks of the fragmentary and elusive divine potencies. In encountering these traces, in nature or art, faith is given content that points beyond the complexes within which these traces appear.

The first dimension of faith is more passive than active. It responds to those traces of God already manifest in nature or human creativity. As such it remains bound to the structures and powers of origin. The second dimension of faith is more volatile and reveals the restlessness within God. If the first dimension is correlated to epiphanies of power (the numinous), the second points toward positive forces of transformation within social orders. We see this dimension most clearly in social eschatologies and their utopian expectations. Faith, unlike belief which relies on cost-benefit calculations, struggles to participate in the evolution of God in human communities. Here God is not so much manifest as the power of Being but as the lure toward justice. Faith is gathered into this lure whenever it transcends given social conditions. Many of our signs of expectation point toward the Kingdom of Justice in which all forms of heteronomy and domination are overcome. No finite set of beliefs can compel us to act and live in the light of the Kingdom of Justice.

Faith is gathered into a social eschatology that points beyond the fragmented structures of community. God holds forth ideals in which finite subjects find the courage and power to move beyond the stagnant forms of interaction. Within the larger communities and their heteronomous powers live the smaller and more focused communities of justice. The members of these communities live in hope of social transformation in which all heteronomous powers will be broken by the divine will. This expectation is not reducible to a teleological belief in progress but lives in the full radicalness of justice that overcomes the demonic distortions of history (Corrington 1988).

The third positive dimension of faith is much quieter than the first two and emerges whenever the self participates in the agapistic love of God that preserves all of the orders of creation from corrosive powers of non-being. As Hartshorne has argued, God preserves all complexes in eternal memory even when they cease to prevail within nature (Hartshorne 1948). No order is ever bereft of divine love, even in the moment of death and destruction. Faith responds to the divine security and remain steadfast against the threat of non-being. The courage required of faith in the second dimension comes only when it penetrates into the mystery of agape in the third dimension. Social expectation can not long prevail without the gift of divine love.

Faith, in this third dimension, is most attuned to the power or Being that is never reticent to show its face. In the words of Schleiermacher, this is the experience of "sheer dependence" on the absolute and underlies the more active forms of faith that respond to epiphanies of power or social expectations (Schleiermacher 1830). All created beings are gathered in the felt "whence" that supports and sustains them against annihilation. Schleiermacher makes this quite clear (1830: 17):

> Now this is just what is principally meant by the formula which says that to feel oneself absolutely dependent and to be conscious of being in relation with God are one and the same thing; and the reason is that absolute dependence is the fundamental relation which must include all others in itself.

All of our dealings with the orders of creation are governed and measured by the God relation in this third dimension. That is, the quiet power of Being, operating in us through sheer or absolute dependence, makes it possible to comprehend and expand the other moments of faith. Our partial dependence on the epiphanies of power and on social expectation is grounded on that dependence which knows no limitation. The finite subject is remade and redeemed through its dependence on the unbounded love of God.

Most difficult to articulate is the fourth dimension of faith. The first three dimensions all relate to the divine itself without explicit reference to the not yet. In the final moment within the life of faith, the tension between God and the not yet emerges in all of its purity (Corrington 1987a). For here faith must learn to experience the movement of God toward its own not yet. Using the language of Tillich, this is the God beyond the god of theism, or, echoing Meister Eckhart, this is the Godhead within which God is embedded. The abyss of the not yet lives as the lure for God's own eternal self-overcoming. While Hartshorne has well understood that God is eternally self-surpassable, he has not penetrated into the ultimate mystery of the elusive not yet. This abyss stands before God as a goad toward divine growth and evolution. The God of process is only made possible by the not yet which is not itself a process.

Faith leaps beyond its first three dimensions by participating in the divine travail. While we live within the gift of agape, the divine stands in need of a counter movement whereby we augment its life by our love and concern. Our own struggles with the not yet serve, by analogy, to awaken us to the divine self-overcoming. In a paradoxical sense, God is both infinite and incomplete. God's incompletion in the face of the not yet is the final reality with which faith must contend.

Our finite existence is sustained and nurtured by the power of Being manifest in nature and great works of culture. Our social existence is quickened and augmented by the lure of the Kingdom of Justice. The core or our being is preserved in the gift of agape that sustains all orders or creation. Yet the lack within God can only be healed when faith returns the divine love. God's lack in the face of the not yet is eased by those of us who live out the full plenitude of faith. In overcoming our own forms of shipwreck we learn of the shipwreck within God as it struggles against the recalcitrance within its own natures. If we assume that God participates in our suffering, through an eternal and responsive sympathy, then it follows that we are obligated to participate in the sufferings of God. Traditional theisms have ignored this aspect of God's life and have thereby misunderstood the true core of faith.

Faith, in all of its dimensions, is made possible by the signs of expectation that point ultimately to the not yet. In theological terms we can say that eschatology is the measure for anthropology. The finite subjectivity of the semiotic self gives way to the expectant self. Yet this quickening of expectation is manifest throughout the innumerable orders of creation. Nature is eschatological through and through and both gives birth to and receives the manifestations of the not yet. Whenever we participate in the divine promise we reach down into the heart of nature and outward toward the Encompassing power of the not yet that most fully serves as the measure for our being.

REFERENCES

CORRINGTON, Robert S.
    1987. "C.G. Jung and the Archetypal Foundations of Semiosis", in *Semiotics 1986*, ed. John Deely and Jonathan Evans (Lanham, MD: University Press of America), 398-405.
    1987a. "Toward a Transformation of Neoclassical Theism", *International Philosophical Quarterly* 27.4, 391-406.
    1988. "Being and Faith: *Sein und Zeit* and Luther", *Anglican Theological Review* 70.1, 16-31.

HARTSHORNE, Charles.
    1948. *The Divine Relativity* (New Haven: Yale University Press).

HEGEL, Georg Wilhelm Friedrich.
    1827. *Vorlesungen über die Philosophie der Religion*, ed. Walter Jaeschke (Hamburg: Felix Meiner Verlag GmbH., 1983). References in the present essay are to the English trans. by Brown, Hodgson, Stewart, Fitzer, & Harris, *Hegel's Lectures on the Philosophy of Religion*, Vol. 1, ed. Peter C. Hodgson, (Berkeley: University of California Press, 1984).

MOLTMANN, Jürgen.
    1965. *Theologie der Hoffnung* (Munich: Chr. Kaiser Verlag). References in the present essay are to the English trans. by James W. Leitch, *Theology of Hope* (New York: Harper & Row, 1967).

OTTO, Rudolph.
    1936. *Das Heilige* (Munich). References in the present essay are to the English trans. by John W. Harvey, *The Idea of the Holy* (Oxford: Oxford University Press, 1958).

SCHLEIERMACHER, Friedrich.
    1830. *Der christliche Glaube*, 2nd. ed. (Berlin: G. Reimer). References in the present essay are to the English trans. by H.R. Mackintosh & J.S. Stewart, *The Christian Faith* (Philadelphia: Fortress Press, 1928).

TILLICH, Paul.
    1963. *Systematic Theology* (Chicago: University of Chicago Press).

PLAYING CARDS WITH THE WITCH
TAROT READING AND PYSCHOTHERAPY

Judith Porges Hollander
Indiana University School of Nursing

The ambiguous symbols of the tarot cards, whose origins lie in the darkness of the middle ages, continue to be used to access the diverse drives and impulses of the psyche, and the cycles of development at work in human life. Current enchantment with the tarot cards is evidenced by the fascination which they continue to hold for individuals despite endless attempts on the part of the skeptic to make fun of them and relegate them to the general wastebasket of tea-leaf readings, crystal balls, and other fortune telling devices.

This study examined the phenomenon of tarot reading with two goals in mind. The first was semiotic, identifying the meaning that "reading the tarot" has for those who use it for direction in life. The information gained from the initial exploration was then used to develop an intervention using tarot reading to enhance the psychotherapeutic experience.

Theoretical Framework

Donnelly's Theoretical Framework (Dougherty, 1984) was the theoretical perspective on which this study was based. The perspective assumes that linguistic representations (descriptions) of events such as tarot reading are homologous to cognitive representations (what goes on in the mind; interpretations). Both are efforts to model the same reality. Since the framework assumes homology between the two representations, linguistic representations can be used to gain access to cognitive representations. Using the terminology of the framework, the task of the initial part of the study was to examine cognitive representations of tarot reading.

Definitions

Cognitive representation. An assumption of the framework is that individuals interact in terms of their cognitive representations. A cognitive representation is a cognitive structure, a network of associations that organizes and guides an individual's perceptions of events, in this case, tarot reading. It influences what is perceived, imposing structure and meaning on the array of events that make up the reading. The interpretations of events are made up of two kinds of meanings: grounded and valuative (Dougherty, 1984).

Grounded meanings. They are "interpretations of activity at the level of recognition or identification" (Dougherty, 1984: 8). They correspond closely to objective meaning. They tend to be interpreted similarly among individuals of the same culture. For example, in reference to tarot reading, the laying of the cards would be the grounded meaning.

Valuative meanings. They are "interpretations of activity at the level of their significance" (Dougherty 1984: 8). They include appraisals and explanations. There is variation in meaning, depending on what the participant valuates the activity in terms of. The valuative meaning associated with tarot reading would be reflected in the reasons why an individual might have her cards read.

Epistemic orientation. An aspect of the cognitive representation, it is the individual's standard of what is desirable. It is the dimension or dimensions around which information is sorted despite the existence of other dimensions that could serve equally well. Donnelly (Dougherty, 1984: 8) likens it to a "lens through which the kaleidoscope of interactional activity is brought into a particular configuration".

Method

The following procedure was carried out to identify the cognitive representations of tarot reading. Two women who consistently resorted to the tarot cards as a guide served as volunteer subjects for this part of the study. Before the reading each subject was interviewed to identify her thoughts about her previous readings. The questioning began in the following open-ended manner. "Tell me about your experience with tarot readings". The subject was then asked to elaborate on issues that she brought up. The goal of the interview was to elicit descriptions of her previous tarot readings without contaminating the descriptions with ideas imposed from without by interviewer-created questions.

Each subject then had her tarot cards read. After the reading each was asked to discuss the reading. Again, the questioning began in an open-ended manner. The interview was audiotaped. Verbatim transcripts were used for analysis.

Subsequently, a list of all the events mentioned while discussing the present and previous tarot readings was generated by reviewing the transcript and identifying each event that the subject referred to while discussing the readings. Each reference to events was identified at the level of its grounded meaning, indicating its recognizable nature. Each event was then identified at the level of its valuative meaning, reflecting the subject's interpretation. The epistemic orientation or perspective from which tarot readings were experienced was inferred from an analysis of the events mentioned and their valuation. The relationship between previous tarot readings and the present reading was also established.

Results

The results indicated that tarot readings had different meanings for each subject. In addition, they suggested that previous experience with tarot reading and interpretations of the present tarot reading were linked. Both subjects interpreted the present tarot reading based on the perspective revealed during the interview discussing past readings.

Susan's Perspective. One subject, referred to as Susan, discussed previous reading in terms of "a TAT, a projective test", which accessed her inner strengths and conflicts. She believed that any card could tap into the psyche because the cards reflected the human condition. Previous readings were summed up as opportunities to resolve or make conscious internal conflicts. "I had my tarot done when I did not know how I felt about continuing or dropping out of school".

Descriptions of the present tarot reading related the reading to internal, conflictual emotional issues. "Oh, that must mean I'm not resolved about the fight I had with Callie". In fact, Susan explained all events that she mentioned in terms of the same perspective that was evidenced when she talked about previous readings. In the terms of the theoretical framework, Susan's cognitive representation of tarot reading could be described as a window to her mind, as she aptly stated: "a projective test". All tarot readings were seen through this lens.

Mary's Perspective. The other subject, Mary, believed tarot cards tapped into universal energy of which she was a part and which became evident when she had the cards read. Previous readings were couched in the following terms. "We are all part of the whole. I have my cards read so that I can find out where I stand in relation to the rest of the universe.... There is information out there that I tap into and use as a guide".

Descriptions of the present tarot reading reflected the same perspective. Mary, as did Susan, explained events that she mentioned in terms of the same perspective evidenced when she talked about previous readings. "I saw that the universal energy centered on my emotional conflicts. Several 'cups' cards (cards representing emotions) were turned over. I guess I better deal with my issues with Jeremy". As is evidenced by her statement, Mary uses the stimuli of the tarot cards to reveal concrete worldly problems. The stimuli are believed to be a reflection of universal energy. In terms of the theoretical framework, Mary's cognitive representation of tarot reading could be described as "a guide to everyday from the vastness that we are all part of".

Summary. Both subjects used the ambiguous symbols of the tarot cards to identify specific personal conflicts and guide future behavior. Although the subjects used tarot reading in a similar fashion, they differed in their explanations and beliefs about the reading itself. For Susan, the guidance originated within her. Tarot simply opened her "window". Mary's guidance came from the universe of which she was a part. Events mentioned about both previous and the present readings were explained in terms of the particular perspective of each subject.

Psychotherapeutic Intervention

A technique qualifies as a projective device when it presents individuals with a series of stimuli so ambiguous that the meaning of the stimuli must come, in part, from within the individuals. Projective techniques such as dream analysis have been used in psychotherapy to access repressed or hidden emotional issues. The study exploring the meanings of tarot reading suggested that tarot could serve such a function. Both subjects used the ambiguous symbols of the tarot cards to identify specific personal conflicts, thereby qualifying the reading as a projective technique. From this perspective, an intervention, using tarot reading to access unconscious material, was developed.

Jane, in therapy with a psychiatric clinical nurse specialist at a community mental health center, volunteered for the intervention. Jane was "stuck" - both in therapy and life in general. She perceived her therapy sessions as superficial and depressing. She was unable to explore any issue in depth. The sessions were punctuated by long silences. In addition, feelings of powerlessness at home and at work were intensifying her moderate depression to the point that she was thinking about suicide.

Jane agreed to have her tarot read immediately before a therapy session. Jane was initially skeptical about the reading. She did not want to waste her time "doing something weird". However, she also realized that she was "stuck" and needed something unusual to move her. She found the reading interesting "and fun". She saw it as a way "to tap into my unconscious and reveal what was important. In that way, maybe I can get at what is shutting me down. I thought of it a key".

The question is, did the key unlock anything for Jane? During an evaluation session immediately after the therapy session Jane stated that she felt better than she had in a while. So little of her life felt like fun, that it was a relief for her to experience fun even in such a controlled environment. She also felt that the issues that evidenced themselves during the reading were significant and that she could no longer avoid dealing with them. One in particular, conflict with authority, was a current problem at work and with her father. She also believed that, in the future, she could use tarot reading to elicit material for exploration when she was stuck.

However, Jane was not transformed. She was still depressed and saw no clear resolution to problems at home and at work. Although the tarot reading lifted some of her depression and provided her with an avenue to promote self exploration, it did not "cure her". Tarot reading was not a miracle.

The therapist also evaluated the session after the tarot reading. She perceived the subsequent session as more lively and fun. She herself felt more in tune with her client and her issues. She felt that the client exhibited less resistance and was more willing to explore painful material. An evaluation, scheduled one month after the intervention, indicated that neither Jane nor the therapist perceived long term effects from the tarot reading.

Conclusions

The subjects in the initial part of this study used the ambiguous symbols of tarot cards to identify specific personal conflicts and guide future behavior. Although they used tarot reading in a similar fashion, the study suggests that their explanations and beliefs about the reading varied.

The ambiguous nature of the tarot reading qualifies it as a projective technique. As such, it can be used, along with dream analysis and other techniques, to access subconscious and unconscious material during psychotherapy. Tarot reading can be construed as a vehicle to the recesses of the psyche. In a lighter vein, tarot reading is fun. As an adjunct to talking psychotherapy it can introduce a joy that energizes the therapeutic process and instills both the therapist and the client with optimism, a necessary element for successful psychotherapy (Yalom, 1976).

Yet for Jane the tarot reading did not significantly access her psyche or initiate any permanent change. She did not accept the reading as meaningful, just entertaining. These results indicate that the intervention is not appropriate for everyone. Future research should explore alternative ways to access the unconscious for such clients. In addition, ways to determine which individuals would benefit from such interventions should be developed.

REFERENCES

DOUGHERTY, Eleanor.
    1984. *Cognitive Models of Face-to-Face Interaction: A Semiotic Approach* Unpublished Ph.D. dissertation, State University of New York at Buffalo.

YALOM, Irvin.
    1976. *Theory and Practice of Group Psychotherapy* (New York: Basic Books).

THE INTERIOR CASTLE AS MYSTICAL SIGN

Felicia E. Kruse
The Pennsylvania State University

The communication of mystical experience inevitably presents a semiotic problem to the mystical writer. Although it is impossible to establish a list of characteristics that can be attributed to mystical states in all traditions, Eastern and Western, one element common to all mystical experience is its ineffability. In *The Varieties of Religious Experience*, William James states (1902: 371) that the subject of a mystical experience "immediately says that it defies expression, that no adequate report of its content can be given in words. It follows from this that its quality must be directly experienced; it cannot be imparted or transferred to others". Since mystical experience includes a sense of the overcoming of human finitude through union with the infinite, the mystic who wishes to attempt to communicate his or her experience to others is immediately faced with the impossibility of language to grasp that which is beyond its reach. What the mystic experiences is beyond signs, but signs must be used if the experience is to be communicated.

Mystical signs signify both directly and reflexively: they serve as symbols whereby the mystic attempts to communicate his or her experience, and they also serve as indices of the mystic's conceptual framework in terms of which she or he interprets the nature of spirituality and the mystical state. In accordance with this twofold nature of the mystical sign, the purpose of my paper is to examine one mystical writer, Teresa of Avila, and one mystical sign, Teresa's image of the soul as a castle in her work *Interior Castle (Las Moradas)*. Through this examination, I hope to indicate, in very preliminary and modest fashion, how the linguistic signs--the images and metaphors--that mystical writers choose to express their experience reflect both the nature of that experience and their interpretation of it. I am not concerned here with the issue of how and whether mysticism can or ought to be validated, nor do I wish to use descriptions of mystical experience as a way to establish aspects of the nature of the sign. The question I am concerned with is: How do signs manifest themselves in mystical experience, and what do the signs that a mystical writer uses say about that writer's approach to mysticism?

Teresa's *Interior Castle* of 1577 develops its description of the spiritual journey as an ascent of the soul to God through its fundamental image of the soul as a castle, which is divided into "mansions" through which the soul progresses. Under the orders of her confessor, Teresa wrote *Interior Castle* as a manual of instruction in the life of prayer for the nuns of her recently reformed branch of the Carmelite order (the

Discalced Carmelites). The work is divided into seven sections, the "First" through the "Seventh Mansions", each containing from two to eleven brief chapters. Each "mansion" (or more properly, set of mansions) represents a condition or stage of the soul in its journey toward God. Teresa describes the soul and its "mansions" as follows (1577: 28):

> I began to think of the soul as if it were a castle made of a single diamond or of a very clear crystal, in which there are many rooms, just as in Heaven there are many mansions.
>
> . . . Let us now imagine that this castle, as I have said, contains many mansions, some above, others below, others at each side; and in the centre and midst of them all is the chiefest mansion where the most secret things pass between God and the soul.

For Teresa, the life of the mystic is the life of contemplative prayer. The life of contemplation is at once an ascent toward union with God and a movement toward a center; it is in the Seventh Mansions, the center of the soul, that the revelation of the divine Trinity takes place.

Since the castle is the soul, Teresa points out, it makes no sense to say that one "enters" the castle in a strict spatial sense. Rather, for the soul to enter the castle is to enter within itself, that is, to attain increasing self-knowledge. The spatial metaphor does hold up, however, with regard to the relation between the soul and the world, or that which is outside the castle. Teresa betrays her Augustinian and Neo-Platonic heritage by likening created beings to "reptiles and other creatures to be found in the outer court of the castle" (Ibid.: 31), "vipers" (Ibid.: 48), "mere refuse" (Ibid.: 91), and "poisonous creatures" (Ibid.: 98). The greatest danger to the soul is that the things of the world, which Teresa almost always describes in derogatory terms, may penetrate the walls of the castle and set the soul astray from its call to union with the divine.

The castle imagery thus serves as an index to us in two respects. First, it points to Teresa's envisionment of the soul as multidimensional insofar as it contains many "rooms" or "mansions", and it enables her to develop the further image of God as dwelling in the seventh mansion, which is also the center of the soul. Second, the castle image underscores the division between the spiritual and the temporal realm that must be made if the person is to live the contemplative life, and this becomes a dominant theme of Teresa's book. "We were saying just now", she states in a discussion of the importance of humble self-knowledge for the life of prayer, "how black and noisome are the streams that flow from souls in mortal sin. Similarly, although this is not the same thing--God forbid! It is only a comparison--so long as we are buried in the wretchedness of our earthly nature these streams of ours will never disengage themselves from the slough of cowardice, pusillanimity and fear" (Ibid.: 39). The walls of the castle provide a barrier set up between the soul, which lives within them, and the things of the world, which are to be abhorred (Ibid.: 58).

Since vipers and other poisonous creatures always threaten the integrity of the castle, it is not surprising that Teresa depicts the ascent of the soul through the mansions as a struggle, even a battle. For Teresa, achieving contemplation is hard work, and the defensive function of the castle comes to the fore in her emphasis on the role of active struggle in attaining the contemplative life. In discussing the Second Mansions, she exhorts, "Let [the contemplative] play the man and not be like those who went down on their knees in order to drink when they went to battle--I forget with whom--but let him be resolute, for he is going forth to fight with all the devils and there are no better weapons than the Cross" (Ibid.: 50). She continues to use battle imagery throughout the chapter, warning the potential contemplative of the war of the faculties that will ensue within the soul once the choice of the life of prayer is made (Ibid.: 51-52). Even in the Sixth Mansions, where the soul has already been granted a degree of union with God, temptations can arise and interior battles can take place (Ibid.: 130).

What is signified in Teresa's symbol of the castle, with its defensive walls that are nonetheless subject to invasion by venomous creatures, is a concept of person in which the soul exists in a relation of deep tension with its own embodiment. The boundary between what is inside and what is outside the castle points to a rending of the soul from the body that Teresa is very much aware is painful to both. Throughout *Interior Castle*, she emphasizes heavily the burden of concrete manifestations of human finitude, especially those involving corporeality. The person who experiences interior prayer is always brought down again by the needs of his or her body. ". . . We are obliged to eat and sleep", Teresa laments, "and we cannot escape from these obligations, though they are a great burden to us" (Ibid.: 78). In addition, she characterizes the embodied condition as a state of exile (Ibid.: 30).

The tension between embodiment and the ascent of the soul is underscored in Teresa's discussions of the role of suffering in interior prayer. Teresa wrote at a time when the extreme forms of physical penance that Christian ascetics of the thirteenth, fourteenth, and fifteenth centuries had often voluntarily undergone were on the decline. During these previous three centuries, it was fairly common for religious individuals, particularly women, to practice severe austerities, including but not limited to self-flagellation and other forms of physical torture, sleep deprivation, and especially extreme fasting, sometimes to the point of death.[1] For complex cultural reasons that I cannot discuss here, the practice of such penances came to have a positive spiritual value for women of the later Middle Ages by providing a means whereby they could achieve a form of autonomy and self-determination in the face of their subjugation by the patriarchal structures of the church (see Bynum 1987: 189-302). By Teresa's time, however, the church was aware that such attempts to establish autonomy constituted a potential threat to its authority, which was already being severely challenged by the Reformation (see Bell 1985: 151-179). In Teresa's Spain, persons who practiced radical asceticism were likely to be classified as demonically inspired *alumbrados* and *alumbradas* ("illuminists"--see Lincoln 1981: 51) rather than as saints.[2]

In accordance with the increasing disfavor into which violent penances were falling, Teresa urges moderation--to a degree. She discusses willful self-mortification as a work of the devil that may not at first be recognized as such (1577: 42):

> He inspires a sister with yearnings to do penance, so that she seems to have no peace save when she is torturing herself. This, in itself, is good; but, if the prioress has ordered that no penance is to be done without leave, and yet the sister thinks that she can venture to persist in so beneficial a practice, and secretly orders her life in such a way that in the end she ruins her health and is unable to do what her Rule demands, you see what this apparently good thing has led to.

Teresa also cautions against the tendency of some religious, "especially women", she notes, to damage their physical health through "severe penances" and thus to experience a delirium that they mistake for a mystical state (Ibid.: 92-93)--behavior which in the preceding few centuries would have been far less likely to have been questioned.

It is important to note that Teresa's admonitions are not against penance and suffering per se, but against *willful* suffering, or suffering which is in any way for the sake of the self. Suffering for God's sake is an entirely different matter. The desire to suffer in imitation of Jesus' suffering is necessary in order to reach the higher stages of contemplation; indeed, as the higher levels are reached, the soul's desire to suffer increases (Ibid.: 48, 84, 106, 129-30). For the most part, such suffering is of an interior kind and is not necessarily linked to physical deprivations, but since suffering can only occur when one is deprived of the condition of wholeness, it points to the finitude of the being (person or otherwise) that suffers. As the contemplative approaches more closely the possibility of attaining wholeness, her awareness of the gap between her finite condition and unity with the infinite increases. Furthermore, since Teresa draws an explicit parallel between the suffering of the contemplative and the physical suffering of Jesus on the cross, embodiment is not altogether left behind even when the contemplative's attention is centered well within the walls of the castle. The sexual imagery that Teresa uses to describe the desire of the soul for union with God underscores the interplay between the ecstatic and painful dimensions of her spirituality (1577: 136):

> ... I know that this distress seems to penetrate to [the soul's] very bowels; and that, when He that has wounded it draws out the arrow, the bowels seem to come with it, so deeply does it feel this love. I have just been wondering if my God could be described as the fire in a lighted brazier, from which some spark will fly out and touch the soul, in such a way that it will be able to feel the burning heat of the fire; but, as the fire is not hot enough to burn it up, and the experience is very delectable, the soul continues to feel that pain and the mere touch suffices to produce that effect in it.

Even in the Seventh Mansions, where the mystical union or "Spiritual Marriage" of the soul with God takes place, the walls of the castle still do not fall entirely away. For Teresa, the mystical union is a condition in which the soul *contemplates* God; there remains a distinction between the soul, which contemplates, and God, who is contemplated. The union in question is noetic rather than ontological, and this is evident from Teresa's use of visual metaphors in the following passage (Ibid.: 209-210):

> [The soul] is brought into this Mansion by means of an intellectual vision, in which, by a representation of the truth in a particular way, the Most Holy Trinity reveals itself, in all three Persons. First of all the spirit becomes enkindled and is illumined, as it were, by a cloud of the greatest brightness. It sees these three Persons, individually, and yet, by a wonderful kind of knowledge which is given to it, the soul realizes that most certainly and truly all these three persons are one Substance and one Power and one Knowledge and one God alone; so that what we hold by faith the soul may be said here to grasp by sight, although nothing is seen by the eyes, either of the body or of the soul, for it is no imaginary vision. Here all three Persons communicate Themselves to the soul and speak to the soul and explain to it those words which the Gospel attributes to the Lord--namely, that He and the Father and the Holy Spirit will come to dwell with the soul which loves Him and keeps His commandments.

It is important to note that even though Teresa's union is noetic, it is nevertheless non-conceptual. The philosophical and theological tradition to which Teresa belongs recognizes a distinction between conceptual knowledge, in which concepts serve as the pure relations whereby objects are known by the mind in its reasoning function, and connatural knowledge, in which emotion or affectivity takes the place of the concept and in which the being known is known not as objectified, but in its subjectivity, although such knowledge is inarticulable. Mystical knowledge is a form of connatural knowledge, as Jacques Maritain describes in his evocative discussion of Teresa's contemporary, St. John of the Cross (Maritain 1932: 370): ". . . the transformation is effected [not] in a 'physical' or ontological manner, but in the order of the relation of the soul to God as object, inasmuch as by grace the soul is made capable of God and turned towards God *to see and to love* as He sees and loves Himself".

The human soul does, however, retain a degree of separateness from the divine nature in the Seventh Mansions, and this becomes apparent when we contrast Teresa's description of union with the divine with that of Meister Eckhart von Hochheim (c.1260-c.1329). Although Teresa and Eckhart come from the same general tradition, that of Western Catholic Christianity, and although both employ the symbolic language of that tradition, Eckhart's approach to spirituality is quite different from Teresa's. For Eckhart, the approach to the divine nature is characterized by the soul's preparing itself for God's entrance into it, which entrance Eckhart calls the "birth of the Son in the soul". The soul's preparation is marked by the attitudes of *Abgeschiedenheit* (detachment, or "letting be") and *Gelassenheit* (releasement, or "letting go"). Although Eckhart's concept of detachment includes detachment from created being, it differs from Teresa's notion insofar as it is not ordered toward contemplation (see Schürmann 1972: 38 for a discussion of this), does not involve a struggle with the demonic, and places the detached soul in a position, once it has received God, to return to the created world in an attitude of equanimity which parallels God's relation to the created world. States Eckhart (i.1280-1329: 127):

> In the soul there is a power for which all things are equally delightful. Indeed, for this power the least important and the best of things are totally one and the same. This power grasps all things beyond 'here' and 'now'. 'Now' means time, and 'here' means place, that is, the place in which I am at present. If, however, I had completely left myself and become quite empty of myself, oh, then the Father would indeed have produced his only begotten Son in my spirit so completely that my spirit would produce him again.

The detached soul is centered in God rather than in particular created things; it simply accepts created being for what it is, which it could not do if its attitude were one of abhorrence.

The birth of the Son in the soul requires a contrasting move, the breakthrough (*Durchbrück*) to the Godhead (*Gottheit*), in which the soul finds its way to its ground, which is also the origin and essence of God. This return to origin constitutes the *via negativa* in its most radical sense, for it reveals the Godhead, the One which is beyond the creator-God and the Trinity and which is "a being beyond being and a nothingness beyond being" (i.1280-1329b: 178). "The final goal of being", Eckhart states (i.1280-1329c: 169), "is the darkness or the unknowability of the hidden divinity, which is that light that shines 'but the darkness has not comprehended it' (cf. Jn. 1:5)". The mystical union involves plunging into the nothingness of the Godhead, its nameless utter beyondness, in order to experience its own unity and the further unity with it of the human soul, which is equally nameless since it is made in the image of God (Fox 1980: 194).

In Meister Eckhart's sermons, the metaphors of birth and flowing out on the one hand, and the breakthrough to the Godhead on the other, develop in a fascinating dialectical tension that I unfortunately do not have space to develop here. But even from what little I have said, it should be apparent that mystical union for Eckhart is more radical than it is for the Teresa of *Interior Castle*. This is in part due to the fact that for Teresa, the distinction between temporality and eternity seems tied to the distinction between bodily life and the life of the soul after death, whereas physical life and death appear to hold little meaning for Eckhart. In Eckhart's view, eternity is now; it is a condition in which the soul can participate in any moment. For Teresa, mystical union is a contemplative experience that offers a foretaste of an afterlife, but for Eckhart, it frees the detached soul from duration so that eternity can be realized in the present instant. In light of this, it is not surprising that Teresa's mystical path finds at its end only a noetic union (a union in knowledge) rather than the ontological union (union in being) that Eckhart's freeing of the soul from duration effects. The walls of Teresa's castle, in addition to signifying the division of soul and body, also signify the division of temporal from eternal life.

The mystical sign constitutes a *sine qua non* for the mystic's communication of his or her experience. In order for this experience to be communicated, it must also be assimilated, and the images and metaphors that mystics use to convey their experiences are also that in terms of which it is assimilated. Thus, although they may not always be a part of the mystical experience *per se*, they do play a role in the interpretation of mysticism and uncover aspects of the framework within which mystical experience is interpreted. In Teresa's case, the symbol of the castle reveals the paramount importance in her spirituality of the sin/redemption theme and the struggle against the finitude of the embodied state. Were we to develop the central symbols in Meister Eckhart--those of the ocean of creation flowing out and of giving birth are particularly important--we would see that they reinforce Eckhart's concern with unity and the transcendence of temporality.

Two intriguing problems emerge from our consideration of Teresa. The first is that of the adequacy of mystical signs. Since the path of the mystic is ultimately one that must transcend signs, no mystical sign can, strictly speaking, be adequate, either to the mystic's own experience or to the ways of other prospective spiritual journeyers. Although Teresa's horror of embodiment may be excessive, for example, it may also be the case that the castle symbol points to a dilemma within the human condition that Eckhart, in his unrelenting drive for unity, neglects.

The second problem is that of reconciling the human embodied condition with the drive toward mystical unity. Teresa's and Eckhart's mysticism emerged in a tradition with a symbolic structure, centered in the Incarnation, which points directly to this tension and carries it within itself. The implications of the Christ symbol for the problem of embodiment in mysticism need to be examined, as does the question of embodiment in non-incarnational mystical traditions. A semiotically sensitive approach to mysticism would contribute greatly to the clarification of these issues.

NOTES

[1] See Bell 1985 and Bynum 1984 and 1987. Bell examines the relationship between the behavior and attitudes of Italian Christian women who practiced self-starvation between the eleventh and seventeenth centuries and those of contemporary anorectics. Bynum's 1987 work is a careful study of the relationship between food and women's spirituality in the later Middle Ages.

[2] This is not to say that in earlier periods ascetic behavior was always interpreted as a sign of sainthood. Severe ascetic practices were commonly discouraged for women, and those who practiced food asceticism and did attain sainthood were generally looked upon as persons to venerate rather than imitate (Bynum 1987: 84-86).

REFERENCES

BELL, Rudolph M.
    1985. *Holy Anorexia* (Chicago: University of Chicago Press).
BYNUM, Caroline Walker.
    1984. "Women Mystics and Eucharistic Devotion in the Thirteenth Century", *Women's Studies* 11, 179-214.
    1987. *Holy Feast and Holy Fast: The Religious Significance of Food to Medieval Women* (Berkeley: University of California Press).
ECKHART von Hochheim ("Meister Eckhart").
    i. 1280-1329. *Breakthrough: Meister Eckhart's Creation Spirituality in New Translation*, trans. of selected German sermons with introduction and commentaries by Matthew Fox (New York: Image Books, 1980). The modern critical edition of Eckhart's German and Latin works is *Meister Eckhart: Die deutschen und lateinischen Werke*, ed. Josef Quint (Stuttgart, 1936-). Lack of access to the Quint edition prevented my consulting it for the present paper. Fox's translation, although rather loose, is the most extensive collection of the German sermons available in English. Page references in the present essay are to the Fox translation as follows:
    i. 1280-1329a. Sermon "Adolescens, tibi dico", 126-129.
    i. 1280-1329b. Sermon "Renovamini spiritu", 176-180.
    i. 1280-1329c. Sermon "Dieses Wort steht geschrieben", 166-169.
FOX, Matthew.
    1980. Introduction and Commentaries to Eckhart i.1280-1329 [q.v.].
JAMES, William.
    1902. *The Varieties of Religious Experience: A Study in Human Nature*, Gifford Lectures delivered at Edinburgh University (New York: Modern Library, 1936).

LINCOLN, Victoria.
    1981. *Teresa: A Woman* (Albany: State University of New Press, 1984). This biography of Teresa of Avila was completed in 1981 but not published until after the author's death.

MARITAIN, Jacques.
    1932. *Distinguer pour unir, ou Les Degrés du savoir* (Paris: Desclée de Brouwer). Page references are to the English trans. of the 4th French ed. under the supervision of Gerald B. Phelan, *The Degrees of Knowledge* (New York: Scribner's, 1959).

SCHÜRMANN, Reiner.
    1972. *Maître Eckhart ou la joie errante* (Paris: Editions Planète-Denoël). Page references in the present essay are to the English translation, *Meister Eckhart, Mystic and Philosopher* (Bloomington: Indiana University Press, 1978).

TERESA of Avila (Teresa de Cepeda y Ahumada).
    1577. *Las Moradas*. Page references in the present essay are to the English translation by E. Allison Peers, *Interior Castle* (New York: Image Books, 1961).

IX

SEMIOTICS OF DECEPTION

LONGING FOR PRESENCE IN THE SEMIOTIC OF DECEPTION

Tullio Maranhão
Rice University

In the concluding chapter to his *Theory of Semiotics*, Umberto Eco raises the question of the subject of semiotics, that is, of "the subject of an act of utterance". Does this subject have an existence outside of the *sēmeion*? Eco's answer is, "No", for "the subject... must be considered one among the possible referents of the message or text", (1976: 314) he writes. In support of his inclusion of the subject into the text he summons Charles Peirce's testimonial. Peirce (1868: 314) writes that the "word or sign that man uses *is* the man itself", that "man is an external sign", and "Thus my language is the sum total of myself". Eco recognizes the existence of a transcendental subject different from the psycholinguistic speaker and living outside the text, but places this subject "beyond the semiotic threshold". Indeed, he contends that by restraining the subject to that one signified in the act of *énonciation*, "semiotics fully avoids any risk of idealism" (1976: 317). This position seems compatible with much of postmodern criticism in its unrelenting deconstruction of the subject as self or author standing outside the text.

The dismissal of the psycholinguistic subject as a source of legitimation of meaning combined with the slighting of the transcendental subject stirs up worrisome concerns. Has the legitimation of meaning been rendered obsolete? The current critique of representation as developed by Derrida and by Lyotard has contributed to enfeeble the justificatory procedures employed to legitimize meaning. After the Kantian uncoupling of meaning and truth, we would be presently witnessing a further debasement of the status of meaning. All authority legitimizing meaning would be constituted by centric interests--ethnocentric, gendercentric, selfcentric, etc. In the scenario of meaning as a free-floating commodity circulating among centric interests impelled by the appetites for appropriation, deception is the paramount semiotic rule. In the absence of a subject to whose intention deception could be entrusted, we are left with the *sēmeion* whose ambivalence constitutes the environment in which deception germinates. In this new habitat deception seems to lose its negative connotations and is perceived as a value neutral tool useful in semiotic analysis. My goal is to challenge this assumption and to reestablish the connections between ethical considerations and deceptive communicative actions even after the subject has been effaced.

Let us begin by looking at Derrida's thoughts about the Saussurean theory of the linguistic sign (see Saussure i.1906-1911, especially 65-100). After proposing Grammatology as a science of *écriture*, that is, as the science of *épistémè* or knowledge, he turns to Saussure's linguistics to see if it fulfills the prerequisites for such a science, and concludes that it does not (1967a). Saussure's notion of sign is contaminated by the metaphysics of presence. The signifier is considered as a representative of sound, and sound in turn as a representative of thought. This smacks of the Aristotelian cosmology which presented thought as internal to the soul and expressed by the sound of voice. Writing comes in as the last link in the chain of representation. Writing is thus the carrier of the longing for the presence of *logos* and its contemporaneity colors the Western thinking about speaking and the sound of voice, about thought itself and meaning. In Derrida's opinion, Saussurean linguistics cannot be the science of *épistémè* because it is caught in the uncompromising dichotomies between image and reality, outside and inside, and appearance and essence. The Saussurean science skirts its epistemological responsibility by invoking the notion of arbitrariness between signifier and signified which helps it circumvent explanations about exteriority and interiority, about presence and absence, thus taking for granted the linguistic sign as present and exterior, and ultimately as coeval with meaning.

Saussure writes that *écriture* veils the appearance of language, that it is not a guise, but a disguise of language. If in writing the gulf between signifier and signified is made wider than in any other media, then writing is a better environment for deception. But Saussure makes a plea for reestablishing the connection between inside and outside, between speaking and writing, and Derrida reminds us of how contradictory this effort is when coming from "the theoretician of the arbitrariness of the sign". Indeed, Saussure writes about the graphic sign "usurping the main role" in its relation to sound. Sound, as representative of thought, is cannibalized by its graphic representation thereby widening the hiatus between thought and representation. The polarization between representation and thought indicates that there is an essence of meaning which cannot be distorted and, furthermore, that the history of the game of hide-and-seek between signifier and signified could eventually be unraveled disclosing the point of origin of the essence of meaning. Bedazzled by writing we would have lost sight of the origin and essence of meaning. Along the lines of Plato's fable in the *Phaedrus*, writing induces forgetfulness and therefore conceals history. Derrida wants to exorcise the nostalgic longing for origin and for essence in those manifestations such as writing in which it cannot be fulfilled, and to start over in the science of knowledge from *écriture* itself, backwards, disassembling the edifice of knowledge. Against Saussure he argues, for example, that history is writing and that historical reconstruction is tantamount to textual deconstruction. He does not deny the "usurpation" carried out by writing; on the contrary, he gives it maximum political use, claiming that history cannot be understood outside the history of domination with writing. For him, speech is already a writing and this fact subverts the order of levels of representation, rendering useless the notion of arbitrariness. Speaking and writing are both unmotivated activities. Hence a grammar of speech or text tells us nothing about *épistémè*.

"Unmotivated but not capricious" (1967a: 46), warns Derrida, in the sense that the choice of signifier is not entirely left to the speaker. Is the signifier more or less natural than the signified? Does naturalness--which stems from the precarious notions of arbitrariness and unmotivation--stand out as guarantee against the ambiguity of meaning, thereby reducing the potential space for deception? Derrida concludes that every instituted level of representation functions as a trace of the ontological difference which is captured by the trace as a historical moment. In this sense, writing conceals the history of metaphysics which is the history of consciousness, of speaking, and of thinking. But writing as trace does not stand witness to history as a still observer; it becomes and thereby dissimulates its self-identity. In Saussurean parlance, the symbol is always becoming a sign. The fact should begin to emerge that the "arbitrariness" of the linguistic sign (in Saussurean language), or the self-occultation of the trace (in Derridean) hardly characterizes deception as something motivated. Indeed, the sleight of hand that blurs the connections between signifier and signified is not of semiological interest, but according to the Grammatology, of historical interest. It is the history of the "becoming unmotivated of the symbol" (1967a: 48).

Derrida contrasts the phenomenology of Husserl to the phaneoroscopy of Peirce. In the first, the radical presence of the thing itself is asserted. The thing shines when the sign as *representamen* is reduced, when in the historical passage from one sign to another the isomorphic relation between sign and thing is broken. For Peirce, the thing is the sign. The *representamen* gives rise to an *interpretant* which is a sign itself. As a consequence of this spiral of sign transformations *ad infinitum*, the sign is rendered imperfect (c.1901-1902: 303). Deceptive? I would say that in both Peirce's semiotics of the sign-thing relation and in Husserl's theory of signs the elusiveness of signification is not semantically deceptive but philosophically meaningful. From a grammatological point of view, semiotic deception is an attempt to justify or to rationalize (in the psychoanalytic sense of the word) the shattering of hope in the presence of the thing. Without hope on the possibility of formulating a theory on the relation between signifier and signified, the idea of a science of signs evaporates. In other words, in the absence of the thing, the science of signs seizes the signifier and claims that deception is the principle of its functioning. Derrida calls our attention to the pervasiveness of ideas of game and play underlying linguistic theories. These theories emerge at the onset of linguistics, when the loss of the thing (in this context Derrida refers to it as the "transcendental signified"--1967a: 50) is already felt as a painful development, as an amputation or a reduction of presence. The semiotic of deception is heir to the game theories of linguistics and arises when in the absence of a "transcendental signified" the gulf between meaning and language is perceived as unbridgeable. The science of the *sēmeion* holds on to the sign following it in its staggering trajectory. But the disconnection of the sign as well as its erratic course cannot be understood by default of a stable background constituted by the signified. Otherwise, if the hypothesis that the only inhabitants in this world are signs were taken in earnest, there would be no reason to talk about deception; the zigzag of signification would not be deceptive but just that which it is.

But let us assume that there is duality in signification, is deception a characteristic of language? And if it is, in what sense is it so? In the sense that language does not do the job of connecting signifier and signified or in the sense that it falls short of a "transcendental signified"? In answering the first part of the question one has to deal with the linguistic games of signification, but the second part of the question calls for a deconstruction of the notions of signifier and signified. Let us run the plow of deconstruction over these axiomatic notions and shift the focus of our discussion from signs to functions of signification. There are two: representation and indication, or metaphoric and metonymic functions. Derrida's analysis of Husserl's theory of signs contains an appraisal of these two functions (1967). In the indicative function the linguistic sign conveys the lived experience of a speaker to another who does not have access to the presen(t)ce of that experience. As an index the sign itself takes on a corporeal inheritance which allows it to be perceived as real and present. It becomes an entity with the same status or reality as that entity to which it points. Derrida writes that, "In this way words act like gestures" (1967: 38). The linguistic categories that exemplify this function are pronouns (pointing to people) and deictic words such as "this", "that", or "here" (pointing to things). Indication contains the prerequisites of a spatial organization of the communicative setting and the presence of a speaker/addressor and of a listener/addressee. The signs used in this function only signify in use and their meaning is contingent to employment. Indication is therefore the function *par excellence* characteristic of dialogue. For Husserl, indication is unwieldy in soliloquy, in "the solitary mental life", because the experience is present to the thinking subject, and so he cannot meaningfully say to himself "It is I", for he is the uttering I.

In soliloquy expression is the emphasized function. Expression or presentation. We must bear in mind that Husserl is not building a typology of signs, but instead is using these types as stepping-stones in advancing his study of consciousness by examining the role of signs in mental life. Proceeding with Husserl's ideas, while expression conveys a meaning, indication is meaningless. The deictic word "here", for example, has signification but not meaning. Hence, indication establishes positions of signification, whereas expression brings forth the identity of things. Evidently, one of the possible meanings to be expressed is that of subject identity, but notice that the subject comes into being transported by a sign. In monologue it is possible to say, "It is I", expressing the meaning of an identity. Consequently the presence of the speaking subject requires expression (identification) and indication (localization) of the sign, and entails a dialogical and monological function, or, in other words, the presence of an other and the witness of the subject/self materialized as sign.

Communication can be effective or represented. In the first case the indicative and expressive functions of the sign have the possibility of being fully realized. Re-presentation finds its place in language not as a picture of effective communication, but as repetition, a presentation again. Most linguistic theories, however, have understood representation as the act of taking the place of something else, that is, the act of substitution. Nevertheless, the representation at stake in communication is the repetitive and not the pictorial one. The comprehension of the linguistic sign demands regularity in its use and not parity in its connection to experience. While Husserl reduces experience limiting the role of pictorial representation in phenomenology, Derrida attacks pictorial representation because it deals in the illusion of the presence of the signified. However, outside of phenomenology and independently of the poststructuralist critique of representation, I would like to note, the regularity of use entails a parity between signifier and signified. This parity is always unstable because the sign is constantly forced into derivation or effacement. Derrida very aptly figures out the game played by linguists which consists in casting the parity into a historical framework by studying the history of sign derivation as correlative of a supposed history of denouement of the signified. He insists that the assumption of parity between signified and signifier is fictitious. It is for this reason that he deconstructs the chain of representation as substitution from writing to speaking, but arrives nonetheless at the most disconcerting notion that at the bottom lies an arche-*écriture* (Cf. Tyler 1987 for a critical analysis of Derrida's hypothesis.).

In Husserl's argument that inward speech addresses no one, the idea of a psycholinguistic consciousness vanquishes, for there can be no self-reflection in indicative speech. The Freudian concepts of conscious and unconscious processes are consequently contradictory to the Husserlian thought. In psychoanalysis, experiences can be unconscious and be brought into consciousness. Memory is a bridge between past and present. Consciousness is precisely a process of retraction from speech deploying an additional layer of signification on top of a previous layer of discourse. But there is one similarity between Husserl and Freud with respect to consciousness. In phenomenological philosophy, the meaning of the subject or of the object becomes an identity when it is expressed. Expression leads to selfsameness, that which is shown is equal to itself, and in being shown repeats itself. Meaning as selfsameness is a concept free from the dimensions of space and time which define repetition as a replication of originality. The original in selfsameness is that which is present and which expresses itself. Likewise, in the Freudian schema, memory is embedded in the present, the existence of the unconscious is acknowledged in consciousness, and in a sense, the past is always an allegory of the present. Where Freud and Husserl differ radically is in the psychoanalytic hypothesis that the atemporal presentation of memory arises out of a dialogue between conscious and unconscious, past and present, ego and superego, or repression and drive. The subject undergoes or instigates a process of decentration by which he becomes two subjects, two selves in dialogue seeking consensual accommodation. Such a subject is all too fitting for the uncritical world of metaphysics in which communication is *écriture* and in which the linguistic sign represents an original signification which although inaccessible to the speakers is still retrievable. Indeed the Freudian consciousness unfolds in a remarkable parallelism to the process of writing (Cf. Derrida 1967b "Freud and the Scene of Writing").

In Husserl's philosophy it is impossible to wedge communication between consciousness and representation. Whether it is the subject, speech, or consciousness these entities only let themselves be known in re-presentation. In Freudian terms it is a "primary process", in phenomenological language, "a principle of principles".

Derrida's project is a continuation of Husserl's momentous program for phenomenological research. The inspirational function Husserl plays for Derrida is unquestionable (1967). Like Husserl, for Derrida the quest for origin is a process of clarification of structures of meaning. He is less wont than Husserl in asserting presence as re-presentation, and in finding in it a sign of being, but he does privilege the arche-trace in a way very similar to the importance Husserl attaches to the Ur-principle. Ironically, although trying to break open the structures he penetrates with deconstructionism, he always ends entrapped in the meshes of the linguistic sign (the written sign) he so much contributes to demystify.

After this brief review of Derrida and his phenomenological heritage, our semiological equation now has the following entities: subject, the thing, signifier, and signified. If the subject was eliminated by being included in the text, later it was devolved to us as an expression of the sign. The signified disappeared under the signifier. We are left with the linguistic sign (containing signification and subject identity) and with the thing. Does this not resemble the ultratraditional Western metaphysical position which discards everything falling short of *logos* and of the thing itself? In his article on the phenomenology of language Derrida concludes that in the same way that Husserl kept the tension between form and meaning going, we may have "to mediate upon the circularity which makes them pass into one another indefinitely" (1972: 173).

We began by promptly disposing of the subject and locating deception in the domain of the linguistic sign alone. Next we realized that in order to talk about deception in this context, a displacement between signifier and signified needed be presupposed. Such a displacement, or more appropriately speaking, mismatch, would be very similar to the duality between form and meaning in the phenomenology of language. But while in that philosophical field there is no dialogue between form and meaning, since these two entities exist as a dyad in consciousness, in semiotics they are perceived as constituting the lining of signification. Thus one can understand the endeavor to discover the rules and principles of this lining in which deception arises as a very captivating explanatory principle, because, if on the one hand it grasps the reality of the mismatch, on the other hand it is asystematic enough not to serve as fountainhead for the flow of duplicity. Deception itself is deceitful.

As I pointed out earlier, the thesis that deception inheres in the sign, thus constituting a trope available for manipulation by the users of language, gives away a longing for the presence of *logos* and of the thing. After ridding us from the subject, cultural and philosophical criticism shook up the status of the thing, without succeeding to remove it. The thing, like god or the totality of meaning, is a stubborn notion perceived by many as indispensable in the preservation of the ethics of discourse. If the thing goes, the sign goes too. The focus on the relation between signifier and signified is a defensive maneuver on the part of those who sense that the thing is in danger. The theories about mismatch between signifier and signified are another step in that same direction. Could we be wrong about this point? Would a semiotics of deception be not a defensive move, but a form of criticism on the way of loosening further the links between signifier and signified? I don't think so because a semiotics of deception needs a stable signifier and a signified that if ever drifting must be anchored to the thing. The case for deception as a process of signification can be made only in the presence of the linguistic sign and of something else that if it fails to represent, the failure only goes to prove that the thing indeed exists. In my concluding observation I would like to leave matters as open as possible, preserving both possibilities of the gross presence of form and meaning and of their dissolution together with the dissolution of the subject. I wonder whether a semiotics of deception gravitates around logocentrism, or disperses itself among the hosts waging the battle without quarters of total criticism. If it is logocentric as I said it is, it needs a name other than "deception" (what about "semiotics of deferment", "of difference", or "of differance"?) and it must substitute the aura of an attack to loosen the links between signifier and signified by the walls of a defense to ward embattled meaning.

REFERENCES

DERRIDA, Jacques.
    1967. *La Voix et le phénomène* (Paris: Presses Universitaires de France). Page references in the present article are to the English trans. by David B. Allison in *Speech and Phenomena and Other Essays on Husserl's Theory of Signs* (Evanston, IL: Northwestern University Press, 1973), 1-104.
    1967a. *De la Grammatologie*, Les Editions de Minuit. Page references in the present article are to the English trans. by Gayatri Chakravorty Spivak, *Of Grammatology* (Baltimore: Johns Hopkins University Press, 1976).
    1967b. *L'écriture et la différence* (Paris: Editions du Seuil). Page references are to the English trans. by Alan Bass as *Writing and Difference* (Chicago: University of Chicago Press, 1978).
    1972. *Marges de la philosophie* (Paris: Editions de Minuit), trans. with additional notes by Alan Bass as *Margins of Philosophy* (Chicago: University of Chicago Press, 1982).
ECO, Umberto.
    1976. *Theory of Semiotics* (Bloomington: Indiana University Press, Midland Book Edition 1979).
HUSSERL, Edmund.
    1913. *Ideen zu einer reinen Phänomenologie und phänomenologischen Philosophie* 3 Volumes (Halle: Max Niemeyer Verlag), Volume 1 trans. by Paul Ricoeur as *Idées directrices pour une phénoménologie* (Paris: Gallimard, 1950).

PEIRCE, Charles.
    1868. "§5. Man, A Sign" in "Consequences of Four Incapacities", originally published in *Journal of Speculative Philosophy* 2, 140-157, reprinted in CP 5.310-317.
    c. 1901-1902. "Sign", entry (with Mrs. Ladd-Franklin) in *Dictionary of Philosophy and Psychology*, ed. J. M. Baldwin (Volume II, New York: Macmillan, 1901-1902, 1911), 527, reprinted as CP 2.303-304.

SAUSSURE, Ferdinand de.
    i. 1906-1911. Lectures delivered at the University of Geneva and published from auditors' notes by C. Bally and A. Sechehaye under the title *Cours de linguistique générale* (Paris: Payot), trans. by W. Baskin as *Course in General Linguistics* (New York: McGraw-Hill).

TYLER, Stephen.
    1987. *The Unspeakable* (Madison: Wisconsin University Press).

THE SIGN OF DECEIT

Floyd Merrell
Purdue University

Sebeok (1976: 147) observes that the capacity for prevarication is not distinctly human, but shared by other organisms, whether by instinct or sundry forms of learning. Lying, which he assigns to the category of prevarication, is "critical of language", though "its semiotic attributes... still remain very imperfectly understood". Eco (1976: 7) suggests that a sign, standing for something else not necessarily existant, is that which "*can be used in order to lie*". By combining Sebeok and Eco, we can provisionally conflate prevarication and lying into the phrase "deviation from what is ordinarily *conceived as* the 'real' or 'true' state of affairs"--deviation implying a straying from, or the enticing of an addressee from, some standard. Another short hop and we arrive at deceit: "a *leading astray* from what is *conceived as* ordinary sign use". What, semiotically speaking, is meant by this "leading astray"?

Let us first consult Macbeth, who asks: "Is this a dagger I see before me?" Since we have it on high authority that he is hallucinating, we would tend to answer with a resounding "No!" He neither sees anything nor was there any real, existent thing to see. This would be the argument of Russell (1905) and Quine (1953: 1-19). Speaking of some-*thing*, they would contend, implicates the speaker: there must be some-*thing* about which her predicate is made. But actually, Macbeth *did* see a dagger; for a moment dagger; for a moment dagger neurons were firing inside his skull producing the effect of a dagger *out there* in the *here, now*, in spite of whether a "real" dagger actually existed or not. If it indeed was not there, then we might say Macbeth was the victim of "naive hallucination"--he was led, he led himself, unintentionally astray. He merely *imagined* he saw the object in question. Yet he was not so "naively hallucinated", for he soon entertained doubt about what appeared before him. Let us call such a state of mind "vacillating hallucination".[1]

An additional facet of the dagger scene is that Macbeth attempts empirically to come to grips with the unexplained appearance before him: "Come, let me clutch thee! / I have thee not, and yet I see thee still" (Shakespeare 1623: 23). It appears that Macbeth wants something akin to positivist verification;or better, Popperian falsification. If he reaches out his hand and does *not* experience a dagger, the dagger-hypothesis is refuted, and the figment can be qualified as "enlightened hallucination" (D. Smith 1983). It must remain as a form of hallucination, however, for the fact is that he previously (thought he) saw it.

It all has to do with perception. But perception is, according to Peirce, elusive: an intentional experience in the sense that it entails consciousness *of* the presentation *of* something. The mode of presentation is *what* something is presented as *to* consciousness. This is the *content* of something perceived. The *object* of presentation is *that which is* perceived, the "semiotically real" not the "actually real" *object* (J. Smith 1983). In this light, to see colors and shapes entails quality, Firstness. To see an *object as object* without its being related to anything else is Secondness. And to see an *object* as part of an *act, event* or *process*, that is, to see *that* such-and-such is the case, is Thirdness. "*This* dagger *here, now*" is essentially *Secondness* when a colored patch of a certain shape is identified. Thirdness, pertaining to symbolicity, on the other hand, is propositional, such as, "This dagger is bloodstained."

When there was the sensation of an elongated and variously colored patch before him, Macbeth was not *yet* consciously aware *of* it. He was *seeing* it but not *yet seeing* it *as* such-and-such in terms of its distinction regarding all other sensations he was receiving at the moment. Identifying the sensation by means of dagger firing neurons in his skull, Macbeth potentially enters into Secondness, *seeing as*, but there is as *yet* no mediary Third interrelating it to other signs, past, present and potentially to come. This rudimentary stage, via Peirce's conception of the interface between "real" and "unreal", is tantamount to dreaming or "naively hallucinating" during which the subject *nonconsciously suspends disbelief* (see Merrell 1985). Conscious willingness to suspend disbelief at an intentional level is possible for Macbeth only *a fortiori*, when he puts his dagger appearance to the test. It is now as if there were a *hallucination frame* marked off and distinguished from the "real".[2]

Quite presumably, after his passage to "enlightenment", Macbeth can now dance in and out of frames, recalling his hallucination *as* hallucination, and reminiscing *about* it from a comfortable distance. This initial passage from hallucination to "reality" was an irreversible event, hence he cannot re-enter his prior "naive hallucinatory" frame--that is, unless he suffers complete memory loss of the event. In other words, if Macbeth disconfirms the existence of the dagger, he is operating at the propositional level of Thirdness as if to say "*This* dagger *here, now*, is *not* really a dagger", thus speaking *about* his dagger sensations. He is now at least tacitly aware of both frames, the hallucinatory and the "real".

Macbeth's condition of Secondness, like *gratuitous play* when exclusively within an appropriate play frame, is *autonomous, self-reflective*, and, with respect to the "real" world frame, *symmetrical* and *atemporally irreversible* (i.e. two children baking make-believe mud "pies" can switch back and forth from their "real" world to their mud "pie" world without jeopardizing either). This situation is structurally comparable to the Epimenidean paradox,

(1) "This sentence is false"

which is the natural language counterpart to a Gödelian sentence (see Merrell 1983, 1985). If conceived as an autonomous unit, the sentence is properly paradoxical, encompassing *contradiction, self-referentiality*, and *infinite regress*. It is likewise *symmetrical* and *atemporally reversible*. On the other hand,

(2) "I am lying"

which is often dressed in Gödelian garb, is another story: it implicates the speaker. Lacan (1973: 138-44) points out that the "I" of the *enunciation* of (2), that is,

(3) *I am deceiving you*

is not identical to the "I" of the *uttered statement* due to the shifter designating it. In Peirce's terms the *uttered statement* consists of an *index* ("I") and an *icon* ("am lying"). The index serves to point toward the other "I", a pragmatic "I" implying (3), which, if then uttered, points to yet another "I" of the next moment, and so on--Peirce's intriguing but enigmatic infinite regress of the self. Consequently, (2), unlike (1), is *irreversible, temporal*, and *asymmetrical*.

Games exist in stark contrast to play and (1), while they share an important feature with (2). The dog nips to mark a gratuitous "This is play" sign, but he doesn't really mean for the nip to denote what it would ordinarily denote: a bite. If his partner in play is rather short-tempered and interprets his nip as a bite, it denotes something other than what he meant it to denote. He now has a fight on his hands. The fight, like football, wrestling, courtship, Wall Street paranoia, and other competitive human war games, is not to be taken lightly. The gratuitousness of play falls by the wayside. Now the stakes are high; the costs are dear. There is a determinate end, and the product is hierarchization, the structure of which is, like (2), *irreversible, temporal*, and *asymmetrical*. During competition between players, a boundary between "game" and life is never entirely closed. The game is played *as if* it were "real", or, in the case of love and war where clear-cut boundaries are rarely set down in the first place, the distinction between "real" and "unreal" becomes totally confused: the meaning of courtship and territorial imperatives are extrapolated far beyond that which is biologically, psychologically, or socially necessary.

It is now *as if* the players in a game of love were to say

(4) "I am sincere"

while implying (3) by way of the other "I"--i.e. the players have become gamers. The "I" of the *enunciation*, (3), is in this case diametrically opposed to that of the *uttered statement*, (4). There appears to be no problem here, no paradox. If (4) is false then (3) is true, it's as simple as that: the utterer is merely deceiving her fellow interlocutor. But this does not tell the whole tale. If the deceiver utters (4) and is lying, it is *as if* she were saying (3). Though the message remains implicit, the fact is that the deceiver meant *it*, rather than (4), which *is* problematical. That is to say, the predicate of (3) doubles back onto the utterer, while the second shifter of the sentence, "you", points outwardly to the deceivee. This two-way indexicality implicates both deceiver and deceivee in a tangle of signification, which will be the focus of the remainder of this paper.

Let us provisionally return to (2). If it is true, it is false, and if so, then it is true, and so on intermittently. Placing the statement within a Tarski-like qualifier--his paradigm sentence was "'Snow is white' if and only if snow is white"--Epimenides could have stated: "'I am lying' is true." The qualifier appended to the utterance confirms it from an "outside" or "higher" frame, which implies a succeeding "I" commenting on the utterance emitted by its predecessor and so on. Russell (1910) performed the service of banning this and all such paradoxes from the kingdom of thought with his Theory of Logical Types, so we should be free of semantic pathologies. But we are not. One problem lies with our penchant for operating along linear, hierarchical pathways with focus resting exclusively on the thought, or the observed as it were, while the observer is supposedly capable of maintaining objective detachment. Such an observer is *set apart from* the world, presumably free to know it, act on it, mutilate and rape it, along unidimensional lines. It is as if the entire act were a monolithic joke: when we get to the punch line, it's all over. Having exploited Mother Nature at will, she loses, and off we go in search of greener fields. Or in the context of this paper, it is as if the deceiver, after becoming bored with the game, were to confess to the deceivee: "I was only joshing, don't believe a word of it." Now the previously "naive" deceivee is an "enlightened" deceiver. Merely another barrier in his road to knowledge has been escalated, and, from a higher perspective, he can joke about the day when she told him that. . . . But we are still caught up in linear, atemporal thinking. From semantic oscillation between true and false as in the case of (1), my example has merely degenerated into a pragmatic quandary without the paradox having been resolved.

And yet, why should there be cause for alarm when such sentences pop up, as they eventually will? The liar and kindred paradoxes, Wittgenstein (1956: III 15) counsels, are of interest only because they have "tormented people, and because this shows both how tormenting problems can grow out of language, and what kind of things can torment us"--even Peirce considered the Cretan liar and other such paradoxes to be "abominations". In this sense, playing the "language-game" of paradoxes is as pointless as thumb-catching, though it can be somewhat more amusing. So if, following Wittgenstein, our paradoxes should create no more than a false-alarm, perhaps we can simply allow them to do their thing and pay them little mind. Then, rather than look upon them as aberrations of thought, we might place them in an asylum, to be occasionally released for the entertainment of the wise of the world. On the other hand, if we pig-headedly persist in our attempt to resolve any and all paradoxes, we remain caught within the classical framework mandating a detached observer, with focus resting squarely on the observed.

But actually, the classical paradigm is not merely perverse, but simply inoperative regarding paradoxes of the Epimenidean sort. The speaking subject of (2) is intimately involved with, indeed, she is "inside", the utterance, and the addressee is dragged into the circularity due to its pragmatic, in addition to its syntactic and semantic, content. Lacan does a tangential dance in order to unpack (2). It is quite clear, he assures us (Lacan 1973: 139), that:

> the *I* of the enunciation is not the same as the *I* of the statement, that is to say, the shifter which, in the statement, designates him, so,. . . it is quite possible for me to formulate in a valid way that the *I*. . . is lying, that he lied a little before, that he is lying afterwards, or even that in saying *I am lying*, he declares that he has the intention of deceiving.

That is to say, even if the "I" of both (3), the *enunciation*, and (2), the *uttered statement*, were considered to be identical, when combined they *would still be* self-referential, *temporally* and *pragmatically self-referential*. It might be contended that the pragmatics of such apparently circular sentences is not the real issue here. In mathematics there are timelessly recursive formal sentences that involve cycles, yet they are considered legitimate, since their recursivity unpacks their circularity. Mathematician Louis Kauffman (1986), following G. Spencer-Brown (1969) refers to this general process as recursive *re-entry* of a form into itself to *re-form*, *re-produce*, itself. One example of re-entry:

$$[1 \underset{\curvearrowleft}{+1}] = \dfrac{1 + 1}{[1 \underset{\curvearrowleft}{+1}]} \quad \ldots n$$

corresponds to the Fibonacci series, in geometrical projection called the "golden triangle", which consists of an infinitely spiraling curve. It is defined as a rectangle with sides of the ratio $1:1/2(1+\sqrt{5})$, which successively re-enters itself. This form of re-entry, graphically defined, is that of a set of concentric circles, or a Chinese box, implying an infinite regress:

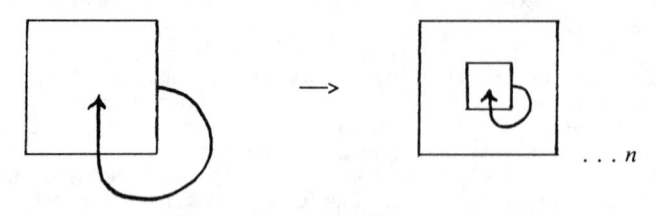

⟶ ... n

Such symmetries can also be seen in, for example, Medieval designs, Arabic tapestries, tessellation patterns, and most strikingly, in Mandelbrot's (1977) fractals. A common example of fractals is the Koch curve, which re-duplicates itself within itself *ad infinitum*:

⟶ ... n

Re-entry is also the case of symmetrical sentences such as (1), the indexical *this* of which "points to" the entire sentence, that is, to itself. Since (1) is undecidable, re-entry re-duplicates the inverse of the form such that there is oscillation between true and false. On the other hand, the temporal and asymmetrical (2) is a horse of a different color. There is no re-entry or re-duplication of a form inside a form in the absolute sense. On the contrary. A difference, however slight, remains after each recursive loop due to the "I"'s eternally changing role as well as that of the "I" of the addressee who is sucked into the equation, by way of (3). In other words, true re-entry can never occur from within the uttered sounds in the air or printed marks on a page. Re-entry in this case demands presence of a text and a pragmatic context such that the sentence re-entering itself and self-reference of the self are one and the same. Quite understandably, Lacan can state with confidence that the presence of both addresser and addressee can validate the paradox in (2) to render it appropriately *decidable*. In this sense, pragmatics *is* the issue here.

The concept of the ongoing self or "I" is fundamentally *dialogical*, which, as the Peircean interaction of the self of one moment with its other of the next, can be written:

(5) $Self_1 \longrightarrow Self_2 \longrightarrow Self_3 \ldots n^3$

Without a determinate "outside", there is no meta-self but only *differences*, more in the sense of Bateson (1972) than Derrida (1968). A non-Tarskian unfolding is also implied here, for neither is there any hierarchical construction, steadily progressing from one linguistic level to the next, which is capable of accounting for, of deciding, any and all levels beneath it. The self system is an unfolding process, nonetheless, the distinction being that, by becoming self-aware, it engages in an open process of describing more and more of itself from "within". In our paradigm case, the "I" of (2) points to "am lying" recursively, but each re-entry produces a not-quite-exact re-duplication of the form:

(6) "I_1 am lying"--> "I_2 am lying"--> "I_3 am lying-->... n

The supposed constant nature of the "I" is thus placed in question. From a particular perspective, a given entity can be determined by some, but not all, of its properties. For example, within a timebound framework, we can speak of Venus as the morning star or the evening star, of a lily as opened in the morning and closed in the evening, or, to use Peirce's example, of Phillip drunk and Phillip sober. That meaning which affords constancy to an entity re-enters itself with each semiotic instantiation representing it, yet though there is re-entry of the meaning into itself, re-duplication is never-quite-exactly faithful to itself. A difference invariably remains. In other words, with each re-entry there is a concomitant unpacking of that particular aspect of one's semiotically "real" world to perpetuate the ongoing stream of *semiosis* by means of which signs are processed and understood through other signs: they explain themselves by themselves (Eco 1979: 198). This implies an n-dimensional acausal, asymmetrical process rather than the cramped, one-dimensional binary model.

Chomsky, of course, obliterated the notion of a linear finite-state Markov chain model for natural languages in favor of a more-or-less binary tree model entailing infinite generativity. But nature, and the nature of sentient beings, are neither linear nor branching. According to Deleuze and Guattari (1980), the Chomskyan "tree" is associated with a base sequence, the "tap root", which sets the ground rules for generation in terms of binary logic. This structure is that of infinitely reproducible principles of *tracing*, of copying, of re-duplicating. Tree logic is a logic of *tracing* and reproduction (Deleuze and Guattari 1980: 11):

> It consists of tracing, on the basis of an overcoding structure or supporting axis, something that comes ready-made. The tree articulates and hierarchizes tracings; tracings are like the leaves of a tree.

Deleuze and Guattari contrast a *map* with a *tracing*: the former is *rhizomic* as opposed to the latter's *arborescence*. The rhizome is a Koch curve taken to the nth degree. The eye cannot see and the mind cannot visualize such minute complexity. This and other Mandelbrot fractals introduce one to the *physics of chaos*, of large-scale disorder. Clouds are in reality not round, mountains are not triangular, faces are not oval and the earth is not spherical. Minute *differences*, infinitesimally variegated *differences*, render such phenomena infinitely complex. And above all, regarding language, words have no predefined and definite meanings. Rather, meaning is *rhizomic*: it is tantamount to topological surfaces and flows, eddies and strange attractors, random wandering rather than bifurcating, rich tapestry rather than bargain basement wallpaper. Flow is shape plus change, motion plus form. A meandering river flows along its constantly changing axis, toward one bank, around a curve, down the river bed, now toward the other bank, up to the surface and down again, now caught in a whirlpool, spiraling like a microscopic particle in a smoke ring. There are recursive rhythms but no absolute repeatability. Heterogeneity and heterarchy are the norm, symmetry breaking to create disequilibria is the standard procedure.

The unceasing flow of words as well marks diminishing returns regarding communication. When language borders on nonsense, on meaninglessness, it is like $\sqrt{-1}$, both meaningful and meaningless. (2) is both true and false, sensical and nonsensical. The sentence can be reputedly solved by distinguishing between levels of communication. But more subtle forms of language use, in literary texts for example, cannot be reduced to such abstraction: consider Lewis Carroll, Laurence Stern, Gertrude Stein, Samuel Beckett, Eugene Ionesco, James Joyce, Jorge Luis Borges. Literature resists binaries and categorical distinctions, it blurs borders, it sets up mirrors placing in question who is speaking and why; words are reiterated but they are never the same, roles change but remain invariant.

So what has all this to do with deceit? Precisely this: without nonsense, without meaninglessness, without lying, that is to say, without *negation*, the possibility of a *distinctly human semiotic*, of existence itself, goes down the drain. (4) can be the *uttered statement* of deceit, while (3) is the model, the *enunciation*. So long as the *uttered statement* exercises its dominance, the deceiver deceives the deceivee upon the latter's interpreting it. Only when the deceivee in "enlightened", by *reinterpreting* (4) (a re-entry of the form into itself), does the model begin to dominate. Now he knows! What the deceiver actually meant was (2). But, logically speaking, that's impossible: he can't know because the sentence is *undecidable*. Perhaps saving grace is to be had, then, by virtue of the fact that the deceiver *was* lying. Or *will be* lying. But that's not entirely it either. Against our logical inclinations "I am dreaming" and "I am hallucinating", like (2), create alternate worlds.

So that's how *we* can know!--by nimbly jumping in and out of different semiotic domains. There was no problem in the first place. And yet,. . . the real quandary--some would call it sublimity--might well stem from the disconcerting fact that the answer lies "outside". As Wittgenstein (1921: 6.41) puts it: "The sense of the world must lie outside the world". That is to says, Just a (4) can emerge and simultaneously pull (3) out of the void, thus implying (2), to create movement, temporality, asymmetry, life itself, so it can also re-submerge into the soup of simultaneity. Mathematician and mystic Nicholas de Cusa (1440: 147) speaks of such dissolution:

> [w]here speech, sight, hearing, taste, touch, reason, knowledge, and understanding are the same, and where seeing is one with being seen and hearing with being heard, and tasting with being tasted, and touching with being touched, and speaking with hearing and creating with speaking.

Or from another angle, Peirce (1891) tells us, not without his own implicit paradox, that:

> [T]he evolution of the world. . . proceeds from one state of things in the infinite past, to a different state of things in the infinite future. The state of things in the infinite past is chaos,. . . nothingness. . . the complete absence of regularity. The state of things in the infinite future is death,. . . nothingness. . . the complete triumph of law and absence of all spontaneity.

This is Derrida's bottomless chessboard, Nietzsche's instantaneous grasp of the eternal return, the nothingness lying behind time. At this apparently inconceivable ground level of *undecidability*--de Cusa's *conjunctionis oppositorum* or Peirce's suspension between nothingness and nothingness--(4) contradictorily *becomes/is* (3), which *becomes/is* (2), and they are all simultaneously thought, said, and heard by deceiver and deceivee. There is an impossible retreat from temporality into atemporality.

Perhaps, over the long haul, deceit is in the eye of the finite and infinitely more humble beholder, that is to say, in the eye of the ignorant. For: "the better a man will have known his own ignorance, the greater his learning will be" (de Cusa 1440: 8-9). In this sense, to disclose hallucination, dream, lie, deceit, is to become aware of one's own ignorance. Such "enlightenment" is a bane and a boon, or perhaps more a bane than a boon, for if hallucination, dreams, lies, deceit, that is to say, *negation*, didn't exist, our knowledge would always remain false to itself, and, unfortunately, our ignorance would remain forever concealed. "Leading astray", it appears, is a necessary step toward ignorance revealed.

NOTES

[1] Regarding such "vacillation" in the reading process, see Todorov's (1970) "hesitation" effect.

[2] I use "frame" in the sense of Bateson (1972) in what he regards as "epistemology", also Goffman (1974) and Uspensky (1970). For more detailed exposition, see Merrell (1983).

[3] This notion of the perpetually altering self is crucial to an understanding of Peirce's "dialogic", which, as Max Fisch (1980-82) rightly points out, pervades his triadic conception of signs through and through.

REFERENCES

BATESON, Gregory.
    1972. *Steps to an Ecology of Mind* (New York: Ballantine).
DE CUSA, Nicholas.
    1440. *On Learned Ignorance*, trans. by Fr. G. Heron (New Haven: Yale University Press, 1954).
DELEUZE, Gilles and Félix GUATTARI.
    1980. *A Thousand Plateaus: Capitalism and Schizophrenia, II*, trans. B. Massumi (Minneapolis: University of Minnesota Press, 1987).
DERRIDA, Jacques.
    1968. "Différance", in *Speech and Phenomena and Other Essays on Husserl's Theory of Signs*, trans. D.B. Allison (Evanston: Northwestern University Press, 1973), 129-60.
ECO, Umberto.
    1976. *A Theory of Semiotics* (Bloomington: Indiana University Press).
    1979. *The Role of the Reader: Explorations in the Semiotics of Texts* (Bloomington: Indiana University Press).
FISCH, Max H.
    1980-82. "The Range of Peirce's Relevance", In *Peirce, Semeiotic, and Pragmatism* (Bloomington: Indiana University Press, 1986), 422-48.
GOFFMAN, Erwin.
    1974. *Frame Analysis: An Essay on the Organization of Experience* (New York: Harper and Row).

KAUFFMAN, Louis.
    1986. "Self-Reference and Recursive Forms", *Journal of Social Biological Structure* 9, 1-20.
LACAN, Jacques.
    1973. *The Four Fundamental Concepts of Psycho-Analysis*, trans. A. Sheridan (New York: W.W. Norton, 1981).
MANDELBROT, Benoit.
    1977. *Fractals, Form, Chance and Dimension* (San Francisco: W.H. Freeman).
MERRELL, Floyd.
    1983. *Pararealities: The Nature of Our Fictions and How We Know Them* (Amsterdam: John Benjamins Press).
    1985. *A Semiotic Theory of Texts* (Berlin: Mouton de Gruyter).
PEIRCE, Charles S.
    1891. A letter dated 29 Aug. In *Collected Papers of Charles Sanders Peirce*, ed. A.W. Burks, vols. 7-8 (Cambridge: Harvard University Press, 1958), 8.317.
QUINE, W.V.O.
    1953. *From a Logical Point of View* (Cambridge: Harvard University Press).
RUSSELL, Bertrand.
    1910. "The Theory of Logical Types", in *Principia Mathematica*, with Alfred N. Whitehead, vol. I (Cambridge: Cambridge Univeristy Press), 31-65.
    1905. "On Denoting", in *Essays in Analysis*, ed. D. Lackey (New York: George Braziller, 1973), 103-19.
SEBEOK, Thomas A.
    1976. "Notes on Lying and Prevarication", in *Contributions to a Doctrine of Signs* (Bloomington: Indiana University Press), 143-47.
SHAKESPEARE, William.
    1623. *The Tragedy of Macbeth*, ed. G.L. Kittredge (Boston: Ginn, 1939).
SMITH, David Woodruff.
    1983. "Is This a Dagger I See Before Me?" *Synthese* 54, 95-114.
SMITH, John E.
    1983. "Community and Reality", in *The Relevance of Charles Peirce* ed. E. Freeman (LaSalle, IL: Monist Library of Philosophy), 38-58.
SPENCER-BROWN, G.
    1969. *Laws of Form* (New York: E.P. Dutton, 1979).
TODOROV, Tzvetan.
    1970. *The Fantastic: A Structural Approach to a Literary Genre*, trans. R. Howard (Cleveland: Case Western Reserve University Press, 1973).
USPENSKY, Boris.
    1970. *The Poetics of Composition*, trans. V. Zavarin and S. Wittig (Berkeley: Univeristy of California Press, 1973).
WITTGENSTEIN, Ludwig.
    1921. *Tractatus Logico-Philosophicus*, trans, D.F. Pears and B.F. McGuinness (London: Routledge & Kegan Paul, 1961).
    1956. *Remarks on the Foundations of Mathematics*, trans. G.E.M. Anscome (New York: Harper and Row).

THE EXPOSED EXOTIC DANCER:
A SEMIOTIC OF DECEPTION IN PORNO-ACTIVE RITUAL[1]

Terry J. Prewitt
The University of West Florida

Exotic dancing in the United States includes diverse performance styles drawn from erotic and burlesque dance genres. Over the past twenty years, exotic dance has undergone a transformation that parallels changing representations of women in magazines like Playboy and Penthouse, as well as in less widely distributed pornographic media. The first stage in this transformation (during the late 1960's) involved the spread of topless dancing throughout the country. Early topless performance comprised burlesque dance patterns but emphasized display of the breasts.[2] Costuming was modest by today's standards; dancers were paid performers or performer/waitresses; dancer-customer interaction during performances was extremely limited. As norms regarding the photographic treatment of nude women became more relaxed, however, dance forms focused more on "genital" presentation, and dancer-customer contact during performances became more intimate. Thus, what had slightly departed from erotic dance forms of the 1940s and 1950s became a highly formalized, direct sexual/social interaction.

Recent elaborations of exotic dance include elements which may be called "porno-active performance". Porno-active performance differs from photographic pornography in at least two ways. First, viewers may become public participants in the dance by involving themselves in the action, creating modifications of performance elements on the part of the dancer. In contrast to privately used graphic representations of nude women, the viewer of porno-active performance is visually accessible to an audience and the dancer. This circumstance imposes social constraints on reactions, and evokes stylized behaviors tied to the male value system guiding the performance. Second, the audience can interrupt the dancer's performance creating a dialogue where viewers and performers are partnered.[3] In many instances, the dancer and audience participants exchange control over the dance "plot", using various postures, facial expressions, or material enticements to shape their interaction.

Contemporary exotic dance incorporates many elements of deception. Deception blurs the difference between dancers' economic motives and customers' sexual/social motives, rendering the performance acceptable for both. On a practical level the dancer must fulfill a narrow range of male expectations or jeopardize her earnings. As one dancer recent put it, "I deliver a fantasy. I look at the man and try to figure out what he wants and provide it on the spot". Such "reading" of the customer creates a social deception and allows self-deception. Similarly, the man may assume diverse personae at the club. For him, the woman is an instrument of social communications to other men, a catalyst in the man's self-deception, and the medium for enacting sexual/social games and rituals.

Deception and Cultural Themes in Topless Performance

Deception in topless clubs protects the privacy of dancers and customers, effectively segregating club relationships from everyday social circles. Thus, regular dancer client relationships may extend for years with neither party knowing significant details about the other's pursuits outside the club. This long-term relationship depends on customer restraint. A customer who becomes too disclosive or too identified with ordinary social interaction risks losing his appeal as a customer. His intentions may be suspect. The dancer may withdraw from interactions that involve taking too much money from "a friend". Customers, nonetheless, are more disclosive than dancers, since their personal circumstances and values are usually central to their motivations and justifications for patronizing the club. Though various psycho-social conditions motivate dancers, economic necessity commonly justifies working in a topless bar. More difficult to answer is the question, "What's a nice guy like you doing in a place like this?"

An answer to this question revolves around a single point: The ties between exotic dancers and their customers remains grounded in everyday social values. The phallocentric notions given such vivid expression in topless clubs pervade most other area of our social life. What differs in the topless context is that males may openly participate in the publicly enacting several phallocentric myths. The result is a paradoxical transformation of personality. Suddenly, the customer can and "should" act in ways prohibited in ordinary social contexts, but acceptable in some all-male social situations involving teamwork or friendly competition. In the topless bar, values verbally espoused in such diverse context as Little-League baseball, hunting or poker parties, and all-male corporate retreats get behaviorally expressed in the presence of women. Given the phallocentric norms of the context, it is not surprising that many regular customers represent many male-dominated blue-collar and white-collar professions (construction workers, servicemen, mechanics, firemen, fishermen, lawyers).

When a man engages in public sexual play with women, the rules of play formally reverse those of everyday where the ideology of male dominance or supremacy is noted. This reversal is by no means a comfortable situation for all men. On first encounters, a customer in a topless bar may find himself at a loss for "appropriate" behavior. The self-conscious cues of the neophyte may make him obviously vulnerable to exploitation. He must learn new rules for social interaction.

By tapping the underlying themes of male dominance in the common culture, men in topless bars may openly compete with each other for control or attention. In order to accomplish this, a man must release himself from the ordinary constraints he places on his sexual reactions to women. At the same time he must enact stereotypic roles consistent with myths of male dominance. In other terms, the club elicits, and to an extent requires, direct behavioral expressions of patriarchal values that idealize masculine control over women, and let men express their own version of a particular "masculine" ideal. Thus, the process whereby a man enters the club scene supports deception in the presentation of self--the customer acts out a role consistent with his cultural values but often inconsistent with his everyday personality.

In some cases, customer deceptions may make dancers economically or psychologically vulnerable. In other terms, some men believe their enactments and may experience little cognitive dissonance when considering their club behavior against their ordinary interactions with women. On the other hand, since dancers usually have a realistic understanding of customer deception, even extreme or obvious customer deception is tolerated or encouraged as a semiosic game an intelligent dancer can use to advantage. The sexual/social game enhances her earnings while satisfying the customer. Such a "positive deceptive" ambience is highly significant when considered against other forms of male-female interaction, such as dating, marriage relationships, work relationships, or even casual social encounters.

The sense in which dancers "fit" their behaviors to male expectations supports economic success, but this aspect of dancer-customer relationships also has a dark side. Some dancers are apparently successful in recognizing the dominance needs of men because their own personalities are complementary to such men's needs. This is suggested by the fact that many dancers have difficulty forming lasting relationships with men in their private lives. The attention dancers receive from men in clubs may temporarily mitigate the low self-images of these women. But the same dependency in private life produces a tendency to fall into abusive relationships, sometimes preceded by abused childhoods. Extreme psychological disorders, especially eating disorders such as bulimia and anorexia, are not uncommon to dancers. On these points, however, it would be easy to overgeneralize. Many dancers lead rather ordinary lives, in some cases more ordinary and well-adjusted than those of the customers they serve.

Spatial and Performance Organization

Space within a topless club varies in layout but usually includes four major public areas: a bar, table areas, a dance runway equipped with counter space and seating, and a game area usually equipped with pool tables. The focal area of the bar is the runway, usually visible from everywhere except the game area. Each section seats different kinds of customers. Most customers are men; when female customers are present, they normally sit in the table areas. Some clubs prohibit unaccompanied females to prevent prostitutes from using the club to solicit.

Regular individual customers occupy every area of the club but most often seat themselves on the runway, but most men on the runway are drop-ins or occasional customers. Finally, special groups associated with bachelor and birthday parties commonly patronize some club during the evenings. Such groups sit along the runway or at tables, depending upon availability of seating group size. Larger groups almost always occupy tables where their interactions are less hampered and tables dances may be performed easily.

Clubs are open from as early as noon through 2:00 A.M. All of the classes of customers except party groups appear among the daytime crowd, though the numbers of customers during the day are usually low. Evening dancing is thus more economically rewarding, since regular customers are augmented by relatively large numbers of drop-ins. Staffing in clubs varies with the size of each establishment. Daytime staff in smaller clubs may include only a bartender and three or four dancers, while in larger clubs as many as eight dancers, two waitresses, two bartenders, and other management staff may be required for normal operations. Evening performances in large clubs may include as many as fifteen or eighteen dancers, several waitresses, and three bartenders. My observations cover all these situations, ranging from times when I was one of three or four customers to those involving as many as 200 people over an evening.

Two kinds of performance occur in most clubs. First, the runway dance features one or two performers who present a set of two or three numbers each. In most clubs the dancers select their own music on a jukebox. Some clubs employ disc jockeys who help establish ambience, assist in music selection, and enforce or make known club rules when necessary. The work of the DJ may include censuring unruly customers and even bouncing them. DJ's and dancers maintain a close public rapport, though frictions sometimes arise over music selection, DJ commentary, or enforcement of club rules. Often, the DJ is the first point of interaction between dancers and club management. Nonetheless the DJ is an important part of some runway dance routines.

The second dance form, "table dances", involve personal performances in the table areas (occasionally along the runway when the club is crowded). The styles of runway and table dancing differ. Since customers request table dances, they converse and react more directly throughout the performance. One or several table dances may be performed for individual customers, the dancer remaining seated with man between numbers. In addition to payment and tips for the dances, the customer usually buys the dancer special drinks, part of the cost going directly to her from the club. These drinks usually have low alcoholic content. Table dances also provide "ritual" performances for groups. The most common ritual performance involves a dance purchased for one man by the group. While the dancer performs, the men in the group observe the reactions of the recipient, and often provide good-natured hooting or other expressions of comradeship. These dances place the recipient in a situation "testing" his manhood, his ability to encounter the dancer at close hand. Nonetheless they are "group performances" distinct from individually requested dances.

One club I have observed features a variation on the ritual performance theme. A key man from one of the party groups--the prospective groom or "birthday boy"--is seated in a chair on the runway. All of the dancers perform on the runway, devoting most attention to the subject. During this ritual, all of the man's clothing is removed except his underwear. These performances draw the entire audience into evaluation of the subject's situation and reactions. The role reversal, involving stripping the male by dominating women, enacts a pure male fantasy. The ritual ordeal of the subject provides for the audience a nearly pure symbolic expression of phallocentric values.

Runway dances place males in competition for the attentions of a dancer. These dances usually involve set routines and a higher regular pattern of dancer-customer interactions. Most dances begin with a "grounding" display. The dancer uses the first part of the music to present herself to the audience, taking advantage of poles, overhead bars, or other equipment to perform relatively complex dance movements and visit all sections of the runway. The "grounding" behavior sometimes includes establishing strong eye contact with men seated along the runway. Eye contact is among the most important "confrontive" mechanisms a dancer uses to elicit tips. After the initial segment of a dance, the dancer usually targets particular customers along the runway through eye contact and dance displays. Direct interactions initiated by the dancer may include lip-singing the words to songs while maintaining eye contact with a customer, imitating a customer's facial expression or posture, directed posing, evocative facial expression directed to an individual, or verbal interactions. The customer in these situations is involuntarily "partnered". Tipping customers are especially targeted with these confrontive tactics. Dancers watch the runway for likely tippers and exchange information on likely and unlikely prospects, as well as "problem" customers.

Customers also initiate partnering using behavioral displays (see Pearson 1987 for a technical discussion of "partnering"). Eye contact is a reliable means of drawing attention from the dancer, even though it is less reliable and direct than a tip display. Tip displays, usually single dollar bills, are presented in various ways. The visible presence of money on the counter usually draws a dance display, but most tippers hold the money to entice the dancer. Bills are often folded lengthwise as a deliberate sign of intent to top; they are held during the resulting display. When the dancer takes the tip, she usually kneels or otherwise makes herself available to the customer, interrupting the flow of her routine. Some dancers integrate tip-taking into the dance; some follow the receipt with brief conversation or a kiss. The interaction during tipping depends on the customer's attitude, whether he is a regular customer or a drop-in, and his manner of offering the tip. Some customers present tips orally, through a female surrogate (another dancer), or through preferred modes of placement. Most tips are inserted in the G-string at a position selected by the dancer, while some are taken in positions dictated by the customer, including orally, between the breasts, or in other places on the costume. Customers who violate house rules for tip placement, touching, or behavior may be rejected by individual dancers, regardless of the mode of tip display.

Tip taking terminates the sequence of individual partnering in the runway dance. Following the tip many dancers make a final presentation or dance display in front of the customer while establishing eye contact with another tipper. Thus, most of the dance consists of a chain of partnering events. Some dancers perform their first number without taking any tips, leaving a few men holding money until the second dance. Only the most established dancers use this technique, though it usually results in a high-yield flurry of tips as the set concludes. Indeed, ignoring a proffered tip is a strategy that often produces competition among several potential tippers to gain the dancer's attention.

The Semiotics of Deceptive Sexual Signs

Throughout all topless dance performances, sexual signs are employed by dancers and customers to create believable interactions. Facial expressions, postures, forms of address, clothing, and various other elements enter into the play of signs employed by dancers and customers. The overall effects of the play are real images of stereotypic gender values. Like photographic pornography, the action in the club invites a personal sexual interpretation. The presence of money and the stated economic motives of dancers do not undermine this effect. Direct male participants in dance club action experience a myth of dominant male sexuality. Dancers create the impression that their actions and motivations are authentic and personally motivated by attraction. Even the confrontive or dominating actions of dancers fulfill male expectations. A man may control and possess a woman, even one he would ordinarily be too timid to approach. From the male perspective, the topless club provides a medium of self-deception.

Reversals from ordinary behavior also promote both cooperative and competitive spirit among some customers. Participants in club rituals, after all, voluntarily allocate women to particular men. This is a central practice in human society, and one at some variance from male sexual patterns in other primate species. From a broad evolutionary point of view, the topless club ritualizes the process through which phallocentrism is culturally expressed in human groups. In another sense, however, topless clubs enact a more universal condition of social affairs. Women in the club initially have equal access to all customers, interrupted only when specific partnering is accomplished during performance. Men placed in competition for women's attentions form groups that are "central" and "peripheral" to the primary interactions between men and women. Thus, the action in a topless club may express real dominance and value differences among males, transmitted through processes of bluff or imposture and carried by the sign content of "masculine presentation". In the end, we find a very fine line between what is "deception" and what is "real".

Of course, women in topless clubs compete with each other for economic rewards. Their success may depend on surface elements of their status as "women", but more directly hinges on how well they "perform" as women. Effective dancer personae, after all, are removed from the "person behind the performance". Thus, failure as a dancer is not the same thing as failure as a woman; nor is success demonstrative of a woman's ideal of "woman-ness". This is in stark contrast to the situation of the customer who, whether observing or participating, is constantly being judged by the male audience through a rigid standard of "maleness". The men are also judging themselves against the standard, which they accept by entering the scene. To fail as a customer is to fail as a man, since it usually means that the person involved has violated the rules of comradeship or decorum. The violation is signaled by social rejection, and may result in the double loss of money and self-esteem. This opens further questions of "male" and "female" interpretations of the visual images created in the club. I am investigating such comparisons through photographic pornography, and plan to include the results in a longer revision of this paper. For the moment, I must stress that dependance of male identity upon "personal performance" suggests that the topless club is not a totally unrestrained scene for men. Indeed, the rules of club behavior, though "permissively" different from the ordinary, are in many respects more demanding on male consciousness. In a topless club a man sometimes confronts his deepest fears.

NOTES

[1] Mary Rogers, Katherine Stephenson, and Charls Pearson each offered especially helpful critical comments during the development of this paper. Also, Karen Haworth aided in club visits and interviews, as well as in discussion of analytical results derived from my primary observations.

[2] Charls Pearson contributed background ideas for this paper concerning the semiotics of dance and the historical transformation from burlesque performance to contemporary topless performance. It is important to note that burlesque dance styles were sometimes formally taught. Far fewer contemporary dancers obtain formal dance instruction than was the case in earlier decades.

[3] I originally began working with interrupted structure in the context of textual studies of *Genesis*, analysis concentrating on transformations of meaning produced by chapter and verse divisions imposed on the text during the medieval period. This application will ultimately appear in my long manuscript "The Elusive Covenant".

REFERENCES

PEARSON, Charls.
    1988. "The Semiotics of Partnering in Ballroom Dancing", in *Semiotics 1987*, ed. John Deely (Landham, MD: University Press of America), 205-214.

PREWITT, Terry J.
    1988. "The Elusive Covenant", manuscript (Pensacola, Florida) detailing analysis of social and literary structures in *Genesis* currently under review for publication.

APRIL FOOL AND HALLOWEEN: A SEMIOTIC ANALYSIS OF THE LIE

Machiko Takayama
Southern Illinois University

Umberto Eco defined semiotics as a theory of the lie (Eco 1976: 6ff., 58, 179). Then what is the semiotic nature and function of the lie in April Fool and Halloween? While for Bakhtin carnival is a social transgression and freedom (Eco 1984: 3), for Eco it is an instrument of social control through the authorized transgression allowed once a year with an implied frame or a presupposition behind it (Eco 1984: 4ff.). In the following, by applying Eco's theory of semiotics and his analysis of carnival, we find out that these lies in April Fool and Halloween function neither as a social transgression nor as a social control: they are a miniature Disney Land, or a socially accepted "G-rated" dream or lie.

Semiotics as a Theory of the Lie

In the technical sense of Eco's semiotics, a lie means the rejection of the referential fallacy of perception and the rejection of the extensional fallacy of judgment, i.e., it is related to the problem of noun and sentence.

In the well known semiotic triangle of Ogden and Richards, the right bottom corner means a referent or an object (Figure 1). The contemporary semanticists at least since Hjelmslev agree that what the theory of code is concerned is a signfunction between the signifier and the signified, or the left side of the triangle (and its complication *à la* Pierce or Greimas) (Eco 1976: 38 ff, Eco 1983: 148). We know an expression /unicorn/ and a content <<unicorn>> without having a real object //unicorn//. Thus sign-function is a cultural phenomenon: the content of an expression is an interpretant, and does not necessarily have a referent. In this sense, it may be a "lie", yet this cultural phenomenon has some significance on our life. Then an attitude to insist on finding a referent of a cultural content is called the "referential fallacy".

Pointing out the cultural relativity of Kantian categories of analytic and synthetic judgment, Eco proposes the usefulness of the classification of extensional and intensional judgment (or statement) (Eco 1976: 62ff, 158). Extensional judgment has to do with the theory of truth-value, and intensional judgment has to do with the theory of code or a semantic structure of a given culture.[1] Even if a judgment (or statement) is extensionaly false, if it is culturally coded, taught at school, and

Figure 1. Semantic Triangle.

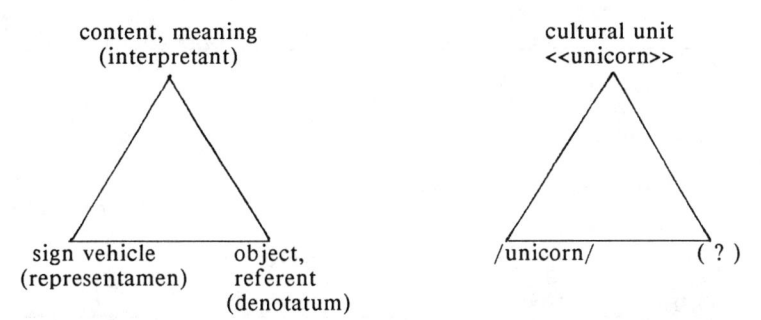

```
     content, meaning                          cultural unit
       (interpretant)                           <<unicorn>>
            /\                                       /\
           /  \                                     /  \
          /    \                                   /    \
         /_____\                                 /_____\
  sign vehicle    object,                     /unicorn/      ( ? )
 (representamen)  referent
                  (denotatum)
```

connotes a <<historical truth>>, it has a social force as a sign. Eco's examples are as follows (Eco 1976: 65, 159). The sentence /Napoleon died at Saint Helena on May 5, 1821/ is true, and the sentence /Ulysses reconquered the kingdom by killing all the Proci/ is false, yet both are coded and have social force. On the other hand, the sentence /Napoleon, after the battle of Marengo, drank a cup of coffee/ is not coded, not taught at school, and has no social force even if it is true. Incidentally, this issue of intensional judgment vs. extensional judgment reminds us of the recent controversy over the movie *The Last Temptation of Christ* (Scorsese 1988) (Leo 1988: 34-36). Extensionally speaking, we do not know exactly what happened to Christ in his last moment. Yet intensionally speaking, we are taught at school or church that Christ was not tempted, and this code of norm of Christianity has a social force to our everyday life. Eco's so-called "extensional fallacy" is an attitude to stick to extensional judgment or theory of truth-value while ignoring the effect of intensional semantics or a cultural code as a social force.

Thus, the condition of signification is not the same as the condition of extensional truth, and an intensional semantics of code is not the same as an extensional semantics. This is why Eco calls semiotics as a theory of the lie.

Eco's Typology of Proposition

A judgment is expressed in the form of a statement or a proposition. Depending upon whether a proposition is referential or not, Eco calls it as an "index-sensitive proposition" or a "non index-sensitive proposition" (Eco 1976: 161ff.). And depending upon whether a proposition is culturally coded or not, he calls it as a "semiotic judgment" or a "factual judgment" (Eco 1976: 158ff.).[2] Now, by these two standards, all propositions could be classified into one of four types (see Figure 2). This typology of propositions is very useful for the later analysis of the nature of verbal and nonverbal proposition as a lie in April Fool and Halloween. Eco shows the difference of these propositions by the example of propositions about the international exchange rate of dollar and lire in 1971 and 1972 under flexible exchange rate system (Eco 1976: 160). But we could pick up a more recent example. Let us take a proposition /Robin Givens married Mike Tyson for money/. Except Robin Givens herself, no one knows whether this proposition is extensionally true or false. Yet this interesting proposition about our cultural hero seems to have a possibility to circulate as a myth (or a culturally shared belief or a code). When this proposition is pronounced for the first time, it is a "standing proposition" of a "factual judgment" which is not coded

Figure 2. Eco's Typology of Proposition.

Coded (Culturally Sedimented) \ Index sensitive (with referent, actual object)	No	Yes
	("statement")	("mentioning", "referring")
Yes — Semiotic Judgement $\begin{pmatrix} A \ldots \ldots A \\ \text{concept type,} \\ \text{percept sememe} \end{pmatrix}$	[Metasemiotic Proposition] Presupposes a performative format <<I state that from now on...>> [Eternal Proposition]	[Index Sensitive Semiotic Proposition]
No — Factual Judgment $(A \ldots B)$	[Standing Proposition] Pronounce for the first time (could be a lie)	[Index Sensitive Factual Proposition] - Predicate $\begin{cases} \text{normal} \\ \text{abnormal} \end{cases}$ - Subject $\begin{cases} \text{misuse} \\ \text{useless} \end{cases}$

yet. When it is stated with a performative format <<I state that from now on --->>, it is a "metasemiotic proposition" of a "semiotic judgment". A movie on the life of Mike Tyson may play this kind of function. And when this proposition settles as a legend, it becomes an "eternal proposition" of a "semiotic judgment".

As for an "index-sensitive factual proposition", Eco suggests the possibility of four subtypes by normalcy or abnormalcy of predicate, and by misuse or uselessness of the subject. Eco's examples (Eco 1978: 162, 168, 169, 170) are as follows:

/This pencil is black/ --- normal predicate,
/This cat is one eyed/ --- abnormal predicate,
/The present king of France is bald/ --- misuse of subject,
/The king of France is bald/ --- uselessness of subject

Eco on Carnival

Eco's analysis of carnival starts as a criticism against Bakhtin's view on carnival. According to Bakhtin, the upside-down world of carnival is a transgression and a liberty. But Eco points out that this performance of upside-down world functions as a social control rather than a liberation because it allows people to inverse the rule of the everyday world only once a year, and it reminds people the implied frame (rule or presupposition) of the world. Eco uses elementary symbols from the symbolic logic to show his argument. Let 'p' be a proposition, then carnival performance '~p' implies 'p' as a frame (or rule) (Eco 1984: 5). Incidentally, we can find a similar controversy as this over the social influence of TV violence and sex. School teachers tend to worry about the transgressional effect of these TV shows on children, but it is possible that these TV shows could compensate these violent desires of the audiences and as a result it might keep them restraint in their actual behavior, i.e. TV shows of violence and sex may have the effect of social control rather than transgression.

Now what is the nature of this proposition '~p' and 'p' in the context of Eco's typology of propositions? If we follow Eco's argument on carnival, 'p' is a social frame or a rule. So this is clearly a "semiotic proposition" which is coded and culturally shared. Then his '~p', negation in a semiotic proposition, is still a semiotic proposition. On the other hand, if we follow Bakhtin's argument, carnival is a transgression or liberty. This means that carnival performance is not merely a negation of 'p' but rather a birth of a new proposition 'q' which is not coded yet. In this sense, Bakhtin's 'q' is a "factual proposition". For example, let us suppose that a social frame 'p' means /The king rules the peasant/. Eco's peasant may perform '~p' as /The peasant rule the king/, while Bakhtin's peasant may perform 'q' as /The peasant ignore the king/. Under a society with the code 'p', 'q' is not coded, or the semantic structure of the sememe <<peasant>> does not include prediction 'q'. So, this 'q' cannot be a "semiotic proposition" but rather is a "factual proposition". Under the frame 'p', prediction 'q' is *abnormal* or transgressional. Yet if 'p' is shakey as a frame, i.e. if the king's head is shakey, 'q' has a possibility of being a *normal* "index-sensitive factual statement" in the context of code switching.

Propositions of the Lie in April Fool and Halloween

Let us first confirm that Eco included in his concept of mention both verbal and nonverbal statements (Eco 1976: 160). Then regarding the lies in April Fool and Halloween as verbal and nonverbal propositions, and using Eco's typology of proposition and his analysis on carnival, what can we find out about the nature and function of the propositions of April Fool and Halloween?

In the United States, Halloween is mainly a festival of children and students performed around a family neighborhood, campus, or shopping center toward the end of the fall season symbolized with the yellow empty pumpkin head which has some connotation with a fool or a ghost. Although the most popular character of costume seems to be still a vampire or a ghost, other characters include from various sources: from comic, TV, movie, animal, politics, space traveller, and so on. These are titled toward the malicious side but not all are so. The children say an eternal proposition "trick or treat" at the door. But this "trick" is nothing substantial. Against this "trick", all kinds of regulations are enforced to protect the part of "ghost"-child: visit only neighbors you know; only where door-light is on; parents stand behind the children; don't eat too much sugar; don't put needles in the candy. For students, the regulations are: don't throw beer cans, drive safely, go home before 1:00 a.m., and so on. These performances are not given at such places as in front of the church, the court house, the government building, or a stock exchange in contrast to what hippies used to do in the sixties. And a Halloween card says, "Have a *happy* Halloween" in just the same manner as we say "have a happy Valentine Day."

If we define these performances as '~p', and search for 'p' as an implied frame or a presupposition, 'p' seems to include all kinds. Although these '~p's from comic, TV and so on are all well known characters, these '~p's are diffused, so are 'p's. Some of '~p' are seasonal, and implied code 'p' itself is also shifting. For example, in the opposition of "Madonna!" ('~p') vs. "mother" ('p'), this 'p' itself shifts to "homemaker" ('q'?). '~p's are not aiming for one particular hyper-anticode '~P' or a new meta-code 'Q', i.e. the Revolution or the Liberation. For example, when a group of family performs "a family of chicken" as a '~p', what could be the implied social frame 'p' which was subverted by *chicken*? 'p's are not converging to one hypercode 'P' or the social norm. The distance between '~p' and 'p' is not wide. For example, the order "Drink beer ('~p') *but* don't throw beer can ('p')" is well obeyed. In summary, the propositions in Halloween performances are all inverted "semiotic propositions", and they function neither as a particular kind of social control nor as a particular kind of social transgression.

Telling a lie on April Fool's Day is practiced generally in informal close circles such as among friends or family. A statement '~p' such as /Today we do not have school. (Don't go to school.)/ is a false "index-sensitive semiotic proposition", and a statement '~p' such as /My chicken got teeth. (Go and look at it.)/ is a false "index-sensitive factual proposition" with abnormal prediction. Both statements as speech acts have illocutionary and perlocutionary forces. The receiver of these messages who react (or being deceived) to these speech acts is called a fool. In another word, these propositions as a lie in April Fool are the speech acts without sincerity condition.

But why do we have only one day of this sanctioned deception? In this context, it is important to realize that we are implicitly required to choose as an April Fool lie only a minor issue and with a good taste. The damage of being deceived should not be more than a minor silly. For example, we should not send friends a false letter with an official-looking stationary warning that they may have been exposed to the deadly AIDS virus (this actually happened in Springfield, Illinois, on April 1, 1988 [*Southern Illinoisan* 1988]). Thus, the frame or presupposition of all these '~p's of April Fool seem to converge to an implied maxim or hypercode 'P' telling that people should be honest to each other. This maxim 'P' is an "eternal proposition" of a "semiotic statement".

Conclusion

The lies of Halloween are inversion of various, diffused semiotic statements without implying any hypercode 'P', and lies of April Fool are minor falsehood of index-sensitive semiotic or factual statement which could converge to maxim 'P' "Be honest". By being diffused or minor, each of these lies function neither as a social transgression nor as a social control.

But, then, is it because we are really tame, obedient, and nice citizens? I don't think so. I guess the reason for the weakness of their effect is that in these days it is very easy for us to become a *real* vampire, a *real* Mafia, a *real* criminal, or a *real* X: these reals just skip these festivals of childish minor lies. They practice lies (or code breaking) 365 days. Then, those weak '~p's of Halloween and April Fool are like fantasies in Disney Land: they are socially accepted G-rated or PG-rated dreams (or lies) of adventure, frontier, future, and fantasy lands. Then, it leads the following question: are '~p's of movies rated-R and rated-X transgressional or social controlling? Why is the movie *The Last Temptation of Christ* so controversial while it is just a fiction (or a lie)? Probably because it is a negation of a hypercode 'P'. For some of us who believe in Christianity as 'P', this movie is '~P' or blasphemous for more than just one day. When Hitler once said that people of mass society are not deceived by small lies but are deceived by big lies, I guess he knew that while people *enjoy* playing 'trick or treat' or April Fool with small lies '~p's, people *need* a hypercode 'P'.

NOTES

[1] /Intension/ should not be confused with /intention/ in phenomenological intentionality.

[2] The expression /factual/ is a little confusing. It does not mean a fact or a real in our ordinary sense. The /factual/ in this context is related to the birth of "facticity" in phenomenological sense. In this context, a factual judgment has to do with the theory of sign production while a semiotic judgment has to do with the theory of code. It should also be reminded that Julia Kristeva's classification of semiotic vs symbolic roughly correspond's to Eco's classification of factual vs semiotic (Kristeva 1974: 19ff.).

REFERENCES

ECO, Umberto.
    1976.   *A Theory of Semiotics* (Bloomington: Indiana University Press).
    1983.   *Semiotics and the Philosophy of Language* (Bloomington: Indiana University Press).
    1984.   The Frame of Comic 'Freedom'" in *Carnival!*, ed. Thomas A. Sebeok (New York: Mouton Publishers), 1-9.
KRISTEVA, Julia.
    1974.   *La revolution du langage poetique*, trans. as *Revolution in Poetic Language* by Margaret Waller (New York: Columbia University Press, 1984). Page reference is to the English translation.
LEO, John.
    1988.   "A Holy Furor" in *Time*, 15 August 1988, 34-36.
SCORSESE, Martin.
    1988.   "Last Temptation of Christ" (film; Los Angeles: Universal Pictures).
Southern Illinoisan.
    1988.   Local news item, 16 April 1988, p. 2.

FIGURES OF DECEPTION IN *A LA RECHERCHE DU TEMPS PERDU*

Inge Crosman Wimmers
Brown University

During a recent forum on fiction devoted to exploring the topic "Why the Novel Matters", David Lodge asked the thought-provoking question "Can a novel be 'true to life,' or does it merely create a 'reality effect'?"[1] The reality effect is one of the figures of deception I will focus on today. I have chosen Proust's novel because in it we find a self-conscious discussion of the uses and abuses of signs in both everyday life and fiction.

Like Lodge, Proust would vehemently disagree with Paul de Man who, in *Blindness and Insight* (1983), categorically claims that fiction should not be confused with reality "from which it has forever taken leave".[2] In reading Proust's novel, we are repeatedly reminded that the dividing line between fact and fiction is far from rigid. Though Proust would agree with de Man that sign and meaning do not necessarily coincide, he would emphatically disagree that signs never lead to meaning.[3] On the contrary, one of the major tasks of the Proustian narrator is to show how, through a variety of indirect means, signs signify. Particularly eye opening is the protagonist's apprenticeship in the reading of signs, social and private, linguistic and other. In turn, his apprenticeship serves as a paradigm for the reader of *A la recherche* who, through unexpected twists and turns, discovers the following paradox, as Genette so aptly put it: "La vérité de la parole est *dans* le mensonge" ("The truth of the word is in the lie").[4]

Examples abound in the hero's initiation into the reading of indirect signs. The most instructive and humorous are those where the protagonist as young boy comes face to face with people of different tastes, habits, and social milieux. One of the most striking examples is his first encounter with the baron de Charlus in front of the Balbec hotel, before discovering who he is. It is a delightfully comic scene as we first share the hero's naive point of view while he interprets the mysterious stranger's penetrating gaze, wondering if he is mentally retarded, a spy, a crook, a thief, a hypocrite or an idiot.[5] The lesson learned from this experience is that there is an obvious discrepancy between appearance and reality, since it is soon revealed that the suspicious-looking stranger is none other than the most venerable member of the Guermantes family, the richest and noblest of aristocrats. Though this much is revealed to hero and reader alike, much remains hidden. How are we to intrepret the strange look with which Charlus sizes up the young hero, and what importance are we to give to the narrator's detailed description of this look and the analogies he introduces to describe it, as, for example, in the following passage: "Il lança sur moi une suprême oeillade à la fois hardie, prudente, rapide et profonde, comme un dernier coup que l'on tire au moment de prendre la fuite" (Proust 1954: 751-752). ("He darted a final glance at me that was at once bold, prudent, rapid and profound, like a last shot which one fires at an enemy as one turns to flee" [Proust 1954a: 807]). While the suggestion of flight explains why the hero thinks of a thief or crook, what is never explained is why Charlus behaves in such a peculiar way.

The situation becomes even more intriguing when the narrator, in describing certain of the stranger's gestures and expressions and in commenting on his clothing, adds interpretive comments that put us on our guard. What he does, in essence, it to let us know that certain aspects of the man's behavior and clothing are indirect signs that function as intentional camouflage. Thus the baron's apparent displeasure, after having impatiently looked at his watch, is unveiled as make-believe by the following disqualifying comment: "[il] fit le geste de mécontentement par lequel on croit faire voir qu'on a assez d'attendre, mais qu'on ne fait jamais quand on attend réellement" (Proust 1954: 752). ("[he] made the perfunctory gesture of annoyance by which people mean to show that they have waited long enough, although they never make it when they are really waiting" [Proust 1954a: 807-808]). This obvious hint that we are dealing with indirect language is reinforced by another example a few lines later: "il exhala le souffle bruyant des personnes qui ont non pas trop chaud, mais le désir de montrer qu'elles ont trop chaud" (Proust 1954: 752). ("He emitted the loud panting breath that people exhale not when they are too hot but when they wish it to be thought that they are too hot" [Proust 1954a: 808]). Communication here is obviously not based on a simple equation between sign and meaning. In fact, in each case, the gesture is not a sign but a false clue that has to be bracketed or written over.

Thus descriptive details and the narrator's undermining metacommentary to the effect that those who really wait do not make such gestures force us to come up with a *second*, derived meaning to be superimposed on the first, a meaning that only becomes clear when we consider the gesture in the context of its use, that is, specifically directed at the child or another possible witness of the scene who is to get the idea that this man is busy, preoccupied, hence indifferent. This second, superimposed meaning functions like an ideogram in that an idea--in this case indifference--is to be derived from a fleeting gesture. However, this second, derived meaning is nothing but a *trompe l'oeil* used to hide yet another, *third* meaning gradually to be inferred by the reader as he comes across similar signs of dissimulation, tipped off not only by conspicuous repetition of such signs, but also by shrewd interpretive comments which obviously come from a more experienced point of view than the young hero's. For instance, particularly revealing is the passage where the narrator comments at length on Charlus' somber clothing, repeatedly stressing that this apparent reserve does not mean that he is indifferent to color, on the contrary, it suggests the very opposite to the experienced eye (Proust 1954: 753; English trans., Proust 1954a: 809):

> d'un peu près on sentait que si la couleur était presque entièrement absente de ces vêtements, ce n'était pas parce que celui qui l'en avait bannie y était indifférent, mais plutôt parce que, pour une raison quelconque, il se l'interdisait. Et la sobriété qu'ils laissaient paraître semblait de celles qui viennent de l'obéissance à un régime, plutôt que du manque de gourmandise. Un filet de vert sombre s'harmonisait, dans le tissu du pantalon, à la rayure des chaussettes avec un raffinement qui décelait la vivacité d'un goût maté partout ailleurs et à qui cette seule concession avait été faite par tolérance, tandis qu'une tache rouge sur la cravate était imperceptible comme une liberté qu'on n'ose prendre.

from close at hand one felt that if colour was almost entirely absent from these garments it was not because he who had banished it from them was indifferent to it but rather because for some reason he forbade himself the enjoyment of it. And the sobriety which they displayed seemed to be of the kind that comes from obedience to a rule of diet rather than from lack of appetite. A dark green thread harmonised, in the stuff of his trousers, with the stripe on his socks, with a refinement which betrayed the vivacity of a taste that was everywhere else subdued, to which this single concession had been made out of tolerance, while a spot of red on his tie was imperceptible, like a liberty which one dares not take.

Though the narrator does not write from an omniscient position, which is evident from the evasive remark "pour une raison quelconque" ("for some reason or other") which reinforces the enigma, the analogies he uses in describing Charlus suggest a hidden message. The insistence, through continued metaphor, on the analogy of the forced diet--which implies a hardier appetite--and the focus on the tie's imperceptible red spot--made doubly conspicuous by thus being pointed out and by the accompanying remark "comme une liberté qu'on n'ose prendre" ("like a liberty which one dares not take")--lead us to suspect some ulterior motive, not only on Charlus' part but also in the narrator's signifying process.

Our suspicion that the narrator's description is motivated is reinforced when, after repeated mention of Charlus' professed virility and open contempt for the effeminate, his voice is described by a series of analogies each of which stresses its feminine characteristics (Proust 1954: 764; English trans., Proust 1954a: 820):

sa voix elle-même, pareille a certaines voix de contralto en qui on n'a pas assez cultivé le médium et dont le chant semble le duo alterné d'un jeune homme et d'une femme, se posait, au moment où il exprimait ces pensées si délicates, sur des notes hautes, prenait une doceur imprévue et semblait contenir des choeurs de fiancées, de soeurs, qui répandaient leur tendresse. Mais la nichée de jeunes filles que M. de Charlus, avec son horreur de tout efféminement, aurait été navré d'avoir l'air d'abriter ainsi dans sa voix, ne s'y bornait pas à l'interprétation, à la modulation des morceaux de sentiment. Souvent, tandis que causait M. de Charlus, on entendait leur rire aigu et frais de pensionnaires ou de coquettes ajuster leur prochain avec des malices de bonnes langues et de fines mouches.

his voice itself, like certain contralto voices in which the middle register has not been sufficiently cultivated, so that when they sing it sounds like an alternating duet between a young man and a woman, mounted, when he expressed these delicate sentiments, to its higher notes, took on an unexpected sweetness and seemed to embody choirs of betrothed maidens, of sisters, pouring out their fond feelings. But the bevy of young girls whom M. de Charlus in his horror of every kind of effeminacy would have been so distressed to learn that he gave the impression of sheltering thus within his voice did not confine themselves to the interpretation, the modulation of sentimental ditties. Often while M. de Charlus was talking one could hear their laughter, the shrill, fresh laughter of school-girls or coquettes quizzing their companions with all the archness and malice of clever tongues and pretty wits.

This passage stands in ironic contrast to Charlus' professed image of virility, which this humorous expansion based on the repeated comparison to the feminine seriously undermines. It functions like a wink at the reader, creating a situation of dramatic irony where narrator and reader know more than the characters. Though the young hero perceives some of the signs that need interpretation, as, for instance, the baron's "theatrical face", and though he correctly concludes that there is a hidden secret ("J'aurais voulu deviner quel était ce secret que ne portaient pas en eux les autres hommes" [Proust 1954: 761]) ("I should have liked to divine what was this secret which other men did not carry" [Proust 1954a: 817]), he has no inkling what this secret is. The narrator obviously does, as he humorously adds another analogy comparing Charlus to a woman, thus exposing him in a situation that becomes more and more amusing (Proust 1954: 764-765; English trans., Proust 1954a: 821):

> A ce moment, apercevant que le mouchoir brodé qu'il avait dans sa poche laissait dépasser des lisérés de couleur, il le rentra vivement avec la mine effarouchée d'une femme pudibonde mais point innocente dissimulant des appas que, par un excès de scrupule, elle juge indécents.

> At that moment, noticing that the embroidered handkerchief which he had in his pocket was exhibiting its coloured border, he thrust it sharply down out of sight with the scandalised air of a prudish but far from innocent lady concealing attractions which, by an excess of scrupulosity, she regards as indecent.

In light of this kind of descriptive overkill, which redresses the balance by juxtaposing signs that blatantly reveal next to those that slyly conceal, the narrator's portrayal of Charlus is clearly ironic and invites the reader to participate in the rewriting of the script. What emerges, through the insistent comparisons to the feminine, is the repressed language of desire whose indices--all partial, metonymic and indirect-- were designed to mislead. Thus the baron's insistent display of indifference is to be reinterpreted, adding a third level of meaning without, however, cancelling the previous one, since the display of indifference does not signify lack of interest. Thus the veil of indifference functions like a negative sign. But why this keen interest and why hide it? The answer, the hidden truth, lies on yet another, the *fourth* level of meaning of this many-layered palimpsest. Yet it is thanks to the dynamics of deception--the convergence of several layers of meaning--that we gradually get there. The final interpretant of this passage, the enigma to be solved, is Charlus' inversion, which, in retrospect, explains why several signs were substituted and inverted, and why cautionary comments and undermining analogies accompanied the various signs.

It is only in a second, retrospective reading, however, that the reader is aware of the full impact of signs and their intentional structure, since he is only gradually let in on the dramatic irony. It is only after having made our way through a number of pages and several layers of meaning that we share the narrator's privileged position of superior knowledge and the pleasure that it provides.[6]

The narrative segment under discussion is exemplary in showing us the complex reading of signs that is inscribed in the Proustian text, and it reminds us that its author is intent on foregrounding the act of interpretation. Proust's concept of the sign is closer to Peirce's triadic structure (sign-object-interpretant) than to Saussure's binary structure of signifier and signified. The way signs are used and interpreted in the Proustian universe forces us to go beyond the semiotics of language as a system of signs to a more pragmatically based orientation. For example, Bakhtin's concept of the dialogic would be more helpful to explain how, in the passage under consideration, language is shaped by the presence of its interlocutors in a given context of use. In the present instance, the Other at whom the discourse is directed includes not only the naive young hero but also any shrewd witness of the scene against whom Charlus has to guard himself, and, beyond that, the reader reading at whom the narrative discourse is directed.[7] Moreover, in a second reading of the novel we realize that the Proustian narrative is designed to teach us how to read, not only the novel but our own lives and the world at large as well. On this, the *fifth* level of meaning, all the intriguing signs we have encountered in the present passage acquire yet another function, reveal another motivation: they are part of an allegory of reading, which I see as the major orientation of *A la recherche*.

Everything in the novel points that way, from enigmatic signs found in the storyworld to the multiple discourses that shape the narrator's text. It is on the level of discourse that we encounter the novel's most disconcerting hurdles.[8] For instance, while the title and the opening paragraphs lead us to expect an autobiographical narrative, this frame of reference is soon transgressed in more ways than one: not only do we come across passages of omniscient narration that stand in sharp contrast to the restricted point of view of first person narration, but a whole volume in third-person narration (*Un amour de Swann*) is interpolated, without explanation, into the protagonist's personal history. More disconcerting yet are two kinds of discourse--iterative and ideological--that constantly shift the focus from the personal to the general. The iterative, a synthesizing narration, places emphasis on the kind of experience described rather than on any one single occurrence. Equally striking are the frequent switches from narrative to ideological discourse when the narrator stops telling his story to generalize or philosophize. As these techniques are repeated and converge, the plot gradually unfolds: we begin to realize that protagonist and other characters alike stand for more than themselves. Once their status changes from person to figure, we can no longer read literally, since we are involved in a double-layered discursive structure that takes us from the primary level of meaning where incidental episodes exist in their own right to an interpretive reading that discloses their significance and expands the frame of reference. Particularly compelling are interpretive remarks disclosing the truths to be discovered through a given episode or character. Thus characters and events begin to function as reading models setting the hermeneutic process in motion.

It is not the quest of time lost, as deceptively announced by the title, that gives the novel its unity, but rather, the constant quest for truth and a gradual process of revelation, which, ironically, leads us through a whole semiotics of deception. As we witness the protagonist's many trials and errors, we, like the hero, undergo a rigorous apprenticeship, with unexpected twists and turns. One of the truths we learn along the way is the paradox, quoted earlier, that Genette has pointed out in studying the many uses of indirect language in the Proustian universe: "La vérité de la parole est *dans* le mensonge" ("The truth of the word is in the lie").[9]

While language is put on trial throughout the novel, the full truth emerges only in retrospect. Not only do we learn, in the last volume, that the protagonist becomes a writer and that metaphor is the crowning achievement of language, we also realize that we have enjoyed the creative powers of language from the start of the novel, and that the time that was supposedly lost and wasted has already been recaptured through style.[10] This is the crowning paradox of the novel: the very text we are reading, by initiating us so successfully into its universe and the problematics of communication, belies its own critique of language. Or, viewed another way, one of the major lessons we learn by reading Proust, as Genette has pointed out, is that indirected language par excellence is the literary work of art.[11]

By making us aware of the problematic nature of sign and referent, Proust teaches us that the ultimate referent of story and discourse is an interpretant, not reference to a person, object or state of affairs, This is made explicit when, in the last volume, Proust's protagonist-turned-writer offers his work as a model for interpretation and introspection: "In reality every reader is, while he is reading, the reader of his own self. The writer's work is merely a kind of optical instrument which he offers to the reader to enable him to discern what, without this book, he would perhaps never have perceived in himself".[12] In the last analysis, *A la recherche du temps perdu* is unveiled as an allegory of reading designed to instruct, not to deceive us. Thus Proust's semiotics of deception leads to a network of associations between reader and text where signification and significance are built on structures of exchange as the narrator takes us from referential illusion to an interaction based on collusion.

NOTES

[1] David Lodge (1988), p. 131.

[2] Paul de Man (1983), p. 17. See Lodge (1988) p. 129 where he attacks de Man's position.

[3] In *Blindness and Insight*, Paul de Man claims "that sign and meaning can never coincide is what is precisely taken for granted in the kind of language we call literary. Literature, unlike everyday language, begins on the far side of this knowledge; it is the only form of language free from the fallacy of unmediated expression . . ." (p.17).

[4] Gérard Genette (1969), p. 249.

[5] Proust 1918. See also Proust 1954, Volume 1, 751-753. In all subsequent citations of quoted material, the French text used is *A la recherche du temps perdu* (Proust 1954); the English translation used in all cases here is *Remembrance of Things Past* (Proust 1954a).

[6] For a description of the reader's privileged position in the reading of ironic texts, see Wayne Booth (1974), pp. 33-39. In the example under discussion, however, the reader has to wait before reaching this position; in fact, the Proustian narrator intentionally misleads him when in passages immediately preceding and following the hero's first encounter with Charlus, Saint Loup praises the latter's masculinity and describes him as a womanizer (Cf. Proust 1954, Volume 1: 750, 751, and 762). However, for the reader familiar with the special connotations now attached to the name Charlus--made famous through the Proustian text--the dramatic irony is more readily apparent.

[7] That a number of indirect signs are directed at the reader is quite clear from Proust's narrative discourse.

[8] I discuss Proust's multiple discourses in more detail in Wimmers (1988) in a chapter entitled "Proust's Palimpset: Multiple Frames of Reference in *A la recherche du temps perdu*", pp. 88-120.

[9] Genette (1969), p. 249.

[10] Proust's famous statement on metaphor, "Je crois que la métaphore seule peut donner une sorte d'éternité au style", appeared first in an article "A propos du style de Flaubert" (Proust 1920: 72-90); cf. *A la recherche du temps perdu* (Proust 1954, Volume 3: 889).

[11] See Genette (1969) p. 294: "C'est le conflit du langage et de la vérité qui *produit*, comme on l'a pu voir, le langage indirect; et le langage indirect, par excellence, c'est l'écriture--c'est l'oeuvre" ("It is the conflict of language and truth that *produces*, as we have seen, indirect language; and indirect language, par excellence, is writing--is the work of art" [my translation]).

[12] Proust 1954a, Volume 3, p. 949; cf. the French text of this quotation (Proust 1954, Volume 3: 911): "En réalité, chaque lecteur est, quand il le lit, le propre lecteur de soi-même. L'ouvrage de l'écrivain n'est qu'une espèce d'instrument optique qu'il offre au lecteur afin de lui permettre de discerner ce que, sans ce livre, il n'eût peut-être pas vu en soi-même".

REFERENCES

BOOTH, Wayne.
   1974. *A Rhetoric of Irony* (Chicago: University of Chicago Press).
DE MAN, Paul.
   1971. *Blindness and Insight*, 2nd edition. (London: Methuen, 1983).
GENETTE, Gérard.
   1969. "Proust et le langage indirect" in *Figures II* (Paris: Seuil).
LODGE, David.
   1988. "The Novel Now: Theories and Practices", *Novel* 21.2/3, 125-138.
PROUST, Marcel.
   1918. *A l'ombre des jeunes filles en fleurs*, later incorporated with other stories published between 1913 and 1927, under the title *A la recherche du temps perdu* (q.v. Proust 1954).
   1920. "A Propos du Style de Flaubert", *Nouvelle Revue Francaise* 14.76, 72-90.
   1954. *A la recherche du temps perdu*, 3 vols., Pléade edition (Paris: Gallimard) represents the first published integration of these stories by Proust, and the first use of the comprehensive title for the included works. The authoritative English trans. by C.K. Scott Moncrieff and Terence Kilmartin as *Remembrance of Things Past*, 3 vols. (New York: Random House, 1981) was used alongside the French edition throughout this paper.
   1954a. *Rememberance of Things Past* (q.v. Proust 1954).
WIMMERS, Inge.
   1988. *Poetics of Reading: Approaches to the Novel* (Princeton University Press).

X

LITERARY SEMIOTICS: CRITICAL THEORY

DEFINING A NARRATIVE SIGNIFIER

Jackson G. Barry
University of Maryland

The present paper engages semiotics to found some basic definitions in narratology, since clearly if one thinks of narrative as a *representation* of something one is definitely in the area of the semiotic. Specifically, I attempt to identify in a given text--my example will be an F. Scott Fitzgerald short story--a narrative signifier and a narrative signified. In pursuing the narrative signifier, three aspects complicate the search. 1. The narrative signifier is much less tangible and much less easily located than the signifier in painting, dance, or even poetry, being, by general consent, a second-order phenomenon. 2. Once located, it is very hard to say with any accuracy what and how this signifier represents. For example, in what sense, if any, is this signifier iconic? 3. Following from #2 and underlying such extensions of narratology as those in communications and cognition, is there a specifically narrative "deep structure" of knowledge? (See Barbara Herrnstein-Smith, "Surfacing from the Deep", 1977). Finally, I want to introduce as a foray of narratology into areas other than the literary story and as an extension of definitions drawn and exemplified in the first part of this paper, a brief analysis from the work in narratology and corrections which is being pursued at the Maryland Correctional Institution for Women by Dr. Norma Procopiow and myself (see Procopiow 1989, this volume, pp. 336-340).

Let me start by defining my three major terms. Narrative will be taken to be an account--hence *told*, not acted--of events with their agents and participants, depicted from a temporal, hence sequential point of view. This is offered with the addendum that sequence or progression need not here be understood as strict clock/calendar chronology. In the simplest sense, the narrative signifier is the story drawn from the text, while the narrative signified is the meaning of that story. ("Story" is used here in its common meaning. Where a technical meaning is intended, "fabula" will be employed.) To flesh out this definition a bit, I should say that I take the narrative signifier to be that second-order meaning which constitutes the narrative chain of events and their agents and participants and which is constructed upon the first-order language of the verbal text. This narrative signifier is a second-order phenomenon in that it is the signified of the language of the text. As we shall see, it in turn becomes the signifier of a further meaning we are designating as the narrative signified.

Certainly the act of isolating a narrative signifier from the story as a whole is arbitrary and artificial, yet isolation is, as with any analytic discipline, absolutely essential if narratology is to claim any specific expertise. While descriptions of place, thematic contrasts, and mention of culture symbols--such as the Ritz Bar and Josephine Baker in our sample story--supply important dimensions of meaning to any story, these essentially synchronic dimensions will be treated in the following analyses as supportive of a narrative code, not as equal and autonomous.

A narrative signifier such as that posited here can be seen to have many connections with what Roland Barthes in his *S/Z* (1970: 18-20) called the proairetic (or actantial) code. For present purposes, I find it much more effective to consider a code of actions and characters (roughly lumping Barthes' proairetic and semic codes) and to subsume under these, as conditions of the action, the codes of theme (symbolic), enigma (hermeneutic), and cultural reference (referential). Barthes wants particularly and properly to hear the many voices in his "readerly" text (20-21). I want particularly to read my texts for their specifically *narrative* content, while acceding that on other occasions they might be read for thematic, poetic, historical, or other contents.

Turning finally to the narrative signified, this will be defined as the meaning of the story which has been constructed as the narrative signifier. This signified will have all the frustrating richness that circles around the meaning of meaning. A story, any story, will signify many things. One of Labov's Philadelphia ghetto stories may signify the educational level of its teller (Labov and Waletzky 1967). The parable of the tortoise and the hare means a steady pace triumphs over erratic bursts. The kind of narrative signified I wish to discuss, however, is that meaning given by the story as exemplum, meaning in other words, through ostention. This is the kind of meaning which story possesses as signifier of temporal dimensions and relations. It is most apparent in literary and historical narratives as defined by Stone (1979), White (1984), and Ricoeur (1983), and is the basis for most claims for narrative as a cognitive instrument (Mink, 1978).

Let me turn here to F. Scott Fitzgerald's short story "Babylon Revisited" (Fitzgerald 1931) and attempt to delineate what I would take the narrative signifiers and their signifieds to be. As illustration we may consider a section at the beginning of "Babylon Revisited" (210) which begins with a brief dialogue between the protagonist, Charlie Wales, and Alix, bartender at the Ritz:

"And where's Mr. Campbell?" Charlie asked.
"Gone to Switzerland. Mr. Campbell's a pretty sick man, Mr. Wales."
"I'm sorry to hear that. And George Hardt?" Charlie inquired.
"Back in America, gone to work."

The fragment of conversation is obviously synechdochic, a part implied by the opening "And" standing for a longer query about Ritz Bar "regulars" now absent. From the literal sense of this conversation we begin to draw a narrative thread that includes a possible protagonist attempting to pick up the pieces of a life he had once known.

Fitzgerald continues with a third-person narration of Wales' impressions of an emptier Paris and a quiet, almost deserted, American Bar at the Ritz. Charlie refuses the second drink proffered by the bartender, and we learn that Charlie has strictly limited his drinking for a year and a half and that he is in business in Prague. A presumably drunken bachelor party is recalled and one of its participants described as having paid off much food and liquor at the bar with a bad check. Finally the bartender asks:

"Here for long, Mr. Wales?"
"I'm here for four or five days to see my little girl."
"Oh-h! You have a little girl?"

The scene is as *told*. Even the bits of dialogue have the effect of being reported by a narrator rather than spoken by actors. The signifier is strictly speaking non-mimetic. As Barthes says "Narrative does not show, does not imitate" (1966: 124). What we have is a naming: a description of states, events, and their relations as the narrator has perceived and arranged them. ("It was late afternoon . . . ." [211]) ("Charlie scribbled an address . . . ." [210]) It is in this sense of perception and arrangement and the verbal skill to convey these that the narrative signifier gains its power. Although the opening dialogue takes place with Charlie settled at the bar, the diegetic passage which follows describes first Charlie's general state ("He was not really disappointed to find Paris was so empty", [210]) then takes him back to embarking from the taxi and passing on into the bar. Thus from sentence to sentence, paragraph to paragraph, or, even from section to section, the discourse does not necessarily follow a chronological order. In this sense certainly, narrative, which we have defined as concerned with time, does not signify that concern through any literal mimesis of its subject. The narrative signified one draws from the text , however, does offer important temporal dimensions. It establishes Charlie at the bar in conversation, then explains the mood in which he arrived there--lonely in an emptier Paris--but strong and not unhappy about the passing of a frivolous age. We learn his purpose, the point of the quest which constitutes the story. The sense of the opening at the bar gains strength at the end of the story, when, in the way described by Iser, we look back to revalue items in light of what we learn as the story progresses (Iser 1972). In this way the bar has special narrative significance because after his disappointment in not gaining custody of his daughter, Charlie returns to the Ritz, framing this visit with an arrival and departure from the same place, significantly loaded with memories of his Babylonian days.

The story picks up in diegesis outside the bar and takes Charlie through the streets of Paris on a late rainy afternoon, from the glitter of the right bank to a more "provincial" and family-oriented left bank, where, at the apartment of his brother- and sister-in-law he greets the daughter they have been keeping for him. The progression is clear in the narrative choices: closing the interior, casual, conversation scene in the bar to move the protagonist out into the late afternoon, to move him geographically on a route traceable on a Paris map to the place of his first important encounter with the adversarial sister-in-law from whom he must win his daughter. Coloring and giving significance to its events, the reader will note in this narrative the sterility and artificiality of the right bank bar, with "a group of strident queens installing themselves in a corner" (211) and its contrast with the five-course bourgeois restaurants on the left bank. Noted also will be the contrast of the empty bar with his in-laws' comfortable salon where "the cheer of six o'clock spoke in the eager smacks of the fire and the sounds of French activity in the kitchen" (212).

The meaning, the signified of the narrative code of Fitzgerald's text, thus hinges very strongly upon the *re*-visit. On the one hand we have a *visit*, a short stay at a place in which one does not presently live. This includes the feeling of transience in a place previously native and includes, as visit, a given beginning and end marked spatially and temporally by an arrival into and a departure from. Here we note that Fitzgerald's signifier has been particularly well drawn since Charlie could logically have been living in Paris all the while he sought the return of his daughter. We note as well the effectiveness of beginning and ending the story at that symbol of transience, the hotel. The meaning of this story as narrative also inheres in the purposiveness of the visit: the protagonist arrives in hope stoked by his sobriety and the fact that he has obtained a very well paying job. On the other hand, the visit as *re*-visit sparks all the overtones mentioned above that each move of this visit, each furtherance of his purpose, is marked by memories of his previous associations with the same place in years past.

If we jump to the end of Fitzgerald's story and consider a total narrative signifier, we can see a meaning which would encompass the idea of failure unjustly inflicted (as Charlie, through no *present* fault loses custody of Honoria almost as that right was in his hands). We see a purposeful movement as Charlie advances his goal in his three visits to the Peters' apartment always maintaining the self-control he lacked in his drinking days, but in each present move through each part of the Paris/Babylon city, haunted by his past behavior there.

The point that I would finally wish to emphasize about the narrative signifier/ signified pair and about the limitations and the value of narrative study is that this pair defines a kind of temporal experience as only narrative can. The well worn notion in aesthetics concerning the "concrete universal" (Wimsatt 1947), which has become in semiotics Eco's ostention, holds well in this case (Eco 1979: 209-211). "Babylon Revisited" is an ostended sign of a particular experience of quest into a previously occupied territory, a quest honestly undertaken but freighted with guilt from previous days. As the New Critics insisted with their "heresy of paraphrase", the meaning cannot be neatly summarized, and any attempt such as mine above will inevitably appear lame. On the other hand, I would insist that a narrative like "Babylon Revisited" does indeed signify, does indeed have a meaning that clarifies and explains hence may be considered a cognitive instrument for a kind of knowledge of experience unique to narrative as signifier of time, agents, and actions.

Some proof and illumination of my thesis may come from the experiment which is described in Norma Procopiow's paper in this volume. In our project for using narrative in correctional education, Dr. Procopiow and I actually assigned "Babylon Revisited" and worked with the inmates exploring in compositions of their own the meanings of the *re*-visit which that story afforded. Clearly the idea of returning to a place one had known before a climactic break like a prison term would be very close to these inmates. We asked them to construct a narrative of their own on a personal revisit. One very moving account told of the inmate's return to the poor neighborhood in which she had grown up and started the street fighting and drug dependence which had placed her in jail. There was excellent material on the omnipresence of drugs and the concomitant brutalization of the neighborhood, on the woman's fear for herself and for her children. Narrative, I would say, had worked well for this inmate. There, on a sheet in front of her she could see a past and a present, a series of steps taken. Where we would use the techniques learned from narrative study in this case would be to point out that connections are generally not clear. The writing tends to be simply accumulative as one might guess from her title, "When I Was Young and My Life". The overwhelming influence of environment on action, which we would recognize as a Naturalistic trait, is not explored. Point of view is unmitigatedly personal.

Though I would want to scale back some of the wider claims for narrative to fit the definitions I have offered, I cannot believe that the signifying powers claimed recently for narrative are *all* chimeral. Properly understood, research in this field should add to our knowledge and prove of practical use in the many areas where story serves as a primary cognitive instrument.

REFERENCES

BARTHES, Roland.
- 1966. "Introduction to the Structural Analysis of Narratives", in *Image, Music, Text*, essays selected and trans. Stephen Heath (New York: Hill and Wang, 1977).
- 1970. *S/Z* (Paris: Éditions du Seuil), trans. Richard Miller (New York: Hill and Wang, 1974).

ECO, Umberto.
- 1976. *A Theory of Semiotics* (Bloomington: Indiana University Press).

FITZGERALD, F. Scott.
- 1931. "Babylon Revisited", in *Babylon Revisited and other Stories by F. Scott Fitzgerald* (New York: Charles Scribner's, 1960).

HERRNSTEIN-SMITH, Barbara.
- 1977. "Surfacing from the Deep", in *On the Margins of Discourse: The Relation of Literature to Language* (Chicago: Chicago University Press, 1978).

ISER, Wolfgang.
- 1972. "The Reading Process: A Phenomenological Approach", in *The Implied Reader: Patterns of Communication in Prose Fiction from Bunyon to Beckett* (Baltimore: The Johns Hopkins University Press, 1974), Iser's English trans. of his *Der implizite leser: Kommunikationsformen des Romans von Bunyan bis Beckett* (Munich: Wilhelm Fink, 1972).

LABOV, William and Joshua WALETZKY.
- 1967. "Narrative Analysis: Oral Versions of Personal Experience", in *Essays on the Verbal and Visual Arts*, ed. June Helm (Seattle: University of Washington Press).

MINK, Louis O.
- 1978. "Narrative Form as Cognitive Instrument", in *The Writing of History: Literary Form and Historical Understanding*, ed. Robert H. Canary and Henry Kozicki (Madison: University of Wisconsin Press).

RICOEUR, Paul.
- 1983. *Temps et récit* vol. I (Paris: Éditions Seuil), trans. by Kathleen McLaughlin and David Pellauer as *Time and Narrative* (Chicago: University of Chicago Press 1984).

STONE, Lawrence.
- 1979. "The Revival of Narrative: Reflections on a New Old Story", *Past and Present* 85, 3-24.

WHITE, Hayden.
- 1984. "The Question of Narrative in Contemporary Historical Theory", *History and Theory* 23, 1-33.

WIMSATT, W. K. Jr.
- 1947. "The Concrete Universal", in *The Verbal Icon* (New York: Noonday Press, 1954).

THE LITERATURE OF SILENCE: A CONCERN OF SEMIOTICS?

Vittoria Borsò
Universität Mannheim (West Germany)

The concern with the so called "literature of silence" is embarrassing in many senses. Not only is the attempt to describe this object a tough enterprise, but, worse, silence seems to imply a univocal relationship to the problem of discourse. Silence appears, at first glance, to be the opposite of discourse, "parole". From this viewpoint, the proposal to consider "literature of silence" in the context of Mexican literature certainly provokes the criticism of more advanced cultural studies refusing to link "mutism" to one of the so-called third world cultures. This is not my aim. I would like to rethink the "literature of silence" as a cultural practice which, on the contrary, should open some "illuminative" viewpoints to our powerfully reasoning Western cultures. In rethinking the line of criticism on "literature of silence", which is represented by Maurice Blanchot and a short remembrance of Roland Barthes, I'll try to discuss a couple of "crucial" points, which in my opinion found little attention in new criticism and even in postmodern era. This quest leads eventually to the problem of pertinence of such literary and cultural approach to semiotics, which, according to its genesis and nature, essentially focuses on communication and plurality of sense, or on its negation.

I. The Place of "Literature of Silence"

The delineation of this literature is not exactly a question of style, epoch or nationality, but rather belongs to a certain *attitude* towards writing. Maurice Blanchot explores the writing *experience*, recalling the old myth of poetry as the siren song (*Le livre à venir*, 1959). He highlights the state of *distance* from the encounter with this *reality* (the "Sea Voyage" akin to the "Drunken Boat" of Rimbaud) which *aside from its illusionary* nature is experienced with a real and unappeasable desire (1959: 10). To be distant from the source of the song means, for Blanchot, being in a continuous state of divergent feeling: on the one hand the feeling of a "real desire" towards the image of the song and, on the other, the awareness that a real representation of this image is not possible. To consider this illusionary image as the representation of reality can only be attained by way of *reason*. Thus, the "*bon sens*" of Ulysses alone was able to vanquish the distance and to destroy the power of the desire which burned when he was exposed to the song. Blanchot distinguishes two attitudes toward this appeal, that is, two attitudes towards writing: The first, which is exemplified by Ulysses, masters the temptation and afterwards finds his own subject as well as his own world confirmed (p. 16). The second, like Melville's Ahab, who has accepted the encounter with the image pursuing him obsessively, is submerged by it and eventually succumbs[1]. This image belongs to the domain of otherness[2]; an otherness which can be of psychological or epistemological nature.

Blanchot's reading of the myth can be interpreted in the sense of postmodern criticism of representation. Nevertheless, the aim of Blanchot is not to see primarily within a philosophical framework. Blanchot insists on the *experience* of those writers who are possessed simultaneously by the feeling of the presence of the "Other" and of its distance, eventually becoming aware that *any representation, that means any signified pretending to grasp "the other", is an illusion*. This kind of writer is like Ahab on the sea, before his encounter with the inconceivable. At the encounter, writing comes to an end.

Blanchot presents various aspects of this writing attitude as he reviews different authors.

1. That this "other" coincides especially with the image of time is, of course, illustrated with Proust. Proust tried to confer to "real" life the "magic simultaneousness" of his own "image of time" (p. 20). In his "novel" objects are immersed in a special light where anything appears as a reflection (p. 27). At the same time the experience of each instant and of its essentiality is powerful. The light of the writings of Proust is compared with the "light of the voids *between* stars" (p. 33). Blanchot uses a myriad of metaphors for explaining this *"écriture"* of lightful void (as an example: Proust's style has "slow curves, a fluid weight" [p. 33] etc.).

2. The sufferance accompanying this practice of writing is evidenced by Blanchot when he reviews Artaud. The criticism against any logocentrical concept of deepness by Artaud provokes a *sufferance* which is *present* in his words almost bodily (p. 56-57). This "deep" physical quality of Artaud's language creates the experience of a *presence*, and it is the sensual force of Artaud's language of "cruelty"--of sufferance--that produces the fascination of his proposal to find another logic, the "logic of the body" in the theater[3].

3. The effort to *say the void*, the *"néant"*, is highlighted in Blanchot's commentary on Joubert, a preromantic French writer. For Joubert, the void is the only palpable reality of language. Even if he does not go as far as Mallarmé later at the turn of the century, Joubert's word can express the *"invisible* fullness of the world"* (p. 82); a metaphor by which Blanchot means the vivid intensity of language in signifying the world and at the same time the distance towards the signified (world). Joubert never wrote a book. He merely concentrated fervently on the search of the exact point where writing is possible (p. 71). Blanchot compares his "contemplations" to a huge *text of silences*, a book like an "immobile sky of moving stars" (p. 84).

4. Virginia Woolf is then, for Blanchot, the writer who represents all the above mentioned aspects. She was reticent in believing to have found the language corresponding to her own experience of "the moment of being"; reticent up to the point and including suicide. Time, as fleeting moments which Woolf calls "reality", are like lightening fragments in a transparent space (p. 139), as she explained, like "something abstract incorporate in the lands, in the sky" (p. 139)[4].

Concerning this kind of experience[5], Blanchot especially underlines the fact that reality is felt as simply existing, even if it exists only exceptionally, as an ephemeral moment of the book (p. 151). This "wonder" occurs as a result of the fidelity of the writer towards this transcendent point of desire (p. 142) opening the language to the "silence", which means a desire charging language with the dolorous consciousness about the incapability of saying[6].

This "experience of desire" is a different attitude towards writing than other authors have. Blanchot exemplifies the latter on Joyce and Musil[7]. These writers are "illuminate". They are aware that any representation of reality is a work of fiction and, playing with the labyrinth of discourses on reality, they discover the "natural condition of being" in the lack of authenticity, originality and truth. Their discourses are polyphonic and deconstructionist. Their assails against Western logocentric beliefs reveal--and inspire in the reader--the pleasure of play with cultural models. The struggle for the "true image", for the transcendent reality, is for them not an impellent sufferance: In the language of the above mentioned authors like Virginia Woolf, this struggle lasts, on the contrary, like a resonance, when a doubt[8] about the reality of their own speech reverberates on words, similar to a silent white light.

In Latin America the existence of these two paradigms of writers can easily be observed. José María Arguedas, who also practiced "literature of silence" up to his suicide, explains in his posthumously published book *El zorro de arriba y el zorro de abajo* (1971) his own incessant struggle for an ideal cultural language of Peru which could vanquish the distance between Western signs and a cultural experience charged with otherness. Arguedas reasons along the above line of thoughts about two kinds of writing attitudes and classifies Latin American writers in (illuminate) cosmopolitans (professionals!)--like Borges, Cortázar, Vargas Llosa, Fuentes etc.--and "provincialists"--like Juán Rulfo, Gabriel García Márquez and others.[9] My objective consists in focussing on this second type of writer maintaining the aim of Blanchot[10] to see this kind of literature as the desire of attaining a real presence through representation and the feeling of its impossibility. That linking of Latin American literature to the suffering struggle for a cultural system, which could be able to represent a real experience of otherness, is fitting, and may be evident if one considers that Latin America is generally classified as a culture of otherness. Instead of highlighting the postmodern viewpoint on alterity leading to the absence of signified (Lacan), to simulation (in the sense of Baudrillard[11]) or to the necessity of conveying discourse to *"différance"*, I like to focus attention on the reading *experience* accompanying such texts.

II. The presence of otherness in reading experience

In some contemporary Mexican novels similar to Rulfo's writing, it becomes immediately evident that the reading experience is supported by the impressive sensuality of discourse. A "strange" presence is produced by the resonance of words carrying the silence like a body[12]. This alienation of usual discourses on reality opens the reader to experience the presence of the other as Merleau-Ponty claims to be the original attitude of human beings. Arguing that perception of the other has a primacy towards constitution of the self, art experience may recover, according to the French philosopher, the state of indeterminacy of the self, where perception "throws" one's being out into the "world", de-centering the self. Nevertheless, in the sense of the above mentioned reading of "silent literature", the supreme encounter with the other, even *in* a language which has been opened to new spaces, is incessantly associated with the presence of the void. The experience remains a desire of the other in as much as its image is seen (perceived) and--as an effect of the "resonance of the void"--is lost at the same time.

The ec-stasis of this writing practice can become the experience of the reader who is also decentered in many senses. It is not only a matter of the epistemological relationship of the subject towards the world, on which deconstructive approaches mostly focus. In this reading, the ec-stasis belongs rather to the ethical mood of the subject, which, experiencing the sensual power of otherness (the silent echoes of the words), places the emphasis not on the self (for instance as subject of knowledge), but on the other. At the same time, the silent echoes of signs reminding of the void, do not allow the subject to grasp the other and to relate it to a signified. On the contrary, it is a *practice of humility* that the subject learns by this kind of reading; it is an ethical relationship to otherness which has been evidenced by the French philosopher Levinas.

Accordingly, the highlight of alterity should be the *presence of the other* in the own experience of desire. Quoting Merleau-Ponty:

> The roles of the subject and of what it sees are exchanged and reversed. I thought I gave to what I see its meaning as a thing seen, and then one of these things suddenly slips out of this condition. The spectacle begins to furnish itself a spectator who is not I but who is reproduced from me (1973: 135).

In Mexican novels this "other presence" is death--the associate image of Proustian time; an image which sometimes appears in the form of deserts, focussing, for instance, on South Mexico's suffering, desiccate landscaping as well as on its white, cloudy sunny sky reflected on a stony uniformity. This lack of visuality--as Blanchot attempts to describe with reference to Jouvert--is not a lack of perception, since language is charged with awakening the reader to the ex-centric perception of low tonalities and sounds, where minimal impulses are painful flashes of light. This perception is supported by vocabulary and syntax as well as by the whole discourse which repeats the uniformity: not only by way of a voice which appears silent despite its polyphonic nature, but also by means of a special treatment of time accompanying the uniformity of space. Fleeting moments have a slow rhythm, conferring a special feeling of time, like the feeling of primordial movements of life[13].

Some remarks on a novel by the Mexican writer José Revueltas, which I will have only a very limited space to elaborate on, may be illustrative: Plot and situation of *El luto humano*, 1943 (Human Mourning), are radically elementary: A child dies in a hut, a man perishes in the outer desert submerged by the storm, somebody--a friend--tries to seduce the anguishing mother. The landscaping is reduced to a river and three houses. As an effect of the primordial situation, the river is perceived as the border between wilderness and civilization, death and life. The odyssey of the father Ursulo crossing "the desert" in order to look for a priest celebrating the funeral of his daughter becomes a voyage to death: Ursulo is accompanied by Adán on the way to the other side of the desert, and in crossing the river, they seem to traverse the limits of life. The presence of death in their boat, although it seems unmotivated, is perceived: one of the two, either Adán (the "first" human [A: beginning of the alphabet]), who is an Indian; or the other, Ursulo (the "last" human [U: the end of the alphabet]), who is a mestizo, has to die. The presence of the primordial necessity of fight between races is experienced simultaneously with its futility. The landscape has cosmic presence, similar to a strange physics which is created by the words of an intensive and elementary peculiarity: Wind, river, storm create a body which envelops everything (*"La noche animal que rodeaba el mundo"* (p. 34 /the animal night which embraced the world). Even metaphors cannot confer a signified, a name to this presence. Any rational solution is undermined by the weak motivational structure of the novel. Informations like the allusions to the cristero revolution are like flashes; they participate in the same movement of the storm. The presence of words of silence which alienate the representation of reality is felt with real intensity; an experience which eventually leads the astonished reader to surrender himself to this other he learned to desire in the low voices, opening his eyes in order to perceive the intensity of shadows: *"Y como hablaban era sólo silencio* (p. 35 /The way of talking was only a silence). The elementary situation of extreme conflicts engenders an atmosphere which remains irreducible to models of knowledge. One can attempt to respond to the astonishing experience giving psychoanalytical or historical answers (about, for instance, the cristero revolution). Nevertheless, the mystery of this image of desert where history and humans are only elements of a whole "animal" atmosphere, remains untouched and valid as the only real presence.

III. Some Conclusions

You will certainly have recognized some aspects which you may relate in a more general way to poetic experience, since the unappeasable desire towards the other is the source of all writing. The particularity of the literature I tried to comment is the simultaneous lucidity about the illusionary nature of sign and the passion towards it. In reading this literature it is possible to attain both: a consistent experience of reality in an artistic moment *as well as* the consciousness about the illusionary condition of representation itself. Especially the cultural context of Latin American literature suggests very much a practice of the sign which is the *simulation* (in the sense of Baudrillard) of discourses on history, origin and subject coming from Western hemisphere and leaped over to the new world. The clash with other cultures, far from having been resolved in form of a homogenous cultural representation, provokes in literature the "feeling of other presence" and reveals the fictional and discursive nature of reality. Nevertheless, the consciousness of the simulation does not weaken the experience of a presence of the other.

This attitude of reading appears as evidence in the kind of Mexican literature I called to your attention. Nevertheless, this reading is not submitted to the history of literature, but it is an attitude, perhaps an ethical mood, which is independent of historical or national classifications.

Perhaps this "evidence" of such a reading can be seen more generally as the recovering of the "Ptolemaic" past into the "Copernican" epoch of illuminate postmodernism, as the German philosopher Sloterdijk predicts, meaning by that the return to the acceptance of the evidence in real experiences, despite of the consciousness about the illusionary status of reality: Only an epoch where criticism takes into account the evidence of artists experience of "rising sun" despite the knowledge that it is an illusion, can now follow (Sloterdijk, 1987: 68-69). I would like to relate this prediction of Sloterdijk to the experience of a "literature of silence" which suggests to sometimes interrupt the polyphonic noise of criticism in order to practice the humility learned in the experience of the other.

Nevertheless, there are more specific conclusions to draw:
The "reticence" of the writing attitude I called "silence" in the sense of Blanchot, is certainly the reason why in some cases, pieces of (literary) art have been first discriminated by the canon of literary history, then neglected by criticism. The reason for this disregard could be the fact that this literature is uncomfortable to a criticism whose principles, more generally, are based on a economic logic, be it of magnitude ("meaning" as "sense plurality") or of its negation or deconstruction. Barthes had himself accepted the premise of language as an institutional discourse and writing as its transgression (1953: 54-57). Literature of silence was seen as the last price of transgression, which is resignation and mutism. Blanchot's proposal is thereby

different from the early Barthes of 1953: In the space between desire and deception Blanchot also looks for the future universe of writing (Title: *"Le livre á venir"*).

What is the role of semiotics, especially semiotic literary criticism, in face of this writing? In the most open practice of, for instance, "plurality of society" (MacCannell 1982) or of intermediary state between methods (Umberto Eco 1987) the theory of semiotics opens itself to other approaches, including to a deconstructive aim (MacCannell 1982). Nevertheless, I wonder whether semiotic practice in literary criticism takes advantage of the literary experience I attempted to present to you before, learning from poetic attitude a practice of reticence--which could be able to question its own role--though desiring the encounter with the image of the text. This could surmount the attitude of "superman criticism", as Hayden White has judged semiotic criticism for having a universal pretention (1978: 277)[14].

Semiotic literary criticism has to question its own practices. The attempt of, for instance, Dominick La Capra to "rethink" (1983) theory of history can be taken as an example. Analogously, literary criticism should face itself with other texts which have been apart and, founded on the consciousness to be a discrete mode of discourse, should attempt also to write another discourse of criticism, creating "other objects" of literary history[15]. This also means that past literary works could be considered not as representation of past cultures, but as the "sign"[16] of a force which can (could) not be represented on the scene of cultural history. In relating the "suffered" experience of otherness to its own practice, *literary critics* could maybe draw more expressively social and ethical consequences. Independently of the knowledge about the reality or its illusionary representation, the "disfiguration of the authoritative status of analytical discourse"[17] could eventually reveal a subject of critics being in the practice of loving the other.

This was my way to recover the crucial moments of past utopias into a presence of simulations.

I beg your pardon for my attempt to face myself with *the other* of my own discourse. Maybe I was inspired by a siren song coming from the other side of the ocean.

NOTES

[1] Blanchots insists on the fact that this discrepancy can never be overcome, and that the work of art is merely a "strange movement", which is akin to "the restless and infinite search for the source" (*"le . . . poème est la profondeur ouverte sur l'experience qui le rend possible, l'étrange mouvement qui va de l'oeuvre vers l'origine de l'oeuvre, l'oeuvre elle-même devenue la recherche inquiète et infinie de sa source"* [p. 269]).

[2] That this "image" belongs to the realm of the "Other" becomes evident when Blanchot makes reference to the myth of Orpheus. The image (woman and death) inspiring the poet is the "Otherness" par excellence: Euridix exists as long as she is not visible to or seen by the poet. Any attempt of looking at her leads to her destruction. Writing is then the desire of this encounter and the passion which enables one to "stay on the side of the image" though knowing the impossible destiny of this sojourn, which, nevertheless, is the work of art itself: *". . . comme un homme qui a rencontré une image, se sent lié à elle par une étrange passion, n'a plus d'autre existence que de séjourner auprès d'elle, séjour qui est son oeuvre"* (p. 127).

[3] Blanchot seems to me to allude to a reversal of the Cartesian logics by Artaud's practice of suffering suggesting with Artaud that "suffering could be the only mode of thinking" (*"Est-ce que souffrir serait, finalement, penser?"* [p. 58]).

[4] Virgina Woolf is quoted in the French presentation of Monique Nathan (*Virginia Woolf par elle-même* [p. 139]).

[5] Blanchot renounces any attempt to define experience, although experience is the main concern in this book. Even in the chapter entitled *"Littérature, oeuvre, expérience"* (p. 270) he only describes a state of anxious search and underscores the movement towards the desire which is the source of writing (p. 271). The renouncing the attempt at a philosophical discourse on "experience" and the trial to move along the line of the desire as suggested by the texts he reviews, is Blanchot's way to deny any other objective than the desire itself. Blanchot's understanding of experience is neither existentialistic/ontic nor phenomenological since no consciousness (of the self or of the other) is the objective of this experience. In order to escape any position of philosophy, he moves along the line of (lightful) metaphors of the void. Blanchot's attempt becomes eventually more evident when he suggests that no eternal truth is associated to this experience, since it is only a demand of coping with the (philosophical) order of essences (*"Ce ne sont pas les vérités éternelles, les types y les caractères . . . une exigence qui s'oppose a l'ordre des essences"* [pp. 271-272]).

[6] This "source of desire" takes different images. For Henry James and Nathalie Sarraute it is, for instance, dialogue. In *The Turn of the Screw* the obsession of a dialogue which is able to establish the community, is at the same time a passion for the inconceivable, i.e., for a transcendental principle (p. 211), whereas for Sarraute the suffered search for a dialogue is a "deep experience" without any ontological deepness, dialogue in her novels being a simple result of casual encounters, e.g. on the square (p. 214).

[7] I am mindful of the fact that I'm simplifying the very sensitive way of Blanchot to be careful in classifying or judging writers. He, for instance, comments extensively Musil's passion for saying the indifference (in *Der Mann ohne Eigenschaften*); it is a passion which, again, is suffered because of the impossibility of its realization since Musil's search for expressing the absence of properties is not a simple negation of the hero, but the attempt to express the void of essentiality without representing it (p. 206). Nevertheless, Musil is eventually incoherent and time and again falls into the trap to fill the void with philosophical verbosity (p. 205). Musil, like others, takes a conflicting position between these two types of attitude towards writing.

[8] With Mallarmé's *Un coup de dés* Blanchot underscores that in poetry doubt and certainty about things coexist, meaning thereby that real things are evoked as present but, at the same time, they are as distant and uncertain as possible. Particularly by recognizing this impossibility of affirming reality one comes closer to the process of writing itself (*"Ce qui pourrait se traduire en disant [inexactement]: Le doute appartient à la certitude poètique, de même que l'impossibilité d'affirmer l'oeuvre nous rapproche de son affirmation propre"* [p. 325]).

[9] See *"Diario del 11 de Mayo y 13 de Mayo"*, in: *"El zorro de arriba y el zorro de abajo"* (1971).

[10] The sensibility of Arguedas and his congeniality with these writers make Arguedas' argument interesting to me despite his own ideological limitation of accepting the indigenistic argument.

[11] In commenting Borges (p. 130) Blanchot alludes to something close to the Baudrillardian "simulation". I am referring to Baudrilliard, for instance, in 1981.

[12] Traditional Latin American studies call this an effect of "magic realism". See, for instance, the more recent study of A. Flores (1985) and a criticism of this concept by Chiampi (1983).

[13] I am thinking, among others, of the short story of Juan Rulfo, "Luvina", which I have discussed in "Metaphor and Myth in Contemporary Theory: Evidence from the Contemporary Novel" (1987) making reference to the role of myth in Latin-American literature.

[14] In this respect I venture to recall Blanchot's definition of "dictatorial" writers in the sense of *dictare*, a writing which is based on a stable consciousness of ones own beliefs (*"On dirait qu'ils [ces écrivains] se ramaissent sur eux-même, ou sur quelque croyance, sur les conscience ferme, mais bientôt fermée et bornée"* [p. 301]). It seems to me that discours of criticism is basically subjected to this risk.

[15] See, for instance, Didier Coste's stating the necessity of writing "a negative literary history" having a similar objective (1988:40).

[16] I am attempting to follow the line of Lyotard's toughts in reading Kant's criticism on history (1986); a criticism which is related to the Kantian idea of "sublime".

[17] This could be the consequence of La Capra's proposal of "transference", as Peter de Bolla points out La Capra's suggestion of "folding back within any historical analysis the tropes and figures, conceptions and preconceptions..." (1986:57). From this point of view, La Capra's proposal seems to me to be more complex than White's approach of history by way of literary analyses (1980), reviewed by De Bolla in the same article). Looking for a "transferential" relation between history and literature, La Capra attempts to apply the concept of dialogue (in the sense of Bakhtinian carnival), also taking serious the Derridian consideration that "the reality" of the text consists in a transcendental quest which controls the subject of critics when it risks to remain imprisoned in the ontology of the text. La Capra also points out the social and ethical responsibility of criticism, missing this aspect in Derrida's writings (1983:26).

REFERENCES

ARGUEDAS, José María.
   1971. *El zorro de arriba y el zorro de abajo* (Buenos Aires: Editorial Losada).
BARTHES, Roland.
   1953. *Le degré zero de l'écriture* (Paris: Éditions du Seuil, 1972).
BAUDRILLARD, Jean.
   1981. *Simulacres et simulation* (Paris: Galilée).
BLANCHOT, Maurice.
   1959. *Le livre à venir* (Paris: Gallimard)

BORSÒ, Vittoria.
    1987. "Metaphor and Myth in contemporary theory: Evidence from the contemporary novel", in *Semiotics 1986*, ed. John Deely and Jonathan Evans (Lanham MD: University Press of America), 328-339.
CHIAMPI, Irlemar.
    1983. *El realismo maravilloso* (Caracas: Monte Avila Eds.).
COSTE, Didier.
    1988. "Pour une histoire littéraire négative" in *L'internationalité littéraire*, ed. Antony Pym, Actes Noesis II (El Prat de Llobregat/Barcelone), 30-41.
DE BOLLA, Peter.
    1986. "Disfiguring history". *Diacritics*, Winter 1986, 49-60.
ECO, Umberto.
    1987. *Streit der Interpretationen* (Konstanz: Universitätspresse)
FLORES, Angel.
    1985. *El realismo mágico en el cuento hispanoamericano* (Puebla: Premia).
LA CAPRA, Dominick.
    1983. *Rethinking Intellectual History* (Cornell University Press).
LYOTARD, Jean-François.
    1986. *L'enthousiasme. La critiue kantienne de l'histoire* (Paris: Galilée).
MACCANNELL, Dean, and Juliet FLOWER-MACCANNELL.
    1982. *Time of the Sign* (Bloomington: Indiana UP).
MERLEAU-PONTY, Maurice.
    1973. "Dialogue and the Perception of the Other". English Translation by John O'Neill: *The Prose of the World* (Evanston, Illinois: Northwestern University Press).
REVUELTAS, José.
    1943. *El luto humano* (México: Ediciones Era, 1980).
SLOTERDIJK, Peter.
    1987. *Kopernikanische Mobilmachung und ptolemäische Abrüstung. Ästhetischer Versuch* (Frankfurt: Suhrkamp).
WHITE, Hayden.
    1978. *Tropics of Discourse* (Baltimore/London: Johns Hopkins UP, 1985)
    1980. "The Value of Narrativity in Representation of Reality", *Critical Inquiry*, 7, 4.

DIALOGUE AND MONOLOGUE

David K. Danow
University of South Carolina

Nearly half a century ago, in an article bearing the same title as the present paper, Jan Mukařovský, the Prague School literary theorist and aesthetician, declares that "The problem of the relationship between monologue and dialogue is one of the urgent questions of contemporary poetics. . ." (1940: 81) Although "contemporary poetics" has since made great strides (at times in a variety of mutually opposed directions), that problem remains only partly resolved today--and that due largely to the writings of M.M. Bakhtin. The distinctions Bakhtin makes between the two concepts, however, are derived at times from the sphere of his projected discipline of "translinguistics", at others from metaphysical or ethical concerns. In both cases, however, questions of dialogic relations remain paramount. At the core of Bakhtin's entire philosophical thought, in fact, is the problem of "dialogism", with its attendant complexities and difficulties. Yet the term appears both ill-defined and overburdened, and, as his biographer remarks: "Bakhtin himself must bear part of the responsibility for the widespread confusion that characterizes appropriations of 'dialogism'" (Holquist in Bakhtin 1979: xiii). That confusion is not likely to be soon resolved, but a clear delineation of the problem is needed for its eventual resolution.

To respond (however belatedly) to Mukařovský's call of nearly half a century ago to meaningfully distinguish between monologue and dialogue would serve well as a first step. However, when Bakhtin's thinking is necessarily taken into account, the problem immediately becomes more complex than Mukařovský appears to have envisioned it, since it must then be extended beyond the realm of poetics, to which the Czech thinker would have seen it applied. It also extends, however, beyond Bakhtin's own translinguistics. Encompassing problems of poetics and especially the complexities of dialogical relations in literary texts, that projected new discipline is conceived to incorporate more broadly the related concerns of quotidian discourse as well. Moreover, ideological considerations that are central to Bakhtin's metaphysics, both further complicate and *enhance* the matter of distinguishing between monologue and dialogue. That question, it seems, is thereby superceded by the need to distinguish between monologism and dialogism, as more broadly encompassing rubrics that extend beyond the sphere of discourse analysis (in literature and life) to that of ideology, as it pertains to these two modes of discourse. Hence the problem as Mukařovský originally posed it becomes more complex even as it remains essentially unresolved. The intention here will be to approach the question on the two levels just discussed: first, regarding its ramifications from what may be viewed as its translinguistic standpoint; and, second, from a certain metaphysical viewpoint.

In his article, "Dialogue and Monologue", Mukařovský defines monologue as "an utterance with a single active participant regardless of the presence or absence of other passive participants" (1940: 81). All that is needed for monologue to take place, in other words, is a single speaker who may be the only one present to hear his own words. (As Bakhtin abbreviates it in his later, unfinished writings: "Monologue as speech that is addressed to no one and does not presuppose a response" 1979: 117). Further, in conformity with Prague School thinking (as articulated in its 1929 "Theses"), Mukařovský posits the alternation of speech between two speakers as fundamental to dialogue. Accordingly, the dialogic mode requires that the speakers undertake roles that are alternately active and passive. This feature, for Mukařovský, represents the principal opposition at play in the distinction between monologue and dialogue. Other Prague School thinkers make a further distinction between "monologue and dialogue language" (Veltruský 1984: 600), although this terminological distinction appears both fruitless and unproductive (as though in either case a certain specific lexicon were employed). Nevertheless such viewpoint serves to heighten the sense of a distinction between monologue and dialogue--but without significantly inspiring a clear sense of the principal differences between them.

In elaborating Mukařovský's 1940 study, a contemporary Prague School apologist observes that some of the characteristic features of "dialogue language" include "the first and second grammatical persons constantly changing places . . . shifts and reversals of meaning [and] the integration of whatever is said in two or more alternating and interpenetrating semantic contexts". But, as the crucial concern, it is unequivocally stated (again in conformity with Mukařovský in particular and with Prague School thinking in general) that "to be read as dialogue, a literary text or segment of a text must be divided into alternating speeches attributed to different speakers". Curiously, the same researcher takes Bakhtin to task when he observes that, in his book on Dostoevsky, Bakhtin (1963) "completely overlooked the crucial importance of the division into speeches when he qualified Dostoevsky's 'polyphonic' novel as a true dialogue" (Veltruský 1984: 599). While that particular censure appears quite undistinguished, Bakhtin in fact defines dialogue in just such fashion--and also in clear conformity with the basic definition proposed by the Prague School--when he declares (1979: 71,72):

> The boundaries of each concrete utterance as a unit of speech communication are determined by a *change of speaking subjects*, that is, a change of speakers. . . . One observes this change of speaking subjects most simply and clearly in actual dialogue where the utterances of the interlocutors or partners in dialogue . . . alternate.

Moreover, in the unfinished essay, "Problem of the Text", he acknowledges in telegraphic manner the same basic suppositions but hints, significantly, at their entirely elementary character (ibid.: 117):

> The narrow understanding of dialogue as one of the compositional forms of speech (dialogic and monologic speech). One can say that each rejoinder in and of itself is monologic (the absolutely minimal monologue) and each monologue is a rejoinder from a larger dialogue.

Dialogue is thus conceived on a fundamental level as being composed of interlarded monologic speech elements. But to suggest that "the division into speeches delivered by alternating interlocutors [is] the ultimate criterion of what is a dialogue and what is not" (Veltrusky 1984: 599), goes but a short distance in providing an understanding of what intricacies are at work in eliciting and maintaining dialogical interaction.

Thus, while crediting that fundamental description of dialogue as alternating speech, Bakhtin argues further, as a way of elucidating those intricacies, that in dialogue neither speaker is ever passive, even when silent. Rather, each is consistently engaged at all times in an effort to convince, rebut, or refute the other, while constantly modifying his position with respect to what has so far been articulated and in anticipation of what might yet be said. Bakhtin's emphasis, in contrast to the Prague School thinker, is therefore jointly focused upon both the speaker *and* the utterance, acknowledging thereby the preeminent role played by the latter in eliciting (further) dialogue. Such emphasis upon not only the role of the speakers but upon that of their respective word serves to focus more sharply upon the complexity of dialogic interaction. For it goes beyond the simplistic recognition of heralding alternating speech as the fundamental dialogical principle, by acknowledging the internal dynamics at play, at each respective pivotal moment, when one speaker's utterance serves to evoke a new considered dialogic response from the other.

Taken a paradoxical step further, for Bakhtin, not only is dialogue carried on between two speakers, whose speech is characterized by responsive alternation. There is also the potential for dialogue between what C.S. Peirce calls "different phases of the ego" (1893: 4.6), specifying, in Bakhtinian terms, the potential dialogical relationship of the speaker to his own utterances. Thus when Peirce notes that "All thinking is dialogic in form" (1909: 6.338), Bakhtin would surely agree. But this raises the question of whether--beyond the previously noted "narrow understanding" of each rejoinder in dialogue being "in and of itself monologic"--there exists any such thing as monologue? Or is it, rather, always the case of a single being--at the least-- engaging in dialogue with himself (as a constantly changing other)? Such would appear to be a reasonable conclusion from the perspective of Peirce and, oddly, for Bakhtin as well.

In at least partial response to what remains essentially an unresolved ambiguity, Bakhtin declares the importance of interlarded monologic speech as framed structures, constituting individual texts of varying scope and dimension. The opening and closing statements of an utterance represent the boundaries of speech that not only initiate and close the argument but also serve as points of tangency, as it were, between the utterances of the one speaker and the other. Within the monologic structures constituting dialogue, opening and closing statements are thus especially significant. "For they are, so to speak, sentences of the 'front line' that stand right at the boundary of the change of speech subjects" (1979: 89,fn.i). Therefore the question of what strategies go into the "framing" of an utterance--that is, how the utterance is initiated and concluded, is deemed crucial to an understanding of dialogic speech.

This same concern, it might be added, is particularly appropriate when attempting to distinguish between the various modes of reported speech, especially when the category of quasi-direct speech comes into play (defined as "discourse that is formally authorial, but that belongs in its 'emotional structure' to a represented character, whose inner speech is transmitted and regulated by the author" 1979: 130, fn.15). A heightened awareness of the making and breaking of frames applies as well to the problem of isolating and distinguishing between various narrative voices and between shorter narratives, or subtexts, incorporated within the greater narrative. Thus Jonathan Culler suggests that "the analyst must determine what shall count as the elementary units of narrative and investigate the ways in which they combine" (1975: 205). Such proposal is tantamount to arguing for a poetics of framing--of establishing the borders of a given text's subtexts or elementary units. As Bakhtin puts it, "In order to understand, it is first of all necessary to establish the principal and clear-cut boundaries of the utterance" (1979: 112).

Within the framework of Bakhtin's translinguistics, as the case in point, this basic unit is the utterance, conceived as the "*real unit* of speech communication" (in contrast to the sentence, which is viewed rather as a unit of language) (ibid.: 73,71). In broader terms, Bakhtin also conceives of "The text as *utterance*", or "work utterances", whose "true essence", like the utterance per se, "always develops *on the boundary between two consciousnesses, two subjects*" (ibid.: 104,76,106). In sum, to analyze the framing of the text and its constituent narrative components is crucial to the critical enterprise, but also serves as analogue to the like endeavor of discerning the borders of an utterance that may constitute a given monologue or dialogue.

On another plane, of *ethical* concern, Bakhtin elaborates broadly, within the entire range of his writings, a metaphysical component inherent in the distinction between monologue and dialogue. Whereas the Prague School distinguishes (in its 1929 "Theses") between "alternately interrupted (dialogic) speech and unilaterally uninterrupted (monologic) speech" (1929: 12), neither, it would seem, is granted a privileged ideological position. In Bakhtin's system of thought, wherein he calls for "surmounting monologism", such is not the case. Instead, the value attached to monologism is potentially negative rather than neutral and is diametrically opposed, in principle, to dialogue. For Bakhtin, the monologic word "is indissolubly fused with its authority--with political power, an institution, a person--and it stands and falls together with that authority . . . . If completely deprived of its authority it becomes simply an object, a *relic*, a *thing*" (1975: 343-344). This in contrast, then, to the "living" dialogic word, which is vitalized and constantly revivified by its varied contextual usage and by the rich abundance of meanings that as a result accrue to it.

In ethical terms, as Bakhtin declares, "What monologism is, in the highest sense, [is] a denial of the equal rights of consciousnesses vis-a-vis truth. . ." (1963: 285) By denying those "rights" monologism may appear in its most extreme (political) form as violence--as the triumph of might rather than the word. In this sense, the potentially bountiful relationship between the self and other--as Bakhtin's most vital meaning producing model--necessarily breaks down, since the word as an otherwise dynamic ideological source is reduced to the level of an unproductive stasis. That the authoritative word itself, as inert object, will inevitably be deprived of its authority may be presumed as certain as the fact that the political, economic, and social fortunes to which it is bound are sure to change. However, the reduction of the potentially dialogic utterance to its monologic counterpart affects negatively the relationship of the self and other as well. For in providing the occasion for such reduction, the one claiming an unassailable position in effect substitutes for the truth-seeking dialogic word a rigidified verbal construct that masks and obfuscates, rather than communicates.

Representing the distinct counterpoint to this possibility in Bakhtin's humanistic philosophy is the ideologically and radically opposed principle of dialogism, which may be understood to embrace a number of interrelated facets of human discourse. Within its expansive rubric it is designed to account for the participants in dialogue, their inevitable role as ideologues promoting one point of view or another, their similarly inevitable mutual influence upon one another implicit in the degree of persuasiveness brought to their respective arguments, their necessarily differing perceptions of the object of discourse, and the implicit task of attempting to at least partially reconcile those perceptions. Ultimately, by divorcing the entire concept from the realm of static linguistic generalization, the term is intended to acknowledge the potential for dialogue inherent in discourse. And in so doing, it is meant to bring into clear focus what Bakhtin conceives to be the "genuine life of the word"--when it actively engages the utterance of another and is itself engaged by that utterance.

In figurative terms, dialogism refers as well to the mutual influence of "work utterances" ("The text as utterance"), whereby a given work is acknowledged to be in "dialogue" with other works and with an entire tradition, from which concept the notion of intertextuality is derived. However, in this related context, the term "dialogue" must necessarily be consistently placed in quotes to designate its figurative aspect. Of related concern, the challenge here amounts to distinguishing between dialogue, as the concrete exchange of verbal utterances between two or more interlocutors, as opposed to its figurative employment regarding problems of intertextual relations. In this respect, the term--with its implications for literary theory and cultural semiotics--is clearly burdened. And yet, it is just this incursion into as yet only partially explored areas and potential disciplines that affords the concept additional promise, allowing Julia Kristeva to remark with a certain enthusiasm typical of her adopted intellectual milieu that "dialogism may well become the basis of our time's intellectual structure" (1967: 89).

In summing up, the Prague School definitions of monologue and dialogue may have appeared inadequate, especially in light of the problems that Bakhtin raises. However, in attempting to get beyond its seemingly simplistic approach to the problem of definition, and by instituting instead the related concepts of monologism and dialogism, we find that the former term (with its moral and ethical implications) is relatively manageable conceptually, even though it is, in effect, a dead-end concept that Bakhtin would surely say leads us nowhere, except to the shutting down of dialogue, a negative potential to be deplored.

On the other hand, our appropriations of dialogism, while seeming to afford grand possibilities, presents a problem that lies in the term's ranging beyond concrete understandings of dialogue *between individuals*--that is, the understanding of the Prague School--to figurative formulations that allow us to commonly equate dialogism with intertextuality. So Jurij Lotman, for instance, and virtually everyone else today, speaks of texts as engaging in dialogues and polylogues. And yet, if we could resurrect for a moment one of the Prague School thinkers, he might articulate in a perhaps strained whisper that only individuals engage in dialogue, not texts.

To extend this seemingly obvious point one step further, the same problem applies to cultural institutions. Mukařovský already speaks of the interrelations among such cultural institutions as literature, law, religion and economics--but he does not slip into the pitfall of regarding cultural operations, or the functioning of culture, as being encompassed under the rubric of the grand workings of dialogism. Are we, then, doing this in his stead? Or, in other words, once we depart from concrete understandings of dialogue and proceed into the murkier, figurative realm of dialogism, do we not burden the concept too greatly, so as to come up with less, when we thought we had more?

REFERENCES

Bakhtin, M.M.
    1963.   *Problemy poetiki Dostoevskogo* (Moscow). Page references are to the English edition, *Problems of Dostoevsky's Poetics* (= *Theory and History of Literature* Vol. 8), ed. and trans. by Caryl Emerson (Minneapolis: University of Minnesota Press, 1984).

1975. *Voprosy literatury i estetiki* (Moscow). Page references are to the English trans. by Caryl Emerson and Michael Holquist, *The Dialogic Imagination: Four Essays by M.M. Bakhtin*, ed. Michael Holquist (Austin: University of Texas Press, 1981).
1979. *Estetika slovesnogo tvorchestva* (Moscow). Page references are to the English trans. by Vern W. McGee, *Speech Genres and Other Late Essays*, ed. by Caryl Emerson and Michael Holquist (Austin: University of Texas Press, 1986).

Culler, Jonathan.
1975. *Structuralist Poetics: Structuralism, Linguistics, and the Study of Literature* (Ithaca: Cornell University Press).

Kristeva, Julia.
1967. "Bakhtine, le mot, le dialogue et le roman", *Critique* 239, 438-465. Page references are to the English trans. by Thomas Gora, Alice Jardine, and Leon S. Roudiez in *Desire in Language: A Semiotic Approach to Literature and Art*, ed. Leon S. Roudiez (New York: Columbia University Press, 1980), pp.64-91.

Mukařovský, Jan.
1940. "Dialog a monolog", *Listy filogiske* 68 (Prague). Page references are to the English edition in *The Word and Verbal Art; Selected Essays by Jan Mukařovský*, ed. and trans. by John Burbank and Peter Steiner (New Haven and London: Yale University Press, 1977), pp. 81-112.

Peirce, Charles Sanders.
1893. "Logic and Mathematics", in *The Collected Papers of Charles Sanders Peirce*, Vol. IV, ed. Charles Hartshorne and Paul Weiss (Cambridge: Harvard University Press, 1933).
1909. "Ontology and Cosmology", in *The Collected Papers of Charles Sanders Peirce*, Vol. VI, ed. Charles Hartshorne and Paul Weiss (Cambridge: Harvard University Press, 1935).

Prague School Writings.
1929. "Theses", *Travaux du Cercle linguistique de Prague* 1 (Prague). Page references are to the English translation in *The Prague School; Selected Writings, 1929-1946*, ed. Peter Steiner (Austin: University of Texas Press, 1982).

Veltruský, Jiří.
1984. "Semiotic Notes on Dialogue in Literature", in *Language and Literary Theory* (= Papers in Slavic Philology No 5), ed. Benjamin A. Stolz, I.R. Titunik, and Lubomír Doležel (Ann Arbor: University of Michigan), 595-607.

POETICS OF ILLUSION: GOGOL'S FANTASTIC STORIES

Erika Freiberger
Glassboro State College

The Russian writer Nikolai Gogol (1809-1852) is an acknowledged master of the fantastic and the grotesque. In his Ukrainian and St. Petersburg stories[1] which date from the first half of the 1830's, witches, wizards, devils, ghosts, pigs, and finally, run-away-noses play havoc with his characters' perception of reality and illusion. Gogol's urge to exaggerate beauty as well as terror and banality serves as a poetic device of the fantastic and grotesque, as does his technique of distortion, disruption and evasion which is basic to his poetics of illusion. This paper will examine how Gogol's Romantic imagination blurs the boundaries between reality and illusion through various semiotic devices: difference and displacement; metaphor and metonymy as verbal means of expressing differences and displacement; exaggeration and dream as expressions of displacement; the use of mirror as a threshold phenomenon;[2] contradiction as a variant of difference or displacement; variants of illusion; and intertextual discourse. Gogol's poetics of illusion is expressed in his verbal art and is closely intertwined with psychological and philosophical undercurrents.

Gogol was born into a world of Romanticism which was distorting reality by fantasy. However, this world was changing psychologically, reflecting the transformation of society which was entering a new age of awakening capitalism. Gogol exposed the banality, vulgarity, and mediocrity of Russian life. He was by nature a comic genius. Even so, his contemporaries found it difficult to understand or trust him since his life and work were so full of contradictions and deceit. Gogol treated the immensely trivial with great earnestness and presented reality as absurdity.

Critics (Fanger 1979: 5, Karlinsky 1976: 280, Erlich 1969: 1-2) have noted the enigmatic quality of Gogol's life and work and have related Gogol's personal crisis to a cultural crisis in Russia. We can find an expression of this cultural crisis in the story, "The Portrait" (1835a), with its depiction of the crisis of an artist which is brought about by the new market in the art world. The artist's new vision is deceptive. He wants to become a famous painter overnight. Gold becomes his passion. He becomes very self-conscious, buys a lorgnette to ogle people and is continually looking at himself in the mirror. The theme of self is central here. When the artist sees the work of a real artist, he tries to regain his talent, but cannot, and goes mad. Gogol's narrator tries to explain what is at the root of the artist's crisis: art lovers no longer exist. Art is now bought up by bankers for investment and the narrator likens art auctions to funeral processions. In his novel *Dead Souls*, the theme of cultural crisis finds its ultimate expression: corrupt people enrich themselves by selling the ownership papers of dead serfs who had not yet been stricken off the census roll. The general cultural crisis became a personal crisis for Gogol and culminated with Gogol's burning of Part 2 of the novel which he was no longer able to continue writing. The destruction of his work, followed by his own self-destruction, is an ultimate act of displacement and evasion.

Fanger (1979: 16) points to *evasion* as a prominent feature in Gogol's life and work. He also mentions Gogol's heightened awareness of the relation between author and reader. He notes that the public was not prepared for the new poetics that Gogol was shaping. The reader gets only a "semblance" of things. The world depicted in Gogol's Ukrainian stories had disappeared, and Gogol was acknowledging this absence. Fanger (1979: 96) views these stories as "essays in evaluation". He notes the theme of misleading appearance in "Nevsky Prospect" (1835a) and the themes of identity, vanity, sensitivity, deception, and illusion in "Diary of a Madman" (1835a). In the Petersburg stories, Petersburg is depicted as the capital of illusion, a "dream symbol of banal glory". In the play, *The Inspector General*, the characters pay homage to this image of Petersburg. Fanger points to *displacement* and the blurring of ontological boundaries in "The Overcoat" (1835-1836) where a coat becomes the displaced object and causes its owner's displacement. Fanger (1979: 256) connects Gogol's technique of exhibition and simultaneous concealment with the philosophical concept of 'The Other', especially in Sartre's sense, as the hidden death of one's possibilities. Fanger views *evasion* as movement to the unknown, as deferral of judgment. Evasion can also function as narrative strategy. Most importantly, Fanger notes the principles of *ne to* which he (1979: 214) explains as a "constant denial of what appears in the represented reality and in the representation itself. . . . Things are not what or where or as they should be: parts usurp the function of the whole. . . ."

Nabokov (1944: 11) called Gogol a "ghoul" or "ventriloquist" who "was not quite real either" and labelled Gogol's muse and his whole world as "absurd". Nabokov pointed to Gogol's "shifting" as the basis of Gogol's art and described Gogol's presentation of reality as a mask. In Gogol's world there is neither truth nor untruth. The correlations between objects and signs alter and this gives rise to the grotesque.

What was this new poetics of illusion that was referred to by these various critics and writers? First of all, we must bear in mind that the rhetoric of illusion is made of words and Gogol's narrators constantly remind us of it. In the Preface to "The Fair at Sorochinsky", (Gogol 1831: 11-16) the beekeeper-narrator wonders where the other narrator picked up all these words. He expresses some doubts about his own capacity to tell stories and mentions "how much stuff gets into print nowadays that one has more wrapping paper than one can use". Secondly, illusion is created through warped perception, deception, exaggeration, transformation, displacement, contradiction, dream, and mirror.[2] Illusion defies all logic and operates with blurred vision and time frame. The fantastic is a mode of illusion and includes the variants of the fearsome and ludicrous. Fear and horror are semiotic reactions to a world full of terrifying signs. Gogol's narrators are good semioticians who describe these signs which Gogol's characters as well as his readers, must interpret.

In *Semiotics of Poetry*, Riffaterre (1978: 2) describes *displacement* as a principle that creates meaning as a sign shifts from one meaning to another. Semantic indirection occurs which "threatens the literary representation of reality, or mimesis". Many examples of displacement can be found in Gogol's stories. In the story "Ivan Fyodorovich Shponka and His Aunt" (Gogol 1832), we have a humorous example: timidity gets new meanings and is displaced by dishonesty and cowardliness. When Ivan was a boy, his teacher thought he was a pupil who was anxious to learn and was never involved in the mischief of the other boys. We note here a degree of timidity which is still unmarked, since the boy wanted to please. Later on, however, when Ivan is made a monitor in the Latin class, he caves in to a boy's bribe of a pancake and is caught by the teacher. The narrator remarks that "the timidity which had always been characteristic of him was more marked from then on". And that was the reason why he did not join the Civil Service, "having learned by experience that one is not always successful in covering up one's misdeeds" (Gogol 1832: 238). More fantastic examples of displacement, aided by exaggeration, occur in Ivan's dream. Ivan is scared to death of marriage, or the thought of having a wife. He dreams that he is married. The undesired wife is displaced by geese who seem to multiply. When he pulls out a handkerchief, he finds a wife in his pocket. The cotton in his ears turns out to be a wife as well, and so on. A wife is pulling him up to the belfry and Ivan is mistaken for a bell. Then he dreams that his wife is a kind of woolen fabric on sale in a shop where the shopkeeper cuts a wife off the bolt. The tailor finds it to be poor quality and out of fashion. When Ivan wakes up, he consults his dreambook but finds nothing in it that resembles his "incoherent" dream.

Riffaterre points out that this transfer of a sign from one level of discourse to another is the domain of semiotics. Semiosis is related to the interpretation of signs from the mimesis level unto the higher level of significance. The process of semiosis takes place in the reader's mind and "results from a second reading". This involves linguistic and literary competence. The second stage is a "retroactive reading" or "hermeneutic reading". Riffaterre notes that the text functions "something like a neurosis". This statement is especially applicable to Gogol's texts. Another splendid example of neurotic displacement can be found in the story "The Nose" (1836) in which a nose is displaced and takes on a life of its own. The missing nose parades on Nevsky Prospekt (1835a) in Petersburg as a high ranking Civil servant and reveals himself as a semiotician in Kazan Cathedral. When Kovalyov, the owner of the nose, tells this high ranking Civil servant that the latter is his nose, the nose/high ranking Civil servant tells him that he is mistaken, that he is himself, and that furthermore, he could see from the buttons of his uniform that Kovalyov was serving in a different department. Although the run-away-nose embodies the highest social aspirations of its owner, the owner discovers to his dismay that he cannot exist without a nose. In the end, he wakes up one morning with the nose back on his face.

Riffaterre (1978: 82) also remarks about intertextual punning ("...the dual sign works like a pun") which is helpful to our understanding of Gogol's poetics. In "The Nose" (1836), for example, the police clerk makes a pun on the word 'nose'. When Kovalyov reports his missing nose, the police calls it 'Mr. Nosov', a strange name for a person and a strange name for a nose.

Intertextuality comes to the fore, especially where there are two conflicting codes. Riffaterre discusses humor as a variety of intertextuality. The implicit intertextuality changes as times and culture change. In "The Nose", an ad for the missing nose is called into question by the agency for the ad contains a clash with cultural sobriety. Furthermore, Riffaterre (1978: 150) views nonsense as intertextual scrambling ("the scrambled text is an icon of intention..."). At the very end of "The Nose", the narrator brings a discourse on "the really strange fact of the supernatural displacement of the nose and its appearance in various parts of the town in the guise of a State Councillor" and "how did Kovalyov fail to realize that he could not advertise about his nose in a newspaper?" It was not that the rates were too high, the narrator notes but that it was "improper, awkward, not nice!" "But what is even stranger and more incomprehensible than anything is that authors should choose such subjects" (Gogol 1836: 231-232), the narrator concludes.

Eco's (1984: 21) discussion of a text as a system of signs which functions as a sign, is also most useful in our discussion of Gogol's poetics of illusion. He views the linguistic sign not just as a system of signification, but, rather, as a "detectable unit in the process of communication". Eco raises the questions whether signs indicate states of the world. He discusses sign as *difference*. He refers to the matrix of something being present and something being absent. Fanger also noted *difference* as the keystone to Gogol's poetics.

To give an example once more from "Ivan Fyodorovich Shponka and His Aunt", the narrator explains the difference between an infantry regiment, which Ivan joins, and a cavalry regiment, which obviously, would have been more prestigious. The difference is obscured by the narrator's remark that "most of the officers drank neat spirit and were quite as good at dragging about Jews by their curls as the hussars; some of them even danced the mazurka. . . ." From this example we can see that it tells, in fact, much about the state of the world in Gogol's Russia. Ivan, however, was a "mild and gentle soul" who kept still drinking only ordinary vodka, did not mistreat Jews, did not dance the mazurka or play cards, and thus "was naturally bound to be always left alone".

Difference is expressed also in the description of Ivan's homeward journey by noting the absence of something: "Nothing of great importance occurred on the journey". The state of Ivan's interior world as well as his standing in the exterior world are described thus: on Saturdays, when the Jewish driver took off, Ivan used to inspect his own trunk, and his undergarments in it, "to see whether they were properly washed and folded". And he removed the fluff from his new uniform, "which had been made without epaulettes". The absence of epaulettes points to a demotion at the end of his service.

Difference can also be expressed as contradiction. For example, the spiteful stepmother in "The Fair at Sorochinsky" (Gogol 1832: 19-20) is described in incongruous terms: she is wearing a "smart green woolen jacket adorned with little tails, to imitate ermine, though they were red in color. . ." and "a flowered chintz cap that gave a particular majestic air to the round face, which betrayed so unpleasant and savage a nature that everyone hastened to turn from it to the lively face of the daughter".

In his poetics of illusion, Gogol uses metaphor, synecdoche and metonymy masterfully. Eco views metaphor in a framework that includes synecdoche and metonymy. He (Eco 1984: 88-89) explains metaphor as a semiotic phenomenon: "The inner nature of metaphors produces a shifting of the linguistic explanation onto semiotic mechanisms that are not peculiar to spoken languages. . ." Eco (1984:141) stresses that metaphors are "always governed by rhetorical rules and controlled by their co-texts". The verbal metaphor is often connected with visual, aural, tactile, and olfactory experience. Examples of such intertextual metaphors abound in Gogol's work. In "Ivan Fyodorovich Shponka and His Aunt" (Gogol 1832: 253), the neighbor's mother is described as a "short old lady, a regular coffeepot in a cap". Eyebrows, which Ivan's aunt regards as the most telling sign in a woman's face, show the character of a woman. The collar of one of the two Ivans in the story about "The Quarrel of the Two Ivans" (Gogol 1835) is so high and stiff that his head rests in it as though in a chaise. In "Nevsky Prospekt" (Gogol 1835a) the pedestrians turn into a parade of whiskers and moustaches with color codes; hats, dresses, kerchiefs; waists and sleeves. The green color of the uniforms of the Civil servants serves as a metaphor for spring. The entire street functions as a channel of communication, with an ever changing collection and movement of metaphorical and metonymical signs. The narrator gives us a reading of these signs. In "The Portrait" (Gogol 1835a), the intertextual references to painting, like the colors red and blue, refer to the colors of dusk and twilight when the fantastic sets in; they indicate some disturbance, an incongruence, a "conflagration".

Eco raises the question whether metaphor has cognitive value. He points out, that in fact, someone who creates metaphors is lying. The person is not speaking literally: he/she "pretends to make assertions, and yet wants to assert seriously something that is beyond literal truth" (Eco 1984:89). Gogol and his characters set out to do just that. In "Ivan Fyodorovich Shponka and His Aunt" (Gogol 1832: 235-236), the main narrator, Rudy Panko, dismisses another potential narrator, the gentleman in the pea-green coat, as too much of a liar. Frequently, the reader is informed that there is a "story about this story" but that the narrator's memory is "incredibly poor". And he apologizes for not always telling the literal truth: "You may tell me a thing or not tell it, it is all the same. It is like pouring water into a sieve". In the same story Grigory Grigorievich interferes during the dinner conversation and warns his guest, Ivan Fyodorovich, not to believe Ivan Ivanovich, that he was "always telling fibs" (Gogol 1832: 257). There is another narrator, a fine young gentleman but when you listen to him, you "begin to get puzzled . . . for you can't make head or tail of it". Another storyteller, the beekeeper-narrator informs the reader, tells terrible stories "that make your hair stand on end" and the narrator has left him out on purpose for the good people might be so scared they "would be as afraid of the beekeeper as they are of the devil" (Gogol 1832: 15).

In addition to Riffaterre's and Eco's approach in which the notion of *displacement* and *difference* figure prominently, Todorov's brilliant analysis of the poetics of the fantastic is immediately helpful in elucidating Gogol's poetics of illusion. Todorov (1970: 168) discusses the fantastic as a product of the 19th century, which he, too, describes as "nothing but the bad conscience of this positivist era". Todorov (1970: 21) views historical genres as a subgroup of complex theoretical genres and distinguishes three aspects of the literary work: the verbal, syntactical, and semantic. The verbal aspect helps shape ambiguous visions as "fantastic"; it is linked to the syntactical aspect "insofar as it implies the existence of formal units which correspond to the character's estimation of events in the narrative"; and it refers to the semantic aspect which includes all the various themes, such as misleading appearance, illusion, displacement, and metamorphosis.

Todorov's definition of the fantastic is most useful: the fantastic occupies the duration of uncertainty, the moment of hesitation in the reader, rather than in the text. It lies in the relation of the real and the imaginary. It happens when mystery, or the inexplicable intrudes into the real world. It constitutes a break in the acknowledged order, an eruption of the inadmissible within the everyday legality. The fantastic can appear in form of the supernatural, the uncanny, or the marvelous. We could give a large catalog of examples from Gogol's Ukrainian and Petersburg stories which would perfectly fit Todorov's definition. But the supernatural does not aid us in defining the genre of the fantastic, Todorov points out. Fear and terror are semiotic reactions of the reader, but not conditions of the genre. Todorov suggests that we define the fantastic in terms of opposition to the faithful reproduction of reality, or in terms of opposition to naturalism. Such a definition would bring us closer to the genius of Gogol who has been labelled a "Realist" by his Soviet critics, in the conventional nineteenth century sense of that word. The ambiguity in Gogol's work that has been noted by various critics, arises, according to Todorov, as a result of two stylistic devices: the use of the imperfect tense and modalization. For example, in the *Evenings on a Farm Near Dikanka* (Gogol 1831: 128), the assessor of Sorochinsky who is described with realistic detail, "would certainly have noticed her, for there is not a witch in the world who could elude the eye of the Sorochinsky assessor". When vision is blackened out by magic--the witch was gathering up the stars and the devil was stealing the moon, "no one in Dikanka noticed that the devil had stolen the moon" (Gogol 1831: 129-130). Furthermore, the witch was really the blacksmith Vakula's mother, "and no one could have told that she had been riding on a broom the minute before" (Gogol 1831: 139).

Todorov distinguishes the supernatural which remains unexplained, from the uncanny--the supernatural explained, and the marvelous--the supernatural accepted, the fairytale being one of the varieties of the marvelous. In Gogol's Ukrainian stories, especially in *Evenings on a Farm Near Dikanka*, all of these variants can be found. The closeness of these stories to Ukrainian folktales and puppet theater, and also to the German Kunstmärchen has been noted by critics (Fanger 1979: 90-91; Setchkarev 1965: 95, 119). Seductive women and stepmothers turn into cats and witches who ride on broomsticks, or who try to kill their stepdaughters; dead maidens inspire necrophilia in admiring men; notes passed in dreams remain after the awakening as tokens of real wishes or intentions; evil is harnessed in the service of good but may also end in murder and horror. The Dikanka stories depict a world as seen in a glittering mirror: a world of fantastic illusion.

Todorov discusses discourses of the fantastic, such as figurative discourse, rhetorical forms (the supernatural originates in the figurative image), and exaggeration. He notes that the supernatural becomes a symbol of language. Devils and vampires exist only in words and images. Todorov (1970: 60) stresses that the fantastic can subsist only in fiction for it requires a reaction to events. He discusses Gogol's story "The Nose" which, in his view, constitutes a border-case. It does not meet the first condition of the fantastic, that of the hesitation between the real and the illusory or imaginary; it is situated within the marvelous. Different perspectives are suggested by the text, including that of allegory (Todorov 1970: 72). Allegory implies the existence of at least two meanings for the same words. The word 'nose' is transformed into a proper name, and finally 'nose' is transformed into the Russian expression for 'non-plussed'. Thus, the word 'nose' takes on other meanings than its literal one. The world Gogol describes is that of St. Petersburg, it is not that of the marvelous. Todorov suggests that we search out an allegorical interpretation. However, the psychoanalytical interpretation of castration would not be allegorical. It does not account for the nose turning into a person. Todorov (1970: 73) also notes that social allegory does not fully explain the central transformation any better than does the psychoanalytical interpretation. At the end, the author addresses the reader directly, stressing the reader's function throughout the text, "thereby even facilitating the appearance of an allegorical meaning", but at the same time asserting that it cannot be found. Todorov concludes that Gogol asserts "non-meaning". He (1970: 73) thinks that the story anticipates "what the literature of the supernatural will become in the twentieth century". Todorov calls Gogol's approach "illusory allegory".

The fantastic is called into question. In the twentieth century, with Kafka and Sartre, the fantastic become the rule rather than the exception; "normal" man becomes the fantastic being.

As Eco had noted, the narrator may lie, and this may shock us "structurally", according to Todorov (1970: 86), for the reader assumes that the narrator's discourse "lies outside of the test of truth". Todorov lists other features of fantastic narrative: directions regarding the role of the reader, the time of its perception, the process of uttering, the time of reading itself. The series cannot be shifted. All of these features can be observed in Gogol's stories. In the Preface to "The Sorochinsky Fair", the narrator describes the road to his cottage near Dikanka and warns the reader that this road to storyland is indeed a bumpy road, that "last year" Foma Grigorievich fell into a ditch, although he himself was driving and "had on a pair of spectacles, too". In other words, vision and time are blurred and the process of fictionality is uneven and treacherous. But once you get to storyland, you will find the best honey, the most perfect pies, etc, "so many good things that you will talk about them to everyone you meet". Aesthetic pleasure is promised to those who go through the semiotic process of listening, reading, and interpretation.

Aesthetic pleasure is what one experiences when reading Gogol's fantastic tales. Gogol's intricate poetics of illusion is as powerful now as it was in Gogol's time. It prepared the way from Romantic poetics to the poetics of the twentieth century of Kafka and Sartre. It was intimately connected with cultural change. The artist was the mouthpiece of that changing reality. The cornerstones of the new poetics that Gogol was fashioning were difference, displacement, shifting, exaggeration, and contradiction. No wonder this new poetic meaning structure was perceived as topsy-turvy.

NOTES

[1] The stories with Ukrainian settings are collected in *Evenings on a Farm Near Dikanka*. Part I was published in 1831 and contains "The Fair at Sorochinsky", "St. John's Eve", "The May Night or The Drowned Maiden", "The Lost Letter"; Part II was published in 1832 and contains a Preface and the stories, "Christmas Eve", "The Terrible Vengeance", "Ivan Fyodorovich Shponka and His Aunt", and "The Enchanted Spot". Other stories with Ukrainian settings are contained in *Mirogorod* (1835), literally meaning 'City of Peace': "The Old-World Owners", "Taras Bulba", "Viy", "The Quarrel of the Two Ivans". Other stories with Petersburg settings were published at the same time in the volume *Arabesques* (1835a) which also contained "Nevsky Prospect", "Diary of a Madman", and "The Portrait".

[2] Eco (1984: 202) understands mirror as "a threshold phenomenon marking the boundaries between the imaginary and the symbolic".

REFERENCES

ECO, Umberto.
    1984. *Semiotics and the Philosophy of Language* (Bloomington: Indiana Univ. Press).
ERLICH, Victor.
    1969. *Gogol* (New Haven and London: Yale Univ. Press).
FANGER, Donald.
    1979. *The Creation of Nikolai Gogol* (Cambridge, Mass., and London: The Belknap Press of Harvard Univ. Press).
GOGOL, Nikolai.
    1831-1832. *Evenings on a Farm Near Dikanka*. Stories published by the Bee-Keeper Rudi Panko, ed. by O. Gorchakov (Moscow: Foreign Lang. Publ.), an early English edition under the same title (New York: A.A. Knopf, 1926). Quotations in this paper are from the 1957 English edition.
    1835. *Mirogorod*, trans. with an introduction by David Magarshack (New York: Farrar, Straus, and Cudahy, 1962).

1835a. *Arabesques*, trans. by Alexander Tulloch with an introduction by Carl R. Proffer (Ann Arbor, MI: Ardis, 1982).
1835-1836. *The Overcoat and Other Tales of Good and Evil by Nicolai Gogol*. Trans. by D. Magarshack (New York: the Norton Library, 1957). Quotations in this paper are from the English edition.

KARLINSKY, Simon.
1976. *The Sexual Labyrinth of Nikolai Gogol* (Cambridge: Harvard Univ. Press).

RIFFATERRE, Michael.
1978. *Semiotics of Poetry* (Bloomington & London: Indiana Univ. Press).

SETCHKAREFF, Vsevolod.
1965. *Gogol: His Life and Works*. Trans. by R. Kramer (New York: New York Univ. Press).

TODOROV, Tzvetan.
1970. *Introduction à la littérature fantastique* (Paris: Éditions du Seuil). Page references in this paper are from the English trans. by R. Howard *The Fantastic. A Structural Approach to a Literary Genre* (Cleveland, London: The Press of Case Western Reserve University, 1973).

INTERTEXTUAL AND INTRATEXTUAL ANALYSIS: THE HOLY GRAIL IN JULIEN GRACQ'S WORK

Michèle M. Magill
North Carolina State University

In 1960, Julia Kristeva said: "each text is built as a mosaic of quotations, each text is an absorption and transformation of another text" (Kristeva 1969: 146).

To point out that to write is to rewrite is not original, nor is it original to state that the Quest for the Holy Grail is a source, among many sources, of Julien Gracq's works, and for many other works.

Long before Kristeva ever introduced "intertextuality" into the vocabulary of literary criticism, Julien Gracq, without ever using the term itself, said in *Lettrines* (1967): "Each book grows on other books". Even earlier, he had noted that in an imaginary work, "all the elements are provided--they are only recomposed in another way" (Gracq 1961: 68). "Each book is nourished, as we know, not only by the materials life provides, but also, and perhaps primarily by the thick literary soil which has preceded it" (Gracq 1961: 26). In his own case, he could have added that each of his books was nourished by his other preceding books. This is a phenomenon Jean Ricardou referred to when he added to intertextuality the idea of "restricted intertextuality", where the literary allusion comes from the author's previous writings (Ricardou 1975: 11, 37).

Narrowing down the scope, we come to the notion of intratextuality, or what Françoise Calin calls: "les emprunts obsessionnels" (an author's obsessional borrowings) of an author, and "the way their distribution and development structure a novel" (Calin 1987: 215). As Gracq once said: "the true creative reverie is a poor, ressassing one, a rather obsessional reverie" (Gracq 1961: 67).

Regardless of wherever this obsession begins, or whenever it occurs in a text, it not only identifies its sources, it also reveals its own progressive weaving.

In this paper, we shall hopefully see how the analysis of intertextuality, restricted intertextuality and intratextuality can help define the creative processes which have absorbed and transformed a medieval text, the legend of the Holy Grail, or various versions of it, into a modern body of work, the plays and novels of Julien Gracq.

I. Intertextuality: the Grail in Gracq's First Works

Before discussing the notion of intertextuality, I would like to say a few words about Julien Gracq's place in French Literature: Julien Gracq is a contemporary

French writer who, for reasons of convenience, has been seen as a surrealist, even though he does not fully belong to that movement. While he shares the surrealists' passion for the beautiful and the fantastic, and strives to reconcile in Man the irrational and the rational, he is also greatly concerned with the themes of salvation and damnation; his poetical and magical universe, where action and dream are closely interwoven, are filled with timeless characters. His style is baroque and sumptuous; his noble, "recherché" language has nothing in common with the "automatic writing" recommended by the surrealists. Rather than "surrealizing" the moment, Gracq "derealizes" it.

This process of "derealization" is helped, by the multitude of literary allusions, quotations and images, among which the legend of the Holy Grail is the most obvious and recurrent. What particularly interests me is to discover what Gracq knew of this legend, and how he interpreted and transformed it in his work. At this point the task becomes more complex because there are so many versions of the legend, each absorbing and transforming the preceding one.

The legend of the Holy Grail

Even specialists of the legend of the Holy Grail do not seem to agree on its origins. The similarity between French poems, which appeared at the end of the XIIth and the beginning of the XIIIth century, and Celtic literature concerning the legend are quite interesting, though not particularly revealing. Whatever its origins, this legend was first told in *Li Conte del Graal*, by Chrétien de Troyes (=1181), but Chrétien died before finishing it, and numerous authors continued the legend. At the same period, the legend joined the Cycle of Arthurian romances. Of all these continuations, there finally emerged a wide ensemble: The Lancelot-Grail (+1220), strongly marked by christian values, (more than in Chrétien's *Perceval*). There were also many translations and adaptations of Chrétien's *Perceval* in Europe during the Middle Ages, particularly *Parzival*, by Wolfram von Eschenbach (=1204) which constitutes the main source of Wagner's opera (1882). Since the Wolfram's version, through Wagner, whom Gracq called his "intercessor and wakener", had a profound influence on Gracq, perhaps it would be appropriate to provide the reader with a short summary (Gracq 1967: 38).

Perceval, a poor and ignorant youth, decides to become a knight. His mother dies of sorrow when he leaves for the court of King Arthur. After many adventures, from which he learns courtesy and honor, he discovers that he is of noble descent. He meets Le Roi-Pêcheur (the Fisher-King/ the Sinner-King) and attends the ceremony of the Holy Grail, in the castle of Montsalvage. Because of his discretion (his mother always told him to be polite), he does not ask the significance of what he sees, and the next day when he wakes up the castle is deserted. Back in Arthur's court, a woman named Kundry, messenger of the Grail, reproaches him for not asking the question which would have delivered Amfortas, Le Roi-Pêcheur, from his suffering. Perceval falls in deep despair and for five years does penance, living like a pagan in the forest, until he meets a hermit who unveils "The Lord's ways" to him and tells him about the mystery of the Holy Grail, and of Amfortas' wound. Perceval, absolved and in peace with God, leaves for Arthur's court where Kundry finds him and announces that he has been chosen as king of the Grail, "in spite of everything". He returns to Montsalvage, asks the question and cures Amfortas.

Although the versions of Chrétien and Wolfram are very similar indeed in their narrative elements, they differ on three essential points:

1) the question: In Chrétien's version, Perceval asks why the spear is bleeding and for what the Grail is used.

In Wolfram's version, Perceval, out of common sense and charity asks why the king is suffering.

2) the Grail: For Chrétien, it is a sacred relic, which probably comes from the Last Supper.

For Wolfram, it is a magical stone, which preserves and restores life.

3) Amfortas: In Chrétien's version, he is simply a Fisherking.

For Wolfram, Amfortas has transgressed the order of the Grail by committing adultery. His hip wound represents punished sexuality. To survive, he has to see the Grail. He is a Sinner-King.

The Grail and Gracq

So now that we have seen these points of reference and comparison, perhaps we can better understand the new meaning that Gracq gives the legend, first in his own version, a play entitled *Le Roi-Pêcheur* (1948), then in his other works.

In his play *Le Roi-Pêcheur* Gracq frees himself from both the traditional interpretation of the Holy Grail legend and from the Wagnerian interpretation, and achieves an entirely original version. Robert Kanters notes that Gracq tries to "deliver the Grail first from the christian enchantment, then from the musical enchantment" (quoted in Francis 1979: 15). The action and setting correspond to Chrétien's Perceval, but the main characters, Amfortas, Perceval, Kundry, and Clingsor play the role that Wolfram has assigned to them (though there are differences in roles' importance among the secondary characters).

The recentering of the legend is revealed by the title itself: It is not Peredur, nor Perceval, Percevans, Parzivàl or Parsifal, but *Le Roi-Pêcheur* and the play indeed isolates one moment of the Quest for the Holy Grail. The castle of Montsalvage is waiting for "the Pure One", who will cure Amfortas. Clingsor, the magician, announces Perceval's arrival to Kundry and Amfortas, reminding the King that while Perceval can cure him by asking the question about the Grail, the King will, as a result, loose the throne of Montsalvage to Perceval. On his way to the castle, Perceval meets Trévrizent the hermit, who vainly tries to stop him from his quest. Later, Amfortas tells Perceval that he too undertook the Quest, saw the Grail and became King of the Grail, but that when he fell in love with Kundry, his life became filled with illness, unhappiness and also a physical and spiritual mutilation. Perceval decides then to leave, but Kundry convinces him to stay and attend the ceremony of the Grail. Amfortas tries one last time to dissuade Perceval, revealing that Perceval's quest is about to end, but also warning him of the consequences of such a success, of the certitude that blinds, the end of adventure, and the beginning of eternal rest and solitude: "Where you enter hope ends and possession begins" (Gracq 1948: 141). Perceval remains quiet during the ceremony and leaves the castle without having asked the question which would have made him King of the Grail.

The play's structure therefore resembles a circle, the end joining its starting point: at the beginning, there is a somber, stagnant world, the world of waiting. Perceval's arrival creates tumult, unrest, uncertainty, and blinds this world with a light it had long forgotten, a light it both fears and longs for. But Perceval, by renouncing his quest, throws the world of Montsalvage back into its lethargy. All that is left, once again, is hope and waiting. The event, which this world so much longed for, does not take place.

In the preface to this play, Gracq says: "Medieval myths are open myths telling about permanent and rewarded temptations". The quest, in Chrétien's version, remained unachieved because the author died before he finished the work, but in *Le Roi-Pêcheur*, the author deliberately leaves the quest unfulfilled. We will now see how Gracq "dechristianizes" the legend, how it remains a story of initiation, of a quest, not particularly for a christian knowledge, but for an ultimate knowledge, which causes an unbearable confrontation between Man and the Sanctity he himself creates.

In Gracq's *Le Roi Pêcheur*, as in Wolfram's version, Amfortas' fault was to love a woman other than the woman destined for him by the Grail; and as in Wagner's version, the fault is also related to adultery, which was not at all the case in Chrétien's version. Likewise in Wagner's version, Kundry, messenger of the Grail, and Orgueluse, who is responsible for Amfortas' wound, are one and the same character. But in Gracq's version, after inflicting the wound, she also tries to cure it. She is a guide for Perceval, a living hope and fighting force for Montsalvage. In Gracq's version, Amfortas is the main character, both priest and guardian of the Holy Grail. His wound is what keeps the castle alive. For Perceval, to live is to desire, which creates privileged ties between him and Amfortas, who once desired and possessed a woman who was not his wife. The two men are opposed but complementary. As for the Grail itself, Gracq never enters the quarrel between specialists over its nature (vase, dish or stone). To him however it is the divine, the sacred and unquenchable desire for perfect knowledge. It means salvation as long as it is desired, but brings about solitude, despair and death, if ever possessed. At the end of the play, Amfortas treats Perceval as a man by letting him choose not to ask the question. Perceval leaves the castle of Montsalvage as he had found it, in waiting. Perceval's own longing, waiting and desire have been unfulfilled, and that is the condition for life and hope. Therefore the play goes back to its starting point, it is its own prelude.

The waiting for an event, desire and quest are very characteristic of Gracq's novels. For the Grail may be only the name that the myth gives to what pushes a human being to outdo and to live beyond herself, and what gives a meaning to her life. The quest for the Grail is the modern adventure of a quest for an ideal, always near but always unreachable, and this how Gracq here joins the Surrealist Movement.

II. Restricted Intertextuality

We find this interpretation of the legend in other works by Gracq, which will allow an analysis of restricted intertextuality.

Gracq's obsession with the Grail appears in his first novel, *Au Château d'Argol* (1938). I will try to summarize the story: Albert, a young and rich aristocrat, buys the castle of Argol without even seeing it. Shortly after his arrival, he receives a message announcing the visit of a childhood friend, Herminien (a man), who is bringing along Heide, a woman Albert does not know. Herminien is a fascinating character, and Heide, a young, beautiful and erudite woman. On the night of their arrival, Heide, inexplicably, but passionately kisses Albert. A strange game begins between these three uncommon people, finally resulting in the rape of Heide by Herminien. Albert finds Heide in the forest, but Herminien has disappeared. Then one day they find him, wounded and bleeding. They bring him back to the castle and Albert discovers, in Herminien's room, an engraving showing Perceval and Amfortas, the bleeding spear and the Grail. Then one night Herminien leads Albert through a secret passage which opens into Heide's bedroom. After this violation of her privacy, Heide kills herself, and is buried by the two men in a grave on which her name had already been engraved, as if her seemingly untimely death had actually been anticipated. That evening, Herminien announces his departure, and exchanges with Albert a solemn promise. As Herminien leaves during the night, he hears a man's steps behind him. Albert knifes him in the back.

Though it is clearly set in modern times, *Au Chateau d'Argol* is the one novel by Gracq which is the most clearly marked with signs of the Grail. Indeed the Grail seems to belong to the very movement of the writing: the structure, the themes and images, characters and objects can all be compared to those of the legend. For example, the objects that Albert contemplates in the chapel are a spear and a helmet, and at the end of the novel, the discovery of the engraving representing Perceval puts all the text in a "mise en abyme". As in the legend, the novel also begins with the journey of the hero and continues with a period of waiting. [This narrative thread can also be found in other novels by Gracq *Le Rivage des Syrtes* (1951) and *La Presqu'île* (1970), as well as *Un Beau Ténébreux* (1945), and *Un Balcon en Forêt* (1958)]. Albert is a man in quest of a lost completeness, which he finds at the castle of Argol, as Perceval did at Montsalvage. These two castles are much alike; surrounded by thick woods, threatening walls, filled with furs and luxury, and a strange silence, they appear as places of either pleasure or torture, with the power to save or to damn, a world unto itself. This dream world is shaken by three events: Heide's kissing of Albert, the rape of Heide by Herminien, and the murder of Herminien by Albert.

The events of *Au Château d'Argol*, as the adventures of the Holy Grail, happen in a fantastic atmosphere. The characters clearly belong to an elite community, strangely free and available, but united by their waiting for a mysterious knowledge. The period of waiting is a suspended time, full of privilege and promise, hope and freedom, while the decisive act, by making one escape from destiny, seals it for ever. Waiting is therefore ambiguous, since it refuses action to better accept it. It is a kind of anti-destiny, though its object is destiny. It is the reverse of an exhilarating, adventurous quest.

The narration of *Au Château d'Argol* closely follows the stages of the quest in the Holy Grail: both works begin with the heroes' (Albert and Perceval) desire for knowledge. Both heroes encounter obstacles: dangers of Nature, self-doubt, transgression of what is forbidden. The role of these obstacles is to serve as experiences of initiation, which always occur trough a woman. In the Holy Grail, Perceval is initiated by the damsel in the tent, whom he kisses forcibly, by his cousin Sigune, who reveals to him his true identity, by Blanchefleur, his virgin bride, and by Kundry, messenger of the Grail.

In Argol, Heide, as initiator and tempter, might be identified to Kundry. She is pleasure (since she allows sexual knowledge), child (when wounded she is tended by Albert), magic (by her alliance with nature). Her wound renders salvation or damnation possible. But she also represents the Grail, which once possessed means death. And this is where the myth changes: the Grail does not bring life but death. Herminien presents Heide as the object of salvation, but Albert does not acknowledge it, nor does he possess her; as for Herminien, he rapes her, and is damned (he is wounded "au flanc") and consequently damns Albert, who becomes his murderer.

The wound, so important as a principle of life and death in the engraving, is therefore the crucial moment of the quest. In the legend, it is Amfortas' wound. In *Au Château d'Argol*, the wound is doubly represented by the rape of Heide, and Herminien's wound.

A third wound could be perceived by the reader when s/he considers the rest of Gracq's novels: since the Grail reappears in each of them, the book itself becomes the Grail, and the ever-bleeding wound can be seen as the act of writing.

Let us consider now, for a further illustration of the restricted intertextuality, a few elements of the legend in Gracq's other novels:

-the passivity: Albert and Heide ignored "ce qu'il sera décidé d'eux" (Gracq: 1938 57). "Tu ne choisiras pas, Perceval, tu es choisi", says Amfortas in *Le Roi-Pêcheur*.

-the endless waiting: "Il ne se passait rien" says Aldo in *Le Rivage des Syrtes* (Gracq 1951: 37) and Grange in *Un Balcon en Forêt* (126).

-It is the wound, already commented upon in *Le Roi-Pêcheur* and *Au Château d'Argol*, which in *Un Balcon en Forêt* gives a certain weight to reality, more than death, because death remains a stranger while the wound is the irreducible contingency. It is only in the alliance of the imaginary and the real that the surreal can be conceived.

- Gracq's places outside of time are a regressus at uterum, an initiation to the kingdom of death: in *Un Balcon en Forêt*, in Mona's house, Grange "se sentait blotti comme dans un ventre"; Marino's temptation, (as Amfortas'), is to remain "roulé dans son cocon", "amarré, ligoté, empaqueté" in *Le Rivage des Syrtes*. But, for fear of irremediably dying, one has to transgress the established order. That is why all of Gracq's characters decide to "lever l'ancre". But the perilous journey needs a guide: in all of Gracq's novels (this is where he unknowingly adopts the vision of the celtic Woman), the guide, the initiator is a woman: it is Heide, as we have seen in *Au Château d'Argol*, or Christel who has the vision of the Grail in *Un Beau Ténébreux*, or in *Un Balcon en Forêt*, Mona, "fille de la pluie, . . . une fadette, une petite sorcière". Aldo expresses very well why Gracq gives the woman such a role. He says about Vanessa in *Le Rivage des Syrtes*: "Je comprenais maintenant pourquoi Vanessa m'avait été donnée comme un guide, et pourquoi, une fois entré dans son ombre, la partie claire de mon esprit m'avait été de si peu de prix: elle était du sexe qui pèse de tout son poids sur les portes de l'angoisse, du sexe mysterieusement docile et consentant d'avance à ce qui s'annonce au-delà de la catastrophe et de la nuit" (Gracq 1951). Death, whether it is brought by war (*Le Rivage des Syrtes*, *Un Balcon en Forêt*, *Le Roi Cophetua*), suicide (*Un Beau Ténébreux*) or murder (*Au Château d'Argol*), is an image of another world, where Eros is linked to Thanatos, Kundry to Amfortas and Perceval, Mona to Grange, Heide to Albert and Herminien, Vanessa to Aldo.

III. Intratextuality

With the time left for intratextuality in the last part of this essay, I will simply show how some elements repeat themselves inside a same narrative.

- In *Un Beau Ténébreux*, for example, the image of a "route d'initiation" becomes significant when it reoccurs: "Ce petit groupe de hasard, . . . , ceux que j'associerai toujours dans mon souvenir, quoiqu'il advienne, à la plus singulière initiation " (The word "initiation" is underlined by Gracq).

- In *Le Rivage des Syrtes* the initiation is related to water in the expression "eau initiatique". But as we have seen, initiation is also related to Woman, and it is not surprising to find initiation, Woman and water all related in this novel: Aldo, first says: "je me sentis m'épanouir sous la douce averse de ce sourire mouillé"; later, during the initiatic cruise towards the forbidden frontier, Vanessa is placed at the prow and " la beauté fugace du visage de Vanessa se recomposait de la buée de chaleur qui montait des eaux calmes". Aldo's souvenir of Vanessa pushes him to transgress the maritime frontiers of his country and consequently provoke the war: "je serrai les lèvres, sur les cheveux sauvages de Vanessa que la nuit reprenait et gonflait dans le lit comme la marée une touffe d'algues . . . ce qui me restais à faire, je l'accomplirais maintenant."

To conclude this analysis, I would like to point out an interesting example of intertextual and intratextual occurrences of the legend of the Holy grail in *Le Rivage des Syrtes*; this novel is a turning point in Gracq's work, because that is where he abandons direct literary allusions and quotations. However, as Ruth Amossy has remarked, there is an endless relation between this novel and some texts by André Breton, the "pope" of Surrealism. She notes: "The borrowed threads weaving the narrative are perfectly integrated, and nothing signals them to an unadverted eye (Amossy 1982: 89). One example she gives illustrates perfectly the inter and intratextual signs of the Grail in this novel. Danielo says to Aldo, right before the moment where he launches the adventure: "Il ne s'agit pas d'être jugé . . . Il s'agissait de répondre à une question--à une question intimidante--à une question que personne encore au monde n'a pu laisser sans réponse, jusqu'à son dernier souffle . . .
-Laquelle?
-Qui vive?"

REFERENCES

AMOSSY, Ruth.
   1982. *Parcours symboliques chez Julien Gracq* (Paris: SEDES).
CALIN, Françoise.
   1987. "'Le Maelstrom' d'Edgar Poe dans *Un Beau Ténébreux* de Julien Gracq: Essai d'analyse intertextuelle", *French Forum* 12.2.
FRANCIS, Marie.
   1979. *Forme et signification de l'attente dans l'oeuvre romanesque de Julien Gracq* (Paris: A.G. Nizet).
GRACQ, Julien.
   1938. *Au Château d'Argol* (Paris, Corti).
   1945. *Un Beau Ténébreux* (Paris, Corti).
   1948. *Le Roi-Pêcheur* (Paris, Corti).
   1951. *Le Rivage des Syrtes* (Paris, Corti).
   1958. *Un Balcon en forêt* (Paris, Corti).
   1961. *Préférences* (Paris, Corti).
   1967. *Lettrines* (Paris, Corti).
   1970. *La Presqu'île* (Paris, Corti).
KRISTEVA, Julia.
   1969. *Recherches pour une sémanalyse* (Paris: Seuil).
RICARDOU, Jean.
   1975. "Claude Simon, textuellement", *Claude Simon* (Paris: Union Générale d'Editions "10/18").

THE ILLUSION OF READING: DECONSTRUCTIVE VS. SEMIOTIC THEORIES

Steven C. Scheer
Saint Meinrad College, St. Meinrad, Indiana

According to a commonsensical yet nevertheless profoundly insightful scheme, writing is a kind of reading, reading a kind of writing. That is, good writers write as if they were reading what they are in the process of writing, just as good readers read as if they were writing what they are in the process of reading. The scheme actually involves four personages two of whom are real while the "other" two are imaginary. Thus, there is always an actual writer and an implied writer, an actual reader and an implied reader. The actual writer is the person writing, the implied writer is a *persona* writing. The actual reader is the person reading, the implied reader is a *persona* reading. In an ideal world we would not have to go any further. I take it that in an ideal world all signs would be transparent and language would be so unproblematic as to be unnecessary. But we do not live in an ideal world. And the actual world we live in, perfused as it is with signs which are always ambiguous at least in the sense of being open to different interpretations, both the acts of writing and reading are problematic in the extreme even if under most circumstances we do not regard them as such. The first problem in the actual world that underpins both writing and reading is that of intentionality. We know that reading, under most circumstances beyond the most basic act of communication, cannot be "merely" the recovery of the writer's intentions. That's because under *some* circumstances at least the writer's intentions may not be clear to the writer him/herself. Last spring, for example, I wrote the following abstract (that is, proposal) for this paper:

> Deconstruction and semiotics are, in a sense, theories of reading. The status of the sign, though, is radically (?) different in each. In deconstruction signs are (always already) signs of signs or signs about signs, that is, meta-signs. In semiotics this is not (necessarily) so. The question is, are "realities" depicted by (conventional) fiction effects of signs? Using J. Hillis Miller's reading of Emily Brontë's *Wuthering Heights* as my case in point, I wish to argue that it is possible both to transcend the deconstructive controversy and to preserve its semiotic implications. Since reading is always, in some sense, a re/covery of meaning and since the re/covery in question is always, in some sense, partial, a reading, to be successful, must always (of necessity) privilege certain (sets of) signs. In a deconstructive reading such

privileging is a violation of the rules. In semiotics, on the other hand, the question remains at least debatable. In arguing my "case," I wish to pay particular attention to Miller's insistence that the 'error [of reading] lies in the assumption that the meaning [of the text] is going to be single, unified, and logically coherent'. The illusory nature of reading (since all reading is partial) can only be both transcended and preserved on the border between the inside and the outside of 'undecidability' and 'unlimited semiosis'. It is here that deconstruction may be seen as an aspect of semiotics and vice versa.

Having waited until this fall to actually write the paper (*this* paper) for which the foregoing is an abstract or proposal--that is, a promise--the first question that pops into my mind is, what on earth does it mean? Of course, there is a sense according to which the abstract or proposal must make sense since it was on its basis that the referees have invited me to the thirteenth annual meeting of the Semiotic Society of America. Nevertheless, reading in the fall what I have written in the spring, I myself detect illogic, incoherence, and inconsistency in it (though not necessarily in that order). The question then remains, what on earth were my intentions last spring? Obviously, I had intended that my proposal be accepted. Obviously, I am grateful that it has been. Obviously, there is nothing wrong with my title either, though I did intend it to be attention-getting. Nor is there anything wrong with the logic of Miller's statement about reading. The point that all reading is illusory so long as it takes itself to be complete and exhaustive is well taken. It is also both commonsensically and profoundly true. Yet reading in the fall what I have written in the spring, I must confess that the only thing which excites me about my own abstract or proposal at this point is the statement that since the re/covery of meaning "is always, in some sense, partial, a reading, to be successful, must always (of necessity) privilege certain (sets of) signs. In a deconstructive reading such privileging is a violation of the rules."

What impresses me about this statement is the (implied) contradiction *within* deconstruction. Rather than doing "damage" to deconstruction, though, the statement in question seems to support the thesis of my title, except that by now it should be clear that it is not just reading but writing, too, which emerges as illusory. Perhaps I may throw a more helpful light on the problematic question of intentionality if I may be permitted to describe that elusive moment when what the writer writes is not yet written but when it is already, in some sense, being formed in his/her mind. But isn't that formation itself always already an example of "writing". I mean, must there be writing in the literal sense (of putting marks on paper or hitting the appropriate keys of a keyboard) for us to speak of writing? According to common sense, yes. But is common sense right here? It may be, yet I continue to be troubled by the fact that even as I write what I write seems to precede, even if ever so slightly, what I write.

For one thing, when I am truly concentrating on what I am trying to say, I seem to become oblivious of the physical act of writing altogether. Yet what I have in mind is not exactly (never exactly) what I seem to be reading as I watch, so to speak, the ongoing and always already partial completion of the physical act which produces what I write in physical form so that it is suddenly readable by someone other than me (even though, during the physical process of writing itself, this other [the reader] is still me [the writer]). If there is always an element of surprise for the writer, then, *whose* intentions does the writing itself carry out? And the same applies to reading as well, for it is somehow not "merely" the intentions of the writer or the reader that find their way, that somehow just happen to stumble into a "reading". This is true even if we distinguish between conventional and anti-conventional readings, on the one hand, and unconventional, that is, idiosyncratic, readings, on the other, which may be further subdivided into the intentionally and the unintentionally nonsensical. In all instances of reading there is an interaction in and by means of the text between the writer and the reader. But if reading as a total and exhaustive re/covery of meaning is an illusion, writing as a total and exhaustive "covery" of (some intended) meaning is an illusion, too.

J. Hillis Miller's (1982) reading of *Wuthering Heights* may well prove to be a good case in point for the alleged conflict between deconstructive and semiotic theories of reading after all. The essay in question begins innocently enough. The first thing Miller tells us is that the novel is an example of "'realistic' fiction". At the same time, however, the novel also provokes "interpretation" by "overtly" inviting "the reader to believe that there is some secret explanation which will allow him[/her] to understand the novel wholly" (1982: 42). So Miller's beginning is not innocent after all. Furthermore, the epigraph/inscription at the head of the essay, a quotation from the novel itself ("I don't care--I will get in!"), Lockwood's "ejaculation" (Brontë's word, repeated by Miller) "when he tries to get back into the Heights the second time", immediately complicates matters because Miller takes it to be "emblematic" of the reader's dilemma (1982: 42). Miller's next move is to quickly rehearse the history of the novel's reading beginning with Charlotte Brontë's prefaces. Charlotte offers four different (at times contradictory) ways of reading the novel. Miller follows his account of Charlotte's interpretation by a breathtakingly quick review of all previous readings (including his own) only to announce, triumphantly, that "[a]ll these interpretations are, I believe, wrong" (1982: 51). This is, of course, the kind of shockingly deconstructive statement that gives deconstruction a bad name. But only if it is taken literally, which is pretty impossible to do, but then anti-deconstructors tend to be capable of the impossible. In any case, the reason why Miller claims that all of the novel's interpretations are wrong is because they all (inevitably/unavoidably) claim to be impartial when they are in fact (inevitably/unavoidably) partial. "No doubt", Miller continues, "my essay too will be open to the charge that it attempts to close off the novel by explaining it, even though the explanation takes the form of an attempted reasonable formulation of its unreason" (1982: 51). The trouble is not, then, with any (good) interpretation per se. "The error lies in the assumption that the meaning [of the novel] is going to be single, unified, and logically coherent" (1982: 51). Almost in the same breath Miller calls this "error" a "fault" and goes on to claim that the "fault of premature closure is intrinsic to criticism" (1982: 51), which means that it is not a "mistake" (my word, notwithstanding the quotation marks) which could have been avoided.

Clearly we are in the midst of deconstruction here. The novel invites interpretation. The critic accepts the invitation. The critic's interpretation, though, is both necessarily impartial and inevitably/unavoidably partial. The reason for this is simply "human", if you will: "The reader has the experience, in struggling to understand the novel, that a certain number of the elements which present themselves for explanation can be reduced to order. [But] [t]his act of interpretation always leaves something over, something just at the edge of the circle of theoretical vision which that vision does not encompass" (Miller 1982: 52). There is, in other words, always already more in the text than any reader/reading is going to account for. It is the very richness of the text, then, that is responsible for the novel's "resistance to theoretical domination. . . . The novel is not incoherent, confused, or flawed. It is a triumph of the novelist's art. It uses the full resources of that art against the *normal* assumptions about character and human life which are built into the *conventions* of realistic fiction" (1982: 52, italics mine). The point is, though, that it is the novel itself which invites the very thing it then frustrates.

How can the deconstructor account for this paradox, for the failure of the "logical mind" which is "so conspicuous"? (Miller 1982: 52). (Note in passing, by the way, that these questions do not simply apply to *Wuthering Heights* alone though they definitely apply to *Wuthering Heights* as well.) Again, the "reason" is not difficult to find (1982: 69):

> The special form of 'undecidability' in *Wuthering Heights* . . . lies in the impossibility, in principle, of determining whether there is some extralinguistic explanatory cause or whether the sense that there is one is generated by the linguistic structure itself. Nor is this a trivial issue. It is the most important question that the novel raises, the one thing about which we ought to be able to make a decision, and yet a thing about which the novel forbids the reader to make a decision.

And where there is "undecidability" (a crucial term in deconstruction), can the question of "origin" (ditto) be far behind? Miller is unabashed about the question in question. He tells us in no uncertain terms that the idea of "origin may [simply] be an effect of language [itself]" (1982: 68). Miller claims that Heathcliff's experience in the novel is, finally, emblematic of the reader's attempt to penetrate its mystery. Heathcliff attempts to compensate for his loss of Catherine (which implies that there was a prior union between them) by amassing everything that once belonged to her or that may be associated with her (the Heights, the Grange, etc.). What Heathcliff discovers, however, is that none of the "signs" of/for Catherine can signify anything other than the separation between them, a separation which had "always already" been in place. "The sense of 'something missing' is an effect of the text itself" (1982: 62). And the fact of the matter is that the "something" in question has always already been "missing" in the *first* place. Thus, the idea of a prior union is nothing but an illusion. And the "illusion [in question] is created by figures of one sort or another" (1982: 68). Of course, Miller knows that we can only speak in figures. Which is precisely his point. Heathcliff's search for a "center" is but a prior repetition of the reader's search for the same. The problem is that "[w]hatever emblem is chosen as the center turns out to be not at the center but at the periphery. It is in fact an emblem for the impossibility of reaching the center" (1982: 60). If there had ever been a union between Heathcliff and Catherine, then why should they desire it so ardently from the *beginning* of their relationship? "As soon as Cathy can say, 'I am Heathcliff', or 'My love for Heathcliff resembles the eternal rocks beneath,' they are already divided. This division has always already occurred as soon as there is consciousness and the possibility of retrospective storytelling. Storytelling is always after the fact, and it is always constructed over a loss" (1982: 61).

As we can see then, deconstruction doesn't solve any problems. Nor does it create them. What it does is bring them into clear focus and reveal them in their very concealedness. And what a deconstructive reading finds is that the very foundation of any ideological structure (whether it is Lockwood's Heathcliff's or the reader's) is simply a base in perpetual need of another foundation, and so on *ad infinitum*. And this is an extremely constructive thing indeed. But what has this extremely constructive (really deconstructive) thing have in common with semiotics as a potential theory of reading? According to Jonathan Culler, a "semiotics of reading" is potentially valuable because it addresses itself not to individual interpretations but to "interpretive conventions" (1981: 67). For Culler, "[a] primary task of the study of reading is to describe the operations responsible for interpretations we find plausible" (1981: 73).

What we find plausible, though, will depend on the conventions we find acceptable. And these conventions carry intentions which are over and beyond us. We are, therefore, still caught in the problematic question of intentionality. Since the etymological meaning of the word "sign" is something we (always already) follow, intentionality implicates the question of priority. It comes down, in the final analysis, to the before-after of writing/reading itself. I have begun this essay by claiming that the one is the other, that writing is a kind of reading, reading a kind of writing. Who follows whom, therefore? Does the reader follow the writer or does the writer (in some sense) follow the reader? The answer is that both follow both. The signs of such following are manifest everywhere in both reading and writing. Both writing and reading are incomplete and inexhaustible. But because each insinuates itself as complete and exhausted, each is illusory. Even as I bring to a conclusion this writing about the illusion of reading, then, I am aware of the fact that my reading of the illusion of writing is just as vulnerable to the same illusion as the other. Thus, deconstruction, which emphasizes "undecidability", is just as "uni/versal" in its potential application as a semiotics which places a stress on "unlimited semiosis". Whether an act of writing or reading falls under the auspices of the one or the other makes no difference. Each makes sense of its own terms in its own terms. And whose terms does my own discourse satisfy? Perhaps no one's. I have a feeling that neither deconstructive nor semiotic theories can finally determine the question of reading and writing in the *first* place. Perhaps (luckily) the sign of the thirteenth annual meeting of the Semiotic Society of America is that reality is itself an illusion, an illusion generated by the illusion of a reality in which signs are and/both rather than either/or. It is, therefore, with the foregoing words that I conclude what can never be concluded.

REFERENCES

CULLER, Jonathan.
    1981.   "Semiotics as a Theory of Reading", in *The Pursuit of Signs: Semiotics, Literature, Deconstruction* (Ithaca: Cornell University Press).

MILLER, J. Hillis.
    1982.   *Fiction and Repetition: Seven English Novels* (Cambridge: Harvard University Press).

ALDO PALAZZESCHI'S :riflessi: RETROSPECTIVE READING AND REVERSE INTERTEXTUALITY[1]

Anthony Julian Tamburri
Purdue University

> A book is not an isolated being: it is a relationship,
> an axis of innumerable relationships.
> One literature differs from another, prior or posterior,
> less because of the text than because
> of the way in which it is read.
>
> -- Jorge Luis Borges --

Introduction

Palazzeschi's :riflessi (1908) is undoubtedly problematic for numerous reasons. The superficial story-line differs radically from what other turn-of-the-century writers in Italy were producing, involving as it does, a one-way, predominantly epistolary novel about two men of an unusual friendship. The first part consists of unsent and, therefore, unanswered letters written by Valentino Kore to Johnny Mare, whereas the novel's second part, epigrammatic in nature, consists of a third-person, at times journalistic-type narrative. In fact, nowhere does one find a straightforward, narrative intervention on the author's part; Palazzeschi does not offer a story-line in the traditional sense. There is no development of action or plot; characterization is kept at a minimum; and, as there is no beginning, so is there no true closure. :riflessi was therefore not at all consonant with the cultural atmosphere of its time, which, ultimately, added to the difficulty in interpretation for its contemporary reader.

Indeed the difference between the novel's contemporary reader and the person who picks up the novel at a significantly later time is fundamental to my paper, since these readers would each approach the same work with a different knowledge of the author's sign-producing repertoire. Within this framework, then, my goal here is twofold. I shall demonstrate first that this novel, as is the case with many literary compositions we consider non-canonical, creates significant problems in interpretation not easily resolvable by engaging in a chronological mode of reading vis-à-vis other works by the same author; and second, that in such cases of interpreting non-canonical texts, one might resort to a *retrospective reading* of the work in question in order to understand further the formalistic and contextual intentionality therein.

Retrospective Reading: A Retro-Lector

In dealing with the relationship between *:riflessi* and Palazzeschi's later manifestoes the necessity of reading retrospectively becomes apparent. This need further distinguishes--for the moment, chronologically--between two different types of readers: the contemporary reader (who may or may not be what some have called the implied reader) vis-à-vis what I shall call the *Retro-Lector* (the person who comes along after the production of [a] subsequent text[s]).[2]

To be sure, an author expresses certain notions, concepts and ideas at various periods throughout his/her literary career. When one reads chronologically, one reads text A, to then pass on to text B, then to text C. This sets up an apparently natural process of the first text "influencing" a later text, in this case the second, both of which then "influence" still another, a third and so on, creating a seemingly neat and linear progression of *dialogue* between texts, as is apparent in the following diagram:[3]

Reading (contemporary reader):

Text A (1908) ---> Text B (1914) ---> Text C (1915)

Naturally, dialogue between texts may not always be so simple and schematic as I have presented above: Text A may not necessarily be an intertext of B. Rather, a rapport may develop between Text A and, let's say, Text C, which in turn may, again, not necessarily dialogue with a subsequent Text D.

Notwithstanding such (ir)regularities in influence, one finds that a problem nevertheless arises in an attempt to conciliate the origin of *images*--signs, codes, referents and the like--of the various texts. It is clear that subsequent texts of an author's production--subsequent to the *first* text, that is--often depend on his/her previously composed works. Analogously, this is also true with respect to the reading process and its concomitant interpretation of the text. In this manner then, the images of the later text (Text C for example) depend on those of a previous text (Text B), which in turn ultimately depend on those of the originating text (Text A), images which appear for the first time:

Interpretation (contemporary reader):

Text C (1915) ---> Text B (1914) ---> Text A (1908)

Surely, images which appear for the first time in an author's *opus* often do not create major difficulty in interpretation. This is primarily true for those works which are created according to canonical exigencies. Where they do, however, it is precisely because they appear in the earlier work, for the first time, where there is no intertextual backdrop against which the reader might compare the material gathered at that moment of reading. The author, that is to say, may have adopted signs, codes, and referents which, when compared to other writers of the same period, differ dramatically and thus seem totally arbitrary in nature. What is important to note at this point is the vastly different and seemingly arbitrary, signs, codes and referents an author has adopted. Such a creative process is clearly in opposition to the accepted norm of artistic invention, and the text produced not only differs dramatically from the norm, but it is by definition non-canonical. It is precisely within this framework --the interpretation of what we consider non-canonical texts--that I retain necessary the notion of a *Retro-Lector*. Thus, as with all texts, so here too the question of interpretation becomes a question of intertextuality: namely, the reader's intertextual knowledge vis-à-vis the literary text. And it is here in this attempt at grounding interpretatively these initial images, that the notion of a second type of reader is born --the *Retro-Lector*.

This new type of reader is not contemporary to the text; and it is indeed this *non-contemporaneity* which distinguishes this type of reader from others:

Reading (post 1915/*Retro-Lector*):

Text C (1915) ---> Text B (1914) ---> Text A (1908)

S/he approaches an earlier text--Text A as in the diagram above--with a *previous* knowledge of a later text--Text B, or perhaps even Text C. In this manner, what to a contemporary reader of Text A (or to someone who reads A as the first text of that author's *opus*) seems a series of ambiguous, difficult, and perhaps even impossible codes to decipher, is instead more readily decipherable to whoever approaches Text A having already read Text B. The following diagram illustrates this process:

Interpretation (Post-1915/*Retro-Lector*):

Text A (1908) ---> Text B (1914) ---> Text C (1915)

For this type of reading, then, I have in mind a type of reader "able to deal interpretively with the expressions in the same way as the author deals generatively with them" (Eco 1979: 7): namely, someone similar to Eco's "Model Reader", or Iser's (1972) and Chatman's (1978) "Implied Reader"--the ideal audience to whom the text is directed. This audience is of course *contemporary* to the text; whereas the notion of *:riflessi* as an outline of the philosophy expounded in "Equilibrio" is reserved instead for what I have called the *Retro-Lector*. A slightly modified version of Chatman's (151) diagram of the narrative-communication situation can help clarify my distinction between the roles of the readers of Palazzeschi's early period. Chatman offered the following:

Narrative Text

| Real Author | Implied Author -->(Narrator)-->(Narratee)--> | Implied Reader | Real Reader |

Appending the *Retro-Lector*, I would modify the second half of Chatman's diagram in the following manner:

Narrative Text (*:riflessi* 1908)

| Real Author | Implied Author -->(Narrator)-->(Narratee)-->(1908) | Implied Reader | Real (1908) Reader | Retro- (1915) Lector |

By *Retro-Lector*, then, I mean that person outside the narrative text, similar to the "Real Reader", who, however, because s/he comes along after the publication of the author's *opus*--or a greater part thereof--also has the advantage of reading with hindsight. Thus, the *Retro-Lector* approaches a text such as *:riflessi* (1908) with a previous knowledge of "Equilibrio" (1915) so that the latter text ("Equilibrio") constitutes "that already" (Barthes 1970: 20) necessary for a complete decoding of the former (*:riflessi*). In this sense, the *Retro-Lector* engages in a type of reverse intertextuality when s/he resorts to "inferential walks in order to gather intertextual support" (Eco: 32) from a later text.

In modern texts such as *:riflessi*, an author's "semantic fields (*key words*)" (Eco: 26) are not always abundantly distributed (nor, for that matter, easily discernible); rather, they are "strategically located" within the text. The reader, then, must first identify such "semantic fields" as s/he proceeds in an attempt to evaluate them and reconstruct eventually the "unformulated text" (Iser: 34). Precisely for this reason, one is "obliged to look backward many times, and in general, the more complex the text, the more it has to be read twice, and the second time" not just "from the end", as Eco (21-6) states, but indeed, in certain cases as I now suggest, also retrospectively: that is from the perspective of a later work.

From the Oedipal to the Androgynous: A Desire for Completion

In "Equilibrio" (1915b: 28), Palazzeschi defines life as a "game of liar's dice" the main goal of which is to alleviate the individual of his/her "sadness". He aims his attack at social conditioning and its stifling effect on the human condition, as he calls for the assertion of an active spiritual involvement. The equation "perfection = conformity", which Palazzeschi had denounced in "Varietà" (1915a), is reflected in "Equilibrio" by a similar formula of "'equilibrio' ('balance') = social conditioning" (28; emphasis added):

> [Y]our little daddies were right, how many times they told you that you had to grow into well-*balanced* people. . . . Friends, if you grab your mother's breast, or that of your wet-nurse, with your left hand, that far-sighted mother of yours, that diligent wet-nurse, *will push it back*, perhaps with infinite sweetness, and they will make you understand, as best they can, that you *must take their breast with your right hand, and always with that one* . . . . We are all one-handed, the other we have for show. Mother, father, teacher, uncle, maid, curate, church-cleaner, doctor, *everyone, everyone against you*, with shoves or with hugs, *they will make you walk the straight and narrow path*, on that spoke of the circle which is directly in front of your nose, *making sure that you don't turn as you walk*.

Whereas for society "equilibrio" is adherence to the conventions of an already existing state, for Palazzeschi, instead, "equilibrio" constitutes 1) the ability to adjust and acclimate oneself to opposing and divergent influences, 2) a strong desire and capability to explore and experience these different forces.

Returning to *:riflessi* after having read "Equilibrio" offers the reader--i.e., the *Retro-Lector*--intertextual knowledge which better aids in the disambiguation of the novel's codes and referents. Such a construction thus requires an integration of the text's various elements. The reader's task of *:riflessi* is to gather the various bits and pieces of information scattered throughout, in order to de̲cipher that which Palazzeschi had en̲ciphered. Through a cross-referential examination of certain letters, one discovers a specific progression which brings about a positive change in Valentino's character. One also comes to understand that *:riflessi* is indeed an *outline* of what Palazzeschi was to expound eventually in "Equilibrio". For this last point, the notion of intertextuality in a broad sense comes into play, since a previous familiarity with "Equilibrio" is necessary so that the reader can pick out from the novel the salient features which lie at the base of the philosophy Palazzeschi was to expound seven years later in this manifesto. Such intertextuality is indeed a type of *reverse* intertextuality in that the reader (a *Retro-Lector*) engages in a retrospective reading of *:riflessi*.

Palazzeschi's notion of "equilibrio" is twofold in meaning. First, it rescues humanity from an urgency beyond his control--God, "paura" ("fear"); in more general terms, the individual is freed from ideological victimization. Second, it refers to the individual's ability to adjust to opposing and divergent forces (i.e., superimposed social codes of behavior thwarted by the individual's instincts), namely, his/her "mental agility". In accordance with Palazzeschi's philosophy the individual now has full rein over his/her own existence to do whatever s/he desires: how, when, and where. Palazzeschi (1915b: 31) thus fittingly concludes this final manifesto with a reaffirmation of his adhesion to the various concepts of individual freedom opposition, diversity, and, most of all, "variety" (*varietà*):

"Look, the very trees of my garden, are dressed a bit in green, a bit in red, a bit in yellow, then they're even a bit nude, just for the sake of change. It has been said that the world is like an orange. Precisely. And you're satisfied to eat a slice of it? Cucù! I'm tempted by the whole thing!"

Both Eduardo Saccone (1977) and Giuseppe Savoca (1979) consider *:riflessi* highly oedipal. A closer examination of the novel, however, demonstrates, among other things, that evidence of a strictly oedipal nature is not infallible; and in this regard one may indeed speculate otherwise. Turning back to "Equilibrio", then, one finds that Palazzeschi's notions of freedom, diversity, opposition, and the like, all aid in creating a truly *complete* individual, one who has the opportunities to experience all aspects of life. Conversely, a sense of lack lies at the base of Valentino's dilemma, and his only hope for resolution comes in the form of a mirror and a portrait of his young mother. Any type of father figure, *complementary* or *adversarial*, is absent from the novel. Indeed, it is precisely this absence which, when reading *:riflessi* with "Equilibrio" as an intertextual backdrop, affords the possibility of another interpretation: to look at the novel not necessarily within terms of the oedipal, but indeed from the perspective of androgyny--"the One which contains the Two; namely, the male (*andro-*) and the female (*gyne*)" (Singer 1976: 6). Moreover, I would substitute the notion of identification (the son with the mother = an androgynous situation) for that of possession (the son's desire for his mother = an oedipal situation). According to Aristophanes in Plato's *Symposium* (p.353BC), this is the eventual re-merging of the two original halves of the androgyne, having been previously cut in two by Zeus.[4]

The reader of *:riflessi* discovers an integration process of the male and female which ultimately results in the *healing* of Valentino's emotional state. This re-unification develops through a series of episodes involving Valentino and a portrait of his young mother, the Princess Kore. Young ("He was fourteen years old at that time and the princess was twenty-nine. Prince Valentino Kore was now exactly twenty-nine years old."), the princess seems more a peer than a mother figure. Similarly, the references made to her throughout do not demonstrate characteristics of a maternal nature.

In front of the portrait in deep contemplation, Valentino expresses an inexplicable need which transcends any physical or sexual desire. When, in fact, he is finally "guarito", we see first of all that the princess's presence did indeed "calm all his emotions in order to *reawaken the purest of feelings*" (121; emphasis added). Again, in Aristophanes's view (Plato p.353BC: 191d), this demonstrates "how far back we can trace our *innate love for one another*, and how this love is always trying to *reintegrate our former nature, to make two into one*" (emphasis added). Throughout this entire process, two important characteristics stand out. First, Valentino speaks of the princess in terms of a "sposa" ("spouse"). However, she does not embody the typical "sposa": rather, she is loved for the simple reason of being present. Secondly, the relationship between the two transcends physicality and nourishes itself of a spiritual love. It is a relationship which again recalls Plato's *Symposium* (192c-e; emphasis added):

> ... the purely sexual pleasures of their friendship could hardly account for the huge delight they take in one another's company. The fact is that both their souls are longing for a something . . . to which they can neither of them put a name, and which they can only give an inkling of in cryptic sayings and prophetic riddles. . . [S]uppose [Hephaestus] were to ask, . . . How would you like to be *rolled into one, so that you can always be together, day and night, and never be parted again*? . . . [T]hen you can live your two lives in one and, when the time comes you can die a common death and still be two in one in the lower world. . . . We may be sure, gentlemen, that . . . not one of them could imagine a happier fate. . . , *to be merged, that is, into an utter oneness with the beloved*.

Hence, the reawakening of "the purest of feelings" precisely because, as Valentino says, "She's still there, and all I have to do is turn around to see her, and when I'm in my easychair, She's in front of me, and we remain thus in an extraordinary idyll" (127). Valentino's transcendence of sexual desires is explicit in the awakening of his "purest of feelings", which, in turn, echoes Aristophanes's claim that "sexual pleasures could hardly account for the delight they take in one another's company". Likewise, Valentino's "purest of feelings", awakened by such an unusual process, recalls the androgyne's "longing for a something else . . . to which [s/he cannot] put a name." The result then, is that both instances communicate the abandonment of the ordinary for the extraordinary. Finally, Valentino's position in front of the portrait recalls Aristophanes's notion of union and oneness. We read above that "not one of them could imagine a happier fate. . . , *to be merged, that is, into an utter oneness with the beloved*". Valentino's declaration figures as a quasi-mathematical formula which, instead of rendering the equation $1 + 1 = 2$, gives rise to $1 + 1 = 1$. Closer scrutiny demonstrates the pronominality of the formula: the *I* of "I'm" plus "She" results in "we". Viewed in the original Italian context, we may indeed find supporting evidence in "mia" "mi" and "restiamo . . . in un idillio", as this final singular noun, underscored by the indefinite article, constitutes the final stroke of our hypothetical mathematician's pencil: "e quando *sono* nella *mia* poltrona *Ella mi* è dinanzi, e *noi restiamo così in un idillio* straordinario" (127).

Valentino's healing thus constitutes a merging of the male with the female. Analogous to Plato's androgyne, he is healed only once he is re-united with his other half; that is, once the re-unification process has been completed. Turning again to "Equilibrio", one sees that in Palazzeschian terms "equilibrio" is synonymous to totality or completion. Considering, now at this point, the relationship between Palazzeschi's first novel of 1908 and his last manifesto of 1915, the notion of retrospective reading vis-à-vis such a relationship proves to be a valid interpretive process indeed. The notion of androgyny as, among other possibilities, a metaphor for completion becomes apparent only once one reads "Equilibrio" and uses it as a backdrop for the further disambiguation of the seemingly arbitrary and ambiguous signs, codes, and referents Palazzeschi adopted in :riflessi. Valentino's healing, his desire to become one, is, to be sure, an antecedent, if not anticipation, of Palazzeschi's later, more apparent notion of completion which one perceives in "Equilibrio". Appropriate, therefore, seem his concluding words to the manifesto: "It has been said that the world is like an orange. Precisely. And you're satisfied to eat a slice of it? Cucù! I'm tempted by the whole thing!" (31).

NOTES

[1] This paper constitutes the first part of a larger study devoted to the notion of a *Retro-Lector* and a re-evaluation of Palazzeschi's *:riflessi*; which, in turn, constitute part of a greater work in progress dedicated to *opera* of other non-canonical Italian writers. In this paper, all translations from the Italian are my own.

[2] This notion first appeared (then, *modern reader*) in Tamburri (1986), now modified in Tamburri (1989?). The term *Retro-Lector* grew out of my discussion of this reading process with Professor Dinda L. Gorlèe. Analogies to this reading process may be found in Lotman's (1971: 285) notion of text and Riffaterre's (1978: 5-6, 90-91) retroactive reader.

[3] For more on this notion of a "unidirectional 'current'" of influence, see Morgan (1985).

[4] Considering the oedipal component in the novel a false, superficial metaphor, Stefanini (1980) stated: "For Oedipus I would almost substitute *Hermaphrodite*. More than a return to his mother, I see his identification with her, the merging of Valentino and the beautiful *femme fatal* (in the oval portrait-mirror he finally contemplates his true image. The princess was Valentino and Valentino is the princess (104: 'It is she!,' better yet 'It is I!' or 'I'm her!')". Stefanini's comments, as he has also stated in conversation, recall other works by Palazzeschi of this period; the mirror, for instance, is an obvious *pre/inter*text of the poem "Lo specchio".

REFERENCES

BARTHES, Roland.
    1970. *S/Z* (Paris: Éditions du Seuil). Page references are to the English trans. by Richard Miller (New York: Hill & Wang, 1975).
CHATMAN, Seymour.
    1978. *Story and Discourse: Narrative Structure in Fiction and Film* (Ithaca: Cornell University Press).

ECO, Umberto.
  1979. *The Role of the Reader: Explorations in the Semiotics of Texts* (Bloomington: Indiana University Press).
ISER, Wolfgang.
  1972. *Der implizite leser: Kommunikationsformen des Romans von Bunyon bis Beckett* (Munich: Wilhelm Funk). Page references are to Iser's English trans. *The Implied Reader: Patterns of Communication in Prose Fiction from Bunyon to Beckett* (Baltimore: Johns Hopkins University Press, 1974)
LOTMAN, Jurij.
  1971. *Struktura khudozhestvennogo teksta* (Moscow). Page references are to the English trans. *The Structure of the Artistic Text* (= *Michigan Slavic Contributions*, No. 7) by Gail Lenhoff and Ronald Vroon (Ann Arbor, MI: Department of Slavic Languages and Literature, University of Michigan, 1977).
MORGAN, Thaïs E.
  1985. "Is there an Intertext in this Text?: Literary and Interdisciplinary Approaches to Intertextuality", *American Journal of Semiotics* 3.4, 1-40.
PALAZZESCHI, Aldo.
  1908. *:riflessi* (Florence: Cesare Blanc).
  1915a. "Variety", *Lacerba* 3.1, 5-7.
  1915b. "Equilibrio", *Lacerba*. 28-31.
PLATO.
  p. 353BC.*Symposium*, in *The Collected Dialogues of Plato, Including the Letters* ed. Edith Hamilton and Huntington Cairns (New York: Pantheon, 1961).
RIFFATERRE, Michael.
  1978. *Semiotics of Poetry* (Bloomington: Indiana University Press).
SACCONE, Eduardo.
  1977. "*Alleg(o)ria di Novembre*: La sublimazione imperfetta di Aldo Palazzeschi" *Modern Language Notes* 92, 79-116.
SAVOCA, Giuseppe.
  1979. *Eco e Narciso: La ripetizione nel primo Palazzeschi* (Palermo: Flaccovio Editore).
SINGER, June.
  1976. *Androgyny: Toward a New Theory of Sexuality* (New York: Anchor Press).
STEFANINI, Ruggiero.
  1980. Unpublished letter to Anthony J. Tamburri (23 March).
TAMBURRI, Anthony J.
  1986. "Palazzeschi's *Il codice di Perelà*: Breaking the Code", *Italica* 63.4, 361-380.
  1989?. *Of* Saltimbanchi *and* Incendiari: *Aldo Palazzeschi and Avant-Gardism in Italy* (in press; Madison, NJ: Fairleigh Dickinson University Press).

SAINT-LOUP AND THE WHITE RABBIT: INTERTEXUAL FICTION AND REALITY

Eva Tsuquiashi-Daddesio
Slippery Rock University

The textual construction in Proust's *A la recherche du temps perdu* (1927) exploits a set of complex and disguised relationships between the mimetic and the purely scriptural aspects of writing. The first appears in its linear development as the production of a fictional world based on the possibility of a singular referential construct whereas the second emerges in the organization of the graphic material in such a way that it negates the possibility of transparent mimesis by producing myriad fragmentary but related effects on the signification system. The only remaining reality becomes then the depths of the surface of the written page where "Ecrire, c'est peut-être amener à la surface quelque chose comme du sens absent" (Blanchot, 1980: 71) [Writing, consists perhaps in bringing to the surface something like an absent meaning].

The description of the character named Robert de Saint-Loup in Proust's text provides a particularly fruitful segment because it will allow us to explore the complexity of this semiotic system in an embedded framework that duplicates and underscores the global structure of the novel. This framework is based on a certain number of correspondences between Proust's text and a specific passage from Lewis Carroll's *Alice's Adventures in Wonderland* that establish Proust's segment as a metamorphosis of Carroll's. This basic relationship is then developed as a stratification of co-existing levels of signification.

The passage constituting our point of departure is the description of the first encounter in *La Recherche* between an almost magical Robert de Saint-Loup and Marcel, the narrator-protagonist, during a hot summer day near the beach (Proust, 1927: 552):

> One afternoon of scorching heat ... I saw, tall, slender, his head held proudly erect upon a springing neck, a young man go past with searching eyes, whose skin was as fair and whose hair as golden as if they had absorbed all the rays of the sun. Dressed in a clinging, almost white material such as I could never have believed that any man would have the audacity to wear, the thinness of which suggested no less vividly than the coolness of the dining-room the heat and brightness of the glorious day outside, he was walking fast. His eyes, from one of which a monocle kept dropping, were of the colour of the

sea . . . . One felt that this so special quality of his hair, his eyes, his skin, his figure, which would have marked him out in a crowd like a precious vein of opal, azure-shot and luminous, embedded in a mass of coarser substance, must correspond to a life different from that led by other men.

As for the embedded inscription of Carroll's text in this paragraph from "Within a Budding Grove" ["A l'ombre des jeunes filles en fleurs"], the following passage from Lewis Carroll's *Alice* proves to be the disguised source (Carroll, 1865: 15):

So she was considering, in her mind (as well as she could, for the hot day made her feel very sleepy and stupid), whether the pleasure of making a daisy chain would be worth the trouble of getting up and picking the daisies, when suddenly a White Rabbit with pink eyes ran close by her. There was nothing so *very* remarkable in that; (. . .) but, when the Rabbit actually *took a watch out its waistcoat-pocket*, and looked at it, and then hurried on, Alice started to her feet, ...

We will start then, by pointing out all the correspondences between this segment and Proust's depiction of Robert de Saint-Loup. To begin with, the general context in both cases is extraordinarily similar. They both tell the story of a first meeting between a protagonist and a character that she or he follows. Both Carroll's Alice and Proust's Marcel are shown in scenes where they are motionless images during a hot summer day when quite unexpectedly they are witnesses to the passage of an arresting appearance. From this point on, the characters described in each text correspond to radically different referents, since one is supposed to be a rabbit and the other a human being. However, the coincidence of the elements chosen to render the description of each character produces a more precise level of identification between Proust's text and Carroll's. In regards to the purely mimetic aspect, the physical appearance of Robert de Saint-Loup is presented as a series of variations from Carroll's text. First, the whiteness that Marcel observes in a young man "Dressed in a clinging, almost white material" (Proust 1927), reminds the reader of the "White Rabbit" that Alice sees. Second, the color of the eyes: Saint-Loup's are "of the colour of the sea", the White Rabbit has "pink eyes". Third, there is "the monocle" that "kept dropping" from Robert's eyes whose round shape, size, and usage brings to mind the White Rabbit holding and looking at a pocket watch ("the Rabbit actually took a watch out of its waistcoat-pocket"). Fourth, Robert's rapid gait (which later on becomes the only identifying element of his presence) is also isolated in Carroll's text in the sentence "a White Rabbit . . . ran close by her" (Carroll 1865). Finally, a fifth identifying element is related to Proust's choice of the character's name: Saint-Loup where "Loup" designates a "wolf" thus linking in a chiasmatic image the depiction of a human being borrowing the characteristics of a fictitious animal with the depiction of a fictitious animal, namely Carroll's "White Rabbit", that displays human characteristics.

This list of resembling narrative details constitutes however, only the most superficial level of associations that a textual metamorphosis can achieve as a repetitive constructive device. The powerful creative possibilities of repetition as a writing technique appear only in the particular developments generated by these intertextual relationships. In this regard, the rules of text production as they have been proposed by Michael Riffaterre (1978) will help us introduce the signification process in Proust's text. Riffaterre's concept of "overdetermination" accounts for the existence of superimposed scriptural structures that produce the intertextual system of signification. In this particular text, "overdetermination" appears in the form of synecdochic figures whose functions are twofold. They set in motion a progressive evacuation of referential meaning by designating gradually reduced shapes, however, in so doing they produce a paradigmatic, discontinuous narrative that fits Riffaterre's concept of "expansion". This expansion creates in its turn, a subversive and catachrestic image stemming from the displaced meaning in the synecdoches that fits Riffaterre's notion of "conversion". This last notion is particularly useful in the sense that it points to the transformational power of this process that will help to account for a complete reversal in meaning. Thus, in Proust's text, the cloaked presence of Lewis Carroll's White Rabbit creates, at an implicit level, a puzzling distortion of the image of Robert de Saint-Loup where the almost mythical male figure represented at the linear surface is doubled by homosexual aspects represented by synecdochic structures creating a humorous catachrestic displacement.

Homosexuality is thus a pertinent undercurrent element in the texts compared. Psychoanalytical studies of Lewis Carroll's life and works have shown repressed, and socially unacceptable erotic tendencies. As for the representation of Saint-Loup in Proust's novel, the explicit text of another segment of the proposed description ostensibly suggests a concealed homosexuality in the sentence: "some even thought him effeminate, though without attaching any stigma, for everyone knew how manly he was and that he was a passionate 'womaniser'" (Proust, 1927: 552). This contradictory suggestion becomes then a divergent signifying thread that guides the reader through a concealed system of signification that can be read in the dissimulated inscription of Carroll's text and that appears as a tragicomical dimension superimposed on the mythical Robert de Saint-Loup.

Saint-Loup's synecdochic representation is gradually established by a progressive reification introduced by a series of metonymic relationships between the character and his surroundings that are designed to produce a number of optical effects. The first element is the light that Saint-Loup absorbs "all the rays of the sun", like the black box of a camera capturing an image; the second, his slenderness which evokes contradictory elements like "the coolness of the dining-room", and "the heat and brightness of the glorious day outside", the inside as well as the outside, freshness as well as warmth; a third element, his eyes, reflect the color of the sea close by. This transformation of Saint-Loup into an optical instrument produces then a synesthetic relationship with the surrounding nature. It also starts a process of reification that takes the shape of a petrification, when Saint-Loup is compared to a "precious vein of opal, azure-shot and luminous". This new metamorphosis repeats certain elements evoked by the metonymic relationships but introduces also new elements that more distinctly announce the synecdochic images that will follow. The "luminous opal", that Saint-Loup becomes refers then, not only to a layer of the earth's crust in which the character disappears again, thus introducing the idea of petrification, but also to a particular type of stone that reiterates essential aspects of the synesthetic description in relation to the surface of the earth. The opal reflects the solar spectre by absorbing its light as Saint-Loup does with "the rays of the sun", in a stone whose name evokes both the words "opaque", and "pale", suggesting at the same time the darkness and light necessary to the function of a photographic camera. Furthermore, the white-bluish tones of the opal repeat the extraordinary whiteness of Saint-Loup's clothes as well as the color of his eyes that reflect the color of the sea.

Through the opal, Saint-Loup appears then in a synecdochic figure as a beautifully petrified white and transparent image. The characteristics of this image facilitate then a further reduction and displacement of the character into an optical instrument in the word "monocle" appearing in the segment "his eyes, from one of which a monocle kept dropping". This image is particularly important because it constitutes as we shall see, a turning point in the glorifying depiction of Saint-Loup. In this segment, the word "monocle" establishes the first distinctive link to the Carrollien text because the White Rabbit, all dressed up and carrying a pocket watch, constitutes precisely the first incongruous and startling image as does the falling "monocle" in the description of Robert de Saint-Loup. This intertextual link is strengthened by Saint-Loup's own name, since a slight variation transforms the wolf in "Loup" into "loupe", a magnifying glass in French, thus achieving the synecdochic metamorphosis of the character into the "monocle" he carries. This displacement is explicitly suggested elsewhere in the text, when one character mispronounces Saint-Loup's name and calls him "Saint-Loupe" (Proust 1927, 268). Furthermore, "loupe" happens to be also a feminine noun, thus reinforcing the series of concealed allusions to homosexuality.

The "monocle" as a synecdochic image of Saint-Loup constitutes then the point of departure of the series of catachrestic effects originated by the etymological displacements that are established in relation to Carroll's intertext. To begin with, this word in French as in English comes from the latin "monoculus" where "mono" means single and "oculus" eye. This connotation immediately brings to mind the single-eye of the monstrous Cyclops, in an image that clashes with Robert's beauty. Furthermore, an anagrammatic reading reveals at the same time "oculus" and "culus", bottom, that becomes "cul" in French. The importance of these associations become clear when one discovers a similar play under the latin form of the word "rabbit" in the intertext. Thus, the word "cuniculus" that overtly designates an animal whose reproductive performance is a symbol of fertility conceals and exposes anagrammatically at the same time "cunnus" the female sex as well as "culus" suggesting the fertile and the infertile alternatives to sexual intercourse, heterosexuality and homosexuality which happen to be the two aspects that define the existence of the character of Robert de Saint-Loup throughout Proust's novel.

More importantly however, Saint-Loup's "monocle" and the White Rabbit's "pocket-watch" embody a couple of pivotal and illuminating associations for the interpretation of Proust's text. On the one hand, the "monocle" functions as one of the many optical instruments (Shattuck 1963) that can be found throughout *La recherche* that suggest at the same time the obscurity of the object to be seen and an emphasis on seeing in a particular way suggested by allusions to underground treasures (1116). The intertextual construction produces as we have just seen, the progressive transformation of Robert de Saint-Loup into the optical instrument, then into Time in the shape of the White Rabbit's "pocket-watch" in the same way Proust considers his book "serving merely as a magnifying glass" (1113) to a text whose existence is closely linked to a particular idea of Time (1120).

On the other hand, the construction of the paradoxical Saint-Loup as an exemplary heterosexual but living as an underground homosexual serves to mirror the development of the whole text. The life story of Saint-Loup up to his premature death as a hero definitely buries his homosexuality to the world and it coincides with the long account of a frustrated literary vocation, but paradoxically constituted by the product we, as readers, have in our hands. We know then that the literary work has been written as Marcel knows about Saint-Loup's homosexuality. Saint-Loup's death seems to trigger the resignation of Marcel to failure as a writer by finishing the seclusion of the artist that the reader sees attending the Matinée de Guermantes (983). Nonetheless, this episode constitutes the beginning of the process leading to the discovery of the possibility of writing precisely through an unexpected, although displaced turn to Saint-Loup's homosexuality. The magic possibility of the artistic recovery of all moments lost in Time finally appears to Marcel in the image of Saint-Loup's daughter, who resembles so much her father that for him "the soul of that Guermantes was gone, but the charming head of the departed bird, with its piercing eyes, had come and taken its place on the shoulders of Melle. de Saint-Loup" (1112), thus exposing, posthumously, the feminine side he hid all his life. Significantly enough, Marcel's contemplation of this reincarnation of Saint-Loup, constitutes the last narrative image of the text and functions as a living metaphor of the possibility of his work of art in the sentence "Time, colorless and impalpable, had, in order that I might, as it were, see and touch it, physically embodied itself in her and had moulded her like a work of art" (1112). The importance of the notion of Time in relation to this development reinforces the one to the Carrollian rabbit.

Proust's writing is thus a recognition of the way reality is shaped by words in the literary work. However, as Leo Bersani recognizes in *Marcel Proust, the Fictions of Life and Art*, more than that "the very point of Proust's novel would seem to be to destroy the illusions novelists usually seek to cultivate" (1965: 247) since the "narrator himself presents his work both as a faithful report on his past and as an exercise of pure invention". The textual reality of Proust's work appears then as the recognition of the impotence of words to recover a pure referent in the past but of its power to build a new, complex and magical one. This reality becomes then "l'espace ouvert à la 'théorie fictive', là où la théorie, par la fiction, entre en danger de mort" (Blanchot, 1980: 73) [the space that opens to 'fictive theory', where theory, through fiction, runs the danger of death]. In *La Recherche* the space of that danger is made up of the multiplicity of non-referential images that words can convey in a scriptural dimension of Time.

REFERENCES

BERSANI, Leo.
    1965.   *Marcel Proust: The Fictions of Life and of Art* (New York: Oxford University Press).
BLANCHOT, Maurice.
    1980.   *L'écriture du désastre* (Paris: Gallimard). All translations are mine.
CARROLL, Lewis.
    1865.   *Alice's Adventures in Wonderland*, *The Complete Works of Lewis Carroll* (London: The Nonesuch Press, 1966).
PHILLIPS, Robert, ed.
    1971.   *Aspects of Alice*, "Lewis Carroll's Dreamchild as seen through the critics' looking-glasses" (New York: The Vanguard Press, Inc.) 279-373 ("Freudian Interpretations").
PROUST, Marcel.
    1927.   *A la recherche du temps perdu* (Paris: La Nouvelle Revue Française). Page references in the present article are to the English edition, trans. C. K. Scott Moncrieff and Frederick A. Blossom, *Remembrance of Things Past*, (New York: Random House, 1934).
RIFFATERRE, Michael.
    1978.   *Semiotics of Poetry* (Bloomington: Indiana University Press).
SHATTUCK, Roger.
    1963.   *Proust's Binoculars* (New York: Random House).

XI

LITERARY SEMIOTICS: DISCOURSE ANALYSIS

THE ROLE OF THE PARATEXT IN *THE NAME OF THE ROSE*

Thomas C. Daddesio
College of St. Benedict

In recent years, critics and theorists have taken a keen interest in what Gérard Genette (1981, 1987) has called the paratext, that is the ensemble of utterances (titles, prefaces and epilogues) that constitute the thresholds through which we enter and exit literary works. This morning I will attempt to demonstrate that the functioning of the paratext in *The Name of the Rose* (Eco 1980) justifies this lavish attention. Although it is not always a simple matter to say where the text ends and the paratext begins, I will suggest that Adso's narration of the events in the monastery be considered the main text; the paratexts that I will be studying are the translator's preface (1-5) that opens the novel and Adso's "Last Page" (495-502) that ends it. These choices are certainly not free from challenge. Some would no doubt contend that Adso's epilogue is actually part of the main text, since it is narrated by the same voice that relates the terrible events that took place in the monastery. Others would probably point out that the main body of Adso's story is not only followed by the section called the "Last Page"; it is also preceded by a "Prologue" (9-18) penned by Adso. Would it, then, not be more appropriate to focus on these two sections? Although a detailed response to this question would exceed the scope of this paper, let me present two reasons for my choice. The first reason is that the translator's preface and Adso's "Last Page" display typical paratextual functions in that they suggest how the main text should be read and what meaning the reader should attach to the narrated events. Furthermore, despite their obvious differences, these paratexts compliment each other. Whereas the translator's preface constitutes a search for the origin of the work, Adso's epilogue seeks its ultimate meaning. Both attempt to ground Adso's tale on an authority that is situated outside the text itself. Thus, I would argue that from a functional point of view, Adso's "Last Page" is paired off with the translator's preface rather than with his own "Prologue".

I

The *Name of the Rose* begins with a preface written by the "translator" of Abbé Vallet's 19th century French translation of Mabillon's edition of a 14th century manuscript of one Adso of Melk. Although this preface contains several references that encourage us to identify the translator with Eco himself, few readers are truly taken in by the ploy, preferring to conclude that Eco is simply following, though with an obvious touch of facetiousness, the time-honored tradition of authenticating fictional events by appealing to the authority of a manuscript written by a witness to said events. Nonetheless, Eco adds a twist to this familiar scenario by endowing his translator with an acute sense of erudition that compels him to attempt to confirm the authenticity of the manuscript. As a conscientious erudite, our fictional translator first goes to the monastery of Melk where he finds no sign of Adso's text. Next he tracks down the *Vetera Analecta*, the alleged source of Adso's tale, but the edition held by the Bibliothèque de Sainte Geneviève does not contain Adso's text. Then he seeks out the Abbaye de la Source, the publisher of Vallet's translation, only to discover that no such book had been published there. Just when he is about to give up all hope of ever finding a trace of Adso's manuscript, he discovers in Buenos Aires a Spanish translation of Milo Temesvar's *On the Use of Mirrors in the Game of Chess* that quotes Adso's manuscript at length. However, Temesvar's source is neither Vallet nor Mabillon, but rather a certain father Kircher whom, the translator has it on good sources, never wrote of Adso of Melk. Our translator's quest for the original manuscript has come full circle; what began as a quest for certainty ends with a set of mutually contradicting clues. For every clue that points to the existence of Adso's manuscript, there is one that suggests that it never did exist. In the end, he is not able to determine whether Adso's tale was a true story or simply the invention of a devious novelist. What seems to be the point here is that we can never recover an original meaning that somehow preceded and was the cause of the text; we can only detect the traces left by the text and on the text as it passed through different hands. Since the authority of erudition is ultimately grounded on our ability to distinguish between original manuscripts and frauds, the inability of Eco's fictional translator to make this distinction constitutes an initial breach in the belief in the univocality of meaning. In this light, the reference to Mabillon takes on a special irony since one of the major contributions of the celebrated Benedictine scholar was his work on the authentication and the dating of medieval manuscripts.

The other paratext that I want to focus on is Adso's "Last Page" which is composed of three temporally distinct segments. The first segment tells of the immediate aftermath of the fire that devastated the monastery and its library. The next segment records Adso's return many years later to the ruins of the monastery where he assembles the remains of the once majestic library. It will be these fragments that will inspire Adso's narration of the events he witnessed. The third segment evokes, as he nears death, Adso's reflections on the meaning of those events. At the center of this last section are the fragments and the desire for transcendent meaning that they unleash. Adso writes "Mine was a poor harvest, but I spent a whole day reaping it, as if from those disiecta membra of the library a message might reach me" (500). All that Adso observed in that monastery, murder, heresy, inquisition and the burning of books, was so patently senseless, so devoid of meaning, so inconsistent with the idea of a benevolent divine plan for humanity, that he could only hope that the discovery of some hidden, transcendent meaning could restore order to the universe. However, in the final analysis, instead of succeeding in gaining access to this higher plane of reality, Adso is unable to determine "whether the letter he has written contains some hidden meaning, or more than one, or many, or none at all" (501). Thus Adso's attempts to find transcendental meaning in the events he witnessed and in his own discourse proves to be illusory and his tale closes not with a burst of illumination but rather upon blindness, silence, and death.

Before proceeding any further, let us draw a preliminary conclusion. Both paratexts are characterized by a desire to ground the validity of Adso's tale on an outside authority, either its origin or its ultimate meaning. Each attempts to frame Adso's tale so as to place it on solider, more credible grounds. This process can be viewed as one that seeks to center Adso's discourse, one that would provide it with a stable focal point from which the heterogenous elements that compose it could be read in a coherent fashion. However, in each case, the quest for interpretative authority proves to be futile and Adso's tale is left to stand by itself.

II

At this point, I would like to consider these paratexts as they relate to the rest of the novel. In *Naming the Rose*, her recent study of Eco's novel, one of Theresa Coletti's (1988) major theses concerns the omnipresence of the theme of the indeterminacy of meaning. Coletti traces this theme in Adso's experience with the language of love, the meaning of heresy and the transgressive effects of laughter. In each of these instances, the question of the interpretation of texts and reality is posed explicitly and in each case the novel undermines the logocentric belief in simple, univocal meaning. Probably the most succinct expression of this theme is to be found in the passage just quoted where Adso admits his inability to know whether the fragments of the library, the events he observed or his narration of those events possess a single meaning, several meanings or none at all. This critique of the univocality of meaning is not simply that a given text can be interpreted in different ways; the stronger claim that is being urged here is that we have no way of knowing in any absolute sense whether a given text possesses meaning that can be isolated so as to give rise to an interpretation.

Coletti also studies how the structure of the novel, its title and the author's disavowals of authorial autonomy make manifest the idea of the indeterminacy of meaning. The sort of functioning that we have just detected in the paratexts takes part in this general strategy. On the basis of these considerations, the view of *The Name of the Rose* that recommends itself is that of an eminently self-reflexive novel where each level presents the notion of the indeterminacy of meaning. What could be more satisfying than for a reading to yield the very same conclusion as it questions the different aspects of a text. While there is no doubt that Eco's novel persistently challenges the univocality of meaning and that this theme arguably furnishes the grounds for its unity, it is my contention that this theme unleashes transgressive forces that the novel's self-reflective frame can not contain and that the paratext constitutes a crucial point in this conflict. The question that we must pose is that of the relation between the novel's thematics and the frame that presents it.

To gain a clearer understanding of this problematic, I would like to consider these two paratexts in light of Derrida's conception of the parergon. In *La Vérité en peinture*, Derrida's (1978) reflections take as their point of departure a passage from Kant's third Critique where it is question of the ornamental accessories to works of art. Kant's three examples of parerga are the frames of paintings, the clothing of statues and the columns of buildings. By definition, a parergon is an accessory, detachable addition to the work of art, in sum, a supplement. But as Derrida has demonstrated time and time again, the nature of supplements is never simple. The parergon is detachable, but that does not mean that it can be considered negligible. In its own way, the parergon is an intrinsic component of the ergon, the work, because it is called to remedy a lack within the ergon. If the work were complete in and of itself, there would be no need for the parergon. Thus, by its very presence the parergon reveals what is absent, what the work lacks.

The question to be raised now is to what extent do the paratexts of Eco's novel participate in the logic of the parergon. If the primary function of the parergon is to respond to a lack within the ergon, then we must determine what is it that constitutes the lack within *The Name of the Rose*. In addition to whatever lacks characterize literary works in general, I would argue that the unity of Eco's novel is undermined by the very theme that would seem to unify it, that is the theme of the indeterminacy of meaning. Any text that claims that meaning is indeterminate undermines in the same gesture its authority to make such a claim. The supreme irony is that Eco's novel runs the risk of being engulfed by the very heresy that it is advocating. If meaning is indeterminate, then on what grounds are we to recognize the authority of the discourse that makes that claim. When we apply the message of Eco's text to the discourse that articulates that message, we lose all reason to accept that message in its unproblematic transparency. Thus, we seem to be faced with a variation of the Liar's Paradox. In order to be convinced of the truth of the claim that the meaning of Eco's novel is that meaning is indeterminate, we need a reason to believe that there can be a single, unambiguous interpretation of the novel, something which Eco goes to great lengths to withhold. If it were possible to draw a conclusion from such an unstable constellation of meanings, it would be that there is simply no way to insulate a discourse that makes this claim from the transgressive effects of the principle that it is announcing.

We can now suggest that the lack that the paratexts of *The Name of the Rose* are responding to is the abyss that the theme of the indeterminacy of meaning opens within the novel. The quest for the true origin or for a divine ultimate meaning of Adso's tale can be read as the gestures of a nostalgia for unambiguous and authoritative meaning. Such gestures, if they were to prove to be successful, would confer upon Adso's narrative a unique status as a text whose meaning be would solidly grounded and, thereby, protected from indeterminacy. These paratexts would then seem to hold some hope for containing the forces that menace interpretation. However, by dint of their failure to remedy the lack that makes them necessary, they merely stand as signs of the fundamental incompleteness of Eco's text. We now see the paradox of the parergon: in that it can not remedy the lack of the text that it is appended to, the parergon can only reveal the presence of this lack. By their very presence, these paratexts point to the inability of Adso's tale to stand by itself; by their failure to ground or center it, they demonstrate that this lack is irreducible.

Let us return one more time to Coletti's reading of *The Name of the Rose*. The above comments should not be construed as implying that her reading of this novel is mistaken and the present reading somehow gained access to the truth of this text. All I wish to bring to light is how Coletti, like many other readers of Eco's novel, glosses over the implications of the themes that her reading discovers. The discursive chain that we have been considering is the following: Coletti's text says that Eco's text says that meaning is indeterminate. Rather than tracing the effects of indeterminacy as it contaminates each of the successive links in this chain, Coletti attempts to place a frame around Eco's text that would keep transgression in its place, that is subordinated to the discourse that announces it. From this perspective, Eco's text is about transgression, but it remains surprising resistant to its effects. Furthermore, the transgressive forces that the writing of this novel sets in motion do not stop at the outer limits of the text, if it were possible to define such limits. These forces can not be enclosed within a discourse that admits to being fiction and be denied entry to the discursive space of criticism that would aspire to truth. The effects of indeterminacy do not respect the boundaries between theory and literature. Thus, the frame that Coletti's reading places around *The Name of the Rose* is not only powerless to stop the authority of Eco's discourse from being questioned, it has at the same time no power to prevent the authority of her own discourse from succumbing to the same forces.

This brings me to the status of the present discourse. I have attempted to provide a glimpse of a certain interplay between text and critic, between literature and theory, but, in doing so, I have allowed myself to make a certain number of categorical statements that appeal ultimately to the possibility of univocal meaning. However, it should be clear by now that the text that I have presented this morning is not exempt from the effects of indeterminacy that have been detected in Eco's novel and Coletti's commentary. The frame of certainty that I have constructed around their texts can and should be questioned at its turn. Such a process of unlimited semiosis would seem then to lead to an infinite regress that at each moment would take us farther and farther away from stable and certain meaning. Reading would seem to have come to an impasse that would make a novel like Eco's literally unreadable. But perhaps it is only unreadable if we continue to conceive reading as it has been conceived up until the present time. Let us entertain the possibility that the very experience of unreadablity could create an opportunity for reading and conceiving reading differently. A passage from Derrida's "Living on/Borderlines" makes this point cogently. Here Derrida (1979: 116) is speaking of the title of Blanchot's *L'Arrêt de Mort*.

> If reading means making accessible a meaning that can be transmitted as such, in its own unequivocal, translatable meaning, then this title is unreadable. But this unreadability does not arrest reading, does not leave it paralyzed in the face of an opaque surface; rather, it starts reading and writing and translation moving again. The unreadable is not the opposite of the readable but rather the ridge (arête) that also gives it momentum, movement, sets it in motion.

This passage does not offer a simple resolution of the conflicts created by the indeterminacy of meaning. Such a resolution would only subjugate us once again to rule of univocality.

REFERENCES

COLETTI, Teresa.
    1988.   *Naming the Rose* (Ithaca: Cornell University).
DERRIDA, Jacques.
    1978.   *La Vérité en peinture* (Paris: Flammarion).
    1979.   "Survivre". Page references are to the English trans. by James Hulbert, "Living On: Borderlines" in Harold Bloom, et al., *Deconstuction and Criticism* (New York: Seabury Press), 75-176.
ECO, Umberto.
    1980.   *Il Nome della Rosa* (Milan: Bonpiani). Pages references are to the English trans. by William Weaver *The Name of the Rose* (New York: Harcourt Brace Jovanovich, 1983).
GENETTE, Gérard
    1981.   *Palimpsestes*. (Paris: Seuil).
    1987.   *Seuils*. (Paris: Seuil).

ROTPETER'S REVENGE: KAFKA'S "REPORT TO AN ACADEMY" AS CRITIQUE OF ANTHROPOCENTRISM[1]

R. Lane Kauffmann
Rice University

Wittgenstein claimed (i.1936-1949: 223) that if a lion could speak, we could not understand him. Even if animals could manipulate a verbal code, the gap between their life-world and ours would still be unbridgeable (Palmer 1984: 145-46). But the thought-experiment need not end there. One may extend the counterfactual premise and ask, what if a lion could speak and we *could* understand him? Such is the enabling premise of the genre of the animal tale. Granting animals the power of speech by fiat, this genre is a language-game in which we imagine ourselves eavesdropping on the otherness of the other (as though speech could somehow be given without disturbing that alterity). Yet, as though to confirm Wittgenstein's point that we are unable to imagine animals using language in a nonhuman way, animal tales commonly anthropomorphize the beast, making it the mouthpiece of human desires and emotions. Not surprisingly, such tales show us less about animals than about that other strange species, *Homo sapiens*. From Aesop's fables to Kafka's animal stories, the genre has worked to explore the human condition by defamiliarizing it, imagining it from a nonhuman perspective (Schwarz 1986: 82).

The genre draws its ideological resonance from the deep ambivalence felt by humans toward other animals (especially primates). Do they represent inferior, once rival, species, to be used as needed for our food, experiments and pleasure? Or are they our own ancestors, primitive versions of ourselves? Heidegger speaks of the "abyss" separating us from other living creatures, and of our "appalling and scarcely conceivable bodily kinship with the beast" (1947: 206). We sense a great distance between them and us, and yet--they are too close for comfort. Since Darwin, we are forced to entertain the hypothesis, if not accept as fact, that when we see an ape we are observing ourselves at an earlier stage of evolution. No wonder we are both amused and put off by the notion of talking simians (witness the *Planet of the Apes* films).

On the other hand, this very "abyss"--the apparent impossibility of interspecies dialogue--makes the thought-experiment enacted by the animal tale an appropriate symbol and limit case of the hermeneutical problems which we encounter in human interaction. The presumed speechlessness of animals enables them to function allegorically as substitutes for voiceless or dispossessed others in human experience: slaves vs. masters, "primitive" vs. "civilized", oral vs. text-literate cultures (the possibilities multiply). By the same token, anthropocentrism in the animal tale becomes a trope for centric or universalizing discourse in general.

Insofar as Kafka's story, "Report to an Academy" (1917), purports to depict interspecies communication--or more precisely, the partial accommodation of an ape to a human language and life-world--it may be regarded as a dialogical experiment which attempts to go beyond anthropocentrism. It thus anticipates recent experiments in ethnography, in which the informant is allowed to speak in person, to appear as subject rather than as mere object of discourse (Marcus and Fischer 1986: 67-73). What sets "Report" apart from the traditional animal tale is, among other things, the fact that in this story, the animal's possession of language is not simply presupposed, but is internally justified. The narrator tells how he, an ape, came to acquire consciousness and the power of speech. This highlights, and allows the interpreter to focus on, the semiotic processes by which the "other" is constituted in the tale. From the outset, we find ourselves, as readers, among the ape's audience--an Academy to whom he makes a report. We are told how he came to be wounded and captured by hunters, why he took the trouble to acquire human language, and how he attained "the cultural level of an average European." The premise of the story is that of Darwinian evolution at fast forward, of phylogeny telescoped onto ontogeny; the premise that in a single lifetime, an ape has become humanized, become *like us*--at least to the point of being able to discuss his differences with us. Except for the initial shock of the premise that we are listening to an ape's monologue--and the residual difficulty of suspending disbelief--the narrative structure of the tale is rather conventional, resembling that of a first-person *Bildungsroman* (novel of education).

But in Kafka's "Report", the truly "other" is not the educated ape, but the savage one, prior to speech; and *this* other--who is the most interesting to the Academy--is unfortunately inaccessible, as Rotpeter himself (to use the ape's given name) points out. He begins his report with the caveat that he cannot fully comply with the Academy's request to give an account of his former life as an ape: the price he has had to pay for his transformation has been the forgetting of his origins. "In revenge, . . . my memory has closed the door against me more and more." The past has become inaccessible; the "opening" through which he might once have returned has narrowed irretrievably. The call of the wild, once a "strong wind", is now only a "gentle puff" wafting about his heels. Rotpeter does not hesitate to remind the august audience of their shared origin: "Your life as apes, gentlemen, insofar as something of that kind lies behind you, cannot be further removed from you than mine is from me. Yet everyone on earth feels a tickling at the heels; the small chimpanzee and the great Achilles alike." Rotpeter regrets that he has been charged with conveying "what with the best will in the world I cannot communicate"; he can only "indicate the line an erstwhile ape has had to follow in entering and establishing himself in the world of men." And he returns to this topos of limited expressibility, noting that "what I felt then as an ape I can represent now only in human terms, and therefore I misrepresent it, but although I cannot reach back to the truth of the old ape life, there is no doubt that it lies somewhere in the direction I have indicated." Kafka cannily suggests that there is no unmediated access to the ape's past; that otherness is mediated by the ape's fallible memory and by the opacity of an alien medium-- human language.

It is now generally accepted that the primary intended target of Kafka's satire in this tale was the historical phenomenon of Jewish assimilation into the mainstream of European bourgeois society (Rubinstein 1952; Kauf 1954; and Robertson 1985: 164-71). The ape's abandonment of his origins and early remembrances, his adaptation through abject mimicry of his captors, and his refusal of sentimentality combine to form an astute and poignant criticism of this phenomenon--a criticism which lets neither the assimilating Jews nor the imitated Gentiles off the hook. But the tale has other levels of meaning. Implicit in Rotpeter's report to an academy is Kafka's parody of the rhetoric of contemporary science (for a more thoroughgoing parody of scientific rhetoric, see his "Investigations of a Dog"). Kafka wrote when Darwin's theory of evolution had taken on the aura of orthodoxy, and it is likely that the ape's dubious progress in "Report" represents the author's doubts concerning the tacit optimism of Darwin's model of human evolution.[2] Without intending to contravene either of these two levels of meaning, I propose to develop yet a third way of reading the tale--a way clearly related to the one just mentioned--namely, as a critique of anthropocentrism.[3]

Rotpeter's testimony is full of potential embarrassments for his audience, the members of the Academy. The behavior of their human compeers is far from creditable. Rotpeter is first wounded by a hunter's "wanton shot", and is then mistreated by his captors. Particularly striking is their presumption of human superiority. This hubris is evident even in those who do not openly mistreat the ape but actually befriend him, instructing him in human ways. Rather than accommodate in any way to Rotpeter, they oblige and assist the animal to become more like themselves, more "civilized". They are delighted by the ape's mimetic talent, and there is something quite narcissistic in the enthusiasm with which they encourage his assimilation, as though the ape's humanization somehow did them credit. Their vaunted civilization is effectively relativized as its highest values are surveyed from the animal's point of view. The ape loses no time in clarifying that his accession to human culture was not voluntary but compulsory. He denies that his decision was motivated by desire for "freedom" as humans define it. Indeed, he scorns their sublime conception of freedom, which he considers exemplified in the "self-controlled movement" of trapeze artists: "What a mockery of holy Mother Nature! Were the apes to see such a spectacle, no theater walls could stand the shock of their laughter." The ape's quest is a more modest one. He seeks not freedom but "only a way out; right or left, or in any direction . . . To get out somewhere, to get out! Only not to stay motionless with raised arms, crushed against a wooden wall." For his human audience, Rotpeter's motive can only diminish the value of his acculturation, since it shows that this path was taken only as a desperate expedient.

By far the most effective deflation of human pretensions is achieved through the ape's account of the acculturation process itself. It is only through "inner calm", great discipline, and heroic sacrifice that the ape can overcome his repulsion for things human. Rotpeter's method of self-transcendence is one of disciplined observation and mimicry of human habits and behavior. His tutelage begins with the imitation of external movements and gestures, and ends with the aping of speech. His apprenticeship involves, to use the suggestive terms of Deleuze and Guattari (1975)--a progressive "deterritorialization" of the oral region, away from its standard simian functions, and its "reterritorialization" to the "human" ones of spitting, smoking, drinking, and, finally, speaking. Throughout, the human creatures he imitates come off worse than the ape by comparison. "It was so easy to imitate these people. I learned to spit in the very first days. We used to spit in each other's faces; the only difference was that I licked my face clean afterwards and they did not." The culmination of his education--his initiation into the human community by yelling "Hallo!"--comes immediately after downing a pint of despised schnapps. The breakthrough to language is accompanied by the senseless gluttony learned from his teachers. Thus, Rotpeter learns the "discontents" of civilization the hard way. True, he is exhilarated by the learning process, but he is careful not to overestimate his attainment of the "cultural level of an average European. In itself that might be nothing to speak of," he notes--and here one imagines the squirming of his audience!--"but it is something insofar as it has helped me out of my cage . . ." Rotpeter's veiled resentment toward his human mentors and tormentors shows through in such comments.[4]

Rotpeter's revenge is to turn the tables on humans, to make them squirm, using the very tools he has learned from them--above all, language, with its resources of irony and objectivity. Deploying both the testimonial and the ironic capacities of speech, he holds up a mirror to his human interlocutors, revealing their true natures to them with merciless accuracy. It is Rotpeter's studied tone of objectivity, and his accurate mimicry of the very rhetoric and genres of science--as in his final appeal, "I am only imparting knowledge, I am only making a report"--which make Kafka's debunking of anthropocentrism so effective in this tale.

But if these instruments of civilization are Rotpeter's means of liberation and of revenge, they are also a kind of open-air cage, a minimum-security prison-house of language. They represent his permanent exile from his original animal state. While the story may be seen as an ironic variant of the "noble savage" myth, the ape is in fact no longer savage, nor is he entirely noble--though he is apparently more noble than his captors, on whom he even takes pity ("They were good creatures, in spite of everything."). The ape is something in between: a lucid but resentful savage. He has exchanged a literal cage at the beginning of the tale for the metaphorical, cultural one at the end; but he is no less "trapped" now than he was at the beginning. Ironically, his virtuoso performance (the delivery of the report) only highlights the distance between the ape and his human interlocutors. Rotpeter repeatedly stresses his full transformation, but the process--as Saki's Reginald once said of human ascent from the apes--is far from complete. The melancholy ending of the tale makes this point clear. The tragedy is that Rotpeter sacrifices his ape nature without ever becoming fully human. He remains stuck in a hybrid, in-between state, neither ape nor human. "With my hands in my trousers pockets, my bottle of wine on the table, I half lie and half sit in my rocking chair and gaze out of the window".[5] This alienated, in-between state is symbolized by the nature of his only intimate relationship: "When I come home late at night from banquets, from scientific receptions, from social gatherings, there sits waiting for me a half-trained little chimpanzee and I take comfort from her as apes do. By day I cannot bear to see her, for she has the bewildered look of the half-broken animal in her eye; no one else sees it, but I do, and I cannot bear it." Such is the price of his assimilation. It is his chosen way out, and he refuses to be pitied or told that it was not worth the trouble. But neither can he be complacent, for he senses that he can never be fully accepted by humans, nor can he himself identify fully with the products of human culture, to which he stands mainly in instrumental relation: they are for him only professional tools, actor's props for his performances. His lucidity and his alienation are inseparable. Kafka's allegorical tale illuminates the dark side of assimilation under duress--whether in primitive or in advanced stages of civilization--while showing the hubris and mystification of pretending that such transformations could ever be entirely successful.[6]

I have concentrated on the internal aspects of Kafka's dialogical experiment --the events narrated by Rotpeter and his attitude towards his audience, the Academy. But it would be naive to treat the conflicting forces at work here as though they were bounded by and enclosed *within* the story. The text may be considered a dialogical move in a language-game in which the reader is also engaged--as one is reminded by the shock of the story's presentational premise. According to Michel Serres (1968: 67), "*To hold a dialogue is to suppose a third man and to seek to exclude him*; a successful communication is the exclusion of the third man. The most profound dialectical problem is not the problem of the Other, who is only a variety . . . of the Same, it is the problem of the third man. We might call this third man the *demon*, the prosopopoeia of noise." But who plays this "Other", and who the "third party", in Kafka's tale--or, for that matter, in the discourse of his commentators? Rotpeter, the talking ape in Kakfa's story, speaks to the Academy about his former wild self and his subsequent capture. From the standpoint of the narrator, the "third party" is in one sense his human captors, while in another sense it is his former ape nature (though Rotpeter uses the first person to refer both to his former and to his present self). Insisting on the distance he has travelled, he tries to convince us that his ape nature is entirely behind him. But his comments reveal that part of it remains, and refuses to be suppressed. Some of the disquieting ambiguity of the ape's situation is transferred to the reader by the end of the tale, as we are subtly reminded that our own evolution is also less advanced than we like to think. The story's full satirical effect is felt only when we realize as readers that we are at once the addressee and the "third party" of the ape's discourse; at once members of the "Academy" who receive his report, and accomplices of his human exploiters-- when, in other words, we recognize something of ourselves in the humans whose barbarous acts are recounted in Rotpeter's report.

NOTES

[1] Much of my argument in the present article appears in different form in Kauffmann (1989).

[2] Margot Norris (1985: 66-72) analyzes Rotpeter's evolution as a series of "adaptive mimetic performances", the most subtle of which is the ape's delivery of the scientific report, which coincides with the act of narration itself. Norris's cogent interpretation--which unfortunately I came across only after writing this paper--at once confirms and provides a richer context for the present reading of "Report" as a critique of anthropocentrism, by placing Kafka's stories in a tradition of "biocentric" literature and art which includes Darwin, Nietzsche, D.H. Lawrence, and Max Ernst.

[3] Prior to Norris (1985), Kafka commentators had recognized the tale's anti-anthropic thrust (e.g., Neider 1948: 81), but without elaborating upon it.

[4] In a Kafka sketch of "Report", Rotpeter confesses to a human interlocutor: "Sometimes I'm overcome with such an aversion to human beings that I can barely refrain from retching. This, of course, has nothing to do with the individual human being, least of all with your charming presence" (1917: 260).

[5] Rotpeter's alienation is also evident in the above-cited sketch (see note 4), where the ape explains: "Actually, it's not the smell of human beings that repels me so much, it's the human smell which I have contracted and which mingles with the smell from my native land" (Kafka 1917: 261).

[6] Schwarz has rightly argued (1986: 84-85) that Kafka draws on the "emotional ambivalence" intrinsic to the traditional animal fable, while departing from the typically unambiguous "moral" of the genre, by infusing his own animal tales with "a profound ambivalence and sense of suffering". This suggests an important qualification to Kauf's interpretation of "Report" (1954) as representing an unequivocally Zionist critique of Jewish assimilation. Kauf's interpretation overlooks Kafka's essential ambivalence as a partially assimilated Jew, which shows in his mixed

sympathy and aversion toward the ape. On the allegorical level, Rotpeter is offered no attractive alternative which would be equivalent to the Zionist option. Robertson (1985: 131-84) provides a thorough discussion of Kafka's ambivalence toward Zionism and the question of Jewish assimilation.

REFERENCES

DELEUZE, Gilles, and Félix GUATTARI.
    1975. *Kafka: Pour un littérature mineure* (Paris: Minuit) Page references in the present article are to the English trans. by D. Polan, *Kafka: For a Minor Literature* (Minneapolis: University of Minnesota Press, 1986).
HEIDEGGER, Martin.
    1947. *Brief über den Humanismus* (Bern: A. Francke Verlag). Page references in the present article are to the English trans. by Frank A. Capuzzi in collaboration with J. Glenn Gray, in *Martin Heidegger: Basic Writings*, ed. David Farrell Krell (New York: Harper, 1977), 193-242.
KAFKA, Franz.
    1917. "Ein Bericht für eine Akademie", *Der Jude II*, 559-65. References in the present article are to the English trans. of "A Report to an Academy" by Willa and Edwin Muir, and to two contemporaneous Kafka sketches, "A Report to an Academy: Two Fragments", trans. Tania and James Stern; both translations in *Franz Kafka: The Complete Stories*, ed. Nahum N. Glatzer (New York: Schocken, 1983), 250-58 and 259-62, respectively.
KAUF, Robert.
    1954. "Once Again: Kafka's 'A Report to an Academy'", *Modern Language Quarterly* XV, 359-65.
KAUFFMANN, R. Lane.
    1989. "The Other in Question: Dialogical Experiments in Montaigne, Kafka, and Cortázar". In *The Interpretation of Dialogue*, ed. Tullio Maranhão (Chicago: University of Chicago Press).
MARCUS, George E. and Michael M. J. FISCHER.
    1986. *Anthropology as Cultural Critique: An Experimental Moment in the Human Sciences* (Chicago: University of Chicago Press).
NEIDER, Charles.
    1948. *The Frozen Sea: A Study of Franz Kafka* (New York: Oxford University Press).
NORRIS, Margot.
    1985. *Beasts of the Modern Imagination: Darwin, Nietzsche, Kafka, Ernst, and Lawrence* (Baltimore: Johns Hopkins University Press).
PALMER, Richard.
    1984. "Expostulations on the Postmodern Turn", *Krisis* 2, 140-49.
ROBERTSON, Ritchie.
    1985. *Kafka: Judaism, Politics, and Literature* (Oxford: Oxford University Press).
RUBINSTEIN, William C.
    1952. "Franz Kafka's 'A Report to an Academy'", *Modern Language Quarterly* XIII, 372-76.

SCHWARZ, Egon.
    1986. "Kafka's Animal Tales and the Tradition of the European Fable", in *Franz Kafka (1883-1983): His Craft and Thought*, ed. Roman Struc and J. C. Yardley (Waterloo, Ontario: Wilfred Laurier University Press), 75-88.

SERRES, Michel.
    1968. "Le Dialogue platonicien et la genèse intersubjective de l'abstraction", in *Hermes I: La Communication* (Paris: Minuit). Page references in the present article are to the English trans. by Marilyn Sides, in Serres, *Hermes: Literature, Science, Philosophy*, ed. Josué V. Harrari and David F. Bell (Baltimore: Johns Hopkins University Press, 1982), 65-70.

WITTGENSTEIN, Ludwig.
    i.1936-1949. *Philosophical Investigations*. Published posthumously in 1953 with facing German and English texts, trans. G. E. M. Anscombe. Page references in the present article are to the third edition of the English text (New York: MacMillan, 1968).

DEELY'S SEMIOTIC AS *DOCTRINA* AND JOYCE'S 'PROCESS OF MIND' IN *ULYSSES*

Mary Libertin
Shippensburg University of Pennsylvania

In the "Editorial Afterword" to *Tractatus de Signis: The Semiotic of John Poinsot*, John Deely offers a clear definition of semiotic as doctrina. He distinguishes *doctrina* from *scientia* (1985: 415), showing how the former "is a department of knowledge belonging to the order of what is not as opposed to what is susceptible of critical resolution at the empirical level". He states (1985: 415): "it is an objective discipline ruled by intrinsic demands indifferent to subjectivity in its individual (though not in its social) dimensions, and grounded in the *signifying* whereby the here and now acquires coherence of structure, and what may be absent or non-existent becomes a part of the texture of present experience--whereby, in a word, the transcendence of the given distinguishing cognitive life from merely assimilative and physically bound processes of material individuality is established". Deely limits the burgeoning field of semiotics from its "foundational doctrine" (416). The importance of Deely's work is in its presentation and elucidation of Poinsot's "unique remedy" for the "split between being and intelligibility that received its classic systematic formulation in Kant and which has perpetuated itself down to our own times" (498-499). The remedy in short is the explanation "of the apparent intersubjectivity of objects in discourse . . . and their partial coincidence in experience with mind-independent beings" (499). Understanding semiotic as *doctrina* allows us to understand how *Ulysses* itself comes to similar conclusions about the contradictory empirical level of information within the novel.

It fits what Joyce, early in 1903, wrote about the cognitive process. He writes in his aesthetic notebook (1903: 145) that "the artistic process is like the natural process", substituting the concepts of system and process for what he finds has been mistranslated as "imitation" in Aristotle's *e tekhne mimeitai ten physin*. Joyce equates the process of signification with the process of cognition in an entry titled "The Act of Apprehension" (1903: 148).

> It has been said that the act of apprehension involves at least two activities--the activity of cognition or simple perception and the activity of recognition. The act of apprehension, however, in its most complete form involves three activities--the third being the activity of satisfaction. By reason of the fact that these three activities are all pleasant themselves every sensible object that has been apprehended

must be doubly and may be trebly beautiful. In practical aesthetic philosophy the epithets 'beautiful' and 'ugly' are applied with regard chiefly to the third activity, with regard, that is, to the nature, degree and duration of the satisfaction resultant from the apprehension of any sensible object and therefore any sensible object to which in practical aesthetic philosophy the epithet 'beautiful' is applied must be trebly beautiful, must have encountered, that is, the three activities which are involved in the act of apprehension in its most complete form. Practically then the quality of beauty in itself must involve three constituents to encounter each of these three activities . . . . [ellipses Joyces']

Joyce wrote about the cognitive process frequently. In *Stephen Hero*, his protagonist says (1901-6: 37; cf. 33, 41-43) "This quality of the mind which so reveals itself is called (when incorrigible) a decadence but if we are to take a general view of //life// the world we cannot but see a process to life". And "the process of the mind", Joyce writes in an early essay "A Portrait of the Artist" (1903a: 60), "liberate[s] from the personalized lumps of matter that which is their individuating rhythm, the first formal relation of their parts". The relation of part to whole, is Joyce's definition of rhythm (1903: 145; 1916: 206). By *Ulysses* Joyce equated the process of signification/cognition with "the first entelechy, the structural rhythm" (15.106-7), which Stephen contemplates in the second episode, Nestor: "It must be a movement then, an actuality of the possible as possible. Aristotle's phrase formed itself . . . . Thought is the thought of thought . . . . The soul is in a manner all that is: the soul is the form of forms" (2.67-75). The antecedent for the pronoun *it* could be either *entelechy* or *art*, for in *Ulysses* Stephen contemplates both. In *Ulysses* Joyce organized a series of eighteen episodes, each written in a different style and divided into three sections, to reflect his conception of the artistic process, wherein the artistic process and the process of the mind embodied in the work and used by readers are equivalent. Subjectivity in its individual dimensions in *Ulysses* (as is clearly demonstrated with use of Deely's discussion of semiotic as *doctrina*) includes what is not capable of resolution at the empirical level within the text. In *Ulysses* the movement from the first to the third section embodies the movement from cognition-dependent to cognition-independent thought, and the drama implicit in the process itself becomes the object of the concluding section of the novel. Joyce realized that there are successive stages of inquiry or thinking, stages which are neither purely subjective nor purely objective, but which can be depicted and reveal more truth than had been thought possible about the boundary between the real and the unreal. As Joyce developed his ability to represent both cognition-dependent and cognition-independent elements within one work, the epiphany was no longer dependent upon the insight within one person's or character's mind. The process of mind and the formal relations of parts Joyce understood finally as equivalent. The relation of parts in a system needs no single mind--no traditional narrator--to reflect or reflect meaning. As Charles Peirce says (6.490): "order is simply thought embodied in arrangement".

Stephen Dedalus's epiphanic "chyrsostomos" ushers in a subjectivity wherein the here and now "acquires the coherence of structure" and "what may be absent or non-existent becomes a part of the texture of present experience". *Chrysostomos*: the word is a symbol of abduction. Abduction begins with a "surprising phenomenon, some experience which either disappoints an expectation or breaks in upon some habit of expectation" (6.469). The surprising phenomenon, for Stephen (and for the reader) is the manner is which the glistening gold points mock the Buck Mulligan, the mocker of transubstantiation who is waiting for a response to his whistle of call, which would signify the completion of the consecration of the offerings in his "mass". The word *chrysostomos* represents the surprise of abduction and, in its polysemy, the conjecturing involved in abduction. It has often and correctly been cited as one-word epiphany; but it has never been connected to the effects of the sun or to the cognitive process of Stephen in the episode or to the use of the sun as a structuring device of the novel.[1] He notices the manner in which the natural process mocks the pseudo-artistic/theological process of Buck. The sun glistens on Buck's gold fillings; the natural process itself transforms the mockery into what has been mocked. What is the "bursting of the startling conjecture" (6.469) or the hypothesis within the abduction which is both in the reader's mind and Stephen's mind, though, true to abduction the hypothesis need not be a conscious one? The hypothesis is that the natural process is like the artistic process. The presence and absence of sun becomes a structuring device in the novel whose character is noticing the principle which makes nature and Homer the same.[2] Stephen's consciousness in the first three episodes of the novel reflects a mind unconsciously pondering the above abductive hypothesis, and we are in a subjectivity wherein "what may be absent or non-existent becomes part of the texture of present experience", as Deely says. An example of this is the appearance in the water of the elderly man and the young man at the end of the first episode. The elderly man could very well be imagined, partly imagined, or real: Stephen's perceptions are still reflecting his process of abduction.

No distinction is made between cognition-dependent and cognition-independent reality until the second section of the novel, when we are in the stage of the process of cognition called deduction, when, for the first time, words are referred to as words, for example, on the page of the book when Molly points to the word *metempsychosis*, when for the first time the words refer to both a metaphoric and literal level, as in the sentence "Kidneys were in his mind as he moved about the kitchen" (4.1-6). Just as a reader of the first section of the novel is placed in the mode of sensation which is structural and wherein the present and absent are included in present experience, the reader of the section is placed in the mode of perception and must proportion the semiotic aspects of presence and absence from a deductive, rather than an abductive point of view.[3]

The result of this upon the reading of the subsequent episodes is equivalent to an exploration of how "transcendence of the given distinguishing cognitive life" is possible from "merely assimilative and physically bound process of material individuality". The third section of the novel shows what has been made possible because of words--everything has been made possible--and what is possible because the process of mind is everyone's (or semiotic as doctrina): a radical elimination of the ability to resolve the textual problems in the basis of "what is physically present in sensation", even though the latter is the basis of both doctrina and scientia. In Eumaeus, like Skin-the-Goat Fitzharris, one can not "vouch for the actual facts which quite possibly there was not one vestige of truth in" (16.324-5). What is present in sensation is "*corruptio per se* and *corruptio per accidens*" (16.759-60) and the episode as a whole is shown to be "quite within the bounds of possibility . . . not an entire fabrication though at first blush there [is] not much inherent probability in all the spoof" (16.826-28). In Ithaca, the reader is much like Bloom, who, reading Shakespeare "more than once for the solution of difficult problems in imaginary or real life . . . in spite of careful and repeated reading . . . derive[s] imperfect conviction from the text, the answers not bearing in all points" (17.386-54). The reader considers the educational careers of Stoom and Blephen (17.386-91); with the text raising its self-consciousness, characters are literalized and words are permutated: *meatpot* becomes "Peatmot. Trumplee. Moutpat. Plamtroo" (17.604-5). Molly Bloom's individual behavior has been the basis of much speculation in the novel, but such speculation because of her subjectivity serves to emphasize the irresolveable nature of textual (and semiotic) matters even when individual consciousness is depicted in the novel.

As Deely and Joyce show, there is an "apparent intersubjectivity of objects in discourse . . . and their partial coincidence in experience with mind-independent beings" adds a dimension of the reality of the here and now as presented in discourse; but this also adds a layer of illusion concerning the ability to resolved in an individual subjectivity what the process of mind (and process of art) insists is everyone's.

NOTES

[1] This has been explained in more detail in my unpublished doctoral dissertation, *The Play of Musement in James Joyce's Ulysses*.

[2] Joel Weinsheimer (1983: 256) explains that "what Peirce suggested is that the beautiful can have this same kind of cognitive import, that literature can be true, that Homer and Nature can be the same". Joyce, who likens the artistic process to the natural process, poses the same relationship with the title of *Ulysses*.

[3] I am using the definitions of sensation and perception as John Deely defines them in *Introducing Semiotic*.

REFERENCES

DEELY, John.
- 1982. *Introducing Semiotic: Its History and Doctrine* (Bloomington: Indiana University Press).
- 1985. "Editorial Afterword" to *Tractatus de Signis: The Semiotic of John Poinsot* (Berkeley: University of California Press), 391-514.

JOYCE, James A.
- 1901-6. *Stephen Hero*, ed. John J. Slocum and Herbert Cahoon (New York: New Directions, 1963).
- 1903. "Aesthetics" in *James Joyce: The Critical Writings*, ed. Ellsworth Mason and Richard Ellman (New York: The Viking Press, 1964), 141-148.
- 1903a. "A Portrait of the Artist" in *The Workshop of Dedalus: James Joyce and the Raw Materials for "A Portrait of the Artist as a Young Man"*, ed. Robert Scholes and Richard M. Kain (Evanston: Northwestern University Press, 1965), 60.
- 1916. *A Portrait of the Artist as a Young Man.* (New York: Viking, 1964).
- 1922. *Ulysses*. A Critical and Synoptic Edition, prepared by Hans Walter Gabler with Wolfhard Steppe and Claus Melchoir (New York: Garland Publishing, 1984), 3 vols.

LIBERTIN, Mary.
- 1983. *The Play of Musement in James Joyce's Ulysses* (Tulsa: The University of Tulsa, unpublished doctoral dissertation).

PEIRCE, Charles S.
    1908.   "A Neglected Argument for the Reality of God". *Hibbert Journal*, 7, 90-112. Reprinted in *Collected Papers of Charles Sanders Peirce*, Volume 6, Charles Hartshorne and Paul Weiss (eds.), 311-339. Cambridge: Harvard University Press, 1934.

WEINSHEIMER, Joel.
    1983.   "The Realism of C. S. Peirce, or How Homer and Nature can be the Same", *American Journal of Semiotics* 2.1/2, 225-263.

THE SEMIOTICS OF NARRATIVE:
NARRATIVE, PRISONERS, AND SOCIAL MEANING

Norma Procopiow
University of Maryland

This paper links two areas of current significance: the rapidly expanding field of narratology and program experiments in correctional education. Research into the nature of narrative, now the focus of wide disciplinary investigation, is pointing again and again to the importance of narrative as the instrument through which persons understand their place in the world and their relationship to others. Such findings can streamline correctional programs to provide a direct, more basic, hence effective approach to developing inmates' life adaptive/learning skills. The reading and writing of stories, including prisoners' own accounts, can form a basis for organizing their experiences into patterns which strengthen perceptual and cognitive skills. Dealing centrally with time and character as signifiers, narratology addresses two of the most important concerns of the prison situation. Taking narrative out of the traditional moralizing and discriminatory teleology, we tested this semiotic approach in the Women's State Prison in Jessup, Maryland during the summer of 1988. The parameters of this pilot program constitute the content of this paper.

The rationale for this project emanates from a needs and problem statement underlying the grant proposal for its funding. It is targeted for women inmates, who presently comprise the greatest need in the inmate population. There is perhaps no population for whom help in thinking skills is more needed, both for the women themselves and for the society they participate in, than female prisoners. In 1976, there were about 11,000 females in our state and federal prisons. A decade later, this figure multiplied to more than 26,000, an increase of 138 percent. While this statistic is alarming, what is more alarming is the paucity of training these women receive to prepare them for productive lives upon release. By comparison with male offenders, the average sentence for adult female offenders is short: 44.5 percent are sentenced for 2 to 5 years. More women return to society sooner than their male counterparts--but with less preparedness for the transition. When they return to the community, over 50 percent of these women will be heading single-parent households; rendered unemployable, many will be forced to go on welfare. They will also be likely to repeat the patterns of abuse and violence that they either perpetrated or were victimized by prior to incarceration.

Competence in independent living requires the ability to understand one's situation, how it came about and where it can lead. Researchers concur that such understanding depends upon the ability to construct and/or comprehend a narrative, to tell one's story accurately and persuasively. Priorities, realities, consequences, and commitment become more clear through the narrative process. Inability to understand them can lead to illegal behavior and subsequent incarceration. Moreover, persons without narrative skills cannot defend themselves in a court of law, or adequately represent themselves in hearings for welfare housing, job discrimination. In the final analysis, teaching the cognitive skills embedded in narratology is the most practical way to train inmates for vocational, social, and independent living on all levels.

We commenced the project with an exercise whereby the inmates could structure a mini-narrative which, while it was personal, would move beyond the solipsistic point of view. Inmates tend to encounter difficulty moving beyond their comprehension of the signifier and the signified of "me" the victim vs. "injustice", "unfairness", in "them", those they blame for their problems. There is also a tendency among these women to identify with the aggressor while at the same time regarding themselves as the victims of the aggressor. Representation, sign, meaning are consequently skewed. Thus the first exercise was to have them write a narrative (their own) from *their* perspective and then to compose that narrative from *another* point of view. This was done by having them complete a sentence and then write a one-page narrative on the subject. Sample sentence fragments were the following:

1. When I was a child...
2. The time I was most scared...
3. I got into trouble when...
4. The worst fear of my life was...
5. My trial was...
6. My first week in prison was...
7. When my family last visited me...

After completing these compositions they were asked to rewrite them from the point of view of another narrator (a spouse, child, judge, lawyer, victim, corrections officer, etc.). They are assisted in how to consider using another point of view. Some of the ways they can do this are to consider what details or facts this other narrator leaves out--and why; to consider what details or facts this other narrator might add--and why; to determine whether this narrative could have another ending; to reflect on how typical or atypical this story is. Several aspects of the process of composition are discussed. For example, it is emphasized that the students made decisions about the contents of their stories and the manner in which they told them. Understanding the motivations behind a given way of recounting a tale suggests that the student can differentiate between controllable and non-controllable approaches to life. If their narratives are brief, this means that they are giving less information to the reader and will therefore get back less, perhaps even hostile, response. Social reciprocity becomes an index of *giving* in the narrative; silence begets indifference alienation, etc.

Moving from this strategy, we attempted to establish the thought patterns which link their personal stories with the stock of narratives running from the simplest fairy tale or, in a contemporary context, soap opera, to the most sophisticated history or novel. They can read their personal narrative as a tool for assessment: a) it employs a specific skill, the art of story telling; b) it is both a process and a product; c) it has standards both linguistic and sociocultural; d) it was determined by the conditions under which it was written; e) it reflects reality from just one point of view; f) a friend, parent, or the inmate herself at another time, might write that narrative differently. The linguistic process by which they wrote these narratives is foregrounded. They are shown the universals operating and are asked for the following: the kinds of pronouns used (e.g., constant use of "I", third person, first person plural); the sequence of the narrative (e.g., linear, chronological, random); the nature of the vocabulary (e.g., realistic, fantasy-like, violent); the words and thought used at the end of the narrative.

Following this autobiographical exercise, we moved on to stories by other writers. It was helpful to start with the fairy tale, which is Structuralist; in an elementary way we were able to bring in some of the theoretical bases of Propp's and Greimas' work. It was stressed that one of the primary criteria of story is that something happens which is slightly different from the conventional day-to-day occurrences in a given society. For example, fairy tales usually begin with a change in routine activities. Here we used *Cinderella*. By habitual pattern, the sisters prepare for fancy parties while Cinderella does all the chores and stays at home. But the change that generates the story is that this time Cinderella does go to a ball; moreover she leaves behind a slipper--an uncharacteristic happening. As result, the prince traces the slipper back to its owner, bringing an unconventional occurrence to a conventional ending for the fairy tale genre. There are several important signifiers in this tale that may be found in other fairy tales: a) virtue is pitted against evil; b) virtue is rewarded; c) virtue forgives evil.

The inmates' response to the story is of course predictable: "This doesn't happen in real life." We then discuss the reasons why it doesn't happen: there is no real place or time in the story; rather than deal with specific characters in a human situation, the signified is a moral message. Yet, we can emphasize that what happens to Cinderella is not related to the goals associated with independent living. There is no goal- setting, decision-making, resource identification, or character development in the tale. Cinderella remains a static character who is acted upon, albeit in a lucky fashion. Also, her support system (so crucial to inmates once they are released from prison) is a fairy godmother. Yet, while there is more fantasy than reality in the tale, we had them write a narrative in which they themselves assumed the role of Cinderella. The results proved quite revelatory to the inmates.

Still working in the realm of fairy tale, we read *Hansel and Gretel*, which delivers a different signifier for women. In this tale Gretel is also triumphant; but unlike Cinderella, who is passive and simply waits for her prince to rescue her, Gretel is an active agent in her victory. Gretel used her resources effectively; self-determination, self confidence, self awareness. These overrode such economic and emotional difficulties as are admittedly only broadly mentioned in the story. Thus, the notion of handicaps, be they social, financial, familial (Gretel's father reluctantly agreed to the abandonment of Hansel and Gretel) become identifiable universals for the inmates.

Subsequent to the fairy tales, we worked with modern texts--an Alice Walker story, "Really, *Doesn't* Crime Pay?", and "Babylon Revisited" by F. Scott Fitzgerald. (See Jackson Barry's analysis of the Fitzgerald story in this volume. He utilized the re-visit narrative whereby the students found parallels in their own lives to that of the Fitzgerald protagonist.) Finally, we chose a TV soap, *Dallas*, to extrapolate from the glittery world of that serial the notion of narrative as mythmaking. Here the purpose was to connect the "myth" of *Dallas* with the students' own habits of mythmaking--ordering stories to explain the world, its heroes and anti-heroes. The timelessness of myth patterns became the thrust of this exercise. It was indicated that there is basically no difference between the romps of Mt. Olympus and contemporary myths, real and fictional (myths of political leaders, sports figures, entertainment stars, vs. the myth of the oil baron in *Dallas*). By situating a narrative in a context (even one as fantastic as Mt. Olympus), we understand behavioral motivation. It was explained that while the Greek myths and fairy tales come to us from no single author and thereby represent a collective set of social values, the team of script writers who produce *Dallas* also represent a collective set of social values. From this, the inmates were encouraged to return to their personal narratives to define their own set of values. Some of the findings that emerged indicated that they wanted easy rewards, that work is to be avoided, that they felt they were the center of the universe, that they lacked impulse control and sense of the consequences of their behavior.

This growth in cognition and self understanding was most apparent in the myth analysis of *Dallas*. We used primitive schematics of archetypes. In effect, that the structure of myth is polar, turning on notions of good and bad (heaven and hell religio-cultural contexts). The primitive mind in early civilizations apprehended the world and being in terms of cycles seasonal, diurnal, human. For example, spring, dawn, and birth were seen as analogous; as beginnings, they represent hope, the creation of a new earth, of a new society, of a new hero. This cycle is embodied in stories where promise is the key signified (e.g., Spring as the time for the resurrection of Christ in the *New Testament*). In addition, notions of death and life are attached to different elements in the world (human, animal, vegetable, etc.). For example, communities of creatures symbolize life (schools of fish, flocks of birds), whereas isolated beasts are more menacing and suggest death (serpents, vultures). When we make or read stories, the abstract association we have is often a way to vivify such notions; or they make them operate in ironic contrast to that universal association. Therefore, prior to analyzing *Dallas* we had the inmates do a little mythical associating themselves. We had them choose a story in which one of these cycles or world elements plays a significant role (the *Bible* is a source from which many of them could draw, since their literary familiarity derived from church related activities). They were asked to write a paragraph on how the myth operates in that particular story; then they were asked to discuss how the myth reveals their own needs and desires.

Returning to *Dallas* as a popular current myth, we talked about the popularity of the program. There is criminal activity evident in many of the characters in the show, but it is on different levels than the sort of street crime most of the inmates know. Drawing the comparison between white collar crime and lower echelon crime brought the inmates into personal narrativizing. On this frame of reference, we explored the interpersonal relationships in the show. Analysis revealed that the characters all form part of a large family, many of whom live together at the family ranch. We discussed the fact that studies have attributed *Dallas'* popularity to its subliminal message--the family as the ideal institution. That is, despite all the feuds and crises that punctuate the series, familial bonds, fidelity, procreation, etc., are held up as the model values. This is reinforced by the environment; the setting is a bucolic family estate, there is constant summer sunshine (this is Texas, after all!), progeny (legitimate and otherwise!) is sacred, connubial love is the cherished human condition. Given this reading of the series, we asked the students to write short narratives on one of the following aspects of *Dallas*:

1) How do you see yourself, or your mother, in the role of Miss Elly?

2) Which character do you identify with, and relate an experience in your own life to demonstrate this.

3) Write a narrative on what it takes (and means) to make it in the world of business or other type of employment. How does watching *Dallas* provide ideas on this subject?

4) Tell about the role of the men in your life as compared with that of the men in the show (e.g., the ruthless J.R.; the sweet Bobby).

5) Tell about the role of the children in your life as compared with those of the children in the show.

6) Do any of the following sayings apply to this show: "nothing lasts"; "the world is not necessarily just"; "being good doesn't pay off"; "each of us is ultimately alone"? If so, how are they reconciled in the show?

When we completed our study of *Dallas* the pilot ended. It was a brief experiment, lasting just two months. The remainder of the project can only be realized if the grant subsidies which we requested are provided. Therefore, we can only remark on the work done thus far. It was our impression that the inmates moved to a higher level of self understanding and, in some instances, toward a stronger sense of self and hope regarding the future. What better use can the semiotics of narrative employ than to develop such important cognitive skills?

XII

ELIAS CANETTI: TRADITION AND TRANSFORMATION

A FICTION OF DETECTION:
THE POLICE ENQUIRY IN ELIAS CANETTI'S *AUTO-DA-FÉ*

David Darby
University of Toronto

The situation at the opening of the police enquiry convened mid-way through Canetti's novel does not augur well. Despite the considerable number of characters offering themselves as offenders, plaintiffs, and/or witnesses, Siegfried Fischerle-- the pickpocket, embezzler, and pimp, indeed the only figure in the story-world whose criminal intent has been established as "fact" in the narrator's discourse--is long gone by the time the hearing begins. As in any detective enquiry--fictional or otherwise--proceedings are initiated with the aim of establishing an objective, factual version of certain prior events. Thus the narrative situation invites a reader's expectations of witnessing the composition of a privileged manifestation of the story at the expense of the lies, misconceptions, and misconstructions which inform the non-authentic belief-worlds of the characters. One critic's discussion of the protagonist Peter Kien's arrival at the police station as a sudden transition from the "world of the lawless to that of the most extreme standardization" (Curtius 1972: 301 [my translation]) applies to the level of narration as much as to that of story, since the change of scene appears to suggest the imminent and authoritative imposition of narrative law and order on an erring discourse.

The account of the investigation is central to the novel not just in the sense of its physical position in the text but also in terms of its function in the overall structure of the discourse. It represents the climax of the process of accumulation of mutually exclusive, semiotically unstable, non-authentic models of reality, all character-generated, which has dominated the first half of the text. At the same time it represents the first of three typological structures suggestive of the possibility of hermeneutic closure. This fiction of detection, an *in machina* attempt to systematize meaning, is followed by a fiction of escape (Fischerle's America-project), and finally by a fiction of *ex machina* deliverance (the intervention of Peter Kien's psychiatrist brother Georges, slayer of metaphorical dragons). The second half of the text depicts the failure of each of these structures. I intend to discuss the resistance to hermeneutic closure offered by Canetti's text in terms of the failure of forensic detection to accommodate unassimilable signifiers in a homologous system. This failure in turn confirms, in Eco's terms, the "openness" (1959: 49) of this text and suggests a metaphysical subversion of positivistic assumptions implicit in traditional detective fiction.

As Todorov notes (1971: 57), the narrative structure of detective fiction is characterized by the existence of two interrelating stories. There is the story of detection--that is, the events of the forensic enquiry--and there is that of the crime which is usually revealed in fragmentary form as the investigation progresses. The narration of the events of the story of detection is usually chronological (Nusser 1980: 35), and access to the earlier story is gained by means of shorter or longer passages of embedded flashback or, in narratological terms, analepsis. The analepsis attempted in the police enquiry differs from previous analepses in Canetti's text in that it is character-motivated, that is, initiated by an actant on the level of story. Previous analepses are by contrast initiated and sustained by authority of the third-person narrator.[1] This authority renders possible the completion of the analepsis, meaning that the return to the principal narrative occurs automatically as the gap between the two time levels closes.[2] However, the attempt made in the police station by the story-world characters lacking narrative authority to separate and rejoin time-levels collapses and with it the fundamental structure of fictional forensic detection.

These character-initiated analepses, which aim to pass off non-authoritative readings as definitive meanings, never fully escape the influence of their narrative context. We witness the impotence of characters, trapped as actants within the principal, non-analeptic story and unable to manipulate its narrative structure. Peter Kien does of course narrate a story--that of his murder of Therese--but this is then a secondary, embedded story and its narration is tolerated only up to a point by the controlling principal narrator. When Kien's analeptic narrative runs into conflict with an element of the narrator's fact-world, he is forced to treat the phenomena of the principal story as "hallucination" (Canetti 1935a: 307), thereby attempting to undermine the semiotic legitimacy invested in them as part of a more authoritative discourse. The collapse of Kien's analeptic account is triggered by the intrusion of an event from the principal discourse, such as the voice of Therese, the very character Kien claims to have murdered (Canetti 1935a: 308-309). Thus the analepsis is interrupted rather than completed and the information contained therein is left neither authenticated nor ordered.

For the other characters present during this episode Kien's discourse contains signifiers which can be incorporated with a consequent change of meaning into the particular codes of their belief-worlds. Thus the attempt to decode a past story leads immediately to a new non-authentic encoding. Peter Hühn sees detective fiction as being concerned with "sign-interpretation, meaning-formation, and story-telling", and argues that "the initial crime--as long as it remains unsolved--functions as an uninterpretable sign, that is, one that resists integration into the established meaning-system of the community . . ." (Hühn 1987: 453-454). Thus, in *Auto-da-fé*, the character Pfaff interprets Kien's claim to the murder of Therese in terms of his own guilt: "The caretaker was seized with terror. . . . The Professor was talking about a wife but he meant his daughter" (Canetti 1935a: 303-304). Kien's wife Therese is similarly compelled to integrate the data she receives into her construct of reality (Canetti 1935a: 303):

> Therese was astonished that she had never noticed anything. So he'd been married when she came into his service, and she'd always thought he was a bachelor; she'd known there was a mystery, the mystery was his first wife, he'd murdered her, still waters are murderers, so that was why he never spoke, and because his first wife had had a skirt like hers, he'd married *her* for love. She cast about for proofs. . . .

Kien's confessions are part of a character-motivated analeptic discourse and as such do not participate in any privileged system of signification which may inform the narrator's principal non-analeptic discourse. They are rendered polysemic as they float between non-authenticated, character-generated readings. The analeptic story to be read in the police-enquiry is confronted by an absence of any "accepted patterns of reality" (Hühn 1987: 454). If such a communal, legitimating pattern is to be found anywhere in the text, it is not in the subworlds produced in the discourses of the characters of the principal story-world, but in the metadiscourse of the third-person narrator. It's existence--even on this level--is, however, neither certain nor necessary.

Kien's analeptic narrative merely baffles and bores the figures present at the enquiry whose function might be expected to be that of specialist detectives: the police. These figures, notably the Inspector, the man with the memory, and the proud father, reveal themselves to be as much inhabitants of private belief-worlds as the collection of plaintiffs, suspects, and witnesses with which they are confronted. The Inspector's obsession with his appearance and with the inadequacy of his nasal profile is perhaps the most remarkable. The proud father appropriates Kien's speech to his own specialized pattern of reality as he grows "anxious at his son's good German composition. This is what book-learning led to" (Canetti 1935a: 310). The attention of these figures is thus clearly concentrated on the world of the story in which they are actants and not on that of the story which they are supposed to investigate. The man with the memory, who burns with zeal at his agreeing with himself on fourteen different points (Canetti 1935a: 310) is able to relate Kien's narrative only to private analeptic time levels and to the proleptic level of "the subsequent interrogation" (Canetti 1935a: 308) which never takes place. Since these detectives' interest in analepsis is at best minimal, Kien's defense concerns them only by virtue of the fact that its discourse is *enacted* on the level of the principal story.

The degree of importance attached to features of the discourse of the secondary, embedded story is suggested by the terms in which the policemen see their own and Kien's performances. The Inspector's interrogation is seen as "an incomparable feat. . . . Pale and excited he rose to his feet, bowed to left and right, sought for words and at length expressed his deep emotion in a simple phrase: 'Thank you, gentlemen'" (Canetti 1935a: 314). Kien's defense has positively theatrical overtones (Canetti 1935a: 305):

> The playing-time was short. They would have liked more for their money. Kien spoke and performed, he took great pains. It was clear how seriously he took his profession. He earned his money with the sweat of his brow. No actor could have done better. . . . His gestures were convincing. Almost, the spectators applauded.

When his defense collapses he makes an error in returning to the beginning when "only a new and striking performance would have saved him" (Canetti 1935a: 308). Unable to maintain the standard of his earlier performance, he is accused of being merely a "Clown" (1935a: 309) and loses his audience. In having to be repeated, Kien's discourse encounters the danger of stasis: As Kien becomes bogged down in the act of reformulating the narrative already begun, the movement toward completion of the analepsis is lost. As Kien's analepsis breaks down, the caretaker Pfaff takes over the defense of his new protégé and his speech serves to terminate the police enquiry. This is not, however, due to its content (that is, to the authenticity of the information it carries) but rather because of its unexpected performative features, not the least of which is its volume (Canetti 1935a: 322).

This emphasis on performance (discourse) over authenticated fact (story) is reminiscent of the various archaic practices of administering justice described by Huizinga in the section of *Homo Ludens* dealing with "Play and Law" (Huizinga 1939:

76-88). Huizinga observes that "in less advanced phases of culture . . . the idea of right and wrong, the ethical-juridical conception, comes to be overshadowed by the idea of winning and losing, that is, the purely agonistic conception" (1939: 78). Thus Kien is engaged in what Jean-François Lyotard--following Wittgenstein--terms "language games" (Lyotard 1979: 10). Lyotard states: "[T]o speak is to fight, in the sense of playing, and speech acts fall within the domain of a general agonistics" (1979: 10). It is of course precisely the priority given to the performative aspect of the discourse--Lyotard's "agonistics of language" (1979: 10)--over its communicative function that in *Auto-da-fé* inhibits the completion of analepsis essential to hermeneutic detection.

Canetti's Inspector lacks virtually all the qualities attributed to traditional detective figures such as Holmes or his predecessor, Dupin (of Edgar Allan Poe's "The Murders in the Rue Morgue"). His blunt facial profile alone offers a marked contrast with that of Holmes. Commentators note the "intellectual superiority" (Nusser 1980: 31 [my translation]) expected of the detective, or see the detective as "the instrument of pure logic, able to triumph because he alone in a world of credulous men holds to the Scholastic principle of *adequatio rei et intellectus*, the adequation of mind to things" (Holquist 1971-1972: 141). When not engaged in analeptic activity Holmes succumbs to his cocaine habit and exists between cases in a state of at best limited animation. Stefano Tani writes of Dupin that once his "creative" faculties are engaged he "thinks so intensely of the crime-puzzle to be solved as to obliterate his usual personality" (1984: 5). The contrast with the inability of the Inspector and his colleagues in *Auto-da-fé* to transcend the story-world which they inhabit could hardly be greater. The complete devotion of the detective's intellectual faculties to the analeptic narrative, the embedded story-level of the events to be investigated, is an essential factor in those detective fictions commonly considered to be paradigms of their genre. If Holquist's description can be applied to any figure in this episode of *Auto-da-fé*, it would be to Kien, whose valiant attempt to reason out the events of the earlier story and to hold to the principle of "*adequatio rei et intellectus*" founders on the priority of the third-person narrator's account of the events of the investigation itself. For Kien, within his non-authentic system of meaning at least, a "super-reader" (Hühn 1987: 459) gifted with "the ability to question preconceived notions and break through automatized modes of perception" (Hühn 1987: 455), "there are no mysteries, there is only incorrect reasoning" (Holquist 1971-1972: 141).

Much has been written on the scientificity of literary detection (e.g. Brecht c.1939: 451-452), and historical studies of modern detective fiction frequently indicate a connection between the inception of the literary tradition and the development of modern science and positivistic thought (e.g. Tani 1984: 11). If, as Nusser suggests, authors of detective fiction are engaged in popularizing "the methods and ethos of the natural sciences" (1980: 47 [my translation]), then this study must take into account the implications of the radical subversion of this fiction evident in Canetti's police enquiry.

Auto-da-fé was written during the so-called Golden Age of detective fiction. It is suggested that the detective tradition in the inter-war era offered, in view of the positivistic world-view it espoused, aesthetic and ideological reassurance. This affirmation of form and reason is central to Kien's willing participation in Canetti's police-enquiry. Kien's belief-world and the science by which he sustains it are under serious threat of disintegration. Hühn's explanation of the popularity of the genre among intellectuals of the inter-war period is particularly pertinent to Kien's situation: "In a time when familiar, clear cut, and finite patterns were starting to disappear from science . . . as well as literature . . . the detective genre . . . may have seemed to offer intellectuals reassuring proof of the validity of the personal story"

(Hühn 1987: 464). Kien sees the police enquiry as the ideal opportunity to reaffirm his rational, scientific constructs of reality. Kien's faith in reason and the fairness of the proceedings reflect the expectation of Hühn's "reassuring proof". However, he is interrupted by the police officers behind whose behavior he senses "an attempt to influence him", and by the suspicion of "movements behind his back" (Canetti 1935a: 314). In fact the "attempt to influence him" is initiated quite literally *behind* the other figures present.[3] This noise (both literal and figurative) invades and disrupts Kien's discourse which has the proposed aim of fixing a semiotically stable reading of the implied analepsis-time crime story. Kien has a story to tell, but its discourse is not privileged above others: he is lost in a world where he has not the authority to narrate and thus his discourse founders, unable to verify itself.

Whether one views Golden-Age detective fiction in terms of "an escape from literature" and from the "smart and easy pessimism" of Modernism (Nicholson 1929: 113-24), or--like Bertolt Brecht--as an escape from a reality and a world of science in which "the law of causality functions at best half-way" (Brecht c.1939: 456 [my translation]), Canetti's subversion of the tradition suggests a fictional world in which philosophical and semiotic "reassurance and conformism" are impossible. Therese in the passage cited earlier adopts a scientific approach in that, having constructed her hypothesis, she sets about the task of "cast[ing] about for proofs" (Canetti 1935a: 303). The existence of proofs presumes however a stable referential network shared by all the characters involved in generating worlds. In the absence of such a communal system of signification, and as a consequence of Therese's being incompetent to generate authentic fictional worlds, the scientific proof--in other words, knowledge--projected by Therese will inevitably lack legitimation.

In its parodying of a current tradition, our police enquiry anticipates a literary tradition usually referred to as anti-detection, "a high-parodic form that stimulates and tantalizes its readers by disappointing common detective-novel expectations" (Tani 1984: xv). Poe's detective stories are discussed in terms of "a rational exorcism of irrationality, a conflict between logic and multiform, mysterious reality" (Tani 1984: 15). In contrast, in Canetti's text, the detective process fails in its function of exorcism and even compounds the multiformity and mystery of reality. The fictional world of Canetti's police enquiry prefigures Tani's depiction of postmodern sensibility as characterized by its "lack of a center, its refusal to posit a unifying system". It is a world which forbids definitive reading, and which "substitutes for the detective as central and ordering character the decentering and chaotic admission of mystery, of nonsolution" (Tani 1984: 39-40).

Until now neglected in the critical literature, Canetti's parodic subversion of formal elements of the fiction of forensic detection foregrounds the problematic status of knowledge by bringing together mutually exclusive narrative models of reality. This episode foregrounds the play of competing non-authenticated systems of meaning which is central to my reading of *Auto-da-fé* as a radically open text. In the absence of a legitimate pattern of reality, the "evidence" constitutes only a labyrinthine accumulation of contradictory, polysemic signifiers. As the rational-communicative project of the investigation proves useless, the language of the episode inevitably adopts an exclusively performative function, whereupon story and discourse become confused, and juridical questions are rendered indecipherable in the noise of the agonistic process. Without a stable, communally recognized--and so legitimate--referential framework, it becomes in *Auto-da-fé* meaningless to ask the most fundamental question of detective fiction, "Whodunit?", and still more so to hope for an answer.

NOTES

[1] For example, the chapter "The Secret" consists almost entirely of sustained analepsis (Canetti 1935a: 26-34). The distinction between narrator-motivated and character-motivated analepsis is made by Rimmon-Kenan (1983: 50-51).

[2] The concept of completed analepsis is developed by Genette (1972: 92).

[3] Wedgwood's translation, "Their strange behaviour seemed an attempt to influence him", does not permit the reading I propose; the German text states: "Hinter ihrem sonderbaren Gehaben wittert er einen Beeinflussungsversuch" (Canetti 1935: 378).

REFERENCES

BRECHT, Bertolt.
    c. 1939.   "Über die Popularität des Kriminalromans", *Schriften zur Literatur und Kunst*, Vol. 19 of *Gesammelte Werke in 20 Bänden* (Frankfurt am Main: Suhrkamp, 1967), 450-457.

CANETTI, Elias.
    1935.   *Die Blendung* (Wien: Reichner).
    1935a.   *Die Blendung* (Wien: Reichner), English trans. by C. V. Wedgwood, *Auto-da-fé* (New York: Continuum, 1946).

CURTIUS, Mechthild.
    1972.   "Das Groteske als Kritik", *Literatur und Kritik* 7, 294-311.

ECO, Umberto.
    1959.   "Poetics of the Open Work", *The Role of the Reader: Explorations in the Semiotics of Texts* (Bloomington: Indiana UP, 1979), 47-66.

GENETTE, Gérard.
    1972.   *Figures III* (Paris: Seuil).

HOLQUIST, Michael.
    1971-1972.   "Whodunit and other Questions: Metaphysical Detective Stories in Postwar Fiction", *New Literary History* 3, 135-156.

HÜHN, Peter.
    1987.   "The Detective as Reader: Narrativity and Reading Concepts in Detective Fiction", *Modern Fiction Studies* 33, 451-466.

HUIZINGA, Johan.
    1939.   *Homo Ludens: Versuch einer Bestimmung des Spielelementes der Kultur* (Amsterdam: Pantheon). The English trans. by R. F. C. Hull, *Homo Ludens: A Study of the Play-Element in Culture* (London: Routledge and Kegan Paul, 1949) was alone used in this work.

LYOTARD, Jean-François.
    1979.   *La condition postmoderne: rapport sur le savoir* (Paris: Minuit). The English trans. by Geoff Bennington and Brian Massumi, *The Postmodern Condition: A Report on Knowledge* (Minneapolis: U of Minnesota P, 1984) was alone used in this work.

NICHOLSON, Marjorie.
   1929. "The Professor and the Detective", reproduced in *The Art of the Mystery Story: A Collection of Critical Essays*, ed Howard Haycroft (New York: Biblo and Tannen, 1976), 111-127.
NUSSER, Peter.
   1980. *Der Kriminalroman* (Stuttgart: Metzler).
RIMMON-KENAN, Shlomith.
   1983. *Narrative Fiction: Contemporary Poetics* (London: Methuen).
TANI, Stefano.
   1984. *The Doomed Detective: The Contribution of the Detective Novel to Postmodern American and Italian Fiction* (Carbondale IL: Southern Illinois UP).
TODOROV, Tzvetan.
   1971. "Typologie du roman policier", *Poétique de la prose* (Paris: Seuil), 55-65.

ABSENCE AS PRESENCE: SIGMUND FREUD IN THE WORKS OF ELIAS CANETTI

Kristie A. Foell
University of California, Berkeley

Elias Canetti has taken a strong position against Freud, both in his autobiographical writings and in his sketches, insisting that his own work not be interpreted in a Freudian manner and challenging many of Freud's basic assumptions. This very negativity, viewed from a Freudian perspective, is a sign that Freud is actually very important to Canetti. In this paper, I do not propose to do what Canetti would most deplore--namely, reduce either his life or his work to the schema of the Oedipal complex. Instead, I would like to point out how a number of omissions and absences in Canetti's work signal the insistent presence of Freud's thought in the author's mind.

Canetti's early life was fraught with events that could have been designed by Freud himself, but Canetti is very careful not to see them that way. The first volume of Canetti's autobiography, *The Tongue Set Free*, begins with his earliest memory: the episode in which he nearly has his tongue cut out (1977:9-10). In psychoanalysis, a person's earliest memory is extremely important, so that it is tantamount to a challenge to Freud when Canetti titles his opening chapter "My earliest memory".[1] Canetti never gives this scene its obvious Freudian interpretation, "castration anxiety"; rather, the tongue is seen as a symbol of linguistic capability and of the profession of the poet. (In the chapter "Storytellers and Writers", from *The Voices of Marrakesh*, Canetti sees the storytellers, the oral poets, as the true prototype of his occupation: "They seemed like my older and better brothers" [1967: 82]). He is not afraid of losing his male organ or potency, but of losing his capacity for communication.

Similarly, in writing about his brother's circumcision, Canetti reports the blood, but records no fear, no feeling that his brother's member is in danger, nor any identification with his brother's situation. Nor does the advent of the younger brother create the feelings of being threatened and of jealousy which Freud expects children to feel vis-à-vis younger siblings; instead, his sense of self is strengthened by his new pants and his new position as first-born son. The pride of gender is directly connected to the pants: "During this entire time I wore skirts *like a girl*. I wanted to go about in pants *like a boy*..." (1977: 25; emphasis added). But, although Canetti is elsewhere conscious of a sexual meaning of pants (the book Kien gives Therese [1935:41-42]), here he is careful not to connect the pants with the organ they cover.

Even more obviously open to Freudian interpretation is the death of Canetti's father, which leaves the son as the sole and most trusted companion of his mother, a position he guards jealously. In the way in which the child immediately identifies himself as his mother's sole support, and vehemently opposes and frustrates all her attempts at forming a new romantic attachment, the reader cannot fail to see that the child has put himself in the father's place. But there is no indication of a wish for his father's death--and how could the child or the man admit such a wish in the face of the father's actual death? Unlike Freud, who, as a tot, attributed a younger brother's death to his own jealousy (Jones vol. 1: 7-8), Canetti blames the outbreak of war for his father's sudden heart attack and traces his pacifism to this moment, while his mother blames her own near-romantic involvement with another man (1977: 85-88).

Throughout his autobiography, Canetti is extremely silent about his own sexual development, a subject other writers of autobiographies are often only too glad to expound upon. Particularly in the later volumes, when Canetti describes his courtship almost exclusively in intellectual terms, and mentions his marriage only after the fact, this silence seems deeper than mere discretion would call for. Of course Canetti is protecting a very private sphere of his life, one which he seems to want to present as irrelevant to his literary development. But could not one reason for this protection be that he wishes to deter from the outset any Freudian interpretation of his own development?

The few unavoidable intimations of something like sexual knowledge or curiosity are carefully framed in other terms. As a child, the young Elias often overhears his parents speaking in the "secret language" of German, the language of their early romance (1977: 37-39). He feels himself excluded, feels that there must be "wonderful things which one could only say in this language" (1977: 38), and longs to understand. One day, imitating his father's voice, he calls his mother by her German nick-name ("Mädi")--and fools her (1977: 38-39)! Still, he wishes he could actually speak the language, and writes: "I cannot explain why I was not angry at my father for this [his knowledge of the secret language]. But I was deeply irritated with my mother, and this irritation did not vanish until she taught me German years later, after my father's death" (1977: 39). Faced with the child's early exclusion from and jealousy of parental relations, Canetti interprets his own curiosity as applying primarily to the language, not to whatever secret, perhaps romantic or sexual, messages might have been relayed in that language (unless we see the "wonderful things" as potentially sexual). And he is careful to disavow any anger against his father in this situation, but offers no explanation for turning his anger against the mother.

In the chapter "Confessions of a Fool", Canetti, then 16, mentions his first exchanges of stories about girls with his male friends. His stories are entirely made up, although he assumes that those of his friend, Jean, are not. The content of these male tall tales is not explicitly sexual (Canetti 1980: 44):

> Everything was in a chivalrous tone; it was a matter of admiration, not grasping. If the admiration was so clever and wellexpressed that it penetrated and was not forgotten, one had conquered; the conquest consisted in the fact that one made an impression and was taken seriously. If the stream of lovely things one thought up, but also articulated, was not interrupted, if the opportunity of delivering them to their destination did not depend only on one's own skill, but also on the expectation and reciprocity of the girl in question, that was evidence that one was taken seriously, and one was a man.

Canetti insists on his lack of knowledge, indeed of interest, in sexuality at this point --"I would not have been able to say what happened between lovers other than kisses" (43)--and yet the language and images he uses in the above passage are decidedly sexual. One might argue that the passage, although it describes a boy of sixteen, is, after all, written by a man of over eighty. But for such an avowed anti-Freudian, Canetti draws the parallel between male sexuality and male linguistic prowess rather neatly. Could this be unconscious? Or is Canetti here attempting to show that communication is the paradigm for sexuality, and not the other way around?

The way in which Canetti presents these few hints of early sexual knowledge (and the latter account cannot even be called early) is always calculated to deny the importance of sexuality. Language or communication in general is foregrounded instead. For Canetti, language is not always or primarily the key to the unconscious, as in Freud's thought; rather, it often serves to conceal meaning and hinder communication. Canetti's theory of the acoustic mask also speaks for this "surface" view of language (1975: 42; 44-45), counterbalanced by his tendency to linguistic mysticism.

Canetti's carefully edited presentation of his own life is mirrored in that of Peter Kien, the main character of *Auto-da-Fé*. Canetti could not very well dispense with an account of his childhood, even his early childhood, in an autobiography, but in his novel, he comes very close to doing so. Kien seems to have no past; Barbara Meili has remarked that this fact alone is enough to bar the reader from a psychoanalytical approach to Kien (Meili 1985: 34). A few fragments of Kien's childhood do come to light, however, and Lothar Hennighaus has elaborated on these (1984: 65-68). But Meili's point--that these memories do not contribute to a specifically Freudian interpretation--still holds, for two main reasons. First, the memories do not go back far enough into childhood; there are no memories from infancy or very early childhood, and no primal scene. Second, many of what could be the most revealing memories are not related by Peter Kien, but by his brother, George (as when George recalls Peter's temporary blindness during an episode of measles, and concludes that this must be the reason for Kien's current condition [1935: 460-462]). A Freudian would find this memory of an outsider useful only in conjunction with memories of the subject himself; thus, George can confirm the early origins of Peter's self-identification with his eyes, but the new information George provides about the family constellation must be viewed more skeptically, since it is not reflected in Peter's own memories.

The fact that so much information about Peter's childhood is absent must have a crucial impact on any attempt at interpreting Kien's dream of the Aztec priests. In the construction of this dream, Canetti both enacts and undermines Freudian theories of dream-interpretation. Kien's dream functions both on the surface level and symbolically, but its symbolism tells us little or nothing we did not already know about Kien. Eyesight and blindness are thematized in the dream, but these symbols "stand for" Kien's actual anxiety about his eyes; eyes are never given their Freudian significance. "Blinded, Kien closes his eyes" (Canetti 1935: 37) in expectation of the sacrifice's blood; although Kien fears blindness for the sake of his books, he is already blind to human suffering and emotion. This thought is even more clearly expressed by Kien's indifference to the mounds of burning human flesh, while the thought of burning books tortures him.

This kind of direct representation is not what Freud would expect from a dream, since Freud assumes that most dreams undergo a distortion by means of which the actual thoughts and wishes expressed in the dream are disguised (Freud 1900: 223). If we look at the "symbolism" in Kien's dream as a one-to-one correspondence --the fire represents fire; the books, books; and the people, people--then the dream has only a literary, not a psychological, function as a foreshadowing of the end of the book; in this function, the dream is not symbolic at all (in the Peircean sense), but iconic. Yet each of the dream elements does point beyond itself, both away from, and back to, the psychoanalytic interpretive model. Freud has given us a detailed interpretation of fire as a dream symbol in the case of Dora (Freud 1905: 225; 230-36); it has a sexual significance. But fire is also the first element Canetti lists as a symbol of the mass in *Crowds and Power*, where he describes in detail a Navajo Indian dance in which the dancers actually go into the fire (as does Kien) in an attempt to equate their human group with the fire's symbolic representation of mass (1960: 82 ff.). Seen from this perspective, the important feature of the hordes of books, and the people into which they are changed, becomes not *what* they are, but *how many* they are. The latent meaning of Kien's dream, then, would be his desire to become part of the mass. Canetti has used the symbol "fire"--seen as a symbol of sexual desire long before Freud--only to reinterpret it. Kien's dream may still be seen as a wish-fulfillment, but the wish is not of a sexual nature.

My beginning of a dream-interpretation is purely symbolic (in the Freudian sense): it avails itself of generally recognizable correspondences between the dream-thoughts and the dream-content. But a symbolic approach leaves out the second prong of interpretation on which Freud insisted: the associations the dreamer himself attaches to the dream-content.[2] Canetti appears to be poised on the brink of giving the reader this information when he writes (1935: 40; apparently from Kien's perspective):

> Divided into its constituent parts, a dream loses its power. . . . He [Kien] had thought of Eratosthenes, the old librarian of Alexandria, a few days ago, upon meeting a blind man on the street. The name Alexandria awakened in everyone the memory of the fire in the famous library. . . . On a medieval woodcut, the naiveté of which always made him laugh, there were thirty or so Jews who were burning like straw and yet stubbornly continued to scream their prayers even at the stake. . . . Out of all this, sleep had brewed a dream.

But here the "interpretation" stops. Apparently Kien believes that these "day residues" are *all* the dream consists of. This is not an interpretation at all, but an academic dissection intended to protect the subject from any coherent meaning the dream might have. This is clearly a critique of the logocentric Kien, who is so blinded to all things human that he can understand his own dream only with a philologist's insight: by snuffling out its textual sources and rationalizing. While Kien's matter-of-fact source citations may still aid the astute reader in discovering more in Kien's dream than he himself is able to (cf. Hennighaus 1984: 78-83), his overly rational and superficial "interpretation" also serves as a caricature of Freudian interpretation and allows Canetti to make his critical point. It is noteworthy, however, that he must criticize the "reductionist" Freud by himself reducing Freud's method to its most mechanistic elements.[3]

We have looked at only a few instances of Freud's absence as presence in Canetti's work. A complete study would not only have to examine the works mentioned here more thoroughly; it would also have to account for *Crowds and Power*, whose apparent independence from Freud Canetti himself calls into question (Canetti 1980: 140). The absence of Freud in strategic places (in combination with the acknowledgment of his importance elsewhere) reinforces Freud's presence in Canetti's works. This state of affairs may be an unintentional, perhaps unconscious, tribute to

Freud, who wrote that the parts of dreams patients forget are often those to which they have the most resistance; these are the most important parts. What is not represented or recalled -- what is absent -- is that which is most present in the unconscious.

NOTES

[1] English translations given throughout this paper are my own. Page citations are to the original German editions listed in the references.

[2] "I must expressly warn the investigator against overestimating the importance of symbols in the interpretation of dreams, restricting the work of dream-translation to the translation of symbols, and neglecting the technique of utilizing the associations of the dreamer" (Freud 1900: 375).

[3] Hennighaus writes: ". . . for Kien, as for Freud, only the causality of the dream formation is important. Like Freud, he believes in the omnipotence of *ratio*, which need only find the right analytical formula in order to reestablish the sovereignty of 'his majesty the ego' over the anarchy of the drives . . ." (81; my translation). This seems to me an extreme over simplification of Freud's method, as is Kien's "interpretation". The question of authorial intentionality thus remains open to at least three alternatives: 1) Canetti himself misunderstood Freud (unlikely); 2) Canetti is deliberately exaggerating as part of his satire; 3) Canetti is not criticizing Freud at all, but only the penetration of an oversimplified, easy, jargonistic application of Freud's thought into all spheres of thinking.

REFERENCES

CANETTI, Elias.
    1935. *Die Blendung*. Originally published by Herbert Reichner Verlag, Vienna; reprinted by Carl Hanser Verlag, Munich, 1963.
    1960. *Masse und Macht* (Hamburg: Claassen Verlag, 1978).
    1967. *Die Stimmen von Marrakesch*, originally published in London by Canetti (Munich: Hanser, 1978).
    1975. "Karl Kraus, Schule des Widerstands". *Das Gewissen der Worte*. 1st ed. (Munich: Hanser) 39-49.
    1977. *Die gerettete Zunge. Geschichte einer Jugend* (Munich: Carl Hanser Verlag).
    1980. *Die Fackel im Ohr. Lebensgeschichte 1921-1931* (Munich: Carl Hanser Verlag).
    1985. *Das Augenspiel. Lebensgeschichte 1931-1937* (Munich: Carl Hanser Verlag).
FREUD, Sigmund.
    1900. *Die Traumdeutung*. The translation cited is that of A A. Brill (ed.), *The Basic Writings of Sigmund Freud* (New York: Random House, 1938), 181-549.
    1905. "Bruchstück einer Hysterie-Analyse". *Gesammelte Werke* 5 (Werke aus den Jahren 1904-05), ed. Anna Freud et al. (London: Imago, 1942) 161-286.

HENNIGHAUS, Lothar.
    1984. *Tod und Verwandlung. Elias Canettis poetische Anthropologie aus der Kritik der Psychoanalyse.* Europäische Hochschulschriften 767 (Frankfurt: Peter Lang).
JONES, Ernest.
    1953. *The Life and Work of Sigmund Freud*, in 3 vols. (New York: Basic Books).
MEILI, Barbara.
    1985. *Erinnerung und Vision. Der lebensgeschichtliche Hintergrund von Elias Canettis Roman "Die Blendung"* (= Studien zur Germanistik, Anglistik und Komparatistik 115; Bonn: Bouvier).

CANETTIAN AND FREUDIAN APPROACHES TO SWIFT

Steven J. Rosen
St. Peter's College

When Gulliver lies tied down and walked over by tiny Lilliputians or slays slimy, monstrous vermin, transformed physical proportions impose the presence of animal and human bodies with shocking vigor. This paper contrasts two ways of interpreting Swift's vivid, inventive treatment of the body, Freud's and Elias Canetti's. I argue that the latter's, less well-known perspective elucidates Swift's physical sensibility more effectively. The Canettian system more accurately reflects the *totality* of Swift's references to the body, better shows what motives *structure* that totality, and thereby better illuminates *Gulliver's Travels*'s artistic unity.

Contrasting Freudian and Canettian interpretations of Swift will also help us appreciate one reason why Canetti opposed Freud: that the latter's preoccupation with *libido* tends to trivialize and distort *literary* values.

A considerable and well-known body of Freudian commentary finds Swift's sexual sensibility disturbingly regressive and misogynistic. It reproves Swift's several anti-sexual scatological poems and connects the considerable scatology in *Gulliver's Travels* to Gulliver's eventual revulsion from his wife. As Freudians see it, Swift not only devises Gulliver's situations to accommodate regressive urges--as when he jumps into a tremendous turd; such indulgences betoken incapacity for adult sexuality. Furthermore, the revulsion Gulliver eventually suffers in his wife's presence apparently reflects Swift's personal flight from sex.

Now that Freudianism is, rightly, widely criticized for sexism, note that Freudian Swift critics consistently reprehended Swift's misogyny. In the most detailed critique of Swift from this standpoint, Phyllis Greenacre not only observed that Swift's "anal fixation" resulted in a "total retreat from genital sexuality" (1955: 114); she *protested* his

> peculiar fascination with and horror of woman's bodies, likening their sexual organs to the lower bowel and seeing them always as dangerously contaminating and yet in some way enticing. (86-7)

Likewise, D.H. Lawrence, Aldous Huxley, and John Middleton Murry deplored what Murry called Swift's "excremental vision" (1955; 432)--his disgust with defecation, sex, and ultimately all of life. As most Freudians and Lawrentans have seen it, Swift's horror at human waste, stench, and general body mess drove him--just as such disgust drove the Yahoo-crazed Gulliver--to misanthropy, misogyny, and madness.

Another Freudian critic, Norman O. Brown, attempted a revaluation of this "excremental vision" by treating Swift as a precursor, not a case, of Freud's idea that anal libido pervades culture. But Brown misread Swift as a precursor in his own attack on *sublimation*. Brown claims, for example, that "What makes man, is Swift's language, a Yahoo, 'with a strange disposition to nastiness and dirt...,' is, ironically, his disposition to rise above the body and negate it" (1959:293). But Yahoos do *not* sublimate their ordure; they employ it directly and uninhibitedly.

There is no good reason to shirk discussing Swift's scatology or sexuality. However, while Swift's genius does inhere in his power to present the body in a variety of startling situations, only a small part of that material is clearly sexual or scatological. Hence, his physical sensibility may well be better interpreted from a non-Freudian focus, and I think that Elias Canetti's *Crowds of Power* supplies that alternative.

By a *Canettian* approach, I mean one which focuses on power; attests to the fascination of crowds; places acquiring, ingesting, and excreting food (as indispensable power-processes) at the core of consciousness; understands madnesses chiefly as power-diseases, more often grounded in food-related than in sexual anxieties; and deplores the extreme likelihood of these power-diseases (*megalomania* and *paranoia*) in rulers. A Canettian perspective connects Swift's scatology to squeamishness about eating rather that sex; it regards Gulliver's eventual refusal to be touched as a disorder of power, rather than libido.

The most promising opportunity for comparing Freudian and Canettian perspectives on Swift lies in the resemblance of Gulliver's adventures to the classic paranoid hallucinations of Schreber, whose *Memoirs* both Freud and Canetti analyzed. Schreber, like Gulliver, felt himself surrounded by "so-called little men--tiny figures in human form" (Canetti 1960: 440). Freud found these delusions grounded in Schreber's "sexual life", specifically, repressed homosexuality (1911: 127). Indeed, Freud claimed, apropos of Schreber, that in general "Paranoia is a disorder in which... the really operative factor...lies in...homosexual components" (1911: 162).

The German judge D.P. Schreber hallucinated a delusionary mission "to redeem the world, and to restore mankind to their lost state of bliss"--essentially, by having sex with God, through penetration by his divine rays (Freud: 1911: 112). Gulliver's first confrontation with the Lilliputians shows a similar penetration motif. Forty bowmen mount him as he lies tied down, with the sun glaring in his eyes. And these Lilliputians--suggestively enough, six inches tall--not only attack the tied-up Gulliver with arrows, but stick a pike up his nose; yet he rather loves the little men, especially admiring the emperor's "strong and masculine features" (Swift: 1726:13).

Another resemblance between Schreber and Gulliver lies in their preoccupation with excretion, in which Schreber took "voluptuous pleasure" (Freud 1911:123). In his *Memoirs*, Schreber asserted that "any one who has been in such a relation as I have with divine rays is to some extent entitled to sh___ upon the whole world" (Freud 1911:123). But he hallucinated that a conspiracy kept him from enjoying his rightful evacuations. Clearly, Schreber's excrement complex resembles Gulliver's Lilliputian experience. Gulliver urinates torrentially; he defecates, not on the whole world, but gigantically, in open air, his "offensive matter...carried off in wheelbarrows", (Swift 1726: 12). He heroically pisses out a palace fire--and he too gets persecuted for this, impeached for treason primarily for "mak[ing] water within the precincts of the Royal Palace" (47-48).

What might the resemblance of Schreber's paranoid delusions to Gulliver's experiences mean? For Freud, the significance of Schreber's hallucinations was their homosexual origin. He analyzed Schreber's *Memoirs* to claim that the root of paranoia was always "an attempt to master an unconsciously reinforced current of homosexuality" (1911: 162). Accordingly, a Freudian critic might likewise regard *Gulliver's Travels* as the product of a repressed homosexual's paranoid fantasies.

However, even if Gulliver's adventures did originate as homosexual fantasies, or were "undertaken out of a lust of the eye" (Greenacre 1955:95), surely few readers experience then as such. In *Gulliver's Travels* the fascinating alterations of perspective rarely generate lust or even disgust, but frequently a thrilling physical *fear* or *triumph*. Typically, Swift's presentations of other bodies enhances their *danger*. Thus, repeatedly terrorized, Gulliver's eventual horror of marital intimacy is an insanely displaced fear of violence. He rejects sex because he feels imperiled by touch; not, as Freudians stress, because he is disgusted by excrement. Swift's anti-sexual scatology is also best understood in this context: a totality of body representations certainly organized by paranoia, but not necessarily by anal libido. And such a sensibility is far better elucidated by Canetti's *Crowds and Power* than by Freudian approaches.

Canetti has also analyzed Schreber's Gulliverian *Memoirs*, chiefly to illustrate similarities in the defensive endeavors of paranoics and absolute rulers. He saw Schreber, who regarded himself as "champion for the German people" as a precursor of Hitler. Consequently, Canetti (1960: 449-50) deplored Freud's

> well-known attempt to find the origin of [Schreber's] particular illness, and of paranoia in general, in repressed homosexuality. There could scarcely...be a greater mistake. Paranoia may be occasioned by anything; the essence of each case is the *structure* of the delusional world and the way it *is peopled*. Processes of power always play a crucial part in it.

in essence, Canetti's "paranoic feels surrounded by a pack of enemies" (1960: 456). And Canetti insists that tendencies to such paranoia lie deep in all human nature, independent of sex, given the necessity of eating and its inherently fearsome brutality:

> We all eat and . . . each of us has grown strong on the bodies of innumerable corpses. Here each of us is a king on a field of corpses.

Canetti grounds consciousness--not, like Freud, in sex or libido, but in eating and associated survival processes. For Canetti, *megalomania* reduces to a mania for prey; *paranoia*, to the dread of being preyed upon. And Canetti explains excremental disgust, *as did Swift*, as uneasy guilt over killing the things we have loved to eat.

Freudian critics have pointed out that Gulliver's size requires him to excrete publically; it generally facilitates exhibitionistic and regressive sexual opportunities. And from a Freudian perspective, I interpreted the Voyage to Lilliput as a masochistic-homosexual fantasy: Gulliver's size transformation affords him disguised homosexual gratifications. Now, a Canettian interpretation of the voyage to Lilliput would focus, as with Schreber, not on the supposed sexual origin of Swift's or his hero's paranoia, but on "its structure" and "the way it is peopled". In Lilliput, Gulliver contends with an ambivalent but fundamentally hostile *crowd* of little creatures. In his one explicit reference to Swift, Canetti compared the hallucinations of drunkards, with their "crowd sensations on the skin" and sense of being "caught up in . . . masses of tiny things", to "precisely the Lilliput effect" (1960: 362). More generally, he regards such imaginations as *paranoid*. The prototype paranoid Schreber was surrounded, assaulted, climbed on, penetrated, and minutely managed in his bodily functions by myriad "little men" he hallucinated. Canetti's description of the physical relationship between Schreber and his crowd, "the one a giant and the others tiny creatures fussing around him", certainly applies to Gulliver (1960: 449).

For Canetti, the most striking characteristic of crowds is their tendency to increase. By likewise noting its tendency to grow, Swift suggests the threatening power of the Lilliputian multitude. At their first confrontation, one Lilliputian mounts Gulliver, then forty. Fifty cut the strings holding down his head, one hundred bring him food, and the crowd, when he eats, "makes a thousand marks of wonder" (Swift 1726: 7). In town, ten thousand Lilliputians mount him on ladders; 100,000 simply view him.

Significant too is the crowd's potent available hostility. At the outset, they overcome Gulliver by sheer numbers, i.e., attacking with "showers of arrows" (Swift 1726:6). Eventually the court conspires to blind, then starve Gulliver, so that by a crowd effort, "five or six thousand...might, in two or three days, cut [his] flesh from [his] bones" (Swift 1726:51). In effect, the crowd, *en masse*, threatens to prey upon Gulliver.

Here is one of the most Canettian aspects of Swift, the readiness with which each imagines power relations in terms of *eating*. "Everything which is eaten", says Canetti, "is the food of power" (1960: 219). To have power is to have another in your mouth, in the grasp of your jaws, about to be rended and devoured. From this perspective, rather than being tied up and sexually penetrated, Gulliver's initial confrontation with the Lilliputian horde would suggest the *Canettian* ordeal: being in the jaws of your predators. From Canettian perspective, the arrows and pike that penetrate Gulliver more readily suggest a predator's teeth than phalluses.

Another Canettian eating concept applies when Gulliver, securely chained in the city, finds that flight is impossible. Then he experiences what both he and Canetti calls "Melancholy", and which, Canetti (1960: 347) says

> begins when flight transformations are abandoned because they are felt to be useless...[the Melancholic is resigned to his fate and sees himself as prey, then as food, and finally as carrion or excrement.

Having survived the Lilliputian's prickings and bindings, i.e., the clutches of their collective jaws, Gulliver proceeds to glory in heroic feats of consumption and excretion. Because he is so prodigiously fed by the crowd, it is a short step to imagine Gulliver feeding *on* them. And that is how Canetti interprets the Gulliverian hallucinations of Schreber, as "a precise model of *political* power, power which feeds on the crowd and derives its substance from it" (1960:441). More particularly, Swift conceived Gulliver's confrontation with the Lilliputians in accord with what Canetti calls "national crowd symbols" (160:169). In Lilliput, Canetti's English crowd symbol--the shop's captain--confronts his polar opposite in the mounted bowmen of the Mongol or Tartar horde (another subject of Canetti's).

Clearly, Gulliver's adventures, i.e., bizarre physical situations, consistently involve, not sex, but power processes associated with eating and being eaten--in Lilliput by the crowd, in Brobdignag by giants.

In Brobdignag the now diminutive Gulliver fears the giant's teeth and knives; feels disgust at their nursing, chewing, and micturating; engages in food fights with a dwarf and monkey; cuts up and tears apart gigantic vermin--having "the good fortune to rig up [a fly's] belly,...lest [he] might have been infallibly torn to pieces and devoured" (Swift 1726: 72); jumps into a gigantic turd; and eventually, escapes from this horror of predation, mastication, and defecation by flight. All these episodes involve what Canetti analyzes as food-related terrors. And when the good Brobdignagian King rejects "secrets of state" and gunpowder for "mak[ing] two Ears of Corn grow...where only one grew before" (Swift 1726: 111), that food image epitomizes rather than transcends the adventure's unifying and disturbing implication: *that life feeds off life*. From the time Gulliver hides from the monsters' scythes among their enormous corn until he is carried away in the talons of a gigantic bird, he has to fear predatory violence--that he might "be a morsel in the mouth of the first among these enormous barbarians who should happen to seize" him (Swift 1726: 66). The presence of giants, however gentle, naturally imposes a vision of life's fundamental savagery. Gulliver's altered perspective forces him to realize the violence of eating.

Gulliver first manifests both excremental and sexual disgusts in Brobdignag, aversions coincidentally evoked when the gigantic Maids of Honor urinate. But the Queen's *eating*, her huge crunching mouthfuls, also nauseates him. Obviously, the Voyage's giganticism generally conduces to disgust. Can we say which of Gulliver's aversion is most fundamental?

Freudian critics, as noted earlier, explain Swift's scatology in relation to sex (or anal libido), noting, as Swift sometimes did, that excrement disgust conflicts with (yet may be evoked by) sexual attraction. However, Swift's excremental vision may be better explained, again, from a Canettian standpoint. After all, excreting always follows eating, the fundamental power-process for Canetti. Our ordure testifies, shamefully, to what we have killed, torn apart, swallowed, and digested. Excrement, Canetti (1960:211) writes,

> is loaded with our whole blood guilt. By it we know what we have murdered. It is the compressed sum of all the evidence against us....and, as such, it stinks and cries to heaven. It is remarkable how we isolate ourselves with it; in special rooms, set aside for the purpose, we get rid of it; . . . . it is clear that we are ashamed of it.

In a long autobiographical poem celebrating his erection of two gendered outhouses, Swift, like Canetti, pondered *why* excrement disgusts (and thereby conflicts with sex); and he answered, like Canetti, that it evinces our gustatory sin--in his term, "gluttony" (1730: 62). The moral horror of eating makes excrement disgusting and sex problematical for both writers.

As noted above, the Freudian critic Greenacre (as well as the Lawrentian, Murry) derived Swift's deplorable misogyny from his association of women with excrement--even to the point of confusing women's genitals with their lower bowels. Granted that association, Gulliver (and presumably Swift) was also disgusted by woman's organ of *feeding*, the breast--not only when a Brobdignagian breast exposes a cancer, but when another one merely nurses. Greenacre also opined that Swift often referred to breasts as "dugs" because that word resembles "dung" (1955: 113). But for Swift the association also worked the other way--that is, to remind us that we excrete what we have eaten. For example, when the Maids of Honor urinate before Gulliver, they discharge, not simply "urine", but "what they had drunk" (Swift 1726: 95). Typically, Swift's terms implicate all food-associated actions. And a Canettian versus a Freudian focus on Swift's "excremental vision" reminds us that Swift's scatology functions primarily, not to degrade women, but to invoke a *disturbing totality of eating processes*.

Reflect upon "A Modest Proposal". For Swift, *eating is preying*, something he can neither forget nor fully accept. Likewise, Canetti stresses the human tendency to a horrified sympathy with what we eat. He sees this in the Sanskrit word for flesh, which etymologically means "me-he", and connotes the basic, natural dread of punishment for eating: being eaten (1960: 326). Swift, similarly, reminds us that human treatment of other animals constitutes a damning collective sin. After the Houyhnhnms learn that the English castrate horses, they resolve to emasculate their Yahoos.

As we would expect, in Gulliver's final voyage the most fully elaborated bodily function is neither copulating nor excreting but eating.

The Yahoos' diet is detestable. Their usual food, which they "greedily devour", is loathsomely smelly "Ass's flesh" (Swift 1726: 199). Furthermore, "they held their Food between the Claws of their Feet, and tore it with their Teeth" (199). To the abstemious and gentle Houyhnhnms, nothing...rendered the Yahoos more odious than their undistinguished appetite...[but] it was peculiar in their temper that they were fonder of what they could get by rapine or stealth at a greater distance, than much better food provided for them at Home" (277-8). Typically, Swift associates, not sex, but the indispensable processes of *eating* with *aggression* and *transgression*.

On the other hand, the Houyhnhnms ingest only milk and vegetables; rather than tear their food apart, they eat "with much decency and regularity" (200). Interestingly, Gulliver notes the privacy Houyhnhnms preserve in their eating while dining together: "each Horse and Mare eat their own hay" (200). Gulliver's own diet among the Houyhnhnms, similarly, minimizes both individual and communal aggression against food. He extensively describes how his prepares his oat cakes, emphasizing their *construction*: Yahoos tear apart their food, Gulliver gently builds his up. Carnivorous by nature, as his teeth betray him to be, Gulliver "traps an occasional Rabbit, or Bird, by Springes made of made of Yahoo's Hairs" (201). There Swift, like Canetti, invites us to feel the horror of predation by projecting humans (as Yahoos) into the situation of their prey--something he most famously accomplished in "A Modest Proposal". Thus among the Houyhnhnms, by eating little, eating gently, constructing rather than destroying his food, and above all, by eating and preparing his food by himself, Gulliver denies the communal guilt of eating.

Hence, when Gulliver must return home and finds himself averse to the mere "presence" of his wife and children and their "smell", what he dwells upon is his refusal to share meals with them (Swift 1726: 254):

> much less could I suffer them to eat in the same room. To this hour they dare not touch my bread, or drink our of the same cup; neither was I ever able to let one of them take me by the hand.

Gulliver's paranoid refusal to be touched, his inability to "suffer a neighbor Yahoo in [his] company, without fearing this teeth and his claws, "derives from a fundamental horror of violence most frequently evoked for Swift by *eating and eating together* (260).

Crazy as they are, Gulliver's attitudes about eating clearly prefigure Swift's. In his final years he also ate alone. As his dementia or insanity gained upon Swift, his caretaker (Murry 1955: 483) wrote that Swift

> would not eat or drink if his servant stayed in the room. His meat was served up ready cut, and sometimes it would lay for an hour on the table before he would touch it, and then eat it walking.

Swift apparently became what Canetti calls a *melancholic*--someone afraid to confront his food and cut it up for fear it might suggest his own eventual end as prey.

In conclusion, it is not Freud's but Canetti's perspective--grounding madnesses, as power-diseases, in the fascination of crowds and fearfulness of eating-processes--that readily shows what deep connections unify *Gulliver's Travels*.

Of course, while Canetti's concerns fit Swift's more closely than Freud's do, one may still appreciate whatever illumination a Freudian perspective on Swift supplies. I contrast Freudian and Canettian focuses on Swift mainly to understand why Canetti opposed Freud. Projecting their rival analyses of Schreber onto Swift shows that Freudianism, unlike Canettianism, tends to distort and devalue much classic *literature*, most of which deals directly with power, not sex. Most of the classical literary genres--adventure, history, tragedy, satire, political oratory--can be readily described in Canettian, not Freudian, terms. When Canetti conflates the concept of *ruler* and *paranoic*, insisting on their mutually irresistible tendency to dissimulate malice and command mass deaths--as Gulliver did in bitterly generalizing about Kings and ministers after the Lilliputian court--he commits dubious exaggerations about politics but exactly describes the laws of a certain literary genre, classical political tragedy. As a more traditionally literary thinker than Freud, Canetti's world view enables us to enjoy the continuity between ancient and contemporary literature; and through such concepts as crowd symbols and the projection of eating processes, Canetti refreshingly reconceives that literature without distorting it.

NOTES

[1] By *Freudian*, I mean an approach which focuses on sexual scenes and allusions; regards sex as a work's organizing subject; interprets fantasized physical confrontations and intimacies, despite their subject's disavowals, as sexual wish fulfillments; and seeks the cause of madness in sexual regression, repression, and dysfunction. See Ferenczi (1926), who supposed Swift impotent, "with a lack of courage in relation to women of good character and perhaps with a lasting aggressive tendency towards women of a lower type" (Brown 1959: 182); and Karpman (1942), who pronounced Swift a "neurotic who exhibited psychosexual infantility, with a particular showing of coprophilia, associated with misogyny" (Brown 1959: 182). Greenacre (1955) and Brown (1959) are discussed above. The present author devised the Freudian interpretation of Lilliput, after Freud's understanding of Schreber (as homosexual); of course, the "Canettian" interpretations of Swift are also formulated by me, not by Canetti.

[2] Lawrence wrote of Swift's "insane...horror" that "Celia shits"; "the very fact...simply devastate[s] his consciousness" (1928: 26). Huxley's well-known essay focuses on Swift's "hatred of bowels" (1931: 110). Murry is discussed above.

REFERENCES

BROWN, Norman O.
    1959. *Life Against Death: The Psychoanalytical Meaning of History* (Middletown, Ct.: Wesleyan Univ. Press). Page references here are to the 1971 third paperback printing.

CANETTI, Elias.
  1960. *Masse und Macht* (Hamburg: Clasen Verlag). Page references are to the English trans. by Carol Stewart, *Crowds and Power* (New York: Seabury Press, 1978).
FREUD, Sigmund.
  1911. "Psychoanalytic Notes Upon an Autobiographical Case of Paranoia (Dementia Paranoides)". Page references are to the uncredited English translation in *Freud: Three Case Histories*, ed. Philip Rieff (New York: Collier, 1963).
GREENACRE, Phyllis.
  1955. *Swift and Carroll: A Psychoanalytic Study of Two Lives* (New York: International Universities Press).
HUXLEY, Aldous.
  1931. *Do What You Will* (London: Chatto and Windus).
LAWRENCE, D.H.
  1928. *Letter* to Lady Ottoline Morrell 28 Dec. Page references to "D.H. Lawrence", *Selected Literary Criticism*, ed. Anthony Beal (New York: Viking Press, 1966).
MURRY, John Middleton.
  1955. *Jonathan Swift: A Critical Biography* (New York: Noonday).
SWIFT, Jonathan.
  1726. *Gulliver's Travels*, ed. Robert Greenberg (2nd ed., chiefly from 1735 text; New York: Collier Books, 1962).
  1730. "A Panegyrick on the Dean", in *The Poems of Jonathan Swift*, ed. Padriac Colum (New York: Collier Books, 1962), 57-64.

XIII

SEMIOTICS OF POETIC DISCOURSE

THE PRAGMATICAL DIMENSION OF RESERVE IN JOHN KEBLE'S *THE CHRISTIAN YEAR*

Beverly Seaton
Ohio State University

> *Those old worshippers of silence,*
> *are they indeed so difficult*
> *to understand?*
>
> -- Charles Morris, "Semiotic" --

John Keble's collection of devotional poems, *The Christian Year*, 1827, was one of the most popular works of poetry in the nineteenth century, selling 158 editions by 1873 in addition to many unofficial and pirated copies (Tennyson 1981: 226). But Keble was famous not only as a religious poet but also as one of the founders, perhaps the main inspiration, of the Oxford Movement, a reform movement in the Church of England which arose largely as a response to the prominence of Evangelicals within the Church and the rights gained by Dissenters without.

Keble's 1833 sermon, "National Apostasy", preached at St. Mary's, Oxford, set forth the call to action for a number of young clergymen at Oxford, most prominently John Henry Newman and Edwin Pusey. These men wrote a number of Tracts setting forth their positions, which gave them the name "Tractarians". Basically, they issued a call for unquestioning support of the national church an a return to more Catholic traditions. Never as influential in the Church as the Evangelical party, the Oxford Movement was critically wounded when Newman, along with some others, "went over to Rome".

One of the most important Tractarian concepts was Reserve. For the individual worshipper, Reserve is the quality of holding back, of controlling, religious emotion; for the Deity, Reserve is the prudent concealment of total knowledge from an unworthy or immature subject. As a spiritual ideal, Reserve is allied with humility and silence, with quiet obedience and acceptance. The principal Tractarian writer on Reserve, Isaac Williams, developed the topic to an extreme, implying that religion should guard its mysteries from the world and not work very hard to bring in converts. Williams' target was the Evangelical Party, which attempted to bring all sinners to Christ through enthusiastic preaching and teaching (Williams 1837). A companion concept to Reserve was Analogy, the gradual revelation of God through his works, which G.B. Tennyson has called, "God's way of practising Reserve" (1981:

47). Both Reserve and Analogy are important aspects of *The Christian Year*, but my specific topic in this paper concerns Reserve.

In his study of *The Christian Year*, G.B. Tennyson suggest that the practice of Reserve is behind many of the difficulties modern readers have in appreciating Keble (1981: 104-5), and my own reading of the poems verifies his observations. More specifically, he writes that "Analogy governs the subject matter of the poetry, Reserve the style" (1981: 93). However, I feel that Reserve is more than *style*, at least in the way that I might define *style*. Semiotic analysis can help clarify the role played by Reserve in Keble's work.

We can begin with the point that *The Christian Year* exemplifies the concept of open text with a Model Reader who can be partially defined by his/her ability to relate to Reserve (Eco 1979). In *Foundations of the Theory of Signs*, Charles Morris writes that the pragmatical dimension of semiosis, governing the relation of signs to interpreters, deals with the "biotic aspects" of semiosis, or "psychological, biological and sociological phenomena which occur in the functioning of signs" (1938: 30). Perhaps we can add "spiritual" to the catalog of the biotic aspects of signs, thus locating the problem of Reserve in the province of pragmatics. Further, when we see that Reserve concerns the relationship of signs to their interpreters, we need to consider the issue of the interpretant.

My view is that Reserve is a habit of religious thought, a tendency to view religious issues a certain way, which fits the definition of *interpretant* given by Morris, following Peirce: "in the end the interpretant of a symbol must reside in a habit and not in the immediate psychological reaction which the sign vehicle evoked or in the attendant images or emotions" (1938: 31). Since I am discussing poem, I will take a broader meaning of the word "symbol" in this definition, namely that the interpretant of a *devotional poem* resides in this "habit". Reserve, thus, is a habitual response to the act of worship; when it is activated in the Model Reader of *The Christian Year*, the Reader is able to locate the significance of the poem's themes more surely than a Reader not similarly equipped.

The central problem, then, is this: how does the poet communicate to his readers the notion of non-communication? If a poem is an act of communication, how can non-communication be put across? To the modern reader, most of the poems seem dull and murky, lacking originality and focus. But this is not because Keble is not a talented poet: while his poems were popular with the mass of readers, they were equally praised by intellectuals of the period. He was named Professor of Poetry at Oxford from 1831-41 (two terms) on the basis of his poetry.

Certain psychological and sociological assumptions about the Model Reader are relevant to the problem. One of these is the underlying assumption, by Keble and other Tractarians, that most people prefer a noisy, exciting life to a quiet, placid one. Tract 29, for example, "Christian Liberty, or, Why Should We Belong to the Church of England", tells of a parishioner who attends a dissenter's meeting and is examined about this behavior by his parish priest. The author explains the appeal of the dissenting preacher: ". . . there was something in the energy of the preacher's manner, in the vehement action by which his teaching was accompanied, and in his seeming earnestness in the holy cause of God . . . ." The priest is contrasted to the chapel minister: "Compared with the fervour of this man, the quiet but sound discourses of his Rector seemed spiritless and tame" ("A Layman" 1834: 1). In *The Christian Year* Keble usually assumes that the choice of quiet and peace is not a popular one, that retirement and silence are burdens.

Likewise, Keble pictures life as a vale of tears requiring much resignation and stoic acceptance for successful passage. While all Victorians do not share this consistent melancholy, it certainly prevails in *The Christian Year*. The poem for the

"Nineteenth Sunday after Trinity", for example, takes its text from the third chapter of Daniel, the story of Shadrach, Meshach, and Abednego in the fiery furnace, and develops the notion that in this life we are all in a similar situation. Examples from life are a woman in the "first lorn hour of widowhood", a father watching at a child's deathbed, and a "Christian Pastor, bowed to earth/with thankless toil, and vile esteemed . . ." (Keble 1827: 129).

These two attitudes could be considered interpretants, inasmuch as they constitute a habitual response to the general situation of life, and they combine with Reserve to model a state of mind receptive to the poet's views of acceptable worship. They are both, however, much more easily identified in the poetry itself than is Reserve.

Two other important aspects of the poems can be explained in light of the intertextuality of *The Christian Year* with the Book of Common Prayer. Keble's book is a companion volume to the prayer book, with poems for every Sunday of the year, other important Holy Days, and various sacraments. The Sunday poem often relates to the scripture reading for the day, usually the Gospel although sometimes the Epistle. This intertextuality predicates knowledge of the prayer book on the part of the Model Reader, which in turn leads to two assumptions about the Reader. First, the Reader is a church member; Keble is preaching to the converted. We find no elementary evangelism here, no invitations to lost souls--the Reader is a communicant member of the church in which Keble is a priest. Thus the poet and the Reader already share a set of spiritual assumptions, which does not need to be specifically communicated in the poems. Second, the Reader is a family member, in the larger sense of nation as family. With such social solidarity, one has no need of explaining oneself.

Thus, both the intertextuality and the two more easily identified interpretants discussed above help narrow the focus of each poem's act of communication so that Reserve can be more easily accommodated. But we still need to see how the habitual response we call Reserve is triggered in the Reader.

First, there are a few fairly explicit references to Reserve, all of which relate to the difficulties humans have in comprehending the Deity. The other part of the definition of Reserve, relating to the worshipper's own reservation of his religious faith, is only indirectly inferred. For example, "Holy Communion" (171) begins with this stanza:

> O God of Mercy, God of Might,
> How Should pale sinners bear the sight,
> If, as Thy power is surely here,
> Thine open glory should appear?

In the next stanzas, allusions to Moses meeting with God on Mt. Sinai appear, implying, however, that modern Faith can see "wonders Sinai never knew" because Christians can look on the body of Christ crucified for mankind. A poem with a similar development is that for the "Thirteenth Sunday after Trinity", which takes as its text part of the Gospel reading from the Book of Common Prayer, "He turned Him unto His disciples, and said privately, Blessed are the eyes which see the things that ye see; for I tell you, that many prophets and kings have desired to see those things which ye see, and have not seen them; and to hear those things which ye hear, and have not heard them" (Luke 10: 23-24). While the prophets beg to see God's glory, God "their aching gaze repressed/Which sought behind the veil to see . . ." (119). However, modern Christians can see God "as in a glass" by looking on the Savior's face; although "The rays of the Almighty's face/No sinner's eye might then receive", humans can look on the face of Christ, "our dear Savior's face benign" (119). In both of these poems, Christ is a less brilliant and more comprehensible *visual* object of worship.

Vision-light imagery, in fact, is the most common sort of imagery Keble employs to suggest Reserve. Many of the poems, while lacking a direct reference to Reserve, manage to suggest it through application of the constant values of the visual equation developed in the two poems discussed, and a few other like them. Keble's use of vision images has a traditional base, for the Judeo-Christian God is not one to be looked on or even portrayed. The iconoclastic bias of much of the Old Testament validates the notion of Reserve on the part of God, at least in the sense of *seeing* God. Keble merely uses a common metaphoric formula implying that God is light, then describes the light as similar to the light of the sun, too strong for us to look at directly. This use of vision-light imagery then becomes an encoded element in all of the poems.

Another sort of imagery is used in the same way, hearing-sound images. Keble's poems are replete with references to the strong *light* of heaven and the *sound* of heavenly music. The voice of God is just as elemental a concept as the face of God, but it does not receive so much attention in Western religious tradition. However, in many New Testament episodes, Christ speaks of those who hear him, as in the passage already quoted in full, "to hear those things which ye hear", or "He that has ears to hear, let him hear" (Matthew 11:15). The strong opposition between light and dark is not paralleled by the sound-silence dichotomy, for its power is not just based on human biological functions of sight and hearing, but on the functioning of the heavens themselves. This union of revealed religion and nature is especially important in poems like these which make great use of Analogy.

A series of eleven poems, from the poem for "Epiphany" through that for "Ash-Wednesday", shows the operation of these two types of imagery in various ways. (Of course, every time Keble uses light or sound imagery he is not suggesting Reserve.) The term *epiphany* means the manifestation of something, just as *theophany* means the manifestation of God. The first poem in the series, that for "Epiphany", refers to the Biblical event which is called Epiphany or Twelfth Night, the manifestation of Christ to the Gentiles through the star in the east. In Keble's poem, the star is clear to us in early life, but "Too soon the glare of earthly day/Buries, to us, Thy brightness keen" (33). This is a reversal of the light equals God image, with worldly things being so bright that we cannot see the star. The star, we discover, is not all that brilliant; we must find our way back to seeing it, perhaps not until "calm old age", by following "waymarks sure" (33). Thus in Keble's way of looking at the Epiphany, God was showing us the way not by an overwhelmingly bright light, but by one we must work to see. (Actually, my use of *work* is probably a heresy of some sort; perhaps *obey* is the better word.

The following poem, for the "First Sunday after Epiphany" (35), is one of those poems in the book which are strongest in developing Analogy, with an emphasis on the domestic aspects of God in nature:

> Needs no show of mountain hoary
>   Winding shore or deepening glen,
> Where the landscape in its glory
>   Teaches truth to wandering men:
> Give true hearts but earth and sky,
> And some flowers to bloom and die,
> Homely scenes and simple views
> Lowly thoughts may best infuse.

Vision and sound imagery complements the theme of humility here, in such lines as these (35):

> Soft as Memnon's harp at morning,
> To the inward ear devout,
> Touched by light, with heavenly warning,
> Your transporting chords ring out.

Words such as "soft", "quiet", and "modest" set the tone. The contrast between the soft sights and sounds of nature which reveal God to us is carried on in the next poem, for the "Second Sunday after Epiphany", where the worldly life is "loud" and Christian joy is "silent". Keble praises the "richest, tenderest glow" of the "autumnal sun", as presaging the sight of God at death. And in the very next poem, for the "Third Sunday after Epiphany", the "autumnal sun" of the first stanza is paired with a rainbow, "Flinging soft radiance far and wide". The sight of the rainbow is paralleled by the sound of a singing lark, but then (37):

> Brighter than rainbow in the north,
> More cheery than the matin lark,
> Is the true gleam of Christian worth . . .

This "gleam" is compared to a "diamond blazing in the mine", because it is "unseen by all but Heaven" (39). Here we have an indirect reference to Reserve on the part of the individual worshipper, one which is typical of these poems.

In the Book of Common Prayer, the Gospel lesson for the Fourth Sunday after Epiphany concerns the story of Christ taming a storm at sea and driving the demons from men by forcing them into the bodies of swine. Keble's poem for the same Sunday is based on that story, emphasizing the peace after the calming of the storm and the peace of mind of the worshipper after his own demons, his own "storms within", have been exorsized. Obedience and devotion lead to quiet, to peace, to calm. The next poem, for the "Fifth Sunday after Epiphany", also opposes noise to quiet, referring to storms within as in the previous poem. The light imagery in this poem shows worldly cares of two sorts with two different characteristics: "high estate" is marked by too much light, or "glare", while poverty and trouble is marked by "gloom". The Cross, however, "makes night of day" by its "radiance" (43).

The next two poems, that for the "Sixth Sunday after Epiphany" and that for "Septuagesima Sunday", stress humility and lowliness. In the first, Keble invests religious devotion with characteristics of those diminished aspects of life such as a flower, "tender" and "frail", or "some dim vision" which we cherish. Humility is characterized in vision and sound imagery: "still voice and closed eye,/Suit best with hearts beyond the sky" (46). The poem for "Septuagesima Sunday" (46) is one his most famous, with Analogy in its theme, comparing Nature to the Bible as a source of knowledge about God.

> There is a book, who runs may read,
> Which heavenly truth imparts,
> And all the lore its scholars need,
> Pure eyes and Christian hearts.

Throughout the poem, vision imagery dominates, although there is sound imagery as well. Sin alone keeps us from seeing the "mystic heaven and earth within". The last stanza (47) is a petition for the "pure eyes" of the first stanza:

> Thou, who hast given me eyes to see
> And love this sight so fair,
> Give me a heart to find out Thee,
> And read Thee everywhere.

Vision-light imagery dominates the poem for "Sexagesima Sunday", in words and phrases like "wandering eyes", "lawless glances", "the light of Christian lore", and "Faith's eye". While "fallen man" stands before God's judgment, he can see the Garden of Eden, which was left in sight so as to remind man of God. The poem for Quinquegesima Sunday" (50), on the theme of the rainbow covenant (Genesis 9:13), develops the notion of the rainbow as one substitute for the brilliance of God's presence:

> What but the gentle rainbow's gleam,
> Soothing the wearied sight,
> That cannot bear the solar beam,
> With soft undazzling light?

Then, Christ's human aspects are paralleled to the rainbow (51):

> The Son of God in radiance beamed
> Too bright for us to scan,
> But we may face the rays that streamed
> From the mild Son of Man.

In the final poem in this series, that for "Ash-Wednesday", again we find abundant vision imagery. The first stanza speaks of the sinner's "swelling eye" and the second of "The loving eye that watches thine" (51). Stanza three has "a pitying eye" belonging to a sympathetic friend. But the important eye is Christ's, in stanza six, when the penitent sinner has withdrawn himself from others to pray, as admonished in scriptures, "in secret". Then, in the final stanza (52), the redeemed souls on their way to Heaven are described:

> With upward eye they float serene,
> And learn to bear their Savior's blaze
> When Judgment shall undraw the screen . . .

These eleven poems are quite typical of the entire volume, in which the twin dichotomies of light-dark and sound-silence are worked in various ways so as to suggest Reserve. Unless the reader is prepared for the poems, not only for their intertextuality with the Book of Common Prayer but also for the prevalence of Reserve as interpretant, the poems cannot function as complete acts of communication. Another aspect of the poems' intertextuality with the prayer book needs to be mentioned, that the poems themselves are often cast in the form of prayer, a specific act of worship which again suggests Reserve because prayer is, by scripture authority, a private act.

When Eco analyzes the many functions of the interpretant in *A Theory of Semiotics*, we find that one of them explains further the role of Reserve in *The Christian Year*: the interpretant can guarantee the validity of the sign (1976: 68). All of this imagery, all the repetition of such words as *silent, solitary, hidden, faint, quivering, veil, quiet, shade, inward, soft, still*--are granted authority by the concept of Reserve. To see that this is true, we only need to consider the other point of view, that of the Evangelicals. From their perspective, these words, this imagery, would be meaningless if not heretical. Their God is anxious to be recognized; their religious emotion spills forth in joyful noises. Their devotion is matched by good works, and their Christ walks among men.

Thus, considering Reserve to be the interpretant, validating the concepts expressed in the poems, I think we can say that Reserve goes beyond style. However, G.B. Tennyson's observation that "Analogy governs the subject matter" is certainly true (1981: 93). I think we can argue that this fact made *The Christian Year* acceptable to readers who were perhaps not so tuned to Reserve. For while to the Tractarian, Analogy shows that God wants us to see him indirectly, in his works, thus reserving complete manifestation from us, to the Evangelical, God's revelation of himself in Nature is just further proof that he wants us to know him more completely. Together with the revelation of the Bible, the book of Nature pictures God for the Evangelical much more overwhelmingly than any metaphor about looking into the face of the sun could possibly express.

But how Analogy functions in these poems so as to suit two very different Model Readers is another topic.

REFERENCES

ECO, Umberto.
    1976. *A Theory of Semiotics* (Bloomington: Indiana University Press).
    1979. *The Role of the Reader: Explorations in the Semiotics of Texts* (Bloomington: Indiana University Press).

KEBLE, John.
    1827. *The Christian Year*. Page references in the paper are from an American edition (Philadelphia: Altemus, n.d.).

"LAYMAN, A"
    1834. "Christian Liberty; or, Why Should We Belong to the Church of England?" in *Tracts for the Times*, Volume 1 (London: Rivington).

MORRIS, Charles.
    1938. *Foundations of the Theory of Signs* (Chicago: University of Chicago Press).

TENNYSON, G.B.
    1981. *Victorian Devotional Poetry: The Tractarian Mode* (Cambridge: Harvard University Press).

WILLIAMS, Isaac.
    1837. "On Reserve in Communicating Religious Knowledge", in *Tracts for the Times* (London: Rivington).

NEGATIVE CAPABILITIES: SHIFTING SIGNS IN KEATS'S "ODE TO A NIGHTINGALE"

Scott Simpkins
South Dakota State University

John Keats's famous "Ode to a Nightingale" (1819) offers a working model of his principle of "Negative Capability", that frame of mind in which an individual "is capable of being in uncertainties, Mysteries, doubts, without any irritable reaching after fact & reason" (1817: 193). Through a text constructed of shifting signs, Keats encourages free, meaning-less production as the most likely way to elicit incalculable associations and interpretations from the reader.

In fact, Keats gives readers no choice; by providing an initiating version, a prototext containing a plenitude of gaps and conflicts, he forces them to produce their own final version. Earl Wasserman observes (1953: 178): "In any reading of the 'Ode to a Nightingale' the turmoil will not down . . . . Forces contend wildly within the poem, not only without resolution, but without possibility of resolution". This fosters a reading which effectively releases the reader from constraints of logic, allowing the decoding process to develop unencumbered by expectations of a definitive result. As Keats (1818: 224) argues in his personal correspondence, "We hate poetry that has a palpable design on us--and if we do not agree, seems to put its hand in its breeches pocket".

The conflicting planes of signification throughout the poem promote unrestricted readings as the speaker, while experiencing a state of "drowsy numbness" (1), reflects upon thoughts prompted by a nightingale's song. Moreover, the conclusion (79-80) challenges *all* of already undecidable reading activity up to that point when the speaker suddenly exclaims:

Was it a vision, or a waking dream?
Fled is that music:--Do I wake or sleep?

This ending offers the major decoding index to the poem. By placing this development at the conclusion, Keats provokes a sublative coding which demands "retroactive reading", to use Michael Riffaterre's term (1978: 5) for the "second interpretation" of the text which he classifies as "the truly *hermeneutic* reading". Riffaterre asserts (1978: 5-6):

As he progresses through the text, the reader remembers what he has just read and modifies his understanding of it in the light of what he is now decoding.... As he works forward from start to finish, [the reader] is reviewing, revising, comparing backwards.

The most important component of this notion, however, is the circularity it enforces, an endless spiral which is grounded by the cues derived from the text. In the forceful conclusion to *Semiotics of Poetry*, Riffaterre (1978: 166) confirms this when he argues that

> The reader's manufacture of meaning is ... not so much *a progress through the poem* and a half-random accretion of verbal associations, as it is a *seesaw scanning* of the text, compelled by the very duality of the signs--ungrammatical as mimesis, grammatical within the significance network. This seesawing from one sign value to the other, this alternating appearance and disappearance of significance, both in spite and because of unacceptable features on the plane of mimetic meaning, is a kind of semiotic circularity characterizing the practice of signification known as poetry. In the reader's mind it means a continual recommencing, an indecisiveness resolved one moment and lost the next with each reliving of revealed significance, and this it is that makes the poem endlessly rereadable and fascinating (emphasis added).

Riffaterre is correct in denying a naive linearity within the reading process, a movement that clearly would presuppose a type of "progress". For, the endless cycle of gain and loss in the semiotic economy delineated in the Nightingale Ode graphically denies such an ideal faith. And it is this crisis of faith that is not only central to Keats's poem, but is also at the center of the Romantic project overall; a give-and-take of signification which denies the security of the letter but simultaneously reaffirms a faith in signification nonetheless. In other words, knowing that linguistic constructs cannot produce calculated and certain responses in decoders, the Romantics tried to exploit this situation through slippery texts which encourage free and undetermined decoding. As Percy Bysshe Shelley observes in his "A Defence of Poetry" (1821: 116), "A Poet is a nightingale, who sits in darkness and sings to cheer its own solitude with sweet sounds; his auditors are as men entranced by the melody of an unseen musician, who feel that they are moved and softened, yet know not whence or why".

The Nightingale Ode serves as an excellent paradigm for this endeavor. Viewed from a generic standpoint, the text appears to exemplify regularity and logical order as the eight stanzas suggest an evenness reinforced by the repetition of line typography, meter and rhyme. But, this implied symmetry is a ruse designed to lure the reader unsuspectingly into a semiotic maze without a clue of the chaotic undertaking that lies ahead.

By describing his mood in the opening lines (1-4), the sender of this message establishes a speaker-context:

> My heart aches, and a drowsy numbness pains
>   My sense, as though of hemlock I had drunk,
> Or emptied some dull opiate to the drains
>   One minute past, and Lethe-wards had sunk:

While providing concrete indications of the speaker's condition, the similes employed additionally indicate a state of mind which conditions the reader's perception of the text to follow. The speaker is feeling distressed and deadened--an unfavorable situation that will obviously be reflected in the text. The elaborate description of this condition attests, furthermore, to a heightened sense of consideration for the reader, as if to dictate that the speaker is being particularly careful to construct a text which will ensure complete and successful signification. And, of course, the speaker discusses himself to comply with both generic expectations of the ode form and the situation implied by the title. Since this is an "Ode *to* a Nightingale", it is assumed that *somebody* will be speaking to or about a nightingale in order for this textual event to take place.

The subject addressed in the remaining lines of the stanza (5-10)--

>'Tis not through envy of thy happy lot,
>   But being too happy in thine happiness,--
>   That thou, light-winged Dryad of the trees,
>   In some melodious plot
>   Of beechen green, and shadows numberless,
>   Singest of summer in full-throated ease.

--similarly fulfills certain requirements by providing the presence, in some manner, of the subject (or object) being addressed. An apparently simple triadic economy is being constructed here: the *speaker* is apostrophizing a *bird* as a vehicle for a message to the *reader*. Yet, this is confusing: what exactly does the speaker mean when he decodes the bird's happiness for us as derived "not through envy of thy happy lot, / But being too happy in thine happiness"?

This sounds like a signifier without, apparently, a signified. Signs begin to shift at this point, a movement which intensifies and fluctuates but never quells as the decoding process accumulates distinct ruptures.

The second and third stanzas establish the speaker's yearning to intensify the pleasing side of the intoxication he experiences, suggesting a desire for non-directed, non-embodied thought--a Negative Capability enhanced through outside stimulants. A necessary result of thought--an awareness of the ravages of mutability--seems to be at the root of this desire as the speaker, in the third stanza (21-30), wants to

>   Fade far away, dissolve, and quite forget
>   What thou among the leaves hast never known,
>   The weariness, the fever, and the fret
>   Here, where men sit and hear each other groan;
>Where palsy shakes a few, sad, last gray hairs,
>   Where youth grows pale, and spectre-thin, and dies;
>   Where but to think is to be full of sorrow
>   And leaden-eyed despairs,
>   Where Beauty cannot keep her lustrous eyes,
>   Or new Love pine at them beyond to-morrow.

Thinking stands as a metonymy here for all types of associative undertakings, activity Keats (1817: 185) refers to in one of his letters as "consequitive reasoning". It is clear, then, that the speaker desires a frame of mind which rises above discursive method and, through an active--albeit artificially influenced--engagement of the imaginative faculty, manages to escape from the oppressive consciousness that has created the heartache mentioned in the first line.

The speaker provides a dramatic apostasy after this point by resisting the urge to partake in artificial enhancement of the senses, deciding instead to channel this urge into poetry. A polar opposition flexes within this statement, offering a counter statement which throws the speaker's activity into disarray (31-34).

> Away! away! for I will fly to thee,
>   Not charioted by Bacchus and his pards,
> But on the viewless wings of Poesy,
>   Though the dull brain perplexes and retards:

It sounds as though he has made a distinct and appropriate decision--until these lines are subverted by admission that this procedure is frustrated because "the dull brain perplexes and retards". His mind balks at the careless acceptance of linguistic surety, thereby drawing attention to the painful loss which attends such an undertaking. For the Romantics, the mind's ground was pre-linguistic, and it was only the ceaseless desire to textualize thought for the pleasure of the reader that led them to accept the limited possibilities of textual communication. The speaker struggles with the sluggish response by his brain, a natural resistance to the insufficiencies of the letter, no doubt, as he remarks (35-37):

> Already with thee! tender is the night,
>   And haply the Queen-Moon is on her throne,
>   Cluster'd around by all her starry Fays;

Yet the speaker is trying to convince himself merely through assertion. By declaring that a certain point has been attained, he believes that it *has* been attained through the ontological agency of linguistic voicing. But this situation is shone to be a pathetically delusive enterprise as the speaker comments (38-45) on the physical context within which his statement is made:

> But here there is no light,
> Save what from heaven is with the breezes blown
>   Through verdurous glooms and winding mossy ways.
>
> I cannot see what flowers are at my feet,
>   Nor what soft incense hangs upon the boughs,
> But, in embalmed darkness, guess each sweet
>   Wherewith the seasonable month endows
> The grass, the thicket, and the fruit-tree wild;

Despite his fevered attempts, the speaker's efforts to forget the tyranny of mutability fail. Trying to turn this into an advantage, however, he celebrates "Death" and associates it with the "ecstasy" of the bird's song. And it is the nightingale's song which assumes the status of the infinite text, one whose temporal frame is unhinged by its engagement with both loss and gain. For the bird's song is not the individual bird's song; rather, it is the generic song of the nightingale which is passed on and reiterated by each nightingale. "Thou wast not born for death, immortal Bird!", the speaker concludes (60-63),

> No hungry generations tread thee down;
> The voice I hear this passing night was heard
>   In ancient days by emperor and clown:

Because this is physically impossible and thus foments confusion through a disruption of logic, the speaker is evidently directing the reader toward a metaphorical decoding: that the speaker means the nightingale's text is neither saturated nor depleted through temporal influences; it shifts throughout time from speaker to speaker without ever losing its ideality.

But, the closing stanza destroys all of this apparent certainty as the speaker acknowledges (71-77) the delusion that has overtaken him.

> Forlorn! the very word is like a bell
>   To toll me back from thee to my sole self!
> Adieu! the fancy cannot cheat so well
>   As she is fam'd to do, deceiving elf.
> Adieu! adieu! thy plaintive anthem fades
>   Past the near meadows, over the still stream,
>   Up the hill-side; and now 'tis buried deep
>   In the next valley-glades:

The speaker has realized that a linguistic charade has been taking place; that this escape from temporality, from loss, has been a self-perpetrated con. This would suffice as an ending to enforce closure and restrict the text entirely--if it were not for the final two lines. Once the reader comes to them, the entire decoding process is recontextualized to a degree of undetermined (and undeterminable) proportions.

With the closing cue operating as a palimpsestic frame, the reader has to revaluate the undertakings of the poem to produce a satisfying decoding. And now that the reader is functioning retroactively, many of the instances of uncertainty within this message reveal themselves as such with heightened emphasis.

Clearly, a literal reading of the opening description of the nightingale's presence "In some melodious plot" (8) comes to mind readily upon rereading the text from the standpoint of its conclusion. If plot is viewed in the sense of arrangement of material in a story, then an entirely different decoding process begins. The poem, in this regard, would possess a "melodious plot" which employs a nightingale to prod the reader to piece together the confusing series of signs that constitutes the text as a whole. In addition, all of the sub-messages within the larger message are now suspect because a dream or vision expresses concerns which differ significantly in status from those voiced in reality. Thus it is clear that through the ambiguous narration and a subversive ending, Keats has designed a text that takes full advantage of the polysemous nature of the sign, enabling readers to produce it to their own satisfaction according to each individual's capacity to engage in Negative Capability--to be willing to forge a path through a confusing and ever-changing terrain.

After all, language functions even more surrealistically than usual when operating within a dream economy (or that of a vision, for that matter) as signifiers and signifieds interact and combine, shifting wildly without underlying logic. Accordingly, in the dream or vision *text* when signs collide, mutate and dissolve, this movement is likely to be pleasing rather than disturbing (with the exception, of course, of bad dreams or unsettling visions). Those readers who can approach a text constructed in this fashion and create a favorable decoding of this swirling jumble through Negative Capability, are able to turn it into a dream; those who cannot do so, end up with a nightmare.

REFERENCES

KEATS, John.
    1817-1818. *The Letters of John Keats*, ed. Hyder E. Rollins, vol. 1 (Cambridge, MA: Harvard University Press, 1958).
    1819. "Ode to a Nightingale", in *Complete Poems*, ed. Jack Stillinger (Cambridge, MA: Harvard University Press, 1982), 279-281.

RIFFATERRE, Michael.
    1978. *Semiotics of Poetry* (Bloomington: Indiana University Press).

SHELLEY, Percy Bysshe.
    1821. "A Defence of Poetry," in *The Complete Works of Percy Bysshe Shelley*, ed. Roger Ingpen and Walter Peck, vol. 7 (New York: Gordian Press, 1965).

WASSERMAN, Earl.
    1953. *The Finer Tone: Keats's Major Poems* (Baltimore: Johns Hopkins Press).

"PAIN IS PERFET MISERY": READING THE MILTONIC DISCOURSE OF VIOLENCE

Sid Sondergard
St. Lawrence University

The Elder Brother in *A Mask* (1634), stoic defender of virtue's power, finally succumbs to his younger brother's insistence on rescuing their sister from the cruel magician Comus, and promises to "drag him by the curls to a foul death, / Curs'd as his life."[1] The Attendant Spirit sent to protect the Lady, however, counsels the philosophical brother that "He with his bare wand can unthread thy joints, / And crumble all thy sinews" (Hughes 1957: 104). The syntagmatic concomitant of the verbs "unthread" and "crumble" here is death, unambiguously encoded to index an essential Miltonic modality: violence breeds violence, a suicidal equation.[2] Analogously, his Sonnet XV (1648), addressed to chief Parliamentary General Thomas Fairfax, rhetorically ponders "what can War, but endless war still breed, / Till Truth and Right from Violence be freed" (Hughes 1957:159-60). These pejorative observations on violence seem ideologically congruent with the Christian moralism conventionally attributed to the poet nicknamed "The Lady of Christ's College" by fellow Cambridge students. Milton hated this imposed signification, and publicly rationalized "because I never showed my virility in the way these brothellers do . . . see how stupid and ill-advised they are to reproach me with a thing upon which I can most justly pride myself" (Wolfe 1953: 284). As if in defiance, a syntactic brutality embedded in Milton's verse and prose functions to reject the feminine connotations associated with poetic practice, asserting instead a self-imposed identity and "virility"--yet it does so while claiming to eschew violence as self-destructive.

The reader attempting to decode Milton's discourse of violence is led to question whether the poet is privileging an aesthetic of cruelty (beyond that rhetorically germane to a given polemic), or whether he embeds elements of violence as didactic markers in the narrative trajectories of his works. Either interpretation necessitates the analysis of a semiotic code not ordinarily associated with Milton. John Rumrich cites the "nearly debilitating horror that Milton appears to have felt at the prospect of death, and at the cavalier treatment of one's corpse by a ferocious, at best oblivious world"[3] (1987: 168-69) as foundation for the poet's attempts to achieve semantic glory through martial encounters on the battlefields of literature. Profanation of the dead was not an unwarranted concern, as demonstrated in a contemporary newspaper account of the disinterment of Oliver Cromwell and other Parliamentarian leaders: "they were pulled out of their coffins, and hanged . . . after which they were taken down, and their heads cut off, and their loathsome trunks thrown into a deep hole under the gallows" (Masson 1880: [VI]123). Apparently as fearsome as the spectres of death and desecration, however, is the humiliating spectre of literary failure, denoted in Milton's annotation of "The Passion" (1630), a lyric on Christ's suffering that does not actually treat the Redeemer's physical torments: "*This Subject the Author finding to be above the years he had, when he wrote it, and nothing satisfied with what was begun, left it unfinisht*" (Hughes 1957:63). Fearing lest he prove an English Hector in defeat and defilement, Milton aggressively counters with a "dynamic conflict" (Loewenstein 1988: 90) between literary or historical archetypes and his ability to appropriate and master them rhetorically, and formulates an experiential discourse with which to implement his strategy. It is predicated on an axiomatic antipathy to pain; it is marked by systemic patterns of dismemberment, of wounding, and of plague (as *un*natural catastrophe); and it is fictionally intensified by the immediacy of graphic expression.

Our semiotic readings of physical trauma--pain--in the discourse of Milton's epic poetry benefit from the kind of hermeneutic reversal advocated by Richard Harland's Superstructuralist methodology, in which "we invert our ordinary base-and-superstructure models until what we used to think of as superstructural actually takes precedence over what we used to think of as basic" (1987: 1-2). Rather than taking spiritual rebellion as our signifier base and reading pain as its concomitant signified, we can privilege our reading of pain (as cued by the poet's emphatic textual references) to interpret it as a universal referent, the systemic signification of shared experience, of human participation in *Paradise Lost* (1667; rev. 1674). The rebel angel Nisroch, speaking from the informed perspective of having had "his riv'n Arms to havoc hewn" during the first day of the War in Heaven, complains to Satan that valor is useless when it is "quell'd with pain / Which all subdues"; *any* compromise with the enemy would be preferable, for "pain is perfet misery, the worst / Of evils" (Hughes 1957:334). Pain *is* "perfet misery," a concrete torment without abstract peer,[4] which is why Milton revises the archetypal scenario of Satan's primal injury even as the epic progresses. If Satan had not experienced pain, he would not have been motivated to seduce Adam and Eve to pain. Satan's pain, self-infecting and self-consuming--"For only in destroying I find ease / To my relentless thoughts" (Hughes 1957: 381)-- initiates the process of semiosis that Eve interprets as semantic justification for her rejection of God's sovereignty, thereby incurring her own pain. As Satan's crimes are unprecedented, so are his punishments; he is both criminal (actant) and crime (referent), hence he must also suffer pluralistically, for pain is both the agency of God's punishment and the punishment itself.

In support of this strategy, Milton reinvents the instance of Satan's first experience of pain periodically throughout *Paradise Lost*, metonymically replacing pain-as-effect with pain-as-cause, while Satan's suffering implicitly signifies the suffering of others. During the family reunion in Book Two, Sin reminds her father of the Athena-like headbirth that delivered her into heaven: "All on a sudden miserable pain / Surpris'd thee" and "on the left side op'ning wide, / Likest to thee in shape and count'nance bright, / Then shining heav'nly fair, a Goddess arm'd / Out of thy head I sprung" (Hughes 1957: 250). Unfortunately, an incestuous union between Satan and Sin culminated in the even more hideous birth of Death, who "breaking violent way / Tore through all my entrails, that with fear and pain / Distorted, all my nether shape thus grew / Transform'd" (Hughes 1957: 250). More unfortunate yet, Death's rape of his mother Sin produces the Hell-hounds, cruelest of progeny, who "when they list, into the womb / That bred them they return, and howl and gnaw / My bowels, thir repast; then bursting forth / Afresh with conscious terrors vex me round" (Hughes 1957: 251). Milton's systemic degeneration of the arch-rebel and his demonic children is structured by horrific images drawn paradigmatically from the poet's imagination--Hjelmslev's expression plane--but its meaning is ultimately derived from reader empathy with the torment of physical pain. Satan reflexively interprets its semantic substance in Book Four, when, alone, he confesses that if God were to forgive him, he would rebel all over again, for "ease would recant / Vows made in pain, as violent and void. / For never can true reconcilement grow / Where wounds of deadly hate have pierc'd so deep" (Hughes 1957:279). Milton textualizes this purely hypothetical proposition (since Satan will *not* be forgiven) to encatalyze the profound "meaning effect" (Greimas and Courtés 1979: 96) of pain.

The myth of the invulnerable Lucifer (a semantic explosive Milton embeds in the first half of the epic, and regularly detonates to connote the defeated Satan) is reconstructed in Book Six. For Adam's edification and entertainment, the angel Raphael narrates the story of Lucifer facing God's warrior-angel, Michael, in one-on-one combat: Michael's sword first cut Satan's in half, and "deep ent'ring shear'd / All his right side; then *Satan* first knew pain, / And writh'd him to and fro convolv'd; so sore / The griding sword with discontinuous wound / Pass'd through him" (Hughes 1957: 331). Archetypal agony aside, Satan takes a measure of comfort in the discovery that angels "Cannot but by annihilating die," and counsels his legions to return better armed the next day. Satan's pain again signifies the imminence of others' even greater pain, as the rebel angels in full battle-armor are crushed by God's mountain-wielding squadrons: "Thir armor help'd thir harm, crush't in and bruis'd / Into thir substance pent, which wrought them pain / Implacable" (Hughes 1957: 339). Imagine being stepped on while inside a tin can. Milton concludes Satan's participation in the discourse of pain by allowing his devil a rhetorical parting shot at Christ in Book Four of *Paradise Regained* (1671), promising his old nemesis a future of "scorns, reproaches, injuries, / Violence and stripes, and lastly cruel death" (Hughes 1957: 524). This syntagmatic string, of course, mocks the interlocutor delivering it, for it marks a diachronic progression parallel to his own, with the exception that his manipulators--Milton and God--deny him an end to the discourse he, too, has been taught to read experientially.

The systemic patterns of dismemberment in Milton's literary discourse function to communicate unity rather than chaos, reflecting the author's strategic transcoding of narrative archetypes to produce and control signification.[5] The pastoral elegy *Lycidas* (1637), seeking to demonstrate the justice of the poet's God in its polemic, imposes the rationale of historic necessity on the drowning of fellow Cambridge student/poet Edward King via analogy to the decapitation of Orpheus, "When by the rout that made the hideous roar, / His gory visage down the stream was sent" (Hughes 1957: 122). Milton encodes the floating head and the sunken head (he curses the flawed ship "That sunk so low that sacred head of thine" [Hughes 1957: 123]) as discrete signifiers of talent and meaningless loss; yet when read conjunctively they argue God's design, and meaning--i.e., a rationale-- is derived from non-meaning. René Girard explains this as the semantic effect of ritual *sparagmos*, a rite "directed toward order and tranquility, not violence. It strives to achieve violence solely in order to eliminate it" (1972: 132). The intertextuality of Milton's mythic analogy functions as a "textual interpretant" (Riffaterre 1978: 109-10), directing the lyric's reader to weigh *inevitability* with loss as the passage's signifieds.

Milton frequently imposes a violent narrative schema as his agency of control when critiquing religio-political structures. Guy Fawkes's failure (transformed by history into an icon of thwarted rebellion, as a visit to Madame Tussaud's demonstrates) to blast James I and his Parliament on November 5, 1605, provides Milton in his first year at Cambridge with the framework for his commemorative Latin polemic, "In Quintum Novembris" ["On the Fifth of November"] (1625). That English proto-nemesis, the Pope, is urged by Satan, "You have it in your power to scatter their dismembered bodies through the air, to burn them to cinders, by exploding nitrous powder under the halls where they will assemble" (Hughes 1957: 18), and Milton transcodes the Gunpowder Plot's threat of historical chaos into the unity of present antipathy toward an enemy common to his university peers. When, in Book Six of *Paradise Lost*, Moloch is "Down clov'n to the waist, with shatter'd Arms / And uncouth pain bellowing," and other rebel angels are also "Mangl'd with ghastly wounds through Plate and Mail" (Hughes 1957: 332), Milton is imposing a private doctrinal emphasis on the mythic model of "War in Heaven," communicating the empowering unity of Heaven's forces as signified through the dismemberment of the (literally) divided and self-interested rebels. John M. Steadman has observed a regular tendency among certain Renaissance writers towards discursive violence, ordinarily characterized by disruptive substitutions, as "for harmony, deliberate dismemberment, a kind of syntactic sparagmos" (1984: 25). What functions as a stylistic device for many writers is employed didactically--i.e., heroically--by Milton to conquer his opponents. He replies in his anti-prelatical tract, *Animadversions* (1641), to Bishop Joseph Hall's defense of Episcopacy; wielding the power of imposed signification Milton declares "your dissever'd principles were but like the mangl'd pieces of a gash't Serpent" (Wolfe 1953: 674). Rhetorically, associatively, he shreds both argument and opponent.

A homologous violence system is structured from patterns of wounding which, like patterns of dismemberment, derive their semantic value from an experiential seme: fear of the body's holistic integrity being violated. Moreover, there is a crucial isomorphic correspondence in Milton's works between the immediacy of a wound being inflicted and the comprehensive significance of that act in the synchronic context of literary/historical time. If reader perception of the isomorphism of discourse encourages interpretation, in A.J. Greimas's terms, "according to the principle of equivalence, [of] all the possible definitions of the lexematic occurrences" (1966: 93), then a writer may encode cues for reader disengagement from a text to stimulate active rather than passive interpretation--as when the reader is presented with the unpleasant scenario of a sympathetic character's suffering and looks to the writer for a philosophical rationale.

Milton's lyric "Upon the Circumcision" (1632-33?) forces a hermeneutic ambivalence upon the reader who considers, with the poet, this painful moment in the life of the infant Christ: "O more exceeding love or law more just? / Just law indeed, but more exceeding love!" The resolution of this ambiguity is revealed in a literary/historical continuum of wounding, for the child who in ritual circumcision "now bleeds to give us ease" prefigures the adult whose death archetypally expresses liberation, whose "Huge pangs and strong / Will pierce more near his heart" (Hughes 1957: 81). Milton evokes painful emotions from his reader through Christian guilt and/or human empathy, but the concomitant disengagement from the text and analytical demand for coherence that this stimulates reveals the isomorphic continuity of wounding and hope and heroic altruism, for the poet also encodes the rationale of a literary/historical context: Christian destiny.

In *Paradise Lost* Milton exercises his power as poet to wound and to heal, making explicit his dominance of his expression form. Adam reports to the angel Raphael that God "stooping op'n'd my left side, and took / From thence a Rib, with cordial spirits warm, / And Life-blood streaming fresh; wide was the wound, / But suddenly with flesh fill'd up and heal'd" (Hughes 1957: 373). The foregrounding of Adam's pain serves to index the human race's pain to be suffered on account of that same rib later, but the graphic violence of the extraction also focuses attention on the poet's ability to effect miracle, as the wound "suddenly with flesh fill'd up". Milton's self-apotheosis continues as he rewards Adam for suffering this torment: in Book

Nine, Satan reveals that prelapsarian Adam, following this primal injury, was "exempt from wound, / I not; so much hath Hell debas'd, and pain / Infeebl'd me" (Hughes 1957: 389). As Teiresias was compensated with prophecy for being struck blind by the gods, Adam is compensated with invulnerability by the same God who first wounded him.[6]

    In a letter to German admirer Peter Heimbach, dated 15 August 1666, Milton laments "so many deaths of my countrymen . . . in a year so poisonous and plague-ridden," and thanks the young man for his concern that the poet, too, had been "borne away" (Kelley 1982: 3). Plague was a regularly recurring commonplace in Stuart England, a quotidian reality in London, and it followed Milton to Cambridge, where, in 1630, Joseph Meade, a Fellow and Tutor of Christ's College, reported "Our University is in a manner wholly dissolved, all meetings and exercises ceasing . . . we live as close prisoners, and, I hope, without danger" (Masson 1858: [I]233). It is not surprising to find this experiential referent functioning as another image pattern in the author's discourse of violence--plague as a natural phenomenon cannot be controlled, but Milton can and does appropriate it for the semantic structure of his literary polemics. His regicide tract, *The Tenure of Kings and Magistrates* (1649), urges the execution of Charles I as a just response to tyranny, and employs plague tropically to taint the monarch: to spare him is to consider the deaths and sacrifices of his opponents as "vile, and no more to be reckn'd for, then the blood of so many Dogs in a time of Pestilence" (Hughes 1962: 235-236). Charles is implicitly vilified as agent of human devaluation, a signification predicated on acknowledged conflict between monarch and subjects, and on the shared cultural conception of plague; this is what Roland Barthes identifies as the connection of "a mythical schema to a general history" (1957: 128), and Milton is precisely such a mythmaker. He similarly transcodes natural catastrophe as didactic vehicle in Book Eleven of *Paradise Lost*. Adam is shown a vision of the varieties of death to be visited on mankind as a result of his disobedience; the violence of man in conflict with man is painful enough, but he is informed that another consequence has been the perversion of nature. When in a kind of "Lazar-house" he sees "Numbers of all diseas'd, all maladies / Of ghastly Spasm, or racking torture, qualms / Of heart-sick Agony, all feverous kinds" (followed by fifteen individual afflictions), while "Dire was the tossing, deep the groans, despair / Tended the sick," Adam weeps and declares of humanity, "Better [to] end here unborn" (Hughes 1957: 444). The vision of Book Eleven is penance that Adam must suffer before being allowed to see the triumphant vision of the Redeemer in Book Twelve. A painful reality of Milton's seventeenth-century world, plague is not an arbitrary sign in his discourse of violence; rather, it is one of many patterns selected from the oppositions, or internal arrangement (Barthes 1964: 73-74) within the paradigm "violence", upon which Milton has imposed his own literary semantics.

    Joel Morkan, examining the curious mixture of violence and humor in Miltonic invective, claims that the author "both psychologically and intellectually" is "the exact opposite of what he seems when wielding the burning scourge of rhetorical vehemence" (1978: 485). While undoubtedly true, this duality indexes methodological syncretism rather than some kind of psychic schism: it is this that empowers Milton's discourse of violence. In his *Commonplace Book*, compiled perhaps over thirty-six years, Milton writes "A man's courage depends, not upon his body, but upon his reason, which is man's strongest protection and defense" (Wolfe 1953: 373). Reason also proved Milton's strongest offense: armed with rhetoric and intellect, he never conceded defeat in literary battle while serving as the Council of State's Secretary for Foreign Tongues. Characterizing his service there, Milton's discourse of violence is never meaningless, and is never casually employed; within its structures, for example, he transcodes historical tragedy as religious affirmation (Sonnet XVIII,

"On the Late Massacre in Piedmont" [1655]) and proposes political equations that metonymically substitute for the semantic weight of many acts of tyrannical violence one crucial *other* act (the retroactive defense of Charles I's execution presented in the *Eikonoklastes* [1649]). The presence of systemic violence through almost fifty years of Milton's literary career indexes his pragmatic implementation of it as a semantic structure--securing his permanent reputation for control and precision while effectively denying the signification of "The Lady of Christ's College."

NOTES

[1] *Editor's Note:* References to Milton's work are drawn from several different collective sources. Titles and dates for each piece are introduced in the text, and citations are listed under the redactor's names and modern publication dates for the published collections used.

[2] This modality serves Milton both as motif and as rationale. Throughout *Paradise Lost* Satan heaps torment upon his own head by seeking to torment others; following the disastrous first day of the War in Heaven in Book Six, the Arch-Fiend suggests "perhaps more valid Arms, / Weapons more violent, when next we meet, / May serve to better us" (Hughes 1957: 334). Their invention of cannons necessitates an even greater escalation by the heavenly forces--who retaliate by crushing the rebels with entire mountains: Satan always receives greater damage than he inflicts. Milton employs the same pattern to justify the execution of Charles I, complaining about vacillators in *The Tenure of Kings and Magistrates* (1649), "As for mercy, if it be to a Tyrant, under which Name they themselves have cited him so oft in the hearing of God, of Angels, and the holy Church assembl'd, and there charg'd him with the spilling of more innocent blood by farr, then ever *Nero* did, undoubtedly the mercy which they pretend, is the mercy of wicked men" (Hughes 1962: 193). How much this text tested Milton's rhetorical might may be measured by noting that it appeared approximately two weeks *after* the King was executed on 30 Jan. 1649, and was "popular" enough to merit an expanded edition in 1650.

[3] Death ("an ontological sink, a black hole of glory" [Rumrich 1987: 78]) is the most terrifying character in *Paradise Lost*, an idiot child with a lust for mass murder, a masterwork of grotesque. When Satan in Book Two promises him a feeding-ground on earth, "Death / Grinn'd horrible a ghastly smile, to hear / His famine should be fill'd, and blest his maw / Destin'd to that good hour" (Hughes 1957: 254). The narrator's ironic tone increases the horrific effect, reinforced tropically by alliteration ("Grinn'd horrible/good hour").

[4] The exception occurs when Milton chooses to restructure the hierarchical values of his poetic idiolect; in *Samson Agonistes* (1671), the discourse of pain isomorphically functions as a metaphorical vehicle of the expression plane, while the content plane addresses Samson's spiritual anxiety: "My griefs not only pain me / As a ling'ring disease, / But finding no redress, ferment and rage, / Nor less than wounds immedicable / Rankle, and fester, and gangrene, / To black mortification" (Hughes 1957: 566).

[5] Milton adroitly structures his polemics with literal or figurative dismemberment, depending upon his didactic intentions, as in *Of Reformation* (1641), the first of his anti-prelatical tracts. To signify the Episcopacy as a corrupt, ambitious entity that

threatens violence to all England, Milton composes (Wolfe 1953: 583-584) the grotesque parable of the Wen (a skin tumor, perhaps etymologically derived from the Old English *wund*, or wound, described as "little lesse then the Head it selfe, growing to it by a narrower excrescency") who claims his right to succeed in place of the head if it "should faile":

> [A] wise and learned Philosopher . . . soone perceiving the matter, and wondring at the boldnesse of such a swolne Tumor, Wilt thou (quoth he) that art but a bottle of vitious and harden'd excrements, contend with the lawfull and free-borne members . . . head thou art none, though thou receive this huge substance from it. . . . [Thy] folly is as great as thy filth . . . and that thou containst no good thing in thee, but a heape of hard, and loathsome uncleanness, and art to the head a foul disfigurement and burden, when I have cut thee off, and open'd thee, as by the help of these implements I will doe, all men shall see.

This patient is already dead, thanks to the semiotic surgery Milton has performed: the Episcopacy/Wen's doctrines/excrements are "cut off" by the writer's rhetoric/implements. He does not hesitate to apply the experiential discourse of violence to literal injustices identified within the same text--as the Episcopacy's ecclesiastical courts are condemned for serving "to tear the flesh from our bones, and into our wide wounds instead of balm, to power in the oil of Tartar, vitriol, and mercury" (Wolfe 1953: 612)--affirming thereby John M. Steadman's observations that Milton's systemic violence is manifested in form as well as in content, "In the frequency and violence of metaphors, the discontinuities or distortions of syntax, and the unresolved tensions within the medium of discourse itself" (1984: 113).

[6] Milton punishes Adam and the reader for original sin by forcing both to watch the angel Michael's vision of the future in Book Eleven: a systemic treatment of violence and corruption which begins with the murder of Abel. Cain "Smote him into the Midriff with a stone / That beat out life; he fell, and deadly pale / Groan'd out his Soul with gushing blood effus'd." The reader certainly shares Adam's repulsion: "O sight / Of terror, foul and ugly to behold, / Horrid to think, how horrible to feel!" (Hughes 1957: 443). R.A. Shoaf reads Milton's discursive violence in *Paradise Lost* as ideology and methodology: "To be precise in his argument to justify the ways of God to men, to be severe in his understanding of the ways of God, to be accurate in his characterization of how it is with men, Milton must cut, chisel, hone language . . . he must practice violence and submit to violence, and he must constantly risk falling into the abyss of confusion" (1985: 60). As a theory of Milton's poetics, this seems just; but to suggest the ambivalence of the poet personally in his practice is to question the degree of his deliberate artistic control, which, as I have attempted to show, the poet repeatedly asserts in the systematization of his violent discourse.

REFERENCES

BARTHES, Roland.
    1957. *Mythologies* (Paris: Éditions du Seuil). Page references in this paper are to the English trans. by Annette Lavers (London: Jonathan Cape, 1972; American edition with pagination unchanged, New York: Hill and Wang, 1972).

1964. *Eléments de sémiologie*, in *Communications*, no. 4 (Paris: Seuil), 91-135. Page references are to the English trans. by Annette Lavers and Colin Smith, *Elements of Semiology* (London: Jonathan Cape, 1967; American edition with pagination unchanged, New York: Hill and Wang, 1968).

GIRARD, René.
1972. *Violence and the Sacred*, trans. Patrick Gregory (Baltimore: The Johns Hopkins University Press, 1977).

GREIMAS, A.J.
1966. *Sémantique Structurale* (Paris: Larousse). Page references are to the English trans. by Daniele McDowell, et al., *Structural Semantics: An Attempt at a Method* (Lincoln: University of Nebraska Press, 1983).

GREIMAS, A.J., and COURTÉS, J.
1979. *Semiotique: Dictionnaire raisonne de la theorie du langage* (Paris: Hachette). Page references are to the English trans. by Larry Crist, et al., *Semiotics and Language: An Analytical Dictionary* (Bloomington: Indiana University Press, 1982).

HARLAND, Richard.
1987. *Superstructuralism: The Philosophy of Structuralism and Post--Structuralism* (New York: Methuen).

HUGHES, Merritt Y., ed.
1957. *John Milton: Complete Poems and Major Prose* (New York: Macmillan).
1962. *Complete Prose Works of John Milton, Volume III: 1648-1649* (New Haven: Yale University Press).

KELLEY, Maurice, ed.
1982. *Complete Prose Works of John Milton, Volume VIII: 1666-1682* (New Haven: Yale University Press).

LOEWENSTEIN, David.
1988. "*Areopagitica* and the Dynamics of History" in *Studies in English Literature 1500-1900* 28, 77-93.

MASSON, David.
1858-80. *The Life of John Milton* 6 vols. Rpt. 1965. (Gloucester, Mass.: Peter Smith).

MORKAN, Joel.
1978. "Wrath and Laughter: Milton's Ideas on Satire." *Studies in Philology* 69, 475-95.

RIFFATERRE, Michael.
1978. *Semiotics of Poetry* (Bloomington: Indiana University Press).

RUMRICH, John Peter.
1987. *Matter of Glory: A New Preface to Paradise Lost* (Pittsburgh: University of Pittsburgh Press).

SHOAF, R.A.
1985. *Milton, Poet of Duality: A Study of Semiosis in the Poetry and the Prose* (New Haven: Yale University Press).

STEADMAN, John M.
1984. *The Hill and the Labyrinth: Discourse and Certitude in Milton and His Near-Contemporaries* (Los Angeles: University of California Press).

WOLFE, Don M., ed.
1953. *Complete Prose Works of John Milton, Volume I: 1624-1642* (New Haven: Yale University Press).

XIV

SEMIOTICS AND GENDER AWARENESS

GALLIC SEMIOTIC SUBJECTS AND FEMINISM: GREIMAS, DURAS, *ET AL.*

Thomas F. Broden
University of Nebraska-Lincoln

In the film *Hiroshima mon amour*, for which Duras wrote the screenplay, there is a scene which figures in the WWII France flashback sequence showing the female protagonist as an adolescent. The scene takes place on a public square of her provincial town of Nevers, under the eyes of a crowd of inhabitants (Duras 1960: 76-77; trans. 61-62). Seated on a chair in a town square, the young woman has her hair shorn off for having had a German boyfriend during the Occupation. The girl's lover is absent from the scene, having already been shot dead in battle. The bald head, a stigma in itself for a youth, will serve as a public brand signifying she was a wartime traitor. To punish her for opening herself sexually to the enemy, society takes away one of her most evident public marks of feminine gender--she will look like a boy for some months.

In the main body of the film the female protagonist, played by Emmanuelle Riva, is a married French actress who has a brief torrid affair with a Japanese man. The encounter between a white French woman and an Oriental man violates strong French racial taboos in France. The flashback points to a pattern of erotic attraction to a socially forbidden Other. At the same time, given the narrative focus of the film as a whole, the scene in Nevers puts into question the process of justice in that French society. The scene of (in)justice is also a spectacle within a spectacle; its editing and framing present it as a show for the people of Nevers and emphasize the drawn-out public moment of shame inflicted on the girl.

The scene from *Hiroshima* is one scene among many in which Duras raises questions of gender and power in a tight scenario presented as a spectacle (within a spectacle). Madeleine Borgomano (1985) has taken advantage of the hauntingly obsessive character of Duras's oeuvre, which returns so often to certain key problems, and even to certain characters, settings, and plot lines, to do brilliant analyses of Freudian scenarios in the texts--the primal scene, the fall of the father, and 'a child is beaten.' One can imagine slightly different starting points--Lacan's study of the triangulation of desire in *Le ravissement de Lol V. Stein* (1964), or René Girard's work with triangles of desire (1972). The intersubjective frameworks serve as models or mini-language games for behavior.

I will focus here on three main scenes, and will start from a loose theoretical framework derived from A. J. Greimas's actantial schema (Greimas and Courtés 1978), a schema which functions as an idealized frozen moment extracted from a narrative development. The paper will work with the narrative actants, or actants of the utterance, which in a typical manifestation can be thought of as realized in two triangles linked in a point. Each triangle consists of a Sender acting on an Object through the intermediary of a Subject/Receiver often syncretized in one actant. The Subject/Receiver is in an immediate relation of desire (or phobia) to an object or end. The Sender, hierarchically superior to the Subject, attempts to transmit a desire or a mission, and eventually an entire set of values, to the Subject/Receiver. The Sender acts as a judge vis-a-vis the subject of performance, passing judgment on the Subject's acts. The doubling of the triangle comes from the polemical structure of discourse in which the two sets of Sender-Subject axes, for example, converge on the same point constituted by the object of desire.

In the above scene from *Hiroshima*, the young girl plays the role of the Subject, here *subjected* to the sanction of postwar French society in the role of Sender. The negative sanction seeks to cast the girl's acts as those of an ant-subject, and to deny the validity of its behavior. Society and the young woman have radically different narrative programs which have come together on the point of the girl's object of desire, the German boyfriend.

This paper will investigate three scenes from Duras concentrating on the nature of the violence entailed, the treatment of gender and the framing of the scenes as a spectacle; attention will also be drawn to aspects of object-choice in the texts. On another occasion, it would be important to pursue as well the direct link between violence and eroticism so clear in other Durassian texts, such as *L'homme assis dans le couloir* (1980; trans. *The Seated Man in the Passage*) and *La maladie de la mort* (1982; trans. *The Malady of Death*). I will proceed by introducing the second scene.

Duras's recent autobiographical novel *L'Amant* (1984; trans. *The Lover*) depicts a French colonial family in Indochina between the two world wars. The focus of the novel is on the young Duras persona's affair with the Chinese man--another violation of the racial taboo. In one scene the girl, who still lives at home, is being interrogated by her mother in a small room of the house (Duras 1984: 72-74; trans: 57-59). She is accused of sleeping with the man; the accusations are hurled in shouts and are punctuated by attempts to slap the daughter. The young girl lies and denies everything.

The scene enacts the same Sender/Receiver relation as in *Hiroshima*; the negative sanction puts the subject in the role of a villain. As in the *Hiroshima* scene the lover is absent and the girl is alone with her accuser; as in the *Hiroshima* scene she cowers before the accusations without making any argument in support of her desires and actions.

In the scene from *L'Amant*, there is a history behind the situation of the mother. The mother has been marginalized and victimized by the patriarchal Indochinese colonial society--a story told in greater detail in *Un Barrage contre le Pacifique* (1950; trans. *The Sea Wall*). Yet in relation to her daughter she plays the role of the Sender, she takes on the responsibility of enforcing the strictures of society, affirming its racism and denying the daughter the same access to sexuality available to her two brothers. The mother thus acts out the classic matriarchal preservation of patriarchy; she takes the place of the father, preserving and enforcing the law of the father on her daughter. The mother inflicts on her daughter the same violent victimization and exclusion that was inflicted on her by the patriarchal administration. She repeats the same scenario but in the role now of torturer and not of victim.

A similar syndrome appears in the text "Albert des Capitales" from the autobiographical *La Douleur* (1985; trans. *War: A Memoir*) set in 1944 Paris. Like the mother of *L'Amant*, the young Duras persona in the text has been victimized and marginalized: victimized in that her husband has been captured and deported to the Nazis, marginalized within her Resistance cell. Yet she accepts to play the role of the Sender, to stand in for the two male co-leaders of the cell, in interrogating a Frenchman accused of gross collaboration. The tables are now turned; the Duras persona is in the role of the torturer, an older male in that of the victim, declared a traitor and a villain. The thematics of the gaze (as studied by Doane 1981) are stressed in the text, and point to the inversion of gender roles. With the help of two strong men, the accused is beaten nearly to death without having provided much information.

The Duras persona follows the mother in *L'Amant* with a vengeance, developing a lust for bloodshed and power in the heat of the scene. "Albert des Capitales" delineates--in an intensely historical, political context--the same hysterical repetition of the cycle of violence. Victimized by the anti-Sender Nazi state, she reproduces its violence; rebuffed by her resistance compatriots she does the dirtiest police work for them and their leaders, her Sender.

The specular thematics noted in the *Hiroshima* scene are prominent in the scenes from *L'Amant* and "Albert des Capitales." Again, the spectacle is both a scene of suffering and a trial and punishment by a makeshift jury or lynch mob. As the mother goes through her interrogation, the girl's two brothers listen to the scene from outside the room and participate verbally. The elder son, equated by the narrator to the war, to the Nazi war machine (Duras 1984: 78; trans: 62-63), wants more punishment, to protect the family honor; the younger son pleads for mercy. Similarly, in "Albert des Capitales" other resistance fighters line up inside the small room like a chorus, women in front, men in back. They chant triadic strings of insults at the accused informer. Yet with the persistence of the violence the group splits. In all, seven members walk out in protest--and seven is a standard number of jurors in a criminal trial in France. In both cases, then, the event is at the same time spectacle or show; the political action is also communal ritual and trial. Emphasizing the motif of show, Duras works a '*cinema mundi*' convention in both texts. She notes that for the mother in *L'Amant* living out in the country such scenes and other tirades took the place of movies (Duras 1984a). In "Albert des Capitales" the Duras persona muses at one point "I'm in a movie theater", to which the narrator agrees (Duras 1985: 144; trans: 125); further in the text the torturer mentions that the victim in the dark room with the light shining on him must feel as if he too were at the movies (151; 130). Throughout the text the lighting, the action, and the characterization suggest parallels with the *film noir* genre.

The specular dimension, the voyeurism in the registers of violence and judgment serve to open up a distance between the reader and the character and to draw attention toward the values at stake and away from the linear plot continuum. The devices are used to make the scenes function as forums for a debate on political values and the process of justice. The spectacles and jurors in the scene point to the actions as sanctions in this two-fold manner, and emphasize that the character in the role of interrogator and torturer is not Subject but Sender in the scenario. The character is hierarchically superior to a Subject and is entrusted with maintaining and enforcing the values of the community gathered about.

Yet the specular dimension and world-as-(movie)-theater device also serve to position the characters as actors at a remove from their own actions. The *Hiroshima* flashback is an image-only scene, with the sound remaining within the scene in the present. The scenario has an unreal quality in which the girl appears--much like Lol V. Stein--to be "not there." In "Albert des Capitales" there is a schizophrenic quality to the sudden transformation of the brooding, unenthusiastic Duras persona into an excited, bloodthirsty torturer. The text is equally divided between notations of the external scene and notations of her thoughts and feelings. The radical disjunction between the two at many points separates the character from the scene and poses the question of alienation.

If the specular devices draw attention to the scenes as sanctions and examinations of social values, the axiological attention must be drawn first to the issue of violence, its nature and justification in the scene. Bonita Oliver (1985) has recently argued that René Girard's notion of "good violence" can be used to study Duras's novel *Moderato Cantabile* (1958) and her film *Nathalie Granger* (1973). Oliver follows Girard's (1972) assertion that transgressing a prohibition in the realm of the sacred is violent, but is a violence which has a therapeutic effect on the community. This "good", externalized violence expressed in ritual can dissipate destructive internal violence pent up within the community. Duras's "Albert des Capitales" seems to set out following the Girardian formula, replete moreover as it is with all the tribal savagery that seems to stalk Girard's communities. The resistance group melds for a moment in triumph and revenge, while the accused makes a constructive use of violence within himself to assert his identity--whether true or not. Yet the protracted refusal of the accused to fulfill his role of villain in the group's narrative program by turning over the sought-for cognitive object of desire brings an end to the therapeutic effects of the violence. The immanence of its pus and tears, blood and cracked skin prevents the accused's body from transcending from corporal signifier to any deferred, resemanticized signified.

Hélène Cixous has cited Duras as one of a handful of writers who would practice an *écriture féminine* which she fosters (Cixous 1975 trans.: 878n3). One would like to apply to Duras's texts Cixous's vision of a revalorized notion of power; Cixous writes (483-484, cited and translated in Moi 1985: 124-125), in an interview with Françoise van Rossum-Guyon:

> I would indeed make a clear distinction when it comes to the kind of power that is the will to supremacy, the thirst for individual and narcissistic satisfaction. That power is always a power over others. It is something that relates back to government, control, and beyond that, to despotism. Whereas if I say 'woman's powers', first it isn't *one* power any longer, it is multiplied, *there is more than one* (therefore it is not a question of centralization--that destroys the relation with the unique, that levels everything out) and it is a *question of power over oneself*, in other words of a relation not based on mastery but on availability.

Yet clearly the texts scrutinized here gesture only implicitly and in Brechtian, counter-example fashion to any utopian revision of power. The victims and would-be-reformers or revolutionaries follow a cycle of remaining immured in their silence instead of contesting the accusations, first, then of occupying the old role of power and repeating the destructive violence. Duras has not recently followed Rochefort (1972), Cixous (1975), or Wittig and Zeig (1976), in creating utopian scenarios.

Instead, these Durassian texts, at least in their treatment of social violence, seem to fit in the syndrome of the first period of the French postwar women's movements as striated by Kristeva in "Le temps des femmes" (1979). The women seek a place within the power structures set up by a masculine society. The darkly ironic view of the possibilities of viable revolutionary action in the texts parallels that of Sartre in postwar dramas and novels. Their acute sense of being tried and condemned by history again matches Sartrean texts (eg. *Les Séquestrés d'Altona* 1960). Duras's texts do not split up the female characters into public and private halves as do the Sartrean pieces, however.

In place of a conclusion I would like to pose a question. The powerlessness and the silence of the Durassian victims, their repetition of the power structures, lead one to wonder whether for Duras the assumption of the Sender's role by women characters goes hand in hand with the frequent murder or effacement of the father of the family in Duras's texts. The first father of the family in Duras's first novel, *Les Impudents* (1973), is dead long before page one; the mother's second husband is a sensitive, work-loving, but confrontation-fleeing man bullied by the elder son. The fatherly uncle of her second novel *La Vie tranquille* (1974) is murdered by his nephew in an Oedipal gesture, while the father himself plays only a marginal role in the family, before going half-mad at the novel's mid-point. The father of Duras's third novel *Un Barrage contre le Pacifique* (1950), as of *L'Amant*, is long dead at the outset of the text. One could continue citing examples at will. Duras envisions a secluded room of one's own for women in *Nathalie Granger* (1973) which can make converts of outsiders who stray in. She does not show women changing a family structure or a society at large. Perhaps for Duras this transformation could only be possible if the father would enter the fray as an ally of the victim, in turn an impossible condition for Duras. The missing father could be linked to the absent masculine object of desire in the scenes of sanction.

REFERENCES

BORGOMANO, Madeleine.
    1985. *Duras: Une lecture des fantasmes* (Petit Roeulx, Belgium: Cistre, Essais).
CIXOUS, Helénè.
    1975. "Le rire de la méduse", *L'Arc* 61, 39-54, trans. Keith Cohen and Paula Cohen "The Laugh of the Medusa", *Signs* 1 (Summer, 1976), 875-899.
DOANE, Mary Ann.
    1981. "Woman's Stake: Filming the Female Body", *October* 17, 3-36.
DURAS, Marguerite.
    1943. *Les Impudents* (Paris: Plon).
    1944. *La Vie Tranquille* (Paris: Gallimard).
    1950. *Un Barrage contre le Pacifique*, Roman (Paris: Gallimard), trans. Herma Briffault *The Sea Wall* (Pellegrini & Cudahy, 1952).
    1958. *Moderato Cantabile* (Paris: Minuit), trans. Richard Seaver (New York: Grove, 1960).
    1960. *Hiroshima mon amour*, Scenario et dialogues, (Paris: Gallimard, NRF), trans. by Richard Seaver as *Hiroshima mon amour* (New York: Grove, 1961).
    1964. *Le Ravissement de Lol V. Stein*, Roman (Paris: Gallimard), trans. Richard Seaver (New York: Grove, 1966).
    1973. *Nathalie Granger, La Femme du Gange* (Paris: Gallimard).
    1980. *L'Homme assis dans le couloir*, Recit, (Paris: Minuit), trans. Mary Lydon *The Man Seated in the Passage* in *Contemporary Literature* 24.2 (1983), 268-275.
    1982. *La Maladie de la mort*, Récit (Paris: Minuit), trans. Barbara Bray *The Malady of Death* (New York: Grove, 1986).
    1984. *L'Amant* (Paris: Minuit), trans. Barbara Bray, *The Lover* (New York: Pantheon, 1985).

1984a. Interview with Bernard Pivot televised on the program *Apostrophes*.
1985. *La Douleur* (Paris: P.O.L.), trans. Barbara Bray *The War: A Memoir* (New York: Pantheon, 1986).
GIRARD, René.
1972. *La Violence et le sacré* (Paris: Grasset).
GREIMAS, Algirdas Julien and Joseph COURTES.
1979. *Sémiotique: Dictionnaire raisonné de la théorie du langage* (Paris: Hachette, Classiques Hachette: Langue Linguistique Communication), trans. Larry Crist, Daniel Patte et al., *Semiotics and Language: An Analytical Dictionary*, with a bibliography by Edward McMahon (Bloomington: Indiana University Press, 1982).
KRISTEVA, Julia.
1979. "Le temps des femmes", *34/44: Cahiers de recherche de sciences des textes et documents Université de Paris 7* 5 (Winter), 5-19, trans. Alice Jardine and Harry Blake "Women's Time," *Signs* 7.1, 13-35.
MOI, Toril.
1985. *Sexual/Textual Politics: Feminist Literary Theory* (New York: Methuen).
OLIVER, Bonita.
1985. "Le thème de la violence de *Moderato Cantabile* à *Nathalie Granger*", *Atlantis: A Women's Studies Journal* 10.2 (Spring), 31-44.
ROCHEFORT, Christiane.
1972. *Archaos ou le jardin étincelant*, Roman (Paris: Grasset).
SARTRE, Jean-Paul.
1960. *Les Séquestrés d'Altona* (Paris: Gallimard).
WITTIG, Monique and Sande ZEIG.
1976. *Brouillon pour un dictionnaire des amantes* (Paris: Grasset).

THE PLAY OF ILLUSION IN A MAP OF LOVE:
LA CARTE DE TENDRE (1654)

Martha M. Houle
College of William and Mary

> *For you men, defeats are only fewer successes.
> In this unequal game, our fortune is not to lose,
> and your unhappiness is not to win.*
>
> -- Choderlos de Laclos (1782: 173) --

The map in *Clelia* is a witty answer to a lover's question: "For pity's sake, my dear Clelia . . . , tell me where I am, I implore you" (1654: 391-2). The context of the *Carte de Tendre*, the *salon*, is the space of play: there is time, games, self-imposed rules, and leisure, a finality without end: the signs of aristocracy (Marin 1977: 63). We find all of these things in *Tendre*: in this spatial representation of a gallant voyage, we see a drawing of a country with small villages to pass one night or several, lightly-suggested paths with the possibility of diversion, frontiers in the form of a lake and a sea, "Countreys undiscovered", yet to be mapped. The pleasure is in the play: Tenderness is to be travelled and retravelled, but no two trips are alike. But this space is not empty: made of figures, it generates language: "Sighs, obligations, *small cares* in love, all of it is language", writes Furetière (1690; emphasis added). And it generates narratives--no one narrative, formalistically patterned. But narratives that, by the consent of the group, abide by or establish conventions. *Questions d'amour*, for example, a common *salon* game, "are the fruit of long collective debates, of lively speeches, of tender confessions, and also of disenchanted reflections. In circles [e.g., *salons*], around the fireplace, during meals, questions arose and answers flew" (Rosso 1985: 220). These *salons* are spaces organized by women to teach men how to converse, love, and be *honnêtes hommes*. This training, however, is not determined by women as subjects: the gaze is male (Kaplan 1983), and women are to perpetuate their own objectification, passively passing on the rules of courtship to new generations of men. We shall see in a minute that her contemporaries reacted to Mlle de Scudéry's map within the year or two following hers. But let us now read *Clelia*'s narrator's description of the *Carte de Tendre* with her.

Clelia proposes the *Map of Tenderness* to teach Herminius, her aspiring lover, something about love--indeed, to tell him exactly where he is on a map, invented for that purpose. Herminius (Scudéry 1654: 394-5) has a reason for wanting to know: he does not want to be unhappy in love, and with a map he will receive much needed guidance:

> As I am unable to go from New Friendship to Tenderness if you do not keep your word, I am asking for the Map that you promised me; but in asking for it I am committed to leaving as soon as I will have received it, to take a trip that I imagine to be so agreeable that I would rather take it than see the whole Earth, even if it were to receive a Tribute from all the Nations of the World.

With this trip, a sort of medieval love-service (Jackson 1974: 17), Herminius plans to decrease the distance between him and Clelia. What he wants is to be situated and to be directed: he wants not to know where he himself is, but rather where *she* is. Anticipating this (Scudéry 1654: 405)--the planned seduction by the male--the woman is absent from the map:

> Also this wise Maiden (*Fille*), wanting it to be known on this map that she had never had love, and that she would never have anything but tenderness in her heart, made the River of Inclination flow into a sea that she called the Dangerous Sea; because it is rather dangerous for a Woman to go a little beyond the last Bounds of friendship. And she then made that beyond this Sea is what we call Countreys Undiscovered (*Terres inconnues*), because in effect we do not know what is there ... In this fashion she found room to make an agreeable moral of friendship by a simple witty game; and to make it understood in a rather particular manner that she had not had love, and that she could not have any.

Parenthetically, Scudéry's *Carte de Tendre* and Lafayette's *La Princesse de Clèves* are the only women's texts canonized today from the seventeenth century--they have a lot in common: inscribing delay and absence in a discourse of women's desire (see DeJean 1985). This *trompe-l'oeil*--the gaze, the *objet a* comes into play, to quote Lacan, "when, in love, I solicit a look, what is profoundly unsatisfying and always missing is that--you never look at me from the place from which I see you. Conversely, what I look at is never what I wish to see" (emphasis deleted)--this map is a woman, but from which the third dimension--*tendre, jouissance*--is absent. Let us now look at what the eye sees before the gaze "triumphs" (Lacan 1973: 103) over it.

In the representation of *Tendre*--and "tenderness", as one heroine defines it, is "A certain sensibility of heart that is almost never found sovereignly except in persons who have a noble soul, virtuous inclinations, and well-turned wit" (Scudéry in Aragonnès 1934: 139)--we see the progression from fashionable and gallant qualities, the *art de plaire* (art of pleasing) in conversation and correspondence, to personal qualities like Honesty, Goodness, or Constant Friendship" (Aronson 1986: 227). Instead of one route to Tender, as Herminius requested and expected, there are three.[1] In this map, Clelia presents an enigma, a trick map, a picture of his desire which will protect herself (that is, where she is absent), an *épreuve* or test in the chivalric and later the courtly tradition.

Tender-upon-Esteem is reached through twelve steps, "because Clelia ingeniously put as many villages as there are small and great things, that can contribute to the birth through esteem of that tenderness of which she has heard speak" (1654: 400). The first village is *Grand Esprit*, "Great Spirit".[2] This step of moral worth and even of great wit is the first step to Esteem, and leads to *Iolis Vers*, "Pleasing Verses". These verses are the agreeable productions of wit, but not necessarily of a poet. The verses evolve into *Billet Galant*, "A Gallant Letter" written to a member of the *beau sexe* by a lover who gives himself over entirely to her service. *Billet doux*, "An Amorus (sic) Letter", is synonymous with *billet galant*: both are *poulets*, short love letters that were sent to *Dames galantes* and called "chicks" because they were folded with two points or wings.[3]

The next village is *Sincérité*, "Sincerity", where one speaks frankly, openly, with no pretence or dissimulation.[4] At *Grand coeur*, "A Great hart" may represent affection, friendship, love, and tenderness. *Probité*, or "Honesty", is a natural goodness or virtue by which one abstains from hurting anyone. The path leaves "The River of Inclination" with the village of *Générosité*, "Generosity", which means an elevated soul, great courage, magnanimity, bravery, and liberality; someone who prefers honor to any other interest.

The last three villages are *Exactitude*, "Exactness", the punctual observance of the least of demands; *Respect*, "Respect", the deference, honor, and submission that one pays to one's superior; and *Bonté*, "Goodness", that refers to virtue, particularly to charity, gentleness, and patience. They lead to Tender-upon-Esteem. *Estime*, "Esteem" is the good or bad opinion one has of the value or merit of a person or thing, for example, "This action or that work have placed this gentleman or that author in [great] esteem" (Furetière 1690). In a moral context, "One cannot overestimate virtue, freedom, sincere people, and good friends" (Furetière 1690).

The second route leads to Tender-upon-Recognisance through eleven steps. The lover begins at the village of *Complaisance*, "Complacency", a deference to the feelings and the wishes of others ("Complacency is normally accompanied by flattery . . ." [Furetière 1690]). *Soumission* or "Submission", the humiliation and obedience of the lover, is followed closely by *Petits Soins* or "Small cares", that particular attachment one has to a mistress to serve or please her ("Sighs, obligations, small cares in love, all of it is language" [Furetière 1690]). "You see," continues the narrator, "one must pass through Assiduity (*Assiduité*), in order to understand that it is not enough to give all these obliging cares for a few days, cares that inspire so much gratitude, if one does not give them assiduously" (Scudéry 1654: 401-2).

The next village is *Empressement*, "Empressment", a witness to the ardor, affection, and diligence with which one completes a task. "After that," explains the narrator, "you see that one must pass by Great Services (*Grands Services*); and to indicate that few People render them, this Village is smaller than the others" (Scudéry 1654: 402). At *Sensibilité*, "Sensibility", one is disposed to receive the impressions of objects on the senses, as in "That woman has a tender and sensitive soul, which is said in love as well as in compassion and in gratitude" (Furetière 1690). "Afterwards", concludes the narrator (Scudéry 1654: 402-3),

> one must, in order to arrive at Tender, pass through Tenderness (*Tendresse*), because friendship attracts friendship. Then one must go to Obedience (*Obeissance*): there being almost nothing that engages the heart of those one obeys more than to do it blindly; and to arrive finally where one wants to go, one must pass through Constant Friendship (*Constante Amitié*), which is no doubt the surest path, to arrive at Tender-upon-Recognisance.

At Tender-upon-Recognisance one experiences gratitude for the services or the good offices of a friend.

The town Herminius requested the map in order to find, Tender-upon-Inclination, is also the town with no landmarks on its path: "Clelia . . . put no Village along the edge of the River: it flows so fast that one has no need of lodgings on its Banks in order to get from New Friendship to Tender" (Scudéry 1654: 400). We encounter here, with Herminius, the paradox of the allegorical (though really enigmatic) Map of Tenderness: a map such as Tenderness relates and interprets a concept or an idea or a desire as topographical space, and this love map therefore puts into representation a theory of love; but the place created by Mlle de Scudéry is the generator of narrative, the description of a fictional world, the story of a romance.

The *Map of Tenderness* appears as a metonymy and not a fixed instance for the romantic love--expressing the uneasiness inspired by the image--in Molière's *Les Précieuses ridicules*. This one-act play was first performed during the most active period of the *précieuse* controversy (1654-1661), beginning with the *Carte de Tendre* and *Clelia* and ending with the whimper of changing fashion, and Louis XIV's personal reign. In 1659 Mlle de Scudéry's long novels were well known, and the debate over who and what the *précieuses* were, well established.[5] Scene four stages two young cousins from the provinces arguing with Gorgibus, the father of Magdelon: he wishes to marry them to two men who have just paid them a visit, and wants to know why they treated the suitors so badly (whispering, yawning, asking the time every minute, and so on).

Magdelon answers with a narrative: courtship must proceed as in Mlle de Scudéry's *Le Grand Cyrus* (1649-1652), with love born from afar and declared, first meeting resistance, then encouragement, continuing with kidnappings, jealousies, persecutions by the fathers, "and everything that follows", in a prolonged and unending courtship. Gorgibus responds to this narrative with "What in the devil is this jargon I hear? This is very high style."

After Magdelon's unintended parodic reading of the courtly tradition found in the novels that Scudéry and others wrote, Cathos reverses the Clelia-Herminius relationship: she pedantically reads the map as a set of rules to be followed, misreading the absence as a presence, turning female mystery and obliteration into a self-referential system. She says:

> Indeed, my uncle, my cousin speaks truly. How can we receive men who are so uncouth in matters of gallantry? I'll wager that they have never seen the Map of Tenderness, and that Amorous Letters, Small Cares, Gallant Letters, and Pleasing Verses are lands unknown to them.

The courtly tradition of women teaching men is undermined by this use of the map, and replaced by the pragmatic and safe arranged marriage. Molière defuses Herminius's masculine anxiety by inserting his dilemma (how to read the map?) into comedy: the humor of the play, and the devastating force of the satire of the *précieuses*, is clearly attributable to the insertion of a romantic novel into a comedy, and to the juxtaposition of two incompatible genres. "Reality" is the frame of the play: as Boileau avers, in a comedy the character "is not a like portrait or image; / It is a real lover, son, or father" (Boileau 1674: III.419-420).

Gorgibus and the two suitors represent, therefore, bourgeois reality. The two aspiring *précieuses*--who later mistake two valets for a marquis and a vicomte--and their romantic ideas are completely rejected and ridiculed at the end of the play, both by the suitors and by Gorgibus. Bourgeois values displace the self-indulgent "extravagances" of valets (scene one) and women (scene sixteen), "and you, who are the cause of their folly, stupid nonsense, pernicious amusements of idle minds, novels, verses, sonnets and *sonnettes*, may you go to the devil!" (scene sixteen). Gorgibus, in this last tirade, pulls together the strands of the satire against the *précieuse*, but especially against the mix of reality and fiction or romance.

Clelia's problem at the end of Molière's play remains, How to translate a masculine perception of love as goal-oriented, as following a well-frayed path, as a conquest perhaps, into an uncertain, multiple, feminine, and (casuistically speaking) more refined structure? As we have seen, Clelia gave him more information than he no doubt wanted, but not the information he expected or thought he needed.

I would now like to suggest some approaches to reading this map. First of all, by citing a contrasting map, that of Tristan L'Hermite's *Le Royaume d'Amour*, published soon after Mlle de Scudéry's and no doubt as a reaction to it. Notice that it has a circular well-defined path, with a capital city, *Jouissance*, or "(Sexual) Pleasure" or "Enjoyment". The woman's body and male desire are inscribed over and over again, not only in the decorative female figures but also in the masculine point of view, that of the conquest (visits, sighs, resistance, *jouissance*, indifference, etc.).

Secondly, it might be useful to consider all of these love maps as political redrawings of France after the Fronde (1648-1652). Whereas before this period aristocrats pursued glory and honor through great deeds, afterwards political power was no longer possible. I. M. Richmond observes that "To satisfy this need for individual distinction [a new source for that personal glory so necessary to their *amour-propre*], they turned towards gallantry, that is, towards the sublimation, verbal at least, of the relationships between men and women" (Richmond 1977: 27). *Épreuves* of love replace military *épreuves*.

Thirdly and finally I would like to point out that Claude Filteau, in his much cited analysis of the *Carte de Tendre* (1979), attempts to add a third dimension to the map: whereas Clelia scrambles, obliterates, mystifies woman's desire--evoking women as mystery, enigma, the dark continent--Filteau makes the woman's text into a *trompe-l'oeil* (see in particular his graphs). As Lacan points out, the *trompe-l'oeil* is the shifting gaze, the shifting object of desire; Baudrillard would refer to the "disturbing strangeness" (1979: 91) of the impossibility of a third dimension. Most commentaries have sought to redraw and defuse this text in an attempt to appropriate a space. A failed attempt, perhaps--but that remains to be seen. Does the enigma empower or disempower? Let me end, albeit cynically, with a quote from Filteau's study where he denies the map allegorical or enigmatic value: "It is a question, on the contrary, of describing [the map] endlessly and exhaustively, setting up contemporary instruments of analysis to make the representation of things conform to a true discourse" (1979: 59).

NOTES

[1] The names of the villages on the *Carte de Tendre* are taken from the original French (using also their English version in the 1678 translation).

[2] In my unpacking of this map I am relying on Antoine Furetière's *Dictionnaire universel* (Paris, 1690).

[3] Furetière adds this illustration of the word's usage: "In the past prudes made a scruple of receiving *poulets*; now they have boxes full of them."

[4] "To speak sincerely is to speak from the depths of one's heart, one's heart on one's lips. To act sincerely is to act in good faith." *Dictionnaire universel*, s.v. *sincerement*.

[5] For two very different points of view on the issues involved in the debate, see Domna Stanton (1981) and Jean-Michel Pelous (1980).

REFERENCES

ARAGONNÈS, Claude.
    1934. *Madeleine de Scudéry. Reine du Tendre* (Paris: Armand Colin).
ARONSON, Nicole.
    1986. *Mademoiselle de Scudéry, ou le voyage au pays de Tendre* (Paris: Fayard).
BAUDRILLARD, Jean.
    1979. *De la séduction* (Paris: Galilée).
BOILEAU-DESPREAUX, Nicolas.
    1674. *L'Art poétique* (Paris: Nouveaux Classiques Larousse, 1972).
DEJEAN, Joan.
    1985. "Sappho's Leap: Domesticating the Woman Writer", *L'Esprit Créateur* 25.2, 14-21.
FILTEAU, Claude.
    1979. "Le Pays de Tendre: L'Enjeu d'une carte", *Littérature* 36, 37-60.
FURETIÈRE, Antoine.
    1690. *Dictionnaire universel* (Paris: Le Robert, 1978).
JACKSON, W. T. H.
    1974. "The Nature of Romance", *Yale French Studies* 51, 12-25.
KAPLAN, E. Ann.
    1983. "Is the Gaze Male?", in *Powers of Desire. The Politics of Sexuality*, ed. Ann Snitow, Christine Stansell and Sharon Thompson (New York: Monthly Review Press), 309-327.
LACAN, Jacques
    1973. *The Four Fundamental Concepts of Psycho-Analysis*, trans. by Alan Sheridan (New York: Norton, 1978).
LACLOS, Choderlos de.
    1782. *Les Liaisons dangereuses* (Paris: Editions Garnier Frères, 1961).
LAFAYETTE, Marie-Madeleine de.
    1678. *La Princesse de Clèves* in *Romans et nouvelles*, ed. Emile Magne (Paris: Editions Garnier Frères, 1961).
MARIN, Louis.
    1977. "Puss-in-Boots: Power of Signs--Signs of Power", *Diacritics* 7.2, 54-63.
MOLIÈRE, Jean-Poquelin.
    1659. "Les Précieuses ridicules", *Oeuvres complètes*, vol. 1 (Paris: Editions Garnier Frères, 1962), 189-220.
PELOUS, Jean-Michel.
    1980. *Amour précieux, amour galant (1654-1675). Essai sur la représentation de l'amour dans la littérature et la société mondaines* (Paris: Klincksieck).
RICHMOND, I. M.
    1977. *Héroïsme et galanterie. L'Abbé de Pure, témoin d'une crise (1653-1665)* (Sherbrooke, Qué.: Naaman).

ROSSO, Corrado.
  1985. "Le Chancelier Séguier et Marie Linage autour des 'Questions d'amour'", in *L'Age d'or du Mécénat (1598-1661)*, Colloque International CNRS, March 1983 (Paris: Editions du CNRS), 219-230.
SCUDÉRY, Madeleine de.
  1654. *Clélie. Histoire romaine*, vol. 1 (Paris: Augustin Courbé; English translation, London, 1678).
STANTON, Domna.
  1981. "The Fiction of *Préciosité* and the Fear of Women", *Yale French Studies* 62, 107-134.

PERMEABLE BOUNDARIES, FEMININITY, AND VIOLENCE

Linda Kintz
University of Oregon

Certain texts of the period of literary modernism are marked by a thematic that recurs, repeats itself, organizes meaning--the usefulness of gendered fluidity as threat. I want first to read from several texts of the period between 1918 and 1925, then turn to what I see as a way to bring together an analysis of their organization of meaning. First, this from Antonin Artaud, in a collection of short pieces called *The Umbilicus of Limbo*, written in 1925. He presents several characters in a very brief play concerned with a Young Man's search for meaning. Other characters include The Bawd, The Wet Nurse, and The Girl, as well as The Knight and The Priest. At the end, a Gigantic Voice turns the Bawd's clothes into glass with its loud thundering, revealing her naked and hideous body. The Wet Nurse then appears, her breasts cut off, and the Girl is carried onstage and dropped, dead. When The Knight asks the Wet Nurse, "Where did you put it?" she replies, "Here". And pulls up her skirt, petrifying the Young Man into rigidity. The Knight covers his face in horror: "Now an enormous number of scorpions emerge from under the Wet Nurse's skirts and begin to swarm in her vagina which swells and splits, becomes vitreous and flashes like the sun." The Young Man and Bawd flee like victims of brain surgery, say Artaud's stage directions. The Girl, coming to life in a daze, says "The virgin! so that's what he was looking for" (1956: 76).

The world was for Artaud, says Susan Sontag (see Artaud 1956: xvii), a "world clogged with matter (shit, blood, sperm), a defiled world". The demonic powers that rule the world "are incarnated in matter--matter is 'dark'", and it is the body as carrier of that matter that arouses profound revulsion; the poet becomes his body and then must transcend it, must seek to become a "body without organs" by means of his theater, a theater that annihilates the body: "a body 'entirely' transparent, skin and flesh of the bone that is the spirit, intact from any pulsational movement, event, opacity", says Lyotard (1969) of Artaud, who produces a theatrics of "space" taken to its widest extension and purified. Language, for Artaud, is thought turned into matter, and constitutes an "obscene identity between the flesh and the word"; the word "becomes loathing and must be transcended". How? By the works of a "physician of culture" like himself who wants to use it change consciousness, to liberate theater from its confinement "in language and in forms", by "sensory violence as embodied intelligence". The aestheticization of revulsion at the body and its transcendence becomes the theatre of cruelty, the obscenity of femininity and carnality here figured by vitreous, swarming masses of scorpions; the obscene body that haunts Artaud is gendered female and transcended by its destruction, a new, transparent flesh produced.

Now juxtapose Artaud's description of bodies with these descriptions from Klaus Thewelheit's study of the writings of members of the Freikorps, volunteer vigilante armies that roamed Germany after the first World War, hired by the socialist Chancellor Ebert to bring order after the war. As Barbara Ehrenreich says in her introduction (Thewelheit 1977: ix),

> [B]etween 1918 and 1923, they fought Polish communists and nationalists, the Russian Red Army and Latvian and Estonian nationalists in the Baltic region, and the German working class throughout Germany.

They were relatively autonomous and well-organized. Thewelheit suggests they may have had more to do with the rise of the Nazis than did "the mass psychological appeal of fascism".

When one looks at letters, journals, and novels written by members of the Freikorps, as did Thewelheit (1977: 24), one looks at how this language functions, not so much at what it signifies or expresses, as at "its role in the man's relationship to external reality, and its bodily location . . . the way the bodies speak of themselves, of objects, and of relationships".

What emerges in Freikorps writings is a particular characteristic of threat (which is simultaneously mesmerized fascination), variously described as "bloody masses", "the Red flood", "the new flood rising before every dam, threatening to pulverize its petrified forms of life". It was the broken dam that allowed Germany to be overrun (Thewelheit 1977: 231):

> The whole world poured out over Germany: Americans and New Zealanders, Australians and Englishmen, Portuguese and French. The bitterest pill to swallow was the stationing of blacks everywhere by the French: Moroccans and Senegalese negroes, Indochinese and Turks. . . .
> The Red flood brought all of the worst instincts to the surface, washing them up on the land.

There were external invasions and internal ruptures--threatening fluidity, wetness, slime everywhere (1977: 233):

> General strike. State of siege. Sees only Germans with hate in their eyes. Hears only curses and swearing. A gigantic, filthy-red wave breaks over him. He feels he's drowning in it . . . . Meanwhile, shame and betrayal, filth and misery rose higher and higher around us; we could practically have drowned in it . . . . The sergeant slowly drags himself down the iron staircase, unbolts the heavy gate, and steps out into the square with his arms up. In an instant, the Red wave sweeps over his corpse and storms up the stairs like a pack of wolves, lips dripping saliva.

But the violent response to such threat produces fluidity as well by producing a particular condition in female bodies: "A blood-drenched mass, silver and blue, lies in the sand . . . .a bloody mass, a lump of flesh that appears to have been completely lacerated with whips and is now lying within a circle of trampled, reddish slush" (1977: 195).

Such descriptions proliferate and are linked by Thewelheit to the inscription of the body in the larger social order, its involvement in the reproduction of the social order that is fascism (Thewelheit 1977: 218):

> The monumentalism of fascism would seem to be a safety mechanism against the bewildering multiplicity of the living. The more lifeless, regimented, and monumental reality appears to be, the more secure the men feel. The danger is being-alive itself.

The similarity between the interpretations of "matter" in both Artaud and these Freikorps men is striking--the problem ultimately is in the being-alive, leading us to Benjamin's concept of the "aestheticization of politics" by the Nazis: "Mankind", says Benjamin (1955:242),

> which in Homer's time was an object of contemplation for the Olympian gods, now is one for itself. Its self-alienation has reached such a degree that it can experience its own destruction as an aesthetic pleasure of the first order. This is the situation of politics which Fascism is rendering aesthetic. Communism responds by politicizing art.

Fascism's aesthetic ritual of self-destruction and Artaud's modernist theater of cruelty aestheticizing the transcendence of "being-alive", through the becoming transparent of the suffering body, are similar enough to require further comparison. (One is also reminded of Nietzsche's becoming the philosopher-womb and giving birth to himself, using femininity in order to transcend it.)

In these instances, the revulsion, disgust, fear of materiality, of the fluidity of bodily processes that transcends bodily boundaries, is involved. As Thewelheit (1977: 409) says of the Freikorps:

> You could almost say that erect, soldierly bodies were the sole reference points for those states and substances (which at times could even surface in, and exit from, the bodies). In fact, all of the anxiety-producing substances introduced in this work have something in common: they could be called upon to describe processes occurring in or upon the human body, especially its orifices

'Floods', 'morasses', 'mire', 'slime', and 'pulp'--this whole battery of terms can describe bodily secretions if you start out with a negative attitude toward them. Pleasurable occurrences have been reversed to produce a panicked defense against the very possibility of their subsequent occurrence. All of these substances flow, are hybrids, moving slow or fast, having to do both with the inside and the outside of bodies. And those fluids occur on the battlefield, where there is mud, slime, blood, liquids; in places where women are: cooking, altering substances, cleaning up babies, cleaning toilets, doing "women's work;" and on and in bodies, in particular female ones.

The hybrid, says Thewelheit (1977: 410), is negativized to stand in for all that is terrifying:

> Included in this category were all of the hybrid substances that were produced by the body and flowed on, in, over, and out of the body: the floods and stickiness of sucking kisses; the swamps of the vagina, with their slime and mire; the pap and slime of male semen; the file of sweat

that settles on the stomach, thighs, and in the anal crevice, and that turns two pelvic regions into a subtropical landscape; the slimy stream of menstruation; the damp spots wherever bodies touch; the warmth that dissolves physical boundaries (meaning not that it makes one body out of a man and woman, but that it transgresses boundaries: the infinite body; the body as flow).

Also the streams of orgasm, of infancy and diapers, of milkstream at breasts, etc.

The body experiences itself in terms of its relation to the cultural logic of the organization of bodily boundaries between it and the world. Here an organizational, logical "fault" becomes signified as dirt, filth, mixture, a point we will return to in Julia Kristeva's (1980) tracing of the logical organization in monotheistic cultures of the body's "clean and proper" boundaries, the sustained development of abomination through which Judaism and then Christianity part with sacrificial religions, the progressive interiorization of "abomination" and the production of a transparent, abstract flesh, or as we might describe it in Foucauldian terms, a technologized "organic" body, the mechanical organic, the "body without organs". Filth and abomination are matters of logical distribution: "the loathsome is that which disobeys classification rules peculiar to the given symbolic system" (Kristeva 1980: 92), classification rules whose effects are the production, organizing, and policing of dirt, the hybrid, and the "feminization" of those categories. The aestheticization of self-destruction can thus be seen more and more as a step in cleaning up the proper body: the destruction of the "defiled maternality" called the "feminine"--and groups gendered feminine: communists, blacks, Jews, proletarians, the proletarian whore, and women in general, except for the White Mother, like the Virgin in Artaud's play: the one woman uncontaminated by matter who comes to be associated with monumentality and with transcendence itself--the one woman separated from "femininity", hollowed out, cleaned up, abstracted.

Mixture, the hybrid, heterogeneity. The terms are familiar because they also occur in a good deal of feminist theory as ways to describe the literary experiments of women trying to resist the language of phallogocentrism. It would seem important to problematize those terms and see them from two different directions, two different discursive subject-positions associated with gender. What are we to make of Virginia Woolf's use of slime and mud to suggest possibilities of resistance to militarism, patriarchy, and imperialism in Between the Acts, written during the Battle of Britain, possibilities of writing differently: "She raised her glass to her lips. And drank. And listened. Words of one syllable sank down into the mud. She drowsed; she nodded. The mud became fertile. Words rose above the intolerably laden dumb oxen plodding though the mud" (1941: 212).

Mud, slime, fluidity in Woolf's texts, as in the texts of many other women writers suggest other possibilities for the hybrid, for fertility, a different construction of maternality, differences in the uses made of fluidity, slime, mixture and the functions they serve in a larger cultural logic. We are seeing in these modernist texts an unacknowledged gendered relationship to heterogeneity. Walter Benjamin (1955) says that fascism was a "parody of revolution', both producing and destroying reality, arising, as does revolution, out of heterogeneity, but in theorizing that heterogeneity and its relationship to fluidity, Adorno steps over the possibilities Woolf sees: "[T]he undifferentiated state before the subject's formation was the dread of the blind web of nature, of myth;' and if the subject were liquidated rather than sublated in a higher form, the effect would be regression--not just of consciousness, but a regression to real barbarism" (Adorno 1978: 79). Thus Man's relation to nature as fluidity is here associated only with the threat of regression to barbarism, fascism; he must move past what we might call the mirror stage toward the symbolic, still indirectly presupposing a gendered domination of nature, a masculine subject. Yet Woolf suggests the usefulness of fluidity in combatting fascism. She, like Kristeva, moves to describe what Lacan leaps over in the mirror stage, what occurs prior to it, that is, the semiotic--pre-linguistic but not pre-cultural, having to do with the territorialization of the body prior to entry into the signification of a developed language system.

Kristeva's semiotics of monotheism traces the development of masculine subjectivity in a Judeo-Christian cultural tradition, a logic of abomination whose effects prove to be the production of "the clean and proper body". She extends Lévi-Strauss' notion of a cultural logic to apply both to the social order and to the ordering of subjectivity by means of the construction of symbolic boundaries that define the body: "[T]he prime role of culture is to ensure the group's existence as a group, and consequently in this domain, as in all others, to replace chance by organization" (Lévi-Strauss 1949: 179) to resist excessive expenditure and ensure regularity, predictability. That masculine subject of monotheism becomes the administered, normalized subject in an economic system based on an absolute right to property for proper subjects.

The important concept that will connect Kristeva's work on what she calls the abject back to Benjamin's observation about aesthetics and politics is the concept of the sacred, which, secularized, becomes the aesthetic. Following the work of Mary Douglas, Kristeva sees the sacred as the effect of a religious system of differences that organizes and orders by means of rituals of pollution and defilement. Topologically, this initially meant that some people were excluded from a certain space or place, such as the temple. But such spatial articulations become interiorized, embodied by means of exclusions and productions inscribed on and in the bodies of those who make up the social group.

Divisions can only be enforced within signifying networks if there are margins that limit the meaning of each of the elements, margins that hold a place between divisions; paradoxically, in the monotheistic semiotic system of abomination which leads us to a way of talking about filth, slime, and floods, these margins are produced by means of historically changing rites of defilement, margins which foreground the weakness of the "imperative act of excluding", an impossible imperative which must always fail in a system of differences. The imperative act of exclusion must produce borders and margins, filth and slime, in order to provide itself a place; the poverty of prohibition has useful effects. As Foucault says of grids of intelligibility, "[I]t is only in the blank space of [the] grid that order manifests itself in depth as though already there, waiting in silence for the moment of its expression" (1966: xx).

In Kristeva's analysis, the divisions are theoretically held in place by the seme of blood, produced as a border that both defines and disrupts the categories it limits. But blood does not signify, as that implies a "clean" separation of blood from its meaning; it thus occupies a very unstable but necessary position, both threatening and tantalizing but inaccessible to circulation as a signifier. Blood is like the corpse, the border that makes "me" possible, "something rejected from which one does not part", "a border that has encroached upon everything" (Kristeva 1980: 3). It might be either the unsignifiable but cultural excess Woolf seeks or defiled maternality, the other excess that "arouses paranoid rage to dominate those improper objects [ab-jects], to transform them, to exterminate them" (Kristeva 1982: 91). Foucault argues that a symbolics of noble blood was replaced by an analytics of sexuality, blood replaced by sex. But because he does not account for a gendered relationship to his site of enunciation, he overlooks the persistence of the seme of blood in the technologies of sexuality, a gendered relationship to materiality and blood.

"Subjection", engenderment within a linguistic system, arises out of "the dispositions of the place-body and the more elaborate speech-logic of differences", in a subject-position constituted retroactively by a phallocentric symbolic system; the place of the phantasmatic mother must be established as not encroaching, so that each subject might learn to speak properly: "The body must bear no trace of its debt to nature; it must be clean and proper to be fully symbolic" (Kristeva 1980: 102). But though Kristeva provides important methodology, her subject, like Foucault's, is masculine. She doesn't develop the implications for female modernists of psychoanalytic descriptions of gendered subjectivity: there are initially two different subject-positions in relation to entry into the symbolic, a binary opposition then embedded into administration and multiple subject-positions. The masculine subject must learn separation on its way to "purity" and is threatened by closeness; the female subject, however, is threatened by separation and simultaneously inscribed as abject. One cannot presume that the two genders can be encompassed by the concept of the "speaking subject" within the history of Western monotheism, a history of "confrontation with the feminine and the way in which societies code themselves in order to accompany as far as possible the speaking subject on that journey" (Kristeva 1980: 58).

The history of monotheistic religions is thus a history of the purification and production of the abject, secularized for Kristeva finally in avant garde aesthetics: "The artistic experience appears as the essential component of religiosity", (1980: 17) its task to "retrace the fragile limits of the speaking body" (1980: 18), "to speak the pre-objectal, pre-nominal", bringing us back to the possibilities of reading the pre-linguistic in a gendered way: as an example of resistance or as (1980: 53) the

> x-ray of the drive foundations of fascism . . . [where] [t]he body's inside . . . shows up in order to compensate for the collapse of the border between inside and outside. It is as if the skin, a fragile container, no longer guaranteed the integrity of one's 'own and clean self' but, scraped or transparent, invisible or taut, gave way before the dejection of its contents.

But as Thewelheit suggests, the masculine body's dissolved boundaries are reconstituted by the violent destruction of female bodies, bloody, feminized masses providing a safe approach to the feminine, the only possibility of closeness without threat, the dissolution of the female body itself and the woman as love object, the organs without body as correlative to the body without organs that transcends it. Though ostensibly gendered feminine, the body proves to be divided--its dejected feminized contents deprived of bodily boundaries, dissolved, while the transcendent "monumental" fascist masculine body reinstitutes its own boundaries by violence against its being-alive. Purity through violence produces the transcendent, transparent body. Are the Freikorps subjects mad? Is Artaud's attempted transcendence abnormal? Or do they, instead, resemble normal subjects produced by the technologies of a logic of purity?

I want to suggest a possible answer by referring to a description from recent political discourse that bears on this. In an article in the Washington Post Weekly, University of Texas communications professor, Kathleen Hall Jamieson describes as "The Effeminate" style of political discourse--"emotional self-disclosure through the use of storytelling and imagery" (Grove 1988: 25). Its best practitioner? Ronald Reagan, whose effeminate style is much preferred over the "manly" style, which is impersonal, rational, direct, and data-based". The manly style, she says, is a "noose", marked by an "inability to disclose some sense of private self on an intimate mass medium".

Carried along in this description is the logic of the appropriation of the feminine and its transcendence by means of that appropriation; the most masculine of political activities, the leadership of the national security state, whose capacities of discipline, surveillance, and technology surpass anything Jeremy Bentham ever dreamed of, can now be gendered feminine but only because that leadership has been made safe from femininity. Ronald Reagan, not women, not gays, can be effeminate. The production of interiority turns inside out, as does language, the effeminate macho politician disclosing "some sense of a private self on an intimate mass medium". (One assumes, unfortunately, that it takes semiotic training to become aware of the duplicity of the "private" and the "intimate" in those sentences.) The transparent body without organs, pure form, pure style, has transcended femininity by appropriating it--by aestheticizing a certain politics.

REFERENCES

ADORNO, Theodor.
   1978. "Subject and Object", in *The Essential Frankfurt School Reader*, ed. Andrew Arato and Eike Gebhardt (Oxford: Oxford University Press).
ARTAUD, Antonin.
   1956. *Oeuvres completes* (Paris: Gallimard). Page references are to the English edition, *Antonin Artaud: Selected Writings*, ed. with an introduction by Susan Sontag (New York: Farrar, Strauss, and Giroux, 1976).
BENJAMIN, Walter.
   1955. *Illuminations* (New York: Harcourt Brace, 1968).
FOUCAULT, Michel.
   1966. *Les Mot et les choses: une archéologie des sciences humaines* (Paris: Gallimard). Page references are to the English trans., *The Order of Things: An Archaeology of the Human Sciences* (New York: Pantheon, 1970).
GROVE, Lloyd.
   1988. "When They Ask If Dukakis Has a Heart, They Mean It", *Washington Post national Weekly Edition* (October 17-23, 1988), 24-25.
KRISTEVA, Julia.
   1980. *Pouvoirs de l'horreur: essai sur l'abjection* (Paris: Éditions du Seuil), trans. by Leon Roudiez as *Powers of Horror* (New York: Columbia University Press, 1982). Page references are to the English translation.
   1982. "Psychoanalysis and the *polis*" in *Critical Inquiry: The Politics of Interpretation* 9.1, 77-92.
LÉVI-STRAUSS, Claude.
   1949. *Les Structures élémentaires de la Parenté* (Paris). Page references are to the English version of the revised French edition (1967) trans. by James H. Bell, John R. von Sturmer, and Rodney Needham, *The Elementary Structures of Kinship*, ed. Rodney Needham (Boston: Beacon Press, 1969).
LYOTARD, Jean-François.
   1973. "La dent, la paume", *Des dispositifs pulsionnels* (Paris: UGE, 1973). Paris: UGE). Page references are to the trans. of Patrice pavis in *Languages of the Stage: Essays in the Semiology of the Theatre* (New York: Performing Arts Journal Publications, 1982).

THEWELHEIT, Klaus.
   1977. *Männerphantasien, Vol. 1: Frauen, Fluten, Korper, Geschichte* (Berlin: Verlag Roter Stern). Page references are to the English trans. by Stephen Conway, *Male Fantasies, Vol. 1: Women, Floods, Bodies, History* (Minneapolis: Minnesota University Press, 1987).
WOOLF, Virginia.
   1941. *Between the Acts* (New York: Harcourt, 1969).

LUCE IRIGARAY: THEORETICAL AND EMPIRICAL APPROACHES TO THE REPRESENTATION OF SUBJECTIVITY AND SEXUAL DIFFERENCE IN LANGUAGE USE

Katherine S. Stephenson
University of North Carolina-Charlotte

Luce Irigaray is known in America primarily for the feminist philosophy she articulates in *Speculum of the Other Woman* (1985) and *This Sex Which is not One* (1985), both 1985 translations of much earlier works (1974, 1977). American feminists became familiar with Irigaray through translations of three essays in *This Sex Which is not One*, originally translated in *Signs* (1980) and *New French Feminisms* (1981). The fact that these first translations were taken out of the larger context of Irigaray's *oeuvre* had the unfortunate effect of focusing attention on a limited aspect of her work--the mother/daughter relationship and the question of autoeroticism--and allowing American feminists to incorporate her into the on going battle at the time about *l'ecriture féminine*. Comparisons with Hélène Cixous and Julia Kristeva led to her being typecast as an essentialist French feminist. Critics are just beginning to reevaluate this reductivist notion of Irigaray's feminist philosophy and the up-coming translations of *Ethique de la différence sexuelle* and *Sexes et parentés*, among others, will do much to inform the American public of the wide variety of subjects Irigaray has incorporated in her feminist critique of Western society and culture.

A large part of Irigaray's career has been devoted to the development and analysis of empirical studies on language use deriving from her work as a psychoanalyst. As early as 1973 Irigaray presented the results of her first language tests in *Le Langage des déments* where she details a grammar of pathological subjects. In this investigation of anomalous linguistic performance, she adopts a syncretic method of analysis combining elements from structural, distributional, actantial, generative, and transformational linguistics. By addressing the two essential constituents of linguistic performance--the model of competence and that of the speaking subject--she attempts to discover if anomalies are due to a disruption on the level of language structure itself, i.e. on the level of *la langue*, or on the level of the structure of communication--of the pathological speaking subject's relation to language, the allocutor, and the referent--leading to the subject's inability to manipulate the semantic and syntactic structures of language. The latter proved to be the principal area of disturbance, directing Irigaray to concentrate not on the content of the utterance, as is the traditional focus of linguistic analysis, but rather on the act of enunciation as the site wherein subjectivity manifests itself by revealing the speaking subject's specific mode of structuring language.

In *Parler n'est jamais neutre* (1985) Irigaray elaborates her continuing analysis of the enunciation into a more far-reaching critique of the universal or generic masculine subject in scientific discourse. Here she assumes the subjectivity inscribed in her own use of the pronoun *I* and revindicates sexual difference as a fundamental component of subjectivity in the system of representation constituted by language. This recuperation of the sexual marking of discourse comprises more than a deconstructive act in its affirmation of a reality covered up and denied by phallocentric discourse. In her preface to *Parler n'est jamais neutre* Irigaray states the irritation and laughter with which she is inspired by the fact that scientific knowledge remains rooted in an unquestioned ideology of platonic truths. Its requisite representational model whereby the scientist states that "X is equal to, greater, or less than Y" presents (Irigaray 1985: 7-8)

> a type of encoding of the world from which the subject is absent and which he surrenders, under the cover of universality, to one or several subjects, leaving apparently no affects, a language stripped of all pathos, absolutely neutral and detached, [which] transmits itself to someone else without any known origin or source. The world thus supposedly finds a perfect translator or translation, an adequate copy of the universe and, today, of the subject. The formula, its mechanics, its machinery suffice. No more creation of life. Everything is realized in a sterilized reduplication. The subject becomes a machine without future evolution.... What is lacking [here] is creation, the affirmation which says: *I live.*

Irigaray demonstrates that the supposed objectivity of scientific discourse is "a question of style", of "a technique which does not state itself to be, or know itself to be distinguished from the supposed truth" (1985: 9). In this sense she relates works of science and art as "fabrications" which tend towards detachment in their desire to be "closer to the world than to [their] producer" (1985: 8), for all "philosophers and scientists are poets in the tranquil exposition of their message ... which is as much a text (*écriture*) as the product of an operation of objectivity, truth, or thought" (1985: 13). This comparison allows her to accentuate the creative nature of these "graphic" products, which is usually occulted in the case of scientific works. Creativity is to be understood here, however, as the localization of subjectivity in language use, of a subjectivity that is sexually marked.

While postmodern philosophy, particularly deconstruction, has legitimized an interdisciplinary focus on subjectivity, it has yet to come to terms with the question of sexual differentiation within subjectivity. For Irigaray, to affirm the subject of discourse as a sexed being is an ethical imperative, a fundamental truth-condition of discourse: "This science [claiming universality] which wants to be more scientific, or the only scientific [discipline], can be so only at the expense of an ethics of the subject itself" (1985: 9). Perhaps nowhere is this occultation of the sexual component of subjectivity more apparent, nor its deconstruction more immediately imperative or productive, than in the field of psychoanalysis. When elaborating the conclusions of her work in the "Questions" essay of *This Sex Which is not One*, Irigaray (1985: 152-153) begins with this issue:

> The fact that Freud took sexuality as the object of his discourse does not necessarily imply that he interpreted the role of sexualization in discourse itself, his own in particular. He did not carry out an analysis of the presuppositions that bear upon the production of discourse

insofar as sexual difference is concerned. Or again: the questions that Freud's practice and theory raise for the scene of representation . . . do not go so far as to include the question of the sexualized determination of that scene. Lacking such an interpretation, Freud's discourse remains caught up in a meta-physical economy.

While Irigaray first dealt with the relationship of subjectivity, sexual differentiation, and their representation in discourse with regard to psychoanalysis, this relationship may be seen as the central issue of her feminist philosophy and its critique of phallocentric discourse's "hierarchization" of difference in its "subordinat[ion] of the other to the same" (1977: 159). Moreover, Irigaray's philosophy never limits itself to a deconstructive agenda, for she continually proposes a complementary reconstructive one based on the recuperation of sexual difference. This emphasis on difference, however, has been one of her most controversial positions, especially in America where the tendency is to minimalize difference in favor of defusing confrontation and of a gender-neutral concentration on the individual, or on a pragmatic rather than theoretical approach to sexual equality. Irigaray's (1977: 161) theoretical focus on discourse, nonetheless, has always had a pragmatic goal:

> Women cannot work on the question of their own oppression without an analysis and even an experience of institutions--institutions governed by men. What poses a problem--a fundamental one?--for the feminine . . . is the operation of discursive logic . . . [the] hierarchical structure [of which] has always put the feminine in a position of inferiority, of exploitation, of exclusion with respect to language. . . . Thus it is necessary to turn again to this 'proper' character of language, analyzing it not only in its dual movement of appropriation and disappropriation with respect to the masculine subject alone, but also in what remains mute, and deprived of any possibility of 'self-affection', of 'self-representation', for the feminine.

The investigation of language's role in the maintenance of sexual inequality has always been seen by Irigaray as fundamental to the feminist agenda. Beginning with *Speculum, de l'autre femme*, Irigaray concentrated her efforts on philosophical discourse, since "[t]he philosophical order is indeed the one that has to be questioned, and *disturbed*, inasmuch as it covers over sexual difference", for it is the discourse that "lays down the law to all the others" (1977: 159). The goal of this questioning was to "go back through the masculine imaginary, to interpret the way it has reduced us to silence, to muteness or mimicry, and . . . from that starting-point and at the same time, to (re)discover a possible space for the feminine imaginary" (1977:164), to "secure a place for the feminine within sexual difference" since that difference "has always operated 'within' systems that are representative, self- representative, of the (masculine) subject" (1977: 159). Since language comprises the most fundamental of representational systems, the concept long held to be true of the neutrality of language must be understood as another political tool of the praxis of sexual indifference under the guise of which female subjectivity has been denied (equal) representation. Thus feminist criticism must deal with the philosophical question of woman as a position in discourse to successfully execute any pragmatic goals.

The writing strategy used by Irigaray to "disturb" philosophical discourse itself offers an initial model for providing a space within which to articulate female subjectivity. Her deconstructive interrogation of master discourses, in order not to reproduce the very values and positions of the phallocratic system upon which they are based, eschews the logic of "discursive coherence". She practices instead a dialogic parody and what I would call an implosive mimicry that, by exposing gaps in the phallocratic system master discourses represent, reveals the vacuous superstructure left by a deconstruction of their presuppositions and causes it to collapse inwardly. Irigaray's discursive strategies have received more critical attention than the theories on language and representation on which they are based, the most accurate and comprehensive analysis of which to date can be found in Elizabeth Gross' article "Philosophy, subjectivity and the body: Kristeva and Irigaray" (1986). Gross does not fail to contextualize her elucidation of the relationship between language, representation, and power relations in Irigaray's thought within its pragmatic, political goals, as demonstrated by her description of Irigaray's "feminine subversion of discursive regimes" (Gross: 138-139):

> To speak *as*, not *for* women, is in itself to begin to undo the reign of the proper, the self-identical, singular phallic organisation. To speak to evoke rather than designate, to signify rather than refer, to overburden oppositional dichotomous categories by refusing their boundaries or borders is to occupy the impossible 'middle ground' excluded by logic and reason in their present forms. This is not to create a discourse *without* meaning, but rather to proliferate many meanings, none of which could hierarchically unify the others, . . . to create a space in which the exploration of many discourses and many women's voices can articulate themselves--and force others to listen.

Irigaray's theories have been informed by her intuitions about how female subjectivity might manifest itself discursively, and her own discursive practice provides an example of how "destabiliz[ing] the presumed norm of masculinity . . . may help establish the conditions necessary for the production of new kinds of discourse, new forms of knowledge and new modes of practice" that successfully transcend phallocentric knowledge's "basic models of representing the two sexes" (Gross 1986: 142-3). Such writing strategies, however, while based on the recuperation of sexual difference and exploration of the creativity inherent in acknowledging the sexually marked subjectivity represented in language, are molded conceptually by a negative reaction to the norms posited by phallocentric discourse. Having reached somewhat of an impasse when it comes to specifying theoretically how female subjectivity might recuperate self-representation in language (I say somewhat because it is not possible for theory to describe such a phenomenon without being prescriptive), Irigaray has returned to the language tests she first developed for pathological subjects to assess the representation of subjectivity and sexual difference in everyday language use by non-pathological subjects. For critical to the diachronic project of social change through a revolution in language and the processes of signification is a synchronic assessment of not only how sexual difference may affect language use but also how gender is itself constructed by language. This is the crux of the social and political implications of Irigaray's focus on language, for, as Gross (1986: 139) states,

> language, discourses, texts, utterances are not simply empirical acts, like all other human actions, but serve to fundamentally ground, represent and make social/natural life meaningful. Neither neutral nor transparent modes of *reflection*, they are active agents of the processes of inscription, '*worlding*', categorising and valuing the world.

An understanding of how men and women represent their relation to language, the world, and the other in ordinary discourse will not only delimit how in the patriarchal order language inscribes gender difference through the "psychic *internalisation* and reproduction of patriarchal power relations" (Gross 1986: 125), but will hopefully reveal as well sexually distinctive patterns of communication or discursive economies and open the way to conceive a different social order, one based on the sexual order of discourse.

This last expression--"the sexual order of discourse"--is the one chosen by Irigaray to entitle two presentations of her latest research on sexual differentiation in language use: the 1987 essay "L'Ordre sexuel du discours" published in a now out-of-print issue of the journal *Langages*, and her July 1987 seminar at the Toronto International Summer Institute of Semiotic and Structuralist Studies. Since the language tests she had previously developed concentrate on localizing the representation of subjectivity in the act of enunciation, they required no methodological changes to apply them to the question of the sexual differentiation of subjectivity. The only modifications made were in the choice of words used to elicit a linguistic performance on the part of the subject.

The originality of Irigaray's method of analysis lies in the focus on the act of enunciation to delimit the speaking subject's particular mode of structuring language. Her hypothesis is that, as sexed beings, the forms we produce are themselves marked by sexual difference; that men and women privilege different communicative structures based on a different discursive or logical syntax. What makes their distinction and recuperation difficult is the fact that they reproduce the syntax of social order which has always "been a means of masculine self-affection . . . or self-representation. Whereas the 'other' syntax, the one that would make feminine 'self-affection' possible, is lacking, repressed, censured: the feminine is never affected except by and for the masculine" (Irigaray 1977: 132). It seems possible, however, that within the different discursive syntaxes used by the two sexes, one may be able to extrapolate from those structures representative of an internalization of social order the more fundamental differences representative of sexually marked discursive economies which could then be explored as a means of allowing woman's self-affection, "a self-affection that would certainly not be reducible to the economy of sameness of the One" (Irigaray 1977: 132).

The results presented so far by this empirical study seem to reveal that women and men occupy some distinctively different subjective positions in their relationship "to language, the object of discourse, the world, and the other" (Irigaray 1987: 108). Their utterances differ in choice of subjects, interplay of pronouns, types of verbs, verb tenses and modes, predicate-transformations, grammatical categories chosen for localizing meaning or connotation, the articulation of the relationship subject/ allocutor, the subject's appropriation--or lack of appropriation--of the message, and so on.

From these discrete formal differences, Irigaray has isolated more general patterns of sexual marking. One such pattern is that women have a tendency in their utterances "to say or experience some relationship to the other and the world", "to link language and reality by communicating a message", while men "speak of themselves, or among themselves", or "are satisfied to simply manipulate the language" (1987: 120). Another pattern she identifies is that "women construct more objective sentences the sense or denotations of which are often based on extra-linguistic contexts", while men "connote their messages more, affirming their subjective mark more intensely" (1987: 108).

While such results certainly seem to confirm her hypothesis, there is still work to be done on mechanical aspects of the language test (i.e. mathematical and observational paradigms) and on the internationalization of the research to ascertain culturally-specific and cross-cultural differences in sexual marking. Nonetheless, it is encouraging to see such a preeminent theorist and philosopher investigate the empirical applications of her theories, though to be precise, Irigaray has always maintained a close working relationship between empirical and theoretical approaches.

Certainly, it is difficult to comprehensively assess the work of such a prolific writer with such breadth of inquiry during her lifetime, or, indeed, while that work is still evolving and much of it not yet translated (though at present there are five separate translation projects on her work). Yet if there is one thread uniting all of her works, it is her critical focus on the representation of subjectivity in language, and the lack of representation of female subjectivity. To disregard the role her empirical studies have played in the formation and development of her theories is to neglect a significant corpus of her work. More importantly, it has caused critics to remain ignorant of what, especially in her latest research, promises to provide a significant evolution in our understanding of the linguistic representation of subjectivity and its sexual marking, and the development of a more comprehensive theory of the enunciation.

REFERENCES

GROSS, Elizabeth.
    1986. "Philosophy, subjectivity and the body: Kristeva and Irigaray", in *Feminist Challenges*, ed. C. Pateman and E. Gross (Boston: Northeastern University Press), 125-43.

IRIGARAY, Luce.
    1973. *Le Langage des déments* (Paris: Éditions de Minuit).
    1974. *Speculum, de l'autre femme* (Paris: Éditions de Minuit), trans. by Gillian C. Gill, *Speculum of the Other Woman* (Ithaca: Cornell UP, 1985).
    1977. *Ce Sexe qui n'en est pas un* (Paris: Éditions de Minuit). Page references in this article are to the English trans. by Catherine Porter and Carolyn Burke, *This Sex Which is not One* (Ithaca: Cornell UP, 1985).
    1985. *Parler n'est jamais neutre* (Paris: Éditions de Minuit). Translations are mine.
    1987. "L'Ordre sexuel du discours", *Langages* 85 (March), 81-123. Translations are mine.

XV

CAMILLO AND THE ILLUSION OF COLLECTIVE MEMORY

THEATER AND ARCHITECTURE: A PARALLEL EXPERIENCE

Curt Dilger
Temple University

Part One: The Memory Theater

Inside the mute exchange between ideas and things there lies a place able to absorb paradox, habitable only by virtue of contemplation. Glimpses of this other territory, perhaps incalculable in dimension, are potentially always available to us, yet only on specific occasions do we read the spectacle of memory theater. Its unexpected appearance provides us with a world far richer than any schema for representation. The memory theater, and its hermetic structure, indicate an opportunity for the figure in the carpet to surface, to give some portion of its secret. When the chance image no longer seems merely arbitrary, and instead presents a fragmented quality of a hidden design, we reach through the gesticulating screen of nature to discover its theatrical identity.

All accidents, events, actions, however ephemeral, leave an ephemeral trace. The atmosphere and the earth both contain these traces and allow them to disperse. Time casts itself on every surface, and embeds things with the imprint of text--history. However, this form of involuntary narration does not appear equal in effect or significance--we must read the particular texts of ordinarily illegible things, those which demand attention in our experience. Through experience we *arrive* at memory, inexplicably hidden before, and participate perhaps not so much in a process of intellection as in inhabitation. We peel away the text of edges so we may dwell in them.

Our daily life describes the topos of forgetfulness. The haze of duties and habits, laws obeyed unthinkingly, seems to threaten life with torpor, and obscures the values we pursue. The world we habitually call the real world is one of confusion and loss. This topography constitutes the labyrinthine plenum of history, the place where texts accumulate, intersect, blur, and disintegrate into mere things, appearances with elusive meanings. History is the sedimentation of vaguely inscribed surfaces. Fragments of this patina will, at times, emerge as significant moments, traces of a larger, invisible world. Memory is the search for a structure which will enable these fragments to cohere. Its process is necessarily one of excavation and retrieval. The horizon is a place of discontinuity, a discovery of the virtual within the apparently homogenous labyrinth. Sediment that obscures and forgets gives way to excavation, in the hope of recovering some status of origin. This process of retrieval is not in any way complete or neutral in relation to the topography through which it searches. Nor can there by any hope of absolute success--only the smallest interior glance can attest to memory's substance. There seems to be no means to verify existence, only an infinite opportunity to speculate upon possible existences. Every attempt to verify becomes lost in the face of a chance refutation in nature. Every foothold can lose way just when we are most certain of its security. When we perceive an emergent structure in the interstitial spaces of remembrance, history and fiction act as conspirators, twins, discourses which question the source of design and intention. Origin is both historical and fictional--it can be read from evident signs, but evidence requires a form of speculation to complete its circumstances. Speculation can indicate not simply a reasonable scenario for origin, but any number of scenarios, fantastic or banal, direct or cryptic, each with an independent authority. The manner in which these motifs are played out, interrupted, or contradicted, is properly the substance and spectacle of the memory theater. Narrative begins when we imagine a world where memories coalesce. Illusion enervates the inactive, and imbues narration with a virtual, or extra-dimensional presence. We then see through the simply serial organization of texts, and divine a *mise en scene*, a place appearing to perform and demonstrate an event. These gestures, illusions of signs hidden in motion, constitute the perceptual horizon of the theater, because a gesture inhibits reading just as it invites it.

Without events, place would not truly exist, no edges would form, and no distinctions could be made. The memory theater, instead of a departure from reality, becomes the place where reality witnesses its own likeness. This performance allows what we call ordinary to be swept away momentarily, and replaced by the ghosts of chance. Significant characters, curious and difficult in form, play seemingly undirected parts; rather, the direction is from an obscure and remote source, and exerts only a fluctuating influence.

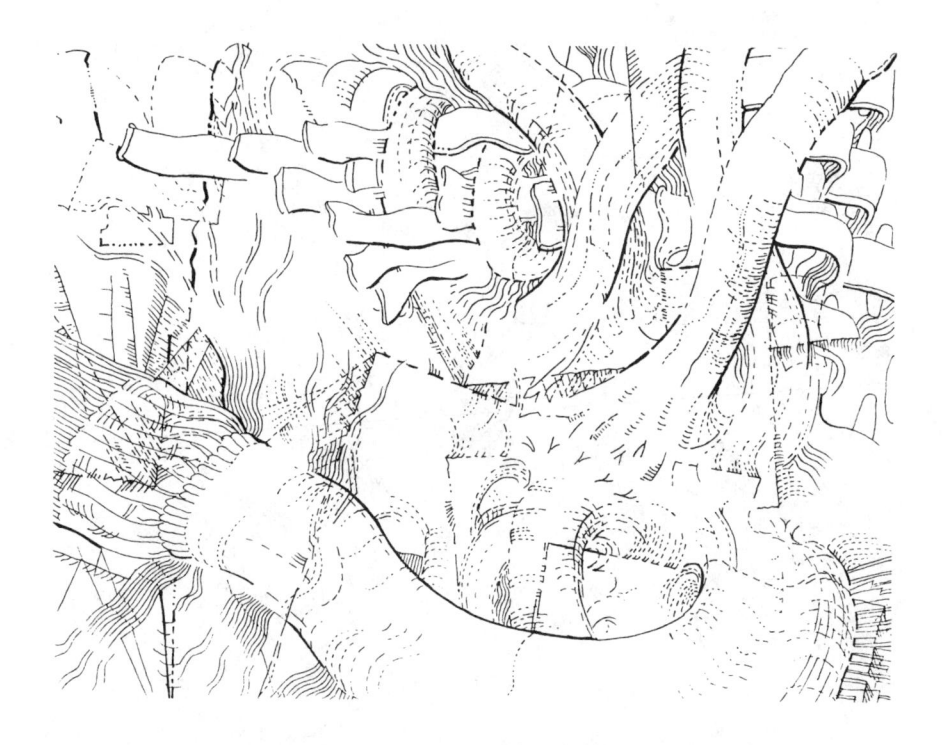

    Conditions like these, despite their unpredictable, rapid and improvised structural changes, make life elude the naive determinism of world as idea, as well as the superficial resignation of world as mute form, and gives it a vital charge, a freshness and potential to experience. Intentions are lost inside the things we make--the belief that works are equivalent representations, transparent vehicles for our desire for meaning, oversimplifies a difficult relation. Meaning wells up in the object, is suddenly lost, found again, articulated with great clarity, and dissolved into other meanings. Interpretations are neither determined facts nor arbitrary structures, but places which age, and attempt to survive the vicissitudes of all threatening elements. It is here, inside the boundaries of an epiphany, that we see life's reflection.

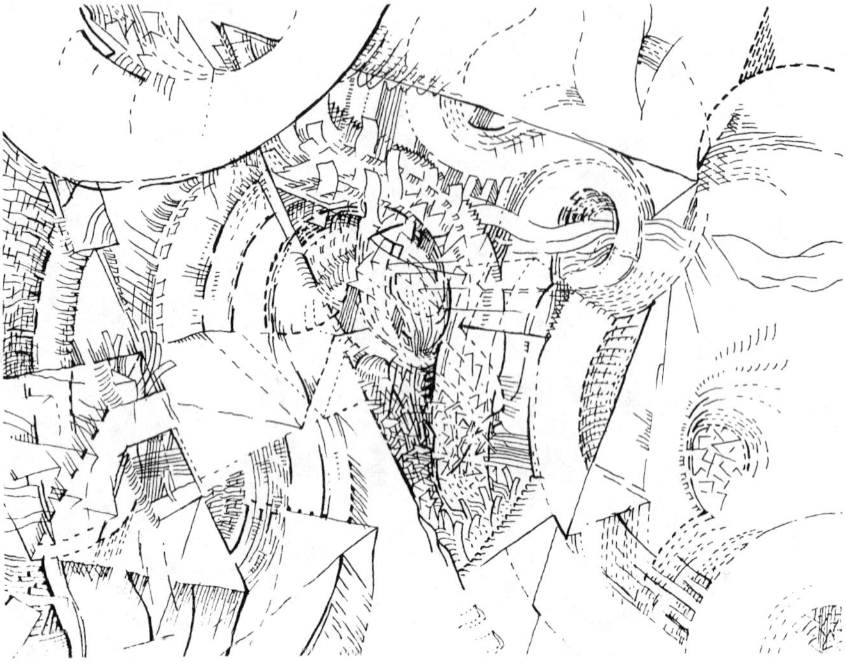

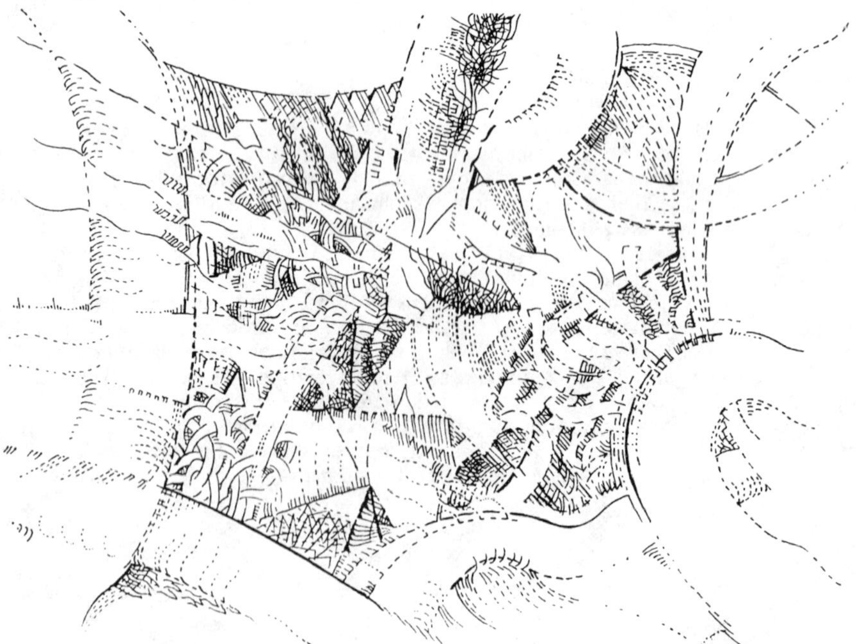

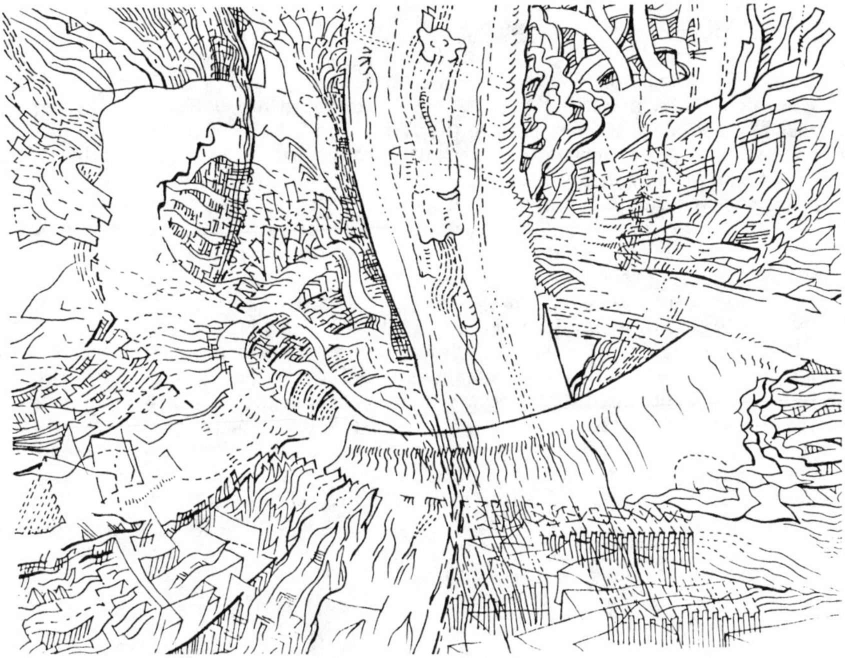

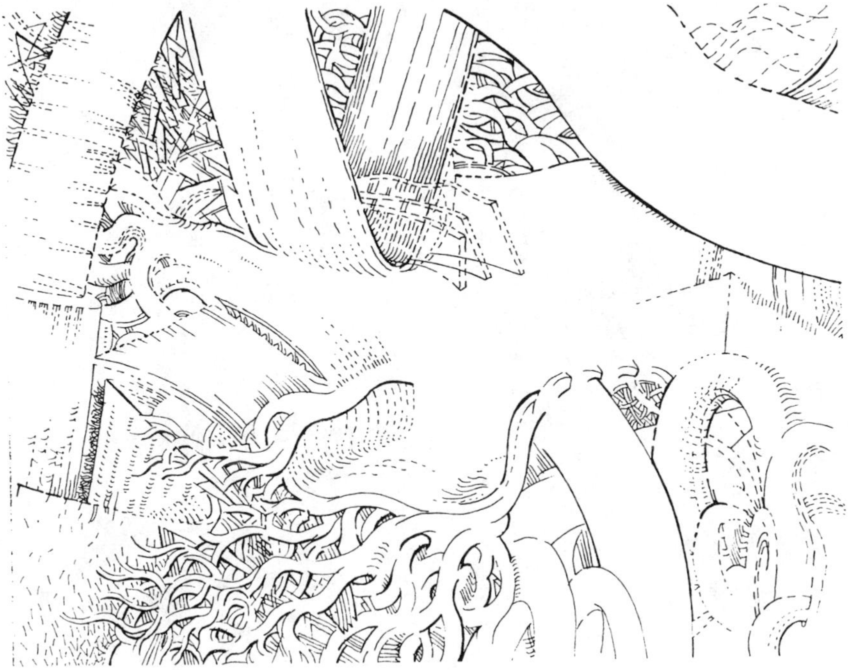

Part Two: Architecture and Its Mirror

The construction of a memory theater runs a precisely parallel course to our original perception in nature, because the original inspires its fictive continuation. Cities are elaborate scaffolds, built to support the hopeful chance for our aspirations to be embodied in one image, one spark of vision. Various factors affect the choice of a site and its use; many seem banal or arbitrary. The activity of architecture requires an effort to reclaim this site, not in the way of correction but in rediscovery. Places in the city are in a constant state of flux; empty lots acquire temporary uses, buildings are built, they change owners almost as quickly as they change function, additions are made, renovations. More importantly, above all of these inevitable but forgettable occurrences, are moments when a hidden identity of the city reveals itself. A valuable aspect of a site must be cultivated, once found.

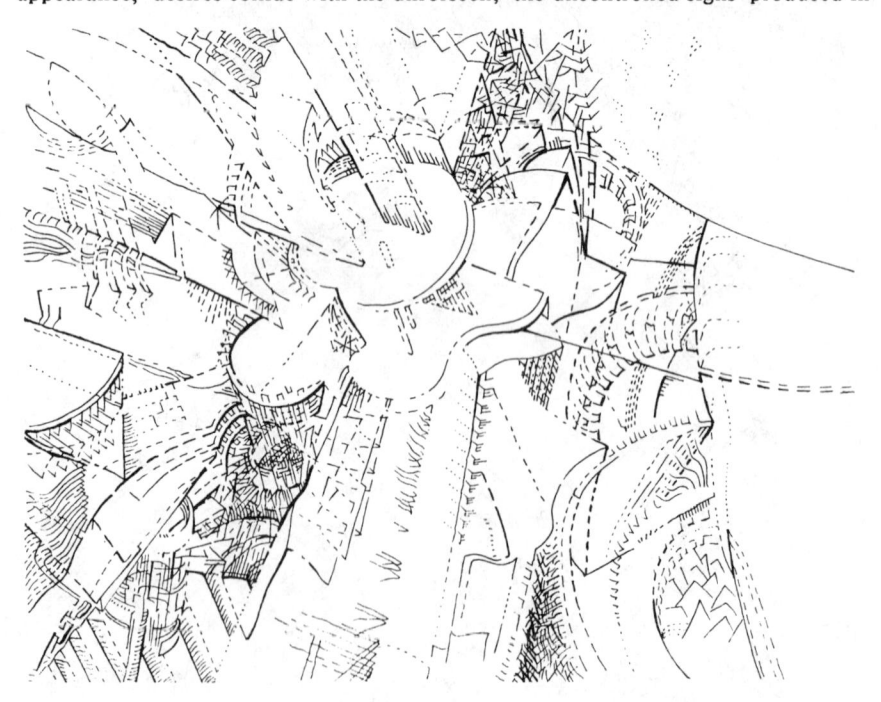

The discussion of type in architectural theory is a search for the text of memory and convention. Types are fragments of the immutable, invisible world. We arrive here by contemplating the traces, gestures left in the visible. Any application of the principle of type in making architecture is problematic because method is always confounded by unimagined criteria. Nevertheless, our intuition of repetition and continuity is an essential step towards architecture. We look for a place of stability through broken, fleeting glances. This stable world has a monstrous appearance; desires collide with the unforseen, the uncontrolled signs produced in nature. From the site grows the monster like an infection, architecture, an intersection of different discourses. A grafted, celibate union of the body with its metaphor, demonstration yields many readings. Its intricacy and difficulty demand a particular attention to the edge made between our expectations and our experiences.

A walk through the city confirms the need to look carefully. Often we discover meanings and places where none had been intended. Perhaps just as often we visit city centers, intended to inspire, that leave us empty. Nor can function offer us true insight; factories are sometimes more exhilarating than monuments. Curiosity guides the mind fascinated by the monster's elusive form. Regardless of its simplicity, any moment is invaded by various effects of light, atmosphere, and season; these elements deform substance, illusions emerge. Decay is one of the most persistently inventive forces. Disruptions allow us to suspend the banal and immerse ourselves in the sublime event, when fire permits psychoanalysis. The horizon of this world is the true proscenium which frames and contains the memory theater. Conventional identities fall away from buildings in the city; parks, markets, squares, empty streets, all participate in an enormous project a spectacle, of tragic, comic, and ambiguous finalities. Here, telephone lines become the traces of birds bearing messages; auguries. Clouds drift through glass office towers. Highways have electric blood coursing through them--veins and arteries of a body whose form and extent are incomprehensible. Stains and cracks in the sidewalk invite reading like some extravagant, foreign inscription. Fictions multiply. The color of the sky can redeem an otherwise ugly and neglected neighborhood. The sun sets on a piece of bread.

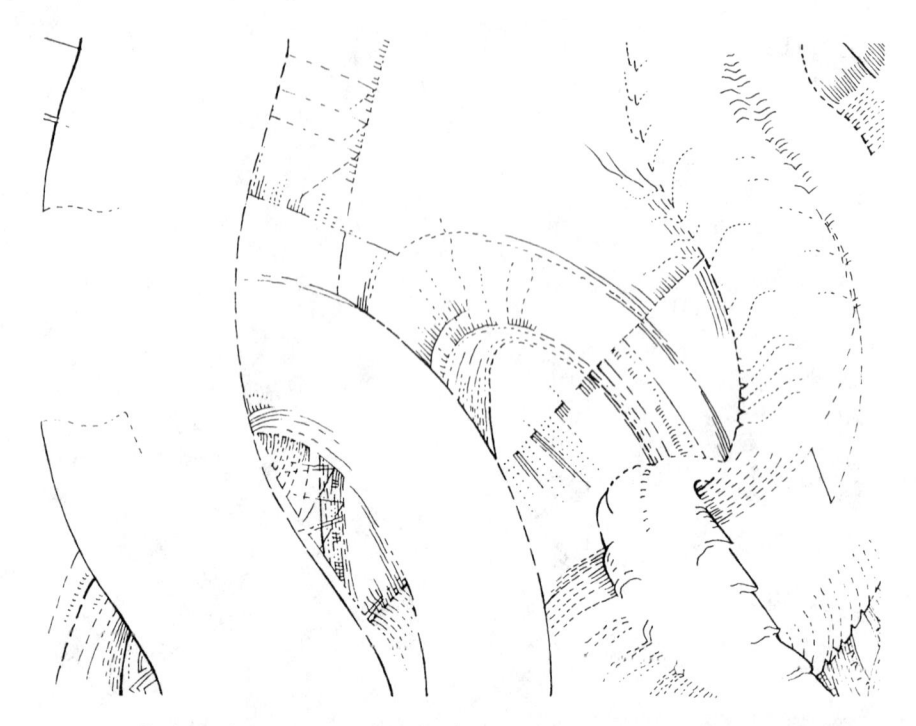

A fictive origin a theory, for architecture is embodied in the memory theater. Unlike the primitive hut or Temple of Solomon paradigms of origin, the making of architecture begins not with the construction of any particular artifact, but in the act of reading a sign. Imagination interprets this chance event, and reads into places. At the first level of making, inspiration is the subtle breath which compels curiosity. We regularly engage in building, an involuntary effort of classification. Architecture, however, must rely on an aleatory response to find its fulfillment and definition. Otherwise, those artifacts built with hopeful intentions, will merely dissolve into the labyrinth; burdensome obstacles to clear vision. In other words, architects do not make architecture; they merely create another potential, with risk of failure. And since meaning does not reside easily in the thing as itself, it seems necessary to revise aesthetic values. Beauty cannot be measured simply by material handling, permanence, or conceptual transparency--its primary value must be its inexhaustibility. The test of any work hinges on its development of an intensely sublime world, where fresh meanings can be continually extracted.

Architecture, and its attempts of monumentality, used to be associated with a desire to outlast decay and firmly establish itself in the world as a constant fact. Despite this noble and quixotic impulse, we can now recognize the fragile, momentary, and undulating pursuit of universality. This world of paper has abandoned the vain conceit of material permanence and embraced the molecular proliferation of experience, where the theater of memory is found once again, in the largest blocks of stone, the smallest grains of sand, or the flickering light of the screen.

CAMILLO'S THEATER AND THE AUTOMATON

Homa Fardjadi
University of Pennsylvania

In looking at Giulio Camillo's 'theatre of memory' my aim is three fold. First I shall offer a reading of Camillo's theatre as a mnemonic device used in the process of active remembrance. This reading involves consideration of the role of the actor/orator in the architecture of Camillo's theatre. Second, on the basis of this reading, I shall attempt to present an analogy between the situation of the architectural project considered as an act of projection and the mnemonic device. This device will not only be seen in terms of its own site but also as a mediator situating and providing the vision of 'another', that is the place outside of the particular problem. The architectural project would occupy the inbetween space of the two sites. Finally, I shall present a brief description of a project which I have recently undertaken with a group of architecture students at the University of Pennsylvania. In it the construct of automata was used to analytically pose the 'other site' in order to disclose aspects of 'machination and mask'.

Vigilus wrote to Erasmus that "he [Vigilus] has been to Venice and has met Camillo who has allowed him to see the Theatre. . . . 'and has diligently inspected every thing'(Yates 1966: 136):

> ... it pretends that all things that the human mind can conceive and which we cannot see with the corporeal eye, after being collected together by diligent meditation may be expressed by certain corporeal signs in such a way that the beholder may at once perceive with his eyes every thing that is otherwise hidden in the depths of the human mind. And it is because of this corporeal looking that he calls it a theatre [Erasmus i. 1532-1534: 29-30; cited in Yates 1966].

As the existing evidence of the exact makeup of the theatre of Giulio Camillo is scant and visual material remains secondary and speculative (it was never recorded from the model presumably produced by Camillo himself) our imaginative reconstruction of the theatre should consider the diagram and the verbal description as the only point of departure. In reviewing such descriptions the following may be noted:

1. In Camillo's theatre the position of the audience-performer is reversed relative to the building of theatres. The orator stands facing the amphitheatrical form in which he places his 'words and things' in an idealized order and where in theatre buildings the audience would normally be situated. The orator delivers his speech in response to places inside the levels and gates of the device of his theatre. His reading does not address the 'audience' of the theatre but draws from these subjects the basis of his act. The act of recounting works reciprocally with what is stored inside the spaces of the amphitheatrical rooms. The theatre, then, is not only to be taken as a metaphor for making things visible through the act but also as an architectural body with a metaphoric construct.

This reciprocal inhabitation of the actor and the world allows the memories of the orator--his 'things and words'--to be equivalent in their degree of corporpality and to find their appropriate order according to the schema of the theatre. I am of course, referring to the diagram representing the hierarchy of territories and beings which the imagery and characterizations of Camillo's theatre present through the use of Hermetic, Cabalic and Biblical traditions.

2. No definition of the stage is given as to its dimensions, form or characteristics. In the Vitruvian theatre the back of the stage, the '*frons scenae*', has five decorated doors, through which the actors make their entrances and exits. Camillo transfers the idea of decorated door from those in the '*frons scenae*' to imaginary decorated doors over the gang ways in the auditorium. Here again the accent is on the speech as the 'act'. It implies that the situation in which the act takes place, the stage, has the auditorium as its form and that this is presented each time the act is performed by the orator. The material of the back drop, the stage doors, would be 'constructed' from characterizations of the imaginary doors in the auditorium which made the setting for his speech. The particular speech would make the form of the stage, the setting for his presentation from, the material present in the auditorium.

3. The orator's musings through the spaces of the different levels seems to be based on his imagination which seeks behind the doors the stored secrets of such territories. As Frances Yates suggests in *Art of Memory* (1978:142): "his memory building is to represent the order of eternal truth; in it the universe will be remembered through organic association of all its parts with their underlying eternal order". The correspondence between the body of the orator and the 'audience' is apparent and is common to the neoplatonic reading of sign in nature. The aim is to transcend the theatre as a structure or device through the function of imagination by grasping it as a figure.

4. The structure of the theatre is given and binding but in it transcendence or 'resistance' seems to be a central theme. It is the seeing of the theatre as the locus or place 'out side' oneself that acts as an imaginary referent against which the self is seen.

The machinations of remembering is structured and what prompts it is given as paradox. The story of the act is rewritten through each speech or projection. In this the role of the orator becomes analogous to that of the interpreter who has to resist structure of his own limits. Such a break with reality seems instrumental in establishing the place of 'the other' in the act of remembering by the orator. This is the sense in which the mnemonic device of the Theatre of Camillo is read not as an object but as an encounter.

The Encounter and the Architectural Project

In the context of teaching architecture a special problem arises which has to do with the condition of designing a project in two respects. The first is the activity that takes place in order to locate the strategy according to which the project is developed. The strategy mediates between the client and the architect. And it is a situation shared by students and practicing architects alike. The second is the setting up of conditions in a particular studio by a teacher for the project to be developed by 'another', namely the students. Here, obviously, the set up involves one more degree of separation. In this process the exercises are, on the one hand, to lead towards the strategy and, on the other, to set up the dialogue between the teacher and the students in the class. Under such circumstances the studio project becomes a device which can provoke and articulate such a dialogue. Considered as such, the studio project may be understood as analogous to Theatre of corporeal looking of Camillo. The Theatre is seen as an encounter in which the audience is taken as the subject of the act and the Theatre becomes the domain of intersubjectivity.

The studio project also needs to have a structure which can both further the original dialogue and yet also be overcome and resisted. This is in order for the project to emerge within a more specific context and in response to the particular vision of the student. The project then, is seen as a catalyst, an exercise situated in the context of one's own interests and that of the students while dealing with an architectural problem. The process enables the project to be legitimized not only through the program/use or themes, that is issues which contemporary architecture seems to have accepted, but one which challenges the physical and historic context or situation and poses them in dialogue with a vision. To set the terms and articulate such dialogue would become the task of the exercises.

With the Theatre of Camillo as the mediating body, a mnemonic device in the process of speech/projection, we assume its role as an analogue to a mediating construct in the process of architectural projection. This thing inbetween the remembered and the known, the vision and the facts, we would pose as a subject in response and in resistance to which the figure of the project will find its visibility. I propose the automaton to be such a mnemonic device with regards to the architectural project as a body in act.

Automaton: The Body and Its Double

The automaton consists of two parts: first is the external body presented as a performance such as in flying, moving or singing objects; second is the internal body of the automaton with its hidden functioning mechanism or secret workings. This secret machine makes us believe that the artificial body we see is engaged in an act repeating, as it were, the actions of the living body in speech and motion. The hidden and visible parts of the automaton, when viewed by an observer together reveal another dimension, which is that of simultaneous conjunction and separation of opposites in an artificial body. A sense of false reality is thus projected which further accentuates the metaphorical character of the automaton and therefore it can be read as a mechanism of doubt.

Another interpretation of this mechanism may be read through the process of anamorphosis. This projection results from viewing not the acting body but from recording a point of view outside the cone of vision projected by the figure. This encounter allows the appearance of 'another reality' which exists parallel to that presented by the appearing subject. The mechanisms of the automaton primarily function by inducing a presentation of motions and effects, but in reading the repetitive acts the idea is not to project the ideal reason but the possibility of reading 'otherwise' or making an alternative interpretation. The outside viewer experiencing the automaton in anamorphosis, therefore, finds reason in conjunction with unreason through the machine that faults its own reasoning, an anti-machine.

The relationship between the process of the architectural projection and the automaton as a mnemonic device may also be seen as analogous in their artificiality. The automaton's playfulness, it's games in tricking perception can reveal the oxymoronic nature of architectural project. Also in the case of the automaton this can be seen in the potential correspondences between mechanism and appearance. In architecture it can be expressed as the dialogical relation between the idea revealed through function, (i.e. the way a building acts in use) and the building's particular material visibility.

Cabinet with a Secret: 'the Other' and the Architecture of an Urban Site

With the schema of the automaton in mind we took up the following process for a studio project on an urban site in Philadelphia:

1. Object in use: Students were asked to construct a small object with a particular use; a cabinet for the storage of things. An example was a tool box designed by a student to contain a set of five wood working tools.

2. The secret: The relationship between the things stored and the particular demand placed by the cabinet on how it could be used was to be seen as a secret. The acts of manipulation of the object would establish it as a body with its workings (machinations) in dialogue with the user. In the tool box example (Figure 1) the five tools were placed in a rectangular box in such a way that each tool functioned as a part of the box itself. They acted as hinge, handle, frame and so forth and transformed the box in various stages of opening for use.

3. The analytic charting: The 'object in use' was to be documented with analytic drawings using orthographic projection. These drawings were seen as registers of various sections through the object/site. Drawn in sequence and repetition, they documented the movements and transformations of the box. In the case of the tool box, the drawings recorded the dialogue between the body of the box and the body of the tool as a new architectural unity.

4. Machine and anti-machine: The oxymoronic nature of automaton, the machine acting as anti-machine, was to find its analogue in the arrest of function or use within the construct. Trapped or forgotten use would thus enable the object to be taken as a 'found object' within a new site/use. In the tool box example the tools were literally what made the normative function of the box in its particular transformations possible. A series of functions of weight, measuring, rotation, locking and release allowed the box to become engaged with these functions. The box thus transformed through use and the tools found a new function in relation to the cabinet/site.

5. The cabinet as subject: Imagining the cabinet as the subject set within the context of the urban site, the students were asked to write a narrative characterizing their cabinet on the new site. The written words were to articulate the encounter between 'the other' and the site.

Figure 1. The 'tool box' by Tom Collins, Fardjadi Studio, University of Pennsylvania.

6. Shadow projection: Next, the members of the studio installed their cabinets within a grided frame (Figure 2) and recorded the shadow projected by the new frame onto the model of the site. This was a means of transferring and spatializing the site with the characteristics of the cabinets acting as outsider inhabitants. The analytic drawing and shadow projections constituted the given. They became the referents-equivalent to the audience stages in the memory theatre of Camillo, and would thus be used in dialogue with the vision of the particular student and interpreted as the new narrative/program for the site.

Figure 2. The Frame with the Cabinets, Fardjadi Studio, University of Pennsylvania.

Through the process described above, the cabinet was situated in the new site, both in its readings of machination and mask, (its functioning body and material representation), and as a 'found object'. It then acted as the 'other', and generated a dialogue between the program and the design of the project--the project as the domain of intersubjectivity. The new vision of the site developed in dialogue with the 'outsider' or cabinet/automaton. This reciprocation allowed the project to take place in the space between its machinations and its own adopted masks. The function and theme of the site became subjected to the 'break' which the vision of the other object/site created. The new project took place in the space between the program/ theme and the vision of the speaker/architect following the dialogue.

REFERENCES

CAMILLO DELMINIO, Giulio.
    1550. *L'Idea del Theatro* (Venice: Baldassar Constantini).
ERASMUS, Desiderius.
  i. 1532-1534. *Opus Epistolarum Des. Erasmi Roterdami*, in 12 volumes, ed. P. S. Allen et al. (London: Oxford University Press, 1906-1958). The letter cited in this paper appears in volume 10.
WENNEKER, Lu Beery.
    1970. "An Examination of *L'Idea del Theatro* of Guilio Camillo, Including an Annotated Translation, With Special Attention to His Influence on Emblem Literature and Iconography", Ph.D. Dissertation, University of Pittsburgh (Ann Arbor, Michigan: University Microfilms).
YATES, Dame Frances.
    1966. *The Art of Memory* (Chicago: University of Chicago Press). Page references are to the 1978 edition (Middelsex, England: Penguin Books Ltd.).

THE CONE OF VISION:
DELIRIOUS HISTORY AND OPTICAL MNEMONICS IN VICO AND CAMILLO

Donald Kunze
The Pennsylvania State University

To my knowledge, Giulio Camillo has never been classed as a historian. Even to consider this possibility seems to raise a contradiction, since his most famous project, the apocryphal "theater of memory", placed its user in an a-temporal, or "eternal", space where origins, events, and ends of the human scene were brought together into a single gaze directed at the *cavea* of a traditional auditorium. Memory was redefined by Camillo (1550), and given a sense opposite that used by most historians. Camillo's memory was not of events arrayed along a temporal continuum but of a set of categories--or better, "places"--into which anything historical might fit at the expense of its historical particularity.
    Neither could it be said that Camillo has ever enjoyed any standing as an architect, although his possible association with Serlio and others seems likely (Wenneker 1970: 68). Even in this architectural-sounding project of a memory theater, architectural form is almost a coincidental fact. Camillo had at first preferred the analogy of the human body, as the best aid for artificial memory. Only later did he choose the form of the theater, perhaps in response to the commonplace use of the term "theater" to describe any systematic discussion or display. There are so few conclusive reports of the actual theater that many doubt whether a physical theater ever existed. And, beyond the seven-by-seven matrix formed by the rows and aisles of the *cavea*, there is little theatrical presence in Camillo's schema that would require a physical building to exist.
    But, given the slim or non-existent ties linking Camillo to historiography or architecture, there are compelling reasons to consider the memory theater as decisive in the development of both fields. There are even good reasons for seeing the memory theater as the first and most important event *requiring* each to be defined in terms of the other. The key to this connection is the Enlightenment model of knowledge, which like everything else of its day strove to define the relation between the subject and object in terms of a distance, and this distance in terms of a cone radiating from the subject as an apex towards the world as a set of objects adumbrated by reason. This cone was known mainly through its optic counterpart, the cone of vision; or through the sections taken through it, which ever since Alberti were representations described as windows.

The Cone Of Vision

It has become possible, even fashionable, to describe diverse aspects of Enlightenment thought in terms of the geometry of this "cone of vision". This analogy is appropriate in that one might regard the entire spirit of Enlightenment science and reflection as "projective". That is, not only did the Enlightenment begin with a radical separation of the subject and object which, played out in terms of contrasting geometries, generated the spectacle of the viewer visually addressing the world as something *to be seen*, but several scholars have recently demonstrated an intimate series of exchanges between the optical and geometric sciences and diverse other institutions of the time such as economics, natural science, philosophy, aesthetics, and political thought. Where the cone of vision was a real and influential analogue for Enlightenment enterprises, post-Enlightenment criticism has focused on the imperialism, neurosis, and tragedy of its geometry. Undoubtedly, Michel Foucault (1975) has done more than any other scholar to advance the thesis that visibility, as exemplified by the cone of vision, transformed the mental and physical space of the European domain and its colonies to allow for an unencumbered flow of authoritarian control ("panopticism").

There are two projects, however, that constitute early and conclusive critiques of the cone of vision and the Enlightenment presuppositions behind it. The first, Camillo's theater of memory, was famous in its time but is either unknown or misunderstood today. The second, created nearly two hundred years later, is the graphic frontispiece of Vico's *New Science* (1744), a work that constitutes the first and still most comprehensive overthrow of Cartesianism in the human sciences. The text of the *New Sciences* is the subject of perennial revivals, but the frontpiece has been ignored for the most part. Yet, in a philosophy that places the image at the origin of human consciousness, this image exemplifies Vico's theory by working as the origin of the *New Science*. There are parallels between Camillo's theater and Vico's image that reinforce the barely visible truths of each.

The Memory Theater of Giulio Camillo

In this context we must first consider Camillo's theater of memory as an optical device which, among many other things, it surely was. The stage was in singular low-point of the structure, but Camillo described it as a "high and incomparable placing", which we as pilgrims climb to reach a final panoramic view. The celestial character if memory's gaze form this point has both a figurative and a literal usefulness. Richard Bernheimer (1956) has documented how, in the Baroque period, the Roman amphitheater was used to represent the Christian idea of the heavens--a tableau of angels and nobles seated, figuratively, in rings of clouds terminating in the zenith of the universe. On the literal side, the seven planets and their movements provided a mathematical analogue for memory's own combinatorial schemas, such as Ramon Lull's system of concentric rings. The gaze towards the heavens was thus not only a symbolic anticipation of the resurrection of the body but also an enactment of the motions of a starry maze constructed out of concentrically arranged emblems. Equally, this optical space was a temple and a labyrinth, with the number seven representing alternatively enigma or perfection.

By giving precedents to the Vitruvian stage, Frances Yates (1966) has become the chief classicist of Camillan scholarship. But the connection between this diagram and Vitruvius is not direct. The importance of the "seven aisles" in Camillo's auditorium comes from the planets, classical mythology, Biblical sources, Hebrew mysticism, and Renaissance magic. Also, Camillo gives an unusual example of the perfection of seven as containing both even and odd numbers. Where most cite the numbers three and four, Camillo uses one and six. Wenneker (1970: 364) thinks this may be a mistake, but I would point out that the combination of one and six may have Kabbalistic significance for Camillo. Seven is an "overdetermined" quantity in Camillo's thinking, while this is hardly the case in Vitruvius. In addition to the traditional and mystical references, Camillo seized on seven as a number of completion. In his book, Camillo recounted (1550: 13) that Moses had, during his conversations with God, passed seven times through the spheres, the Sephiroth, surrounding God.

But how was this number of completion useful as a metaphor? Camillo's theater was a means of penetrating beyond things ordinarily visible, into the mysterious fabric of a memory externalized. Camillo compared external memory to a divine ray, "outside of us" (1550: 59-60). To explain this, he introduced the image of the three Gorgon sisters who, being blind, share a single eye which they pass around from one to the other. This symbol of prophecy is also emblematic of the human soul, particularly that part of the soul called the "active intellect", or *Nessamah* in the Hebrew of the Kabbala. To free this soul from the other two souls, the *Nephes* and the *Rauch*, a metaphor of cutting was used, as in the Christian image of "knife of the word of Christ", or the more erotic image of the kiss. Camillo had written (1550: 74-75) that:

> without the death of the kiss we cannot unite ourselves in a true union with the Celestial, nor with God .... Therefore, since the body is that, which holds us apart from a true union, and from the kiss which Celestial things would like to give to our souls, gathering them to themselves, it follows that by the dissolution of it (the body), one might come to this kiss.

This kiss brings together the themes that Freud was to memorialize as the hallmarks of eternity, love and death. Camillo used the (then) well known myth of Diana and Endymion, a mortal Diana lured to the top of a mountain and put under a spell of perpetual sleep in order to enjoy his kisses forever. Endymion, in the Renaissance use of this myth, stands for the highest part of the soul; Diana for the celestial and supercelestial voyage the soul must make in departing from its body.

The "outside" of the active intellect, the externalized vision of wisdom, is given form by the planetary spheres in their pre-Copernican symmetry. But it is also clear that Camillo regarded this passage as difficult, a puzzle. And, in order of the seats of the auditorium, Camillo planted a mystery. The first rank of images arrayed in his auditorium are planetary, except for the central seat, which instead of being named after the fourth "planet", the sun, was given the designation of "the banquet". Beneath this door, Camillo placed four rather mysterious objects related to the passage of the higher soul through its forty-nine steps: an image of Virgil's golden bough; "the soul in its three parts"; and a pyramid which Camillo characterized by its "indivisible point, which must symbolize for us the Divinity" (1550: 15-16).

A remaining object is hardly ever discussed, but I find it intriguingly connected to other images of the soul and its relation to vision. This is the image of Pan, whose head is "celestial" because of the upward-pointing horns, whose hide is celestial and "starry", and whose goat legs suggest the inferior world. This apparently was a well known image, one of those anamorphic iconographic commonplaces that is easy enough to pass over. It is the image of "the girl with hair streaming upwards" (Camillo 1550: 45,52,74,78). The girl, like Pan, is an embodied soul. The hair streaming upwards to heaven stands for the *Nessamah*, just as Pan's horns had indicated heaven through their upward gesture. In several places of the theater, a girl with *cut hair* is used. Cut hair signifies a loss of the divine in most cases. But where the cut refers to the death of the kiss, where the head and its celestial associations are allied with the separation of the *Nessamah* from the lower soul, the *Nephes*, a decapitation is a fragmentation of the cone of vision: a chipping-off of the very apex, creating a triangle that is something like vision itself, the "circle of fire" that Camillo found as the source of divine illumination. Whether this is inside the eye, as the optical model of the cone-of-vision suggests, or outside, as Camillo's arguments suggest, is the question. The key lies in what this symbolic decapitation might mean.

Clouds about the Head

The antiquity of the soul and its relation to the head is great. We know from excavations of graves that the head was regarded as a special seat of procreation, genius, and divinity. Often, the head was severed and placed in a special position in relation to the body. In war, decapitation and intraposition of the head between the thighs was regarded as the means of "laying the ghost" of the slain.

The head, the seat of the *psyche* and the part of the body corresponding to the highest part of the soul, was additionally associated with a curious image: that of the head surrounded by a cloud. Richard Onians (1951: 422-23) elaborates that: "Darkness was believed to be substantial, mist. The darkness which veils the eyes in swoon or death seems to be outside, to envelope the victim . . . . It was thought of as a veil of mist enwrapping the head". The cloud of death, like the "death if the kiss", opens the highest part of the body to the liminal realm, and when this metaphor of the body is taken as a memento of the soul, this death becomes a line between two kinds if visibility, we can see how Camillo's optics was formed out of a series of carefully worked paradoxes. The first paradox is a metaphor of irony, the exchange of . . .

Life for Death

It is very likely that Camillo was aware of the structural identity between his position as a viewer on an "incomparably high" mountain and the well-known image of Scipio gazing down on earth from the celestial heights of his dream, which he cites in *L'Idea del Theatro*. The transposition of the dead for the living and *vice versa* was Neoplatonic. Scipio sees souls at their healthiest: that is, when their bodies are dead (Macrobius c.410: 81-89). In contrast, the soul endures the live body as its tomb on earth. One's mortal life is a temporary death for the soul, relieved finally by the body's death or by the insights of the mind in reflection.

The trope of death-for-life, or "life-in-death", is more common than one might think. The boundary between life and death was commonly guarded by monsters, such as the sphinx, or by dogs or dog-headed gods. The shared feature of these creatures was their propensity to eat human flesh. This was for the reason that many cultures employed animals to consume the corpse as a means of proper burial. Anubis, the dog-headed god of the Egyptians, was sacred as both a Hermes figure and as an eater of the dead. Otto Rank (1922: 62) made an intriguing connection between this practice and vision:

The official devourer of corpses among the Persians was originally the dog, an animal that nowadays plays only a mute role in the ceremony. The Parsi is supposed to die while in the sight of a dog who has been brought into the room of the dying person in order to strike the fleeing soul with his glance.

Interesting for our purposes is the easy transition from the act of devouring to the gaze as a *substitute*. The Parsi ceremony was called the Sagdid, literally, "the dog has seen".
We might at this point take an excursus into the rich realm of lore associated with the evil eye, whose relation with vision and death touch at many points on Camillo's mythology of the gaze. Even a cursory view of this material would reveal significant tangencies. The most important is, as the funerary custom of the Parsis suggests, the equivalence in mythic thought between the verbal curse or blessing and the visual gaze. We find this equivalence not only in Camillo' visualized memory system but in the emblem tradition in general, where text and image were traditionally set in a poetic counterposition, each complementing the other.
The curse and the gaze, the compact dyad of the evil eye, translate into the exchanges between vision and divinity in Camillo's theater. The dog devours the body of the corpse with his glance, which is the substitute for material consumption. For Camillo, this funerary custom is transformed into a kind of method, which we have encountered in the two images of the "death of the kiss", drawing from the myth of Endymion, and the "cloud about the head", present in the Kabbalisitc image of the soul and the use of the Sephiroth as Janus-faced guardians ringing the entry to the images of the theater. The guest at the banquet of the gods is Camillo--or the idealized rhetorician--himself. But the question of who is eating and whom is being eaten is an ambiguity worth resolving.

The Dipintura as Memory Theater

Donald Phillip Verene (1988), in a comprehensive analysis of the frontispiece of the *New Science*, recounts that in the course of publication of a completely rewritten version of the *New Science* in 1730 Vico withdrew materials from the Venetian publisher, due to an affront involving the architect, Friar Carlo Lodoli. Intending to publish letters concerning the controversy in a *Novella*, Vico was persuaded by further communications from Venice to suppress these materials, leaving a gap of eighty-six pages. To fill the space, Vico commissioned an allegorical engraving or *dipintura*, designed by Domenico Antonio Vaccaro and engraved by Antonio Baldi. Vico wrote an explanation of the "Idea of the Work" by annotating each of the items in the engraving.
Vico himself called the *dipintura* a memory device, inspired by the so-called "Tables of Cebes". This Table itself, famous in Vico's time and before, contained an apotropaic device, in the form of a curse introduced in the text before a description proper of the *mons delectus*--"mountain of choice"--which was pictorially a labyrinth expressed topologically as a pyramid or mountain with a spiral path, truncated at the top by a temple. The pilgrims to the temple of Saturn see a painting of this mountain displayed at the threshold and inquire about its meaning. An old priest tells them that the image carries with it a curse, that whoever looks upon it and misses its meaning will be condemned to ignorance and despair; while anyone who understands its significance will be granted wisdom. The curse and the mountain are not accidents of an anecdote.

The *mons delectus* has its origins in the "cosmic mountains" of mythology: both a center (*omphalos*) and an extremity; an axial pyramid ending in a "wholly-shining" summit, or burning sky. This image is found in more mundane settings, where relationships are somewhat clearer. At the top of the Egyptian obelisk, a small pyramid represents the "seed of the sun". The column below is the mountain simplified, but it also serves in related images as the *enclosure* of Saturn, which was held by ancients of several cultures to be the "sun" of the night-time sky, the "northern sun". Saturn, the soul of the world, is held, contained, or imprisoned by a circular or spiral structure that is its lower soul (*Nephes*), or shadow. Its radiant light is masked by the enclosure, which in Kabbilistic tradition is the set of "broken lights" of the Sephiroth as well as the veil of enigma taken into the "broken" images or emblems which, as riddles, surround divine wisdom. The crescent form of this container has two meanings. The first is that the bottom half is the most illuminated portion of the circle, the part that shields the brightness of the ether from penetration from below. The second is the iconographical relation to the crescent of the moon, which by reflecting the light of the sun, is the "planet" functionally closest to the *Nephes* and, as a female deity, the mediator between earth and the triune eye of heaven.

The crescent may be pictured as the horns of the moon, or as wings. In this transposition, the idea that the head is uppermost--and hence most soul-like--part of the body suggests that the form of death associated with enlightenment is decapitation. But this brutal image is ordinarily reworked into the image of the kiss, and its function as a standard trope denoting the escape of the soul was a common theme of poets since Classical Greece.

But we might expect to find at least one image where the euphemism of the kiss is omitted and the idea of decapitation is given directly. Such an image (Fig. 1) occurs in a source historically and circumstantially close to Camillo: Curione's commentary appended to Valeriano's *Hieroglyphica* (1614: 908). Justice is "decapitated" as an image, but this hypotyposis holds the "truth" that her head is concealed by the divine cloud which renders it invisible. In Vico's frontispiece (Fig. 2), the winged temples of Metaphysic accomplish the same iconographic relationship, confirmed by the connection of Metaphysic's breast-jewel with the divine eye.

A few other details point in this direction. Metaphysic stands on the belt of the Zodiac above the signs of Leo and Virgo, the approximate position of Justice in Curione's emblem. Like Camillo's centrally placed "banquet" on the first rung of the planetary deities, Metaphysic's body is divided with the same logical partitioning as Pan, with horns pointed upwards. The globe of heaven is placed perilously on the edge of the altar, a banquet table of the gods. It is my conjecture that this placement is intentionally present as a swerve, or *clinamen*, from an expected meaning. As a kind of flag to the alert reader, it is equivalent to Camillo's unexpected substitution of the banquet for the sun at the level of the planets.

The column's capital in Camillo's case is the collective architectural entity of the auditorium. In Vico's case, it is the figure of Metaphysic, "decapitated" by her winged temples and head turned towards the divine eye. Metaphysic standing on a sphere, or a sphere acting as the "head" or "capitol" or a female column in this case convey the same message. In the first instance, Metaphysic *is* the separation of the divine from the earthly part; in the second, the separation occurs with the ambiguity between etymologically identical ideas of host, guest, and ghost as expressed as the threshold between stage and auditorium of Camillo's theater.

I might offer a token confirmation of this identity by examining closely the jewel on Metaphysic's breast. Of its concavity, Angus Fletcher (1986: 38) has argued that "This mirror, and particularly its convexity, holds the secret to the inner life of

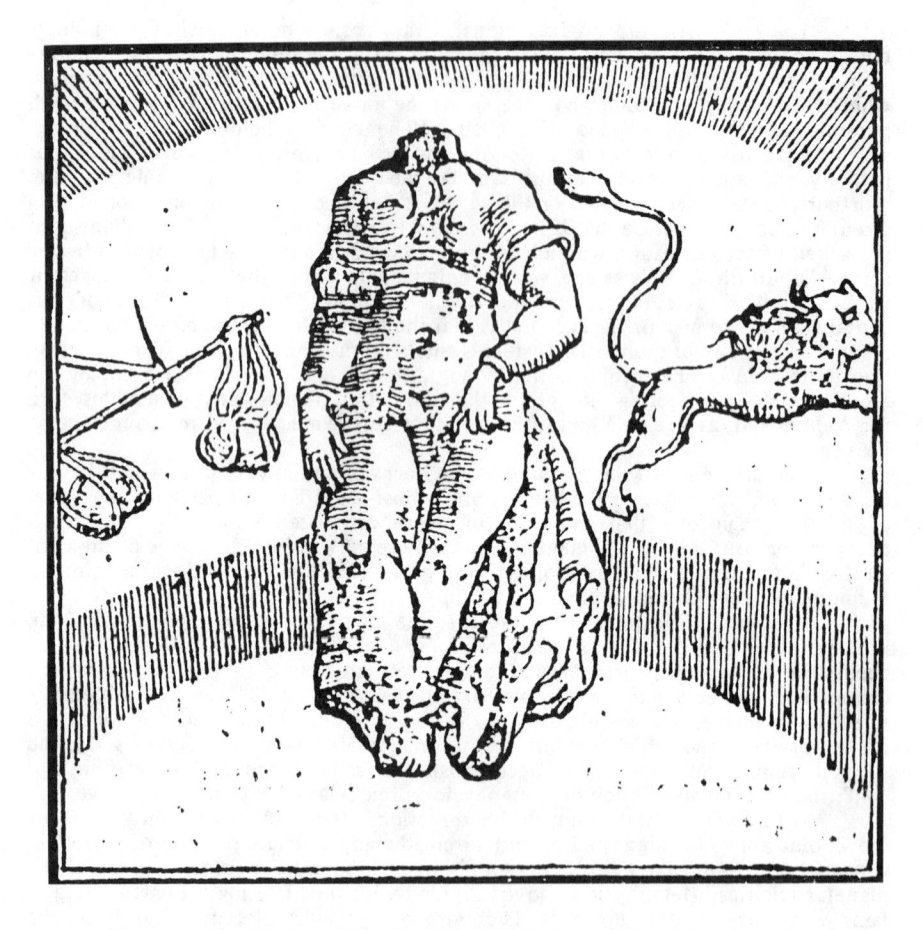

Figure 1. The Figure of "justice" from Valeriano's Hieroglyphica (1614: 908).

Vico's method, both in its range and power and in its ultimately enigmatic withdrawal". The jewel drawn by Vaccaro shows itself to be not simply convex, however, but a composite structure. Looking above the point where the divine ray strikes it, one can just barely make out the shape of a crescent enclosing a circle or shadowy sphere. Here, in miniature, is the idea of the frontispiece *in toto*: that of a head (vision) concealed in a cloud. When this cloud is transformed into the crescent of the moon, Diana/Metaphysic becomes the agent of a *kiss*, drawing out the soul of the Endymion, asleep at the top of a truncated mountain, the object of a divine and erotic spell.

Figure 2. Frontispiece of Vico's *New Science* (1744), the "dipintura".

The Cone Of Vision Revisited

The problem of history's dependence on the Enlightenment cone of vision was the necessity to define the apex as a discontinuity, a lookout point shielded by the representation, immune to contamination by the object--history--that the historian himself held to be ubiquitous. One means of isolating the apex was for the historian to claim to be the "last man", the one who has seen it all. Spengler, Gibbon, and Toynbee made this claim indirectly by painting history in the broad strokes of tragedy. Nietzsche and Hegel did this philosophically, by pushing the metaphor to the point it shared with madness.

But the search for a spot outside history, which claims our attention precisely because it is seamless and offers no such spot, leads in both cases beyond the logic of historical method and into the domain of rhetoric. Here, there are two kinds of tropes available to the expression of the ineffable: silence and incompleteness. For Camillo, it was the silence of the emblem and the riddle; for Vico, the incompleteness of an image that requires the reader to take his place within the composition.

Vico's discussion of the images that appear in his frontispiece is remarkably thorough (1744: 3-26). The history of each subject is described and given a place in the *New Science* to follow. Each, that is, except the winged helmet of Hermes, which lies at the foot of the statue of Homer. The helmet is mentioned later in the *New Science* but curiously is given no consideration in the otherwise complete discussion of the frontispiece. Other circumstances suggest that this omission was purposeful. Homer stares intently at the helmet; his right hand open, its palm turned down towards the helmet. The winged helmet of Hermes enables an ordinary head to take on powers that Metaphysic enjoys permanently. From the associations of the head with the divine, with the breath of the upper-most soul, and with the invisibility imparted by the clouds about the head, we know that Hermes' helmet is symbolically close to the helmet of Hades, which also imparted invisibility to its wearer. Its wearer is both invisible and symbolically dead, conducted by Hermes himself, the dog-god. In the frontispiece, the helmet is both present and absent. It is present as the last of a series of objects denoting the development of human culture; and absent from the text.

In Vico's discussion of the "method" of his New Science (1744: 100-06), he asserts that the external facts of history are reflected internally, in the mental development of the individual. The reader, who is outside the text in a literal and theoretical sense, proves the truth of the *New Science* by an anatomical method, so to speak. He becomes the object of the ideal eternal history, and his reading--which moves from the literal to the allegorical to the analogical meanings--confirms this. The final moment of proof, however, is "anagogical". The separation between past, present, and future--essential to any idea of historical development--collapses into the mind of the reader. The historian himself is contaminated by his subject in the final moment of realization. The moment is both awful--for how can meanings be stabilized in such a moment?--and pleasurable: the kiss of Diana. "The reader", Vico predicts (1744: 103), "will experience in his mortal body a divine pleasure as he contemplates in the divine ideas this world of nations in all the extent of its places, times, and varieties". Further (1744: 104): "He who meditates this Science narrates to himself this ideal eternal history so far as he himself makes it for himself by that proof 'it had, has, and will have to be.'" The reader becomes Vico, becomes history itself, in a final collapse of text, author, and reader.

If the reader finds himself in the *New Science*, he reaches into the frontispiece and takes out the winged helmet. Donning it, he asserts a kinship with *la Donna Metafisica*. But I assert that this is more than a token act of sympathy. It is adoration of a lover for a loved, an Acteon for a Diana, a troubadour for his noble lady: his muse, Memory. The gaze of his lover is found in the frontispiece by inverting the relationship between Jove and Metaphysic, by cutting an eyehole in the frontispiece precisely at that point where the divine eye casts its ray towards the jewel of Saturn. The reader must see the entire frontispiece through a mirror. The vanishing point is brought forward and embodied. It is the place of irony and contamination. It is final and without end.

REFERENCES

BERNHEIMER, Richard.
    1956.   "Theatrum Mundi", *Art Bulletin* 36, 225-47.
CAMILLO, Giulio.
    1550.   *La Idea del Theatro* (Venice: Baldassar Constantini).
FLETCHER, Angus.
    1986.   "on the Syncretic Allegory of the *New Science*", *New Vico Studies* 4, 25-44.
FOUCAULT, Michel.
    1975.   *Surveiller et Punir; Naissance de la prison* (Paris: Editions Gallimard).
MACROBIUS, Ambrosius Theodisius.
    c.410.   *Somnium Scipionis Expositionis*. First ms. edition 1472, BMC V.172 (IB 19655); HCR 10426; St.M4; Jan,I,lxxxviii, Editio princeps (Venice: Nicolaus Jenson). English trans. William H. Stahl, *Macrobius, Commentary on the Dream of Scipio* (New York: Columbia University Press, 1952). Page citations in this article are to the English translation.
ONIANS, Richard B.
    1951.   *The Origins of European Thought About the Body, the Mind, the Soul, the World, Time and Fate; New Interpretations of Greek, Roman and Kindred Evidence, Also of Some Basic Jewish and Christian Beliefs* (Cambridge University Press).
RANK, Otto.
    1922.   "Die Don Juan-Gestalt", paper given at the Vienna Psychoanalytic Association, April 26. Published as an article in *Imago* 8, 142-96. Subsequently published in book form as *Die Don Juan-Gestalt* (Vienna: Internationaler Psychoanalytischer Verlag). English trans. David G. Winter, *The Don Juan Legend* (Princeton: Princeton University Press). Page citations and quotations in this article are from the English translation.
VALERIANO, Ioannis Pierii.
    1614.   *Hieroglyphica* (Frankfurt).
VERENE, Donald P.
    1988.   "Vico's 'IGNOTA LATEBAT'", unpublished ms. Forthcoming in *New Vico Studies* 5.
VICO, Giambattista.
    1744.   *Principi di scienza nuova di Giambattista Vico, d'intorno alla comune natura della nazioni*, 3rd edition (Naples: Stamperia Muziani). English trans. Thomas Goddard Bergin and Max Harold Fisch, *The New Science of Giambattista Vico* (Ithaca: Cornell University Press, 1968). Page citations and quotations in this article are from the English translation.

WENNEKER, Lu Beery.
    1970. "An Examination of *L'Idea del Theatro* of Giulio Camillo, Including an Annotated Translation, With Special Attention to His Influence on Emblem Literature and Iconography", PhD. Dissertation, University of Pittsburgh (Ann Arbor, Michigan: University Microfilms).

YATES, Frances A.
    1966. *The Art of Memory* (Chicago: University of Chicago Press).

ARCHITECTURE AND THE ILLUSION OF PERFECT MEMORY

David Leatherbarrow
University of Pennsylvania

Plato, in one of his attempts to define true knowledge, compared opinions (*doxa*) to unfettered slaves, who, when not tied down, can be neither permanently held nor possessed, as it is in the nature of both to eventually escape. To prevent escapes of this sort he advised binding opinions to solid grounds or rational principles, which like shackles, make true opinions permanent possessions. Memory images are, it seems to me, also likely to escape when not shackled. Escapes of this sort are experiences of forgetfulness, which can be overcome by siting the images to be remembered in the places that make up a mental map of an architectural enclosure.

The importance and usefulness of spatial frameworks for binding and grounding mental images in the memory was well known to ancient writers on the art of memory. Practitioners of this art, public speakers generally, lawyers and politicians particularly, tied the images of their speeches to a mental framework that conformed to the architecture of an actual place. I propose to use the ancient rules for "finding" or "designing" such a framework to describe both the nature of rhetorical topics and the characteristics of a theater of memory, an example of which is the theater "designed" by the "divine" Camillo Delminio. Dame Frances Yates has, in the first chapter of her classic text on the *Art of Memory*, summarized the rules for the formation of memory places: these places were to be: 1) arranged together in an unbroken sequence or continuous series, 2) sited in an isolated region, 3) not too much like one another, 4) dimensioned of moderate size, neither as large as a public square nor as small as a crack in a wall, 5) well lighted, and 6) spaced apart by distances of moderate length, about 30 feet on average. With these rules in mind one necessarily forms an image of a rather elaborate architectural setting with considerable variety and little repetition. In fact, some ancient writers argued for the utmost variety in memory architecture, observing that regularity, symmetry and repetitive layouts caused confusion, just the opposite of what this art was meant to promote. Place identity, so important in the practice of this art, presupposed place difference. While Yates found it odd to imagine an orator trying to memorize the order of speech topics in a "disorderly" architectural layout, both the regularity of the ensemble and the repetition of places were thought to prevent the practice of orderly recollection.

Not so odd then might seem the memory theater designed by Camillo Delminio. Its layout of places was quite simple; there were seven levels, seven gangways, seven gates and seven pillars, all of which were laid out along the lines of the radii of a semi-circular amphitheater. It was a work of "stupendous labor and divine skill" that Camillo accomplished, so magnificent thought his contemporaries, that it caused his reputation to be known throughout Europe until the eighteenth century.

The actual construction of the theater is not altogether certain. Presuming its actuality, it was made large enough for two spectators to view its marvelous contents. Upon entry, one was confronted by what Camillo called a "window to all the contents of the soul". These were contents previously unseen but always desired by those who wanted to know things in truth. Camillo's aim was to unify and make complete all that an orator might want to remember. He also wanted to establish a permanent or eternal framework that would tie down these memorable things, "to store up eternally the eternal nature of the things to be expressed in a speech". This meant that he had to order and find places that were both capacious and distinct, places that would, when viewed together, keep the mind awake and the memory moving. He thought ancient orators wrongly confided the parts of the speeches they wanted to remember to "frail places". His attempt, on the contrary, was to ensure permanence by locating rhetorical images in places that would never move--the kind of binding Plato recommended for opinions. The desire to tie down and permanently possess true knowledge is what is most evident in Camillo's Project.

This intention explains the use of the number seven in Camillo's design and its semi-circular form. The seven pillars that defined the limits of the lowest level of his theater were named the columns of Solomon's House of Wisdom. The seven levels also signified the Sephiroth. Evident above the steps at the perimeter were the twelve signs of the zodiac. The spectator confronting this layout of memory places stood against a framework that reflected the macrocosm; it was, when articulated by images, meant to show the eternal and encompassing order of all that is.

Very different then is Camillo's theater from the layouts described in the ancient texts on the art of memory. Instead of variety, difference and irregularity, there was unity, repetition and sameness. In his aspiration to signify wholeness distinctions between places were eliminated, or at least suppressed. Camillo's theater was certainly a consistent articulation of Renaissance neo-Platonic hermetic cosmology, but it was probably not a very good framework for binding together the images that might make a persuasive and a memorable speech. In his focus on the symbols being bound, he overlooked the problem of binding. I think one can establish an inverse ratio between the formal consistency of his memory theater and the mnemonic efficiency of its use, as consistency was perfected recollection was probably confused. While I am not sure that this ratio can be used in reverse, with respect to inconsistency and mnemonic efficiency, I do maintain that one must not forget the importance of difference and irregularity when finding or designing the layout of memory places.

More helpful then might be some of the other "theaters" that were built as a result of Renaissance speculation on architecture and memory. I have in mind a case that might appear to be quite far removed from Camillo and Renaissance Italy; namely, the theater designs of Inigo Jones. Given the well-known connections between Jones and Scamozzi, however, and the latter's ties with Palladio and Barbaro on the one hand and Bruno on the other, the case of Jones' theaters as examples of the architecture of memory may not be so unlikely. I hope to show that his designs for theaters can be seen as layouts wherein images one would like to remember could be ordered, stored and made available for recollection precisely because they were not perfectly unified nor built of repetitive parts.

Theater is a term that had a wider range of meanings in Elizabethan England than it does today. In point of fact, there was then no necessary connection between this type of architectural setting and the performance of a play or drama. Nor was there a necessary connection between the idea of the theater and architecture. The completeness, unity, wonder and truth of theatrical contents did not presuppose walls, columns and windows. Furthermore, it is a well known fact that dramas of a sort were performed then in settings that were not shaped as we would shape a theater nowadays. As the architect of the Stuart court, Jones designed, staged and managed court masques in Whitehall Palace for example. The space used there for these performances was a long rectangular hall used commonly for meeting and banqueting. Another site for performances was an open courtyard in the palace, under a temporary tent covering. Theatrical events also occurred outside the palace, in open squares and on certain streets. Furthermore, as dramatic performance did not depend upon theater architecture, theaters were places for non-dramatic events. The architecture of the theater was in fact a polyvalent form, its meaning embraced medical, political, sacred, and only sometimes dramatic events. When considering the mnemonic potential of these forms it is necessary to acknowledge the fact that they had non-dramatic purposes too.

The first "theater" I want to describe is the Barber Surgeon's Anatomy theater built in London by Jones in 1636. Significant characteristics of the design are its oval plan geometry, amphitheater section, orientation towards the operating table, seven windows, and its domed ceiling ornamented with signs of the zodiac. The second floor entry porch was joined to the main hall of the Surgeons by an open arcaded gallery. Certainly the space of the operating theater is singular and uniform. The five levels of its auditorium, for example, repeat the geometry of the perimeter oval, just like the seven levels of Camillo's theater. This same oval geometry, formed by drawing four arcs around two overlapping circles, was used by Robert Fludd to illustrate the formal correspondence between the human body and the heavens. This is significant for two reasons: the first is that the plan of this building drawn by John Webb, Jones' assistant, shows a body on an operating table underneath the image of the heavens on the ceiling (the two being joined at the center of the theater), and the second reason is that Camillo first described the form of his macrosomic image as a body revealed in dissection. If, however, the levels or windows of the anatomy theater were to be used as memory places there is every reason to believe there would be some confusion of memory images, as the differences between places that is presupposed in the mental movement through their sequence have been suppressed, excepting the uniqueness of the so-called Serlian window opposite the entry. In fact, it is the axis that joins together the entry, the body on the table and the only real source of light in this cramped site that interrupts the perfect uniformity of the place. I take it that this axis is what is memorable about this theater. The only place in the interior that perfect uniformity was evident was in the dome, which was a place viewed best when lying on the operating table. There is something pathological about a view that remains fixed on a vision of perfect uniformity .

The second theater I want to describe is Jones' reconstruction of Stonehenge. While Jones never referred to this reconstruction as a theater, its similarity to and dependence on the Vitruvian description of the Roman theater is obvious. In fact, he referred to the Vitruvian description in the margins of the published version of his reconstruction. His plan was based upon the centralized combination of four equilateral triangles within a circle, as was the theater described by Vitruvius. The lines and intersections of these figures were used by Vitruvius to position all the component parts of the theater: the *frons scaenae*, its openings and thicknesses, the stage, the size of the orchestra, the limits of the auditorium and its gangways and stairways. All of this is clear in the plan designed by Palladio for Barbaro's edition of the treatise. Significant for Jones, no doubt, was the fact that this method of combining triangles within a circle was described by Vitruvius as the method astrologers used when they mapped the twelve signs of the zodiac and computed the musical harmony of the stars. Jones thought the architecture of Stonehenge mapped the heavens. Its plan was circular, its section was open to the sky, and its hexagonal perimeter was entered from three points. After rejecting the supposition of it being dedicated to gods such as Diana, Pan or Juno, Jones concluded that it embodied the Roman symbolism of Coelus, the sky god who rules the beginning of all things. This was clearly evident he thought in the openness, circularity and tuscan simplicity of the construction, but it was also signified by the pyramidal, upward reaching, and flame-like form of the stones. Like the Vitruvian theater, it located the twelve signs of the zodiac. It was an image of the celestial crown of the stars. For this reason it can be judged as approximately identical to the theater proposed by Camillo. Especially significant is the fact that Jones also compared Stonehenge to the Temple of Jerusalem, as it was adorned with the twelve figures of the celestial Cherubim. I have noted already that the lowest level of Camillo's theater was defined by the seven pillars of Solomon's House of Wisdom--wise Solomon being the hero to whom medieval philosophers credited the origin of the art of memory. Jones' reconstruction of Stonehenge is certainly his most economical and integrated symbolic form, but it also is, for this reason mainly, his design that is least plausible as a memory theater --it resembles Camillo's very closely.

I have mentioned Jones' work at Whitehall Palace already. My next example is from the set of ceiling paintings that adorn Jones' Whitehall Banqueting House. Jones did not execute these paintings, however; they are the work of Rubens. Let me describe the painting in this group called "James I Recreates the Empire of Great Britain". The painting can be seen as a theater of British imperial politics. James I is seen on the right hand side of the canvas seated upon his throne. With an orb in his left hand he points his scepter over a space at the bottom of the canvas that is filled with weapons and armor being set aflame by a putto. His scepter is directed toward two women and a child on the left side of the canvas. The women personify England and Scotland, the child standing between them can be taken as either the young Charles I or the personification of the new United Kingdom. England and Scotland have also joined together to crown the youth, and they are aided in this task by a figure that represents either wise Minerva or Pallas. In the background of the scene a circular temple is represented. Its paired columns are masculine, its coffered dome caps the heavens.

Clearly, the temple that contains this event is a sacred site. And this event re-enacts Biblical myth, the Judgement of Solomon. That story tells how two women who contended for a child appealed to the wisdom of Solomon. They were surprised by the brutality of his judgement when he decreed that the child be split in half --thus teaching them the short-sightedness of their request. In this new version of the story, however, the two women suffer no brutality, just the reverse; the crowns of England and Scotland were unified.

The Solomonic theme runs through the Whitehall ceiling panels generally. In the "Golden Age of James I" for example, the King is seated in a niche that is framed by a pair of twisted or Solomonic columns. The paired columns in the judgement scene repeat this theme. I would like to recall the fact that Jones restored the broken fragments of Stonehenge in pairs of pyramidal uprights. One is not surprised then that he compared Stonehenge to the Temple of Jerusalem. Significantly, the suggestion that a restoration even be attempted came from Britain's new Solomon, James I.

In fact, Whitehall Palace as a whole was thought to be a version of Solomon's House of Wisdom. Quite clearly, Jones's design for the Palace derives from Villapanda's reconstruction of the Solomonic Temple, which was published shortly before his design and certainly known to him. It can also usefully be compared to Juan de Herra's design for the Escorial. Herra saw his King, Philip II, as Jones saw his--a new Solomon. Both designs combine a series of courtyards grouped around a central church, in imitation of the Villapanda reconstruction. In Whitehall a circular space like that of Stonehenge has been made into the main entry forecourt, ringed on its inside with twenty-four (that is twelve times two) columns. Perhaps one can even read the seven bays of the facade of Jones' Banqueting House as a flat wall equivalent of the seven pillars of Solomon's House of Wisdom, or alternatively, a filled out version of the seven windows that make up the interior of the Barber Surgeon's Anatomy Theater.

But there was another design for a circular memory theater in Whitehall Palace; namely, the Cockpit Theater. This theater got its strikingly memorable name from the site of the Royal sport of Henry VIII. It was originally a free standing two story octagonal building which was later surrounded by rear extensions of the Palace. Even having been absorbed into the body of the Palace, its original autonomy and form cannot be forgotten. Jones was commissioned by either James I or Charles I to transform the old Cockpit into a theater for the performance of court masques-- although it had been used for the purpose before Jones undertook the project. Jones rebuilt the roof in pyramidal form and had its inner surface, the ceiling within the space of the theater, decorated with a map of the heavens. For this purpose he used blue velvet cloth painted with stars in the pattern of the zodiac. The cloth was held up at regular intervals by ropes the length of which could be adjusted during the course of the masque in conformity with the sites of its events. The *frons scaenae* of the theater consisted of two stories, the lower with five openings, like the Vitruvian stage, or Palladio's Teatro Olympico, and the upper level had one major central opening like the Barber Surgeon's Theater. The plan of this wall was made semi-circular, its limits were defined by lines that preserved the form of the original octagon. The auditorium was enclosed within this latter figure but that too was interrupted by the side of the King's box, which was placed on the central axis of the whole composition--just like the operating table in the anatomy theater.

While there is much in this design that points to the integrity and coherence of Jones's other theaters, its final form is clearly the result of his encounter with the memory of figures established before his design was undertaken. Can the Cockpit Theater be taken as equivalent to Camillo's theater of memory, or can it be taken as equivalent to the Teatro Olympico--which was clearly used by Jones as a precedent --or is Jones' design to be judged a failure on this account because of its lack of perfect regularity and integrity?

Let me return to the inverse ratio I proposed earlier. I have said already that the perfection of formal consistency leads to the confusion of recollection. On this account Jones' Cockpit Theater would seem a more likely site for the practice of the ancient art of memory than Camillo's theater. Certainly the design is more memorable, both as a piece of the city and as a place for performance. I want to suggest that this is precisely because it acknowledges the presence of contents and forms that were not part of an already defined system of symbolic forms--like the forms of Camillo's neo-Platonic, hermetic cosmology. In proposing this inverse ratio I have had in mind a quotation from Ben Jonson, Jones's contemporary, sometime collaborator and sometime arch-enemy. In his *Explorata* Jonson (1641: 2281-2300) wrote:

some will say variety breeds confusion, and makes, that either we lose one or hold no more than the last. Why do we not persuade husbandmen, that they should not till land, help it with marl, lime and compost, plant hop gardens, prune trees, look to bee hives, rear sheep, and all other cattle at once? It is easier to do many things, and continue, than to do one thing.

Following Jonson, I conclude that I would prefer a theater of memory that allowed me to "do many things", than one that allowed me to always do only one thing--no matter how perfect that One thing might be presumed to be.

REFERENCES

CAMILLO DELMINIO, Giulio.
   1550. *L'Idea del Theatro* (Venice).
JONES, Inigo and John WEBB.
   1725. *The Most Notable Antiquity of Great Britain called Stone-Heng, Restored* (London).
JONSON, Ben.
   1641. *Explorata: or Discoveries; made upon men and matter* (London).
YATES, Dame Frances.
   1966. *The Art of Memory* (London and Chicago: The University of Chicago Press).

XVI

SEMIOTICS OF FILM, TELEVISION, AND THEATER

MAX HEADROOM: TELEVISUAL INVENTION AND EDISON CARTER

Ian C. Henderson
Southern Illinois University at Carbondale

We all know Max Headroom. Just as he ironically predicts at the end of the first episode of his eponymous prime-time series (1987), he has become assimilated into U.S. Culture as a star. Max merchandizing assails us from the supermarket shelves (he has even written a guide to life!), his face has fronted the recent Coca Cola advertizing campaign, and the correlation has been posited between Max and the American president (Ron Headrest) in the syndicated cartoon, Doonesbury. Commuting between England and America over the last three years, I have been able to watch the meteoric rise of Max Headroom from interesting and enigmatic idea to iconic media event in two countries. He has hosted his own rock video show, has reached the cover of Newsweek, and has now turned his hand to the role for which he was created, that of talk show host (Waters, 1987). All this to say, that the U.S. TV series *Max Headroom* serves to introduce American audiences to Max's alter ego and correlational functive, Edison Carter, rather that to Max himself. The problem that I address in this paper is how this introduction is made, given that on the face of it, Edison is the model for Max. The analysis will be grounded in Eco's conception of invention as a mode of sign production, detailed in his (1976) *Theory of semiotics*, and to which I will now turn.

Eco's Invention as a Mode of Sign Production

The bulk of Eco's theory of semiotics is directed toward explicating both a theory of codes and a theory of sign production. In general, the theory of codes accounts for the structure of communicative acts (signification), while the theory of sign production accounts for content (communication). Eco offers a typology of four modes of sign production: recognition, ostention, replica, and invention. Invention is the most radical form of sign production. It proposes a *new* correspondence between an expression and a content. Eco (1976: 245) succinctly elaborates the differences between invention and the other three modes of sign production:

> Everybody recognizes an expression produced by a recognition because a previous experience has linked a given expression-unit with a given content-unit. Everybody recognizes an expression produced

by choice made on the basis of a common mechanism of abstraction, such as the acknowledging of a given item as representative of the class to which it belongs. Everybody recognizes an expression produced by replica, because the replica already replicates an expression type which has already been conventionally correlated with a given content.

Invention differs from recognition, ostention or "choice", and replica in that a person posits a correlation between an expression and a content that does not already exist. What is inventive is not the expression nor the content, but the physical labor of connecting them. This labor is particularly evident to us in those cases in which the invented correlation is seen to fall short, in which it is seen to be forced. One thinks particularly of the televisual advertizing of political campaigns. Invention can take place in one of two ways, one moderate and one radical. Eco's conception of radical invention is more problematical than moderate invention. Eco likens radical invention to the advent of Impressionism as a totally new way of seeing (the perceptual model is bypassed). As such it represents "a radical code-making, a violent proposal of new conventions" (1976: 254) that may not be accepted for centuries! As such an investigation of radical invention is beyond the scope of this paper. Here, I concentrate upon the physical labor involved in the production of the character of Edison Carter in the first episode of the networked series *Max Headroom* (Deguere, 1987) as an example of moderate invention.

Moderate invention occurs when a perceptual representation is projected directly into an expression continuum (1976: 252). From the sender's point of view this is achieved through the accepted rules for similitude. On the other hand, from the addressee's point of view, it is simply an expressive structure. As Eco makes clear, the new sign-function cannot afford to be entirely the result of an inventive transformation, it must offer the interpreter some clues drawn from the other modes of sign production. This analysis will show how this is worked out in the case of the posited correlation between the computer generated Max Headroom and the reporter Edison Carter.

This correlation is, as I have stated, achieved through the physical labor of moderate invention. I shall describe some of the particular manifestations of this physical labor, showing how the labor requires a reworking of both expression and content planes under the rubric of similitude. This description will show how the sign-function operates to constitute a reflexive or reversible relationship between the content and expression planes (between "signifier" and signified" in the more familiar Saussurean terminology). After all, Eco is not providing a typology of signs, but an outline of the modes of production of sign-function. However, before I turn to the description, I offer a brief plot summary to contextualize the following analysis.

Plot Summary

The Channel 23 action news reporter, Edison Carter, stumbles on a plot by his own network to cover up the explosive side-effects of the revolutionary Blipverts. Blipverts are 30 second commercials reduced to 3 seconds, developed by the network employee and computer whiz-kid, Bryce, under the direction of the network head, Grosman, for their leading advertizer, the Zik Zak Corporation. When his live broadcast is pulled from the air, Carter attacks his controller (the studio based employee who directs a reporter on location through extensive use of computer technology), and demands a replacement. Theora is that replacement. When he breaks into Bryce's secret quarters and views a tape recording of the Blipvert effect (a sedentary viewer literally explodes), he is discovered. In his efforts to escape, Carter is thrown from a motorcycle into a barrier that has the legend "Max Headroom 2.3 m". His battered body is captured by Grosman, and Bryce recreates his memory as a computer-generated image and personality in order to find out what he knows. In a coma, Edison is sold to a Body Bank, where Theora finds him and buys him back. With Bryce's aid, Carter challenges Grosman on live television showing the world the tape recording that is in Max's memory, and the cover-up is exposed. With the plot outlined, let us now turn to the problematic of the analysis.

Edison Carter and Max Headroom

The title and promotional trailers have already informed us that this is Max's show and that, despite what the narrative may imply to the contrary, it is Max that is the model for Edison and not vice versa (would the Canadian actor have had a part in a major U.S. prime-time series if it were not for Max?). The narrative plays upon this paradoxical relationship between originator and originated (between signifier and signified). My perspective, then, is the invention of TV reporter Edison Carter, which is achieved on the basis of similitude. This constitution is achieved in a number of ways, and is centered around the Cartesian problematic of mind and body, and modified here as the problem of technology. In order for it to be understandable to the viewer, the invention of Edison Carter is achieved by offering clues drawn from the other modes of sign production, in this case particularly from Eco's third category, that of replica. The transformations of invention exist as a mode of semiotic production "in which something is mapped from something else which was not defined and analyzed before the mapping took place" (1976: 250). In other words, the invention of Edison Carter occurs concurrently with the invention and replication of Max Headroom. Accordingly, the structure for my discussion is provided by the twin notions of "person as machine" and "machine as person"; a structure which allows a bi-directional approach. The structure provides both for the complex process of segmenting a new material continuum and for the process of mapping those elements that are constituted as pertinent. This analysis will take place after an examination (albeit sketchy) of how our understanding of Edison and Max is grounded by the opening credits and by the expressions (signifiers) that designate them.

We initially meet both Max and Edison in the opening credits. After the camera moves upward through a dawn cityscape toward a tall faceless skyscraper which bears the neon number 23 on the two visible sides of its summit, we see swiftly juxtaposed clips of a man walking, running, and hitting the top of a car in apparent frustration. There is a brief shot of Max, before we view a still representation of the same man, accompanied by the text "Max Frewer --- Edison Carter/Max Headroom". Next, the other cast members are similarly presented and we return to Edison vigorously pushing open a door and striding purposefully toward us. We are given another brief glimpse of Max, before we view Edison in a more sedentary pose. After the jumbled chaos of what turns out later to be a "Blipvert", the opening of the show *per se* is marked by the legend "20 minutes into the future". The opening credits serve to frame our reception of the show that follows: Max Headroom pops up twice in still frame, while Edison is represented as a man of action. Also, the unconventional cinematography signals the technological theme of the show.

Our understanding is also predicated on the nomenclature of the two characters. On the one hand, Max Headroom is a name that adheres to the conventional Western form of christian and surname. Viewers with a British cultural background would immediately recognize the name as the designation for the amount of headroom available for vehicles. On the other hand, the name Edison Carter can be broken down into its constituent parts. His first name is the surname of the inventor of the phonograph and microphone, technological devices that displace sound from the locus of production to a different locus of reception. Common knowledge also suggests to us that Thomas Edison was an innovator in television technology. "Edison" as originator/inventor is counterposed to the connotation of "Carter" as a mere carrier (a signifier without a signified) of technology.

Person as Machine

On the face of it Edison Carter represents a person and Max Headroom, a machine product. This simplistic interpretation flies in the face of certain textual evidence. Edison Carter is constituted as machine-like in a number of ways. First, he is seen to inhabit a machine, a machine that can go wrong. During the mid-section of the show, Edison's body is put out of action. His body is regarded and treated (sold) as a set of spare parts, available for re-sale at Nightingale's body bank, where Florence (the receptionist) evaluates him according to strict criteria. His frail body is seen as a disadvantage on the streets: Edison shouts "It's my neck out there!" We might imagine that, in future episodes, he will wear armor. Further, his brain is regarded as a complex circuit ("a binary computer") that can be replicated as another circuit or program by a knowledgeable kid. The spatial location of this circuit is thereby unimportant. Second, Edison is seen to be at the beck and call of a controller, who is able to "pull him out" when the going gets tough. Although framed in the opening credits as a man of action, Edison is now seen as an unthinking reactor to situations, rather than as an initiator of events. When the technical support of his controller is lost, Edison is unable to escape on his own. Interestingly, in the original British television version, Edison manages to escape from the body bank on his own initiative. On the other hand, in the American version, Theora rescues him. Only once in the program does Edison offer a useful suggestion, when he asks about the possible existence of another elevator, but this path only leads to his motorcycle accident. Third, he is seen to have set reactions to certain stimuli; we know that he will make a sexual advance toward Theora, and finally, we are able to repeat his unvarying on-air introductions. Fourth, Edison is hardly seen without his technological extension, the camera, which much of the time is our point of view on the action. In one fight sequence, Edison's camera is explicitly utilized as an extension to his fist. When Edison holds (is at one with) the camera, he is in control of events. Without his camera, events control him.

Machine as Person

The treatment of Max, on the other hand, is more as a person than as a machine. First, he has both perceptual and expressive capabilities. Indeed, after Max's first word ("Ma-Ma"), development is swift; as the computer whiz-kid states, "he is learning, Mr. Grosman". Second, there is both physical and vocal resemblance to Edison (a person). However, Max has the addition of a particularly human frailty, he possesses a speech impediment (he stutters). Interestingly enough, this facet of his character is almost lost in the Coca-Cola advertizing campaign. Third, despite the presence of a controller or programmer and contrary to the impression created by his stillness in the credits, Max is seen to be able to travel at will. He is able to "get lost inside the system", to escape when necessary. The capability for movement does not seem to be impaired by the apparent lack of a lower body. Also, in contrast to Edison, whose camera (i.e., his communication) can be shut off, Max is seen to be able to escape any threat to his ability to express his speech freely, that personal value that we hold so dear. Fourth, he is referred to throughout as "he" rather that as a thing or an "it". The one exception was made by Mr. Grosman (after all, he represents the major villain of the piece), who was swiftly corrected by the kid when he made such a juvenile mistake. Fifth, the comparison that we are offered, between the computer-generated parrot and Max, shows just how far in advance of that creature he is. And after all, aren't animals of higher value than machines?

Conclusion

The tension between the notions of person and machine, based around the complementary notions of similarity and difference, constitutes the reflexivity of the sign-functions ("person as machine" and "machine as person") in the processes of invention and replica. With Eco, I do not want to suggest that these readings are immediately available to the addressee (the viewer), but that these implicit notions structure the sender's sign production under the rule condition of similitude between person-machine and machine-person (Edison/ Max, Max/Edison), which must itself be predicated upon the concomitant notion of difference. The series of defining coordinates, described above, operate enthymematically to constitute a convention, and thereby to initiate understanding on the part of viewers. This represents the code condition, explicated by Eco as overcoding.

There are never cases of total moderate invention: "Texts are maze-like structures combining inventions, replicas, stylizations, ostentions and so on" (p. 256). This analysis has concentrated upon the paradoxical or dialectical relationship between the processes of invention and replica in the construction of character, in order to explicate the complexity of sign production.

REFERENCES

DEGUERE, Philip.
    1987. *Max Headroom* (Television program, ABC, March 1987).
ECO, Umberto.
    1976. *A Theory of Semiotics* (Bloomington: Indiana University Press).
WATERS, Harry.
    1987. "Mad about M-M-Max", *Newsweek*, 20 April 1987, 58ff.

THE ILLUSION OF REALITY AND THE REALITY
OF ILLUSION IN ANIMATED FILM

Richard J. Leskosky
University of Illinois, Urbana-Champaign

Most discussions of motion pictures and their sign systems routinely ignore a significant portion of the cinema--documentaries, experimental films, and animated films. This oversight is particularly ironic in the case of animated films, since they are arguably the most purely cinematic form of the motion picture. In fact, the term "animated film" is, in a sense, redundant, since all films are animated--that is, all films produce their illusion of motion by virtue of presenting a rapid succession of static serial images to the viewer's eye and brain, which forces or allows the brain to reinterpret them as a single moving image.

The animation process, moreover, was known and used long before what we know as the cinema was invented. The birth of the cinema is traditionally dated from March 22, 1895, when the Lumiere brothers projected their first films for a private audience or from 1889, when William Kennedy Laurie Dickson of the Edison laboratories invented the Kinetoscope, which allowed a single individual to view a fifty-foot strip of sequential pictures producing a moving image of under a minute's duration.

From 1832 on, however, a host of inventions involving spinning slotted discs or revolving drums with sequential images mounted on or in them had been entertaining children and adults with moving pictures. In 1868, the printer John Linnett created the first linear moving picture (one which did not continuously repeat its apparent action as did the others) with his Kineograph (or flipbook, as it is most commonly known today), a booklet of sequential pictures which, when the pages were riffled past the thumb, produced the illusion of motion. And, without the benefit of photography, Emile Reynaud projected animated cartoons for theatre audiences in 1889 with the most sophisticated version of his praxinoscope (a device involving a rotating drum and a system of mirrors). Thus, even if the photographic process had not been invented, modern viewers would still be seeing projected motion pictures today.

Indeed, animated images are regularly encountered today quite apart from film (or television). Flipbooks are still being made by novelty companies, animators, and other independent artists. And the lightboards which adorn Times Square and function as scoreboards in most professional ballparks provide more spectacular examples of camera-less (and projector-less) animation. Even though the animation process functions as the underlying principle of the cinema yet also exists apart from the cinema, it is not entirely improper to speak of animated films as a subset of the cinema since this would certainly reflect the common belief of most filmmakers and critics. Animated films, moreover, have had relatively little impact on mainstream filmmaking. Conversely, live-action films have influenced animated films in several ways. American animated cartoons have frequently parodied live-action films and performers, for example, and the classic Warner Brothers cartoons of the 1930's and 1940's obviously borrowed much of their pacing, gag structure, and physical comedy from silent slapstick comedies. Finally, though all films depend on the same psychological and physiological processes as animation for their perception by viewers,[1] no live-action films (aside from those few which incorporate animated elements, such as the recent *Who Framed Roger Rabbit?*) are made with the same frame-by-frame technique as animated films.

In the remainder of this discussion, I shall be referring to live-action and animated films in their most basic forms and shall be concentrating primarily on their visual aspects after some brief remarks on their aural component.

The cinematic sign system is highly complex and involves a myriad interdependent visual and aural codes. The soundtrack of even the cheapest commercial film, for example, includes language, music, and sound effects; and each of these separate tracks has its own rich system of codes.[2] Superficially, the soundtracks of live-action and animated films would seem to be identical in their structures, coding, and production. This, in fact, is not the case: supplying appropriate dialects, voices, and language varieties for beings which do not ordinarily speak and creating sounds for impossible events present challenging problems in the generation of aural signs. Just how does a rabbit--or for that matter, a doorknob--talk; and what sound does a coyote's body make as it is propelled through thirty feet of solid rock? A further consideration is that sound, as well as pictures, can be animated on film--that is, a filmmaker can create an artificial music track photographically on a film rather than merely recording a musical performance.

By the very way they are made, animated films stand apart from live-action films. Live-action films, at their most primitive level, are made by turning on the camera, letting it run for a while, and then turning it off. The result, when processed and projected, is a record of what went on in front of the camera during the time it was in operation. The first motion pictures by the Edison and the Lumiere studios were exactly this sort of crude, unedited documentary; and most of us have probably sat through (or live in fear of having to sit through) home movies made in this fashion.

Animated films, on the other hand, are specifically made one frame at a time. A single frame of film is exposed in the camera; the filmmaker then makes appropriate changes in whatever is in front of the camera; another frame is exposed; and so on, until the end of the film.[3]

Assuming, then, that all things are equal in the actual projection and perception of live-action and animated films, the essential difference between the two can be characterized as follows. Live-action filming analyzes the event in front of the camera (the pro-filmic event) into twenty-four still pictures per second, and then these pictures are subsequently synthesized into a moving representation of that event. Live-action filming thus in a sense re-creates the pro-filmic event. Animated film, on the other hand, depends on making a series of still photos of inanimate and unmoving objects. There is no pro-filmic event as such, although there is (usually, but not necessarily) a pro-filmic object. Animation thus creates an event where none had existed before.

In terms of C. S. Peirce's second trichotomy of sign categories (icon, index, sign) the differences in the way the two sorts of film are made entail corresponding differences in the way the Peircean categories interact and operate within the animated sign.

A motion picture film, whether live-action or animated, is a photographic sign produced by a photographic process (with certain exceptions among animated films which will be discussed later). A viewer may be seeing a picture by virtue of light passing through a celluloid strip and then bouncing off a screen in a dark room rather than seeing a picture because the light reaches the eye directly after bouncing off a photograph held in the hand, but the sign is nonetheless photographic. It has, after all, been produced by light reflecting off an object and striking raw film stock to create a representation on the film of that object. As such, the cinematic sign is inherently an idexical sign. It is also iconic and symbolic.

If I film the action of raising and lowering my arm, the moving picture of it which I eventually see projected is actually an index of a variety of separate but interrelated objects. The first is, of course, my arm in motion. Every point of the screen arm is there because a ray of light had struck a specific point on my real arm and then the exposed film. Through various stages of processing, printing, and projecting, this physical connection may become more attenuated, but it is not negated. The second object is the photographic process whereby the original picture is captured. The third is the individual strip of film itself as it is being projected. And the fourth is the projection mechanism and process. The list could be extended perhaps indefinitely, but these are the most pertinent objects for consideration here.

The projected image is also an iconic sign. In some obvious ways it looks like my arm, or at least all its parts seem to be in the same relationship to one another as the parts of my arm. This is generally how we think of the cinematic image, but this is not the way things necessarily have to be. I could, for example, place the camera in such a relation to my arm (too near, too distant, at too odd an angle) that a viewer could not identify what was being filmed. Or I could tamper with the lighting, the shutter speed of the camera, or the lens aperture to remove virtually all recognizable details. The indexical aspect of the sign would be preserved in all these cases, but the iconic aspect would be obscured, if not annihilated.

Finally, the projected picture of even such a simple action has a heavily symbolic component. What a viewer would see even in this simple film represents three dimensions in two, has a rectangular border, might be in black and white, has a beginning and an end, and would have a sense of spectacle about it (however faint, given the total banality of the subject) which my original action would not. Moreover, the only reason viewers are able to read a film is because of their cultural background and exposure to other films and filmic conventions.[4]

Now, if instead I animate a bit of film about an arm in motion, categories and relationships begin to shift.

I have a very large number of choices in making my animated film. I might draw a series of pictures of an arm in various positions on pieces of paper or celluloid and photograph each individually. I might make a model of an arm in wood, clay, cloth, etc. and reposition it slightly for each frame of my film (I might even use my own arm in this fashion). I could even forgo using a camera at all and draw or paint a series of tiny pictures of an arm on the filmstrip itself (direct animation, as it is called). In fact, with each of these methods of animation there are specific variations from the live-action standards of the cinematic sign.

As an indexical sign, the projected animated film continues to have as its objects the filmstrip itself, the projection process, and the photographic filmmaking process. But the indexical relationship to the object before the camera changes. First, it is no longer a moving object or at least not an object which is moving in the manner represented on the screen. It may even in actuality be a series of static objects each replacing its predecessor (the individual cels of an animated cartoon provide the best example of this), or it may not exist at all (if the drawing, for example, is made directly on the film stock).

What happens here is that the animated filmic sign has paradoxically separated the object represented from the object's apparent motion. The projected picture is an index of the object (which in this case is itself a representation) but not of the actual motion of that object.

On the other hand, the iconicity of the animated motion picture increases, most markedly in animated cartoons since they resemble the pro-filmic object even more closely than other sorts of animated films by virtue of both the filmic sign and its object being two dimensional in nature. In fact, in terms of the filmstrip itself (rather than the projected image of an animated cel cartoon), the iconicity approaches a sort of isomorphism since the filmstrip consists of miniature reproductions of the original cels, which are made of the same substance as the filmstrip. The only material differences in this case are that the frames on the filmstrip are most probably smaller than the originals and are all physically joined.

Since the object (the drawing on the cel) is itself an iconic representation, the animated sign becomes an even more complex icon. It is more iconic of its object (the drawing) but less of its object's motion (since the individual drawing is static). Simultaneously, though, it is more iconic of the motion of the object of its object (whatever is represented by the drawing on the cel) than is the sign which is its immediate object (that is, the individual static drawing).

With respect to animated cartoons in particular, the symbolic component takes on an overwhelming force. All the conventions of drawing (in whatever style) blend with filmic and cinematic conventions and, in the case of certain cartoons, with specific animated cartoon codes: squash and stretch (deformation of shapes) to suggest mass in Disney characters, for example, or Daffy Duck splitting into several tokens of himself to denote speed and anxiety.

In fact, the symbolic sign has a certain primacy in animated films (particularly, but not exclusively, animated cartoons) while the iconic sign holds sway in traditional live-action films. Thus, no matter how outlandish or fantastic the subject of a live-action film may be, it has to maintain a certain plausibility in order to be accepted or enjoyed. The things presented may never have existed or may never be possible, but they must give the appearance of being real, of looking as though they resemble something in the real world (or some possible world). They must, at the very least, be consistent in their presentation of a possible world. The illusion of reality created by a live-action film is destroyed by any obvious fakery (or rather any fakery which calls attention to itself): the miniature set which is obviously a tiny model on a tabletop, for example, or the ineptly painted backdrop or the rear-screen projection that shows mountains out the back window of a car driving through central Illinois. In part, this is owing to what the viewer knows of the (indexical) nature of the photographic image and to the viewer's underlying assumption that photos do not lie (even though he or she may be aware that they do lie all the time).

On the other hand, as soon as one sees the opening credits of an animated cartoon (or sees a singing raisin), one knows that the normal rules of physics (or anything else) do not necessarily apply any longer to what is seen on the screen and that anything is now possible. In fact, this rule-breaking behavior is especially appreciated in animated films, and in this setting any move toward more realistic representations (a sign with a greater iconicity) becomes less acceptable, more distracting, or even tedious. The nature of the sign in this context affects the viewer's aesthetic sensibilities. This is why the more straightforward (in terms of visual rendering) human Snow White is far less interesting to the viewer than the more whimsical and humorous dwarfs in Disney's *Snow White and the Seven Dwarfs* (1937). The Fleischer Studio's animated feature version of *Gulliver's Travels* (1939) foundered at the box office in large part because Gulliver was rendered in a far more realistic style than the Lilliputians, and viewers found this discrepancy jarring. Gulliver's relative realism was achieved through rotoscoping, a process whereby the cartoon drawings are made by tracing over live-action footage (and often the closer to the original the drawing gets, the duller the cartoon). The tracing procedure augments the iconicity of the sign and simultaneously reasserts its indexicality.

This interaction of the semiotic and the aesthetic is still evident in the contemporary feature films of Ralph Bakshi. His *Lord of the Rings* (1978), for example, was marred by (among other things) scenes in which rotoscoping had degenerated to simply splashing a color wash over black and white live-action figures. Bakshi's more modern stories, such as *American Pop* (1981), have been almost entirely rotoscoped, leading critics to ask why he bothered with the drawings at all since he had made a complete live-action feature which he had then traced over virtually in its entirety.

Who Framed Roger Rabbit? (1988) by director Robert Zemeckis and animator Richard Williams, on the other hand, succeeds artistically because it is very careful to keep its real and its cartoon characters true to their own respective natures. In fact, the only scenes which do not work well in this film are those in which a live-action character is made to behave according to cartoon conventions (as when the human hero is briefly flattened in an accelerating elevator).

Animation, however, is the most protean of the arts, and new techniques may well challenge even the basic points made here. Three-dimensional computer animation, for example, is at the point of producing images that could be mistaken for live-action footage, but these images have no pro-filmic objects or, more precisely, have as their objects iconic signs produced by a collection of symbols known as a computer program. This in turn means that one primary indexical object of such a film is a highly abstract set of symbols, which takes the animated filmic sign into new areas of complexity.

NOTES

[1] Most writers about film have ascribed this whole process to persistence of vision. Nichols and Lederman (1980) and Anderson and Anderson (1980) present evidence that other phenomena are at work and that persistence of vision has a relatively minor role in the process.

[2] In the early 1930's, linguist Roman Jakobson was already examining some of the questions posed by film soundtracks (Jakobson 1933).

[3] It might also happen that the animator, for reasons of economy or speed, may choose to expose more frames at a time. This is referred to as animating by two's, three's, or whatever. Some of the more inept and static Saturday morning cartoon shows have gotten up to eight's and even worse.

[4] Forsdale and Forsdale (1966) present anecdotal accounts of the reactions of people of technologically primitive cultures to their first film viewings and their difficulties in reading the films in the manner intended by the filmmakers.

REFERENCES

ANDERSON, Joseph and Barbara ANDERSON.
   1980. "Motion Perception in Motion Pictures", in *The Cinematic Apparatus*, ed. Teresa DeLauretis and Stephen Heath (New York: St. Martin's Press), 76-95.

FORSDALE, Joan Rosengren and Louis FORSDALE.
   1966. "Film Literacy", *The Record* (May), 608-617. Reprinted in *AV Communication Review* 18.3, 263-276.

JAKOBSON, Roman.
   1933. "Upadek filmu?", *Listy pro umění* I (Prague). Translated as "Verfall des Films?" by Gustav Just in *Sprache im technischen Zeitalter* 27.1 (1968), 85-191.

NICHOLS, Bill and Susan J. LEDERMAN.
   1980. "Flicker and Motion in Film", in *The Cinematic Apparatus*, ed. Teresa DeLauretis and Stephen Heath (New York: St. Martin's Press), 96-105.

THE SEMIOTICS OF VIOLENCE

Milan Palec
Scenographer

The semiotics of violence on the stage and the contribution of scenography depicting this reality requires an investigation of how violence may be pictorialized by all sign systems that create the complex system of scenography. This task cannot be fulfilled without a clarification of the term--scenography.
Scenography is a component in a structure of the theatrical system. If perceived as a sign system, components of its structure are voluntarily participating representatives of the system of the visual arts (painting, sculpture, graphics, photography, architecture, interior design, etc.), the performing arts (cinematography, music, etc.), and audio-visual systems, not to mention scenography's dependence on extra-artistic areas such as technology, economics, and philosophy.
Internal forms of all systems are communicated by a medium known as the sign. The sign system of scenography is very complex because it contains the sign systems from all of the participating arts. If the participation of components within the system of scenography would have a mechanical character, and if the target of the components would be to fulfill the task of their "maternal" arts, then the evaluation of a quality of iconic signs of a painted picture in a frame and the same image painted on the backdrop on the stage would require an identical approach and the use of the same criteria. Similarly, iconic signs of a projected image on the screen of a movie theater, and iconic signs of the same image projected on a plane backdrop on the stage would not differ, and if evaluated, they would have shown the same quality.
Scenography is a component of the theatrical system. It is not a component of the visual arts. Scenography's involvement in a visual part of the theatrical performance indicates its double mission--the visual and the dramatic. The fact that in some countries scenography is taught at Schools of Fine Arts and in others at Schools of Theater underlines the early mentioned double mission and it also indicates for many people an unresolved question of where scenography properly belongs. This problem also exists for the audience who usually evaluate the set or costumes by the criteria of visual aesthetics. Looking back into the history of theater, a theatrical set or costume not only served a visual aesthetic purpose, but it also had a more or less hidden dramatic purpose. The task for a visual aspect of a theatrical performance was always fulfilled by representatives of the visual arts. The painter, or sculptor, or architect arrived on stage to paint backdrops and coulisses and to sculpt scenic object, or to create architectural spaces. Due to their presence in the theater, a design for

theater often reflected the level of the development of visual arts. A stress on the dominance of the visual aesthetics approach in the theatrical production appeared in certain periods of theater which were noted for the isolation among scenographic disciplines: scenic, costume and lighting designs. They rarely met during the preparation of a production and although during a performance those traditional disciplines acted side by side, they were evaluated as such and very often they literally substituted for the artistic disciplines to which they formerly belonged. Therefore, the décor sank to the level of painting, and architectural details were brought on the stage from the streets and interiors on stage copied our kitchens and living rooms. Costume design fell under fashion design or clothing "industry". At its best costumes had been aesthetized by the quantitative over-dimensioning of the historic costume. This was all done in passive, illustrative manner. Lighting design had just been illumination or, at its best, it created the impressionistic atmosphere, mood, or illustrated the time of the day, or yearly season or weather conditions.

A dependence of scenography on the visual arts leads to a dead end. When coming into the theater all participating components of scenography are voluntarily losing their "maternal" arts. The visual arts participating in the scenographic system are not controlled by the principles of visual aesthetics--the visual. But the remaining components of the theatrical system are controlled by the theatrical law--the dramatic.

If the mission of art is to depict reality from different angles then the complex sign system of theater which is created by interdependent structures of *dramatis personae* and *dramatic space* offer the artist a nearly infinite number of perspectives in the depiction of violence on the stage. When components of the structure of the theatrical system act separately, or without any significant relationships, or any intergrational efforts, then the *actor's figure* is solely responsible for the depiction of reality--on our case--of the "violent act" and then scenery is alone responsible for the creation of a "violent environment". The pictorialization of violent nature--storms, the eruptions of volcanos, images of fire, hell and purgatory, etc., from the Baroque period to the period of realistic theater have been treated in an illustrative and illusionistic manner. Images were painted and, in our century, projected onto the stage.

Expressionistic painters who negated realism and impressionism defied illusion realizing that the principal difference lay between empirical life and theatrical reality. Expressionism pictorially formed the scenery, so that it would not be an accidental slice of nature or an insensitive descriptive coulisse, nor that it might be a moody element missing the dramatic target. Expressionism on the stage aimed at the dramatic essence of individual acts of a play by painting devices in order to create a "symbol" which would connect individual acts into a whole. The discrepancy between painted scenery and the actor-man would be reinforced if for the same reason they would not also reshape the *actor's figure* by costume and mask thereby removing a small realistic detail from it and giving it a larger line and scale. Scenery and *dramatis personae* which covered an actor therefore become adequate components. Visually treated shapes were transformed into dramatic shapes--a shape and color were a cast of the dramatic tension of the action. If for the first act of Emile Verhaeren's play "The Dawn" the task of the designer Vlastislav Hofman in collaboration with the director Karel Hugo Hilar (Vinohrady Theatre, Prague; 1920) was to create the background of an outline of a factory city with chimneys--realistic motif--, then the design could not use gray or brick colors, but only color through which the drama could speak. "The Dawn" is a drama of revolution, of class violence, and therefore the scenery had to shine with fire, hence it had to be a picture of the factory city that was red, violently lit and reflected in the darkness of empty space.

Color had to play its part in *mise en scène* and production. There could be no realistic color which belongs to an object, but only dramatic color.

The change of an expressionistic painter to a constructivist architect was another step toward contemporary features of modern scenography. In the period of Constructivism scenery was semantically changed by an actor's action without its material foundation being altered. Violence on the stage was pictorialized in this way by V.E. Meyerhold (The First Theatre RSFSR, Moscow, 1922) in his production of Sukhovo-Kobylyn's play "Tarelkin's Death". The atmosphere of a dying czarist regime was created by the transformation of an abstract fixed construction into a prison and windmill or by an ability of this scenic object to evoke in the spectator the feeling that the scene was actually occurring in a meat grinder.

From the period of the Futurist theater through to Oscar Schlemmer's Bauhaus period, and Jacques Polieri's abstract or kaleidoscopic theater to Mark Paulini's performances with self-destructing machines, we can trace the kinetic principles and an admiration for dynamism. And we can also see separatistic tendencies of scenography which depart from the conventional model of theater and lead toward ever closer ties with the latest trends in the visual arts.

Despite separatistic tendencies in scenography, this component of the theatrical system significantly contributes to the development of the theater. Every structural component of the theatrical system (acting, directing, dramaturgy, literature, music, scenography, etc.) is an active participant within the structure of the theater. This structure expresses the method of relationship and mutual activity for its components. All components are carriers of their own sign systems. All components can be further divided into their elements which are perceived as signs. The relationships of components and their elements make the system of theater and its internal form--a structure, alive. Without an understanding of possible relationships, an artist, who is a theater practitioner, would be limited and insecure in his decisions. A consecutive addition of the components or their elements by which the whole of an artwork originates called *Addition* is even now the most frequently used relationship in theatrical practice. The main axis of a dramatic artwork is the verbal manifestation of *dramatis personae* to which in a mechanical way is added mime, gesture, movement, costume, scenery, lighting, and occasionally even music.

A more sophisticated relationship is the *Parallel Functioning of Components* based on Richard Wagner's *Gesamtkunstwerk* theory. K.S. Stanislavsky developed a doctrine of *General Pause* during his "psychological period" as a reaction against a morphological addition. *Transgression* is based on Stanislavsky's "fore-play" (*das Vorspiel*) and V.E. Meyerhold's contrasting functioning or stressed dissociation. On the principle of *Antinomy*, Meyerhold built the entire theory of his developmental stages--the Stationary theater.

There exists many so called "theatrical antinomies". One of them is characterized as "dialectic antinomy" which is based on a dialectic tension. The *Substitution* of components and their elements served as a base for an avant-garde theater of the 20s and 30s. The *Contamination* is expressed by the dissolution of the limitations of individual components in regard of their "maternal" arts. The *Extension of Components* is a working method built upon immaterial semantic extension which corresponds to and, to certain extent, was raised by the "double image" developed in the paintings of Josef Šima. The *Complete Composition of Components* means that one component completes the other component rather than merely being an addition to it. The *Transformation of Components* has an optical as well as a semantic category. The *Divisional Relationship of Components* is based on antagonism. Components can come close together for a moment, or they can be integrated or distanced from each other. In turn they can look upon themselves as two self-contained facts existing independently of each other. The *Simultaneous Functioning of Components* presupposes the function of components in one temporal moment, whereas *Counterpoint Relationships* exist between components in which they exchange their places and overlap or switch themselves. The *Logic-Causal Relationship* corresponds to correlation especially if it regards time, space and action and their frame as integral regarding the development of *dramatic personae*. For example, its psychological development is an obvious illustration of this principle. The point of departure for logic-causal chain reaction is anecdotality--the logical linear time line regardless of its being essential to the unity of place, time and action. The *Conditional Functioning*, in contrast, is signified by the breaking of the time axis and by melting present with past and future, either in the frame of the one demarcation of the place of action, or in the actual transformation of the place. The place transformations are proverbial in our contemporary films. *Structural Relationships* are based on a dialectic unity of antithesis. The intentional analysis is the possibility of fusing fundamental elements into several fundamental series. The direction of those elements leads to their reciprocal analysis and synthesis.

It would be beyond the scope of this paper after the enumeration of several possible relationships among components and their elements to try to differentiate and signify internal qualities of these unities. Our target--the pictorialization of violence on the stage by scenographic means, reinforced by theoretical investigation, leads us to an illustration of how it can be used in theatrical practice.

Let us select one sequence from Tennessee Williams' play "A Streetcar Named Desire" (Palec, 1988, McLeod Theater, Southern Illinois University). This sequence contains an extremely violent act. In film as well as in realistic theater, the scene of a rape depends solely on the actor's portrayal of realistic characters of Stanley and Blanche. A director's decision of how authentically to depict a rape depends variously on the audience's taste and the actor's individual abilities. The signs communicating this action would act in the first degree if the relationship of components would be an addition or if it would have a form of the parallel functioning of components. An *actor's figure* would be solely responsible for a portrayal of the character of Blanche which might be shaped by an evening dress, and, say, by Stanley's red pajamas. The lighting design could contribute by creating a violent atmosphere using red colors to support a "bordello" mood, a support which in turn would evoke notion that Blanche is a whore and Stanley is an adulterer. The set would offer a bed. Music would add a gradual rhythmic *fortissimo*. All of these participating components would be led to one goal that is to maximize the effect of a violent act on the stage in the manner of *Gesamtkunstwerk*. An integration of components and their elements, however, offers stronger dramatic possibilities. If in the "party scene" during the fight a ceiling lamp in the kitchen were to be put into motion, then the space would seem to be "drunk". The ceiling lamp in the kitchen as a representative of lighting as well as of scenic design would substitute for the characters' "drunkenness"--task of the actors. If during the rape scene the ceiling lamp were again moving wildly then it would serve as a signal for the audience to indicate Stanley's drunkenness in the present scene. This is much stronger dramatic effect might be achieved if Stanley Kowalski--in his rage--were to smash his fist through the Chinese paper lamp covering the naked light bulb in Stella's bedroom. The Chinese lamp is the sign of Blanche's Southern-belle "noble" taste and would be destroyed by the brutal fist of a Northerner--Polish immigrant. The rape which is usually played as realistic would, in our case be substituted for by the actor's action--the penetration of the Chinese lamp by Stanley's fist. The Chinese lamp is a part of the scenery and at the same time a proverbial lighting instrument. This presentation of a rape would not be a copy of a real life act but rather it would be a metaphor for rape, unique and usable only for the violent scene of Tennessee Williams' "A Streetcar Named Desire".

REFERENCES

HOFMAN, Vlastislav (designer), Karel Hugo HILAR (director).
    1920. "The Dawn" (Emile Verhaeren, dramatist; theatrical production; Prague; Vinohrady Theatre).
MEYERHOLD, Vsevolod Emilyevich (director), Varvara S. STEPANOVA (designer).
    1922. "Tarelkin's Death" (Alexander Vasilievich Sukhovo-Kobylyn, dramatist; theatrical production; Moscow; The First Theatre RSFSR).
PALEC, Milan (designer), John STANIUNAS (director).
    1988. "A Streetcar Named Desire" (Tennessee Williams, dramatist; theatrical production; Carbondale, Il.; McLeod Theater at Southern Illinois University).

MURDER AS SIGN AND CYCLE IN *LES NÈGRES*

Mary Ann Frese Witt
North Carolina State University, Raleigh

> ". . . une levée en masse de morts on s'en remettra.
> . . . mais pas de mort du tout, cela pourrait nous tuer.
>
> -- *Genet 1958: 139* --

Genet's novel *Querelle de Brest* (1947) opens with the following sentence: "L'idée de meurtre évoque souvent l'idée de mer, de marins". The sentence encapsulates much of the function of murder in Genet's texts. First of all, it is not so much murder as its idea, or its sign or trace, that interests him in his writing. In spite of the (even today) shock value of Genet's subject matter, both his narrative and dramatic works retain on one level an almost classical *pudeur* in that there is little mimetic violence in either.[1] Murder on the whole occurs on the diegetic level, told rather than shown, or as one of the characters in *Les Nègres* says, the definitive gesture takes place, as in Greek tragedy, offstage. In Genet's fiction, this reported narrative level can encompass a domain that the reader accepts as "true", so that in terms of the fiction we "believe" the stories of murder committed by Notre Dame, Harcamone, Erik, and Querelle. Genet's theater, on the other hand, postulates a domain of unreality, of events that take place in an anti-world. In *Haute Surveillance*, where murder is exceptionally committed onstage, the act is de-realized, becoming an "histoire entre quatre murs" (Genet 1946: 193) through the commentary of the characters. The theater, like the brothel and like the prison, is a world closed within itself, and thus a world in which genuine action is impossible. "Ici nous sommes dans le domaine du mal", says the make-believe Bishop in *Le Balcon*. "On ne peut pas commettre le mal dans le mal" (Genet 1957: 54). The maids can only succeed in virtually murdering Madame; we cannot verify even the existence of the queen and her court in *Le Balcon*, much less their assassination; when the "dead" reappear in *Les Paravents* (1961) to discuss the living we become aware that their killing was theatrical. The theatricality of murder is even more marked in *Les Nègres* when the blacks masked as whites are "killed" onstage, then make comments while in the role of dead bodies, then take off their masks to assume their roles as "real" blacks. This mimetic/theatrical murder is one of the factors that problematizes the diegesis of the previous murders of whites and that of the contemporaneous execution of the black traitor offstage. I shall examine the function of these signs of murder in more detail.

To return for a moment to the second part of the quotation from *Querelle*: why should the idea of murder evoke the idea of the sea? Images of the sea in Genet's writing occur almost exclusively in conjunction with the penal colonies on Devil's Island and on Guiana. Pilorge, in Genet's early poem "Le Condamné à mort" (1947a: 54), fantasizes escaping from prison not to "our" world but across the sea to what is conceived as a Baudelairean utopia:

O la douceur du bagne impossible et lointain!

O le ciel de la belle, o la mer et les palmes. . .

In *Miracle de la Rose* (1943), Genet describes the idea of attaining Guiana as the sea crossed and death vanquished. In *Journal d'un voleur* (1949) he elaborates on the paradox of the penal colony: "Ce lieu semble contenir la sécheresse et l'aridité la plus cruelle et voici qu'il s'exprime par un thème de bonté: il suscite, et l'impose, l'image d'un sein maternel. . .(Genet 1949: 270). An ideal sequence, perhaps most evident in *Journal*, emerges: 1) the act of murder as transgression, as definitive separation from "your" (the reader's) ordinary world 2) the crossing of the sea and 3) rebirth and eternal life in an earthly "paradise". Naturally the paradise is an inverted one, peopled by society's damned rather than God's elect, and furthermore, since the French government abolished penal colonies in 1945, the sequence has become not a possible series of acts but a myth at once sustaining and nostalgic. As we know from the rite of baptism, from linguistic associations such as *la mère*-mother and *la mer*-sea, and as Mircea Eliade (1959) has shown with examples from preliterate cultures, water plays a crucial role in ritual death and rebirth, and the sea is often represented as a cosmic mother. Eliade, like René Girard, also shows how the sacrificial murder of a chosen victim (or a ritual mimetic murder) functions in the process of initiation as a means of dying to the profane world to be reborn in the sacred. It is in this sense then--as transgression, death and rebirth; as transposition from profane to sacred time--that the idea of murder evokes the idea of the sea.

Les Nègres, arguably the most theatrical of Genet's works for the theater, is concerned with the desire for transgression and rebirth through murder. What is the nature of this murder and what is its function in the dramatic text? In attempting to answer this question, it will be useful to look at the Soviet semiotician Jurij Lotman's theory of plot as developed in *The Structure of the Artistic Text* (1971) and an article entitled "The Origin of Plot in the Light of Typology" (1979).[2] Lotman conceives the notion of plot in essentially spatial terms. Every character in the fictional work has an assigned space; an action in the plot sequence occurs when one character trespasses, as it were, into another's space. Lotman also sees the most basic sequence of what he calls the modern "plot text" as a chain of "entry into a closed space and emergence from it" (Lotman 1979: 168). By means of this sequence, the great mythological events of resurrection and rebirth--those that are eternal and cyclical and that have no temporal beginning and end--are, as it were, translated into a narrative form. What we have in Genet's text, however, is a constant subversion of narrativity, or plot closure, by theatricality as well as a continuous removal of the signified and the referent from the sign. In Lotman's terms, the entry into the alien space occurs, but the (triumphant, definitive) return after the "rebirth" does not. *Les Nègres* partakes of conventional drama, primitive ritual, and metatheater, while unclassifiable as any of the above. The metamorphosis of mimetic, diegetic, and referential murder into the *idea* of murder ultimately and paradoxically makes a political and social statement.

The primary sign of murder on stage is the catafalque draped in white around which the blacks dance to the minuet from Mozart's *Don Giovanni* in the opening scene. Archibald, who serves as narrator/m.c. indicates the significance of this object through word and gesture: "Ce soir, nous ne songerons qu'à vous divertir: nous avons donc tué une Blanche. Elle est là. (Il montre le catafalque.)" (Genet 1958: 86). Speaking to the masked "whites" above as well as to the audience (intended as real whites), the designated murderer Village recounts, after much interruption, a brief narrative of his strangulation of an old *clocharde*, now presumed to be the corpse. We are even led to believe that such a woman is killed every evening, as Village prefaces his remarks with "comme d'habitude". It then appears that a dramatic performance, in addition to the narrative, is necessary because required by the "whites". The judge proclaims: "Vous nous avez promis la représentation du crime afin de mériter votre condamnation. La Reine attend. Dépêchez-vous" (Genet 1958: 93). The preparation for the re-enactment would seem to involve the apotheosis of Félicité as Queen of Africa, among other lyrical, non-dramatic events, as well as the "casting" of Samba Graham Diouf, an elderly black clergyman with conciliatory views toward whites, in the female role. The play-within-the-play then proceeds to represent and narrate the story of the murder of Marie, a young girl who lives with her mother, by Village. At this point, the catafalque as theatrical signifier indicates two contradictory signifieds: the body of an old woman; the body of a young girl.

The murder of Diouf-Marie, much anticipated but never performed, gives rise to the comment by Bobo (in her role as part of the onstage "audience") that the ultimate gesture, as in Greek tragedy, is performed offstage. But the comparison with Greek tragedy turns out to be misleading, for there is no messenger to bring us a tale of violence, no diegesis of murder. Instead, we have the following dialogue (Genet 1958: 129).

Archibald: C'est fait? Vous n'avez pas eu trop de mal?

Village: Autant que d'habitude.

Neige: Il ne s'est rien passé, n'est-ce pas?

Village: Rien. Ou, si vous voulez, tout s'est passé comme d'habitude, et très proprement. Quand il est entré derrière le paravent, Diouf m'a aimablement aidé à m'asseoir.

Neige: Et ensuite?

Ville de Saint-Nazaire: Rien d'autre. Ils ont attendu sur
un banc, dans la coulisse, en échangeant un sourire amusé.

Not uncharacteristically, Genet changes fictional and theatrical levels in the midst of Village's speech. Whereas the audience or the reader, as well as, presumably, the Blacks on stage, expect the narration of a murder taking place in a "diegetic" space (Marie's room), they receive instead the account of a non-event (waiting) and a reference to actual theatrical space (the wings). The fictive universes behind the theatrical event on stage have become even more problematic. The figure of Diouf becomes, like the catafalque, a theatrical signifier whose signified is unstable. Sacrificial victim of the black community, Diouf is "raised" to the level of the whites where he plays the part of the white female victim who will instigate their desire for revenge. We have then an elderly, black, live man playing his opposite on all four counts. Because of the very theatricality of Diouf as sign, the public becomes aware that it is not an individual act of murder that the "whites" feel compelled to avenge but instead the concept of murder as a transgression of boundaries: what they call "murder of the color white".

Diouf's arrival in the realm of the whites and the subsequent "voyage" of the whites to Africa would seem to be classic examples of Lotman's plot text: invasions of space by "aliens". Indeed, these two movements are the only actual dramatic events in the play. A moment after the whites arrive in the Blacks' space, what we might call a negative event, or a consummate theatricalization takes place: Ville de Saint-Nazaire (the character who is responsible for reporting on the trial of a black traitor said to be going on offstage) lifts the sheet off what we had accepted as the theatrical sign of the catafalque, revealing that there is nothing there but two chairs. (This prompts the white queen to exclaim "Mes chaises!") The signified had already been problematized; now the signifier is whisked away. What remains is an empty sign: precisely the *idea* of murder. The governor's comic use of the negative verbally corroborates the empty sign: "Pas de caisse!...Ils nous tuent sans nous tuer et nous enferment dans *pas de caisse* non plus". And the judge speaks the words I have used as epigraph: "pas de mort du tout, cela pourrait nous tuer" (Genet 1958: 139).

One murder, or a mass of murders, could lead to a dramatic counter revenge, a plot that the whites have initiated by their "invasion" of Africa. The linear plot is however aborted by the emptying of the sign. We witness not a battle between blacks and whites, Africa and Europe, but a comic and pointless struggle against a ritual attempt to obliterate whiteness. The theatricality of the struggle is further emphasized by the fact that the "whites" are masked blacks. The removal of the masks is another example of emptying a sign.

Given the ostentatious theatricality of the goings-on onstage, are we to postulate a referential "real" world of blacks offstage? Many critics of *Les Nègres* take Archibald at face value in assuming that the theatrical event is merely a device to "divert" the audience from the "real" event narrated by Ville de Saint-Nazaire: the execution of a black traitor. But Ville de Saint-Nazaire (whose name explicitly suggests the sea and seafarers) becomes himself another empty sign, or a sign of the idea of murder. Twice he has to be told which way to exit, and it is not to a diegetic, extra-theatrical space that he is sent but "dans la coulisse" (Genet 1958: 96). It is true that he suggests (but does not describe) the occurrence of a "real" execution, but the theatricalized context, as well as the "play" we have already seen, makes his narration suspicious. His description of the new black leader who will replace the traitor-- "comme vous l'imaginez"--should be taken quite literally. The diegetic persons and places are entirely in the realm of the imaginary.

The world of the theater is for Genet articulated with other anti-worlds (*l'immonde*): prisons, the underworld, the third world. Just as prisoners kill prisoners, maids kill maids, Algerians kill Algerians and blacks kill blacks, actors can only perform with each other. Transgression into what Genet calls "your world" (audience/reader, white, bourgeois, Western) can only be enacted ritually and cyclically, not in real time and space. (When he stopped writing for the theater, Genet of course pursued other strategies.)

What is finally at stake in the idea of murder as it is worked out in *Les Nègres* is not so much killing as the desire for rebirth through transgression. The passage of Diouf from black to white and from male to female, his "giving birth" to the white dolls representative of white power, and his ultimate designation as "worthy Mother" are indicative of the desire to usurp the life-giving power of the female and maternal domains. The fact that both Africa, in the persona of Félicité, and Europe, in that of the Queen, are ruled by women represents not Genet's portrayal of history but his sense of the archaic source of power. The theatrical murder of the white figureheads is a sequel to the play's lyrical climax: a kind of duet between Félicité and the Queen resulting in the absorption (or re-absorption) of the European Mother into the African. Africa, in Félicité's words, is "la nuit ou vient sombrer le jour". And again, " . . . la nuit en personne. Non celle qui est absence de lumière, mais la mère généreuse et terrible qui contient la lumière et les actes" (Genet 1958: 143). Transgression, as we have seen, has been accomplished not by a fictive act of murder but by the creation of its signs. It is this "murder of the color white", enacted in Félicité's (verbal) victory over the white queen, will engender the rebirth of Africa.

The idea of murder thus functions not only as sign but also within a cycle; in Eliade's *illo tempore*, the non-time of ritual death and rebirth. Since there is no dramatic closure to the play, the audience cannot even be assured of the symbolic victory of the blacks. The "white" Queen's last words--"Nous partons, nous partons, mais dites-vous que nous resterons engourdis dans la Terre comme des larves ou des taupes, et si un jour. . .dans dix mille ans. . ."(Genet 1958: 155-156)--and the stylized minuet around the catafalque, repeating the opening of the play, suggest that the act of transgression is part of a cyclical process and that the mythical text has absorbed the abortive plot text. And yet, something has happened, dramatically and theatrically speaking: we are not simply back where we started. Through ritual transgression, a return to Mother Africa has been accomplished ("Entrez en moi, Nègres, Félicité chants on several occasions) along with an usurpation of the life-giving, maternal, "hatching" property of white civilization. "L'idée de meurtre (we may now gloss the sentence from *Querelle*), évoque l"idée de la *mère*."

That this ritual return to Mother is part of the process of rebirth and renewal is postulated by the love duet between Village and Vertu with which the play's dialogue ends. Yet this is no marriage affirming comic closure, fertility, and racial continuity: the expressions of a black love are tentative; the other blacks are still dancing to white music. Genet's cyclical ending leaves open the question of whether or not the blacks have succeeded in murdering the color white as a means of renewal, or whether they will themselves be obliterated in the cycle by eventually donning white masks. What emerges in the end is the ideological power of the theatrical sign: no corpse at all *could* kill.

NOTE

[1] Nor was Genet a violent man. Harry Stewart's findings (Stewart: 1987), while revealing in their historical information, do not, as he claims, significantly alter our perspective on Genet's "ethical views". Surely it is oversimplifying matters to state that current consensus on Genet holds that his interest in crime is "simply literary vengeance upon a bourgeoisie that rejected him" (Stewart 1987: 642). Any attempt to "excuse" Genet's admiration of crime in sociological terms contravenes the psychological violence that his texts would work upon their audience. Conversely, Stewart's revelation that Genet really did admire real, horrible crimes (and thus cannot be "excused") also seems to suggest that we are justified in ignoring the impact of his writing. But perhaps the greatest danger to the thrust of Genet's work comes from its co-option as a "classic".

[2] Additional expansions of Lotman's critical perspective are to be found in *Analysis of the Poetic Text* (1976).

REFERENCES

ELIADE, Mircea.
   1959. *Naissances mystiques, essai sur quelques types d'initiation* (Paris: Gallimard).
GENET, Jean.
   1943. *Miracle de la Rose*, in *Oeuvres Complètes de Jean Genet*, Vol. 2 (Paris: Gallimard, 1951).
   1946. *Haute Surveillance*, in *Oeuvres Complètes de Jean Genet*, Vol. 4 (Paris: Gallimard, 1968).
   1947. *Querelle de Brest*, in *Oeuvres Complètes de Jean Genet*, Vol. 3 (Paris: Gallimard, 1952).
   1947a. *Poèmes* (Lyon: L'Arbalète).
   1949. *Journal d'un voleur* (Paris: Gallimard).
   1957. *Le Balcon*, in *Oeuvres Complètes de Jean Genet*, Vol. 4, (Paris: Gallimard, 1968).
   1958. *Les Nègres* (Décines, Isère: Marc Barbezat), republished in *Oeuvres Complètes de Jean Genet*, Vol. 5, (Paris: Gallimard, 1979). An English trans. by Bernard Frechtman appears under the title *The Blacks: A Clown Show* (New York: Grove Press, 1960).
   1961. *Les Paravents* (Décines, Isère: Marc Barbezat). Reprinted in *Oeuvres Complètes de Jean Genet*, Vol. 5 (Paris: Gallimard, 1979).
LOTMAN, Jurij M.
   1971. *Struktura khudozhestvennogo teksta (Moscow)*, trans. from the Russian by Gail Lenhoff and Ronald Vroon as *The Structure of the Artistic Text* (= *Michigan Slavic Contributions*, No. 7; Ann Arbor, MI: Department of Slavic Languages and Literature, University of Michigan, 1977).
   1976. *Analiz poeticheskogo teksta* (Moscow), trans. from the Russian by D. Barton Johnson as *Analysis of the Poetic Text* (Ann Arbor: Ardis Press, 1976).
   1979. "The Origin of Plot in the Light of Typology", *Poetics Today* 1.1/2 (1979), 168.
STEWART, Harry J.
   1987. "Genet's Favorite Murderers", *French Review* 60.5 (April), 635-643.

# XVII

SEMIOTICS OF ART

PERCEPTUAL SEMIOTICS: FUNCTIONS OF REPETITIONS IN AN IMAGE

Lev Manovich

A Program for Visual Poetics

As (self-appointed?) children of Saussure, we are left with an ambiguous gift. "Linguistics is only a part of the general science of semiology; the laws discovered by semiology will be applicable to linguistics . . . " (Saussure i.1906-1911: 35); but few pages later (Saussure i.1906-1911: 38) we encounter a crucial modification:

> Signs that are wholly arbitrary realize better than the others the ideal of the semiological process; that is why language, the most complex and universal of all systems of expression, is also most characteristic; in this sense linguistics can become a master pattern for all branches of semiology although language is only one particular semiological system.

Unfortunately, it is the latter interpretation of the relationship between linguistics and semiotics which led many to look for the equivalents of syntagm, paradigm, phoneme, etc. in the signifying domains, different from the verbal language. But why should other types of signs (for instance, images) be organized as speech? Speech is parsed linearly, while an image is in parallel; speech and images are processed in functionally different brain hemispheres.

To say "semiotics of images" is to imply that images function as a kind of language in a culture; but it does not mean that images are actually organized as verbal language. However, if in order to develop semiotics of images we cannot borrow terms developed to describe verbal language, where do we start? One way would be to follow the strategy of literary poetics which is concerned with general structures of literary discourse realized in individual texts. In 1967 Todorov defined the goal of structural poetics "to propose a theory of the structure and functioning of literary discourse, a theory that affords a list of literary possibilities, so that existing literary works appear as achieved particular cases" (1973: 7). In the same manner visual poetics should use the existing multitude of images of different cultures and epochs treating them as "data" from which general principles of image signification are to be abstracted. Such poetics will be structural because it studies the general features of visual "languages", treating individual images as manifestations of visual "langue" of a culture. However, we can avoid the abstractness of "classical" structuralism by assuming that the "syntaxes" of various visual languages are ultimately determined by the roles the images play in different societies.

Thus, provisionally and cautiously: poetics of visual discourses should specify *general* modes of pictorial organization, relating them to *historically and culturally* different functions of images and modes of their perception. It should also show how the internal structure of an image constrains its possible meanings (interpretations). The images under study are not necessary artistic but visual discourses in general, all images created in different societies.

Concerned with describing image organization, visual poetics is radically different from the Marxist, psycho-analytic or deconstructive analysis, all of which essentially reduce any cultural sign to its signified. They are concerned with "what and why is represented in a image" while visual poetics asks complimentary questions: "what is the organization of an image, how it allows us to decode the image, how image organization relates to the functions of images in a particular society and how this type of organization emerged. "Similar questions are raised in linguistics. Chomsky founded the idea of a universal grammar in the fact that any chid could potentially learn any human language, thus the grammars of all languages should have some common denominator. Different modes of visual representation, culturally bound, are more difficult to decode for an outsider; the grammar can hardly be inferred from representation itself. Then do different images still have anything in common on the level of their organization? Functions of images, materials, modes of production and cultural perception change . . . is there anything which stays invariant?

What does not change is that images are *perceived* rather than read and heard. This implies that all the diversity in organization of images is limited by the structure of the decoding apparatus, i. e. by the structure of the human nervous system. The fact that an image will be decoded by another human being, with particular perceptual and cognitive apparatus, limits what organization the image can have. This is one reason to bring the theories of psychology of perception to the project of visual poetics. Moreover, just like a reader of an artistic text has a tendency to interpret everything as significant, as intentional, the student of images will tend to see everything in an image as "meaningful. "By explaining some of the features of image organization as being caused by the structure of perception itself we can counteract this dangerous tendency.

Unmotivated Repetitions in Images

As an exercise of combining perspectives of semiotics and psychology in the project of visual poetics I will look at perhaps the most general features of images: their reliance on *repetitions*, or, in other words, the redundancy in their organization. Of course, semiotic theories of literature already emphasized roles of repetitions in a text. Thus, we will use literary theories of Shklovsky, Jakobson and Lotman to see if repetitions in images may have the same functions as in texts. But first I will clarify what I mean by "organization" of an image and by "repetitions" in images.

Rather than talking about an image in general we will limit ourselves to the large class of hand-made and representational images. I will call an image "representational" simply if it contains recognizable objects: Egyptian fresco, 19th century naturalistic paintings or childrens' drawings all fit into this definition. Any image, including representation one, can be approached as a field of colors, lines and textures and other abstract visual elements. (Of course, it was the visual art of modernism which first deliberately looked at pictures in this way.)The term "organization of an image" refers to the description of an image on this level. For instance, we may ask what colors are contained in the image, and are they distributed.

Understood in such way, the organization of most images in the considered class turns out to be highly redundant. A typical image consists of only a limited number of colors, tones, and textures which are repeated over and over.

While a Mondrian painting seems to explicitly define its units, in most images colors, tones or textures change continuously. In order to persuade ourselves that many photographs or illusionistic paintings heavily rely on repetitions also, we may consider histograms of various perceptual dimensions of an image. For each dimension a histogram shows how frequently a value occurs. The advantage of using histograms is the possibility of describing image structure on those perceptual dimensions for which language does not provide words. For instance, we can look at the distribution of different line orientations, or the distribution of sizes and character of shapes used. Histograms can also be used to analyze the patterns of change of various pictorial qualities, for instance how color changes in different parts of an image. Histograms are "blind" to what the lines or shapes can stand for and thus can serve as a tool of formal analysis: they can be constructed for any image, be it an abstract painting or a photograph.

Formally, the notion of redundant organization means that on some of the perceptual dimensions only a limited number of values is used. For instance, out of all possible types of lines an image contains only a few. The point to note is that perceptual dimensions are not only the distributions of discrete pictorial elements such as color or texture, but also the *rates of change* of surface properties. In this sense such "continuous" images as realist paintings also have very redundant organization.

Some repetitions are required for an image to represent certain objects. I will call such recurrences motivated. For example, in a drawing of a cube, the lines that represent parallel edges are also parallel or slightly converging. Such recurrence in line orientations is required, since otherwise the drawing can't be read as a depiction of a cube. However, most images also contain other kinds of repetitions, the unmotivated, which are not required for the depiction. It is these unmotivated recurrences which we can call repetitions proper and whose functions in images we want to understand. For instance, in a particular image an apple and a face were painted with the same color. If different colors would be used instead, the apple and the face will still be recognizable. Therefore, the recurring color has a function other than simply to make objects recognizable. To reiterate: *repetitions* proper are those recurrences in the organization of an image which are not required (not motivated) by what an image represents.

Why unmotivated recurrences, or repetitions are possible at all in representational images? This question can be answered by referring to the process of image perception. In order to be recognizable, the pictorial representation of an object does not have to match all its visual qualities. Some qualities can be given arbitrary values that can be then repeated elsewhere in the image. For instance, to represent a figure the contour is often sufficient; color or texture can be selected relatively arbitrary (depending upon the style) and the selected values can be used again for other objects. This flexibility in our ability to recognize representations makes pictorial repetitions possible. For example: compositionally, the depicted objects are often arranged so that repeated visual movements, often called "visual rhythm", emerge. As far as the recognition of depicted objects goes these movements are not at all necessary: semantically the scene would not change if objects are slightly moved and the visual rhythm is destroyed.

To summarize: most representational images have repetitions in their organization. Some of the repetitions are required to depict the objects, others are not. These latter repetitions (which I called "unmotivated") are possible because the representation of an object does not have to match completely our visual memory of it. Since most images contain an abundance of unmotivated repetitions they are likely to be functional. What can these functions be?

Function 1: A Pictorial Device

Victor Shklovsky first pointed out that literature operates through a number of specific devices, or techniques. For instance, narrative rarely presents us with the description of events in chronological order; it proceeds through flashbacks, in parallel, with digressions or repetitions. "The idea of *plot* is too often confused with the description of events--with what I propose provisionally to call the *story*. The story is, in fact, only material for plot formulation. The plot of "Evgeny Onegin" is, therefore, not the romance of the hero with Tatyana, but the fashioning of the subject of this story as produced by the introduction of interrupting digressions" (Shklovsky 1921: 57). The examples of poetic devices are the techniques of phonetic instrumentation (such as rhythm or meter). For Shklovsky, it is such devices that constitute the unique character of literature, its *literaturness* (rather than the content which can vary with culture and time). In traditional literature these devices only exist to support meaning; they are concealed and do not exist on their own.

Shklovsky's idea that modernist literature brought attention to the literary devices themselves points to the following parallel. Just as Futurist poetry "lays bare" the poetic devices by not connecting them with semantic meaning, modernist visual art reveals the devices of representational painting by not connecting them with mimesis. The word "representational" is used deliberately: Formalists insisted that each new artistic movement can be best understood as a reaction to the preceding one. The modernist artists' activity may be best interpreted as the reaction to the previous leading artistic discourse of the 19th century academism. Thus, modernism laid bare not some universal language of art of all ages but the pictorial devices typical of 19th century painting, such as the centered position of main subject and hierarchy of importance among parts of a painting. The most important contribution of modernism is perhaps the awareness that an image, as an abstract field, has its own life, that is it first of all a system of relations between units, regardless of whether units have denotations or not (compare abstract art of the beginning of the century with 19th century realism). Consider a work by Mondrian. First, there are no denotations in the traditional sense: visual elements exist on their own. Second, because so few elements are utilized, the structural relations between them (i. e. repetitions) can be clearly seen. Moreover, the elements themselves (lines of different colors) can be verbally described. To sum it up: in modernist visual art repetitions, which previously were the devices to support the meaning, became the subject. If we follow Shklovsky, modernist painting is, in some sense, about the formal structures of realist paintings, about the fact that even realist paintings are not just copies of visual reality but a pictorial material organized in an ordered way.

Function 2: To Motivate Visual Signs

"Poetics deals with problems of verbal structure, just as the analysis of painting is concerned with pictorial structure" (Jakobson 1960: 148). Starting with Formalists,

Jakobson shared their search for the uniqueness of poetry; later this project was redefined as the uniqueness of poetic function, one among other functions of speech. But the essence of Jakobson's answer as to what constitutes literaturness did not change. First, for Jakobson, "the poetic use of language is distinguished from other uses through the fact that, in poetry, language is perceived in itself and not as a transparent and transitive mediator of "something else" (Todorov 1977: 272). Second, if Saussure emphasized the arbitrary nature of the linguistic sign, Jakobson pointed out that while linguistic signs are arbitrary in normal use, they become motivated in poetry. This motivation is achieved through repetitions which emphasize the internal coherence of the text. As summarized by Todorov, (1977: 279) "the poetic rhythm attests to the fact that discourse finds its finality in itself, and . . . owing to such mechanisms, language ceases to be arbitrary. "Todorov traces the idea of coherence of art object (which Jakobson takes for granted) back to the Romantic understanding of art as having no outside purpose. The logic is as follows: 1) artistic object has no outside purpose; 2) its purpose is internal; 3) it has to be internally completed, thus harmonious, thus coherent; 4) internal rhythm separates the object from the environment and makes it coherent. Thus the idea of motivation of verbal signs in art can be a side product of Romantic aesthetics, which became naturalized "common sense" of the present century.

Jakobson, implicitly following the Romantic belief in the unique essence of art, juxtaposes the use of signs in poetry and in normal speech; but what is the equivalents of "normal" speech for images? The notion that in poetry the language exists for its own sake does not directly translate for visual realm. However, we can find a parallel to Jakobson's idea of motivation of verbal signs. Recall that the pictorial signs are partly motivated and partly arbitrary: to be recognizable, some visual qualities of the object have to be matched, others can in principle be given arbitrary values. But if the chosen value is repeated elsewhere in the image, the choice becomes motivated. Thus visual repetitions may serve to achieve the internal coherence of the image just as poetic rhythm makes a poem coherent.

This function, however, can't be universal since the idea of internal coherence of "art object" can be traced back to recent historical understanding of art. Therefore, repetitions in artistic images of modernity may function to make these images coherent and complete, according to the romantic ideal. But what about repetitions in images of other cultures--and outside of "art"?

Function 3: To Construct "Artistic Meaning"

There was another reason why Roman Jakobson was concerned with repetitions in a text throughout his life. "The poetic function projects the principle of equivalence from the axis of selection into the axis of combination. Equivalence is promoted to the constitutive device of the sequence" (Jakobson 1960: 155). This means that "words similar in sound are drawn together in meaning" (1960: 167). This idea was fully developed by the Soviet semiotician Yury Lotman.

Lotman's "Structure of the Artistic Text", published in 1970, is perhaps the most systematic and positivist application of semiotic principles to the analysis of art ever attempted (Lotman, 1970). The theories of Formalists, Saussure's semiotics and structural poetics are blended with the notions taken from cybernetics, information and communication theories. For the western reader, the positivist rigor of Lotman and his insistence on the uniqueness of art can appear questionable. While in the West the idea of Sign was used to bare the mythologies of the society and to attack scientific discourse, Lotman draws upon scientific language to further mythologize the idea of art by explaining its unique character scientifically. As long as the word "art" is taken to designate a unique object, a set of cultural practices hierarchically above the rest of culture in value, the search for the essence of art becomes inevitable. The romantic belief in the supreme nature of art, reflected in Formalist's *literaturness* and in Jakobson's *poetic function*, takes a scientific turn in Lotman's theory. For Lotman, artistic text is a message organized in a special way; in art, everything is meaningful, everything has a function; art is the most economical way to transmit information; and so on. However, recently we have realized that a text or an image does not become "art" by possessing some unique qualities but when it is legitimatized by the Art institution and discourse. If any arbitrary text can in principle be legitimized as artistic, it is difficult to accept Lotman's conviction that there is some special mode of organization, common to all artistic texts. As we already saw with Shklovsky and Jakobson, behind the attempts of poetics to empirically discover the unique qualities of art or literature lies a culturally and historically local understanding of art of modernity. Thus, it is meaningful to map Lotman's literary poetics only on the images which can be described by modernist aesthetics. Since we are also concerned with non-artistic images Lotman's analysis of repetitions can't be exhaustive.

Implicitly following the modernist notion of an artist challenging the accepted view of reality Lotman claims that each artistic text creates a unique semantic universe. Repetitions are crucial in this process. The idea of Jakobson that "words similar in sound are drawn together in meaning" (1960: 167) is generalized to be one of the main ways, in which the artistic text forms its meanings. On each level, from phonetic to stylistic, repetitions make the reader form equivalences between syntagmatically and semantically distinct elements of a text. Semantically distinct elements, grouped together, become associated in meaning. If Jakobson insists that art motivates signs, Lotman adds that the artistic text makes equal semantically what can't be equal in everyday language. Each artistic text creates its own hierarchies of oppositions, its own semantic categories. Very similar idea is expressed by Benveniste: "The artist creates his own semiotics; he sets up his oppositions in features which he renders significant in their own order . . . The signifying relationships of any artistic language are to be found within the compositions that make us aware of it. Art is nothing more than a specific work of art in which the artist freely sets up contrasts and values over which he assumes supreme authority" (1969: 238-239).

Lotman's model directly translates to the realm of images. All signs, similar in some respect, are perceived as belonging to one structure. Such structures, rather than direct references of signs, create the unique semantic universe of an artistic text. In a nutshell, the model implies that the viewer perceptually groups visually similar signs and in this way constructs the meaning of an image.

However, do groupings of visually similar elements always take priority over the references of signs? The two modes of interpretation can be best considered as supplementary. Out of many conceptual dimensions on which a visual sign is situated I will concentrate on just one complimentary pair. To avoid confusion with the terms "syntagm" and "paradigm" (which Saussure defined in relation to speech) I will call them "vertical" and "horizontal. "The "vertical" dimension of a pictorial sign is its reference, it is what the viewer, given her/his codes of interpretation, takes the sign to represent. The "horizontal" dimension is the relation of sign to other signs based upon perceptual similarities/differences. Only in the mode of interpretation, corresponding to the "horizontal" dimension the perceptual similarities between signs are used in the manner, suggested by Lotman and the repetitions become important. One would think that most images operate on both dimensions, and that both perceptual groupings and conventional references contribute to meaning.

Function 4: To Create Illusion

The interpretation of repetitions in the spirit of literary poetics has led us to consider them as a semantic device. As Lotman notes, the reader takes everything in the text to be intentional and meaningful. It is, first of all, the theorist of the text who takes everything in a text to be related to semantics. Considering repetitions from the point of view of perception reveals, however, that they can also play a very different role, the one which has nothing to do with semantics. If previously considered functions would only apply to the artistic images of a certain period, this function is much more general.

What I have described earlier as the redundancy of a pictorial organization was a more formal way to say that most images have a homogeneous stylistic appearance. In a typical image smooth shading is not mixed with flat planes of saturated colors, and once the level of detail is chosen, it is followed throughout the image. But why?

At least for the Western culture this stylistic unity is in itself functional, allowing illusionistic images to be read as representations of coherent three-dimensional scenes since the majority of images in Western culture are illusionistic, acting as windows into hypothetical spaces. Western images can be interpreted in this way because they follow linear perspective *and* because they have stylistic unity. On the map, the different symbols are explicitly provided--green triangle means forest, and so on. After familiarizing yourself with the symbols you can easily read the whole map. When you look at an illusionistic drawing, the style of depiction (the pictorial code, so to speak) is not given explicitly but is inferred from the image itself. For instance, you infer that black lines stand for contours of three-dimensional objects. By inferring the code of representation from the illusionistic image, the viewer can effortlessly interpret the whole image as a three-dimensional scene if the code is consistent. If different codes are used in the same image, the illusion breaks down. In the case when one object is rendered with great detail and another one is drawn very schematically, the two objects are not longer seen as belonging to the same space, having the same degree of reality.

If this illusionistic function of repetitions does indeed exist, it testifies to the fact that the organization of an image is not arbitrarily chosen by the imagemaker but is dictated in part by the structure of perceptual apparatus. Since images in Western visual culture function as illusions of space, they have to have a redundant organization in order for perceptual system to read them as these illusions. We see how the reference to psychology of perception can explain a feature of image organization which we may have been tempted to view as a semantic device.

Conclusions

The attempt to transfer semiotic theories of literature to visual poetics suggested that repetitions in artistic images of modernity act as a pictorial device, that they make an image internally coherent and that they also create special "artistic" meaning of the visual text. However, paying attention to the psychological process of image perception revealed that repetitions in both artistic and non-artistic Western images are inevitable if the images function as illusions of real scenes. In summary, there are different kinds of repetitions and what visually can look as the same effect may be a result of very different intentions. Any Western imagemaker makes an image organization redundant because s/he (and his/her viewers) approach images as illusion of space, a convention in Western visual culture. An artist of modernity can also purposely set arbitrary repetitions to create a special "artistic" semantic universe. Finally, some repetitions (which I have called "motivated") are simply required for an image to depict an object.

A semiotic analysis of images should break the pictorial organization and the imagery of any visual sign into separate components. Some components will turn out to be the result of the unique choice of the imagemaker; some will be the conventions of a particular visual language; some will belong to the common web of signifieds of the society; finally, others will be a reflection of the structure of human perceptual and cognitive system, thus a common feature of all images. As I tried to demonstrate in the analysis of repetitions, it is crucial to separate such levels; and without thinking about how the images are perceived it is simply impossible.

REFERENCES

BENVENISTE, Emile.
    1969. "The Semiology of Language", *Semiotica* 1, 1-12 and 127-135, trans. by Genette Asby and Adelaide Russo, in *Semiotics: An Introductory Anthology*, ed. Robert I. Innis (Bloomington: Indiana University Press, 1985), 228-246.

JAKOBSON, Roman.
    1960. "Linguistics and Poetics", in *Style in Language*, ed. Thomas A. Sebeok (Cambridge: The MIT Press). Page references in this article are to the reprint in *Semiotics: An Introductory Anthology*, ed. Robert E. Innis (Bloomington: Indiana University Press), 147-175.

LOTMAN, Yuri.
    1970. *Struktura khudozhestvennogo teksta (Moscow)*, trans. from the Russian by Gail Lenhoff and Ronald Vroon as *The Structure of the Artistic Text* (= *Michigan Slavic Contributions*, No. 7; Ann Arbor, MI: Department of Slavic Languages and Literature, University of Michigan, 1977).

TODOROV, Tzvetan.
    1973. *Poetique*, trans. as *Introduction to Poetics* by Richard Howard (Minneapolis: University of Minnesota Press, 1981).
    1977. *Theories du symbole*, trans. as *Theories of the Symbol* by Catherine Porter (Ithaca: Cornell University Press, 1982).

SAUSSURE, Ferdinand de.
    i. 1906-1911. Lectures delivered at the University of Geneva and published from auditors' notes by Charles Bally and Albert Sechehaye under the title *Cours de Linguistique Générale* (Paris: Payot, 1915), trans. as "Course in General Linguistics" by Wade Buskin (New York: Philosophical Library, 1959). Page references in this article are to the reprint in *Semiotics an Introductory Anthology*, ed. Robert E. Innis (Bloomington: Indiana University Press, 1985), 28-46.

SHKLOVSKY, Victor.
    1921. "Sterna i teorya romana", trans. as "Sterne's *Tristram Shandy*: Stylistic Commentary" by Lee T. Lemon and Marion J. Reis, in *Russian Formalist Criticism*, ed. Lee T. Lemon and Marion J. Reis (University of Nebraska Press, 1965), 27-57. Page citations are to the English version.

ART HISTORY VS. ART MYTHOLOGY: THE SEMIOTIC TENSION

Deborah L. Smith-Shank
Vincennes University

Whether we want to admit it or not, the artistic sensibility of our culture at large is the result of our program of public art instruction. If we despair over 49-million-dollar Van Gogh's and acres of black-velvet Elvis paintings, we have no where else to put the blame except in our traditional elementary, middle school and high school art classrooms.

What is the fundamental problem with public art instruction? Recently, art educators themselves have admitted that too much emphasis has been placed on the production of art at the expense of aesthetics, criticism and an understanding of art history. To address this problem they have created a theoretical model of instruction called *Discipline-Based Art Education* (Getty Center 1985; Eisner 1980). The purpose of this paper is to uncover the hidden tension between art history and art mythology that is buried in this (and any other) model of art and art instruction. The resolution of this tension at both the theoretical and practical level is a case of applied semiotics.

Discipline-Based Art Education has four components production, aesthetics, criticism and art history. One of its problems is the sense that all components have equivalent natures. By looking closely we see that production, aesthetics and criticism are acts whereas art history (at least at the public school level) is less something we do as it is a knowledge base which we use to make aesthetic and critical judgments and produce art. We can say art history is the knowledge base of the Discipline-Based Art Education Model.

We hit a snag by assuming art history is an adequate base upon which to build a program of art instruction. In doing and understanding art, an historical approach is necessary, but when you look historically at art you force yourself into looking and understanding in a sequential way. It is important to understand art in a mythic way as well, nonsequentially and ahistorically. For example, Fauve painter Maurice Vlaminck who, when asked what he thought about the current movement in "young French painting" and what he was working on, wrote (Vlaminck c. 1923):

> ...I try to paint with my heart and my loins, not bothering with style. I never ask a friend how he makes love to his wife in order to love mine, nor what woman I ought to love, and I never worry about how women were loved in 1802. I love like a man and not a schoolboy or a professor. I have no one but myself to please.

Vlaminck, for all his mythic insight, is not so much rejecting art history as going beyond it. That is, if Vlaminck did not understand the historical roots and consequences of his own art and his own training, he would not be able to be so freely in touch with its mythic center.

Perhaps the best way to understand the relation of history to myth is to compare that relation to another important relational system. History is to myth as technology is to nature. At its best, technology works with nature to improve the quality of human life, and history works with mythology to expand our fundamental mythic consciousness in an evolutionary way. At its worst, technology conquers nature, history conquers myth. When technology attempts to replace nature our environment is in trouble. When art history attempts to replace myth our humanity is in trouble (cf. Campbell 1988).

There is a less glamorous but equally important problem with the Discipline-Based Art Education model. That is the problem of going from theory to practice. Most art teachers have not been trained to teach anything but production techniques. The Discipline-Based Art Education model requires these teachers to address aesthetics, criticism and art history. In order to do this there needs to be a clear way to coordinate these components into do-able instructional activities. As we discussed earlier, there is an implied equivalence among the components of the Discipline-Based Art Education model. This has practical consequences as well. For example, if we look at production, aesthetics, criticism and art history as equal units to use in creating instruction, we have no clue as to how these components interact and relate to each other. We need to chart out the relational natures of these components taking into account the fact that they are not equivalent. If we expand the model to include myth, then we can use the inherent tension between history and myth as the energy source behind the artistic doings that we call aesthetics, production and criticism.

In short, while the Discipline-Based Art Education model is a vast improvement over current art instructional practices, it needs to be expanded in two ways to realize its full theoretical and practical power. First of all, the role of myth in art needs to be brought in explicitly. Second, the relational characteristics of these (now) five components need to be identified in a structural way. These two tasks can be addressed by looking at the Discipline-Based Art Education model as a semiotic phenomenon. In this way we can conceive of every act of art instruction as a semiotic event that unfolds from a general Discipline-Based Art Educational model which coordinates the roles of art history and art mythology and which incorporates production, aesthetics, and criticism, in a relational way.

Figure 1 outlines the basic structure of the modified Discipline-Based Art Education model. First of all, the model is built using a series of relations. The act of criticism occupies a central position in the model, not because it is more important than any of the other components, but because critical acts involve direct links to most of the other components of the model. In other words, the model states, by virtue of its organization, that it is possible to react critically in a direct way to public myth, to statements of art history, to aesthetic judgments, and to one's own art productions. When we consider aesthetic judgments, though, we find that these judgments are linked directly to our critical acts, to our own productions, and to our private myths. Production of art is related directly again to critical response, to aesthetic judgement, and to that part of myth we call cliche', or dead myth. Likewise, we can chart out the other direct links that are part of the map of the model.

The second key factor of this modified Discipline-Based Art Education model is the fact that we have expanded the component of myth into the three types of myth that we referred to above. This is due to the fact that there are three fundamental

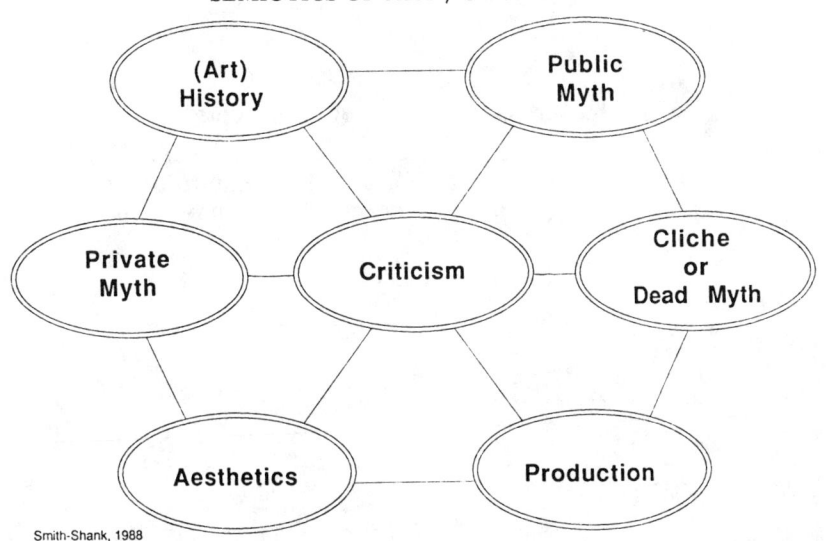

Figure 1. Directional Model of Art which Includes *Myth* as a Necessary Part of a Discipline-Based Art Education Program.

mental sources of myth. Private myth comes from within, and is our basic motivational source. Public myth belongs to the culture as a whole, and shapes our basic understanding of that culture. Cliche', or dead myth, is simply the mythical analogue of dead metaphor. That is, people respond to dead myth in art in much the same way that they respond to dead metaphor in language. That is why we can give a cursory glance to couch art (e.g., "barn painting in the fall"); it means no more to us artistically than does the notion of a "table leg" metaphorically.

No one understood the idea of cliché as dead myth better than Andy Warhol, who observed (Warhol 1975: 96):

> I loved working when I worked at commercial art and they told you what to do and how to do it and all you had to do was correct it and they'd say yes or no. The hard thing is when you have to dream up the tasteless things to do on your own.

Warhol (1975: 144) also said:

> Business Art is a much better thing to be making than Art Art, because Art Art doesn't support the space it takes up, and Business Art does. (If Business Art doesn't support its own space it goes out-of-business).

The third key function of the modified Discipline-Based Art Education model, and the last one that we will discuss here, is its role as a powerful source of instructional ideas. The foundation for those ideas can be found in Figure 2. Notice that all of the instructional "pieces" in the chart are the result of constructing triads from the model. In other words, we can take any three nodes of the model that are

Figure 2. Examples of Sign Patterns Derived from the Model.

Object (Referent)	Sign (Manifest Presence)	Interpretant (Consequence)
Private Myth or Criticism	›› Aesthetics	›› Production
Public Myth or (Art) History or Aesthetics	›› Criticism	›› Production
Criticism or Cliché	›› Public Myth	›› (Art) History
Aesthetics	›› Private Myth	›› (Art) History
Public Myth or Production or Aesthetics	›› Criticism	›› (Art) History
Criticism or Cliché	›› Production	›› Aesthetics
(Art) History or Public Myth or Production	›› Criticism	›› Aesthetics
(Art) History	›› Private Myth	›› Aesthetics

Smith-Shank, 1988

linked, and create a semiotic component from them (see Percy 1983, for an extended discussion of the role of semiotics and consciousness in the artistic process). We do so by determining what instructional consequence we are looking for, and then assigning that consequence to the role of the interpretant (Shank 1982). By doing this, we then automatically determine which node of the triad becomes the sign, and which one becomes the object. This "erector set" approach to semiotic creativity works because of the fact that all signs are resolved, in terms of other signs. So, it does not matter structurally where we begin. All we need to have is a concrete educational purpose.

Let us clarify the previous statements by creating an example of the model at work. Suppose an elementary art teacher wants to expose his or her students to Vincent Van Gogh. There are many ways the teacher can use this model to create a unit within the modified Discipline-Based Art Education approach. In general, Van Gogh can be explored as a public myth (either critically, or as the cultural cliché he has unfortunately become), in terms of the student's aesthetic judgments about their own private myths, and through specific critical acts. These components, while they sound theoretical on paper, can be quite concrete and quite appropriate for elementary students. Let's take a group of third graders and show them a print of Van Gogh's "Starry Night". We ask the students to copy the painting on their sheets of paper with colored crayons and to make their crayon marks as much like the ones they see in the print as possible. When the drawings are finished, they are all displayed in the front of the room and the children are asked to talk about 1) the process involved in making the specific marks like Van Gogh's, 2) the colors they used and the colors he used, 3) the type of person they feel painted the original painting, and 4) what the artist meant for them to understand about this particular "starry night". As we can see, there are no right or wrong answers, only rich and detailed insights into the artist and his work. And we have our targeted consequence; namely, an understanding of a selected goal in Art History.

This modification of the original Discipline-Based Art Education model has both theoretical and practical consequences. By simply acknowledging and exploring the inherent semiotic nature of this process we have a more sophisticated theoretical model and we have a set of specific suggestions to teachers of art on how to make the model work in their classrooms. Perhaps after the third graders in our example understand Van Gogh, they will realize that using 49-million dollars to turn his work into dead myth is just as destructive to art as would be painting Van Gogh's portrait on black velvet and hanging him next to Elvis.

Let us conclude with the words of Van Gogh himself, in a letter he wrote from Arles to his friend and fellow painter, Emile Bernard (Van Gogh 1888):

> ...[they] see the soil of the South as colorless, and a lot of people see it like that. My God, yes, if you take some sand in your hand, if you look at it closely, and also water, and also air, they are all colorless, looked at in this way. There is no blue without yellow and without orange, and if you put in blue, then you must put in yellow, and orange too, mustn't you? Oh, well, you will tell me that what I write to you are only banalities.

REFERENCES

CAMPBELL, Joseph (with Bill Moyers).
    1988.   *The Power of Myth* (New York: Doubleday).
CHIPP, Herschel B.
    1968.   *Theories of Modern Art* (Berkeley, California: University of California Press).
EISNER, Elliot W.
    1980.   *The Role of Discipline-Based Art Education in America's Schools* (Los Angeles: The Getty Center for Education in the Arts).
GETTY CENTER for Education in the Arts.
    1985.   *Beyond Creating: The Place for Art in America's Schools*
PERCY, Walker.
    1983.   *Lost in the Cosmos* (New York: Farrar, Straus, and Giroux).
SHANK, Gary.
    1982.   "Stalking the Elusive Interpretant", paper read at the Annual Meeting (October) of the Semiotic Society of America at Buffalo, New York.
VAN GOGH, Vincent.
    1888.   Letter to Emile Bernard of Paris, cited in Chipp, 1968, 33.
VLAMINCK, Maurice de.
    c. 1923.   "Lettre-Préface", cited in Chipp, 1968, 144.
WARHOL, Andy.
    1975.   *The Philosophy of Andy Warhol* (New York: Harcourt, Brace, and Jovanovich).

XVIII

SEMIOTICS AND POSTMODERN CULTURE

GARBAGE PAIL KIDS: RECOGNITION AND ADAPTATION

Jay A. Knaack
The University of West Florida

Garbage Pail Kids are colored drawings on bubble gum cards, showing nasty, bruised and bewildered children who are depicted as, among other things, a bandaged bowling ball, a urinating dog, an insect eating garbage, a helpless plucked flower, and as diseased, disfigured and socially isolated children. They have such names as "Prickly RICK", "Creepy CAROL", and "MARCEL Parcel". They are obviously drawn by adults to entertain children for commercial purposes. These drawings can be related to childhood development of neurological processes of recognition and perceptual coordination as well as to cultural adaptation.

The cards, which playfully satirize what we often consider to be the more gross, difficult, and common elements of childhood experience, deal with injury, rejection, rebellion, helplessness, and sickness which constitute the more painful rites of passage a child must live through. As such, they represent the reverse image of popular stylized dolls and cartoons on the market which emphasize sweetness and uniqueness (e.g., Cabbage Patch Dolls), beauty (Barbie Dolls), and superpower (Masters of the Universe).

Structural analyses reveal that the messages on the cards are relatively simple and redundant. Following Piaget's theory of childhood development (1932, 1945), we can view the drawings as caricatures of distressful situations children encounter, caused by lack of coordination and clumsiness, which result in punishments, socially negative self-images, rebellion and the inability to understand what is happening to them or to communicate their feelings and experiences. These caricatures are also playful, and are analogous to ways in which children might similarly caricature themselves in imaginative play. For example, the drawings may show children either deliberately or non-deliberately eating in a dirty manner.

The bubble gum cards are caricatures, which many parents detest, because of the way they treat taboo or unacceptable subjects. However, they were highly appealing to children who one presumes were of school age and could buy them. A statement accompanying the cards announced that the purchaser could "trade them". In some cases, the drawings were removable decals, which children could "stick on" lunch boxes, clothing and so on. In reviewing these cards with a number of parents, it was suggested that the cards may have, intentionally or unintentionally, conveyed messages which children could openly use to a) publicize their egocentric predicament (in which case they believe that they alone suffer through these rites of passage), and share these general predicaments with others, thereby rendering these predicaments social and acceptable, and b) that they may have been used by children to illustrate their desire to be treated as humans in an over-structured environment (school, nursery, little league, being hauled from place to place in cars, vans, and buses), and because of the lack of parental camaraderie in families where both parents work, or in one parent families where the parent works, and in which case television has become the new "child sitter". The pictures are of semiotic interest, because they serve to create purely visual metaphors which clarify the children's predicament to themselves, and which words alone cannot do.

The deep structure consists in three relatively fixed elements.

The first is the stylized baby's face, which is uniform and can be altered to show anger, hurt, smiles, doubt, confusion, and so on. There is also the artist's careful attention to the split face image, often half happy and half sad, which correspond to the personal or emotional side of the face and the public side of the face (Rivlin and Gravelle, 1984). Thirdly, adolescents who buy these cards can laugh at infants and infantile problems though they are laughing at the infant within themselves.

Secondly, is the "outer" and "inner" distinction, which some observers claim infants do not make between their own feelings and bodies and the outer world until they gain objective concepts of themselves and the world.

The overlap between the outer and inner worlds is most easily observed in the imaginative play of children. Dolls, toy animals, and even objects and clothing may have feelings and thoughts just like children do. In this case, the world is viewed in anthropomorphic terms, that is, children project their own feelings into other things. On the other hand, they may try to imagine what it would actually be like to be another thing and project themselves into things. For example, children swimming may imagine themselves to be a fish and act like a fish; children may stand stationary and play at being a clock by nodding their heads and saying "tic toc". In one case I have gathered, two little sisters, when occasionally allowed by their parents to sleep together, played at being modelling clay. Each would take turns at rolling up into a ball, while the other pulled and manipulated their limbs to create interesting figures and creatures. This is similar to the game "statues" as well as to using the body or hands to project interesting shadows on a wall. So, children not only imagine there is an inner life like their own in outer things, but also that they can become the outer things and act like or feel like they imagine the outer thing acts and feels.

Adults are aware of this, for in elementary schools, children may be asked to stand and wave their bodies like flowers in the wind to the accompaniment of music. You may also remember children playing at being a dog and biting their parent's ankles.

Imaginative and symbolic play is plastic and is eventually unlearned as we become adults, after which such play appears "childish".

The third fixed element is that of the adult contrast between nature and culture, or the human and the animal or object. These distinctions produce well known metaphors (which are also applied to children) in which humans are favorably or unfavorably compared to things and animals. For example, someone may be as clever as a fox, big as a bear, eat like a pig, or be as dirty as a pig, be hairy as an ape, sharp as a razor, or dead as a door nail.

A fourth element consists in regular contrasts using variables. There is the contrast between children who make noise, scream, and cry, and the pursed lips and silence demanded by adults (even though adults are allowed to scream at children all they like). Other contrasts are between the child who is clumsy, uncoordinated, and ignorant, and the adult who is controlled and knows everything. There is also the contrast between the child who is forbidden to strike back and the adult who has absolute power to punish, isolate, or exclude the child from affection. Finally, we have the sick child who cannot comprehend sickness any better than they can sometimes understand why they are being punished or isolated.

These four elements are worked into visual catastrophes, which employ and create metaphors of childhood anxieties and difficulties.

The Topps Chewing Gum Company logo shows the fixed element in all of the pictures, of the round baby face. The logo shows a closed-mouth boy in a neat suit and tie, seated on the ground with fat baby legs sticking straight out, pushing a remote control button he holds in his lap, which is igniting an atomic bomb exploding out of the top of his head. The contrast here is between the neat and groomed appearance of the boy and his cheerful silence and discipline, while his inner head is shown to be exploding outwardly.

Marcel Parcel shows a boy packaged like a carton, or a box for mailing. Part of the wrapping of the package has been torn revealing his face, and his feet and hands stuck tightly to his body. The right half of his face is smiling, while the left half which is the private side in which emotions are more intensely expressed, has an enlarged and bruised eye looking upwards and a cancelled postage mark on the left cheek. An adult hand above is in the act of stamping the parcel. Here the metaphor is of a child, battered like a postal package and sent away from home, suggesting a child's fear of being abandoned or rejected by its parents. The inner bruised feelings of the child are expressed by partially revealing the child in the package. The right side or public side of the face is smiling and expresses desired social acceptance. The drawing also contrasts the silent child with pursed lips and the noise suggested by the adult postal employee stamping the package.

In a similar vein, *Dizzy Dave* shows the child's body as a string of putty twisted like a rubber band. Little stars over his head are cartoon conventions for suggesting dizziness. While the right side of his face is smiling, the left side appears disoriented with his tongue hanging out. The metaphor is that he is tied in knots, which adults say of people who have too many problems to contend with.

Three 'kids', *Messie Tessie, Slimy Sam*, and *Buggy Betty*, satirize children's lack of motor control and their bad eating habits as judged by adults.

Messie Tessie is a drawing showing a little girl with sticky effluence running from her nose and forming a large uncontrollable mess which she holds between her hands. The effluence is pulled apart to resemble an uncontrollable mass of taffy or gooey swiss cheese. This satirizes the fact that children often catch colds and have runny noses which they cannot control as adults demand.

Slimy Sam is a drawing of a baby in diapers and wearing a bib, depicted as a plump green lizard with claws and fangs and a long curving tail, seated on the floor at a little table. He holds a knife and fork in his hands, while a large fly lays before him on the table. His enlarged eyes and protruding tongue and smile suggest he will relish eating the fly. The suggestion here is that the child is a dirty, animal-like eater, eating forbidden things. Another suggestion is that the child's "animal" stage is normal in so far as other young animals can be imagined to go through this stage.

Buggy Betty is similar to Slimy Sam. Here a fat fly with huge eyes is dressed in a little girl's dress, and hovers over garbage, while hearts are drawn above the head representing conventional symbols of love. This suggests that she loves to eat garbage. Here a child and its wrongful eating habits are compared to the unwanted house fly who frequents the garbage can. The love symbol also suggests purposive rebellion by the child pretending to eat nasty things.

The next group, including *Patty Putty, Disgustin Justin, Crankie Frankie*, and *Fritz Spritz*, portrays childhood rebellion against the demands of the parent.

Patty Putty is drawn as a pudgy baby in diapers, seated on the ground with a fat stomach and prominent navel. Her baby's face is contorted like plastic; the mouth is pulled open to about ten times it's width, one eye is pulled side ways, and one eye protrudes above the top of her head. The tongue is extended and drips saliva. The drawing suggests the playful contortions children like to make with their faces which sometimes anger their parents. The open mouth suggests insuppressible noise and gleefulness.

Disgustin Justin employs the rounded child's body and face in creating an unshaven hell's angel, or social rebel, seated on a motor cycle and drinking a can of beer. The cycle is drawn with dust clouds around its wheels suggesting that it makes a great deal of noise which is obnoxious to proper adults. Here the child rebel is relishing his open display of defiance and is portrayed as a member of a social sub-group.

Crankie Frankie is shown as a boy with horns, a long forked tail and sharp animal teeth, a conventional sign of wickedness, who is grinding up his school books in a hand cranked grinder, again suggesting rebellion against the adult world.

Fritz Spritz portrays a round puppy dog with a baby-like face, smiling, one rear leg raised as though he was going to urinate into the bell of an old fashioned hand-cranked record player. The adult pun intended is to satirize the advertisement for phonographs which shows a dog dutifully seated in front of a phonograph bell listening, as the ad stated, "to the voice of his master". Here the dog is reversed into an attitude of playful disrespect for the redundant sounds or messages issuing from the adult or master world. The act of urinating suggests real problems children have in controlling their bladders and their desire to conceal and hide what they learn to call "accidents" involving their bodily functions. The battered bell of the phonograph speaker and broken records suggest the dog-child is clumsy and as messy as a dog.

The next two 'kids', *Potty Scotty* and *Drippy Dan*, directly reflect problems infants and young adolescents have with controlling their bladders and bowels.

Potty Scotty shows a baby boy barely sitting on an adult toilet and half falling in, smiling and holding a toilet cleaning brush. Next to the toilet lie a can of cleanser and a toilet plunger or plumber's helper signifying cleanliness. They may also signify well cleaned and cleared bodily pipes as well as mechanical pipes. The child is clearly out of control trying to sit on the adult toilet seat, and the cleaning brush also seems to be too big for it, suggesting that for all of the symbols of cleanliness, the child is actually messy and smelly.

Drippy Dan is a portrait of a standing baby in diapers, happily smiling and drinking from a glass. His entire body is full of holes from which streams of liquid pour. The direct comment here is on the inability of infants to control their bladders. The metaphor is that the child is leaky as a sieve.

Three of the 'kids', *Virus Iris*, *Ailin Al*, and *Haley's Vomit* illustrate children's confusion and isolation when they are ill.

Virus Iris is shown sitting in a tub of water, looking miserable, an ice pack on her head, a thermometer in her mouth, and flannel wrapped around her neck. The face also has the appearance of being frightened, and drops of perspiration are drawn on the forehead and her nose is running. On the floor are medicines, Kleenex, and a hospital chart on the wall has a downward curve on it.

Ailin Al shows a crying boy on a crutch, one arm, one leg and his head bandaged, with stars surrounding his head. The stars are cartoon conventions for indicating pain in this context. There are also spirals drawn, a convention indicating dizziness. A little box of gauze with the red cross symbol next to him suggests he has been injured. The comment appears to be on the fact that children often fall and hurt themselves, not having yet acquired full coordination.

Haley's Vomit shows an infant floating in a space capsule dressed in a space suit, terrified and vomiting. The vomit goes up instead of down, suggesting weightlessness. The vomit also contains inner bodily organs, and garbage, which suggests the adult slogan for sickness: "Puking one's guts out". Through the window of the space capsule, we can see planets and stars. Here the child's inner body is brought to be visually outer, while the child is in a space suit and in a space capsule which is in outer space. The visual metaphor is that of the feeling of vertigo one experiences when convulsed with vomiting. The comment is probably on children often getting sick, especially for eating the wrong things, and on the feeling of exclusion sick people experience. The name "Haley's Vomit", is a pun on Haley's comet.

The two 'kids', *Creepy Carol* and *Unstitched Mitch*, reflect the bad self-image children may have of themselves, due to adult comparisons of physical beauty and ugliness, or adult reactions that exclude them, deny them affection, or punish them.

Creepy Carol is a picture of a little girl standing, sucking her thumb, her face and body covered with growths or pistules. There is a large bolt extruding from her head like a Frankenstein monster. A mirror on the wall is hopelessly cracked, suggesting the metaphor that she is ugly enough to crack a mirror. A fish bowl is in the process of being overturned at her feet and the goldfish in the bowl is looking at her in fright. Here the frightening aspect of her appearance to the fish is also reflected in the fright one might feel for the fish who is about to be dumped out of its water. In one arm, the girl carries a book entitled, "How to Win Friends and Influence People". Above her head a large question mark is drawn, a cartoon convention suggesting she is puzzled. The drawing suggests childhood anxiety over social acceptance. The question mark, along with the thumb sucking, suggest she has not yet acquired necessary adult social graces. Her socially inept behavior, breaking and upsetting things, is equated with physical ugliness.

Unstitched Mitch is a drawing of a seated baby boy, with a split face expression; one half is smiling and the other half appears battered. His arms are extended as though he desires to be picked up. His stomach is drawn as an open or split cavity from which stuffing resembling cotton is falling out between his legs. The drawing suggests that the child is not in one piece or is too messy to be picked up, either because he has been naughty and had the metaphorical stuffing knocked out of him, or because his bodily effluence renders him socially unacceptable or unclean and untouchable. Here, the inner feelings of the child are portrayed through the face, the extended arms and the extruded stuffing. The smile and the stuffing suggest the child is like a socially acceptable doll that can be picked up or abandoned at will. This was the most graphic parallel with dolls I could locate, equating the helpless child with a cute and mistreated doll.

The next two 'kids', *Prickly Rick* and *Tee Vee Stevie* are more complex drawings that draw parallels between childhood difficulties and the often onerous or impossible demands of adults.

Prickly Rick represents a stylized and solitary green cactus, isolated in a desert, with the face of an apparently angry boy with a tightly closed mouth. The cactus has a round body, two upright appendages or arms, and a rounded top representing a head. The first parallel is between the angry boy and the prickly cactus. Secondly, the boy is isolated in the cactus which is isolated in the desert, and a poisonous Gila monster or lizard is drawn next to it suggesting danger. Thirdly, the drawing brings our attention to a contrast between the boy's possibly hurt feelings, and the cactus spines which hurt one when touched. This suggests that the boy is isolated and is being punished for having touched or handled the wrong sort of thing. The fact that the cactus spines are extruding from the surface of the cactus suggests the pain one feels at one's skin when touching a cactus. A further suggestion is that the punished child is angry or bristling, and refuses to let anyone touch him or he will hurt them. The cactus spines also represent a visual and outer representation of the pain or anger the child feels, which seems to be extruding from his body.

Furthermore, the upraised arms that are immobile suggest that the boy would like to strike back, but he cannot. The arms also suggest the upraised arms of the punishing parent which cannot be circumvented, parallel to the boy's anger which cannot be placated. The image is a visual metaphor for an angry person whom adults call "bristling", a metaphor which children may not understand verbally, but only in pictorial terms. Furthermore, another cactus arm protrudes in an upright arc where the boy's penis would be located, suggesting childhood difficulties with and failure to understand sexuality, as well as adult sexual touching taboos imposed upon children before the children understand sexuality or the reasons for the taboos. Hence, the title Prickly Rick, appears to be a euphemism for "prick", adult slang for penis.

Last of all I will mention the drawing of Tee Vee Stevie. This is a picture showing a baby sitting in front of a battery of television sets. The baby's eyes are made up of concentric circles suggesting the baby is dazed and non-directional. His face is actually drawn on the screen of a TV set which makes up his head. A video camera is recording the child, and is in turn wired to the television sets, so that the child is presumably watching reflections of itself on the television screen.

There are a number of interesting interpretations possible here. First of all, one can think of endless television viewing as a source of the child's being dizzy or disoriented. Also, the dazed expression suggests the child can no longer see itself or has seen too much of but one likeness of itself. It is as though the child had been chained to television and could only see its own image as a television viewer, in which case the television has been substituted for its head, brain, and motor abilities. The idea seems to be that if a child watches too much television it will turn into a television, or that the television takes over the child's mind. Hence, if we presume that television exposure may also serve an instrumental purpose, in structuring the developing child's mind, then the television provides a circular reflection of that structuring process. Furthermore, we can interpret the television as noisy and full of redundant messages, suggesting the child has become immune to messages directed at it from the mechanical adult medium. This redundancy is also apparent in everyday life in which children are endlessly told to not do certain things. Therefore, the redundant messages from the mechanical television seem to be brought into parallel with largely redundant and negative adult messages. We might view the child as being under a hypnotic trance in an isolation ward. Here, isolated television viewing and the television are substituted for parental closeness, attention, and communication.

REFERENCES

PIAGET, Jean.
    1932. *Le Jugement moral chez L'enfant* (Paris: Librairie Felix Alcan). The English trans. by Marjorie Gabain, *The Moral Judgment of the Child* (New York: The Free Press, 1965), was alone used in this essay.
    1945. *La Formation du symbole chez L'enfant; imitation, jeu et rêve, image et représentation* (Neuchâtel: Delachaux & Niestlé). The English trans. by C. Gattegno and F. M. Hodgson, *Play, Dreams and Imitation in Childhood* (New York: Norton Library, 1962), was alone used in this essay.

RIVLIN, Robert and Karen GRAVELLE.
    1984. *Deciphering the Senses* (New York: Simon and Schuster).

POPULAR POLITICAL SIGNS: JESSE JACKSON'S PRESIDENTIAL CANDIDACY AS DEPICTED IN EDITORIAL CARTOONS

Richard L. Lanigan
Southern Illinois University

Editorial cartoons in major newspapers serve a full range of axiological purposes--political, ethical, and aesthetic--as a popular form of communication. In fact, the editorial page cartoon functions as both a rhetorical and ideological apparatus (à la Roland Barthes) to blend levels of popular memory (aesthetic condition) into arguments for or against the decision (ethical condition) to support voting for (political condition) a particular candidate. A number of typical cartoons featuring Jesse Jackson's presidential campaign in the Democratic Party primaries are analyzed using a phenomenological version of the standard Hjelmslevian semiotic model as interpreted primarily by Barthes (Lanigan 1988: 223).

Contemporary phenomenologists, whether French or German, make use of the relationship that developed historically between (1) the *trivium* of logic, rhetoric (grammar), and poetic, and (2) the philosophical discipline of axiology, namely, politics, ethics, and aesthetics. The modern conjunction of these two disciplinary traditions is especially apparent in editorial page cartoons where newspapers are recording the events of the current 1988 presidential election in the United States. This is to say, the analytic pairs (1) logic/politics, (2) rhetoric/ethics, and (3) poetics/aesthetics become especially useful in analyzing the connotation, denotation, and reality levels of meaning in a semiotic system of discourse. In Barthes' terms the Signifier or "Rhetoric" system entails the logic-rhetoric-poetic component, while the Signified or "Ideology" system entails the politics-ethics-aesthetics category.

The candidacy of Jesse Jackson within the Democratic Party primary elections offers a unique situation for analysis. The candidacy invokes and evokes a popular memory of civil rights, racism, nonviolence, and the right to vote itself. This memory is a cultural artifact that embodies a semiotic system of values that emerge empirically in the editorial cartoon. It is in the cartoon that (1st) picture and (2nd) writing become a "rhetoric" (in the order of experience, the cartoon is an oral representation of power; it is Foucault's rupture of discourse). Also as a reversibility, it is in the cartoon that (1st) writing and (2nd) picture become an "ideology" (in the order of analysis, the cartoon is an inscribed representation of desire; it is Foucault's birth of discourse). In short, political memory is the popular and one of its *monuments* is the editorial cartoon (Lanigan 1984: 31-33).

Before turning to the actual analysis of several representative cartoons, let me say a word about the conjunction of theory and methodology as they bear on the analysis of political cartoons. As you may know from reading volume 69, numbers 1/2 of *Semiotica* published this year, Ray Morris (1988) wrote an excellent article entitled "English-Canadian Cartoons on Relations with France, 1960-1979". In this essay, Morris (1988: 4) covers the traditional theory of the political cartoon. He says,

> Cartoons generally appear on the editorial page, at the point of transition between the front pages, which are mainly political news, and the latter sections, which are mainly publicity material. They offer a commentary on the news, and 'domesticate' [in Goffman's sense] distant persons and events by showing them to be analogous to well-known characters, local scenes, and familiar stories.

Here, cartoons *are* popular memory! Unfortunately, this type of theoretical summary description blindly follows the journalistic ideal model of separating facts, found on the front page, from opinions, found on the editorial page, and from fantasy, found in the advertisement pages.

While Morris conveniently ignores the revolution in journalism wrought by the "new journalism" movement of the 1970s that ruptured the fact/fantasy distinction, I do not. Not only does journalistic prose blend fact and opinion on all its pages, but, journalistic page layouts, graphics, and cartoons are as opinionated as they are factual (Lanigan 1988: 103). The visual coding of prose and picture is not innocent, and it is hardly meant to be objective. As a current example and proof in point, we all chuckle at frustration of American newspapers with a Republican Party editorial view who are moving the Doonsbury cartoon strip of Gary Trudeau from the cartoon page, with high visibility, over to the editorial page with its smaller public.

In the context of Hjelmslev's theory, my point is simple. While the journalist can make efforts at separating the front page facts from the editorial page opinion, and thereby adjust connotative meaning, the same journalist cannot control the denotations. The connotative signifier will always remain a combination of fact and opinion while the connotative signified will combine fact and fantasy. There is a certain journalistic advantage in this semiotic condition, since prose must be used to decode and deconstruct the opinion or fantasy--for both are accessible only through popular fact, the stuff of prose! It is precisely to this enticing theoretical context that Morris falls victim. He constructs an elaborate digital logic model based on information theory and a modification of Riffaterre's hypogram so that prose possibility can always explain the cartoon he is analyzing. Pictures become sentences and the hypostatization is complete.

Against this prose model of cartoon reconstruction, I shall be describing the Jackson cartoons as visual icons. We shall not be concerned to formulate explanatory sentences that redescribe the message of the cartoons. Rather, we shall use the words and phrases in the cartoons as visual parts of the picture. Words in cartoons are visual memories. These words evoke visual signifiers and then invoke the related signifieds as values in those memories. Words in cartoons are, in Foucault's sense, ruptures of an ongoing discourse which specify the social desire to judge others. The graphic, pictorial part of the cartoons are likewise the birth of the social power to be the person who does the judging. In short, we are dealing with the transposition of structures, with a semiotic phenomenology. The best simple thesis for this analysis is that offered by Todorov (1970: 174) in his provocative book *The Fantastic: A Structural Approach to a Literary Genre*. He says of the fantastic made fact, "what in the first world was an exception here becomes the rule". In the journalistic context we may reformulate the thesis to read that "what is a fantastic exception announced with a page one headline or in a backpage advertisement becomes the rule of the editorial page". So, we come to the appropriateness of Barthes' model of semiotic analysis in which the "rhetoric" of the signifier plane is combined with the "ideology" of the signified plane in one system of signification. That is to say, we come to the editorial page cartoon that blends the prose of fantasy in the headlines with the pictures of fantasy in the advertising section.

In terms of a concrete analysis, I am going to discuss two cartoons that illustrate the theoretical thesis I am advancing. One cartoon is simply a picture without words. It invokes a discourse of meaning at various levels of connotation, denotation, and reality signification depending on the viewer's cultural archive of discursive referents, i.e., those everyday practices of visual and verbal signification that can be called upon for phenomenological reduction and interpretation. The second example cartoon is the reverse situation in which the complex presentation of language in the cartoon forms a universe of discourse by which to interpret the picture and, thereby, constitute a new description of experience; and, its subsequent future possibility for reduction and interpretation in the phenomenological style of embodied signification (Lanigan 1988).

The first cartoon with which I am concerned appeared in the *Star-Tribune* newspaper published in Casper, Wyoming on its editorial page for July 24, 1988. This is a simple cartoon consisting of a large image measuring seven by seven inches and printed in black/white contrast. The image is combined front face and profile of an animal head initially perceived as two donkeys head to head; one is black and the other is white. Reconsidered as a frontal view, the image is that of a horse whose face is black on one side and white on the other. This image would look like mere gray shading were it not for the image reversibility where the necks of the two profiles remind us that the black/white contrast is not for one "head" image alone. This cartoon is an example of Barthes' "rhetoric" model of signification where the connotation and reality signifier is mediated by a denotative signifier/signified (see the schema of Figure 1).

The donkey cartoon has a simple level of connotation in which the two profiles of a black donkey and a white donkey in face-to-face contiguity represent the racial conflict of Jesse Jackson as a black candidate and any of the competing white candidates. At the denotation level of analysis, the signifier of the black/white profile donkey takes on a new signified. For anyone knowledgeable about the western Unites States, the front face view of the cartoon represents a horse. The resulting reality level of signification as a signifier/signified on the expressive plane of "rhetoric" is a jackass, i.e., quite literally a half-donkey (*either* half black *or* half white is the "racial" tension) and half-horse (*both* half one political "animal" *and* half another). From the simple presentation of the image without verbal language, a discourse is invoked as a practice of choice and its meaning evoked as a context of reality. Jesse Jackson is the experiential signification of the jackass, a familiar animal specifically bred for strength but inadvertently denied a clear identity of attitude. Hence, the popular memory knowledge of the jackass as stubborn, as an unexpected form of uncontrollable strength, as the best and the worst of two possibilities, as more problem than solution, and so on. The rhetorical force of the reality signification is quite clear to the viewer. You are better off without the jackass, the combination of uniqueness that is unpredictable. You should retreat back to the donkey (allusion to smart, but weak white candidates like Wallace) or to the horse (allusion to dumb, but strong black candidates like Jackson).

The second cartoon with which I have a concern illustrates the Barthian notion of "ideology" or the place of content where perception forms an explicit discourse of value judgments. The cartoon by the editorial cartoonist MacNelly appeared in the *Chicago Tribune* and is printed in black/white and is approximately five inches

Rhetoric   **Ideology**

Connotation - Sr		Connotation - Sd	
"Wallace" [left side > "red"> revolution]		"in 68" ["red" > redneck > no revolution]	
Denotation - Sr	Denotation - Sd	Denotation - Sr	Denotation - Sd
[Candidate > truck-'in > down the road]	[for President > "Some Red" > precedent]	Reagan [center > middle of road]	"in 80" ["rainbow" > storm over > red-again > re*aga*n]
Reality - Sr		Reality - Sd	
"Jesse" [right > truck-in']		"88" {no "in"} [? red > black > revolution {on the left, the rear-view mirror has no face}]	

Figure 1. "Some Red in the Rainbow"

square. Let me describe it visually and then detail the verbal language which contextualizes it.

The image consists of an old fashion pick-up truck with rounded driver's cab and a traditional long bed with exterior fenders. The truck shows age, but endurance and utility. We see the truck from the back as it heads down a country road with trees and shrubs framing the road. There is a single male driver whose plain white neck is visible under a baseball hat and whose head is distinguished by large protruding white ears. In the cab window, we see a shotgun pointed from right to left (a dangerous practice that signals this is no ordinary driver; the gun should point the other way, left to right). The truck has one mirror on the left side with an obvious reverse of visual field to show the right; there is no image in the mirror.

The language in the picture consists of the caption for the cartoon that reads "Some Red in the Rainbow". Within the image itself, there are three bumper stickers. One is on the left side of the bumper and reads "WALLACE in '68". The other bumper sticker is on the right side and reads "Jesse '88". Both of these bumper stickers are black letter on a white background. In the middle of the truck's tailgate (a functional location displaying the up or down possibility of practice, yet designating a "view from above" as it were), there is a third "bumper" sticker that reads "REAGAN in '80". It is half black and half white; the word REAGAN is printed in white letters on a black background, while the "in '80" is in black letters on a white background. Here, the black/white color combination functions both paradigmatically (letters or numbers versus background field) and syntagmatically (one side of the bumper sticker versus the other as a reversible ground and field).

As is illustrated in Figure 1, the ideological formation of discourse constitutes itself as a combination of signifier and signified planes of connotation, denotation, and reality reference. The discursive formation in semiotic terms is quite apparent. The archive of discourse contains the semantic fields associated with the concept of a southern "redneck", that of previous presidential candidates, the idea of "color" as a factor in elections, and the general notion of re-evaluation, revolution, "reds".

At the level of connotation the "WALLACE in '68" bumper sticker functions as a connotation in which Wallace signifies (via the left side position on the bumper) the general concept of "red" as in "redneck", but a particular redneck--namely one who tried to lead a revolution in American politics not unlike the failed revolution of the southern states in the American Civil War. As a signified ideology, however, Wallace failed in 1968 (just as the southern civil war cause failed, but is remembered in popular memory). He became a redneck who could not stimulate a re-evaluation on the part of the general American voter.

At the semantic level of signifier denotation, the cartoon visually specifies that we are dealing with a "candidate for president". Candidates are people who travel down many roads in their campaigns for the country. They get out into the country to see people; the media constantly tells us where they are going, how things look "down the road" for them. Within the denotative signified, we also have the concept of the "precedent" for the "president". With a kind of phonological code of homonyms, we understand the force of the cartoon caption in which "some red in the rainbow" trades on the "some red" precedent for president, namely, George Wallace as well as allusion to the *Wizard of Oz* where one finds the rainbow at the end of the road. Fantasy offers the fact of reality as that "which will have been" to borrow a phrase from the semiotic phenomenologist, Alfred Schutz (Lanigan 1988: 203).

Turning to the ideological denotation, we have the "REAGAN in '80" bumper sticker. Recall it is positioned not on the bumper, but in the middle of the tailgate. "Reagan" is the denotative signifier and in "in '80" is the signified. Some simple contrasts inform this presidential "position". First, Reagan was elected, Wallace was "left" behind. Reagan is a middle moderate by comparison to Wallace's extremism. REAGAN in white letters reminds us of a "white" success, the positive assertion of rednecks, and contrasts with WALLACE in black letters, the negative assertion of rednecks in racial prejudice against "blacks". Reagan is middle of the road and Wallace is to be appropriately "passed on the left". Is it appropriate for Jesse to pass on the left? In the context of the signified "in '80", we are asked to recall that the 1980 election was the end of a storm, the end of the Carter administration where a southern "redneck" as president failed. The presidency is red-again (note the phonological homonym again where red-again is "reagan" and is red-again/re*--aga*n).

At the reality level of signification, we turn to the "Jesse '88" bumper sticker. As a rhetorical signifier/signified, "Jesse" is immediately differentiated from REAGAN and WALLACE; lower case letters versus capital letters. Past reality of success (REAGAN) and failure (WALLACE), both big and obvious results, are compared with the "small" possibility of "Jesse's" chance for success, for being chosen a candidate. Jesse's bumper sticker on the right side of the bumper signifies a possibility, he has a "right" to try. He can keep on "truck-in" down the presidential road--he may arrive or he may not!

In terms of the ideological reality of the signifier/signified, we have the designation of "88" on the bumper sticker. In contrast to the other two bumper stickers, the word "in" is conspicuously absent. The absence signals the presence of the current situation, of the reality that Jesse is not going to be JACKSON. The formality of MR. PRESIDENT (à la REAGAN) is not going to happen to Jesse. Yet, we do not yet know if the negative effect will also occur in which Jesse becomes just plain REVEREND JACKSON, to be held in reverence with a fond memory of a good try (à la WALLACE). In "'80" we are left with a question: Can the colors of evaluation (America's flag of Red-White-Blue) signify a new reality, the new rainbow of Red, White, and Blue/Black? Can Jesse be the first black president? The implication is no; black-blood is not blue-blood (=white). White did not change to red (Wallace failed). White returned to white (Carter failed and Reagan succeeded).

The summary of the rhetoric of ideology and its ideology of rhetoric as discursive reality is imaged in the rear-view mirror on the truck in the cartoon. The mirror has no image in it; we do not see the driver; the driver has no color, neither red nor black! The blank mirror is the image of a white person; white is the absence of color. The political message is quite unmistakable! While there is *some* red in the rainbow, there is *no* black in the rainbow!

REFERENCES

LANIGAN, Richard L.
    1984.   *Semiotic Phenomenology of Rhetoric: Eidetic Practice in Henry Grattan's Discourse on Tolerance.* (Washington, D.C.: Center for Advanced Research in Phenomenology & University Press of America).
    1988.   *Phenomenology of Communication: Merleau-Ponty's Thematics in Communicology and Semiology.* (Pittsburg: Duquesne University Press).

MORRIS, Ray.
    1988.   "English-Canadian Cartoons on Relations with France, 1960-1979," *Semiotica* 69.1-2, 1-29.

TODOROV, Tzvetan.
    1970.   *Introduction à la littérature fantastique* (Paris: Éditions du Seuil). Page reference in this papaer are from the English trans. by R. Howard *The Fantastic: A Structural Approach to a Literary Genre.* (Ithaca: Cornell University Press, 1975).

SEMIOTICS IN THE STREETS: HYPERREALISM AND THE STATE

Thomas E. Lewis
University of Iowa

> It would be <u>meaningless</u> *[to say]* that it is possible to "paint"
> "living conditions", to paint social relations,
> to paint relations of production or
> the forms of class struggle in a given society.
> But it is possible, through their object, to "paint"
> visible connections that depict by their disposition,
> the <u>determinate absence</u> which governs them.
>
> -- *(Althusser 1971: 236-237)* --

No doubt everyone will recall that for Umberto Eco there are no "signs"--only "sign functions" (1976: 49). By this Eco means the "signs" as well as their meanings result from transitory correlations established by abduction between expression planes and content planes and not from biconditional relations of equivalence and identity between signifiers and signifieds (Eco 1984: 1). Eco's shift of theoretical focus from "signs" to "sign functions" thus opens semiotics to a robust concern with context, one which, at least in principle, saves it from turning out as a formalism. Still, something more is required to fully avoid formalism, and, as Teresa de Lauretis (1984), Kaja Silverman (1983), and others have indicated, it is not to be found in Eco's *Theory of Semiotics* (1976). That "something" is a conceptual place for the subject of experience within semiotics.

In the sections of *Theory* devoted to the semiotics of communication, for example, Eco often assumes the guaranteed effects of individuals' "intentions" in his theory of sign production. Yet, in the sections devoted to the semiotics of signification, he often ignores the relevance of individuals' "experiences", "beliefs", and "desires" in his theory of codes. Eco in fact reproduces a dual*ism* of "subject and structure" in *Theory*, with "subjectivity" being represented and promoted by his theory of sign production and "structure" being represented and promoted by his theory of codes. While a certain dual*ity* of subject and structure is necessary in order to avoid reducing one to the other in an unhelpful way, only a perspective that simultaneously theorizes the "subject" as "structured" and the "structure" as "subjected" can avoid the twin *empistemological* traps of idealism or empiricism, on the one hand, and the twin *political* traps of voluntarism or economism, on the other.

To avoid these traps requires that semiotic theory recognize that *some* (one or more) "subject-form" traverses--"supports", as it were, though never in an *a priori* fashion--all instances of meaning. I take this insight of Michel Pêcheux's in *Language, Semantics and Ideology* (1975) as reminding us that "discourse" is the proper object of semiotic analysis. Here the term "discourse" registers the necessity of the subject's involvement and stake in meaning at the same time as it remains consistent with an understanding of meaning as arising processually through the interpretantial chains sparked by sign functions. Just as the impossibility of detaching meaning from context is rendered explicit by Eco when he subverts the traditional separation of semantics and pragmatics, so also the ultimate impossibility of subtracting the subject from meaning is implied (if inadequately theorized) by a number of arguments in *Theory*.

Though not derived from Eco, and certainly not without problems of its own, Pêcheux's represents one of the most successful attempts at demonstrating the impossibility of subtracting the subject from meaning. Pêcheux draws extensively on Althusser's concept of "ideological interpellation" (Althusser 1971: 127-186) in order to argue that there is no meaning independently of the "subject-form"(Pêcheux 1975: 110-129). The "subject-form" itself does not appear in Pêcheux's work as anterior (or pre-given) to meaning; that is, Pêcheux does not consider the empirical subject as the origin of meaning. Rather, Pêcheux views the subject-form as the effect of the operations of what he calls the "preconstructed" and "articulation" in various discursive formations (Pêcheux 1975: 115). By the "preconstructed" Pêcheux means the representation of the world of objects and things in discourse, and by "articulation" he means the process whereby the subject's identity is taken up in discourse insofar as the subject constitutes a necessary if not sufficient support for meaning. One easy way of understanding this distinction is to recall that for Pêcheux all meaning arises as a function of the subject-form (Pêcheux 1975: 136-137); thus, both the preconstructed and articulation entail this form. In any concrete discursive situation, however, some meanings--those of the preconstructed--represent already bound or "embedded" relations between subjects and the experiential world, whereas other meanings are put into a process of "construction"--this process entailing, among other things, the articulation of a subject-form as a support for meaning. On this view, representation is always by, to, and for a subject by means of another representation.

Clearly, such a view does not readily square with a critical problematic organized--as the announced theme of our 1988 SSA meeting, "Sign as Reality/Sign as Illusion", seems to be--around the binary opposition "realism"/"illusionism", as if the question of sign confronted us with the empiricism of pure objectivity, on the one hand, and the idealism of pure subjectivity, on the other. Rather, what it required is the philosophical perspective that has come to be known as a "strong realist" view. By *strong* realist view, and following Jeffrey C. Isaac in *Power and Marxist Theory*, I do not simply mean that things are real "in the *epistemological* sense of existing independently" of the knowing subject but that "they are real in an *ontological* sense, in that they are not necessarily isomorphic with experience at all" (1987: 45). In insisting not only upon the independence of the real but also upon the lack of isomorphism between the real and experience, "strong realism" encourages an understanding of representation and of meaning in which objectivity and subjectivity are effectively imbricated.

Thus, whatever its other problems, Pêcheux's understanding of the subject-form in relation to meaning at least enjoys the significant virtue of embodying this kind of robust philosophical realism. I find such strong realism to be fully in keeping with a semiotic understanding of representational processes as well as with

Figure 1. Richard Estes, *Hot Foods* (1967).
Oil on canvas, 48x30 in. Private collection, West Germany.

a contemporary Marxist understanding of ideological processes. Moreover, I believe that it is only from some such viewpoint--one that recognizes not only the independent existence of the "real" but also its lack of isomorphism with "experience"--that an adequate approach can be made to the study of the genre of "hyperrealism" in North American postmodernist painting.

I have always been fascinated by Richard Estes's urban landscapes, or cityscapes, and have always been disappointed by mainstream critical accounts of them. One of the better attempts at understanding what occurs in an Estes cityscape--though we shall see later why I think it misses the point--is the one offered by Charles Jencks in his book *Postmodernism: The New Classicism in Art and Architecture* (1987: 129, 132):

> An early [Estes] painting, *Hot Foods*, 1967 [Figure 1], contrasts the reflection of centrally disposed architecture with an ephemeral background of lights, advertisement and urban squalor. . . . The overall meaning of this and other urban scenes is to emphasize the rather baneful triumph of monumentality over the contingent, of frozen beauty over life. . . .

In *Alitalia*, 1973 [Figure 2], Estes has given an ultra-real New York airline agency a classical, frontal composition, a geometrically controlled layering and symmetry, one point perspective, and a host of traditional signs of stasis such as the column. . . .The urban realist accepts the ephemeral squalor of the city and presents this with monumentality, alienation, and humor.

Let me note in passing that there is very little "squalor" in Estes's cityscapes and certainly none--at least by what I understand the term "squalor" to mean--in *Alitalia* or *Hot Foods*.

Figure 2. Richard Estes, *Alitalia* (1973). Oil on canvas, 30x40 in. Smithsonian Institution, Washington, D.C. Stuart M. Speiser Collection.

Jencks's observations in fact echo a number of Estes's own statements about his cityscapes. In this light, it is worth recalling how Estes generally works. He walks around New York City photographing extensively. He then blows up his prints, selecting several to serve as "studio models" on the basis of their various strong features. Estes does not simply "paint in" the photographs, however, as a photo-realist would do; rather, he often will move a lamp post, change a shadow, etc., for the sake of composition, and he almost always intensifies colors. The most interesting thing to me about Estes's way of working is that he usually photographs on Sundays, that is, when there are not many--or, ideally, *any*--people in the streets. Thus, Estes's paintings are primarily representations of human-made environments and objects: glass, metal, concrete, automobiles, etc. As Estes himself remarks in an interview with John Arthur, his environments are "still, . . . dead. What do the French call it? . . . *Nature morte*" (Estes 1978: 19).

Significantly, Estes explains the general absence of people from his canvasses, as well as their reduction to a minor role whenever they do appear in certain works, by saying that he cares to avoid any possibility of attributing narrative qualities to his paintings (Estes 1978: 26). In particular Estes does not "want any kind of emotion to intrude" (1978: 26), since emotion would provoke identifications on the part of viewers with his painted environments: "When you add figures then people start relating to the figures and it's an emotional relationship. The painting becomes too literal, whereas without the figure it's more purely a visual experience" (1978: 26). Such identifications, of course, would likely lead to the projection/representation of a subject or subjects within the environment, which then would lead in its turn to the possibility of "narrating" his paintings. As far as I can tell, Estes eschews narrative because he desires his paintings to be exclusively about "objects" and about "painting". Notwithstanding Estes's desire on this score, I shall want to argue that his paintings are also "about" social relations.

Indeed, I am quite willing to take Estes at his word concerning his efforts to eliminate the subject from the "subject" of his paintings, just as I think that we should view Jencks as not wholly misguided in his observations about Estes's cityscapes. After all, Jencks does pick up on what he calls the "alienation" that Estes somehow "paints", and this insight maintains a certain resonance with the interpretation of the paintings that I wish to advance. There is an implication in Estes's and Jencks's interpretations of Estes's work, however, that I believe must be thoroughly resisted: namely, that the *meanings* of these paintings are unsupported by a "subject-form". I shall suggest rather that the meanings of Estes's cityscapes are in fact supported by a quite specific subject-form which, following Nicos Poulantzas in *Political Power and Social Classes* (1968), I will call the "isolation-effect" achieved by the ideological role of the capitalist state. In order to be able to claim plausibility for this suggestion, however, I must first attempt to offer a different explanation of the depopulation of the streets in Estes's cityscapes.

A promising first approach to the problem of the representation of the ideological role of the state in Estes's painting consists of recalling that much of what has been regarded as the romantic portrayal of peasant life in nineteenth-and early twentieth-century French (also Spanish) painting from the late 1850s onward can also be regarded as the portrayal of lower-class urban street life (Reff 1987: 145-146). Here the human subjects of such painting have been pictorially displaced from their urban contexts and symbolically returned to the countryside. Urban space itself is thus represented as populated by the hegemonic class subjects of the nation-state and of finance and industrial capital. These representations perform a compensatory reterritorialization of the urban or town-form as it undergoes increasing deterritorialization by the State-form during the period of industrial development of capital and resubjugation of the towns.

In *A Thousand Plateaus* (1980), for example, Gilles Deleuze and Félix Guattari appropriately suggest that capitalism triumphs through the State-form and not through the town-form. The nation-state is, in their language, a model of "realization for a general axiomatic of decoded flows" (Deleuze and Guattari 1980: 434); that is, the nation-state encodes the multiple migrations of naked labor and independent capital and thereby effects a collective subjectification (nation) which is simultaneously a process of subjection (state) (Deleuze and Guattari 1980: 456). Yet, in making their suggestion, Deleuze and Guattari also indicate the superior power of deterritorialization enjoyed by capital over the State-form itself. Thus the way is opened toward understanding the depopulation of urban space in Estes's paintings in relation to advanced capitalism, or, as Deleuze and Guattari define it, a "worldwide axiomatic that is like a single City, megalopolis, or 'megamachine' of which the States are parts, or neighborhoods" (Deleuze and Guattari 1980: 434-435).

Understanding this relation entails analysis of the formal processes of stratification operated in the depopulated environments portrayed by Estes's cityscapes. For Deleuze and Guattari (1980: 433), the State-form proceeds by making

> points *resonate* together, ... very diverse points of order, geographic, ethnic, linguistic, moral, economic, technological peculiarities. ... In other words, it forms a vertical, heirarchized aggregate that spans horizontal lines in a dimension of depth. In retaining given elements, it necessarily cuts off their relations with other elements, which become exterior, it inhibits, slows down, or controls those relations. ... In this case deterritorialization is a result of the territory itself being taken as an object, as a material to stratify, to make resonate.

I can think of no better overall description of the formal organization of Estes's *Alitalia* and *Hot Foods*.

By way of illustration, "diverse points of order" are made to resonate in each of these paintings. Geographic: Europe vs. USA in *Alitalia*; New York State vs. New York City in *Hot Foods*. Ethnic: Italian, Italian American, and (implied) all other "species" of North American in *Alitalia*: the subsumption of ethnicities in the (implied) act of consuming "fast" or "generic" food in *Hot Foods*. "Linguistic": in the case of Estes's paintings, I would point to the multiplicity of representational modes (written language, advertisements, "mirror" reflections, seeing "through" the "window", the [inferred] sounds of street traffic, the visual in general, the "painterly" in particular). Moral: "Do I want to visit Italy?" vs. "Ought I to visit Italy?" in *Alitalia*; "Is this really good for me even though it saves me time?" in *Hot Foods*, a dilemma emphasized by the ironic "storefront ad" that asserts "We're concerned with decorating your interior. Not ours." Economic: "Can I afford this?" or "Am I just on the outside lookin' in?" in *Alitalia*: the Bowery Bank, hot foods = cheap foods, the capital resources represented by the Empire State Building vs. the Bowery itself in *Hot Foods*; walking vs. riding the bus vs. taking a cab vs. owning my own car vs. flying to Europe vs. (implied) taking a European cruise (an amalgamation of both paintings). Technological: feet, wheels, and wings; glass walls supporting concrete floors and ceilings (both paintings again).

"Subjectivity" in these paintings, moreover, apparently belongs to buildings and their surfaces. Especially through there presentational interplay of surface-as--window and surface-as-mirror, it is they "who" "disseminate" "signs", ignite the sign functions. As far as represented characters are concerned, either "they" are virtually "unrepresented"--that is, "they" are represented *by their absence*--or "they" are reduced to minor roles. Those figures you can see are difficult to identify with: for example, the man in the right-to-left horizontal flow in *Hot Foods* is seemingly "intense", as Jencks has remarked (1987: 129), but it is impossible to construct a story answering the question "why?" from the painting itself. Of course, you can begin--in a *political* way that I'm not sure Estes's canvasses do much *on their surface* to encourage--to inquire into other positions of subjectivity that simultaneously are and are not represented in the paintings: who's driving the cars and buses? who's riding as passengers? who's working in the offices behind the windows of the buildings? Equally as important, or even more so: why--given that the windows seem to reflect everything else and that the original photographs must have reflected the photographer--does *my* reflection not appear? Am *I* not in the street looking at, in, and back at you/myself?

So it is that, if they achieve direct or even partial representation at all, subjects of experience in Estes's cityscapes are confined to quite limited, enclosed spaces. Subjects do not and, despite the horizontal lines that suggest their movement, cannot move because they are frozen by the compositional features of stasis and the lack of narrative qualities. And if and when they are, as it were, "represented" in the modality of an absence--which happens at the very least with the erasure of the reflected image of the viewing subject--subjects of experience are not only frozen but also absolutely isolated in and through the perspective that is offered to them.

Indeed, the representational techniques through which Estes's paintings are constructed impose fixity on the position of the viewing subject. Estes suggests, of course, that one difference between his paintings and the photographs that *inform* them is that "painting is trickery, because you can make people respond by guiding their eyes around the picture. The photograph doesn't do that . . . " (Estes 1978: 27). Yet this particular insight too easily obscures the fact that viewers' eyes may be able to move while their feet are symbolically cemented to the street or sidewalk. The difficulty of narrating the paintings, the vertical lines that serve as so many *points de capiton*, one point perspective, the erasure of the viewing subject's own image that otherwise "should" appear in the reflections (since it definitely would appear in a photograph), etc.--all these features determine that the horizontal and depth flows end up contained in a vertical dimension that offers only one position to the viewer: universalized *isolation*. You must take all this in at once while standing still: although you are in the street and on the sidewalk, you cannot move your body in, around, or through these paintings, since that would require narrative. Thus you are simultaneously omniscient and alone *in the streets*. You are God: unique, and without companions. Mr./Ms. Lonely. An individual without (a) class. (Not to mention without [a] gender or [a] race.)

Poulantzas (1968) offers a suggestive framework through which to interpret the subject-form that, along with the photographs, I am alleging to inform Estes's cityscapes. Contemporary Marxist theories of the state recognize the growing autonomy of the state owing to the differentiation of the political and the economic under capitalism. Thus, while the state performs narrowly legal functions as well as clearly repressive functions, it also performs ideological functions. The most important of these, on Poulantzas's view, it the production, dissemination, and reproduction of the "isolation effect". Isaac (1987: 173) accurately glosses Poulantzas as arguing that

> the isolation effect . . . involves three specific processes: (1) the isolation of individuals through private law, as bearers of legal rights; (2) the isolation of individuals through public law, as formally equal subjects/citizens; and (3) the "reconstitution" or "representation" of the unity of the individuals so isolated. "This means", Poulantzas writes, "that the state represents the unity of an isolation effect which is, because of the role of the ideological, largely its own effect." The political consequence of this is what Poulantzas calls the disorganization or disunification of the working class.

I believe that the same argument applies to the systemic tendency under capitalism (as well as under so-called Eastern-bloc "state capitalism", but through different modalities) to reproduce the disorganization or disunification of race, gender, and other oppressed groups.

You are a viewer of an Estes cityscape. You have an individual right to be in the street. You are not represented as such, however, because "everyone"--abstract subjects/citizens--has a right to be in the street. Would not the meaning of *Alitalia* "differ" (to be understood here in the doubled sense of *différance*) dramatically if there appeared the reflected image of a Black woman looking straight on into the airline *agency* (I have emphasized "agency" here because of the pun involved in its conceptual link to the notion of subjectivity, that is, to the site of experience and action). Would not the meaning of *Hot Foods* similarly "differ" if there appeared the reflected image of a "Bowery Bum" in the mirror/window, a homeless person who could not afford even a Double Whopper with Cheese and who might spend--at I certainly would--my last $2.35 on muscatel anyway? It would indeed *make a difference* if the subject-form supporting the meanings of these paintings were not the abstract bourgeois humanist subject--that is, the subject constructed in the form of isolated individual--and were instead the figure of the human "detritus" created as the "by-product" of the superior power of capital over the State and the towns.

And "to what?", I would reply, if it is objected that this "stylistic" change would reintroduce the body and emotion through establishing the possibility of narrative? The possibility to escape from *meaning* and thus from the *subject-form* is illusory anyway. Ultimately, precisely because the very possibility of meaning depends on the imbrication of a subject-form and an object-form as given in the variably articulated and contingent unities of subject/object that Pêcheux would call "discursive formations", you can narrate anything--even the phone book. Even more to you can narrate the phone booth, and especially the phone booths portrayed in such paintings at Estes's *Telephone Booths* (1968), *Diner* (1971), and *Hotel Lucerne* (1976). Which is why it *makes a difference* what kind of critical discourse surrounds Estes's paintings. Indeed, depending upon the interpretive frameworks that are brought to bear upon them, these absolutely marvelous cityscapes can be made to effect meanings that either conceal or reveal--reproduce or challenge--the subject-form that they themselves inform and which, in its turn, informs them. Which, as you may well imagine, is why I want to conclude with these four propositions.

In their organization of urban space-time, Estes's paintings depopulate urban streets. Subjects of experience disappear from the streets while attributes of agency are ascribed to buildings, their surfaces, and their interiors. This phenomenon could conceivably be related to the disappearance of the abstract humanist subject, but it also and more concretely can be related to the deterritorialization of production and to the compensatory articulation of a new "politics of interest" in the contemporary conjuncture of advanced capital. Ultimately, such representations may be seen as capable of generating interpretantial chains that present arguments for challenging the state on ethico-political grounds--in addition to purely economic grounds--as one of the goals of popular-democratic struggle.

REFERENCES

ALTHUSSER, Louis.
    1971.   *Lenin and Philosophy and Other Essays*, trans. Ben Brewster (New York and London: New Left Books and Monthly Review Press).
DE LAURETIS, Teresa.
    1984.   *Alice Doesn't. Feminism, Semiotics, Cinema* (Bloomington: Indiana University Press).

DELEUZE, Gilles and Félix GUATTARI.
   1980.   *A Thousand Plateaus. Capitalism and Schizophrenia*, trans. and foreword Brian Massumi (Minneapolis: University of Minnesota Press, 1987).

ECO, Umberto.
   1976.   *A Theory of Semiotics* (Bloomington: Indiana University Press).
   1981.   "The Theory of Signs and the Role of the Reader", *Bulletin of the Midwest Modern Language Association* 14.1, 35-45.

ESTES, Richard.
   1967.   "Hot Foods" (painting; reproduced as color plate in Jencks 1987 courtesy of Louis K. Meisel Gallery, NYC).
   1973.   "Alitalia" (painting; Washington, DC: Smithsonian Institution; reproduced at color plate in Jencks 1987 courtesy of Louis K. Meisel gallery, NYC).
   1978.   *Richard Estes: The Urban Landscape*, essay by John Canaday with catalogue and interview by John Arthur (Boston: Museum of Fine Arts and New York Graphic Society).

ISAAC, Jeffrey C.
   1987.   *Power and Marxist Theory. A Realist View* (Ithaca: Cornell University Press).

JENCKS, Charles.
   1987.   *Post Modernism. The New Classicism in Art and Architecture* (London: Academy Editions).

PÊCHEUX, Michel.
   1975.   *Language, Semantics and Ideology*, trans. Harbans Nagpal with references, index, and bibliography by Ben Brewster (New York: St. Martin's Press, 1982).

POULANTZAS, Nicos.
   1968.   *Political Power and Social Classes*, trans. and ed. Timothy O'Hagan (London: Verso Editions, 1982).

REFF, Theodore.
   1987.   "Manet and the Paris of Haussmann and Baudelaire", in *Vision of the Modern City, Essays in History, Art, and Literature*, ed. William Sharpe and Leonard Wallock (Baltimore: The Johns Hopkins University Press).

SILVERMAN, Kaja.
   1983.   *Subject of Semiotics* (New York: Oxford University Press).

STAMPING OUT HISTORY: NATIONAL IDENTITY ON POSTAGE STAMPS

William Pencak
Pennsylvania State University, Ogontz Campus

I decided to have some fun by entitling my paper "Stamping Out History". I could imagine people expecting some radical deconstructionist theory that history is dead, unknowable, or meaningless, only to find I am merely talking about how nations portray themselves on postage stamps. Stamps are small messages, emblems of ruling groups' self-perceptions to be conveyed to the population at home and correspondents abroad. The stamp is also a means of selectively remembering those aspects of a nation's culture it deems valuable: what is not on stamps can be an indication not only of what is unimportant, but of what the powers that be are trying to hide.

For about half the history of the modern postage stamp--which began with the famous "penny black" issued by Great Britain in 1840 bearing the likeness of Queen Victoria--that is, from the 1840s until the early twentieth century--postage stamps were for the most part small, one-colored designs bearing the images of symbols of national unity. The Queen of England, famous patriots in the United States, and imperial eagles in Germany and Russia were images found on letters in these nations decade after decade. The stamps were much like the clothes of the bourgeois gentlemen who invented them--functional, unelaborate, and in their stability reflecting the nineteenth century's belief in an order which admitted change reluctantly and believed it had found good government in the contemporary nation-state.

But even with nations issuing only a handful of stamps over much of a century, patterns emerge. Russia, with its ethnically diverse population and unpopular monarchy, never put a czar on a stamp before 1913, when a series of former monarchs appeared. The incumbent Nicholas II was only depicted on a high, seldom-used denomination. Did the avoidance of the contemporary ruler reflect timelessness, Russia the nation, or the need to downplay antagonism against the contemporary monarchy? In nineteenth-century France, too, republicans and monarchists (who could not even agree on the same flag), avoided any depiction of persons or politically loaded symbols after the demise of Louis Napoleon removed his image from stamps. The head of Ceres, symbol of the nation's agricultural productivity, and other icons representing commerce, peace, and freedom satisfied French postal needs. And although Prussia had issued stamps bearing images of its king before German unification, after 1871 the national symbols (the eagle and Germania) replaced him.

They emphasized that this was a German, and united monarchy, not merely a Prussian one--which, for the most part, it really was.

Austria and the United States did not hesitate to use people in controversial ways to appear on stamps. Emperor Franz Josef served as a symbol for uniting a dual monarchy with two different flags, governments, and sets of icons. His personal popularity as he aged was an unexpected bonus, but still one can imagine reactions to his image among the nationalists of the Balkans and Czechoslovakia. Before the Civil War, the United States kept its stamps politically neutral. Only Franklin, Washington, and Jefferson adorned the early issues--none had belonged to a contemporary political party and all had mythic status as national unifiers. In 1861, however, the Union proclaimed its idea of what the South ought to do by issuing a stamp of southerner Andrew Jackson, who had threatened to hang disunionists thirty years earlier. The Confederacy responded with an Andrew Jackson of its own, accompanied by states righters Thomas Jefferson, John C. Calhoun (the man Jackson threatened to hang), and its own President Jefferson Davis. In 1866, the nation proclaimed reunion with an Abraham Lincoln stamp, and the next thirty years witnessed the appearance of deceased Civil War heroes including Generals Winfield Scott, William Sherman, Ulysses S. Grant, and Lincoln's cabinet members Edward Stanton and William Seward. This selection reflected Northern and Republican hegemony over the Democratic South. Only with the triumph of the Democratic Party during the administration of Franklin D. Roosevelt, in 1936, did rebel leaders Robert E. Lee and Stonewall Jackson finally appear on a stamp, and in the midst of a larger series honoring the United States Army at that. If European nations usually adopted a single symbol of their more united and bureaucratized lands, the more pluralist, decentralized United States similarly employed a wider variety of symbols of unity.

Two other remarks about the early stamps. First, with very few exceptions, only the head or bust of the ruler or other figure is visible. The ruler thus appears literally as the head, or figure-head, of the nation: it is the symbol, not the individual person, which matters. Similarly, many of the early figures are portrayed using idealized Roman-style busts, sometimes wearing laurel wreaths, further depersonalizing them and investing them with the timeless, classical, and imperial Roman values which resonated deeply with the nineteenth century bourgeoisie. The United States is particularly interesting in this respect. Washington, Jefferson, Franklin, and Jackson sometimes appear realistically, sometimes as heroic busts, whereas more modern figures (except for one series of 1870-1871) are given photographic representation. Two series (1894 and 1922 to 1925) have classical busts of Jackson, Washington, and Franklin amid more modern portraits. One can argue such depictions unconsciously reflected Americans' belief that the founders were somehow members of a different, more stable, and perhaps better age.

The colonies of major powers usually issued imitations of the mother country's stamps. Congolese natives opened letters with King Leopold's image, those in India with Queen Victoria's, while Africans under French rule looked at the same symbols of agriculture, commerce, and navigation as Frenchmen at home. By the early twentieth century, however, especially after World War I as the movement to decolonize accelerated, the imperial powers granted on stamps the sort of token representation they hoped would suffice in government. It was not until 1931 that anything Indian appeared on Indian stamps--and then it was British government buildings. Only in 1935 did a non-British symbol finally appear. On one occasion, this took a significantly comic form. The first series with Philippine sites issued by the United States in 1932 contained what ought to have been the image of Pagsanjan Falls in Laguna; instead, Vernal Falls from Yosemite Park in California was substituted, but allowed to stand for the duration of the series to complete the insensitivity. Some colonies did not even have the dignity of their own stamps, especially smaller territories, but had to make do with a special imprint added to stamps of the mother country or a neighboring colony. Ever reminding Ireland of its inferior status, Britain issued no stamps for Ireland but used the regular series there. After independence, Eire took revenge by overprinting images of King George with Gaelic proclamations of independence. Such overprinting also signalled domestic revolution. Portugal and Austria, for example, temporarily blotted out the king's image as they became republics; Nasser's Egypt announced itself in 1952 with three heavy lines superimposed on the face of King Farouk.

Commemorative stamps first appeared at the end of the nineteenth century, but did so infrequently. The United States' first series was an elaborate 16-issue set in honor of the Columbia Exposition of 1893, its next in 1898 to honor the Trans-Mississippian Exposition. These early series, like those honoring the 1901 Pan-American, 1903 Louisiana, and 1907 Jamestown Expositions, honored the contemporary commemoration rather than the event itself, and were sold in connection with the expositions. Perhaps because the United States was a new nation, its identity forged in a history most Americans regarded with pride rather than as a symbol of oppression or controversy, it could issue commemoratives as the monarchies did not. Aside from the World War Victory issue, a plain three-cent purple Victory Allegory, the first commemorative in the United States strictly honoring a past event was the three-issue series of 1920 for the Pilgrims' three hundredth anniversary. Other major nations only began to print special issues in the 1920s. Britain honored the Empire in 1924, but its next commemorative, other than royal jubilees, was to rejoice at the end of World War II. Britain, the last monarchy remaining of the nineteenth century great powers, has also adopted perhaps the world's most conservative approach to issuing stamps. Commemoratives are few, always bear the ruler's image, and in many cases honor the royal family to symbolize apolitical national unity. Not until 1964 did someone outside the royal family appear on a British stamp, and it took the four hundredth anniversary of Shakespeare's birth to accomplish this. In 1965, the Labor Party buried its partisanship to recognize the contribution of Winston Churchill to the cause of civilization. France's first commemoratives honored the 1924 Paris Olympics, Spain's the hundredth anniversary of painter Francisco Goya's death in 1928. Germany entered the world stage in this respect by honoring its lost colonies at the beginning of the Nazi era, in 1934.

But it was Soviet Russia which inaugurated a new era in stamp issuance, much as it marked a new type of society. As the bourgeois democracies continued to stamp out prominent historical figures, rulers, and honor fairly innocuous and conservative patriotic events, the Communist state poured out dozens of large, colorful stamps proclaiming the message of the new regime to the nations of the world. Allegories "Severing the Chain of Bondage", of agriculture, industry, science and art, and "Russia Triumphant" replaced a 1913 series honoring the czars soon after the Revolution of 1917. Under Stalin, Russia honored contemporary workers, women, ethnic groups, soldiers, and revolutionary heroes with great frequency. Russia pioneered in "people's stamps" which hid the reality of Stalinism--the dictator did not appear on a stamp until 1946, then in tandem with Lenin--stamps as both propaganda and yet symbols of what Communism hoped to accomplish.

Sometimes stamps hide things. Stalin's pre-eminence could never have been guessed at from Russian postal history. Mussolini never adorned an Italian issue--Julius Caesar, Augustus, and Victor Emmanuel hid the dictator's hand. He finally achieved postal immortality on a German stamp of 1940 where his image joined Hitler. Hitler, on the other hand, regularly issued stamps to commemorate his birthday, among other events, a practice followed by Ghana's Kwame Nkrumah.

Spain's Franco, Indonesia's Sukarno and Suharto, and Nicaragua's Somozas have all portrayed themselves shamelessly as the essence of their country on the regular, long-term, issues of their nations.

One of the most interesting phenomena in the world of stamps is what I call postal neo-colonialism. Third World and small countries issue unnecessary commemoratives (for postal purposes) to sell to collectors in First World Countries. The stamps frequently honor First World achievements and figures. For example, Mali, one of the world's poorest lands, has honored Konrad Adenauer, Leonardo da Vinci, Louis Braille, and Pierre Curie. Mali has publicized such diverse activities as the 1979 Judo Championship in Paris, horsebreeding, contract bridge, and domimoes. Mali also honors numerous medical and technological achievements most of its population have no idea of. Guatemala honored the fiftieth anniversary of Lindbergh's Trans-Atlantic Flight, Eleanor Roosevelt (in 1973, a year of no special importance for her), and the United States moon landing. Liechtenstein and Tonga are perhaps the most famous purveyors of stamps designed for philatelic rather than postal use. The former, a small European country with 24,000 inhabitants, issues twenty to thirty stamps a year depicting art works, scenery, and the royal family, especially geared to promote tourism. Tonga, a kingdom of Pacific Islands under British protection, issues enormous stamps edged in gold leaf in various odd shapes. Someone with a sense of irony must have designed the five-issue set of 1976 honoring Tonga's friendship with Germany in the form of the Star of David.

It is possible to trace political trends within a nation such as the United States using its stamps. The first American Indian--other than Pocahontas, also the first woman on an American stamp in the 1907 Jamestown series--appeared on a 14-cent stamp in 1923, one year before Indians became American citizens and at the height of anti-immigrant sentiment. A variety of stamps honoring the 150th anniversary of the American Revolution brought forth a protest from Polish-Americans concerning the omission of their contribution. In 1931, a belatedly issued commemorative honored the 150th anniversary (in 1929) of Casimir Pulaski's death. A 1933 stamp with a group of workers (one of whom may have been President Roosevelt with a moustache) was the government's first use of a stamp to promote a contemporary program, in this case the National Recovery Administration and the New Deal. Susan B. Anthony was the first woman to appear on a stamp thanks to her own achievements--Martha Washington had previously appeared along with Pocahontas. But the timing--1936, honoring the sixteenth anniversary of the women's suffrage amendment--suggests the political clout of Eleanor Roosevelt more than a real anniversary. George Washington Carver was the first black American on a stamp; the date, 1948, fell between the integration of major league baseball in 1947 and the armed forces in 1950. American stamps now reflect the diverse wishes of the nation's interest groups, but timing can be significant. Both conservatives like Robert Taft and Dwight Eisenhower and liberals like Mrs. Roosevelt and Lyndon Johnson all had stamps within a year of their deaths, but it took until 1979 for Martin Luther King Jr. and Robert Kennedy, a decade after their assassinations, and the Democratic Presidency and Congress of Jimmy Carter's administration, to receive postal recognition.

As postage stamps have become big business throughout the world, colorful emblems to attract tourists and put a cheerful face on almost any government, it is salutary to note that stamps have made, as well as reflected, history. A Nicaraguan stamp with the image of the nation's active volcano Mt. Momotombo was distributed to United States senators at the turn of the century to encourage a Panama Canal route by supporters of the latter. In 1900, the Dominican Republic issued a stamp showing its boundary extending far into the territory of neighboring Haiti, which promoted intermittent conflict between the nations costing 15,000 lives for four decades.

(Grossman: 114). One can only wonder whether a militant image of Theodore Roosevelt in Rough Rider garb issued months before the 1959 Cuban Revolution may have unnecessarily reminded Cubans of their land's excessive dependence on the United States. Today, Sandinista Nicaragua issues stamps depicting Lincoln and Washington along with Lenin and religious leaders to convince the world it is indeed a pluralist society. Incidentally, Cuban stamps since 1962 are no longer listed in United States catalogues and cannot be legally bought, sold, or possessed in the United States. Similar non-recognition was accorded to the People's Republic of China for years. Recognition of a nation and its stamps go together semiotically.

REFERENCES

GROSSMAN, Samuel.
    1981. *Stamp Collecting Handbook* (New York: Grossman Stamp Company).
SCOTT.
    1984. *Standard Postage Stamp Catalogue* (New York: Scott Publishing Company). This standard reference on stamps is the source for most of the information in this paper.

XIX

SEMIOTIC ACCOUNTS OF LINGUISTIC CONCEPTS

"LANGUAGE AS WORK AND TRADE" AS METAPHOR

Alexander F. Caskey
The University of Chicago

To scholars working within the current theoretical frameworks of linguistic science, the ideas of Ferruccio Rossi-Landi are likely to provoke disbelief and perhaps astonishment. To give the most obvious example from Rossi-Landi's writing: that an abstract element like the phoneme could be seriously compared to the handle or the head of a hammer (Rossi-Landi 1975: 107; Rossi-Landi 1983/1968: 131-147) in the sense that both may be "worked on" to produce a more complex object (hammer, morpheme) runs counter to the theoretical advances of approximately three quarters of a century's research. To put it plainly: phonemes are not objects of contemplation for ordinary speakers; in the course of ordinary discourse, they do not (and cannot) will them into becoming morphemes or anything else. The process of speaking is at this level is purely cognitive, and thus inaccessible to introspection. On this account, the homology between language and economic activity which Rossi-Landi proposes suffers from a basic misconception about language, which linguists practicing in this decade would rush to point out. Moreover, in terms of source materials, Rossi-Landi has been highly selective and perhaps even somewhat self-serving in his reading of linguistic scholarship. It is important to note that in 1968 when *Il linguaggio come lavoro e come mercato* first appeared, that linguistic science had advanced considerably beyond Saussure and even beyond the more recent work of European structuralists, such as André Martinet, on whose work Rossi-Landi bases his homology between material and linguistic "production". While the work of Sapir and Whorf continues to be noted and cited, and deservedly so, entirely new paradigms of research, linked with what has become known as cognitive science, have surged to the forefront. The result is that, with certain noteworthy exceptions, it is not only the case that most linguists are content to look at language as a system in and of itself (*où tout se contient*, to remember the words of Meillet), they are steadfastly insistent in doing so. Such is most certainly the case of the research paradigm known as generative grammar and its several cousins, such as Generalized Phrase Structure Grammar and Lexical Functional Grammar. Other schools of thought, notably that of William Labov and his followers, have attempted to show correlations between linguistic performance and social status but never abandoning the central notion of mental representations made popular by Chomsky. Thus the idea that language could also be studied from the point of view of its actual employment or use has not found a prominent place of the agenda of linguistics in the past few decades.

This should by no means be taken to mean that such questions are without interest. Although the notion of language use, which we can with some confidence assume to be Rossi-Landi's main concern, has, to a large degree, remained outside the domain of inquiry of scholars working within most current theoretical approaches, it is a well known fact that when Chomsky first conceived the distinction between competence and performance, his intention was to derive a theory of linguistic performance, not competence. For reasons that remain in the realm of speculation, this approach was abruptly dropped with the resulting (and well-known) insistence on a rationalist (Cartesian) paradigm of inquiry. From that point on, it simply became a matter of faith among generative linguists that language as a faculty of the human mind must necessarily (and ideally) be explained as a function of cognition. To go beyond that domain would be to ask questions that were at best premature. A prime example of this kind of thinking can be found in the works of Wexler and Cullicover (1980), Berwick (1985), Pinker (1984), and other investigators whose notion of "learnability" has strong mathematical underpinnings. We are dealing in these instances and in many others similar to them with the formulaic, with highly abstract models that attempt to explain what we do without thinking, without introspection.

At the same time, however, language certainly *is* used and the study of how it is used (in the many senses of the word) constitutes, I will argue here, a legitimate domain of inquiry. Following Austin and Searle, we might strengthen our position by claiming that language, from a pragmatic standpoint, has undeniable force in the determination of real world events and that underlying that ability is a capacity, whether innate or learned, for organizing utterances into expressions which are potentially able to "get us what we want". I will leave aside here the much debated question of communication as the main function of language, noting simply that if language as it is used can have that application (and that this use can be appropriately classified) then it is perfectly legitimate to ask how language use (i.e. *communication*, or, in Rossi-Landi's term, "linguistic messages") is related to social and cultural behavior and vice versa.

This notion is by no means new; I am simply restating, in a simplified way what Boas, Sapir, Whorf, and before that, Humboldt have asserted. But I justify the restatement in the face of a disciplinary jaundice toward probings into the less than purely cognitive. The question which most eagerly calls for our attention, then, is how can there be any understanding of the ways in which an "internal" linguistic mechanism (cognitive) relates or inter-relates with the external world when the "internal" is seen as isolated and distinct? We might begin to answer if we recall, with Ferguson (1959) and Brown and Gilman (1960) that there are moments in which linguistic signs are quite consciously manipulated, and deliberately so, with the (tangible) result we are producing something. Clearly language is the tool which we are using to do this. Whether or not this type of production can rightfully be called "work" as Rossi-Landi would have it, is at this point of lesser importance. What we need to know first is how this capacity for applying linguistic expressions links to our (simple) ability to speak. Even if the phoneme in and of itself is not a "tool" and cannot be used as such, this does not preclude the possibility that there are other levels of expression which are accessible to deliberate use.

Following this notion, I would like to suggest that the phenomena studied by Ferguson (diglossia) and Brown and Gilman (pronominal address) are actually somewhat more complex than they may initially appear: in each case, we are witnessing a special form of coding and decoding which presupposes an ability to complete a communicative act. To change languages does no good if we know that our listeners will not be affected; to employ a pronoun which stresses social inferiority will have no affect unless the addressee shares the same belief about that linguistic form. This leads us to the same crossroads at which Rossi-Landi launched his language/economic production homology: it is obvious that there is an interaction but not at all apparent how to capture generalizations about a type of interaction that seems to leap across distinct categories.

One answer, with possible appeal to the cognitive scientist/linguist, would be to posit a modular conception of speech activity (language use) in which output could be defined as the interaction of several distinct, independent modules, each with their own independent organization. This is precisely the orientation which Sadock (1985) has followed in developing Autolexical Syntax which has shown promising results in explicating hitherto opaque relationships between complex morphological structures and syntax. Following this kind of thinking, we could say that "social awareness" (left in this loose definition for the time being) could in principle share a modular relationship to a particular linguistic form or structure. The form in question, for example, an informal pronoun, functions simultaneously as a "pure" linguistic unit (in terms of sound segments, morphological constitution) but when used in a specific social context gains a special meaning. The choice of forms is not altogether arbitrary; the speaker knows that some are appropriate and that others are not. Thus the linking that takes place when the form is chosen is the collaborative result of several operations, not just one.

Quite obviously, as is the case with any linguistic model, memory is an important component: forms and structures must be remembered and applied in a similar way for meaning to be preserved. Similarly, in the instance of Brown and Gilman's work on pronominals, it is clear that a correlation between a determined form and its social impact must be learned, and learned in a different way from which the (linguistic) form itself was acquired. Consider also that the values which underlie language choice themselves may be highly complex, fluctuating or even idiosyncratic to a certain extent. Yet despite this complexity, the modularity of language use is quite simply the product of several inter-relating forces, and we relieve ourselves of the need to explain them all as social or all as purely linguistic (cognitive). What matters is the interface and it is to the rules or principles governing that interaction that our attention should ideally be directed. While it is beyond the scope of this paper to advance a complete set of principles which might comprise a modular theory of language use, it seems reasonable to suggest that such a goal could be attained.

For the purposes of what I am arguing here, it should be apparent that a conception of "linguistic production" (Rossi-Landi's term) in which an (abstract) linguistic process is forced to fit into a (concrete) schema (material production) with which it has very little in common is in fact an unnecessary and even uncomfortable form of gymnastics, given the essential formal and structural divergence between the two processes. It would be far more productive to consider the interface between linguistic behavior and socioeconomic behavior, rather than to force equivalence when they are essentially disparate. To give a relevant example, Rossi-Landi's transference of terms from the world of material production to the domain of language use ("linguistic worker", "linguistic money", "linguistic need", etc.) follows the well-known procedure of metaphor: transposition from source to target. But these metaphors are at best only marginally acceptable (in the linguistic sense) in that they lack a reliable or familiar mediating term at any level of analysis (conceptual, semantic, etc). Thus, at the simple level of metaphor, Rossi-Landi's homology has already gotten into trouble, words in our lexicon are not like money in the bank (as he claims) since we can't manipulate lexical items the way we can our balance, nor can we count them by ourselves with any sort of accuracy. It may not be then a simple coincidence that felicity conditions do not obtain for the (metaphoric) correlation *Language = Work and Trade;* their absence can be seen as representative (inversely metaphorical?) of other flaws in the basic presuppositions Rossi-Landi makes about his subject.

But it is precisely in the interaction between the "goal-directed" and "indexically signifying" functions of language, as Silverstein (1979) has identified them, that we can find a clue to what may be a highly representative case of modular nature of language use: the felicitous instantiation of metaphor. Metaphoric process as I have called it (Caskey 1987) draws on many human capacities: the ability to recognize, analyze, and compare distinctive traits and features in disparate types of phenomena, and finally to "translate" them into language. Whether the categories involved are always available for introspection is certainly a question which Whorf raised for non "SAE" languages, in my own findings, it appears possible at least that metaphoric process may indeed be operative at levels beyond our immediate awareness. To say that someone is "up in the air" may be one thing; to say (as frequently seen in computer magazines) that "our new product will be shipping soon" is quite another. In the second instance, it is understood quite clearly (even if not universally applauded as correct stylistic usage) that the new product will be shipped by the company in question. The noun phrase "our new product" clearly occupies the subject position in the sentence, yet it is obviously intended to be the object of the transitive verb ‚to ship.' Consider another example, collected from WLAK Radio in Chicago in May of 1987: "The Cadillac test-drives spectacular." Here again, the subject position is filled by the logical object, in perfect violation of our real-world knowledge of the fact that cars simply do not drive themselves. That the verbs 'to ship' and 'to drive' lend themselves to this kind of transformation suggests that the subject-object relationship has been mediated by their lexical properties and that this is a kind of metaphorical process which has the potential to illustrate, perhaps with some degree of success, that our different kinds of knowledge, analytic capacity, and reasoning ability, in complementation to purely cognitive components, function in modular combination, that they interact with categories, both linguistic and extra-linguistic, and that language use in its social sense may find a more natural explanation than that which Rossi-Landi's pioneering effort has left us.

REFERENCES

BERWICK, Robert C.
    1985. *The Acquisition of Syntactic Knowledge* (Cambridge, MIT Press).
BROWN, Roger and Albert GILMAN.
    1960. "The Pronouns of Power and Solidarity", in *Style in Language*, ed. T. A. Sebeok, (Cambridge: MIT Press), 253-276.
CASKEY, Alexander F.
    1987. "Linguistic Perspectives on Metaphor" Manuscript (Chicago).
FERGUSON, Charles.
    1959. "Diglossia", *Word* 15, 325-40.
PINKER, Stephen.
    1984. *Language Learnability and Language Development* (Cambridge: Harvard University Press).
ROSSI-LANDI, Ferruccio.

1968. *Il linguaggio come lavoro e come mercato*. The English translation, *Language as Work and Trade* (South Hadley: Bergin & Harvey, 1983) was used in this work.
1975. *Linguistics and Economics* (The Hague: Mouton).
SADOCK, Jerrold.
1985. "Autolexical Syntax: a Proposal for the Treatment of Noun Incorporation and Similar Phenomena", *Natural Language and Linguistic Theory* 3, 4.
SILVERSTEIN, Michael.
1979. "Language Structure and Linguistic Ideology", in *The Elements: A Parasession on Linguistic Units and Levels*, ed. Paul R. Clyne, W. Hanks, and C. Hofbauer (Chicago: Chicago Linguistic Society).
WEXLER, K. and P. CULLICOVER.
1980. *Formal Principles of Language Acquisition* (Cambridge, MIT Press).

THE SEMIOTICS OF MAYAN IMPERATIVES

Joseph DeChicchis
University of Pennsylvania

Wittgenstein's allegory of the slab in the *Investigations* (1945) convincingly illustrates the dichotomy of form and function in language. Having accepted the author's invitation to embark on a cognitive journey, the reader experiences the changing role of *slab*, ostensibly an English noun, which sees duty as a request, an order, a report, and an assertion. The full functional range of a word is difficult to foresee, much as is the importance of a chesspiece, which may change dramatically throughout the course of a single game.[1] We are struck by the multiplicity of use for linguistic forms. How does a semioticist characterize this essential fact about language? The Peircean linguist recognizes the multiplicity of phonetic shapes qua representamina which mediate the relation between a particular pronunciation and the linguistic form it signifies. Similarly, each linguistic form is situated in a network of situational usages which mediate the relation of form to function.

Today, we shall consider some linguistic forms which are often presented under the rubric of imperative. Beginning with a short explication of imperative function, we will proceed through a short presentation of Spanish and English imperative forms to a description of the Mayan imperative system, using examples from Kekchi and Chorti.

Many different linguistic forms have been called imperatives, and they are usually described vaguely, often by inviting an analogy with an open list: a command, request, suggestion, consent, entreaty, etc. (Pei and Gaynor 1954: 97). Such lists hardly count as definitions, but by reviewing them and by considering tokens of prototypical imperatives, we come to recognize certain characteristic functional features. First, every imperative is a stimulus initiated by the speaker in the hope of eliciting a particular response (verbal or nonverbal) from the hearer (Jespersen 1933: 248, paragraph 23.8_4, calls this a "request"). Second, an imperative has deontic force in that it charges the hearer with the responsibility of responding appropriately. We may contrast this with a question, which merely conveys the speaker's desire for information, without encumbering the hearer with the onus of providing that information. To be sure, a question charges the hearer to reply (one should not ignore a question), but the reply need not supply the information sought by the speaker (one may excuse oneself for a lack of knowledge). On the other hand, an informative reply is only sometimes an appropriate response to an imperative, whereas at other times it is not (contrast 1 and 2).

(1) *Tell me about the Dodgers.*

(2) *Shut up!*

The nature of the imperative as a stimulus for a hearer's response explains a salient formal characteristic of Spanish imperatives. As in other Romance language, many Spanish verbs show Imperative Mood forms which are unique within the verb paradigm.

(3) *¡Ve!* "Watch!"

(4) *¡Bebed!* "Drink!"

(5) *¡Vámonos!* "Let's leave!" (Contrast: *¡Vamos!* "Let's go!" and *¿Nos vamos?* "Shall we leave?")

The uniqueness of these forms within the Spanish verb system permits us to say that in Spanish the imperative is grammaticized. All speakers, of course, are capable of imperative utterances, but not all languages are like Spanish in providing specialized forms for this purpose. It is noteworthy that such forms exist only in the second person singular and plural and in the first person plural, which are precisely those categories which can mark the hearer of an utterance, for Spanish does not have separate pronouns for inclusive and exclusive senses of "we". In addition, Spanish is routinely said to have polite (or formal, as opposed to familiar) imperatives, but the forms are not distinct within the verb paradigm. The *usted* and *ustedes* forms of the verb, which are identical to the third person singular and plural forms, are used (euphemistically) in polite or deferential address, and the third person subjunctive verb forms are used similarly in polite imperatives.

(6) *¡Vaya!* "Go."

(7) *¡Véanme!* "Watch me."

Unlike Spanish, the English imperative does not constitute a separate grammatical category. In other words, no English verb form is necessarily imperative in meaning. English imperatives are often thought to be subjectless second person forms.

(8) *Don't (you) be seen!*

(9) *(you) Feel better.*

Such an analysis of English imperatives is incorrect, for we can find examples of imperatives which do not show reduced second person subjects.

(10) *(God) Bless you!*

(11) *Confound you!*

As in the analysis of polite imperatives in Spanish, we must recognize an identity of form in the face of functional multiplicity. In his profound study of English verb constructions, Martin Joos (1964) identified the verb form featured in common

English imperatives as the "presentative". The presentative is formally distinguished by its optional coöccurrence with object pronouns in subject position (as in 14 and 15).

(12) *Ask me no questions, I shall answer none. Prove your case.* (p.34)

(13) *... here was a man ..., come to think of it, brave enough to refrain from tidying up the ambiguities of fact.* (p. 34)

(14) *What we can do is John leave and me pick it up.* (p. 34-35)

(15) *What, me worry?* (p. 35)

(16) *Feed a cold and starve a fever.* (p. 36)

The presentative is not imperative in meaning; rather, the presentative is available for use with imperative meaning (p.35). In English, the imperative is a functional notion; the imperative is not a grammaticized verb tense. The presentative, which is used to show imperative function, is also available for other uses in English. In fact, the broad usage of the presentative may be attributed to its noncoding of temporal and participant information, much like the infinitive. In this regard, we note that the English presentative is less deictic than the Spanish imperative: the distinct singular and plural forms of Spanish partially code for the number of addressees in an utterance situation, whereas the invariant English form is in this respect situationally independent.

Like Spanish, Kekchi has a grammaticized imperative. The thematic, or conjugation, class of every Spanish verb can be determined from its second person plural imperative form. Proto-Mayan had a thematic system which governed the derivational patterns of verb roots. The best illustration of this thematic system is in Chorti Mayan.[2] Chorti verb stems divide into two categories, called U and A. The two categories are distinguished formally in terms of the inflectional and derivational affixes which their verbs take, and they are semantically distinguished in terms of the participant structure of the events which they denote. The Chorti imperative form suffices to determine the category of every Chorti verb. A root imperative which ends in *en* is of category A. The rule is trickier for imperatives which are based on derived stems: a causative imperative, which ends in *sen*, is a U verb: all other stem imperatives ending in *en* are of category A. Although its thematic system is less robust and it has lost the U/A category distinction, Kekchi preserves many of the thematic endings found in Chorti.

The description presented here reflects data from two sources. First, 223 imperatives have been confirmed by a native speaker of Kekchi from Belize (DeChicchis and Tush 1988). Second, I have reviewed imperative tape-recorded forms which occur in folk tales and in life narratives.[3] Kekchi imperatives occur without pronominal prefixes (much as second person singular Spanish imperatives lack the normal *s* suffix), although they can have absolutive suffixes. Based on their phonological shape, the formations which function as imperatives in Kekchi fall into six rough categories:

(i) CVC verb roots: *ban* "cure him!", *top* "mash it!"

(ii) Derived stems ending in *h*: *abih* "listen!", *bitoh* "carry it!", *moq'oh* "hold it!"

(iii) Derived stems ending in *n: ajen* "wake up!", *cunlaan*, "sit down!", *hilan* "rest!", *kutlan* "stand up!"

(iv) Derived stems ending in *b: cirib* "stretch it out!", *lukub* "hang it up!", *pec'eb* "open it!"

(v) Derived stems ending in *s: k'iires* "nurse it!", *tolk'os* "turn it over!", *z'aqobres* "complete it!"

(vi) Forms with final *q: abiomaq* "listen!", *buybutq* "fill it to the rim!", *nimaq* "make it big!"

Hereafter, I shall refer to these imperative formations as Root, H, N, B, S, and Q, respectively. The characteristic suffix consonants, in the case of the H, N, B, S, and Q formations, may be preceded by various vowels, but I will not here go into the details of these minor morphophonemic alternations. In the remainder of this paper, I shall identify the meaning associated with four of these categories (Root, N, B, and S). The status of these meanings as artifacts of general Mayan cosmology will be suggested by my identification of cognates in Chorti. Also, I will show that the Q imperatives are not grammaticized imperative forms, but that they are optative forms which are often pressed into service as imperatives. Finally, I will point out the difficulty of giving a unified semantic analysis for the H imperatives, and I will advance a comparative hypothesis as to why this is so.

All Root imperatives are transitive in meaning. The hearer is told to affect something. A Root imperative which is not embedded in a direct quotation is a deictic; it points out the object which is to be affected. Moreover, the degree to which the utterance compels the hearer to respond accordingly is greater than for any other locution. In Peircean terms, we might call this the indexical force of the imperative, assuming that the hearer's response to an imperative is more causal behavioral than cognitive. The first person singular absolutive can be suffixed to a Root imperative in order to indicate that the speaker is to be the "affected" object,

(17) *il*
see
"look at it"

(18) *il-in*
see-me
"look at me"

The N imperatives are intransitive in meaning. The hearer is told to do something. Because it makes no third person reference, its deixis is limited to relations of the addressee. The force with which the hearer is compelled by an N imperative is comparable to that of the Root imperative. The Kekchi N suffix corresponds generally to Chorti's A stem imperative suffix *en*, but a certain amount of misfit has still to be explained analogically.

(19) *taq-en il-on been li-kabl*
go.up-N look-N top the-house
"go up and see upstairs!"
(or better: "go! look! upstairs!")

All B imperatives are transitive. The sense of a B imperative is more molecular than that of a Root imperative, and the semantic feature which all B imperatives share is the notion of serving as an instrument for something. The hearer is told to "make it be so". The B forms are cognate with the Chorti instrumental suffix *p'*.

The S imperatives are also transitive. Again the sense is molecular, and the common feature is causality. The causal notion which the S forms encode is weaker and less direct than that of the instrumental B forms. An S imperative tells the hearer to "have it be so". In addition, a B imperative implies a state change in the affected object, whereas the S imperative suggests that the affected object is internally intact. Perhaps a better way to state the difference would be to say that a B, but not an S, imperative implies an essential change in the object. Compare the following B and S formations:

(20) *ac'ab*
reduce-B
"make it (the fever) be lower!"
(A lowered fever is no longer a fever.)

(21) *k'ipib*
bend-B
"bend it!"
(The straightness or the particular curvature of a bar may be an essential characteristic.)

(22) *balq'us*
roll.over-S
"roll it over!"
(A rock which has rolled remains a rock.)

(23) *k'iires*
nurse-S
"nurse him!"
(An infant is an infant before and after it is fed.)

This difference in causal notion is difficult to express in English, but it is important to realize that this difference is grammaticized in Kekchi, By way of illustrating a dimension of meaning which many English speakers (but not Kekchi speakers) find basic, we note that the Kekchi pronominal system shows no sex or number distinction parallel to English *he, she, it, they*. Still, Kekchi marks a nuance of causal meaning which English speakers may find difficult to grasp. The Peircean may profitably parallel the distinction between efficient (kind of like B) and final (kind of like S) causation.

Kekchi's Q imperative is not a true imperative formation. Frequently, it is used as an imperative, especially when the speaker is addressing more than one person. In fact, the use of the Q forms in this latter sense is so widespread that a reputable grammar of Kekchi analyzes *ilomaq* as a second person plural imperative of *il*, "see", without discussion (Stewart 1980). A review of actual speech reveals that Q formations can be addressed to both singular and plural addressees, that they can take second person absolutive suffixes, and that they have functions other than imperative. The Q suffix is actually an irrealis marker, and the suffix *om* in *il-om-aq* is a completative suffix meaning "it has been done". The proper analysis of *ilomaq* is given in 24, and supporting examples follow.

(24) *il-om-aq*
see-COMPLETATIVE-IRREALIS
"may it be seen"

One person speaking to another in an enchanted cave:

(25) *il-om-aq   can*
see-COMPLETATIVE-IRREALIS QUOTATIVE
"'may it be seen', he said"

il
see
"look at it!"

a'in   ooro   can
this   gold   QUOTATIVE
"'this is gold,' he said"

Having heard about a new student, a teacher said:

(26) *k'am-om-aq   caq   arin*
bring-COMPLETATIVE-IRREALIS back here
"may he be brought here"

x-in-ko'o
PAST-I-go
"I went"

Other examples include:

(27) *us-aq-at*
good-IRREALIS-you
"be good!"
(literally: "may you be good")

(28) *kam-q-at*
die-IRREALIS-you
"may you die"

(29) *kutlan-q-ex*
die-IRREALIS-you.PLURAL
"stand up!"

    The H imperatives are semantically diverse. Nearly all are transitive in meaning, but a few are clearly intransitive. In addition, a handful of these formations are causative and have an embedded S suffix; one even has an embedded B suffix. The identity of the Chorti cognate is less certain, but we may speculate that it is the U stem imperative suffix. The Chorti form consists in most cases of a root vowel copy suffixed to the verb; however, an *n* is occasionally suffixed. Speaker confusion and a general correspondence of Chorti *n* to Kekchi *y* may figure into the ultimate explanation of the H forms, but further comparative research is needed to assess these possibilities.

The semiotic categories of the imperative field can vary from language to language. Counting only grammaticized categories, we note that there is none for English, that there are two for Spanish, and that there are at least four for Kekchi. We observe functional extension for each of these languages, whereby a form from a nonimperative category is used as an imperative in context. For English, this is the only way to utter imperatives; for Spanish, it is the polite way; for Kekchi, it is also a euphemistic alternative. The feature of variation in the grammaticized Spanish imperative is the plurality of the addressee. In Mayan, the primary dimension of variation involves transitivity and the essential nature of the agent's affect on the object, which is all the more intriguing to the extent to which the Mayan distinction cleaves according to the distinction of efficient and final causation.

In emphasizing functional equivalences, contemporary linguistic theory tends to miss the striking dissimilarities of English, Spanish, and Kekchi categories. On the other hand, previous biases in American linguistics concentrated on structural differences to the exclusion of function. Wittgenstein came to recognize that the structural conclusions of the *Tractatus* (1922) were not wrong but pointless outside a context of usage. Similarly, we must look for a middle ground in linguistics. Speech act theories seem to ignore clear evidence of Whorfianism in language, while structuralist descriptions seem to deny the very threads of universalism which make linguistic comparison interesting. The recognition and the evaluation of these extreme traditions of linguistic analysis is enabled by a semiotic perspective.

NOTES

[1] John Searle, who objects to Wittgenstein's statement that there are countless different kinds of word use, has proposed that there are only five kinds of "illocutionary acts": assertives, directives, commissives, expressives, and declarations (1979: vii-viii). In fact, Searle appears to be kicking a straw man, for he allows an unspecified number of distinct acts to be categorized according to this taxonomy. Accepting his invitation to compare his research program with taxonomic biology, we note that there are now over 3,000 named species of beetles (*Scarabaeidae*) and that entomologists believe that more will be discovered. Speech act research may similarly continue to discover new speech acts. Considering that the major categories of lifeforms have been reworked by biologists faced with new facts and better understanding, we may further suppose that the present taxonomy of speech acts will change as our knowledge of illocutionary acts improves overall. It is this open-endedness which is the point behind Wittgenstein's characterization and which lay behind the analogy he drew with mathematics.

[2] John Fought, who described the Chorti thematic system in great detail (1967), has long suspected that the Chorti thematics were reflexes of the protolanguage. My work on Kekchi imperative formations turned up "cranberry" morphs cognate with the Chorti thematics. This past winter, in a fortuitous evening's discussion, the significance of my discovery as evidence for his comparative hypothesis became clear to us. Professor Fought's spring seminar on American Indian languages directed a search for cognate thematics in other Mayan languages. So far, good cognates have been identified for Kekchi, Yucatec, and Ixil, and their distribution rules out the possibility of borrowing. We are now preparing a listing of these items, together with our full argument for a thematic system in Proto-Mayan, for publication.

[3] Transcriptions of these tapes are in the computer text base of the University of Pennsylvania Center for Language Analysis. It is a pleasure to acknowledge the Institute's support of my Kekchi research.

REFERENCES

DeCHICCHIS, Joseph and Faustino TUSH.
    1988. *Kekchi-English English-Kekchi Dictionary* (Philadelphia: manuscript).
FOUGHT, John.
    1967. *Chorti (Mayan): Phonology, Morphophonemics, and Morphology* (New Haven: Yale University Ph.D. dissertation).
JESPERSEN, Otto.
    1933. *Essentials of English Grammar* (University, Alabama: University of Alabama Press, sixth printing, 1981).
JOOS, Martin.
    1964. *The English Verb: Form and Meanings* (Madison: University of Wisconsin Press).
PEI, Mario A. and Frank GAYNOR.
    1954. *A Dictionary of Linguistics* (Totowa, New Jersey: Littlefield, Adams, and Co., 1980).
SEARLE, John R.
    1979. *Expression and Meaning: Studies in the Theory of Speech Acts* (Cambridge: Cambridge University Press).
STEWART, Stephen.
    1980. *Gramática Kekchí* (Guatemala: Editorial Académica Centroamericana).
WITTGENSTEIN, Ludwig.
    1922. *Tractatus Logico-Philosophicus* (London: Routledge and Kegan Paul, 1981 edition of original German with facing-page English translation by C. K. Ogden).
    1945. *Philosophical Investigations: Part I* (New York: MacMillan, third edition of English translation by G. E. M. Anscombe, 1958).

SPEAKING AS SIGNS OF EMBODIMENT:
JAPANESE TERMS FOR SELF-REFERENCE AND ADDRESS

Michiko Hamada

Speaking: from Substitution to Embodiment

The topic of language has been the central focus in various fields such as philosophy, psychology, sociology, anthropology, artificial intelligence, literature, and so on, not to mention speech communication and linguistics. And, most of us agree that language is essential to successful human communication. Then, we should question in what sense it is essential? Our common knowledge says that if we do not have language, we cannot transmit events or our thought, and, thus no smooth communication is possible. The point we should not overlook in this common knowledge is that some kinds of events or thoughts exist for themselves prior to the act of speaking. To put it another way, there is a clear separation between "signifier" and "signified", and the "signifier" has only the function of substituting for the "signified" which we already have.

Let us see two views of communication which are based on this common knowledge. If we assume that there is a practical event preceding the act of speech, on the one hand, human communication is degraded to communication between machines or at best between guinea pigs barely living in a laboratory setting. The famous linguist Bloomfield bases his linguistic theory on a Skinnerian-like behavior psychology and holds that our linguistic behavior can be explained without any internal factors. Here, the act of speaking is a part of stimulus-response relationship. We human beings are dominated by principles of causality in the natural world. Accordingly, there is not subjectivity involved in this view of communication. On the other hand, what would happen to our communication if we consider language as a transmitter of our thought? Suppose John and Mary are communicators. John has his own thought in his mind and sends it to Mary by using language. Mary listens to what John says and tries to understand his meaning. In this process, all Mary can do is to *guess* at what John's thought is by using an analogy between what John says and Mary's own experience of having a thought when she has said the same thing. Communication in this sense gives the listener no more than what he or she has already had in his or her own mind. Therefore, no new signification occurs. All we have is only a monotonous repetition of the same thinking. Language becomes just a clothing of thought.

A first glance, these two views of communication seem to be opposite each other. However, they share the same ground, which is, the static view of language. The former model has the orientation of "empiricism" where there is no speaking subject. The latter has the orientation of "intellectualism" where we have only thinking subjects. Merleau-Ponty (1945: 177) criticizes both of them by saying that they ignore the significance of the act of speaking. Since they only deal with already sedimented language, they miss the moment when the genesis of the meaning takes place, which prevents them from seeking open possibilities for communicating with others.

To break up this closed communication and recover human nature in our communication, we should recognize the existence of the speaking subject in Merleau-Ponty's concept of "embodiment". The "body", for Merleau-Ponty (1945: 141, 203), is not a physical object, but "an open system of an infinite number of equivalent positions directed to other ends", and "the theory of the body is already a theory of perception" in his philosophy. The "body" operates as the field (sign system) connecting the core (signified system) which is myself as consciousness or my experience and the horizon (signifier system) which is the other or the other's experience. Thus, the "body" as the "anchorage" (1945: 144) (sign) is "inhabiting" (1945: 139) the world (signified) and "aiming at" (1945: 144) the world (signifier). There is no meaning of the world without the operation of the "body". This condition of the "body" is called the "embodiment" of a person.

To see how Merleau-Ponty's concept of "embodiment" gives us a way out from the static view of communication, we should look at the communication phenomenon of imitation in young children. For instance, let us think of a baby smiling back when someone smiles at the baby. Does the baby "reproduce" the smile he or she sees in the other by depending on the analogy between the other's visual face and the feeling which the baby has of his or her face? No, he or she does not. For it is impossible for the baby to have "the other's internal motor feeling of his or her face" and "an image of him/herself smiling" (Merleau-Ponty 1960: 116). The only way to solve this problem is to consider that, in the act of imitation, the baby *embodies* and *realizes*, with his or her own body, the other's conducts or gestures. The other lives in the child's smile and the child lives in the other's smile. Here, the body becomes "one system with two terms (my behavior and the other's behavior) which functions as a whole" (Merleau-Ponty 1960: 118). As the child grows older, he or she learns to distinguish himself/herself from others and adopt his or her own perspective. However, even in adult life, the lack of differentiation is never completely eliminated and remains as the latent corporeal condition of conscious experience (Merleau-Ponty 1960: 138).

When we comprehend the meaning of an other's gesture, this "corporeal schema" plays the essential role, in the sense that we actually *embody* the person who is making the gesture. Seeing an other's angry gesture, I do not have to think what the gesture represents, or what motivates it. I do not recall the feelings I had when I used the same gesture and "guess" how the other feels behind the gesture (Merleau-Ponty 1945: 184). For, the other's trembling fist becomes mine in the "embodiment" experience. Here, the anger as meaning and the angry gesture are an inseparable signification. "The gesture does not make me think of anger, it is anger itself" (Merleau-Ponty 1945: 184). This *oneness* of meaning is expressed (signified) and expression itself (signifier) is the very essence of the practice of speaking. That is why Merleau-Ponty (1945: 184) argues that "the spoken word is a gesture, and its meaning, a world."

To grasp the relationship between speech and gesture in more detail, we most note Merleau-Ponty's two existential modalities of speech (1945: 178); "speech speaking (parole parlante)" and "speech spoken (parole parlée)". They are also called "authentic speech" and "sedimented speech" respectively. The former is the speech which "formulates for the first time" and the latter, "second-order expression, speech about speech, which makes up the general run of empirical language." Merleau-Ponty's concept of "embodiment" experience takes place in the modality of "speech speaking" or "authentic speech". At this existential level, the gestural notion of sign, which is based on our latent corporeal force, is extended to the level of speaking. And, we face the genesis of new meaning by transcending already available meaning. It is this authenticity of speaking that gives birth to the rapture and fulfillment of human life. On the other hand, the "speech spoken" or "sedimented speech" consists of "constituted systems of vocabulary and syntax, empirically existing 'means of expression'" (Merleau-Ponty 1945: 196). It is nothing more than "the repository and residue of acts of speech" (Merleau-Ponty 1945: 196) and "the opportune recollection of a pre-established sign" (Merleau-Ponty 1960a: 44). Since there is no creative aspect to this modality, it allures us to the static view of language.

According to Merleau-Ponty, the dialectic between these two modalities of speech actually exists in the act of speaking. The moment we have a "speech speaking", we destroy the modality of "speech spoken" while fulfilling a new signification simultaneously, and the next moment, this "speech speaking" loses freshness and leaves its residue in the "speech spoken". In brief, sedimentation occurs. Here, the "speaking subject", neither the "functional object" nor the "thinking subject", witnesses the genesis of the prodigious meaning; the "speaking subject" outstrips what he or she has thought before and accomplishes a new thought. That is why we often have such experiences as being choked with tears, feeling like jumping around with joy, or bursting into laughter by spoken words. As we have already discussed, this process is the experience of "embodiment" and, thereby, the new signification it creates is the gestural meaning.

Thus, our view of communication completely runs counter to the static view of communication. The language we are focusing on is neither a connection between a stimulus and a response in causal relations nor a tool to transmit ready-made thought. The reason why we attach great importance to language in human communication is that it provides us with the possibility for overcoming the dichotomy between subjectivity and objectivity. Speech is "a total structure, a system by which one can attain communication with other:" "I exist through language in a relationship with other" (Merleau-Ponty 1964: 69). Next, we will see whether communicators actually have the experience of "embodiment" by observing how Japanese referential terms are used in daily interpersonal communication.

Japanese Terms for Self-Reference and Address

"Who am *I* and who are *you*?" We hear the voice of a confused person who has started learning to speak Japanese. In the Japanese language, the definite and stable *I* as in English does not exist anywhere. Its equivalents seem to be always in flux as if Japanese people's identities are floating. According to Suzuki (1973: 115), Japanese terms for self-reference and address can be divided into three categories; (1) "terms for self-reference": "words used by the speaker with reference to himself", (2) "address terms": "words used by the speaker with reference to the addressee", (3) "terms of reference": "words referring to others who appear in dialogues". The reason why these terms are not called pronouns is that Japanese people do not necessarily use pronouns when they refer to themselves and address somebody.

To take a brief look at the actual use of the referential terms, let us see the following dialogue in a daily communication situation:

Dialogue[1]

Taroo, who belongs to a baseball club in his high school, receives a telephone call from his *koohai* [junior], Takashi.

Takashi: *Senpai* [Senior}, *boku* [I] am now calling from a public telephone close to (my) house. Ø HAVE lost the key for (our) house and have been waiting for somebody to come home for more than two hours.

Taroo: Oh, (that's) terrible! *Senpai* [Senior] can do something (for you). Soon *ore no* [my] family is going to have supper, so come to *ore no* [my] house. Ø can eat together. Later, Ø can call *omae no* [your] home.

Takashi: But, (is it) all right?

Taroo: Of course.

Takashi: *Senpai* [Senior] is kind. Ø will be on ONE's way to *senpai* [senior]'s home soon.

After talking with Takashi, Taroo talks to him mother, Keiko.

Taroo: *Okaasan* [Mother], *koohai* [junior] has lost (his) house key and is in trouble, so Ø told him to come here and have supper together.

Keiko: Oh, that's good. *Okaasan* [Mother] made too much stew tonight forgetting *otoosan* [father] is going to be home late tonight, and was wondering what to do with it. Then, *oniichan* [elder brother], would (you) bring Hanako back because Ø will have supper soon? Ø BE at Miyo-chan's house now.

Figure 1 shows how Japanese referential terms are used in the interpersonal communication situation above.

	Taroo (*Senapai*) ⇄	Takahi (*Koohai*)
Self-Reference	*senpai* [senior] *ore* [I]	*boku* [I]
Address	*omae* [you]	*senpai* [senior]
	Taroo ⇄	Keiko
Self-Reference		*okaasan* [mother]
Address	*okaasan* [mother]	*oniichan* [elder brother]
Reference to Tsutomu		*otoosan* [father]

Figure 1. Illustation of the Dialogue

In Japanese society the ranking order based on the *senpai-koohai* relationship is overwhelmingly important. *Senpai* is a member of a group who is usually older and has a longer period of experience in the group than *koohai*. *Senpai* [Senior] should take care of *koohai* [junior] while *koohai* must pay respect and loyalty to *senpai* at all times. In the dialogue between Taroo and Takashi, Taroo refers to himself by *senpai* [senior] or *ore* [I]. When he uses *senpai*, he looks at himself at Takashi's standpoint. *Ore* is a first-person pronoun and normally should not be used towards superiors. Takashi refers to himself by *boku* [I] towards his *senpai*, Taroo. *Boku* is more polite than *ore* and can be used towards superiors. In addition to *boku* and *ore*, there are a variety of first-person pronouns in Japanese, whereas English has only one, namely "I". Taroo calls Takashi by a second-person pronoun, *omae* which shows casualness and informality. Thus, every time a Japanese uses a first-person pronoun and a second-person pronoun, he or she selects the most appropriate one depending on his or her relation to the listener and the interpersonal context. Takashi addresses Taroo by a ranking term, *senpai* [senior], which clearly shows their role relationship and Takashi's respect for Taroo.

In the dialogue between Taroo and his mother, Keiko, Keiko calls herself by *okaasan* [mother], instead of using a first-person pronoun. Clearly she sees herself from Taroo's viewpoint here. This use of kinship terms for self-reference is made not only towards young children, but towards adult listeners in Japanese daily conversations. And, Keiko addresses Taroo by *oniichan* [elder brother] even though he is her son. Here, she puts herself in Hanako's shoes. This implies that Taroo as Hanako's elder brother has a responsibility to take care of his sister. When she refers to her husband by *otoosan* [father], she assimilates herself with her listener, Taroo. This usage is very common even in conversations among adults.

We have had a glimpse of the way in which "terms for self-reference", "address terms", and "terms of reference" are used in a concrete situation. In addition to terms we have seen, the Japanese referential system includes other pronouns, kinship terms, occupational terms, titles, ranking terms, and the name of the speaker or listener. The common thread we find in all the cases is the assimilation of the speaker and the listener (in some cases, the third person). Without this assimilation, we cannot understand how the Japanese referential system works. Suzuki states (1973: 167, 164) that "there is the assimilation of the self, who is the observer, with the other, who is the observed, with no clear distinction", and the "self-designation in Japanese is relative and other-oriented".

I believe this assimilation in Japanese interpersonal communication is nothing but Merleau-Ponty's concept of "embodiment". For example, when an adult happens to see a little boy crying in a park and says to the boy, "why am *boku* [I] crying?", the distinction between the adult's body and the boy's body disappears and the two lived-bodies become reversible. It is the same as the lack of a differentiation of the self and the other that we have in our childhood experience of speech. This shows the way in which this non-differentiation remains as a latent corporeal force and become the essence of speaking.

The essential point in the embodied act of speaking is that there is always the dialectic between "speech speaking" and "speech spoken", in other words, the fulfillment of a new signification by modifying already available meanings. In the dialogue we have seen, Keiko says to Taroo, "*Oniichan* [Elder brother], would (you) bring Hanako back because Ø will have supper soon?" One day before, she might have said to him, "*Oniichan* [Elder brother], stop watching TV and finish (your) homework!" in an angry voice. Just as we continue to encounter the generation of a new meaning when we read the same book again and again, "*oniichan* [elder brother]" in the dialogue has a unique meaning. If we assume only the existence of the sedimented modality of "speech spoken", we cannot account for this moment of new signification. In brief, the existence of the dialectic between "speech speaking" and "speech spoken" or expression and perception is recognized in all the examples we have seen, which is the moment when the "speaking subject" is experiencing the "embodiment".

Structural Co-ordination of Experience in Communication

So far we have seen how the communicative use of the Japanese referential terms is based on the embodied act of speaking and how the dialectic between "speech speaking" and "speech spoken" is essential at the moment of speaking. Now, we have to ask how it is possible for this dialectic to take place in the practice of speaking. If we suppose the world consists of the collection of individual entities which exist for themselves and that language functions as mere labels of them, we can never account for the dialectic between the two existential modalities. Then, what is it that helps us to understand this dialectic? Merleau-Ponty believes that it is the structure based on the "diacritical" meaning of signs about which Saussure talks. In the middle period of his philosophy Merleau-Ponty started focusing on Saussure's view of language, which helped the development of his philosophy of communication. According to Merleau-Ponty (1960a: 117), the "structure" is not a system of positive ideas but "a unity of coexistence"; "signs function only through their differences". And, it is the speaking subject that establishes "differences" in a sign system and, thereby, the signification of the signs. In other words, there is no "structure" without the viewpoint of the speaking subject. A change takes place in so far as we, as the speaking subjects, have a total configuration of signs as the basis for a new system of signification. In short, the concept of "structure" directs us to outstrip the already sedimented and fixed structure.

Then, we should inquire how the "diacritical" meaning in the "structure" leads to a genesis of a new meaning in the actual practice of speaking. First, let us focus on the state which the speaking subject has prior to the act of speaking. Merleau-Ponty calls this state the "primordial silence" (1945: 184), the "significative intention" or the "speechless want" (1960a: 89). It is a "determinate gap to be filled by words-- the excess of what I intend to say over what is being said or has already been said" (Merleau-Ponty 1960a: 89). To look at this gap in terms of the concept of "structure" or a sign system, it is the gap between our lived-experience of the world and already-available signs. To put it in another way, the "signified", the existential meaning of the experience which I have here and now slips out of the already sedimented "signifier". Here, the "structure" of a system has been pressured and has some kind of tension in it. This primordial state is very attractive in the sense that it has multiple possibilities and a miraculous power, yet, at the same time it is dangerous and dreadful because it has chaotic and unstable aspects. These paradoxical views exist simultaneously because it is the moment immediately before a rupture takes place.

In fact there is an action which breaks up the primordial silence, namely, the act of speaking. Of course, it is not the "speech spoken" but the "speech speaking". And, each time a practice of speaking takes place, communicators experience the generation of a style. The style, here, means the manner in which a new structure is established on the basis of the non-thematic state where the self and the other invade each other. When Merleau-Ponty (1945: 193) states that language is "the subject's taking up of a position in the world of his meanings", he focuses on the way in which the speaking subject structures the nonsignifying world in his or her existential speaking as "embodiment", that is, the way of "singing the world's praises" (Merleau-Ponty 1945: 187).

At last, we come to a position to approach how the style is related to our human communication. When I communicate with an other, I share, with him or her, the style, the manner in which the world is restructured. By applying it to Japanese terms for self-reference and address in interpersonal communication, we can grasp, in a deeper sense, the meaning of the assimilation of the speaker and the listener which we have discussed. Each time one utters a referential term and the other listens to him or her, they share the style; one exists as a style of coexistence for the other, and vice versa. In the dialogue, when Taroo says to his junior Takashi, "*Senpai* [Senior] can do something (for you)", they actually restructure the world in which they are living at the moment, based on their senior-junior relationship; Taroo, in speaking, stands at Takashi's perspective and simultaneously feels that he, as Takashi's senior, should take care of him, while Takashi, in listening, stands at Taroo's perspective and simultaneously recognizes what he is supposed to do as Taroo's junior. What they do at this moment is to make "a choice that establishes a context" in communication (Lanigan 1988: 73). Even in the daily use of a referential term, the speaker and the listener co-witness a new structure and a new signification being originated. Since they form a totality at the point of communicating, we can say 'one' communicates, not that 'I' or 'you' communicates. It is only this positive ambiguity of expression and perception which makes communication possible.

In this research, my argument mainly has focused on the empirical example of the Japanese language. Yet, it does not mean that only the Japanese language has the authenticity of speaking. For, other human languages also have a similar concrete aspect of the assimilation of the self and the other, even though there are greater or lesser degrees of theoretical application. The implication is that no matter which language we speak, our act of speaking is the "embodiment" and that we are able to maintain and will maintain our languages owing to the authenticity of speech.

This study of Japanese terms for self-reference and address has a possibility of opening doors in a variety of directions, such as, foreign language education and intercultural communication. For, it shows evidently that discourse in everyday communication does have the dialectic between "speech speaking" and "speech spoken", although unfortunately the Japanese referential terms has been studied mainly from the viewpoint of "sedimented speech" and we have a tendency to see the "authentic speech" only as e.g., an artistic expression as in literary works. In brief, this study sheds light on this dialectic as the key to the problem of communication. What we must not forget in exploring the possibilities of communication in various directions is to grasp the genesis of meaning as the "prodigy of expression".

NOTE

[1] I translate the original Japanese dialogue which I have made into English, leaving "terms for self-reference", "address terms" and "terms of reference" as they are. And, I try to keep the original Japanese meaning of other parts of the dialogue as much as possible to the extent that they do not sound too strange in English. The symbols I use in the dialogue are given in this legend:

[ ] : English translation of the underlined Japanese words
Ø : Ellipsis of the subject
VERB in capital letter: Because there is no subject in the sentence, the verb is left in its original form.
( ) : The inside of the parenthesis was added when the Japanese original sentence was translated into English.

REFERENCES

LANIGAN, Richard.
   1988. *Phenomenology of Communication: Merleau-Ponty's Thematics in Communicology and Semiology* (Pittsburgh: Duquesne University Press).

MERLEAU-PONTY, Maurice.
   1945. *La phénoménologie de la perception* (Paris: Gallimard). Page references in this paper are from 1986 reprint of the English trans. by Colin Smith *Phenomenology of Perception* (London: Routledge & Kegan Paul Ltd., 1962).
   1960. "Les relations avec autrui chez l'enfant", from the series *Cours de Sorbonne*. Page references in this paper are from the English trans. by William Cobb "The Child's Relations with Others" in *The Primacy of Perception* (Evanston: Northwestern University Press, 1964).
   1960a. *Signes*. Page references in this paper are from the English trans. by Richard McCleary *Signs* (Evanston: Northwestern University Press, 1964).
   1964. *Consciousness and the Acquisition of Language*. Page references in this paper are from the English trans. by H.J. Silverman (Evanston: Northwestern University Press, 1973).

SUZUKI, Takao.
   1973. *Kotoba to Bunka*. Page references in this paper are from the English trans. by A. Miura *Words in Context* (Tokyo: Kodansha International Ltd., 1978).

INTERNATIONAL PLANNED LANGUAGES: AN ESSAY ON THEIR DEFINITION AND LIMITATION

Alicja Sakaguchi[1]

1. Introduction

Semiotics is understood as the science of sign processes in any kind of communication or interchange of information. It treats all forms of *human* and *non-human* sign processes. This article deals with a certain class of human languages which contemporary linguistics and semiotics have given relatively little attention, *consciously created languages* or world auxiliary languages (Welthilfssprachen).

Hardly any other matter of linguistic research has drawn such strongly expressed but small public appreciation as the case of planned auxiliary world languages, such as Volapük (Schleyer 1880), Esperanto (Zemenhof 1887), Ido (Couturat; de Beaufront 1907). The layman usually regards such languages as nonviable *Homunkuli* and as primitive versions of "proper" languages.

Artificial languages are normally contrasted to natural languages, and understood as language manifestations which came into existence more or less as a consequence of intensive alterations at the level of speech structure. Thus, in artificial languages (Ammon and Hübler 1985: 23):[2]

> [wird] jedes zugehörige Element und jede Regel des sprachlichen Ausdrucks geplant, d.h. bewußt ausgewählt und per Beschluß festgelegt. Natürliche Sprachen enthalten dagegen ungeplante Sprachausdrucksbestandteile; sie haben sich--wie man sagt--quasi naturwüchsig (aufgrund von Kommunikationsbedürfnissen) herausgebildet. Neben ungeplanten Bestandteilen können natürliche Sprachen allerdings durchaus auch geplante Bestandteile enthalten.[3]

One need consider only the various forms of language planning, such as orthographic conventions, standardization of terminology, or formation and modernization of national languages. The term "artificial language," moreover, is intended to point out the uniqueness of linguistic phenomena which have been called into existence merely by a group of people (or even by a single person). The phenomena in question usually did not emerge in a remote time barely accessible to research, but in a way 'right before our eyes' (Martinet 1946: 39).

2. The Semantic Scope of the Term "Artificial Language"

In specialized literature the term "artificial language" is actually used to express many different things. Although this expression is most commonly used for the consciously created auxiliary world languages, it may also be understood as the following:

(i) formalized languages such as machine-codes in computer technology, machine oriented prrogramming languages (e.g. Assembler), as well as problem-oriented programming languages (e.g. Cobol, Fotran).

(ii) highly idealized, completely closed code-systems, such as the formal languages in mathematics and mathematical logic as well as in other fields of the "exact" sciences.

(iii) intermediate languages, so called "Interlinguen," for the purpose of automatic translation.

In the broadest sense the term "artifical language" can also stand for a number of other linguistic phenomena. These refer to ethnic languages, which are distinguished by more or less intensive regulations in various areas of language structure, e.g.:

(iv) "literary" standard-languages, which distinguish themselves--contrary to everyday languages or dialects--by a cultivated, "very elevated" linguistic usage, which is closest to the norm.

(v) languages which were brought under regulating influences for the purpose of maintaining certain stages of development (e.g. Sanskrit, Church Latin).

(vi) languages which have been altered systematically for the purpose of standardization, innovation, or enlargment in various fields (e.g. Pilipino, Bahasa Indonesia, modern Hebrew).

In addition, 'artificial language' can sometimes also be understood as:

(vii) the product of an artistic-innovational behavior, which is characterized by conscious changes in word structure, as well as the violation of grammar and syntax. This holds primarily for an avant-garde conception of language in the field of poetics.

This rough listing should be sufficient to show that "bewußtes Sprachschöpfertum . . . sich gleichermaßen auf beide Aspekte der Sprache, den der *Mitteilung* und den des *emotionalen* und *künstlerischen Ausdrucks* erstrecken [kann]" (Bausani 1970: 19).[4] Thus, it is possible to create languages (or parts of languages) which entirely or primarily serve the purpose of *expressive functions*, such as poetic or esoteric utterances. On the other hand, entire languages have been created to provide for comprehensive *"international" communication* and *information* needs.

It remains to be said that all "artificial languages", other than planned auxiliary world languages, have an explicitly instrumental, special-purpose character. Thus, because of their nature, they are insufficient means for everyday communication. Consequently they are not languages in the strict sense of the term, such as Esperanto or Ido, but merely limited languages, such as Algol or Cobol.[5]

Let us now ask whether there is a simple feature (or better a number of features), which distinguishes natural and consciously-created languages from other semiotic systems.

An exclusively structural linguistic approach is by no means sufficient to penetrate the nature of planned auxiliary world languages. This is because the differences between natural and artificial languages are not primarily based on their structural nature, but rather, in a broad sense, are socially caused. The various expressions occurring in the context of *planned auxiliary world languages*, such as "planned languages", "artificial language", "world language", "auxiliary world language", "vehicular languages", "international language", "universal language", "situational language", minority language", "teaching language", and others, ultimately point to a term that cannot be grasped with the instruments of structural linguistics alone. On the other hand, the oppositional pairs occuring in the examination of planned languages such as "homogeneous" vs. "heterogeneous languages", "naturalistic" vs. "autonomous languages", "*a priori* " vs. "*a posteriori* languages", "open [language] systems" vs. "minimal languages", primarily refer to the connections with structural linguistics. The attempt to define an international planned language must always take into consideration three aspects: *society*, *history*, and *linguistic system*. Non differentiation of these aspects, as well as the absence of unequivocal terminological definitions, allow us to detect irrelevant approaches and emotional or ideological influences. The following list of criteria was set up with the intention of eliminating such deficiencies.

2.1. The Specificity of Emergence (Genesis)

A *planned language* is a system which has been consciously created by man to optimize international communication for various purposes. At the root of the emergence of such languages is the theory of linguistic universals. Of great importance also is the language-critical view which asserts that a language must be constructed according to the principles of simplification (ie. economics, convenience). This manner of proceeding, however, should by no means result in a decrease in the expressiveness of the language. Languages of this kind are still to be conceived as the product of one or several indentifiable individuals; the circumstanses and the time of emergence are known, and *that* in a different sense than, for example, the history of the romance or germanic languages, which at least partly is based on reconstruction.

2.2 The Manifestation

Manifestation is concerned with the quantity of optically and acoustically perceptible forms admitted by the language in question. In the majority of ethnic languages one basically finds two basic manifestations: a phonological and a graphemic level. Likewise, international planned languages can, in comparison with ethnic languages, feature two manifestations (e.g. Volapük, Schleyer 1880; Esperanto, Zamenhof 1887), or only one (*Pasigraphien*, as for example in Näther 1805, Bachmaier 1868) or, in special cases, several manifestations (e.g. Solresol, Sudre 1866).

2.3 Degree of Complexity

The lexikon of a living, natural language constitutes an *open* or *unlimited inventory*. As with the natural languages, most planned auxiliary languages represent unlimited dimensions. In this respect the two types of languages hardly differ from each other. The concept "closed system" stands in opposition to "open system".

2.4 Quality of the Language Norms: Autonomy vs. Naturalism

Of particular importance in planned languages is the opposition of "automony" and "naturalism". In this respect, in the main, two different principles of construction can be distinguished. One concerns the demand for *naturalism* (e.g. Occidental-Interlingue, von Wahl 1924; Interlingua, Gode 1951), the other for *autonomy* (e.g. Volapük, Esperanto, Ido).

2.5 Development: Relation between Spontaneous and Programmed Language Dynamics

Development deals with the embedding of international planned languages in a temporal-spatial-social relationship. In approaching this topic, the following questions should be particularly considered: (i) How does the relationship between spontaneous and directed language development present itself in planned languages? (ii) In what way does the procedure of standardization, relating to linguistic norms, differ in ethnic languages and in planned languages?

2.5.1 Language Varieties

Planned languages, even if one only considers their functions, reveal only to a limited degree the social differentiation which is so typical for ethnic languages. D. Blanke (1985a: 277) suggests a division of planned languages into three functional language varieties:

(i)   the *standard variety*
(ii)   the *colloquial variety*
(iii) a *learner variety*

2.5.2 Development, Stability, Norm

We are today able to state, on the basis of the near one-hundred-year-old history of the development of Esperanto as a generally proven means of communication, that the factor of a *consciously controlled further development* is absolutely necessary to guarantee a relative stability and homogeneity in the development of a planned language.

2.6 Targets

It was the main aim of several language creators to offer a means of communication which would *reduce communication problems of the multilingual world and make intercultural exchange more effective*. A critical examination of languages is of fundamental importance in the consideration of desirable performances, qualities, and structures. Language evaluation and language planning, of course, are dependent upon a fixed language ideal. The problem is to *achieve a maximum of performance with a minimum of means*. In language construction, we should add the postulate of the greatest possible "universality".

2.7 The Communicative-Functional Specificity

Here the question to be asked is: What is the communicative function of ethnic and planned languages in everyday human life (in der Lebenswelt des Menschen)? One of the most important forms of communication with a pronounced social functionality is the *national language*, e.g. English or Polish. A planned language, then, may complement national languages whenever they do not offer sufficient means of intercourse. A planned auxiliary language may exist beside the mother tongue, and may support written and oral communication in everday life, and particularly in areas of science and technology, between peoples who speak different languages. Planned auxiliary languages thereby coplement the national languages. In such a case an international planned language is just an *auxiliary language* and will remain chiefly a *second language* for generations.

2.8 The Specific Regional Function

A necessary determinative element of the concept "auxiliary language" or "auxiliary world language" is the function of communication between communities in which different languages are normally spoken. This criterion shall here be called *supra-regionality*. Languages used as means of communication between different nations shall then be designated as *international languages*.

3. Conclusion

The criteria noted above should help (i) to differentiate planned auxiliary world languages from other linguistic systems, and (ii) to distinguish different kinds of planned auxiliary world languages from one another (see Sakaguchi 1989). Although there are at present over 900 planned auxiliary world language projects, only a very few of these (see table 1) have come into practical usage in written and oral situations.

Table 1. The Present Communicative Realization of Auxiliary World Languages.

Language	Communicative Realisation (written language)	Communicative Realisation (spoken language)	Number of Users
Volapük (1880)	X	X	ca. 10 (Golden 1980:89)
Esperanto (1887)	X	X	ca. 1,000,000 (Blanke 1985a: 289)
Ido	X	X	? (a three-digit number)
Occidental-Interlingue (1924)	X	X	? (a two-digit number)
Interlingua (1951)	X	X	61 (Blanke 1985b: 107)

NOTES

[1] This paper was presented in German, and translated with the aid of notes from the author by Hermine Kraßnitzer and Franz Rulitz at the University of West Florida.

[2] *Editor's Note:* Both of the long quotations in this paper are in German. We provide translations in each instance through endnotes. For some special or unusual terms the original German appears parenthetically in the text.

[3] " . . . each pertinent element and each rule of linguistic expression is planned, i.e., consciously chosen and determined by resolution. Natural languages, on the contrary, contain unplanned constituents; they have evolved, as is said, *quasinaturally* (based upon communication needs). Apart from unplanned constituents, natural languages can certainly also contain planned components."

[4] " . . . conscious language construction can likewise extend to both aspects of language, the aspect of *information* and the aspect of *emotional* and *artistic expression*."

[5] *Translators' Note:* "Sie sind daher keine '*Vollsprachen*' . . . sondern lediglich '*Teilsprachen*'. . . ." Literally "full languages" and "part languages", though we note from context that most specialized artificial languages are *complete* or logically well-defined *wholes*.

REFERENCES

AMMON, U. and A. HÜBLER.
    1985. "Sprachplanung und Plansprachen: Zukunftsvisionen einer Welthilfssprache", in *1984: Visionen und Revisionen*, ed. K.H. Börner (Duisburg: Duisburger Universitätstage), 17-43.

BACHMAIER, A.
    1868. *Pasigraphisches Wörterbuch Deutsch - Englisch - Französisch* (Augsburg).

BAUSANI, A.
    1970 *Geheim- und Universalspachen: Entwicklung und Typologie* (Stuttgart: Kohlhammer).

BEAUFRONT, L. de.
    1907 *Grammaire compléte de la langue internationale* (Paris: Chaix).

BLANKE, D.
    1985a. *Internationale Plansprachen: Eine Einführung* (Berlin: Akademie-Verlag).
    1985b. "Kiom da Interlingua-anoj?", *Der Esperantist* 21.5, 107.

GODE, A.
    1951. *Interlingua* (New York: International Auxiliary Language Association). A grammar of the international language, prepared by A. Gode and H. E. Blair of the research staff of the International Auxiliary Language Association.

GOLDEN, B.
    1980. "Memorigo pri pioniraj hungaraj volapukistoj", *Hungara Vivo* 20.3, 89.

HOGBEN, L.
1943. *Interglossa* (Harmondswort). A draft of an auxiliary language for a democratic world order, being an attempt to apply principles to language design.

MARTINET, A.
1946. "La linguistique et les langues artificielles", *Word Journal of the Linguistic Circle of New York* 2.1, 37-47.

NÄTHER, J.Z.
1805. *Versuch einer ganz neuen Erfindung von Pasigraphie, oder die Kunst zu schreiben und zu drucken, daß es von allen Nationen der ganzen Welt in allen Sprachen eben so leicht gelesen werden kann, als die Zahlencharakter 1, 2, 3; in Form einer Sprachenlehre* (Görlitz).

RUSSEL, B.
1957. *Suma, the 1000-word Universal Language* (Gordena). Page references in this paper are from the Third Edition (Pleinview, 1966).

SAKAGUCHI, A.
1987. "Welthilfssprache", in *Sociolinguistics: An International Handbook of the Science of Language and Society*, ed. U. Ammon, N. Dittmar, and K.J. Mattheier (Berlin: de Gruyter), 365-370.
1989. "Towards a Clarification of the Function and Status of International Planned Languages", in *Status and Function of Languages and Language Varieties*, ed U. Ammon (Berlin: de Gruyter).

SCHLEYER, J.M.
1880. *Volapük, die Weltsprache: Entwurf einer Universalsprache für alle Gebildeten der ganzen Erde* (Sigmaringen).

SUDRE, J.F.
1866. *Langue musicale universale* (Paris: Double Dictionnaire).

WAHL, E. von.
1924. *Occidental: Unic natural, vermen neutral e max facil e comprensibil lingue por international relationes* (Tallinas).

ZAMENHOF, L. (Dr. Esperanto)
1887. *Mezdunarodnij jazyk: Predislovije i polnij učebnik* (Varšava).

XX

"PROXEMIOTICS"

JOKES, TRANSGRESSION, AND LAUGHTER

Rui-hong Guo
Southern Illinois University

Many people who speak a foreign language may have found out that, even when one has a fluent command of the language, understanding and being able to laugh at a joke is very hard, if not impossible. Our daily experiences show that even among natives, this ability is not a gift equally bestowed upon everyone. In the present paper, I explicate the analysis Julia Kristeva would give to the working of jokes and laughter, by using her theory of the dialectic relationship between the semiotic and the symbolic, the *chora* and the thetic, which constitutes the signifying practice. I argue that the inability to laugh is due to the lack of one modality of the heterogeneous signifying process: the semiotic, the actual organization, or disposition, within the body, of instinctual drives as they affect language and its practice, in dialectical conflict to the symbolic.

Kristeva calls the signifying practice "the establishment and the countervailing of a sign system" (Kristeva 1977: 18) which calls for both the identity of a speaking subject within a social framework and the challenging of that social framework. This is Kristeva's subject in Process/on Trial, "a split subject--divided between unconscious and conscious motivations, between physiological processes and social constraints" (1977: 6). To account for such splitting, Kristeva posits a signifying process which consists of two heterogeneous components, the semiotic and the symbolic.

The semiotic refers to "the facilitation and the structuring disposition of drives, and the so-called primary processes which displace and condense both energies and their inscriptions" (Kristeva 1974: 25). Postulating that which precedes the imposition of the symbolic, it is prior to signification, syntax, denotation, grammar, and is the primary structure of drives. The semiotic functions through the activities of the *chora*, "a nonexpressive totality that is as full of movement as it is regulated" (1974: 25). The *chora* is not a sign, nor a signifier either; it is a preverbal and pre-Oedipal phase when the child perceives the world through vocal or kinetic rhythm, and depends on a semiotic relationship with the mother's body (1974: 27) which mediates the imprint of social and family structures. The semiotic's meaning process is still tied to drives; thus it is not cognitive because it is not yet "assumed by a knowing subject" (1974: 27). The symbolic designates the establishing and functioning of the sign and signification. It consists of all cultural codes, such as grammar, syntax, denotation, logic, social constraints, symbolic law. It is produced through the Oedipal process, starting with the mirror stage and the separation from the mother's body and the adoption of the paternal authority (1974: 149). The symbolic is the domain of all communicative activity which emerges as a function of positionality, a positing of identity and difference. In a word, the signifying process results from a particular articulation between the semiotic chora and the symbolic device and possesses a split nature.

The arrival of the symbolic is marked by a break, which is called by Kristeva a thetic phase. Kristeva argues that signification is impossible without the completion of the thetic, a threshold between two heterogeneous realms: the semiotic and the symbolic which exist simultaneously in constant tension and unity. The thetic involves the subject's separation from an object which is attributed a signifier and becomes signifiable, and the constitution of an other is necessary for communicating with an other. As the thetic is the precondition for denotation and communication, it becomes the domain of intersubjectivity, and of all human relations. The relationship between the *chora* and the thetic is not static. The *chora* constitutes the precondition for the symbolic, and it is previous and necessary to the acquisition of language, but cannot be unified by a meaning initiated by a thetic break. The *chora*, being mobile and irruptive, constantly returns to the thetic and tears it open, producing various transformations in the signifying process. It is this flux of the semiotic that remodels the symbolic order and brings about creation and revolution in poetic language. Thus, the semiotic *chora*, though theoretically previous to symbolization, exists in practice within the symbolic and comes after the symbolic thesis as the transgression of that thesis.

"Poetic language" as a signifying practice is a semiotic system generated by a speaking subject within a social framework. It stands for the "infinite possibilities of language", and all other language acts are merely partial realizations of the possibilities inherent in poetic language. Containing a heterogeneity to meaning and signification, this kind of language is an unsettling process of the identity of the speaking subject and meaning. In Roudiez's words, it is the "language of materiality as opposed to transparency" (Kristeva 1977: 5), a language in which the writer deals more with the sounds and rhythms of words than with the objects or concepts words seem to denote; in other words, more concerned with the semiotic breach of the symbolic rules. Thus, the influx of the semiotic is particularly evident in poetic language since, for there to be a transgression and subversion of the symbolic, there must be an irruption of drives in the universal signifying order. But the semiotic always presupposes the positing of the thetic without which signification would be impossible. The semiotic functioning is part of a signifying practice which includes the symbolic agency and is a permanent struggle to show the facilitation of drives within the linguistic order itself (Kristeva 1974: 81). The *chora* is raised to the status of a signifier, which may or may not obey the norms of grammar.

Kristeva believes that the semiotic transgression of a symbolic law allows the subject to enjoy and renew a literary practice that explores and discovers the infinite possibilities of language. The subject experiences "jouissance", a totality of joy or ecstasy. This is true particularly in the writings of avant-garde writers, such as Artaud, Bataille, Joyce, Lautreamont, Mallarme, which exemplify the presence of poetic language. With Kristeva, I believe that poetic language also appears outside the field of great literature, and specifically, I argue that the language of jokes partakes of poetic language and the nature of jokes is closely related to the semiotic transgression of the symbolic within the signifying practice.

The semiotic disposition in poetic language shows up in various variations from the grammatical rules of the language. This is one of the ways in which jokes work. Common experiences show that a joke or any statement that makes people laugh depends on making free with the symbolic system, breaking up the inertia of language habits, and re-ordering the psychic drives which have not been harnessed by the dominant symbolization systems. This last point is very important because jokes arouse laughter only when they are told for the first time, when something is said in a new and unfamiliar way. Jokes work on the ambiguity of words and the multiplicity of conceptual relations. Specifically, these include multiple use of the same material, play upon words, similarity of sounds, nonsensical reasoning, diversion of the train of thought, among others. In his book *Jokes and Their Relation to the Unconscious* (1976), Sigmund Freud refers the main mechanisms of jokes to the primary processes of the unconscious: condensation and displacement. Jokes are linguistic condensations and displacements and constitute as the intrusion into conscious thinking of mechanisms that belong properly to the unconscious.

The process of condensation refers to the tendency to compression, one outcome of this peculiar process being the brevity of a lot of jokes. Jokes usually say what they have to say in few words, sometimes too few to be sufficient by strict logic or by common modes of thought and speech. Listen to this joke:

He has a great future behind him. (Freud 1905: 58)

This is an example of condensation with a slight moderation. On the surface, the words "future" and "behind" seem to contradict each other, but it is this very apparent incongruity that renders the statement a joke, because the combination comes as a surprise, but not one so unreasonable as to be unintelligible. It does not take much imagination to figure out that it is a compressed version of a statement like: "He has had a great future before him, but he no longer has it," which is not only a longer sentence, but certainly not a joke any more. This tendency to use as few words as possible is described by Freud as the "principle of economy" (Freud 1905: 167) which is related generally to the economy in psychical expenditure. We take pleasure and bring about a great relief in psychical work when we focus on the sound of a word instead of its meaning, because when we use words seriously we are obliged to hold ourselves back with a certain effort from this pleasant procedure. This enjoyment is to be contributed to the economy in psychical expenditure.

The following two jokes play upon the double meaning of words.

> A doctor, as he came away from a lady's bedside, said to her husband with a shake of his head: "I don't like her looks." "I've not liked her looks for a long time." The husband hastened to agree.
> (Freud 1905: 71)

> Singer: "Now that you've heard my voice, whom do you suggest to accompany me?" Impresario: "A bodyguard."
> (anon. 1986)

Sometimes words that have lost their original meaning in certain connections, regain their full meaning in other contexts.

> "How are you getting along?" The blind man asked the lame man.
> "As you see." The lame man replied to the blind man.
> (Freud 1905: 68)

This case also depends on the multiple use of words, but differs from the above one in that words whose derived meaning seems to be more often used than their original meaning regain the full power of their original meaning under certain circumstances.

Another category of jokes Freud describes as "displacement" jokes since their "essence lies in the division of the train of thought, the displacement of the psychical emphasis on to a topic other than the opening one" (1905: 88). Freud uses the following joke to illustrate.

> "Have you taken a bath?"
> "What? Is there one missing?"
> (1905:85)

The answer is diversed from the question by displacing the accent from "bath" to "taken".

Displacement jokes tend to make use of deviations from normal thinking, of faulty reasoning. For a moment, we are deceived by the seemingly brilliance of a joke and only after the joke has been analyzed do we become conscious of its false judgment, but the joke has achieved its purpose at that precise moment.

> One person to another in front of a science-museum exhibition: "It says here that oxygen was discovered over 200 years ago."
> "Wow! What did people breathe before that?"
> (anon. 1988)

At first sight, the second speaker seems to be asking a legitimate, even insightful question, especially when accompanied by a seriously questioning look, but on further look, the statement is almost nonsensical in taking advantage of our momentary confusion over fact of science and fact of life.

Freud's argument that jokes are formed as a result of a conscious releasing of the energy repressed in our unconscious illustrates perfectly Kristeva's notion of the semiotic *chora* as irruption of unconscious drives in the conscious symbolic system. As children, we take pleasure from play with words, nonsensical talking; we give full play to certain lustful or hostile drives. After the stage of play, with education and civilization, we are taught to repress and censor these primary possibilities of enjoyment. But human beings cannot renounce the pleasure principle; instead, they develop new techniques of expression, in this case, jokes, which provide a means of undoing the renunciation and retrieving what was lost.

> A husband and wife drove for miles in silence after a terrible argument in which neither would budge. The husband pointed to a mule in the pasture. "A relative of yours?" he asked. "Yes," she replied. "By marriage."
> (anon. 1988a)

This joke helps achieve in a roundabout way the enjoyment from calling the enemy some kind of animal, which is a childish play. Jokes purport to continue pleasurable play and attempt to protect it from the criticism of reason, by choosing to work in occasions where the play for pleasure can at the same time appear acceptable and sensible. Jokes avoid an obstacle that stands in the way of the satisfaction of an instinct and pleasure is drawn from a source that has been made inaccessible by the obstacle. Repression is thus released and freed into laughter, and the subject experiences jouissance.

According to Kristeva, laughter "lifts inhibitions by breaking through prohibitions (symbolized by the Creator) to introduce the aggressive, violent, liberating drive" (1974: 224). Laughter is produced by the semiotic *chora* "that arrests and absorbs the motility of the anaclitic facilitations" (Kristeva 1977: 283). A sense of humor seems to build upon the tension between the inhibition prescribed by parents and its removal within childhood situations where parental authority is weakened, and the ego bursts into laughter by suddenly making a leap, a shattered movement, creating a space. "Lautreamont makes laughter the symptom of rupture and of the heterogeneous contradiction within the signifying practice" (Kristeva 1974: 223).

By considering laughter as always an indication of aggression against and rejection of the Creator, Kristeva points to the atheological nature of laughter. Baudelaire treats laughter as profoundly human and incompatible with absolute knowledge. He emphasizes the contradictory structure of laughter which embraces an infinite human pride in the face of misery and rebels against theological authority. To the all-powerful and all-knowing Creator, the comic does not exist. "The Word Incarnate never laughed" (Baudelaire 1855: 450); "Laughter is 'one of the numerous pips contained in the symbolic apple' (Baudelaire 1855: 453), and as a result, it is 'generally the prerogative of madmen' (1855: 450) precisely because it designates an irruption of the drives against symbolic prohibition" (Kristeva 1974: 222). The theological antagonism towards laughter is also depicted in Umberto Eco's novel *The Name of the Rose* (1980). To Jorge, laughter is a blasphemy against the Incarnation, a summoning of the dark powers of corporal matter" (Eco 1980: 477), against which there is no weapon. In laughter, the "villain" does not have any fear; even death does not matter. The "villain" overturns his/her position with regard to the Lord and feels he/she is the Master. It is this lack of fear in the "villain" that scares the theological authority.

Jokes, poetry and other literary devices, bring about an explosion of laughter, because they employ the semiotic rhythm within the language and apprehend in language that which belongs with play, pleasure and desire. For a creative user, language poses a problem, imposing various constraints established by a society, an ideology. The speaking subject, in order to get pleasure, is capable of renewing the symbolic order, even endanger it, though he is inescapably caught up in it. In other words, the speaking subject engages in practice: "the acceptance of a symbolic law together with the transgression of that law for the purpose of renovating it". For Kristeva, laughter is a practice that produces something new. When there is nothing new practice is not laughter; repeated practice does not provoke jouissance. Jokes make people laugh because they are meant only for the first time. They are funny only when they come as a surprise that strikes the audience as unfamiliar, as twisting and transgressing grammatical rules and play with words. With this in mind, it is easier to understand why it is hard to catch the humor of a joke told in a foreign language. People who learn a foreign language usually start with grammar, the syntax, and the right diction, and the major concern is to organize a sentence grammatically correct. Thus the signifying process is more or less constrained by the symbolic, and becomes static because there is no negativity involved, no semiotic transformation which realizes creative originality. This greatly reduces the subject's capacity for enjoyment in a foreign language.

Through my argument that jokes produce jouissance by lifting symbolic repression, I intend to follow with the thesis that when I use language creatively and personally, I embody the linguistic system to express my lived embodiment in the world. Only when I subvert language and exercise heterogeneity do I break the rule and achieve the existential moment, for discourse is authentically meant for the first time. The voice of the "I" is the voice of the speaking subject, who constantly engages in new practices. Kristeva's subject in Process/on Trial is not a unitary entity, but a split subject, forever constrained by the symbolic, but in whom the semiotic continually overruns and negates the symbolic, and through the dialectic of contradiction, the subject renews a practice and arrives at a new position.

REFERENCES

ANONYMOUS.
- 1986. "Laughter, the Best Medicine", in *Reader's Digest*, November, 98.
- 1988. "Laughter, the Best Medicine", in *Reader's Digest*, January, 66.
- 1988a. "Laughter, the Best Medicine", in *Reader's Digest*, July, 56.

BAUDELAIRE, Charles.
- 1855. "On the Essence of Laughter", in *Comedy: Meaning and Form*, ed. R. Corrigan. (San Francisco, California: Chandler Publishing Company, 1965), 448-465.

ECO, Umberto.
- 1980. *Il nome della rosa*. Page references in the present article are to the English trans. by William Weaver, *The Name of the Rose* (New York: Harcourt Brace Jovanovich, 1983).

FREUD, Sigmund.
- 1905. *Der Witz und seine Bezie hung zum Unbewussten*. Page references in the present article are to the English trans. by James Strachey, *Jokes and Their Relation to the Unconscious* (Penguin Books, 1976).

KRISTEVA, Julia.
- 1974. *La révolution du langage poétique*. Page references in the present article are to the English trans. by Margaret Waller, *Revolution in Poetic Language* (New York: Columbia University Press, 1984).
- 1977. *Desire in Language: A Semiotic Approach to Literature and Art*, English trans. by Thomas Gora et al (New York: Columbia University Press, 1980).

THE "CLASSICAL" PROXEMIOTICS OF THE ENCOUNTER:
HOW THE STAGES OF INTERACTION, AS DEMONSTRATED BY MEDIEVAL
AND RENAISSANCE ALLEGORY, PROJECT A TOPOCOSM FOR THINKING

Richard A. R. Watson
Chapman College

> *Without attention being exchanged and distributed, there is no social life. A unique social resource, attention is created anew in each encounter and allocated in ways deeply affecting human interactions.*
>
> -- *Charles Derber 1979* --

Proxemiotics (proxemic semiotics) is a study of the ways we enter into, and exit from, encounters, thusly exchanging and distributing attention through gestural-/sensory duals--a basic give-and-take that defines the stages of entrance and exiting. In this manner, we bargain our way through life, a bargaining process that sometimes becomes more abstracted--into the exchange of more abstract symbolic tokens, objects or work involved in barter or in monetary exchange. A strong argument can be made that, no matter how abstract, or displaced, attention remains the basic unit of exchange. But, as such, the exchange of attention is caught in the "ineluctable" modalities of the senses, and it is the exchange of spoken words, looks, touches and smells--a realm of gestures, body language and verbal language--symbolic action defined by senses--that forges the stages of the encounter.

Sensemiotics, the semiotic study of the sensory modes, deals with these sensory units of exchange. Certainly literature has always shown how encounters proceed through sensory/gestural stages, more or less displaced (compare rape with the rites of courtship), moving from external fringes of contact 'inwards', if one is given the right to proceed to the next stage inwards, and then out again. The "classical" sensory/gestural shift--from mutely visual perception at a distance (which may be one-sided at first but becomes mutual with Sartre's The Look), to oral/aural communication, to smelling, touching, tasting--reminds us that the senses are socially defined by these hierarchic stages (hence the proxemiotics of kinesis, perception, communication, and communion). And, these stages further provide a paradigm for the abstract cognitive quest, so that a young boy who is told "Don't touch," later as the mature Kenneth Burke writes tomes on the Negative.

This is a paper about how the sensory and gestural modalities define the stages of the immediate encounter and, by analogy, the abstract cognitive quest--using literary examples from Chaucer & George Chapman (although literature is replete with examples). Encounters, of course, provide the units of personal relationships, and relationships the units of institutional life, and of society in general. As encounters change, so does the society.

A. The Handling of the Social Commodity of Attention: Primary In-Out Rituals of Victimage

We are constantly negotiating, in encounters with others, the business of rights and obligations. We talk about use of signs in communication--but Peirce, with his 'sinsigns', suggests a sign-form that emerges in perception. On the other hand, there are obviously group signallings that may inhibit crucial forms of communication, such as we find in what Malinowski calls "Phatic Communion". Indeed, I take "communication" as a form caught between two 'radical forms'--"perception", a radical form that allows the individual an awareness of what Buber called the "I-It" relation, & "communion", a radical form allowing the "I-Thou" relation, which at least implies an "Us". However, the merging in the group "Us," in turn, may move into a kind of Sartrean 'bad faith' that betrays a genuine "I-Thou" relation--so, in many cases, social communion may become very superficial. Communication tries to mediate these radical forms, but the radicals themselves suggest a purity that frequently tries to inhibit the other use of signs. Caught in the semi-autism, or indeed (if we go all the way) the autism of perception, we may move away from communion, and even communication with Others. Hence, a person who "sees" too much may be considered asocial. On the other hand, if one is caught in the group awareness of the "Us", then one may put on social blinkers that prevent one from seeing too much. In this latter case, communion betrays both perception and its own radical "I-Thou" relation, and becomes phatically, or emphatically, autocratic. Communication, in mediating these semiotic radicals, finds itself moving between the semi-autistic & the semi-autocratic.

There is presumably a balance of power between these two radicals which is what is invoked when two people encounter each other. And, if an individual encounters two or more people who already define themselves as a group, then the dynamics of this balance frequently becomes even more entrenched. In fact, groups--or, indeed, individuals--tend to treat individuals who approach them (or wish to deal with them) in rather set ways. The "Us" (or the entrenched "I") refuses the possibility of an "I-Thou" relation, making a victim of any outsider. This may happen in war--where the approaching individual is treated as a member of another group. But if there is at least the possibility of the Other joining--then one of four basic in-out rites of victimage are invoked:

(1) *Initiation* (the outsider is allowed in): But, in being allowed into the group, the group assumes the responsibility of hazing--transforming the identity of the outsider into that of an insider (if he or she can survive the test), rewarding the initiate with communion with the inside.

(2) *Discrimination* (the outsider is kept out): Some people, by definition, may be excluded from the group--but as a society develops rules of equity, then such racism or sexism (etc.) may be hidden by ambiguous behavior (see below).

(3) *Henpecking* (the insider is kept in): We don't seem to have an adequate generalized term here, so, in spite of its 'sexist' overtones, I use "henpecking"--but armies use similar kinds of pressure to keep in their members, as do fraternities, cults, etc.

(4) *Expulsion* (the insider is thrown out): If one does something "wrong" in terms of the group, one may be punished (demoted in a hierarchic system of up/down) and even, if bad enough, expelled. Sometimes, as with heretics, a person makes a fundamentally radical choice (Gr. *hairein*, to take , choose) from which the

heresy emerges (*hairesis*, a taking, selection, school, sect, heresy), leading to expulsion. Given group- dynamics, it is perhaps understandable that one would be thrown out for having achieved too much clarity.

Individuals as well as groups can use these four rites. Presumably, in the famous comic strip of several decades ago, Maggie used all four rituals on Jiggs, the long-suffering archetype of the victim-husband, initiating him, henpecking him, discriminating against him, and throwing him out of the house. What pulled Jiggs down was the mental gravity of the situation. Clearly, as tribes join together in the empires of more extended societies, the in-out rites are given an up-down tilt that sometimes confused their primary clarity (Watson, 1985). In fact, the evolution of Babel, with its hierarchies, allows these primary rites to become much more ambiguous. In the Kafkean world of bureaucracy, where one is caught in the middle of a hierarchy, a person cannot separate the hazing of initiation from that of discrimination, or henpecking from punishment. (Note Kafka's "Before the Law" for one treatment of this ambiguity).

Perhaps, as Kenneth Burke has implied, this ambiguity goes back to the origins of these rituals. But, it is in the encounter with others that we try to determine whether we are to be allowed into the next stage of the encounter, or not. This determination occurs in terms of the gestural/sensory duals.

B. The Encounter Has "Internalizing" and "Externalizing" Levels of Action, Each with Its Negotiated Rights and Its Obligations

The following proxemiotic stages apply hypothetically to all encounters--including the (very hypothetical) human encounter with intelligent aliens. The "if allowed" is crucial in defining whether we are moving through initiation, expulsion, discrimination, or henpecking.

(1) *Proximation* (kinetic transit-forms such as walking, driving, etc.) *vs. stasis*: Proximation may lead to an Entrance, through the liminal stage of a threshold, into the Encounter--if allowed. Here one approaches the territory of the Other, or the Other approaches one's realm, or both approach each other--to move into the same space-time locale as the other; this is an important pre-encounter stage, and if difficulties are met here, one may never enter into the encounter. But if allowed in, one may later be allowed to exit out of the encounter. (Of course, the act of proximation itself may involve encounters, with their own intrinsic stages.)

(2) *Perception vs. Apperception*: if allowed, then one may perceive the Other. (Here emerges the classic Wittgensteinian question concerning "Other Minds".) The Encounter itself doesn't start formally until the commencement of two-way communication, but perception and kinesis continue. If one were dealing with a stranger from another culture, or an alien, one would try to find some basis for communication--but, in fact, all such attempts might themselves be considered communication.

(3) *Communication (word to word) vs. Non-Communication*: if allowed, after introductions, one may move into open coded interaction, taking turns. In communication, we still use perception, of course, but perception is not the prime motivation. And, in fact, if one sees too much, perception can get in the way of communication. The social obligation of communication (don't stare) is that one mustn't see too much--one puts social blinkers on.

(4) *Communion (flesh to flesh, individual to group, spirit to spirit) vs. Non-Communion*: If allowed, one may move into feasting, sexual coupling, and presumably forms of mystical identification, allowed by the four primary in-out rites, some of

which re-invoke kinesis, but in this case the kinesis of contact. Insofar as the communal bond is based on an otherness that is involved in rending, or rendering, then community is based on victimage. In such moments, communication and perception may be allowed, but also may indeed be inhibited--hence the proprieties of silence (no talking) and darkness (no seeing) during the sexual act.

Once in, one may move out of the encounter by steps, if allowed to thusly exit, moving down through the various thresholds of communion, communication, perception, etc. Traditionally, one might expect the exiting steps to be much more cursive than the in-going steps--but life is sometimes much more complicated than that. Also, as Bluebeard makes clear, going in does not necessarily mean coming out.

The sequence may apply to mediated as well as immediate encounters. To make a phone call, one uses the mediation of electronics to reach through to a distant person--the phone company provides the proximation. The threshold is broached by the phone ring (perception), which is perceived by the insider, and allows the insider to choose whether to enter into an encounter or not. However, and this is crucial, it is without knowing who one is talking to. The problem for insiders is that they must answer first ("Hello")--and, if they are dealing with a prank caller, this can put them in a vulnerable situation. The dilemma can be alleviated by the use of an answering service, or even a secretary--but, in spite of such devices, the social dynamic created by the phone puts the insider at risk. Perhaps, ultimately, with computerized pictophones, the problem will be resolved in some way. Clearly, technology can change the balance of power that governs our personal boundaries, simply because it affects the politics of interaction in very deep ways.

Each encounter provides its unique twist of the rules--and literature has always focussed on the unique twist. But, before we look at one or two of the twists, let us look at a fairly normative act-hierarchy, which proceeds through sequential stages of body-boundaries, and works for immediate encounters and (with certain compromises) for mediated encounters. The sequence proceeds from outside in. . . . As people move more and more into the encounter, they move more and more "into" each other.

C. An Allegory of Courtship: The Romance of the Rose

In fact, the concept of "Going into an encounter" connotes courtship as a territorial intrusion that must be ritualized. Certainly, as men have often visualized the process of courting a woman, the proceeding into the encounter is visualized as going into the woman, who was seen as a fixture, passive. Hence, the traditional image of the woman as a Rose in a garden, waiting for a suitable suitor to come along--and, as we shall see in Chaucer, the use of a crucial synecdoche: the suitor who is allowed in the walled garden is allowed in the woman. In this manner, Chaucer's translation of the *Roman de la Rose* treats very seriously what, later, in his fabliaux, he treated very funnily--the sexual encounter. (There is some question whether or not Chaucer actually did the translation, and the time frame of the writing is tentative, probably between 1370 and 1380 A.D.). It starts with the hero walking through the meadow, and happening across a garden. He walks around the garden, eventually finding an entrance ("a wiket small"), but can't get in (Chaucer, c.1375, ll.525-530):

> Tho can I go a full gret pas
> Envyronyng evene in compas
> The closing of the square wall,
> Tyl that I fond a wiket small

> So shett, that I ne myght in gon,
> And other entre was ther noon.

So, we start with (1) *proximation* (using the obligation of motion towards another's presence). When we move into the proximity of an other, and become aware of this presence, we then are faced with a decision--go ahead or go back. This liminal stage of intrusion into presence (where the perception of the other is brought into play) invokes the next right or non-right--Can I intrude on your presence? A door may be the cue here. Shall I knock or ring? Hence, the power to say "Come in" in response to a signal, e.g. a door-bell. (Here we get the crucial distinction between actus and status which emerges sometimes, where one person moves in on another who is statically involved with a physical compartment. The latter may have the power to exclude, since higher status suggests a static identity, but may also, under different circumstances, suggest powerlessness in the face of a blitzkrieg.)

Finally, in "The Romance of the Rose," a 'mayde' named Idelnesse opens the door of the walled garden to the hero, telling him about the Lord of the garden (l.601), Myrthe--who built the wall (ll. 645-654).

> And whan I was inne, iwys,
> Myn herte was ful glad of this,
> Ful wel wende I ful sikerly
> Have ben in paradys erthly.
> So fair it was that, trusteth wel,
> It semede a place espirituel.
> For certys, as at my devys,
> Ther is no place in paradys
> So good inne for to dwelle or be
> As in that gardyn, thoughte me.

(2) *Perception* (using the obligation of recognition rights)--Especially, the Look. Here we have the basic distinction between a beginning which is one-way perception and starting with two-way perception. At a buzz or ring, you look through your screen at the intruder. (One crucial function of perception, then, is recognition. Of course, cognition is the radical act of perception--but in the social context one tries to pigeon-hole, and type-cast, identities and motivations as much as possible--so the kind of recognition-process entertained tries to avoid primordially radical cognition.) You may query about who it is, deciding upon whether acceptable to enter or nonacceptable, stranger or friend, etc. Here, usually, the insider has the right to preview the outsider, before proceeding into the encounter proper, with its two-way communication. The meaning of this preview differs, depending upon whether the context is public or private, but, in a normal situation, the visual mode dominates.

In the Rose allegory, a bargaining process now occurs, not as a literal communication, but as an allegorical battle between two sides--one side opposing the lover's suit to gain his lady (Chastity, Danger, Shame, and Wicked-Tongue), and one side favouring the suit (Franchise, Pity, and Fair-Welcoming). This probably mimicks the realism of a situation where the lady was surrounded by people who would take sides concerning the validity of the suit. So, in this case, the courtier communicates, not with the lady, but with significant others who may lead to the lady. One remembers Troilus, who must be introduced to Criseyde by means of an intermediary, Pandarus. Only then can he enter into the formal phase of communication with her--of course, in a garden.

(3) *Communication* (using the obligation of communication rights)-- especially "Talk"--works by two-way interaction, particularly through gestures and through the symbolic action of language. People working in proximity with each other may go through a number of interactions--but, if the formalities of the encounter are adhered to, the entrance into this proximal relation starts with an introduction ("Hello") and the exit with an ending rite ("Goodbye"). It is possible, especially in a mediated context, to have a one-sided communication (as in broadcasting--e.g. SOS) --but such "blind" message-sending takes place under special circumstances, and communication does not occur unless the message is received. In a normal two-way interaction, the auditory sense dominates the *formal* transmission process (although the other senses may actually cue much more significantly).

One of the interesting questions raised by "The Romaunt of the Rose" is the meaning of the Rose. Certainly, the rose stands for the woman, who is surrounded by a hedge that allows the rose to be seen but makes approaching difficult, even for the sake of communication (ll. 1833-1842):

> Toward the roser fast I draw,
> But thornes sharpe mo than ynow
> Ther were, and also thisteles thikke,
> And breres, brymme for to prikke,
> That I ne myghte get grace
> The rowe thornes for to passe,
> To sen the roses fresshe of hewe.
> I must abide, though it me rewe,
> The hegge aboute so thikke was,
> That closide the roses in compas.

But just as there is a double wall protecting the Rose--the outer wall of the garden, and the inner hedge which surrounds the Rose itself--one can posit here a double meaning to the Rose itself--it is the whole woman, but it is also that part of the woman that the courtier desires most fervently--the genitalia, the rose within the Rose. In this latter case, the hedge around the rose 'bristles' (to use Henry James' term) with meaning that can be the source of jokes as well as of awe. It is the hedge that prevents communion, unless one is allowed through. But, as pubic hair, as the "berd" that Chaucer's Absolon discovers in the dark when he kisses Alison's "naked ers" in "The Miller's Tale," it can indicate a short- circuiting of the rituals of courtship. So the fabliaux take the very things that are ritualized (doubled) in the high romance forms, and they cancel the doubling. In this manner, the Boolean logic of G. Spencer Brown's *Laws of Form* (1972) can be applied to the joke, and to literature in general.

(4) *Communion* (using the obligation of communion rights) is a shared event, such as sharing a meal (where the taste sense may dominate), sharing a joke, or, more intimately, having sex (where the tactile sense may dominate). The Rose, here, is the whole woman--but also, part of the joke in Eco's title, "The Name of the Rose", the part that shouldn't be named, the mysterious part that represents the whole. If we name the part, talk about holy things from below, as Chaucer does in his tales, and as Henry Miller does in his modern allegory of the "Land of Fuck", then we may experience a shock that (if we accept the joke and don't just remain shocked, hence cancelling the awe-filled, awful doubling) leads to a release of cathexis, a reflex-shunt that concludes with a shudder of laughter.

At the onset of the sexual act, for the woman especially, there is control over the entrance, and the right to say "Come in". And, since communion is the arena of release, where one lets go of guarded places, the crucial question is whether consummation, which is the end of communion, occurs. Before such completion, there are earlier stages of communion--e.g. a very careful checking of the credentials of the lover, who must "open up" his heart before he can expect the woman to "open up". Hence, in our allegory, the God of Love comes to the hero, shows him "A litll keye, fetys ynowgh," (1.2088) with which Love opens up his heart to see if he is true--since a false heart will steal the treasure of love.

Human relationship "peaks" at the most internal stage of communion, but even in the midst of the most intimate sex, talking (communication) may occur--even though it is a step down. And, of course, perception (the Look) may occur. And a couple may go out for a little 'proximizing' walk.

These are rites of in and out which define the stages of an encounter, and each of these involves "rights". Of course, the formality of these entrances and exits may be violated, or may be abbreviated. A lover may come behind his beloved and kiss her, entering directly into the rite of communion. But that is because he has gained the "right" to do this. If he doesn't have this right, a violation of decorum has occurred. Stories are filled with such shifts & abbreviations, displacements & condensations.

D. The Sensemiotics of Displaced Ritual: Each Stage of the Encounter in the Walled Sensory Garden Emphasizes Specific Sensory Modes

Literature, and film, provides a wealth of information about the encounter's stages of entrancing and exiting, and their sensory shifts--A normative set of stages might proceed as follows, after (1) moving through the threshold to (2) perception of the Other, which is, in most normal situations, visual in a one-way mode. Then, if it becomes reciprocally two-way, we may move into communication, although Sartre's Look can jump right to communion. The Encounter itself starts officially with (3) Communication, which is reciprocal. And, insofar as the main mode of communication is usually verbal (auditory), it involves turn-taking. Perception is still allowed in this first stage of the encounter, but (as with staring) there are usually proprieties against making it too intrusive. (4) When one moves to communion, the senses of touch and smell may become dominant. Frequently we move back into the physical, involving kinetic movement, but, in communion, one may restrict perception (one-way looking) and communication (talking), because these intrude. Note the scene from Malraux's *Man's Fate*, where the man insists on leaving the light on so that he can look at his mate while he makes love to her, clearly an intrusion. The social commandment is "Don't intrude"--particularly in communion, not to see too much. We put blinkers on. Obviously, the function of the non-participant observer is exactly that--to perceive as much as possible (hence don't participate). But a participating observer has to function socially, and seeing too much intrudes.

So Perception/Communication/Communion are hierarchic, building on each other, allowing crucial ratios between these emerge in each encounter--allowing dominance of one or another, moment by moment.

Certainly, the normal sequence of stages is easily undercut. Note the following subversion of order in George Chapman (1962 [1595]: 53):

> Ovid, newly enamoured of Julia, daughter to Octavius Augustus Caesar, after by him called Corinna, secretly conveyed himself into a garden of the Emperor's court, in an arbour whereof Corinna was bathing, playing upon her lute and singing; *Auditus* which Ovid overhearing was

exceedingly pleased with the sweetness of her voice, and to himself uttered the comfort he conceived in his sense of Hearing. *Olfactus*. Then the odours she used in her bath breathing a rich savour, he expressed the joy felt in his sense of Smelling. *Visus*. Thus growing more deeply enamoured in great contentment of himself, he ventures to see her in the pride of her nakedness; which doing by stealth, he discovered the comfort he conceived in Seeing, and the glory of her beauty. *Gustus*. Not yet satisfied, he useth all his art to make known his being there without her offence; or, being necessarily offended, to appease her, which done, he entreats a kiss, to serve for satisfaction of his Taste, which he obtains. *Tactus*. Then proceeds he to entreaty for the fifth sense, and there is interrupted.

This extraordinary Renaissance analysis of the sensory progression of the encounter probably, as Douglas Bush (1963) notes, goes back to Ficino. It is something that contemporary small-group analysis can learn from. We start with Overhearing, which displaces a normal ritual progression, since it has not been permitted by the Lady, and then proceed into smell (reserved very much for the communing stage) and then into the sight of her nakedness. Only at this stage, when Ovid uses his "art" to reveal his presence and to get the lady's acceptance, does the ritual order resume its proper form (but then there is an outside interruption!).

The proper courtly ritual form makes use of synecdochic doubling--in the *Roman de la Rose*, the walled garden provides a double wall around the Rose. And, since the Rose itself is (implicitly) double, that double wall (specifically the hedge) is compounded. In Chaucer's fabliaux, however, we find a cancellation of such doubling. Even so, as long as we have a walled garden, the equation remains the same: for the courtier to get into the walled garden is to get into the woman. And, as we see in George Chapman, even to see into the garden implies the opening up of further rights. So, in the Knight's Tale, Palamoun, a prisoner up in the tower looks down upon a garden in which Emelye walks, blanches, and cries "Ah", immediately falls in love, and this presages a consummation. The joke of Chaucer's "The Merchants Tale" makes use of the same dynamic (ll. 2029-2033, 123):

> He made a gardyn, walled al with stooon;
> So fair a gardyn woot I nowher noon.
> For, out of doute, I veraaily suppose
> That he that wroot the Romance of the Rose
> Ne koude of it the beautee wel devyse;

What Chaucer's fabliaux show is how, in real life, and certainly in the middle class parody of the high class courtship, a crucial step is skipped. In the romance, to enter the garden doesn't mean that one has been given permission to get by the inner hedge--which requires several tests, including the troth of Love. Everything in its due order. But, in the fabliaux, to enter the walled garden means that (1)the male has already been given such permission by the wife, and (2)such skipping of a step is simply an indication of "cheating". The breaking of troth, for the blind January's May is the counterfeiting in wax of the key, which allows her lover Damyan in. Once in, Damyan and May climb the pear tree. Courtly love, when it has lost its doubled ritual stages, simply becomes "cheating"--and this is what makes the stories so hilarious, since the joke is almost always on the person who is cheated against. Perhaps, with humour, we find a reversal of the kind of cultural internalization that

Gregory of Tours, in his *History of the Franks*, talks about, where the earlier lusty behavior the Franks becomes overlaid with Christian guilt.

One last transformation of the equation: In the fabliaux, for a man to enter the walled garden means to enter the woman. However, it should be noted that, whenever the garden is *not* walled, something that occurs a few times in Chaucer's work (such as "the Franklin's Tale," with its "enforced" relationship), then the equation is subverted.

E. A Conclusion on the Proxemiotics of Conceptual Thinking: How the Stages of the Encounter Have Been Used to Create a Model Defining the Stages of Thought

The sensory/gestural duals that we have been talking about do much more than define the encounter with the Other. As we attend to something (L. *attendere*, to stretch toward, from *ad-*, to *+tendere*, to stretch), or involve ourselves in intention (a stretching into), we invoke a cognitive version of the four in-out rites, including our own expression (a pressing out of 'e-motions'). This model appears to go back to Indo-European roots, but is developed & intensified as an extended metaphor through progressive elaborations of language. Certainly, in the model, cognitions aim inward; feelings are expelled. The metaphor defines many aspects of the abstract cognitive quest for us:

Physical Enactment:	**Mental or Cognitive**
running	course-work (L.*cursus*)
steps of walking	steps of thinking
standing	understanding
("*A sign stands for something....*" C.S. Peirce)	
setting down	cognitive set
lying down (I.E. **legh*)	lying to (I.E.**leugh*)
("*Every time there is a possibility of lying, there is a sign function.*" Umberto Eco, 1976)	
conceiving	concepts

In thinking, we move also from a kind of proximation (steps of thinking) to a place where we understand, which in turn allows statements to be made, wherein people or signs "stand for" other things--Kenneth Burke (1945: 21) notes here the generalizing of the Indo-European **sta* root to a crucial family of terms. Here, we set ourselves down (with apologies to Bishop Berkeley, who was rightly suspicious of homunculi doing these things) into the inner perception of cognitive set. Are we then ready to move to the stage of communication, where signs might be used for lying? Finally, we achieve a 'communal', perhaps mystical, moment of seeding or conceptualization.

To fit together these metaphors from our language creates an allegory of cognition. In fact, the reader might feel that I am merely forcing etymological images together--but, I would like to argue, there is a consistency in the etymology of our cognitive terms that suggests much more than an arbitrary connection. As Wittgenstein has made clear to us, we use these images to think with.

It is amazing how consistent remains the parallelism between the etym-roots for physical action and for cognitive action--but I should make clear that lying to somebody (I.E.**leugh*) is etymologically different than lying with someone (I.E.**legh*). Clearly, our language has played a joke by giving the two terms the same current morphology.

Finally, the parallelism explains a crucial development in our concept of representation. The fact is, representation (standing for) started as a ritual moment of dramatically physicalized action, wherein one person represented another, or others, by literally standing for them--a 'personal sign' that stood for others. This then was generalized to all cognitive action, where an abstracted sign "stood for" or "represented" something else. Hence, C.S Peirce's famous definition (1.339):

> A sign stands for something to the idea which it produces, or modifies .... That for which it stands is called its object; that which it conveys, its meaning; and the idea to which it gives rise, its interpretant.

Representation thus goes through a metaphoric juncture which, as with many metaphors in the language, tends to forget its political origins.

The interesting question here, as with each of the other cognitive shifts (to steps of thinking, cognitive set, etc.) is--what remains the same, and what is changed? But that lies beyond the scope of this essay.

Certainly, the generalized sign replaces the person as sign, creating a new kind of representation, a reified typesetting, a new *episteme* for thinking. Here we begin to make use of extended planes as the basis of all representation--hence, as G. Spencer Brown notes, "explanation"--as well as Burke's "stance family of words". What has intruded into the rites of the encounter here is a hierarchic order of planes created by culture, an order which, through the medium of writing and print, accentuates the visually abstract--something that, in its generalizing of the vertical homological yoke (Watson, 1985), has changed the whole dynamic of representation, and indeed the dynamic of the encounter. And, with the new model of representation, so does our concept of the encounter itself change, and indeed our concept of character. We end up being living characters imitating the written characters we scan--Mr. Typus, James Joyce calls us, governed by a new kind of upstanding/fallen self-consciousness that confuses the primary in-out rites.

What do we, as personal signs in this new allegory, stand for now?

REFERENCES

BROWN, G. Spencer.
    1972. *Laws of Form* (New York: The Julian Press).
BROWN, Norman O.
    1966. *Love's Body* (New York: Vintage).
BURKE, Kenneth.
    1945. *A Grammar of Motives* (New York: George Braziller, 1955).
BUSH, Douglas.
    1932. *Mythology & the Renaissance Tradition of English Poetry* (New York: Norton, 1963), 211-212.
CHAPMAN, George.
    1595. *Ouids Banquet of SENSE. A Coronet for his Mistresse Philosophie, and his amorous Zodiacke* (London: Richard Smith). Collected in *The Poems of George Chapman*, ed. Phyllis Brooks Bartlett (New York: Russell & Russell, 1962).
CHAUCER, Geoffrey.
    c.1375 (1370-80). "The Romaunt of the Rose," in *The Works of Geoffrey Chaucer*, ed. F.N. Robinson. (2nd ed; Boston: Houghton Mifflin Co., 1957 [1933]).

DERBER, Charles .
   1979. *The Pursuit of Attention: Power and Individualism in Everyday Life* (Oxford: Oxford University Press, 1979)
ECO, Umberto.
   1976. *A Theory of Semiotics* (Bloomington: Indiana University Press, 1976), 58.
PEIRCE, C.S.
   1931-1958. *Collected Papers of Charles Sanders Peirce*, 8 volumes, 1-6 ed. Charles Hartshorne and Paul Weiss, 7-8 ed. Arthur Burks (Cambridge: Harvard University Press).
WATSON, Richard A.R.
   1985. "Upside-down Perception and the 'Sense' of Right-Side-Up: A Problem in Projective Semiotics", in *Semiotics 1985*, ed. John Deely (Lanham, Maryland: University Press of America, 1986)

XXI

SEMIOTIC HISTORIOGRAPHY

HORKHEIMER, ADORNO, FOUCAULT:
THE TERM "SUBJECT" IN THE ENLIGHTENMENT

Stephan Bleier
University of Cincinnati

Introduction

In an interview shortly before his death Michel Foucault regretted not having read the authors of the School of Frankfurt earlier. With this statement Foucault proved that the attitude of voluntary self-restriction on one's own national traditions in philosophy is indeed an international phenomenon. To avoid such a contraction of the perspective of scholarly research it is necessary to constantly confront different traditions of though with one another. This paper lists a couple of preliminary considerations for a comparison of advanced approaches in German and French social theories. Attempt has been made to promote dialogue between these approaches which have long since not confluenced. The topic of this analysis is the term "subject" in Max Horkheimer's and Theodor W. Adorno's *Dialectic of Enlightenment* and Michel Foucault's *Discipline and Punish*.

Max Horkheimer and Theodor W. Adorno: *Dialectic of Enlightenment*

Horkheimer/Adorno ramify their analysis of the subject into various historical investigations. I would like to address the three most important aspects of their argument: the history of the subject as the history of perception, history of the body and history of labor. There is no doubt that the above factors are essential to a definition of individual. The central problem of the *Dialectic of Enlightenment*, however, lies in the following: what is the force that unifies these three aspects of the individual, what brings about their appearance in history, what determines their historical development to the present day. In a word, the *Dialectic of Enlightenment* centers on the problem of power.

Horkheimer/Adorno define the Enlightenment in the most general sense as "progressive thought" (Horkheimer/Adorno 1947: 3), and they find its effects as early as in Greek epos. "Myth intended report, naming, the narration of the Beginning; but also presentation, confirmation, explanation" (Horkheimer/Adorno 1947: 8): the Enlightenment begins with the history of mankind. In the *Odyssey* the subject still is a function of non-identical and diverse coherence of nature. Subjectivity forms itself only in opposition to this coherence. The ritual of sacrifice exemplifies this development. Sacrifice consists in a surrender and partial dissolution of the ego. However, this component loosens its impact in comparison to the strengthening of subjectivity through rational domination of the ritual-technique, which baffles the gods and nature (Horkheimer/Adorno 1947: 51). The consistent emancipation of the ego from ancient rituals remains external and ostensible: through the denial of its nature components subjectivity becomes an eternal self-sacrifice that results in the destruction of its own essence. "The history of civilization is the history of the introversion of sacrifice" (Horkheimer/Adorno 1947: 55).

The ritual of sacrifice is used to deceive the gods. Being involved in the ritual, however, always presupposes acceptance of their power. "The awakening of the self is paid for by the acknowledgement of power as the principle of all relations" (Horkheimer/Adorno 1947: 9). In his god-likeness man internalizes the power of the gods as law; through his control over other individuals the privileged perpetuates the old hierarchy by profaning it.

At some point in history, philosophy supersedes myth as the privileged model in the explanation of the world. Philosophy inherits this division between subject and object from the Age of Myth and amplifies it. Horkheimer/Adorno demonstrate, how Kantian philosophy inseparably connects the emancipation of the subject with its impoverishment. The ego of transcendental apperception synthesizes nature as sensual appearances, which it subsumes to categories. The status of subjectivity is thus greatly enhanced in comparison to the world of objects, but at the same time the identity of the self is reduced merely to a formal principle lacking contents. The transcendental subject eliminates its natural and physiological remnants and becomes a point without extension. Something very similar happens to the objects perceived. Sensual material of perception is organized by the a priori intuitions of space and time. This principle neglects the reflection of knowledge on its social basis and its historical dimension (Horkheimer/Adorno 1947: 22). "What appears to be the triumph of subjective rationality, the subjection of all reality to logical formalism, is paid for by the obedient subjection of reason to what is directly given" (Horkheimer/Adorno 1947: 26). When thought finally becomes subservient to industrialization, it gives up all claims of dialectical negation (Horkheimer/Adorno 1947: 24) and becomes more and more an instrument of production of operative procedures.

The negative, self-destructive elements of the Enlightenment increase in the 20th century, the Positivistic Age. While nature is being lowered to the levels of mere matter, society as a pure factuality takes upon itself the appearance of a natural force. Thought administers and reproduces the existing, sciences and criticism collect the given facts and data.

During its evolution the subject retains traces of its natural origins as well as those of its separation from nature, which it experienced at various historical levels. These traces reveal the violent conditions of the genesis of subjectivity. They revert the subject to earlier stages of its evolution, despite all its partially liberating factors this evolution has brought about. In the 20th century this retrogressiveness is among the determinants that lead to fascism.

Subjectivity arises out of its separation from nature. This opposition splits nature into external and internal nature. The growing distance towards external nature corresponds to the problematic relation of the ego with its own body. The identity of the subject results from two delimitations against non-identity: delimitation against the diverse external world and delimitation against the various emotions of the body (Horkheimer/Adorno 1947: 46-48). The former subjugation to natural forces is internalized as the subjugation of the body and its emotions to the subject. "Europe has two histories: a well-known history and an underground history. The latter consists in the fate of the human instincts and passions which are displaced and distorted by civilization" (Horkheimer/Adorno 1947: 231). During antiquity and during feudalism body-culture is simultaneously a privilege and a necessity of the ruling classes. Industrialization introduces a change in exertion of power. It substitutes direct command by mechanisms of industrial production that forcibly incorporate the body and discipline it to operate the machinery (Horheimer/Adorno 1947: 36). In the 20th century the fascists' cult of physical fitness is only an apparent paradox. The fascists' exercising of the body rises from their hatred against life and is eventually applied to its ultimate destruction (Horkheimer/Adorno 1947: 249).

Evolution of subjectivity is a subjugation of external and internal nature. This process is by no means autonomous; it is inseparably connected with the exercise of labor. The technique of sacrifice is rationalized by its inclusion in work processes. Sacrifice, which on the one hand determines the form of labor, renders itself thereby controllable through its inclusion in these work processes. Labor has always been organized in its division. Antiquity already sees labor's division into production and the control thereof. The pressure of work "joins the individual to a specific social function and, ultimately, to the self" (Horkheimer/Adorno 1947: 105). "The universality of ideas as developed by discursive logic, domination in the conceptual sphere, is raised up on the basis of actual domination" (Horkheimer/ Adorno 1947: 14). It is economic necessity that creates subjectivity. During economic liberalism the self-made capitalist serves as a model for the modern ego. In the 20th century, however, the role of the entrepreneur pales into insignificance before the gigantic established cartels. An unfathomable machinery takes over the position of the one that originally set it up. Together with its bourgeois role-model subjectivity itself dissolves into 20th century mass-society.

Michael Foucault: *Discipline and Punish*

The main theme of *Discipline and Punish* is the same as in the *Dialectic of Enlightenment*: the production of subjectivity by social power. Foucault's analysis, published almost 30 years after Horkheimer's and Adorno's, is empirical in its approach. Foucault's area of research focuses itself on Enlightenment in a more conventional sense; his *Discipline and Punish* investigates the production of subjectivity in the 18th and early 19th century.

In the Middle Ages individualization takes place in a framework of traditions and rituals (Foucault 1975: 193). Foucault does not describe these circumstances, but the terms "tradition" and "ritual" prove that they occur within the social system and its power. Nevertheless the relationship between the individual and power in the Middle Ages is significantly different from what it is in the Enlightened Age. In the Middle Ages power unfolds in the individuality of the monarch. Power personifies itself at the top of the social hierarchy and thus becomes visible (Foucault 1975: 192/3). However, the individuals that constitute the bulk of the population are subjugated to close observation only when they defy the law. Since medieval court systems base themselves on certain outstanding spectacles of punishment, they tolerate a wide range of minor delinquencies. These crimes, mostly minor theft, become incompatible with the new economic order introduced by early capitalism. Economic change leads to a change in the procedures of punishment, which then thoroughly transforms individualization.

Horkheimer/Adorno depict the evolution of subjectivity as an aggravating body-mind-dualism and as a mutilation of nature in man. Foucault, in the tradition of the Materialist French Enlightenment, describes the mind as a function of body. Subjectivity arises from a body that is disciplined. For the first time these disciplinary actions are realized as a totality in the construction of late 18th century prisons. The "Notes and Drafts" by Horkheimer/Adorno already include a very similar thought: "The rows of cells in a modern prison are monads in the true sense of the word defined by Leibniz [...] Absolute solitude, the violent turning inward on the self, whose whole being consists in the mastery of material and in the monotonous rhythm of work, is the specter which outlines the existence of man in the modern world . . . Man in prison is the virtual image of the bourgeois type which he still has to become in reality" (Horkheimer/Adorno 1947: 226). Foucault gives a long and detailed description of the Panopticon, a round or semi-circular prison with a central tower. This central point of the Panopticon introduces a highly effective method of surveillance. The tower allows the monitoring of all prison-inmates in their single-cells as well as those guarding them. This new method of imprisonment enforces individualization of its inmates by isolating them from each other and by collecting information about changes in each individuals character. The human body is subjugated into an object of knowledge. Subjectivity results from these procedures of subjugation (Foucault 1975: 28). During the 18th century the panoptical model of exerting power disseminates widely into society. Elementary-schools, colleges, hospitals, barracks, workshops and factories are built as architectural variants of the Panopticon, which thus increasingly engulfs a greater part of the population (Foucault 1975: 205). These institutions combine the new model of surveillance and classification with "disciplines" (Foucault 1975: 175). The principles Foucault describes as disciplines organized the distribution of the body in areas. They tie the body to functions and assign it to a strict time schedule. Foucault's analysis of elementary schools in the late 18th century demonstrates that division and categorization by disciplines works through individual factors like achievement, skills, and character (Foucault 1975: 175/6). The disciplines amplify individualization by assigning to people a position in a hierarchy made up of individual criteria.

Together with disciplinary punishment the status of power undergoes severe change. Feudalistic power was concentrated in the monarch. Disciplinary power, however, disseminates into every element of society. Feudalistic self-representation is replaced by abstract principles of standardization and examination. Power becomes autonomous; it is no longer dependent on its exercise by the privileged. "The power in the hierarchized surveillance of the disciplines is not possessed as a thing, or transferred as a property; it functions like a machinery" (Foucault 1975: 177). Power is at its most effective when internalized (Foucault 1975: 202/3).

Foucault does not conceptualize power as prohibition. His concept is not negative, rather positive: power produces reality. Horkheimer/Adorno describe power as dialectics: it is productive and destructive at the same time. Power creates subjectivity through destruction of the subject's natural components. Foucault's concept differs completely: "subjectivity, personality, consciousness" (Foucault 1975: 29) are developed while the body is invaded by power and knowledge. The more the individual is subjugated to power-knowledge, the more individuality is produced.

The *Dialectic of Enlightenment* keeps alive the hope of a possible liberation despite all its pessimism. Thought certainly is an instrument of power. Nevertheless, thought can also attain independence by negating power. This critical and anti-authoritarian tendency of the Enlightenment, "the self-conscious labor of thought" (Horkheimer/Adorno 1947: 194), has the potential of initiating collective liberation. Dialectic criticism can reconcile thought and nature by referring thought to society as its real subject (Horkheimer/Adorno 1947: 37).

In his lectures on *The Order of Things* Manfred Frank points out a self-reflective principle in the works of Michel Foucault (Frank 1984: 161-164, 188/9). Knowledge that arises from this type of self-reflection transcends power-knowledge. Foucault's self-reflection has the same transcending quality that Horkheimer/Adorno ascribe to dialectic criticism. Foucault describes the practical consequences of these discourses which oppose power as uprisings in *Discipline and Punish* and as "the forces that resisted" (Foucault 1976: 144) in *History of Sexuality*. What, however, distinguishes Foucault's critique from that of Horkheimer and Adorno, is his refusal to found his criticism on nature through some ideal subjectivity. It is this refusal to refer to an Absolute which differentiates the French critique of Enlightenment from its German counterpart.

REFERENCES

FOUCAULT, Michel.
    1975. *Surveiller et Punir. Naissance de la Prison*. Page references in the present article are to the English trans. by Alan Sheridan, *Discipline and Punish. The Birth of the Prison* (New York: Pantheon Books, 1977).
    1976. *Histoire de la Sexualité, I: La Volonté de Savior*. Page references in the present article are to the English trans. by Robert Hurley, *The History of Sexuality. Volume I: An Introduction* (New York: Pantheon Books, 1978).
FRANK, Manfred.
    1984. *Was ist Neostrukturalismus?* (Frankfurt: Suhrkamp Verlag, 1984).
HORKHEIMER, Max and Theodor W. ADORNO.
    1947. *Dialektik der Aufklärung*. Page references in the present article are to the English trans. by John Cumming, *Dialectic of Enlightenment* (New York: Herder and Herder, 1972).

THE QUESTION OF THE SUBJECT IN SEMIOSIS: PEIRCE AND LACAN

Julio Pinto
Universidade Federal de Minas Gerais, Brazil

> *No signification can be sustained other than by reference to another signification.*[1]

So said Jacques Lacan in his most baroque "The Agency of the Letter in the Unconscious" (1957) in a discussion of the algorithm proposed by Saussure for the sign, i.e., the relationship between the signifier and the signified. Lacan goes on to say that the attempt to grasp the "constitution of the object" in language will lead to the discovery of such a constitution "only at the level of concept."[2]

A sophisticated thinker such as Lacan would, of course, not claim that the word refers to the thing and in this he seems to echo Charles S. Peirce. One of Peirce's foundational conceptions is that the object and the interpretant of any sign in a semiotic chain is always another sign. Indeed, the several definitions of the representation relation in Peirce's writings emphasize the fact that a sign is always interpretable in another sign.[3]

Nor is it only in this connection that Lacan echoes Peirce. His triadic organization of the real, the imaginary, and the symbolic is remarkably similar to Peirce's three categories of experience--firstness, secondness, and thirdness--not only in its formal aspects but also in conceptual terms. Common to both thinkers is also the dynamic conception of semiosis: Lacan's chain of signifiers is as dynamic as Peirce's semiosis. In fact, the notions of semiosis and chain of signifiers are substantially identical concepts.

It is, however, at this very point that a significant difference seems to emerge. One of the most startling statements in "The Agency of the Letter" refers to the notion that the signifier is an empty form, a signal devoid of meaning. The Lacanian discourse is such that it seems to be conducive to the inference that the signified is a slippery entity, in the sense that the signifier's activity is one of pushing signification forward. The act of interpreting is thus defined as the search for an interpretation--a signified--that insists on not being where the interpreter would like it to be.[4] What seems to be available to the subject is thus an endless chain of signifiers with no signifieds attached to them, which means that the only way of attaining some kind of signification is through the interpreter's act of *assigning* a signified to the slippery signifier. Signification is, therefore, essentially the result of the subject's *fiat*.[5]

To put it differently, what seems to have happened to Lacan results from the fact that for him, as for the structuralists in general, the point of departure is a linguistic view--and a dyadic one at that--of the phenomenon that we call sign. Given the baroque style of Lacan's writing, a non-naive but hasty reading of it could lead to the conclusion about the logical quality of the text that, had Lacan had a philosophically more comprehensive view of the phenomenon of representation, he would not have reasoned thusly:

- a sign may point to several different meanings.

- there is no explicit reason why a sign should have a one-to-one relationship with a signified.

- therefore, the sign is devoid of meaning and meaning is provided by the interpreter.

There is no denying that Lacan's view of the sign is based on a binary framework which, due to its very binarity, is conducive to a clearly defined presence, making the sign a static entity and lending it the character of Being a Sign. Leaving aside this ontological aspect of the sign--which is strange, to say the least, since anything can be a sign of anything, and conversely, every sign is also something other than a sign (this business of representing something being a question of function, not of being)--there is something about Lacan's theory that does not quite cut it. If we think a little further we will be able to see that the weak spot lies in the fact that the chain of signifiers--and it is worth remembering that for Lacan this chain is never linear and syntagmatic, but also organizes itself around a paradigmatic axis--has a dynamic character. Being dynamic it cannot presuppose a two, dyadicity, but it needs a three: in order to be a chain--i.e., a syntax--it has to observe some kind of organizational principle and every organizational principle has a mediating character and is, therefore, a third.

What I mean by all this is that Lacan's openly binary view of the sign makes his theory, or rather, the way in which his theory is formulated, unable to explain the obvious fact that signs exist for the purpose of signifying. Lacan certainly accepts this fact, for the text of "The Agency of the Letter" tries to show, on the basis of the notions of metaphor and metonymy, that the signified can be reached at the interval between two signifiers. Or, not so differently, the signified occurs at certain nodal points, certain *loci* of the signifier chain network. It is clear, therefore, that the signified is a third, and the incoherence in the theory seems to be that, overtly, the representational structure is *said* to be dyadic when in fact it is presented as being triadic.

In spite of the incongruity of the reasoning and the excessively privileged position that the subject is forced to occupy in the processing of semiosis, and given that the theory is, after all, a psychoanalytical one, it is conceivable that, in an exclusively psychoanalytical context, such a view is adequate and even empirically applicable if one has in mind that the signified that the signifier is provided with is one dictated by a hermeneutics that antecedes the sign and therefore creates boundaries for it. However, this is not a debate about whether the theory is effective in the setting of the psychoanalyst's office. What is being called into question is a two-fold point of a theoretical nature: (1) the use of a binary theory to explain a clearly triadic phenomenon; and (2) the role of the subject in the representation relation.

The idea that I wish to present here is that, from the point of view of a general theory of the sign--one in which the verbal sign is NOT paradigmatic--the dyadic stance is not tenable. In other words, a general theory of the sign must consider its object from a standpoint that is more comprehensive than that of linguistics, if it intends to be explanatorily adequate. Since the verbal sign is one class of signs among several other classes, and because the word is a law (which Lacan himself asserts), the word is necessarily a third. Furthermore, every specific semiotic must account for its object in terms of a general theory that includes it.

This requirement is met by Peirce's general theory precisely because it has a general character, and portrays representation within the sign as a triadic relationship in which the interpretant is a fundamental term. The interpretant is the term that is responsible for signification, in the sense that it contains both the sign and its object.[6] The signification achieved by the interpretant is never complete. Actually, semiotic truth would be achieved only in an ideal situation in which the sign, its object, and its interpretant are the same entity, because every sign is indeterminate to a degree, i.e., no sign is capable of fully representing its object.

The sign's indeterminacy is a direct consequence of the way in which the sign is most often characterized in Peirce's writings. A paraphrase of one of the by now standard characterizations would be that the sign represents an object *in some respect* and *creates* in the mind of the observer an equivalent or more developed sign (the interpretant) which refers to the object *in the same way*, the interpretant becoming a sign, and so forth.[7]

Some important inferences may be drawn from such a characterization of the representation relation. First, the fact that a sign and an interpretant represent an object in some respect means that some aspects of the object are not present in signs of it. In other words, signs are faithful to their objects only partially, and every sign has an area that is opaque, as it were. Furthermore, signs can be interpreted in several ways, i.e., they offer a certain number of interpretational possibilities. To the range of interpretational possibilities of a given sign at a given moment in the semiotic chain Peirce gives the name of immediate interpretant. From this range the interpreter will draw an interpretant for that sign. The choice of this interpretant depends upon contextual implicatures, the history of the person who chose it, and so on, and the interpretant thus chosen receives the name of dynamic interpretant.

A dynamic interpretant is, therefore, chosen from among the possible interpretants that a sign *already has*. This leads to two conclusions: (1) it is not possible to speak of a one-to-one relationship between the sign and its object, i.e., between a signifier and a signified, as Lacan correctly noted; (2) the interpreter does not endow the signifier with a meaning, but singles out one possible meaning. The role of the subject is still an active one in the processing of semiosis, but it is by no means an act of "divine" creation.[8] There is a limit to the potential revelatory power of a sign (and this is another import of the phrase "in some respect"), for every sign is a cultural product and public property. The so-called "private symbols" always utilize this public potential for particular use. This does not preclude the subject from being linguistically free but it certainly guarantees the reality of the linguistic fact *qua* law, which is what one actually finds in Lacanian thought as well.

It seems that the hypothesis set forth about the intrinsic thirdness of Lacan's theory is confirmed in terms of the very structure of the representation relation and also in terms of the subject. Lacan seems, therefore, to move away from the static binarity that he so obviously advocates. The only thing that this dyadicity achieves is the concealment of the truly triadic nature of his conceptions. Thus, what he asserts as being the void of signification is nothing more than the opacity that is present in every sign, which makes the interpreter, upon choosing an interpretant, seem to be creating a meaning. In other words, we may say that from a semiotic point of view, Lacan is right. The problem is that he is right for the wrong reasons, which does not invalidate his theory as an empirically applicable one, but makes it easily falsifiable as a theory, and even its empirical applications are bound to be skewed in undesirable ways by its theoretical misconceptions. Thus, the empirical richness of a theory's applications redounds also to its theoretical adequacies, and conversely. It is not enough to have a theory that "works" clinically. The *desideratum* is a theory that works for the reasons we think it works, not in spite of them. The applicability of Lacan's ideas can only be enhanced by removing from them their own unconscious antinomies.

NOTES

[1] Lacan 1957: 150. For the purposes of this paper I will discuss Lacan's theory as expounded in this article only.

[2] Lacan 1957: 150.

[3] The sign that interprets another sign is called an interpretant. It contains the sign that generated it and refers to the sign's object in the same way that the sign itself does. Peirce's well known characterization of the sign in CP 2.228 (1897) produces two very interesting ideas. (1) Semiosis is a dynamic process: if the interpretant is itself a sign, then it is capable, by definition, of generating a further interpretant, which is itself a sign, and so on in a recursive way. (2) The interpreter is not excluded from the process, while at the same time it is clear that the agent of signification is the sign, not the interpreter.

[4] This is clear, for example, in a sentence from "The Agency of the Letter" that speaks of desire as "forever extending towards the desire for something else" (1957: 167).

[5] An extensive discussion of this point is in Ransdell 1979.

[6] When one speaks of object in semiotic one does not mean "thing". The term is used logically here and means "reference".

[7] Peirce 1897.

[8] By this I do not mean that it is not possible to create a new meaning for a verbal sign. However, the creation of such a meaning is done in terms of a stipulation that makes the code available to other potential interpreters.

REFERENCES

LACAN, Jacques.
    1957.   "The Agency of the Letter in the Unconscious or Reason since Freud" in *Écrits* (Paris: Éditions du seuil, 1966). Page references in the paper are from the English trans. by Alan Sheridan *Écrits: A Selection* (New York: Norton, 1977), 146-78.

PEIRCE, Charles Sanders.
   c. 1897.   "Ground, Object and Interpretant", which appears in the *Collect Papers of Charles Sanders Peirce*, in 8 volumes, 1-6 ed. Charles Hartshorne and Paul Weiss, 7-8 ed. Arthur Burks (Cambridge, Ms.: Harvard Univ. Press, 1931-58). Referred to as CP followed by the volume and paragraph numbers. This piece is CP 2.227-229.

RANSDELL, Joseph.
   1979.   "Semiotic Objectivity" *Semiotica* 26.3/4, 261-288; reprinted in J. Deely, B. Williams, and F. Kruse, eds. *Frontiers in Semiotics* (Bloomington: Indiana Univ. Press, 1986), 236-254.

THE SEMIOTIC OF MAURICE BLONDEL'S LOGIC OF ACTION

Anthony F. Russell
Loras College

I. Blondel's Problem of the Divorce between Logic, Ethics and Life

John Locke's proposed new logic and critic, semiotic, the doctrine of the sign, was to mediate between the scientifically articulated objective world and the actions of the human agent, the subject matter of the science of ethics. Maurice Blondel (1861-1949) elaborated on human action itself as the dynamic, concrete mediator between the situated human subject and the environing world, exercising a concrete ethico-logic of its own, the logic of life, which, according to Blondel, is more fundamental than any abstract logic or science of the practical and which is presupposed by, and is the living source of, abstract, theoretical thought, logic and moral science. Since his whole thought is in fact a semiotic of action it is worthy of consideration.

Blondel sought to bring about a *rapprochement* between thought and life which he held to be sundered by the priority given to abstract thought and to the logic of abstract ideas. He blames the ruptures in logic, between science and art, formal and material, major and minor, theoretical and applied, on the separation of thought and its abstract ideas from their living roots in human action (Blondel 1894: 9). He points to a hidden collusion between the positive and exact, mathematical sciences which indicates the presence of a mediator hidden from both those sciences. The qualitative, heterogeneous data of positive science and its method of observation and experiment are exceeded when by induction an ideal universal law is sought to make the phenomena intelligible. And mathematics exceeds itself when its ideal calculus is presumed to be and found to be confirmed in the qualitative heterogeneity of factual data (Blondel 1893: 59-93; Somerville 1968: 77-94).

This rift also results in an antinomy between logic and moral science. Logic means "an unbreakable chain unfolding its links according to a necessitating law" (Blondel 1900: 57). But for Moral Science (Morale) there has to be an "original insertion of autonomous actions, contingency in the world and liberty in man which would be exempt from logical, as well as every other determinism" (ibid.). But "right down to the popular mind there is the conviction of a justice immanent to life" which derives, among other things, from the evident solidarity of historical events and from the influence of "an art and literature which keeps close to the complexities of life," such as is found in the novels of G. Eliot, all of which "display the vegetation of actions sown by the human will in the world and in consciousnesses which is like a blind force of nature and, at the same time, as intelligible as an unfolding theorem" (Blondel 1900: 51-52).

II. Origin of the Fundamental Notions of Thought

According to Blondel, the fundamental notions and laws of thought such as the notions and principles of identity and contradiction, etc. could not have been acquired by thought abstracting them from objective data. Thought cannot abstract the notion of the contradictory from the world of fact since the contradictory is never given in fact. Therefore the principle of contradiction is not found in facts (Blondel 1900: 56-58).

Our ability to alter things according to our desires leads us to spontaneously think that they can be 'other.' 'Others' are also 'opposites' to the extent that they are adequate to or are discordant with our demands, or that our conflicting desires themselves oppose one another. "Contraries are contraries among themselves, never first of all in virtue of an intellectual abstraction, but the result of a totally concrete and qualitative opposition that not only differentiates the series of 'others' but buffets them one against the other according to their fitness or unfitness in relation to the orientation of our tendencies." Thus, "the very principle of the idea of 'contrariety' is not in things nor originally and immediately in our speculative knowledge, but in the subjective determination of our activity" (Blondel 1900: 60-62).

The principle of identity is also acosmic, not realized in the world. It arises "by the subjective precision of the singular intention and [it is] by it alone that we are able to attain or to specify something as one and identical" (Blondel 1900: 59, 62).

The notion of the 'contradictory' which all the other logical notions at least implicitly presuppose, arises in us from our feeling of the irreparability of the past and then only inasmuch as the past is what 'has been done', has been realized by an activity which willed it, not as it is thought to be possible or conceivable. It does not apply to the future. A child breaks a piece of straw and wants to repair it. This is impossible for "it is contradictory that this piece of straw has and has not been broken. If we could not thus want to put things back as they were before we did something we would never come to think that something done could have been done otherwise, or that what is posited is posited without being able to return on the very being of the past" (1900: 63). This irreparability of the past in willed activity is acutely felt when one wants to get rid of an addiction, such as to drugs. This contradictory which we suppose to underlie the real is insinuated by a subjective initiative (Blondel 1900: 63; see also 1893: 341-343, 429; Somerville 1968: 208-209, 235).

III. The Law of Contradiction and of Being

The awareness of the definitiveness of the past in what we have willed and done is simultaneously an awareness that phenomena are more than merely phenomena. Reflective thought will identify this 'something more' as 'being' (Blondel 1893: 312, 342; Somerville 1968: 211, 235). The first law of thought is also the first law of being. Fear of the uncertainty of the future puts us on notice that this being of phenomena is contingent (Blondel 1893: 355; Somerville 1968: 243-244).

The radical absoluteness which attaches to this principle comes from the demands of our ultimate human destiny which it at the root of the tendency of the will precisely as it is a will and so is present in every act the will does, even the most free. The realization of being beyond phenomena leads to the awareness that the will's primordial willing can never be adequated by anything of the purely phenomenal order. The contingency of phenomenal being points to an all pervading being transcending, though immanent to, phenomena whose sustaining action necessitates their being for as long as they are (Blondel 1893: 314, 399-402; Somerville 1968: 211, 306).

Blondel's thought is structured in terms of a three way interplay between thought, being and action. Each can be looked at as a mediator between the other two but none can be thought correctly in abstraction from the others. For Blondel, being is not an underlying substrate, a static absolute, substance, as it is in Blondel's reading of Aristotle, but a relational activity, essentially tied to thought and action. It is the dynamic bond, the vinculum, by which everything is through being-together-with-all-the-others in the whole, in the universe of being. All are one dynamically, by a unity in diversity, a concrete universal (Blondel 1893, translator's preface to English edition: xvi), through the active presence in each and all of the one supreme pure act (Blondel 1893: 399-411; Somerville 1968: 307:316).

The will is thus confronted with an intentional term that it necessarily wills as 'the necessary unique' but cannot realize of its own finite capacity to act. It is faced with a radical either/or choice: either to put itself at the disposal of this transcendent but immanently operational presence for the attainment of its adequately fulfilling end, or to seal itself up in itself as master of itself and of all it surveys. A negative option has the effect of derealizing phenomena as far as the will is concerned, of reducing them to mere phenomenal extensions of itself and treating them as mere means to its own ends, effectively denying, negativizing as far as the will is concerned, their autonomous being which compels us, in the form of moral obligation, to treat them as ends in their own right and not as mere means to the will as if it itself were the only end.

An option against 'the uniquely necessary', which is exercised once the obligation to act imposed by the being character of phenomena by which they are ends in their own right is violated, imbibes into all subsequent willing a negativizing of being in totality, whether within or beyond phenomena. The agent is aware of 'being', the being of phenomena and of the transcendent agent effecting being wherever it is, but wills that it 'be-not.' So, the being of things ceases, not to 'be' but to 'be for the agent' in its willings. So, without self annihilation, in willing to find its adequation without being which is the active bond (vinculum) of solidarity in the universe, the will faces only an infinite void in which to deploy its willing of the infinite (Blondel 1893: 333-344; Somerville 1968-228-236).

In doing what ought not to be done, the negative of the act omitted remains forever as a quality of all subsequent willing and acting. I can't undo by my will what I have effected by my will; the past is forever. But this negation is not an absolute nothing; it is something I have to live with; it abides in my willing as a lived omission. Like blindness, it is not just an absence but a defect of what has it; a privation in Aristotle's terminology. The will lives a contradiction of total being that cannot itself be in reality or in our thought. "Being conscious, at least confusedly, of the conflict of our tendencies and of the demands of our destiny, we find ourselves faced with an option which concerns our being. That is, we have the idea of being and of contradiction only because we are virtually put in the position of resolving the alternative upon which depends the orientation of our life and of our entry into being" (Blondel 1900: 63). "The principle of contradiction preliminarily implies in order to be known the spontaneity of desires, of postulates, of frustrations and successes of our initiative oriented by nature and clarified by reflection, and is finally indispensable to the distinct knowledge of and deliberate usage of our whole intellectual and moral dynamism. The use of the speculative reason is tied solidly to the real and actual usage of the practical reason which determines its true meaning and legitimate bearing" (Blondel 1900: 64; see also 1893: 342).

IV. The Logic of Privation and Possession

Every action involves both centripetally interiorizing the exterior to self in a consolidating self constructive moment and centrifugally exteriorizing the self to the world in a self expressing moment, an immanent-transcendent give and take uniting efficiency and finality, idea and reality. The inward movement, in sympathetic coordination with the actions of environing things, and the outward movement, which is not just a deployment of energy but includes a tacit seeking of the cooperation of external things in realizing their own goals, is explained by Blondel in terms of a sign function which is found in action as such. His understanding of action is thus thoroughly semiotic (see Blondel 1893: 200-205, 269-272; Somerville 1968: 149-152, 186-187). Each being thus has its being in active intercourse with all the others (Blondel 1893: 409-411; Somerville 1968: 314-316). In everything which acts there is a 'within', something akin to a 'self', a synergizing center which develops through the synergizing mediation of action 'inhaling' and 'exhaling' from and to the outside world (Blondel 1893: 99-100; Somerville 1968: 98, 157, 183). This interaction between the *a priori* and the *a posteriori* explains why the exact and empirical sciences are able to borrow one from the other in regard to method (see problem noted above, Section I).

Blondel accuses Aristotle of prioritizing abstract, ideal logic, what he (Blondel) calls a logic of affirmation and negation, regulated by the supreme principles of identity and contradiction as absolute and self evident immediately to thought, because Aristotle, says Blondel (1900: 65-67), took as his point of departure the substantializing way we use words. This, according to Blondel, led to conceptually substantializing other categories whose being was then thought in an absolute, substantialized way, in terms of contradictory affirmation and negation. Blondel characterizes the concrete, dialectical logic operative inherent to life and action prior to reflection, the logic which makes possible moral science as a science of the practical (*la science de la pratique*) by first making possible a 'science of practice' (*la science pratique*), as one of possession and privation rather than of affirmation and negation (Blondel 1893: 426-431; 1900: 53, 64; Somerville 1968: 348-352). The affirmations and negations in this context are then not contradictorily exclusive but dialectically mutually implicatory and principles of concrete implication rather than of abstract exclusion. Human willings in free choices include also the rejections that go together with what is affirmatively chosen. If I choose to do wrong, the absence (non-being) of the good I rejected in so choosing continues as a quality of my choice; my act is not just the negative of what was rejected but the privation of it. The 'absent' has a continuing 'presence' in my consciousness and in my whole subsequent life (Blondel 1893: 473; 1900: 73-75; Somerville 1968: 342-348). When my free choice touches 'the necessary unique' which alone is adequate to satisfy the primordial strive of the will, and which is co-operative in every willing (even the act of rejecting it), and is implicated as affirmed or negated in every act freely willed; if my choice is such as to affirm it I am adequating my exercised freely chosen will act (the will willed; *la volonté voulue*) to what my will wills necessarily as a will primordially in every act it does (the willing will; *la volonté voulante*); I am adequating myself to myself, the self that I am by choosing as I do to the fullness of self to which I necessarily tend in virtue of simply willing, that is, by the primordial bent of the will (the will willing) (Blondel 1893: 321, 467; Somerville 1968: 52, 123).

The dialectical logic immanent in life has as its basic principle this strive of the self to adequate itself to the self in the fullness of being in possession, there then being no privation at all in my will acting. All human freedom operates as subordinated to this iron law of determinism; every choice includes the contradictory either/or of all or nothing, being or non-being.

Furthermore, each act of the will is exercised as a moment of freedom constricted between two determinisms, the determinism of the moment immediately preceding the act, constituted from past causes whether necessary or free, and the determinism inevitably operative in the world and in the self consequent on the insertion of that free act into reality. The realization of an act, and its result, is irrevocable and its consequences inevitable, because realization puts the act done into being with the autonomy, independence of the will, being an end not just a means, that goes with being put into being (Blondel 1893: 146-147; Somerville 1968: 126-127). Individual and world events thus unfold according to a rigid determinism in which free actions are deployed not as necessitated but necessarily freely (see problem noted above, Section I).

Moral obligation, whether complied with or violated, asserts its peculiar type of determinism which is not only consistent with freedom but a condition of its possibility. We could not freely will this or that if we did not necessarily will, and willing necessarily implicates that what is willed simply in willing (whether this or that) be adequate to the will's primordial tendency as a will. If what is willed as adequate is in fact not adequate the will continues its necessary willing in a pseudo-world voided of being while itself living in the real world of being. It thus inevitably lives a contradiction that can neither be nor be thought.

REFERENCES

BLONDEL, Maurice.
    1893.   *L'Action: Essai d'une critique de la vie et d'une Science de la Pratique* (Paris: Bibliotheque de Philosophie Contemporaine, Felix Alcan). Reprinted as Vol. I of *Les premiers écrits de Maurice Blondel* (Paris: Presses Universitaires de France, 1950); not to be confused with *L'Action*, Vol. I (Paris: Alcan, 1936); Vol. II (Paris: Alcan, 1937), which form part of the trilogy *La Pensée, L'Être et les êtres, L'Action* (1934-1937). Page references in this paper are from the English trans. by Olivia Blanchette *L'Action (1893): Essay on a Critique of Life and a Science of Practice* (Indiana: University of Notre Dame Press, 1984).
    1894.   (date drafted; published 1960). "Ébauche de logique générale", *Revue de Métaphysique et de Morale*, Tome 65, No. 1 (Jan-Mar) 1960, 7-18.
    1900.   "Principe élémentaire d'une logique de la vie morale." Paper delivered at the Congrès international de Philosophie, Paris 1900. First published in *Bibliothèque du Congrès international de Philosophie de 1900*, Vol II (Paris: Colin 1903), 51-85. Reprinted in *Les premiers écrits de Maurice Blondel*, II (Paris: Presses Universitaires de France, 1956).

SOMERVILLE, James M.
    1968.   *Total Commitment: Blondel's L'Action* (Washington D.C.: Corpus Books).

INDEX

-- A --

ADAMS, D.: 82
ADORNO, Theodor: 407, 410
AESOP: 324
ALBERTI: 436
ALMEDER, Robert: 112, 114
ALTHUSSER, Louis: 169, 507, 508, 514
AMMON and HÜBLER: 544, 549
AMOSSY, Ruth: 297
ANDERSEN, E.: 41, 48
ANDERSON and ANDERSON: 464, 465
ANDERSON, Henning: 150, 155, 158, 169, 161
ANDERSON, Myrdene: 3, 6, 7, 10-12, 14, 15, 22, 23
ANDERSON, DEELY, KRAMPEN, RANSDELL, SEBEOK and von UEXKÜLL: 11
ANDREWS, Edna: 158, 161
ANONYMOUS: 558
AQUINAS, Thomas: 138, 140, 180, 187, 188
ARAGONNÈS, Claude: 398, 402
ARGUEDAS, José María: 270, 275
ARISTOTLE: 103, 116-118, 331, 332, 585, 586
ARONSON, Nicole: 398, 402
ARTAUD, Antonin: 269, 274, 404-407, 409, 410
ARTHUR, John: 510, 515
ASIMOV, I.: 82
AUGUSTINE: 118
AUSTIN: 524

-- B --

BACHMAIER, A.: 546, 549
BAKHTIN, M.M.: 248, 251, 257, 277-282
BAKSHI, Ralph: 464
BALDI, Antonio: 440
BARBARO: 448, 450

BARBIERI, Marcello: 5, 11
BARRY, Jackson G.: 263, 338
BARTHES, Roland: 53-56, 157, 161, 165, 169, 171, 196, 200, 264, 265, 267, 268, 272, 273, 275, 306, 309, 384, 386, 501, 503
BATES, E.: 44, 47, 48
BATESON, Gregory: 236, 239
BATTISTELA, Edward: 158, 161
BAUDELAIRE, Charles: 557, 558
BAUDRILLARD, Jean: 270, 272, 275, 401, 402
BAUSANI, A.: 545, 549
BEAUFRONT, L. de: 544, 549
BEAUGRANDE, Robert, de: 27, 32
BECKET, Samuel: 238
BEETHOVEN: 57, 60-65
BELL, Rudolph M.: 217, 221
BENJAMIN, Walter: 406-408, 410
BENVENISTE, Emile: 124, 125, 128, 129, 484, 486
BERNHEIMER, Richard: 437, 445
BERNSTEIN, Leonard: 67, 70
BERSANI, Leo: 315
BERTILLON, Alphonse: 192, 194
BERWICK, Robert C.: 524, 526
BLAKE, William: 150, 155
BLANCHOT, Maurice: 268-275, 311, 315
BLANKE, D.: 547-549
BLEIER, Stephan: 573
BLONDEL, Maurice: 583-587
BLOOMFIELD: 526
BOAS: 524
BOILEAU-DESPREAUX, Nicolas: 400, 402
BOON, James: 157, 161
BOOTH, Wayne: 259, 260
BORETZ, Benjamin: 67, 70
BORGES, Jorge Luis: 238, 270, 275, 303
BORGOMANO, Madeleine: 391, 395
BORSÒ, Vittoria: 268, 276
BOUISSAC, Paul: 190, 193, 194
BOVÉ, Carol: 36, 37

BRAKEL, George: 158, 161
BRECHT, Bertolt: 346-348
BRETON, André: 297
BRODEN, Thomas F.: 391
BRONTË, Charlotte: 300
BRONTË, Emily: 298, 300
BROOKS and WILEY: 5, 11
BROWN and GILMAN: 524-526
BROWN, G. Spencer: 564, 568
BROWN, Norman: 357, 362, 568
BRUNER, Jerome: 158, 161
BRUNO: 448
BURKE, Kenneth: 559, 561, 567, 568
BUSH, Douglas: 566, 568
BUSS, Leo W.: 5, 8, 11
BUZZELLI, Donald E.: 93, 101
BYNUM, Caroline Walker: 217, 221

-- C --

CAJETAN, Thomas de Vio: 139, 140
CALIN, Françoise: 291, 297
CAMILLO DELMINIO, Giulio: 429-431, 434, 435, 436-441, 444-446, 447-452
CAMPBELL, Jeremy: 5, 11
CAMPBELL, Joseph: 488, 492
CANETTI, Elias: 343-348, 350-355, 356-363
CARROLL, Lewis: 238, 311-315
CARTER, Jimmy: 505, 506
CASSIRER: 191
CASKEY, Alexander F.: 523, 526
CASTI and KARLQVIST: 5, 11
CHAITIN, Gregory J.: 20, 22
CHAPMAN, George: 559, 565, 566, 568
CHATMAN, Seymour: 305, 309
CHAUCER, Geoffrey: 559, 562, 564, 566-568
CHIAMPI, Irlemar: 274, 276
CHIPP, Herschel B: 487, 491, 492
CHOMSKY, Noam: 67, 70, 190, 237, 480, 523, 524
CHRYSIPPUS: 117
CICERO: 118
CIXOUS, Hélène: 394, 395, 412
COLAPIETRO, Vincent: 165
COLETTI, Teresa: 321-323
COLLINS, Tom: 433
COMRIE, Bernard: 158, 161

COMTE: 104
CONE, Edward T.: 59, 62
CONRAD, Michael: 5, 11, 15, 22
CORRINGTON, Robert S.: 203, 205, 207-209
CORTÁZAR: 270
COSTE, Didier: 275, 276
CREWS, Frederick: 169, 171
CULLER, Jonathan: 197, 200, 279, 282, 301, 302
CUNNINGHAM, Donald: 27, 32
CURIONE: 441
CURTIUS, Mechthild: 343, 348
CUTSFORTH, T.D.: 42, 48

-- D --

DADDESIO, Thomas C.: 319
DANOW, David K.: 277
DARBY, David: 343
DARWIN: 324-326, 328, 329
DAWKINS, Richard: 8, 11
DE BOLLA, Peter: 275, 276
DECHICCHIS, Joseph: 528
DECHICCHIS and TUSH: 530, 535
DE CUSA, Nicholas: 238, 239
DEELY, John: xi, xii, 27, 30, 32, 33, 133, 140, 141, 173-179, 189, 194, 331-334
DEELY and EVANS: xii
DEELY and WILLIAMS: ii
DEELY, WILLIAMS, and KRUSE: 179
DEFOTIS, William: 53
DEGUERE, Philip: 456, 459
DEJEAN, Joan: 398, 402
DE LAURETIS, Teresa: 507, 514
DELEDALLE, Gerard: 116, 157, 161
DELEUZE and GUATTARI: 237, 239, 326, 329, 511, 512, 515
DE MAN, Paul: 254, 259, 260
DERBER, Charles: 559, 569
DERRIDA, Jacques: 151, 154, 155, 165, 167, 169, 196, 200, 225-230, 236, 238, 239, 321, 323
DESCARTES: 154, 168, 171, 184
DES PRES, Terrence: 171
DETIENNE, André: 93
DEWEY, John: 169, 171
DICKSON, William K.L.: 460
DILEO, Jeffery R.: 143
DILGER, Curt: 421

INDEX

DISNEY: 463, 464
DOANE, Mary Ann: 393, 395
DONNELLY: 210, 211
DOUGHERTY, Eleanor: 210, 211, 214
DOUGHERTY, William P.: 57
DOUGLAS, Mary: 408
DURAS, Marguerite: 391-395
DRAY, William: 20, 22

-- E --

EAGLETON, Terry: 169, 171
ECKHART, Meister: 208, 219-221
ECO, Umberto: 27, 33, 68, 70, 81, 82, 124, 127-129, 192, 194, 225, 230, 232, 237, 239, 248-251, 253, 266, 267, 273, 276, 286-289, 305, 306, 310, 319-323, 343, 348, 368, 372, 373, 455-457, 459, 507, 508, 515, 557, 558, 564, 567, 569
EDISON, Thomas: 458
EHRENREICH, Barbara: 405
EINSTEIN, Albert: 186
EISNER, Elliot W.: 487, 492
ELIADE, Mircea: 472, 475, 476
ELIOT, G.: 583
ERASMUS: 429, 435
ERLICH, Victor: 283, 289
ESCHENBACH, Von Wolfram: 292-294
ESPOSITO, Joseph L.: 93, 101
ESTES, Richard: 509-515

-- F --

FANGER, Donald: 283, 284, 286, 288, 289
FARDJADI, Homa: 429, 433, 434
FARDON, Richard: 10, 11
FERENCZI: 362
FERGUSON, Charles: 524, 526
FILTEAU, Claude: 401, 402
FISCH, Max H.: 101, 166, 167, 171, 239
FISH, Stanley E.: 59, 62
FITZGERALD, F. Scott: 263-267, 338
FLETCHER, Angus: 441, 445
FLORES, Angel: 274, 276
FLUDD, Robert: 449
FOELL, Kristie A.: 350

FORSDALE and FORSDALE: 464, 465
FOUCAULT, Michel: 165, 166, 169, 171, 408-410, 437, 445, 573, , 575-577
FOUGHT, John: 534, 535
FOX, Matthew: 220, 221
FRAIBERG, Selma: 38, 48
FRANCIS, Marie: 293, 297
FRANK, Manfred: 576, 577
FRASER, Colin: 184, 188
FREIBERGER, Erika: 283
FREUD, Sigmund: 78, 160, 161, 165, 168, 169, 192, 194, 350-355, 356-358, 360, 362, 363, 413, 414, 438, 555, 556, 558
FRISCH, Karl von: 137, 141
FUENTES: 270

-- G --

GALILEO: 124, 125
GALLIE, W.B.: 153,155
GATLIN, Lila L.: 5, 11
GENET, Jean: 471-476
GENETTE, Gérard: 254, 258-260, 319, 323, 348
GETTY CENTER: 487, 492
GIBBON: 444
GIBSON, J.: 27, 28, 29, 30, 31, 32, 33
GIDDENS, Anthony: 166-168, 171
GINZBURG, Carlo: 192, 194
GIRARD, René: 382, 387, 391, 394, 396
GODE, A.: 547, 549
GOETHE: 58
GOFFMAN, Erwin: 239
GOGOL, Nikolai: 283-289
GOLDEN, B.: 548, 549
GOULD, Stephen Jay: 5, 8, 11, 22, 23
GRACQ, Julien: 291-297
GREENACRE, Phyllis: 356, 358, 360, 362, 363
GREIMAS, A.J.: 248, 338, 383, 387
GREIMAS and COURTÉS: 382, 391, 396
GROSS, Elizabeth: 415-417
GROSSMAN, Samuel: 520
GROVE, Lloyd: 409, 410
GUO, Rui-hong: 553

-- H --

HABERMAS, Jurgen: 167, 171
HALL, Edward T.: 191, 194
HAMADA, Michiko: 536
HARDWICK, Charles: 129
HARLAND, Richard: 381, 387
HARPER, Douglas: 4, 11
HARRIS, Roy: 157, 161, 197, 200
HARTSHORNE, Charles: 106-108, 207-209
HAWKING, Stephen A.: 182, 186, 188
HAWORTH, Karen: 246
HEDIGER, Heini: 190, 194
HEGEL, Georg Wilhelm Friedrich: 14, 103, 203-205, 209, 444
HEIDEGGER, Martin: 324, 329
HENDERSON, Ian C.: 455
HENNINGHAUS, Lothar: 352-355
HENROTTE, Gayle A.: 66, 70
HENSON, Keith: 8, 11
HERRA, Juan de: 451
HERRNSTEIN-SMITH, Barbara: 263, 267
HILAR, Karel Hugo: 467, 470
HJELMSLEV, Louis: 66-71, 248, 382, 501, 502
HOFFMEYER and EMMECHE: 7, 12
HOFMAN, Vlastislav: 467, 470
HOGBEN, L.: 550
HOLENSTEIN, Elmar: 34, 36, 37
HOLLANDER, Judith Porges: 193, 210
HOLQUIST, Michael: 277, 282, 346, 348
HORKHEIMER and ADORNO: 573-577
HOULE, Martha M.: 397
HOUSER, Nathan: 103, 106, 107
HUGHES, Merritt Y.: 380-387
HÜHN, Peter: 344-348
HUIZINGA, Johan: 345, 346, 348
HUMBOLDT: 524
HUME, David:165, 171
HUSSERL, Edmund: 151, 154, 227-230
HUTCHINSON, G. Evelyn: 5, 10, 12, 22, 23
HUXLEY, Aldous: 356, 362, 363

-- I --

IONESCO, Eugene: 238
IRIGARAY, Luce: 412-417
ISAAC, Jeffrey C.: 508, 513, 515
ISER, Wolfgang: 265, 267, 305, 306, 310

-- J --

JACKSON, Jesse: 501-503, 506
JACKSON, W.T.H.: 398, 402
JACOB, François: 191, 192, 194
JAKOBSON, Roman: 36, 37, 57, 62, 158, 160, 464, 465, 480, 482-484, 486
JAKOBSON and HALL: 150, 151, 155
JAMES, Henry: 274
JAMES, William: 215, 221
JAMIESON, Kathleen Hall: 409
JAMMER, Max: 182, 188
JENCKS, Charles: 509-512, 515
JERNE, Niels: 189, 193
JESPERSEN, Otto: 528, 535
JONES, Ernest: 351, 355
JONES, Inigo: 448-452
JONES and WEBB: 449, 452
JONSON, Ben: 451, 452
JOOS, Martin: 529, 535
JOUBERT: 269
JOYCE, James: 35, 238, 270, 331, 332, 334, 568

-- K --

KAFKA, Franz: 288, 289, 324-330
KANT: 93, 94, 103, 106, 107, 110, 111, 331
KANTERS, Robert: 293
KAPLAN, E. Ann: 397, 402
KARLINSKY, Simon: 283, 290
KARPMAN: 362
KAUF, Robert: 325, 328, 329
KAUFFMAN, Louis: 235, 240
KAUFFMANN, R. Lane: 324, 328, 329
KEATS, John: 374-376, 378, 379
KEBLE, John: 367-371, 373
KELLEY, Maurice: 384, 387
KENT, Beverly: 104, 107

INDEX

KESSEL, Edward L.: 137, 141
KING, Edward: 382
KING, Terrance: 150
KINTZ, Linda: 404
KNAACK, Jay A.: 495
KOBYLYN, Sukhova: 468, 470
KOCH, Walter A.: 7, 11, 12, 22, 23
KRAMER, Lawrence: 59, 62
KRAMPEN, Martin: 137, 141
KRISTEVA, Julia: 34, 35, 36, 37, 56, 253, 281, 282, 291, 297, 394, 396, 407-410, 412, 415, 417, 553, 554, 556-558
KRUSE, Felicia E.: 215
KUNZE, Donald: 436

-- L --

LABOV, William: 264, 523
LABOV and WALETZKY: 264, 267
LACAN, Jacques: 34, 37, 169, 233, 235, 236, 240, 270, 391, 398, 401, 402, 408, 578-581
LA CAPRA, Dominick: 273, 276
LACLOS, Choderlos de: 397, 402
LAFAYETTE, Marie-Madeleine de: 398, 402
LAKOFF and JOHNSON: 81, 82
LANDAU, Anneliese: 58, 62
LANGER, Susanne K.: 59, 62
LANGTON, Chris: 6, 12
LANIGAN, Richard L.: 501-503, 505, 506, 542, 543
LAUTRÉAMONT: 35
LAWRENCE, D.H.: 356, 362, 363
"LAYMAN, A": 368, 373
LEATHERBARROW, David: 447
LECKY, Prescott: 192, 194
LEIBNIZ: 576
LEO, John: 249, 253
LESKOSKY, Richard J.: 460
LEWIS, Thomas E.: 507
LEVINAS: 271
LÉVI-STRAUSS, Claude: 166, 169, 408, 410
LIBERTIN, Mary: 331, 334
LIDOV, David: 173
LINCOLN, Victoria: 217, 222
LINNETT, John: 460
LISZKA, James Jakob: 150, 155, 156
LLOSA, Vargas: 270
LODOLI, Friar Carlo: 440

LOCKE, John: 117, 118, 173-179, 583
LODGE, David: 254, 259, 260
LOEWENSTEIN, David: 381, 389
LOHKAMP, Richard J.: 93, 101
LOTKA, A.J.: 5, 12
LOTMAN, Yuri: 309, 310, 472, 474, 476, 480, 483-486
LOUNSBURY, Floyd G.: 22, 23
LOVELAND, Katherine: 38, 39, 41, 43, 48
LOVELOCK, James E.: 19, 23
LULL, Ramon: 437
LUMIERE: 460, 461
LUNDY, James C.: 34
LYONS, John:
LYOTARD, Jean-François: 225, 275, 276, 346, 348, 404, 410

-- M --

MACROBIOUS, Ambrosius Theodisius: 439, 445
MAGILL, Michèle M.: 291
MALINOWSKI: 560
MALLARMÉ: 35, 269, 274
MALRAUX: 565
MANDELBORT, Benoit: 236, 237, 240
MANOVICH, Lev: 479
MARANHÃO, Tullio: 225
MARCUS and FISCHER: 325, 329
MARGULIS and SAGAN: 6, 10, 12, 189, 194
MARIN, Louis: 397, 402
MARITAIN, Jacques: 219, 222
MARQUEZ, Gabriel Garcia: 270
MARTINET, André: 523, 544, 550
MARX, Karl: 165
MASSON, David: 381, 384, 387
MAXFIELD, K.E.: 42, 49
MAXWELL, Nicholas: 8, 12
MACCANNELL and FLOWER-MACCANNELL: 273, 276
MEADE, Joseph: 384
MEDAWAR, Sir Peter Brian: 190, 193
MEILI, Barbara: 352, 355
MEILLET: 523
MELVILLE: 269
MERLEAU-PONTY, Maurice: 34, 35, 36, 37, 270, 271, 276, 537,

538, 540, 541, 543
MERRELL, Floyd: 232, 233, 239, 240
MEYERHOLD, Vsevolod Emilyevich: 468, 470
MILLER, J. Hillis: 298-302
MILOSZ, Czeslaw: 170, 171
MILTON, John: 380-387
MINK, Louis O.: 264, 267
MOI, Toril: 394, 396
MOLIÈRE, Jean-Poquelin: 401, 402
MOLTMANN, Jürgen: 204-206, 209
MONDRIAN: 481, 482
MONTAGU, Ashley: 5, 12
MONTAGUE, Richard: 67, 70
MOORE and ROBIN: 107, 108
MORELLI, Giovanni: 192, 194
MORGAN, Thaïs E.: 309, 310
MORKAN, Joel: 384, 387
MORRIS, Charles: 367, 368, 373
MORRIS, C.W.: 193, 194
MORRIS, Ray: 502, 506
MOZART: 473
MUKAŘOVOSKY, Jan: 277, 278, 281, 282
MULFORD, Randa: 38, 49
MURPHEY, Murray: 105-108
MURRY, John Middleton: 356, 360-363
MUSIL: 270, 274

-- N --

NABOKOV: 284
NÄTHER, J.Z.: 546, 550
NAUTA, Doede, Jr.: 5, 6, 12
NEIDER, Charles: 328, 329
NEWMAN, John Henry: 367
NEWTON, Isaac: 181, 182, 185
NICHOLS and LEDERMAN: 464, 465
NICHOLSON, Marjorie: 347, 349
NIETZSCHE, Friedrich Wilhelm: 55, 171, 238, 406, 444
NORRIS, Margot: 328, 329
NUSSER, Peter: 344, 346, 349

-- O --

ODUM, E. P.: 5, 12
ODUM, Howard T.: 5, 12
OEHLER, Klaus: 111, 114

OGDEN and RICHARDS: 248
OLIVER, Bonita: 394, 396
ONIANS, Richard B.: 439, 445
OTTO, Rudolph: 207, 209
OYAMA, Susan: 5, 12

-- P --

PALLADIO: 448, 450, 451
PALAZZESCHI, Aldo: 303-310
PALEC, Milan: 466, 469, 470
PALMER, Richard: 324, 329
PARRISH and OHL: 68, 70
PAULINI, Mark: 468
PEARSON, Charls: 245-247
PÊCHEUX, Michel: 508, 514, 515
PEI and GAYNOR: 528, 535
PEIRCE, Charles S.: 32, 93-102, 103-108, 109-115, 116-123, 124-130, 133-135, 138, 140, 141, 143-149, 150-155, 156, 157, 160-162, 156-162, 166, 169-172, 173, 174, 176, 178, 184, 188, 191, 197, 200, 225, 227, 231, 233, 234-240, 248, 257, 279, 282, 332, 334, 335, 353, 368, 461, 560, 567-569, 578, 580-582
PELOUS, Jean-Michel: 402
PENCAK, William: 516
PERCY, Walker: 491, 492
PHILLIPS, Robert: 315
PIAGET, Jean: 495, 500
PIAGET and INHELDER: 43, 44, 49
PINKER, Stephen: 524, 526
PINTO, Julio: 578
PLATO: 117, 123, 143, 145, 146, 154, 226, 307, 308, 310, 447, 448, 451
POE, Edgar Allan: 346, 347
POINSOT, John: 133, 138, 140, 141
POLIERI, Jacques: 468
POPPER and ECCLES: 191, 194
POULANTZAS, Nicos: 511, 513, 515
POWELL, Ralph A.: 133, 141, 180, 185, 188
PRAGUE SCHOOL WRITINGS: 277-282
PREWITT, Terry: 241, 247
PRIGOGINE and STENGERS: 5, 12
PROCOPIOW, Norma: 263, 266, 336
PROPP: 338
PROUST, Marcel: 254-260, 269, 271, 311-315
PUSEY, Edwin: 367

INDEX

-- Q --

QUINE, Willard Van Ormand: 180, 183, 185, 187, 188, 232, 240
QUINTILIAN: 118

-- R --

RABBITT, P.A.M.: 184, 185, 188
RANK, Otto: 439, 445
RANSDELL, Joseph: 581, 582
REAGAN, Ronald: 504-506
REFF, Theodore: 511, 515
REVUELTAS, José: 271, 276
REYNAUD, Emile: 460
RICARDOU, Jean: 291, 297
RICHMOND, I.M.: 401, 402
RICOEUR, Paul: 168, 169, 172, 264, 267
RIFFATERRE, Michael: 284, 285, 287, 290, 309, 310, 312, 313, 315, 374, 375, 379, 382, 387
RIMMON-KENAN, Shlomith: 348, 349
RIVLIN and GRAVEL: 496, 500
ROBERTSON, Ritchie: 325, 329
ROCHEFORT, Christiane: 394, 396
ROGERS, Mary: 246
ROSEN, Robert: 15, 20, 23
ROSEN, Stephen J.: 356
ROSSI-LANDI, Ferruccio: 523-526
ROSSO, Corrado: 397, 403
ROUDIEZ: 554
ROUSSEAU: 154
ROWLAND, C.N.: 38, 49
RUBENS: 450
RUBINSTEIN, William C.: 325, 329
RULFO, Juan: 270, 275
RUMRICH, John Peter: 380, 385, 387
RUSSELL, Anthony F.: 583
RUSSELL, Bertrand: 232, 234, 240
RUSSEL, B.: 550

-- S --

SACCONE, Eduardo: 307, 310
SACKS, Oliver: 34, 35, 36, 37
SADOCK, Jerrold: 525, 527
SAFRAN-NAVEH, Gila: ii
SAKAGUCHI, Alicja von: 544, 548, 550
SAKI: 327
SALTHE, Stanley N.: 5, 6, 8, 12, 14, 17, 18, 22, 23
SAPIR: 523, 524
SARRAUTE, Nathalie: 274
SARTRE, Jean-Paul: 284, 288, 289, 394-396, 559, 560, 565
SAUSSURE, Ferdinand de: 67, 124-130, 165, 166, 172, 173, 174, 191, 196-200, 225-227, 231, 479, , 483, 484, 486, 523, 541, 578
SAVAN, David: 116, 121, 123
SAVITCH, Walter J.: 77
SAVOCA, Giuseppe: 307, 310
SCAMOZZI: 448
SCHEER, Steven C.: 298
SCHER, Steven: 59, 62
SCHILLER: 93
SCHLEIERMACHER, Friedrich: 208, 209
SCHLEMMER, Oscar: 468
SCHLEYER, J.M.: 544, 546, 550
SCHREBER, D.P.: 357-359, 362
SCHÜRMANN, Reiner: 219, 222
SCHUTZ, Alfred: 193, 194, 505
SCHWARTZ, Egon: 324, 328, 330
SCORSESE, Martin: 249, 253
SCOTT: 520
SCUDÉRY, Madeleine de: 397, 403
SEARLE, John R.: 524, 534, 535
SEATON, Beverly: 367
SEBEOK, Thomas A.: 67, 68, 70, 71, 116, 124, 130, 136-138, 141, 173, 175, 184, 188, 189, 193, 194, 233, 240
SEBEOK and ROSENTHAL: 193, 194
SEBEOK, LAMB, AND REGAN: 32, 33
SERLIO: 436
SERRES, Michel: 327, 330
SETCHKAREFF, Vsevolod: 288, 290
SEXTUS EMPIRICUS: 117, 123
SHAKESPEARE, William: 232, 240
SHANDS: 189
SHANK, Gary: 30, 33, 491, 492
SHANNON and WEAVER: 191, 195
SHAPIRO, Michael: 150, 155, 157, 158, 162
SHATTUCK, Roger: 314, 315
SHELLEY, Percy Bysshe: 375, 379

SHKLOVSKY, Victor: 480, 482, 484, 486
SHOAF, R.A.: 386, 387
SHORT, T.L.: 109, 115, 124, 126, 128, 130
SILVERMAN, Kaja: 507, 515
SILVERSTEIN, Michael: 526, 527
ŠÍMA, Josef: 468
SIMONS, Geoff L.: 6, 13
SIMPKINS, Scott: 196, 374
SINGER, June: 307, 310
SINGER, Milton: 193, 195
SLOTERDIJK, Peter: 272, 276
SMITH, David Woodruff: 232, 240
SMITH, John E.: 233, 240
SMITH, Paul: 165, 167, 168, 170, 172
SMITH-SHANK, Deborah L.: 487
SOBER, Elliot: 5, 13
SOMERVILLE, James M.: 583-587
SONDERGARD, Sid: 380
SONTAG, Susan: 404, 410
SOUTHERN ILLINOISAN: 252, 253
SPEISER, Stuart M.: 510
SPENCER-BROWN, G.: 235, 240
SPENGLER: 444
SPERRY, Roger Walcott: 186, 188
STANISLAVSKY, K.S.: 468
STANIUNAS, John: 470
STANTON, Domna: 402, 403
STEADMAN, John M.: 383, 386, 387
STEFANNI, Ruggiero: 309, 310
STEIN, Gertrude: 238
STEPANOVA, Varvara S.: 470
STEPHENSON, Katherine S.: 246, 412
STERN, Laurence: 238
STETTER, Christian: 157, 162
STEWART, Harry J.: 475, 476
STEWART, Stephen: 532, 535
STONE, Lawrence: 264, 267
STRAWSON, Peter: 180, 183, 188
SUDRE, J.F.: 546, 550
SÜSKIND, Patrick: 192, 195
SUZUKI, Takao: 538, 540, 543
SWANK, Robert T.: 83
SWIFT, Jonathan: 356-363

-- T --

TAKAYAMA, Machiko: 248
TAMBURRI, Anthony J.: 309, 310
TANI, Stefano: 346, 347, 349

TEILHARD DE CHARDIN, Pierre: 21, 23
TENNYSON, G.B.: 367, 368, 373
TERESA of Avila: 215-220, 222
THEWELHEIT, Klaus: 405, 406, 409, 411
THOM, René: 191, 193
TIEDGE, Christian August: 60, 61
TILLICH, Paul: 203, 208, 209
TODOROV, Tzvetan: 192, 195, 239, 240, 287, 288, 290, 343, 349, 479, 483, 486, 502, 506
TOYNBEE: 444
TRABANT, Jürgen: 67, 71
TREISMAN, Ann: 159
TROYES, Chrétien de: 292-294
TSUQUIASHI-DADDESIO, Eva: 311
TYLER, Stephen: 228, 231

-- U --

UEXKÜLL, Jakob von: 5, 7, 13, 191, 193
UEXKÜLL, Thure von: 189
ULANOWICZ, R. E.: 4, 5, 13
URWIN, C.: 38, 49
USPENSKY, Boris: 239, 240

-- V --

VACCARO, Domenico Antonio: 440, 442
VALERIANO, Ioannis Pierii: 441, 442, 445
VAN GOGH, Vincent:
VELTRUSKY, Jirí: 278, 279, 282
VERENE, Donald P.: 440, 445
VERHAEREN, Emile: 467, 470
VICO, Giambattista: 436, 437, 440-445
VILLAPANDA: 451
VITRUVIUS: 449, 450
VLAMINCK, Maurice de: 488, 492
VOLOŠINOV, V.N.: 136, 142

-- W --

WAGNER, Richard: 292-294, 468
WAHL, E. von: 547, 550
WALKER, Alice: 338
WALLACE, George: 503-506
WARHOL, Andy: 489, 492

WASSERMAN, Earl: 374, 379
WATERS, Harry: 455, 459
WATSON, Richard A.R.: 559, 561, 568, 569
WEBB, John: 449, 452
WEBER, Max: 165
WEDGWOOD: 348
WEINSHEIMER, Joel: 334, 335
WENNEKER, Lu Beery: 435, 436, 438, 446
WESLEY, James Paul: 6, 13
WEST, Donna: 38, 43, 49
WEXLER and CULLICOVER: 524, 527
WHATELY, Richard: 120, 121
WHITE, Hayden: 264, 267, 273
WHORF: 523, 524
WICKEN, Jeffery S.: 5, 13
WILLIAMS, Isaac: 367, 373
WILLIAMS, Richard: 464
WILLIAMS, Tennessee: 469, 470
WIMMERS, Inge: 254, 259, 260
WIMSATT, W.C.: 3, 13
WIMSATT, W.K., Jr.: 266, 267
WINANCE, Eleuthère: 138, 142
WITT, Mary Ann Frese: 471
WITTGENSTEIN, Ludwig: 143, 184, 188, 197, 200, 235, 238, 240, 324, 330, 528, 534, 535
WITTIG and ZEIG: 394, 396
WOLFE, Don M.: 380, 383, 384, 386, 387
WOOLF, Virginia: 169, 269, 270, 274, 407, 408, 411

-- Y --

YALOM, Irvin: 213, 214
YATES, Dame Frances: 429, 430, 435, 437, 446, 447, 452

-- Z --

ZEMECKIS, Robert: 464
ZAMENHOF, L.: 546, 550

SUPPORTING SUBSCRIBERS

To make the Proceedings a self-sustaining publication program within the Society, over and above the support of the individual contributors, a strong base of institutional support is essential. As a gesture of appreciation, we list here by subscription date the institutional libraries which have placed a standing order for the series of Proceedings volumes directly through the Semiotic Society of America Annual Proceedings Editorial Office (in the list, Richard Lanigan is to be understood as an honorary institution):

4 April 1986:	Cornell University Library Ithaca, New York
25 March 1987:	Richard Lanigan Southern Illinois University, Carbondale
19 April 1987:	Wahlert Memorial Library Loras College Dubuque, Iowa
27 May 1987:	Carleton University Library Ottawa, Ontario
17 September 1987:	Indiana University Libraries Bloomington, Indiana
2 October 1987:	Falvey Memorial Library Villanova University Villanova, Pennsylvania
28 October 1987:	University of Iowa Libraries Iowa City, Iowa
13 November 1987:	Archabbey Library Saint Meinrad Archabbey St. Meinrad, Indiana
17 May 1988:	University of South Alabama Mobile, Alabama

COLOPHON

Layout & Design:	Letterheads to Books Dubuque, IA
Keyboarding:	University of West Florida Pensacola, FL
Text:	12 point Tms-RmnII proportional drop 7, 12, 20
Page Output:	Hewlett Packard LaserJet Series II under WordPerfect 5.0